Zwingli

G. R. POTTER

formerly Emeritus Professor of Medieval History
University of Sheffield

The right of the
University of Cambridge
to print and sell
all manner of books
was granted by
Henry VIII in 1534.
The University has printed
and published continuously
since 1584.

CAMBRIDGE UNIVERSITY PRESS

CAMBRIDGE

LONDON   NEW YORK   NEW ROCHELLE
MELBOURNE   SYDNEY

CAMBRIDGE UNIVERSITY PRESS
Cambridge, New York, Melbourne, Madrid, Cape Town, Singapore, São Paulo, Delhi

Cambridge University Press
The Edinburgh Building, Cambridge CB2 8RU, UK

Published in the United States of America by Cambridge University Press, New York

www.cambridge.org
Information on this title: www.cambridge.org/9780521209397

First published 1976
Reprinted 1978
First paperback edition 1984
Re-issued in this digitally printed version 2008

A catalogue record for this publication is available from the British Library

Library of Congress Cataloguing in Publication data
Potter, George Richard, 1900–
Zwingli.
Includes index.
1. Zwingli, Ulrich, 1484–1531.
BR345.P68   270.6′092′4 [B]   75–46136

ISBN 978-0-521-20939-7 hardback
ISBN 978-0-521-27888-1 paperback

ZWINGLI

Contents

Maps

Preface

The first volume of the critical edition of the writings of Huldrych Zwingli was published in 1905, and although two wars and many changes of editors have made progress slow, it is now so nearly complete that it has served as the basis for this study. In almost every case the printed text has been compared with the original manuscript or first printed edition, but in general the work of the editors was so correct as to make direct reference superfluous. In particular, the depth and thoroughness of the many contributions of Walther Koehler have been exploited.

The Librarian of the Zentralbibliothek, Zurich, and successive Directors of the Staatsarchiv have allowed a foreign visitor easy access to the mass of materials under their control, and special thanks are due to them and to the librarians of the Bürgerbibliothek at Bern and other Swiss libraries. The original suggestion that I should turn to Swiss history came thirty years ago from Sir Herbert Butterfield. I have profited by conversations with the late Dr Leonhard von Muralt, with the late Dr Fritz Blanke, and with Dr Ulrich Gaebler in Zurich. Professor A. G. Dickens has helped, especially with the section on Luther, and Professor E. G. Rupp has made valuable suggestions. Professor James Atkinson has frequently assisted one who is no theologian on a number of technical points, and Professor F. P. Pickering has advised about many an otherwise unintelligable German word and phrase. I have also benefited from discussions with Professor R. Walton, now of Wayne University, Detroit, and Professor H. W. Pipkin, who allowed me to read his unprinted study of the nature and development of the Zwinglian Reformation to August 1524. For help in making many journeys to Zurich and elsewhere grateful thanks are due to the research fund of the University of Sheffield and to the Leverhulme trustees. A three months tenure of a fellowship at the Newberry Library, Chicago, enabled further checking to be done. All that the book owes to the indefatigable encouragement of my wife, who has copied, typed and read every word, often several times, cannot be properly stated in a preface, but in more senses than one it has been a labour of love.

Hathersage, September 1975   G.R.P.

Abbreviations used

QFRG	*Quellen u. Forschungen zur Reformationsgeschichte* hg. v. Verein für Reformationsgeschichte (Halle, 1883–).
QSG	*Quellen zur Schweizergeschichte*, hg. v. der Allgemeinen Geschichtsforschenden Gesellschaft der Schweiz, Basel 1877–1907, NF (Basle, 1908–).
QSRG	*Quellen u. Abhandlungen zur schweizerischen Reformationsgeschichte* (Basle, 1901–5; Leipzig, 1912–42).
RTA	*Deutsche Reichstagsakten (Jüngere Reihe): Deutsche Reichstagsakten unter Kaiser Karl V.*, Bde. I–IV, VII, 1. 2 (Gotha, 1893–1935 reprinted Göttingen, 1963).
SKR	*Schriften zur Kirchen- u. Rechtsgeschichte. Darstellungen u. Quellen*, hg. v. E. Fabian (Tübingen, 1956–).
STC	*A Short-Title Catalogue of Books printed in England, Scotland & Ireland and of English books printed abroad 1475–1640*, ed. A. W. Pollard and G. R. Redgrave (London, 1926).
SVR	*Schriften des Vereins für Reformationsgeschichte* (Halle, 1883–1907; Leipzig, 1907–39; Gütersloh, 1951–).
SZG	*Schweizerische Zeitschrift für Geschichte* (Zürich, 1951–).
ZKG	*Zeitschrift für Kirchengeschichte* (Gotha, 1877–).
ZRG	*Zeitschrift der Savigny-Stiftung für Rechtsgeschichte*, Kanonistische Abteilung (Weimar, 1880–).
ZSG	*Zeitschrift für Schweizerische Geschichte*, Bde. 1–30. Continues as SZG (Zürich, 1921–1950).
ZSK	*Zeitschrift für Schweizerische Kirchengeschichte* (Stans, 1907–; Fribourg, 1945–).
ZT	*Zürcher Taschenbuch*, Jg. 1–3 (Zürich, 1858–) NF 1– (Zürich, 1878–).
ZWA	*Zwingliana, Beiträge zur Geschichte Zwinglis, der Reformation und des Protestantismus in der Schweiz* (Zürich, 1897–).

ORIGINAL SOURCES

Allen	*Opus Epistolarum Des. Erasmi Roterodami* denvo recognitum et avctum per P. S. Allen, H. M. Allen et H. W. Garrod, 12 vols. (Oxford, 1906–58).
Anshelm	*Die Berner-Chronik des Valerius Anshelm*, hg. vom Historischen Verein des Kantons Bern, 6 Bde. (Berne, 1884–1901).
Blaurer	*Briefwechsel der Brüder Ambrosius und Thomas Blaurer*

1509–1548, hg. v. der Badischen Historischen Kommission, bearb. v. T. Schiess. Bd. 1 (Freiburg, 1908).

Bosshart   *Die Chronik des Laurencius Bosshart von Winterthur 1185–1532*, hg. v. K. Hauser, QSRG III (Basle, 1905).

Bullinger, *Ref.*   *Heinrich Bullingers Reformationsgeschichte nach dem Autographon*, hg. auf Veranstaltung der vaterländisch-historischen Gesellschaft in Zürich, v. J. J. Hottinger u. H. H. Vögeli. 3 Bde. (Frauenfeld, 1838–40).

EA   *Amtliche Sammlung der ältern Eidgenössischen Abschiede*, Serie 1245–1798, bearb. v. A. P. von Segesser (Lucerne, Berne, 1874–86).

Egli *1*   *Actensammlung zur Geschichte der Zürcher Reformation in den Jahren 1519–1533*, hg. v. E. Egli (Zürich, 1879).

Kidd   Kidd, B. J. *Documents illustrative of the Continental Reformation* (Oxford, 1911, reprinted 1970).

Nabholz-Kläui   Nabholz, H. und Kläui, P., *Quellenbuch zur Verfassungsgeschichte der Schweizerischen Eidgenossenschaft und der Kantone von den Anfängen bis zur Gegenwart*. 3. Auflage (Aarau, 1947).

Muralt/Schmid   *Quellen zur Geschichte der Täufer in der Schweiz*, Bd. 1, hg. v. L. v. Muralt u. W. Schmid (Zürich, 1952).

S   *Huldreich Zwingli's Werke*. Erste vollständige Ausgabe durch M. Schuler u. J. Schulthess – *Huldrici Zuinglii Opera*, Completa editio prima curantibus M. Schulero et J. Schultessio, 8 Bde. (Zürich, 1828–42).

Sabbata   *Johannes Kesslers Sabbata, mit kleineren Schriften u. Briefen. Unter Mitwirkung v. E. Egli u. R. Schoch*, hg. vom Historischen Verein des Kantons St Gallen (St Gallen, 1902).

Salat   *Chronik der Schweizerischen Reformation, v. deren Anfängen bis u. mit Ao. 1534, im Auftrage der katholischen Orte verfasst v. Johann Salat* (Freiburg, 1869). Archiv für die schweizerische Reformations-Geschichte, Bd. 1, 1–487 (Solothurn, 1869).

Sprüngli   *Bernhard Sprüngli, Beschreibung der Kappeler Kriege*. Auf Grund des 1532 verfassten Originals erstmals hg. v. L. Weisz (Zürich, 1932).

StaZ   Staatsarchiv des Kantons Zürich.

Steck & Tobler   *Aktensammlung zur Geschichte der Berner Reformation 1521–1532*, Bd. 1 u. 11, hg. v. R. Steck u. G. Tobler (Berne, 1923).

Strickler   *Actensammlung zur Schweizerischen Reformations-*

geschichte in den Jahren 1521–1532 im Anschluss an die gleichzeitigen eidgenössischen Abschiede* bearb. u. hg. v. J. Strickler, 4 Bde. (Zürich, 1878–84).

Stumpf *1*   *Chronika vom Leben u. Wirken des Ulrich Zwingli,* 2. ed., hg. v. L. Weisz (Zürich, 1932). Quellen u. Studien zur Geschichte der helvetischen Kirche, Bd. 1.

Stumpf *2*   *Johannes Stumpfs Schweizer- und Reformationschronik,* hg. v. E. Gagliardi, H. Müller u. F. Büsser. QSG NF 1 Bde. 5 u. 6 (Basle, 1953, 1955).

Tschudi *Chronik*   *Valentin Tschudi's Chronik der Reformationsjahre 1521–1533,* hg. v. J. Strickler (Berne, 1889). Jahrbuch des historischen Vereins des Kantons Glarus, 24 Heft (Glarus, 1888) 1–249.

Usteri, *Initia*   Usteri, J. M. *Initia Zwinglii; Beiträge zur Geschichte der Studien u. der Geistesentwicklung Zwinglis in der Zeit vor Beginn der reformatorischen Thätigkeit.* Theologische Studien u. Kritiken, Jg. 58 (1885) 607–72, Jg. 59 (1886) 95–159 (Gotha).

Vad.Br.   *Die Vadianische Briefsammlung der Stadtbibliothek St. Gallen,* hg. v. E. Arbenz u. H. Wartmann, MVG XXIV, XXV, XXVII–XXX (St Gallen, 1890–1913).

WA   *D. Martin Luthers Werke.* Kritische Gesamtausgabe bearb. v. J. K. F. Knaake, G. Kawerau etc. (Weimar, 1883–).

WA *Br.*   *D. Martin Luthers Werke, Briefwechsel.* 12 Bde. (Weimar, 1931–67).

Wyss   *Die Chronik des Bernhard Wyss, 1519–1530,* hg. v. G. Finsler. QSRG 1 (Basle, 1901).

Zeller-Werd-   *Die Zürcher Stadtbücher des XIV. u. XV. Jahrhunderts,* müller   hg. v. H. Zeller-Werdmüller u. H. Nabholz, 3 Bde. (Leipzig, 1899, 1901, 1906).

Z   *Huldreich Zwinglis Sämtliche Werke,* hg. v. E. Egli, G. Finsler, W. Köhler, O. Farner, F. Blanke, L. v. Muralt, E. Künzli, R. Pfister, J. Staedtke, F. Büsser. Corpus Reformatorum 88ff (Berlin/Leipzig/Zürich, 1905–) (in progress).

ZH   *Zwingli, Hauptschriften,* bearb. v. F. Blanke, O. Farner, R. Pfister, Bde. 1–4, 7, 9, 10, 11 (Zürich, 1940–63). The Latin writings are translated into German.

SECONDARY SOURCES

Baur   Baur, A. *Zwinglis Theologie, Ihr Werden u. ihr System*, 2 Bde. (Halle, 1885, 1888).

Bender, *Grebel*   Bender, H. S. *Conrad Grebel c. 1498–1526, the founder of the Swiss Brethren, sometimes called Anabaptists* (Goschen, Indiana, 1950).

Bender, *Ref.*   Bender, W. *Zwinglis Reformationsbündnisse* (Zürich/ Stuttgart, 1970).

Bergsten   Bergsten, T. *Balthasar Hubmaier, Seine Stellung zu Reformation und Täufertum 1521–1528* (Kassel, 1961) Acta Universitatis Upsaliensis. Studia historico-ecclesiastica Upsaliensia 3.

Blanke *1*   Blanke, F. *Brüder in Christo. Die Geschichte der ältesten Täufergemeinde, Zollikon 1525* (Zürich, 1955).

Blanke *2*   Blanke, F. *Ort u. Zeit der ersten Wiedertaufe* (Basle, 1956) Theologische Zeitschrift, 8 Jg. 74 ff.

Blanke *3*   Blanke, F. *Täufertum u. Reformation*, in: *Aus der Welt der Reformation* (Zürich, 1960).

Bluntschli   Bluntschli, J. C. *Staats- und Rechtsgeschichte der Stadt und Landschaft Zürich*, 2 Teile. 2nd ed. (Zürich, 1856).

Bornkamm   Bornkamm, H. *Martin Bucers Bedeutung für die europäische Reformationsgeschichte* (Gütersloh, 1952).

Brändly   Brändly, W. *Geschichte des Protestantismus in Stadt u. Land Luzern* (Lucerne, 1956).

Bucher   Bucher, A. *Die Reformation in den Freien Aemtern u. in der Stadt Bremgarten (bis 1531)* (Sarnen, 1949–50).

Büchi, *Schiner*   Büchi, A. *Kardinal Matthäus Schiner als Staatsmann und Kirchenfürst. Ein Beitrag zur allgemeinen u. schweizerischen Geschichte von der Wende des XV.- XVI. Jahrhunderts* (Zürich, 1923) I. Teil (bis 1514) Sonderabdruck aus *Collectanea Friburgensia*, NF 18. II. Teil (1515–22) (Fribourg/Leipzig, 1937) Collectanea Friburgensia NF 23.

Büchi, *Korrespondenzen*   *Korrespondenzen und Akten zur Geschichte des Kardinals Matthäus Schiner*, gesammelt u. hg. v. A. Büchi. 1. Bd. v. 1489–1515, in QSG NF 3/5, 1920; 2 Bd. v. 1516–1527, in QSG NF 3/6, 1925.

Buck/Fabian   Buck, H. u. Fabian, E., *Konstanzer Reformationsgeschichte in ihren Grundzügen.* I. Teil: 1519–31 (Tübingen, 1965) SKR 25/26.

Clasen   Clasen, C. P. *Anabaptism. A Social History, 1525–1618* (Ithaca/London, 1972).

Egli 2	Egli, E. *Die Schlacht von Cappel 1531* (Zürich, 1873).
Egli 3	Egli, E. *Schweizerische Reformationsgeschichte*, Bd. I, 1519–25 hg. v. G. Finsler (Zürich, 1910).
Egli 4	Egli, E. *Analecta Reformatoria*, I. *Dokumente und Abhandlungen zur Geschichte Zwinglis und seiner Zeit* (Zürich, 1899). II. *Biographien* (Zürich, 1901).
Escher, Glaubensparteien	Escher, H. *Die Glaubensparteien in der Eidgenossenschaft und ihre Beziehungen zum Ausland...1527–1531* (Frauenfeld, 1882).
Fabian	Fabian, E. *Die Entstehung des Schmalkaldischen Bundes und seiner Verfassung 1524/29–1531/35. Brück, Phillip von Hessen und Jakob Sturm.* 2nd ed. (Tübingen, 1962).
Fabian *Q*	Fabian, E. *Quellen zur Geschichte der Reformationsbündnisse und der Konstanzer Reformationsprozesse 1529–48* (Tübingen, 1967).
Farner I.	Farner, O. *Huldrych Zwingli, seine Jugend, Schulzeit und Studentenjahre 1484–1506* (Zürich, 1943).
Farner II.	Farner, O. *Huldrych Zwingli, seine Entwicklung zum Reformator 1506–1520* (Zürich, 1946).
Farner III.	Farner, O. *Huldrych Zwingli, seine Verkündigung und ihre ersten Früchte 1520–1525* (Zürich, 1954).
Farner IV.	Farner, O. *Huldrych Zwingli, Reformatorische Erneuerung von Kirche und Volk in Zürich und in der Eidgenossenschaft 1525–1531*, hg. v. R. Pfister (Zürich, 1960).
Farner, *Jud*	Farner, O. 'Leo Jud, Zwinglis treuester Helfer', ZWA X (1955) 201–9.
Feller	Feller, R. *Geschichte Berns*, 4 Bde. (Berne, 1946–60, Frankfurt, 1974) Bde. 1 & 2.
Gedächtnis	*Ulrich Zwingli Zum Gedächtnis der Zürcher Reformation 1519–1919. Textbeiträge* v. G. Meyer von Knonau, W. Koehler, W. Oechsli, O. Farner, H. Lehmann (Zürich, 1919).
Geiser	Geiser, S. H., *Die Taufgesinnten Gemeinden*, 2nd ed. (Courgenay, 1971).
Goeters	Goeters, J. F. Gerhard, *Die Vorgeschichte des Täufertums in Zürich. Studien zur Geschichte und Theologie der Reformation. Festschrift für Ernst Bizer.* (Neukirchen, 1969).
Gussmann	Gussmann, W., *Quellen und Forschungen zur Geschichte*

	des Augsburgischen Glaubensbekenntnisses. 2 Bde. (Kassel, 1930).
Haas,	Haas, M., *Zwingli und der Erste Kappelerkrieg* (Zürich,
Kappelerkrieg	1965).
Handbuch	*Handbuch der Schweizer Geschichte*, Bd. 1 (Zürich, 1972).
Hauswirth,	Hauswirth, R. *Landgraf Philipp von Hessen und Zwingli*
Philipp	(Tübingen/Basle, 1968). SKR 35.
Historischer	*Historischer Atlas der Schweiz*, hg. v. H. Ammann u.
Atlas	K. Schib (Aarau, 1951).
Jacob	Jacob, W. *Politische Führungsschicht und Reformation: Untersuchungen zur Reformation in Zürich 1519–1528.* Zürcher Beiträge zur Reformationsgeschichte. Bd. 1. (Zürich, 1970).
Kägi	Kägi, U. *Die Aufnahme der Reformation in den ostschweizerischen Untertanengebieten: der Weg Zürichs zu einem obrigkeitlichen Kirchenregiment bis zum Frühjahr 1529* (Zürich, 1972).
Knittel	Knittel, A. L. *Die Reformation in Thurgau*, 2 Bde. (Frauenfeld, 1929, 1946).
Koehler, *Buch*	Koehler, W. *Das Buch der Reformation Huldrych Zwinglis.* (München, 1926).
Koehler,	Koehler, W. Huldrych Zwinglis Bibliothek, 84 NblW
Bibliothek	143 (Zürich, 1921).
Koehler,	Koehler, W. *Züricher Ehegericht und Genfer Konsis-*
Ehegericht	*torium*, 2 Bd. QSRG VII., X. (Leipzig, 1932, 1942). Bd. 1. *Das Zürcher Ehegericht und seine Auswirkung in der deutschen Schweiz zur Zeit Zwinglis.*
Koehler,	Koehler, W. 'Zum Religionsgespräch von Marburg
Festgabe	1529', in: *Festgabe für Gerold Meyer von Knonau* (Zürich, 1913) 359–81.
Koehler,	Koehler, W. *Das Religionsgespräch zu Marburg, 1529.*
Marburg	Sammlung gemeinverständlicher Vorträge und Schriften aus dem Gebiet der Theologie und Religionsgeschichte, 140 (Tübingen, 1929).
Koehler,	*Das Marburger Religionsgespräch 1529. Versuch einer*
Rekonstruktion	*Rekonstruktion.* SVR, 148 (Leipzig, 1929).
Koehler, *Zwingli*	Koehler, W. *Huldrych Zwingli* (Leipzig, 1943; 2nd ed. Stuttgart, 1952).
Koehler, *Z&L*	Koehler, W. *Zwingli und Luther. Ihr Streit über das Abendmahl nach seinen politischen und religiösen Beziehungen.* Bd. 1 (Leipzig, 1924). Bd. 11, hg. v. E.

	Kohlmeyer und H. Bornkamm (Gütersloh, 1953) QFRG 6, 7.
Krajewski	Krajewski, E. *Leben und Sterben des Zürcher Täufer-führers Felix Mantz. Über die Anfänge der Täuferbewe-gung...in der Reformationszeit.* 2nd ed. (Kassel, 1958).
Kühn, *Speyer*	Kühn, J. *Die Geschichte des Speyrer Reichstags 1529.* SVR Jg. 47. No. 146 (Leipzig, 1929).
Largiadèr	Largiadèr, A. *Geschichte von Stadt und Landschaft Zürich,* 2 Bde. (Erlenbach-Zürich, 1945).
Lenz	Lenz, M. 'Zwingli und Landgraf Philipp', ZKG III (1879) 28–62, 220–74, 429–63; IV (1881) 136–61.
Locher	Locher, G. W. *Huldrych Zwingli in neuer Sicht. Zehn Beiträge zur Theologie der Zürcher Reformation* (Zürich/Stuttgart, 1969).
Lüthi	Lüthi, E. *Die bernische Politik in den Kappelerkriegen,* 2nd ed. (Berne, 1880).
May	May, G. *Das Marburger Religionsgespräch 1529.* Texte zur Kirchen- und Theologiegeschichte, hg. v. G. Ruhbach. 13. (Gütersloh, 1970).
Mörikofer	Mörikofer, J. C. *Ulrich Zwingli nach den urkundlichen Quellen,* 2 Bde. (Leipzig, 1867, 1869).
Müller	Müller, T. *Die St. Gallische Glaubensbewegung zur Zeit der Fürstäbte Franz und Kilian, 1520–1530* (St Gallen, 1913) MVG 33.
Muralt, *Abtei*	Muralt, L. v. 'Zwingli und die Abtei St. Gallen', *Festgabe Hans von Greyerz zum sechzigsten Geburstag 5. April 1967* (Berne, 1967) 295–317.
Muralt, *Baden*	Muralt, L. v. *Die Badener Disputation 1526.* QSRG III (Leipzig, 1926).
Muralt, *Berger*	Muralt, L. v. 'Jörg Berger'. *Festgabe des Zwingli-Vereins zum 70. Geburtstage Hermann Escher* (Zürich, 1927) 98–126.
Muralt, *Glaube*	Muralt, L. v. *Glaube und Lehre der schweizerischen Wiedertäufer in der Reformationszeit.* NblW, 101. 1938.
Näf, *Vadian*	Näf, W. *Vadian und seine Stadt St. Gallen,* 2 Bde. (St Gallen, 1944, 1957).
Oechsli *1*	Oechsli, W. 'Die Benennungen der alten Eidgenossen-schaft und ihrer Glieder'. I u. II. JSG 41 (51–230), 42 (87–258) (Zürich, 1916, 1917).
Oechsli *2*	Oechsli, W. *Orte und Zugewandte. Eine Studie zur Geschichte des schweizerischen Bundesrechtes.* JSG 13 (3–486) (Zürich, 1888).

Oechsli *3*	Oechsli, W. 'Zwingli als Staatsmann'. *Gedächtnis* c. 75–200.
Ranke, *Ref.*	Ranke, L. v. *Deutsche Geschichte im Zeitalter der Reformation*, hg. v. P. Joachimsen. Gesamtausgabe der Deutschen Akademie (Munich, 1925–26).
Ringholz	Ringholz, O. *Geschichte des fürstlichen Benediktiner-stiftes U. L. Fr. zu Einsiedeln* I Bd. (Einsiedeln, 1904).
Schmid	Schmid, F. *Die Vermittlungsbemühungen des In- und Auslandes während der beiden Kappelerkriege* (Basle, 1946).
Schubert, *Bekenntnis-bildung*	Schubert, H. V. *Bekenntnisbildung und Religionspolitik 1529/30 (1524–1534) Untersuchungen und Texte* (Gotha, 1910).
Spillmann *1*	Spillmann, K. *Zwingli und die zürcherische Politik gegenüber der Abtei St. Gallen.* MVG 44 (1965).
Spillmann *2*	Spillmann, K. *Zwingli, Zürich und die Abtei St. Gallen.* ZT (1966) 86. Jg. (Zürich, 1965).
Spillmann *3*	Spillmann, K. *Zwinglis politische Pläne in der Ost-schweiz* (Rorschach, 1962).
Staehelin, *Briefe*	Staehelin, E. *Briefe und Akten zum Leben Oekolampads zum vierhundertjährigen Jubiläum der Basler Reforma-tion*, 2 Bde. I, 1499–1526, II, 1527–93 (Leipzig, 1927, 1934) QFRG X, XIX.
Staehelin	Staehelin, R. *Huldreich Zwingli. Sein Leben und Wirken nach den Quellen dargestellt.* 2 Bde. (Basle, 1895, 1897).
Tardent	Tardent, J.-P. *Niklaus Manuel als Staatsmann. Archiv des Historischen Vereins des Kantons Bern*, Bd. 51 (Bern, 1967).
Vasella *1*	Vasella, O. *Abt Theodul Schlegel von Chur und seine Zeit, (1515–1529)* (Fribourg, 1954) ZSK, Beiheft 13.
Vasella *2*	Vasella, O. *Österreich und die Bündnispolitik der katholischen Orte, 1527–1529* (Fribourg, 1951).
Vasella *3*	Vasella, O. *Reform und Reformation in der Schweiz* (Münster, i.W., 1958).
Vasella *4*	Vasella, O. 'Ulrich Zwingli und Michael Gaismair, der Tiroler Bauernführer'. ZSG 24 Jg. (1944) 388–413.
Wackernagel, *Basel*	Wackernagel, R. *Geschichte der Stadt Basel*, 4 Bde. (Basle, 1907–24).
Wernle	Wernle P. *Der evangelische Glaube nach den Haupt-schriften der Reformatoren.* Bd. II, *Ulrich Zwingli* (Tübingen, 1919).

Williams   Williams, G. H. *The Radical Reformation* (London, 1962).

Wirz   Wirz, H. G. 'Zürcher Familienschicksale im Zeitalter Zwinglis'. ZWA VI (1935–38), 194–222, 242–71, 470–99, 537–74.

Yoder *1*   Yoder, J. H. *Täufertum und Reformation in der Schweiz. 1. Die Gespräche zwischen Täufern und Reformatoren 1523–1538* (Karlsruhe, 1962) Schriftenreihe des Mennonitischen Geschichtsvereins 6).

Yoder *2*   Yoder, J. H. *Täufertum und Reformation im Gespräch. Dogmengeschichtliche Untersuchung der frühen Gespräche zwischen schweizerischen Täufern und Reformatoren.* Basler Studien zur historischen und systematischen Theologie, 13 (Zürich, 1968).

An exhaustive bibliography of Zwingli's printed works and of books relating to him is G. Finsler, *Zwingli-Bibliographie. Verzeichnis der gedruckten Schriften von und über Ulrich Zwingli* (Zürich, 1897). This has been continued by Dr Ulrich Gaebler of the Institut für Schweizerische Reformationsgeschichte, Zurich. A helpful guide is *A Zwingli Bibliography compiled by H. Wayne Pipkin* (Pittsburgh Theological Seminary, Pittsburgh, Pa., U.S.A. 1972).

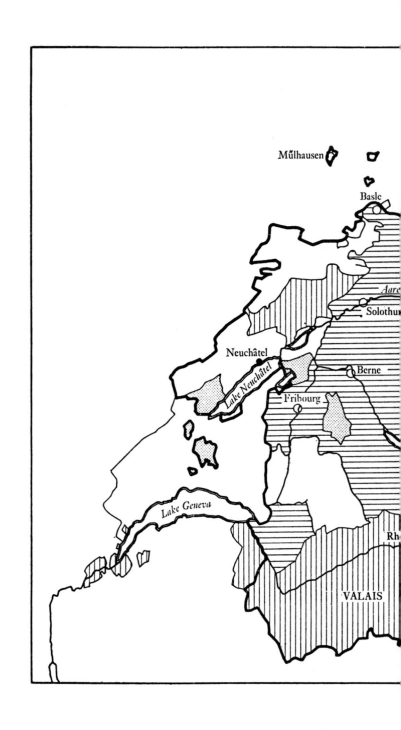

Mülhausen

Basle

Aare

Solothu

Neuchâtel

Lake Neuchâtel

Berne

Fribourg

Lake Geneva

Rh

VALAIS

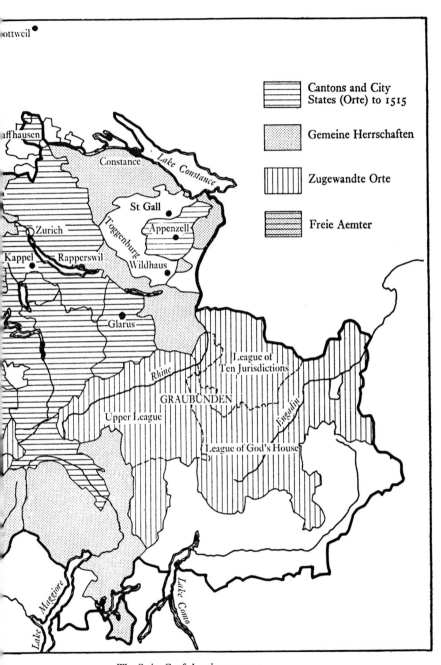

ottweil

Cantons and City
States (Orte) to 1515

Gemeine Herrschaften

Zugewandte Orte

Freie Aemter

affhausen

Constance

Lake Constance

St Gall

Zurich

Toggenburg

Appenzell

Kappel

Rapperswil

Wildhaus

Glarus

Rhine

League of
Ten Jurisdictions

GRAUBÜNDEN

Upper League

Engadin

League of God's House

Lake Maggiore

Lake Como

The Swiss Confederation, c. 1515

1

Early years

The plain statement that Ulrich Zwingli was born at Wildhaus, Switzerland on 1 January 1484, conceals as much as it states. Royalty apart, it is relatively seldom that a birthday can be so surely stated as this, for in the fifteenth and later centuries evidence of date of birth was hard to come by; in some cases a good deal of guesswork is involved. In Zwingli's case however, that New Year's Day, 1 January, was his birthday, and that this was in 1484 can be demonstrated from adequate documentary evidence.[1]

Almost the most unusual thing about the early years of life in the middle ages was survival; most mothers had many children, relatively few of whom grew up. Many were born and died, leaving almost no trace of their existence. The perils of babyhood over, the chief risk was plague and epidemic, less virulently dangerous, obviously, in small villages, but constantly anticipated. When they survived, most children grew up at home with their parents, very much in the open air, and were treated with natural affection combined with a good deal of conventional neglect. Farmyard life was normal, even for city dwellers, and these were relatively few. Parentage, of course, mattered enormously, place of birth rather less, at a time when defined frontiers were almost unknown and even political allegiance was often uncertain. Nowhere in the small civilised world of western Europe was this more apparent than in Switzerland. This predominantly German-speaking area was as difficult to define as the Low Countries or the Indies, and no one was much concerned that this should be so, in an age when areas of territorial uncertainty were not unusual. That 'the Swiss' inhabited part of the Holy Roman Empire was obvious, and if the young Zwingli had a sovereign temporal lord this was the Emperor Frederick III, followed in 1493 by Maximilian I. This, however, was very far from meaning that the Habsburgs ruled in Switzerland, and the extent of their property south of the Rhine and any rights deriving from it were matters of considerable debate. Memories of former hostility, the

[1] For a discussion see Farner, *Zwingli* I, 68–9, II, 309 n. 23; ZWA II, 74–5. Zwingli himself used the spelling Huldrych which may be preferable.

existence of undefined frontiers and unresolved claims to jurisdiction, had led to fighting in 1499, followed by a tacit acceptance of the Rhine as a frontier south of which the imperial writ did not run.

The rulers of western Europe were by now well aware that groups of German-speaking peoples formed a Swiss Confederation, a working alliance or league of communities which had been forced into cooperation by the necessities of existence and of which there were parallels elsewhere. The men of Uri, Schwyz and Unterwalden had some two centuries previously learnt to agree among themselves about pasture for the cattle which provided for their bare existence, and about defence of their persons and possessions against external interference. At first ignored as insignificant, then attacked by their Habsburg overlords as recalcitrant subjects who would not render service or accept jurisdiction, they later became respected because of their proved ability to defeat on their own ground the hitherto almost invincible mailed horseman. In learning self-defence, they learned aggression as well; the direct north–south route between Germany and Italy lay over the St Gotthard once the Devil's bridge had been constructed in the thirteenth century. The control of this passage was of obvious strategic importance and gave the people of central Switzerland a base for, and an incentive to, further expansion.

Larger communities watched and profited, so that Lucerne, Glarus, Zug, Zurich and Berne, with their subjects, allies and friends, joined the original nucleus to form a coherent and self-confident grouping, which demonstrated its efficiency at Morgarten (1315), Sempach (1386) and Näfels (1388). Very poor, simple, rough and self-confident, the Swiss of the later middle ages lived in a bewildering world of local, disorganised semi-anarchy. They are best thought of as forming small, often isolated, independent communities which were reluctantly compelled by circumstances to enter into intermittent ceremonial and formal relationship with one another. Some were primitive democracies where everyone knew that members of the greater families would be chosen to manage affairs; others were growing city-states dominating their own countryside and controlled by nobles or organised craftsmen. Great variety, singular complexity and underlying similarity were distinctive features of this society of very diverse elements. The most obvious characteristic, which explains so much, was poverty. The ideal countryside of the fifteenth century was flat and well watered by navigable rivers leading to the sea. Switzerland was the opposite of this, although to think in terms of 'the Alps', or of an entirely mountainous terrain, is a well-known misapprehension. Mountains were deserts in the middle ages, but even on the lower ground the soil was poor, relatively little grain could be grown, salt for the animals and iron for the primitive tools had to be brought in from outside, and the livelihood which was gained, mainly from pastures which were adequate for little more than half the year, was very thin.

Whenever an insult was hurled at a Swiss, it was about a cow; this useful animal was to them all that the pig and the goat were elsewhere. In these Swiss valleys it was not possible for a large, or even an increasing, population to live off the land, and starvation was all too close to the resourceful men who scraped a bare existence on a monotonous diet of milk soup and cheese. Horses were relatively few and expensive; men travelled great distances on foot to keep up with their scraggy herds. Poverty and population pressure inevitably led to local rivalries for the better pieces of fertile land and to the search for an easier way of life. The struggle for existence bred a race of strong, virile men who had learnt to make and keep agreements with one another, to work and fight together and to respect their territorial integrity and differing institutions. By the mid-fifteenth century, it had become apparent that fighting, relentlessly cruel, with hand-weapons, bows, knives, long spears and the battle-axe in its many forms, could bring employment as well as security. There was always a large element of organised robbery about medieval warfare: then and much later, armies stole in order to keep alive, and their leaders hoped to secure land, loot and ransoms. In the early fifteenth century, the Emperors had notoriously ceased to exercise effective authority even in Germany, while France and England were engaged in the debilitating hostilities of the Hundred Years War combined with great uncertainty at home. After the return of the Popes to Rome and the end of the Great Schism, a state system had developed in Renaissance Italy in which mercenary armies played a notorious part. Orderly detachments of determined and disciplined men could achieve much, and governments were both able and willing to pay for their services. To be hired as a mercenary was normal in this age when armies had ceased to be feudal and had not yet become national. There was no German nation, and the professional hired soldiers of Europe were to be predominantly German-speaking for a very long while.

If Swiss land-hunger was to be satisfied, it must be at the expense of their immediate neighbours, the principalities of the north Italian plain, the Free County and Duchy of Burgundy, the Duchy of Savoy and the districts of the valley of the Rhine. To well-armed marauders, each of these offered temptation; there was loot to be carried off, and there might be opportunities for annexation of fertile farm land. In the 1470s, during the lifetime of Ulrich's father, Charles the Rash, Duke of Burgundy, potentially the most powerful prince in western Europe, had failed disastrously in his attempt to make the Swiss his subjects, chiefly because of the local resistance organised so effectively by Berne, and encouraged by Louis XI of France.

The Burgundian war marks a real turning point in Swiss history. The inhabitants of central Switzerland saw portable wealth unknown before. After the battles of Grandson (1476), Morat (1476) and Nancy (1477), the Swiss forces were recognised as invincible on their chosen ground. In self-defence, the Confederation could send into the field at least 10,000 incomparable soldiers, and self-defence might easily imply attack. It was difficult to differentiate between security, seen as keeping open the supply route over the St Gotthard, and aggression south of the Alps, and in any case such notions meant little at that time. What was certain was that any band of thirty or more armed men from Schwyz or Lucerne could at any time after 1450 obtain regular and well-rewarded employment with the Pope, the King of France, the Duke of Savoy or of Milan. Killing fellow men was profitable, bloodshed paid, and participation in war became an industry that could secure a favourable Swiss balance of payments.

Of much of this the inhabitants of Wildhaus, whose centre for marketing and justice was St Gall, forty difficult miles to the north-east, were only vaguely aware. Such consciousness of a wider world as penetrated to this remote village was likely to be chiefly of the land across the Rhine ruled by the Austrian Habsburgs. Their immediate western neighbours were Glarus, Schwyz, Zug and Zurich, for whom the appeal of mercenary service was less strong than elsewhere since the demand for it came more from the west and south than from the east and north. The pull of the west was only beginning. Basle and Schaffhausen were not accepted as members of the Confederation until 1501,[1] and Zurich was interested mainly in trade with Baden and Württemberg. The city of St Gall was seeking for independence from the Prince Abbot who ruled the wide monastic estates and was himself a member of the Imperial Diet and a prelate of the Empire. He was, however, only an ally (*Zugewandt*) of the Swiss Confederation. Toggenburg, Zwingli's much-loved homeland, had only comparatively recently come under the abbot's control and his connection with the Toggenburgers, of whom Zwingli was emphatically one,[2] was of recent date. In 1436, after the death without direct heir of Frederick VII, last of the hereditary counts of Toggenburg, Zurich had been prominent among the claimants for the inheritance. This claim was unacceptable to the other partners in the Confederation; war followed, and after some twenty years of struggle Zurich had been forced to relinquish its claims.

Thus, the county of Toggenburg was secured by the abbey of St Gall, which, in 1451, entered into a perpetual alliance (*Burg- und Landrecht*) with Zurich, Lucerne, Schwyz and Glarus.[3] Toggenburg itself, however,

---

[1] Handbuch I, 346–7.   [2] Z I, 166, 578.
[3] EA 2, 864–6.

had a separate pact (*Landrecht*) of its own, renewed in 1469, with Schwyz and Glarus only, and was not, like the remainder of the abbot's territory, under the protection of the other two states.[1] The free imperial city of St Gall was a separate entity, and one of growing importance. Abbot and city were thus reckoned as allies, fellows (*socii*) or associates (*Zugewandte*) of the Confederates but not part of the Confederation. Even Glarus, although accepted as a full member (*Ort*), was in a slightly inferior position as far as external relations were concerned.

It was also partly as a result of the Toggenburg dispute that relations between the Confederation and its immediate neighbours were complicated by the collective occupation and administration of the areas which came to be known as 'Mandated Territories' (*gemeine Herrschaften*). These included the districts round Lugano, Locarno and Bellinzona, Thurgau, Sargans, Rheintal, Baden, Bremgarten, Mellingen, and the 'Freie Aemter' west of Zurich.[2] There were also Protected Districts (*Schirmorte*) like Rapperswil and Engelberg, completely self-governing but restricted in external relations. In addition, there were subject territories (*Untertanengebiete*) like the Bernese Oberland, over which city states like Zurich and Berne exercised complete control.[3]

Thus in modern terms Ulrich Zwingli was 'Swiss' only by naturalisation after he became a full citizen of Zurich in 1521; in his early youth he had been brought up outside the Old Confederation, the Thirteen States in many ways so parallel to, yet so different from, the Thirteen Colonies of another century and a New World. The Zwingli family were well aware of the Abbey of St Gall, whose abbot had legal jurisdiction in Wildhaus and, in the last instance, rights of life and death over his subjects. Monastic officials administered the customary law of the county with its feudal undertones and local applicability. Beyond, in theory, lay the imperial courts to which an appeal might perhaps be tried but was unlikely to have any direct effect, the rights of the former Imperial vicar (*Reichsvogt*) being vested in the abbot.[4] The latter used the services of local agents like the Ammann of Wildhaus to administer his land; these agents, anxious to secure the maximum local autonomy, could also appeal for support from the Protecting powers, Schwyz, Glarus, Lucerne and Zurich, and thus

---

[1] Oechsli 2, 97.
[2] Oechsli *1*, 208ff. The correct rendering of Swiss terms into English has always been a difficulty: technical terms are seldom easily transferred into another language. *Ort*, for example, becomes 'canton', but for the sixteenth century the use of 'state' is more meaningful. Some of the conventional translations of *gemeine Herrschaften* (common lordships), *eidgenössische Vogteien* (federal bailiwicks), *Freie Aemter* (free offices), *Leutpriester* (people's priest), are not very meaningful or successful. 'Mandated territories' and 'stipendiary priest' may convey the meaning a little better. See below, 45 n 3.
[3] Swiss constitutional history abounds in exceptions and qualifications which any summary must overlook. [4] Näf, *Vadian*, I, 53–63 esp. 55.

play off Abbot and Confederation against one another. The Toggen-burgers were understandably concerned to emphasise their status as allies of the Eidgenossen, practically *as* Eidgenossen,[1] to enhance their claims to independence. It was in this atmosphere of active local political discussion that Zwingli was reared.

The Benedictine Abbey of St Gall was one of the earliest founded in Switzerland, a notable example of monastic tradition across the ages, and wealthy from landed endowment originally derived from early Carolingian monarchs. Although some of this property had been alienated, the Abbot of St Gall, chosen by his fellow monks, was a remote but powerful figure to whom the villagers reluctantly made customary payments in service, cash or kind. The abbot from 1463 to 1491 was Ulrich Rösch, son of a baker from Wangen, domineering and aggressive, and much disliked locally.[2] As allies and protectors of the abbey, Zurich, Glarus, Schwyz and Lucerne took it in turn to appoint a local resident agent or commissioner to reinforce security and to watch over their interests. This provided another link with the wider world. There was also the Bishop of Constance, to whose officers payments might have to be made, whether for the chrism which the bishop alone could consecrate, for absolution from graver sins, for release from excommunication incurred, for example, by non-payment of tithe, and many other incidents. The episcopal courts were constantly active. For the rest, the scanty inhabitants were secure in their remoteness and worked hard in the upland open air for a meagre liveli-hood.

In the village of Wildhaus, where a few score families built themselves wooden shelters for their livestock and homes for their children, the Zwingli family was well known.[3] Hard work, reasonable luck with herds and crops, and an occasional marriage alliance which was profitable to both sides in more ways than one, had brought financial competence and local influence. The father was well enough off to be able to hire occasional assistance, and was a successful farmer who, as Ammann or chief local magistrate, was expected to speak for the physical needs of the little community just as the parish priest would for its spiritual welfare. Life was rough and simple enough, but the boys and girls were not even on the borderline of poverty. There was always food and clothing available. Family relationships were well known, cohesive and significant; from uncles and cousins help and sympathy could be confidently counted upon. Among the Zwingli relations were some literate, educated men who under-stood Latin, had been to school, had taken holy orders and served as

---

[1] ZWA XIII (1969), 19. [2] Näf, *Vadian* I, 54–8. See below, 272.
[3] The much-visited and illustrated house in which Zwingli may have been born is vouched for only by late and unreliable (but reasonable) tradition.

secular priests or monks. It all helped the family prestige; it meant a certain amount of travelling about to visit them and contacts with the hierarchy of the church as well as with the local cattle-raisers.

Young Ulrich, the third of the family, turned out to be an unusually gifted boy, surpassing his numerous brothers and sisters[1] who seem happily to have accepted the undoubted existence of his superior abilities. We wish we knew more about them. Intellectual gifts meant a little less work on the farm for Ulrich and a little more attention to schooling. It was also apparent that the little boy had a good voice and an ear for music just at a time when choir boys were being sought for and appreciated. Everything, in fact, suggested an ecclesiastical career, and young Ulrich was sent to learn the rudiments of Latin from his clerical uncle, Bartholomew.[2] There was no school in Wildhaus, but there was a small one at Wesen (Weesen) on the Lake of Walen, where his uncle was dean.

School teaching in the fifteenth century, at any rate north of the Alps, was remarkably stereotyped. The same basic need, to secure a working knowledge of Latin, produced the same results. Instruction was necessarily verbal and individual. Paper was, indeed, now becoming available, but it was expensive and not much easier to obtain than was parchment in a sheep-rearing community. In both cases a good deal of processing was necessary, and school books of any kind were rare. Hence memory had to be relied upon almost exclusively, and learning in its earlier stages consisted very largely of repetition of the teacher's words. All over western Europe pedagogues were beating the elements of Latin grammar into their pupils as soon as these had learnt their letters. Declensions, conjugations, tenses, agreements, terminations, quantities and the rest were taught on traditional lines from the *Ars Minor* of Donatus, the *Distichs* of Cato and the hexameters of the *Doctrinale* of Alexander of Villa Dei, along with passages from the Breviary, Missal, Vulgate and Lives of the Saints. Grammar was the basis of the liberal arts; trivium and quadrivium, the

---

[1] Zwingli's brothers were Bartholomew, Claud, Henry, John (Hans), Wolfgang, Andrew and James. There were two sisters, Anna and Catherine, who became nuns at St Maria der Engeln, Pfanneregg (near Wattwil), but later left the convent. One of them was married in Glarus. Ursula, wife of Liehnard Tremp of Berne, was almost certainly not, as is sometimes stated, a third sister. Andrew died in 1520 at Glarus, James died in 1517 as a student at Vienna. ZWA IV, 21–6; Z I, 391. Farner, I, 71–5.

[2] Bullinger, *Ref.* I, 6. Heinrich Bullinger, whose eldest daughter Anna married Zwingli's son Ulrich, succeeded as chief pastor (Antistes, a word used only once by Zwingli) in 1531 and late in life wrote *Historia oder Geschichten, so sich verlouffen in der Eydgnoschaft, insonders zů Zürych mit enderung der Religion, und anrichten Christenlicher Reformation, von dem Jar Christi 1519 bis in das Jar 1532*. He wrote from personal knowledge, assiduously collected local evidence and quoted original documents. He was naturally concerned above all to place his predecessor in as favourable a light as possible. There are a few obvious errors of fact and some significant omissions. A critical appraisal of the *Reformationsgeschichte* could be of great value.

conventional grouping which came to mean what school and college examinations were to mean later, was something inescapable even if not always relevant. Grammar, dialectic, rhetoric; music, astronomy, arithmetic, geometry – the names never vary and were the foundation of the 'arts' courses at the university.

After learning to construe, parse and write simple sentences, Ulrich's contemporaries were expected to proceed to dialectic or logic, the arrangement of an argument or exposition in standard form; and to rhetoric, the embellishment of simple prose. The semi-mathematical disciplines of the quadrivium were supposed to be useful for reckoning dates, including Easter, for grasping the movements of heavenly bodies and for understanding the notation of the choral services. Basically, however, for Zwingli to be put on the road to the university, a working knowledge of Latin, written and spoken, which he could hardly acquire at Weesen, was indispensable.

At the age of ten or under, Zwingli was transferred to the care of a distant relative, Gregory Bünzli, also from Weesen, who lived in the suburb of Basle, Kleinbasel, across the river.[1] There, for two years, he received further and more regular schooling and saw something of the Carthusian monastery with its renowned library. Then, probably in 1496, the lad was moved to Berne, where the learned young Heinrich Wölfflin (Lupulus, the little wolf) had the reputation of being the best schoolmaster south of Strassburg.[2] He was also a musician who could not fail to notice the special talent of his new pupil; he was something of a humanist, and he had travelled to the orient. Environment may not seem influential at thirteen, and for the young Zwingli Wildhaus in the country was home. But he was no longer a country boy; he was literate, and he was becoming acquainted with city life. Berne was to feature considerably in his later life, and it was well that he knew thus early something of its proud and turbulent background.[3] This fortified walled city on the bend of the Aar, with less than 5000 inhabitants, was also at the extreme western boundary of the diocese of Constance, and its territory spilled over into the dioceses of Basle, Lausanne and Sion (Sitten).

From a consciously founded artificial new town built by Berthold of Zähringen in 1191, it had become a free imperial city, rough and small perhaps, but by consistent relentless pressure the centre of a powerful political group. Bit by bit the countryside had been dominated, and when the young Zwingli was there in 1496–8, the boundaries of Berne marched with those of Schwyz and Uri. Burgundy had been defeated, some of the Vaud already occupied, there were shared rights in Aargau, and to the south

[1] ZWA XI, 317-18.
[2] Z VII, 534 n. 10. He wrote some verses in praise of his former pupil after Zwingli's death.
[3] See below Chapter 10.

a moving frontier with Savoy. There were also strained relations with the chieftains of the valleys of Valais.

The new boy was welcomed by Wölfflin, and seems to have liked the place and the people, in spite of an unfamiliar dialect. We know almost nothing of his studies there, but there is good testimony that a serious effort was made to persuade him to become a Friar Preacher. From the thirteenth century onwards the leaders of the Dominicans had constantly kept prominently in mind the need to recruit promising material while young: complaints of enticing or kidnapping boys had been heard often before. Choral services were also generally being developed in large collegiate churches like that of St Vincent's, Berne. For the Dominicans to secure an intelligent scholar who could sing well and had a real talent for music[1] was an opportunity not to be missed.

It would not be an enclosed life in a secluded monastery cut off from the world that they offered, for the Dominicans lived by begging, preaching and hearing confessions in the towns, although by the sixteenth century they were popularly regarded as monks, Religious. They nearly succeeded in their attempts, and there is a distinct possibility that Ulrich was received as a novice. News of this was heard in Wildhaus by his parents and by his uncle with marked disapproval. They were not prepared to lose him to a Bernese friary of not very good reputation. If a church career was now resolved upon, it must be as a secular. The approach must be the normal one through a university, supported if possible by a benefice, then ordination and employment, maybe, as a chantry priest until a parochial cure of souls was available. And so Ulrich was recalled.

It is notable that we know so little about the young Zwingli; there are a few casual references implying normality, but no child psychologist has turned with profit to elaborate the scraps of information available into a convincing explanation of his later mental development.

None the less, the fourteen years between 1484 and 1498 cannot be left on one side as irrelevant: home, parentage, environment, upbringing, are too significant for that, and, in fact, reflections of these appear in the most unlikely places in Zwingli's writings. Relatively well-to-do parents and a stable home background; this he both received and provided for his own children when he lived in a considerable house in Zurich. He never lost his country accent and he wrote naturally in the vigorous Swiss-German of his native Toggenburg, disliked and despised by speakers of good high German like Luther. In addition to the local dialect, Zwingli knew from

[1] ZWA IV, 355–6. Zwingli became later a talented instrumentalist. He once said, 'I know something of the lute and the fiddle, and this is useful in trying to put the children to sleep.' Z V, 54–5; C. Garside, *Zwingli and the Arts* (New Haven, 1966), 9–10, 15, 68. H. Reimann, 'Huldrych Zwingli – der Musiker', *Archiv für Musikwissenschaft* 17 (1960), 126–41 collects a number of references and discusses Zwingli's later rejection of musical services in church.

the closest personal contact his people and their way of life. He often spoke of himself as a peasant or farmer, exaggerating, perhaps deliberately, his rough breeding and ancestry. He was well equipped to understand the needs and outlook of the 'common man'. There were few birds that he did not know by sight and by note, few animals whose feeding, breeding and characteristics he could not expound accurately and fully, few crops he could not identify at a glance, knowing whence the seed came, how it was sown and gathered. He could use earthly metaphors and comparisons with telling exactitude, and he loved the countryside. Again and again he alludes to the conventional virtues of the countryman – simplicity, honesty, fair dealing, hard work, rough fare and trusting faith. What he knew of the relatively narrow world of his boyhood he later applied to his countrymen as a whole. If the Swiss people would but be satisfied with their milk and cheese and not call for dainty victuals, delicate luxuries, elaborate clothes, ornaments, jewels, silks, tapestries, carriages, then they could stand alone. They did not, and should not, need foreign gold and the corrupting luxuries of France and Italy. Such patriotism – for Zwingli can truly be reckoned one of the first of Swiss patriots in the best sense of that overworked word – was comparatively rare. It was almost incomprehensible to the Italians, although Machiavelli might have understood.

All roads led to Rome, and the Pope of the eleven impressionable years between eight and nineteen was the Borgia Alexander VI (1492–1503), whose son Cesare was ever ready to seduce Swiss soldiers to die for the consolidation of the Papal States. As a scholarly young man anxious to improve his knowledge of the external world by contact with travellers, Zwingli can hardly have failed to hear something of the extravagant exhibitionism of the Renaissance Popes and of the drain of money and men southwards. There was danger that the Swiss soil might not be tilled and the hard labour of field and vineyard might be neglected if men left their homeland. Perhaps if he had lived in the harsh highlands of Unterwalden and if he had heard his brothers and sisters cry for bread, his feelings might have been different.

For Zwingli, it was the tightly-knit community of a Swiss valley where every man knew his neighbour, where cooperation was essential for survival and where the leadership of the more prosperous element was taken for granted, that formed the basis of society. Such was the *Gemeinde*, in ecclesiastical terms the parish, with priest, church and common worship; and this, too, was to be the basic unit of the Zwinglian religious organisation much later. Zwingli had, as we have seen, relatives among the Swiss clergy. The village church with its ceremonial, ornaments and obligations had been there all the time, and the boy absorbed all the usual Catholic dogma without, apparently, any difficulty or questioning. In some of the more remote townships usages, and even books, which reflected a much earlier tradition could be found, and later he remembered some of these. In his neighbourhood, too, there were semi-hereditary ecclesiastical families of whom he saw something. Everyone knew that by paying an appreciable annual sum to the bishop's official at Constance, a priest might cohabit with his housekeeper and raise a family without further action being taken. Some might disapprove, but the whole issue aroused little feeling. Church attendance was in practice compulsory; mass was said and heard regularly; the seven sacraments were known and available; confession, if infrequent, could not be omitted. The church as a building was the only place where the whole community could meet under cover, and there was no hesitation about using it, and also about maintaining, adorning and improving it.

There might be criticism of some practices; the payment of tithe was felt to be burdensome and possibly misapplied; the exactions of the archdeacon in the church court were unpopular; the resort to distant Constance for so many purposes connected with wills, contracts, oaths and matters matrimonial was disliked, but none of these things affected acceptance of not only the creeds but also transubstantiation, the resort to the shrines and relics of the saints, whose intercession on behalf of their devotees was expected, the elaborate ceremonial of the church services, pilgrimages and even payments for crusades or indulgences. Ulrich Zwingli grew up in a stable, conventional environment even if a New World was discovered when he was eight and French troops permanently altered the balance of power in Italy when he was twelve or thirteen.

In the autumn of 1498 'Udalricus Zwinglij de Glaris' paid over the money required to have his name so written in the matriculation roll of the University of Vienna. Against this entry in another hand is the one word *exclusus*, 'sent down'. That this refers to our Ulrich is reasonably certain, and from the brief notice some secure deductions can be drawn,[1] while speculation naturally enough has been busy about the addition. Glarus, one of the Swiss states which protected and helped to administer his home, was a natural enough designation of place of origin, about which medieval Registrars were properly curious but not unduly concerned.

Long, lanky, eager boys were moving towards many university cities in 1498: the wandering scholar was a well-known phenomenon, and some, like Johann Butzbach[2] and Thomas, John and Felix Platter,[3] have left

---

[1] *ZWA* II, 466–71, XII, 167 n. 10.
[2] *Des Johannes Butzbach Wanderbüchlein. Chronika eines fahrenden Schülers...übersetzt von D. J. Becker* (Leipzig, n.d., c. 1924). An English version is *The Autobiography of Johannes Butzbach, a wandering scholar of the fifteenth century*, translated by R. F. Seybolt and P. Monroe (Ann Arbor, 1933).
[3] Thomas Platter (c. 1499–1582) was employed at the age of eight as a goat-herd in Valais. He became a wandering scholar, wrote an entertaining, if not entirely reliable, autobiography,

moving accounts of their experiences. They travelled on foot but in company: no one would be foolish enough to move about alone across central Europe, for he would be unlikely to get far without being relieved of his purse and clothes by robbers and outlaws. The potential student was treated as what he usually technically was, a cleric. From monastery to monastery, inn to inn, accompanied by someone who had moved over the ground previously, a boy begged or paid his way to the walls of the town which contained a *studium generale*.

These international institutions had multiplied fast in the second half of the fifteenth century; in Germany alone, Trier (1454), Greifswald (1456), Freiburg (1456), Pressburg (1465), Basle (1460), Ingolstadt (1459), Mainz (1476), Tübingen (1477), Wittenberg (1502) and Frankfurt-on-the-Oder (1506), indicated how the tide was running. The alternative to a German university was one of the older Italian *studia* where, in any case, the study of civil law was likely to predominate, or the mother University of Paris, where theology and scholastic philosophy flourished exceedingly. Paris was far distant, the French king talked of war with the Emperor, the German 'nation' at that university was falling in numbers and prestige. A north Italian university, Pavia especially, had its attractions but scarcely offered advantages that would appeal to an intelligent country lad from Wildhaus who had no intention of joining the legal fraternity.

Vienna was a fine city, and the university founded there in 1365 by Rudolf IV stressed both in its statutes and its practice the philosophical studies of the Faculty of Arts.[1] Thanks to the early recruitment from Paris of Heinrich von Langenstein, it was 'modern' in the technical sense, and some attention was paid to 'poetry', elegant Latinity, after Thomas Ebendorfer of Haselbach (d. 1464) had been Rector.

Humanism, as represented by Aeneas Sylvius Piccolomini, had made an early appearance there, and the cult of Ciceronianism was forwarded by George Peuerbach.[2] Students could also meet Conrad Celtes (d. 1508), the exponent of the latest theories of the art of elegant expression and indefatigable producer of Latin verse. Celtes also appealed to a kind of incipient German nationalism; he edited the early dramatic effusions of the nun, Roswitha of Gandersheim, and was the first to draw attention to the *Germania* of Tacitus. One of his missions in life was the formation of

was taught by Myconius and himself taught Greek in Basle as well as correcting proofs for the press. An English version appeared as *The autobiography of Thomas Platter, a schoolmaster of the sixteenth century*. Translated...by [Elizabeth Anne McCaul afterwards Finn] (London, 1839). The standard edition is *Thomas Platter, Lebensbeschreibung* hg. v. Alfred Hartmann (Basle, 1944). Cf. *Thomas und Felix Platter. Zur Sittengeschichte des* XVI. *Jahrhunderts* bearb. v. H. Boos (Leipzig, 1878).

[1] R. Kink, *Geschichte der kaiserlichen Universität zu Wien*, 2. Bde. (Vienna, 1854), with documents and statutes.

[2] A. Lhotsky, *Die Wiener Artistenfakultät 1365-1497* (Vienna, 1965), 133-60.

literary societies; he was chairman of the *Sodalitas literaria Danubiana*, to which the young were much attracted, and where the plays of Terence and Plautus were produced to admiring if somewhat bewildered audiences. A new approach to geography and mathematics had already been made by Johann Müller of Königsberg (Regiomontanus) and Johann Cuspinian. There was a good university library,[1] which admitted printed texts as early as 1474, and a printing press was in operation by 1492. These slightly unusual features should not disguise the fact that here was a perfectly normal university institution of its age, with the higher faculties of medicine, law and theology in full operation, with chancellor, conservator, rector, nations, proctors, privileges, endowments and degrees. It was normal also in the immorality, superstition and traditionalism which were surface features here, as elsewhere.

In Vienna the young Glarner almost certainly lodged, as possibly did his cousin, Joseph Forrer, in a small, cooperatively run student residence where he was obliged to keep regular hours and always speak Latin. Two close friends were his fellow-countrymen, Arbogast Strub[2] and Joachim Vadian.[3] The latter, of almost exactly Zwingli's own age, came from a wealthy family of linen-merchants of St Gall. In later life, as humanist, geographer, medical practitioner, politician and religious reformer, he showed a breadth of interests and scholarship in which he was surpassed in Switzerland only by Erasmus and Zwingli himself. They all owed something to an Italian Franciscan humanist, Giovanni Ricuzzi Vellini from Padua, and they were all exposed to the scholasticism of the 'via antiqua', the 'realism' of Aquinas and Duns Scotus.[4] Vienna was an exciting place.

Whether, or why, or for how long, Zwingli was rusticated from the University, or whether he left of his own accord, is uncertain. He returned in 1500 and re-matriculated.[5] The Swabian war had intensified passions, and there may well have been a Swiss–German fracas, and some cooling-off period imposed as a result. There is much force in the argument that had there been any serious lapse Zwingli's later enemies would not have

---

[1] Walter Pongratz, *Geschichte der Universitätsbibliothek* (Studien zur Geschichte der Universität Wien) Bd. 1 (Graz-Köln, 1965).

[2] His promising career was cut short by his early death on 15 August 1510. Z VII, 5 n. 2; E. Brandstätter, *Arbogast Strub* (St Gall, 1955), 14–22.

[3] Näf, *Vadian*, supplemented by *Vadian-Studien, Untersuchungen und Texte* hg. v. W. Näf (St Gall, 1945–); H. Ammann, *Die Diesbach-Watt-Gesellschaft* (St Gall, 1928); W. Näf, *Die Familie von Watt* (St Gall, 1936).

[4] C. Bonorand, *Die Bedeutung der Universität Wien für Humanismus und Reformation, insbesondere in der Ostschweiz*, ZWA XII (1965), 162–80, and *Aus Vadians Freundes-und Schülerkreis in Wien* (St Gall, 1965) where the university friendship of Zwingli and Vadian is shown to be inferential only; W. Koehler, *Die Geisteswelt Ulrich Zwinglis* (Gotha, 1920), 15–18.

[5] Egli *4*, 8–10.

failed to give it publicity, nor would he have matriculated for a second time in 1500, even if he did not stay long.

There is no documentary evidence about the young man's movements in 1500–1; from insignificant passing remarks of later years, it is possible, but rather unlikely, that he visited Paris, Cologne and Tübingen.[1] He certainly continued his studies before moving to the most convenient and obvious university of one born in the diocese of Constance, Basle. Here, during the rectorate of Johannes Wentz (May–October 1502), 'Udalricus Zwingling de Liechtensteig' matriculated, paying the usual six shillings.[2] How he supported himself during these years is a matter of conjecture; later in life he reminisced a little about begging for lodging and being refused,[3] and there is better evidence that he earned some money by teaching Latin at the school attached to St Martin's Church, Basle.

At eighteen his real life began within the walls of the 'incomparable Basle', imperial city, seat of a bishop and centre of a patrician-ruled state which only in the previous year had decided to cast in its lot for all time with the Swiss Confederation. It can scarcely have been strange territory; he had been there as a boy, among his earlier teachers had been the Basle graduate, Gregory Bünzli, and its renown was considerable. There had been a General Council of the church there within living memory before the University of Basle had opened its doors to 122 members in April 1460.

There were many and obvious advantages in founding the first, and for long the only, Swiss university in Basle. Communications, most obviously by water along the river Rhine, were easy; there was the security provided by the city walls, there were wealthy citizens and powerful gilds; there was a cathedral, collegiate churches, hospitals, monasteries and mendicant establishments. The university, as it were, added another dimension to the already pullulating clerical population there. There were grammar schools (for boys of course) attached to St Peter's Cathedral and to St Leonhard's, and there was an intelligent and sometimes literate citizenry. There were libraries at the cathedral and in the Charterhouse across the river, as well as manuscripts owned privately. There were also scribes and illuminators who prepared the ground for the printers who could find the indispensable paper on the spot, since the first paper mill had started work in Kleinbasel in 1440.[4] There were block-cutters, book-binders, painters of saints,

---

[1] ZWA III, 414–17; Koehler, Buch, 14; F. Büsser, Die Erforschung der Reformation in der deutschen Schweiz. NZZ 7 November 1971, No. 519 p. 53.
[2] H. G. Wackernagel, Die Matrikel der Universität Basel, I. Bd. (Basle, 1951), 266.
[3] On his way home via Innsbruck and Lindau in the winter of 1502, but this probably meant little more than might failure to 'thumb a lift' to a twentieth-century counterpart. The episode was recorded in a note, now lost, in the margin of his copy of Josephus. Koehler, NZZ No. 2145, 4 December 1938; Farner I, 184; Koehler, Zwingli, 19.
[4] Wackernagel, Basel II, 2, 604.

calendars and cards; and Mainz, the cradle of printing, was conveniently situated down the river. It was from there, probably, that Berthold Ruppel had brought the new art before 1467, and this was to bring scholarship with it. The early printers were their own publishers and correctors; at Basle they had what they needed – men with capital, a good distribution centre and specialists at the university who could help to ensure accurate texts.

The presence, among others, of John Heynlin, Sebastian Brant and the expert in Hebrew, John Reuchlin, was invaluable to Froben, who became a citizen in 1490 and printed in 1491. He was followed by the brothers Petri and the cultivated Amerbach family of scholar-printers. Printing was to be to the glory of God, the spread of knowledge of the kingdom of heaven and the regeneration of Christendom, as well as a new, profit-making enterprise.

When Zwingli reached Basle, the university with the usual four faculties was small but securely founded, the printing presses were active, and the name of Erasmus was already known within the city which was to be the chief centre of his future activities. In later years it was Erasmus who was to be the most influential of living scholars for Zwingli, and it was the printing press which was to make the reputation and to extend the fame of both. In Switzerland, as in Germany, the press was to be indispensable for publicity as well as for accurate and speedy duplication.

The curriculum at Basle in 1500 was still dominated by 'the master of those who know', Aristotle. Aquinas had shown how the Aristotelian texts could be reconciled with scriptural revelation, and out of this synthesis came 'scholasticism'. The study of the liberal arts, obligatory upon all before proceeding to law, medicine or theology, had become almost ex-clusively an exercise in logic, culminating in the verbal dexterities of 'quodlibet' and 'determination'. The relations of faith and knowledge, authority and reason, dogma and opinion, certainty, inference and deduc-tion, were never allowed to be far from the mind of the medieval student. Discussions still went on over the unending problem of the nature of 'universals', of the relationship of facts and words, of realities and ab-stractions. Thus had developed in the arts faculties the dichotomy of realists and nominalists, Thomists and Occamists, later even fancifully aligned with Latins and Teutons. The new University of Basle certainly could not escape the prevailing passion for argumentation and taking sides. The modern 'way' was that of the Nominalists, the ancient that of the Realists, and there was no third 'way' yet of reconciliation.[1]

---

[1] G. Ritter, *Studien zur Spätscholastik* II: *Via antiqua und via moderna auf den deutschen Universitäten des XV. Jahrhunderts* (Sitzungsberichte der Heidelberger Akademie der Wissenschaften, philosophisch-historische Klasse) (Heidelberg, 1922).

Basle was a border city between France and Germany and a border university between realist and modernist. Each school of thought, it was arranged, might be represented by four professors, and thus the path of progress through the philosophical faculty to the highest of all, that of theology, could be by either school of teaching. At first it seemed as if the nominalist influences, deriving from the University of Erfurt (which was so powerfully to influence Luther) might predominate. This was prevented by the arrival of a man who combined conviction with exposition and personality with great ability, John Heynlin von Stein[1] (de Lapide), who had studied at Louvain, Tübingen and Paris and secured a permanent place for his ideas within the recognised curriculum. His eloquent sermons were long remembered, and his excellent library went first to the Carthusians and later to the University. He was supported and followed by others – Geiler of Kaisersberg, Christopher of Utenheim, Matthias of Gengenbach, Sebastian Brant, among them, while John Reuchlin became a leading representative of the nominalists.

The young Zwingli may have picked up from his Vienna days some comprehension of at any rate the existence of such schools of thought, just as a student of a later age would know of a Marxist or Whig interpretation of history without being able fully to define either. To some extent the considerations involved in these debates about universals were to endure throughout his life. What was 'substance'? What was 'reality'? What was the meaning of 'real'? What lay behind words and names? Was nominalism basic to Lutheranism, realism to Zwinglianism?[2] At any rate both sides of a fundamental division of opinion could be heard at Basle. Further, in addition to the commonplace disputes of the schoolmen there was the new learning of the humanists confronting the old learning of scholasticism. Basle offered access to this as well.

Two figures had been seen in the Basle streets while the theologians of Eugenius IV were conducting the debates of the oecumenical council – Aeneas Sylvius Piccolomini and Poggio Bracciolini. One of the many qualities which secured the papacy for Aeneas was the elegance of his Latinity, ability to use a language recognisably similar to that of the age of

---

[1] M. Hossfeld, *Johannes Heynlin aus Stein*. BasZG, Bd. 6 (1907), 309–356; Bd. 7 (1908), 79–219, 235–431.

[2] Zwingli, who read and annotated Duns Scotus' Commentary on the Sentences of Peter Lombard (*Quaestiones super quatuor libris sententiarum* (Venice, 1503) very carefully, was a man of the *via antiqua*, well acquainted with Aquinas. Essentially Aristotelian in outlook, he was later often regarded as a rationalist because he was not prepared, as the 'modernists' were, to despise reason and to see the wisdom of God as necessarily incomprehensible to the human intellect. One conviction remained with him as a result of his philosophical training at Basle – a material thing could not have, induce or bring about, an intellectual or spiritual operation. Luther's different nominalist and 'modernist' training at Erfurt accounts in some degree for later differences.

Virgil and Cicero. Poggio dredged Europe for new classical texts and helped to give the learned world something new to bite upon. Clerics and business men from Basle could hardly avoid visits to Italy, where, too, the sons of some of the wealthy patricians had studied, and both learnt something of the ferment in Rome, Florence and Pavia. They trusted their new university to be 'with' the newest thought, and among the handful of lecturers who were there from the beginning was one whose appointment was 'in poetrye'.[1] In 1464, that 'most elegant professor of Poetry', Peter Luder, the peripatetic exponent of versification from Heidelberg, had expounded classical literature in the intervals of acting as medical adviser to the city. Although there was no professor of Greek until 1538,[2] Luder was succeeded by others who found some hearers for lectures on 'eloquence' in the new cult of Ciceronian Latinity. There was Sebastian Brant (1458–1521), who saw no incongruity in combining attention to style with lectures on civil law. He is indeed remembered chiefly for a rather slight piece of satire, the *Ship of Fools*, which caught the imagination of the age and was translated into Latin by Locher and illustrated with woodcuts by Dürer. If his other verse contributions were mediocre in the extreme, he was still a precursor of better exponents in the future.

Although there was no place for the study of Greek within the lecture-framework of the fifteenth-century university, even here supply was followed by demand. John Reuchlin of Pfortzheim (1455–1522), who matriculated in 1474, had already shown singular linguistic aptitude, and at eighteen had started learning Greek at Paris from fellow students who had themselves picked up a little there from Gregory of Tiferno. He now discovered, living in Basle, a Greek, Andronicus Kontoblatas, otherwise unknown, who offered the equivalent of 'extra mural' classes in classical Greek, perhaps to only two pupils, one of whom was Wessel Gansfort.[3] Good Ciceronian Latin, active versification, rudimentary Greek, the cult of the ancient world – through these, the University of Basle was tinged, we may say, with the Renaissance earlier than any other German seat of learning. Even the study of law was affected, and with some special emphasis on civil law went a renewed contact with Italian scholars, for whom Rome meant the centre of classical learning and memories.

Here, from 1502 to 1506, Zwingli learnt his Aristotelian texts, repeated exercises, argued and 'distinguished' in scholastic fashion with a small number of fellow scholars and teachers. He also understood that the round earth was the centre of the universe. Around it circled the stars in *primum mobile* and above this the heaven, *coelum empireum*, where Christ sat at the right hand of God

[1] E. Bonjour, *Die Universität Basel von den Anfängen bis zur Gegenwart* (Basle, 1960), 95.
[2] Bonjour, *Universität*, 124.   [3] Bonjour, *Universität*, 97.

God to remove his wayes from human sense,
Plac'd Heav'n from Earth so farr, that earthly sight,
If it presume, might erre in things too high,
And no advantage gaine.

Later in life, like many another of his generation, he made fun of the narrow, twisted and conventional learning of the schools. He rightly scorned the slavish adherence to prescribed authority, the needless logic, the meaningless struggles about the implications of words and phrases, the readiness to propose subjects for debate and to answer any put forward by others. The aim was triumph according to the rules of the logical game, not increase of knowledge or attention to truth. All this, of course, was in Latin. Any successful inceptor in arts had a verbal fluency in this language, which he spoke as well as wrote. It was scarcely necessary for a scholar to know anything else. To the Basle student the French language was a closed book.

While he laughed at the '*sophisterey*' of his university training, Zwingli was later to make good use of it. The milestones along the road to the Reformation in Switzerland were marked by the public debates which invariably preceded action. For such exercises, a good memory, quick perception, lucidity of explanation and above all the ability to point out the inadequacies of the other side were invaluable assets. And these were just the qualities that the years in the faculty of Arts at Basle taught the rapidly maturing young man. He was much attracted by what he heard of the scholarship of John Heynlin, and he learnt something from John Gebwiler[1] (c. 1450–1530) from Colmar. More influential was Thomas Wittenbach[2] of Biel (1472–1526) who came to Basle from Tübingen in 1505. The breadth of his knowledge and the unusual grace of his diction evidently fascinated his younger hearers. His lectures in the Faculty of Theology on the New Testament, and particularly on the Epistle to the Romans, were striking, but there can be no certainty that Zwingli, whose biblical knowledge was then sketchy, heard them.

Among Zwingli's contemporaries were Conrad Schmid from Küssnacht,[3] Caspar Grossmann (Megander) and probably Conrad Grebel. There was also John Dignauer, who invited him to his 'promotion' feast in 1514 and who later became preacher at Winterthur and Kilchberg.[4] From Alsace came Leo Keller (1482–1542) better known as Leo Jud. He was of Jewish extraction, the son of a catholic priest and intended

---

[1] Wackernagel, *Matrikel* I, 78–9.
[2] Z v, 718–20, VIII, 84–9. Little certain is known of him.
[3] ZWA II, 65–73.
[4] Z VII, 30 n. 1; Wackernagel, *Matrikel* I, 262; K. M. Sieber, *Die Universität Basel und die Eidgenossenschaft 1460 bis 1529* (Basle, 1960), 71.

at first to be a student of medicine. He was ordained, succeeded Zwingli at Einsiedeln and followed him to Zurich in 1519.[1] Either while he was in residence or shortly after, Zwingli came into contact with the humanist group in Basle which included Beatus Rhenanus,[2] Heinrich Loriti,[3] Conrad Pellican,[4] Conrad Zwick and Caspar Hedio.[5]

With Thomas Wittenbach Zwingli may have discussed the nature of the authority of the Pope and validity of indulgences, but the evidence for this is flimsy; later in life, certainly, Zwingli believed he owed much to these conversations.[6] There is also some likelihood that Wittenbach first suggested to Zwingli that he must learn Greek if he would read the New Testament and the church Fathers in the original. Again, it can have been no more than a passing suggestion. Zwingli was indeed disappointed with the logic-chopping that accompanied his Aristotelian studies, and his knowledge of the two 'ways' of university thought left him working things out for himself, but even in 1506 he had not seriously applied himself to any biblical, still less patristic, studies, and for these latter, Augustine and Jerome in particular, there was much yet to be read and assimilated in Latin.[7]

[1] Z I, 529, V, 718–20, VII, 119–20, X, 201–9; ZWA II, 161–6, 198–208. The biography by C. Pestalozzi, *Leo Judä* (Elberfeld, 1860), needs revision; and L. Weisz, *Leo Jud, Ulrich Zwinglis Kampfgenosse 1482–1542* (Zürich, 1942), adds little to it.

[2] Beat Bild (1485–1547) from Schlettstadt where his library remains. He actively assisted Amerbach and Froben in their publishing activities and corresponded with Erasmus. Allen II, 60–1; *Briefwechsel des Beatus Rhenanus* hg. v. A. Horawitz u. K. Hartfelder (Leipzig, 1886).

[3] 1488–1563. Known from his birthplace, Mollis, in Glarus, as Glarean. He was M.A. (Cologne) 1510, crowned 'poet' by Maximilian 1512, taught in Basle, Paris and Freiburg and was one of Zwingli's earliest correspondents. His best known publication was the versified *Helvetiae Descriptio* (1511, 1515), geographical and historical, highly 'patriotic' in its implications. His knowledge of the classics matched Zwingli's. Glarean remained a Catholic. Allen II, 279; Z VII, 1.

[4] 1478–1556. Franciscan and Hebrew scholar. He assisted Froben in 1516, was professor of theology at Basle in 1523, taught Hebrew at Zurich from 1526, married, and published Bible commentaries. ZWA II (1908), 193–8; Allen VI, 207–8.

[5] 1494–1552. M. A. Freiburg 1516. He was impressed by Zwingli's preaching at Einsiedeln, came to Basle in 1517 and taught theology there from 1519. He later moved to Strassburg. Z VII, 213; Wackernagel, *Matrikel* I, 332.

[6] 1472–1526, Farner, I, 230–3; Z VIII, 84 n. 1; Z V, 718–20; ADB (44), 434–6; H. Türler, 'Dr. Thomas Wyttenbach 1472–1526', *Bieler Jahrbuch 1927* (Biel, 1927) 107–29 esp. 113–15. Wackernagel *Basel* III, 320. Wittenbach later became the reformer of Biel.

[7] There existed across the river, connected somewhat irregularly with the Carthusian monastery, a Basle Literary Society (*Sodalitas Literaria Basiliensis*), a private association which included John Heynlin, John Ulrich Surgant and the printers Froben and Amerbach. Little is known of its meetings, but that Zwingli was present is more than probable. Surgant was best known for his book of advice to preachers *Manuale Curatorum*, frequently reprinted (e.g. at Basle in 1502). He set out the faults the successful preacher will avoid, stressed the importance of the sermon and urged the need for instruction in faith, the avoidance of sin, preparation for death, and personal devotion.

The introductory Greek grammar that was then available in Basle was the *Erotemata*, which had been printed in 1478, and, with his thoughts already towards the fashionable humanism, it may have been in his hands.[1] Zwingli was 'baccalaureus' on 18 September 1504, and early in 1506 was 'promoted' master of arts. His path was now open to the study of theology,[2] the queen of the sciences. For law or medicine he manifestly had no inclination. He was now 22, a mature man by the standards of his age.

How he had been able to support himself for the previous seven or eight years is unknown: he was the only scholar in a family of ten or eleven; his brothers remained farmers, his two sisters became nuns (which required a dowry for each), so that parental help, while assuredly willingly available, cannot have been his sole support. He received a small sum charged on to St Peter's, Basle,[3] in addition to payments for teaching Latin; there are slight hints of begging, to which the age attached no stigma; and he had some pupils. At any rate, he paid his way, and almost immediately after being admitted to the society of the masters, just before the earliest canonical age, he sought ordination at the hands of the Bishop of Constance.

It was all perfectly normal and understandable: there was at least one clerical uncle to encourage his nephew, and the priesthood was almost the only career open for a master of arts. There were no seminaries at the beginning of the sixteenth century; the bishop's delegate assured himself that the baptised male applicant knew sufficient Latin and could repeat and understand the creeds, and was competent to say mass, hear confessions and perform the ceremonial duties to which he had in any case been accustomed all his life. Apart from the very youthful and transitory flirtation with the Bernese Dominican fathers, there was for Zwingli no suggestion of entering a cloister. The church almost alone provided a career and an income by which one with scholarly inclinations could hope to pursue his studies.

What was decisively fortunate was that Johann Stucki, the incumbent at Glarus, had died, and the benefice was available for Zwingli. Somewhat unusually, it was the local custom that the people of Glarus, which meant the leading males of the parish, could put forward the name of an accept-

---

[1] Zwingli claimed in 1523 that he had started to learn Greek 'ten years ago' (Z II, 147 and note 2), but the reckoning need not be taken too precisely. J. F. G. Goeters, *Zwinglis Werdegang als Erasmianer* (Reformation und Humanismus. Robert Stupperich zum 65. Geburtstag. Witten, 1969), 261.

[2] Bullinger *Ref.* I, 7 says explicitly that after he became master of arts he turned to theology; and F. Blanke, *Zwinglis Theologiestudium* (Theologische Blätter, 15. Jg. (Leipzig, 1936) coll. 94–5), notes that he could have studied in the Faculty of Theology for one term (cf. Z v, 719 n. 2), and have attended lectures on the *Sentences* of Peter Lombard.

[3] Z VII, 12 n. 3.

able rector.[1] In practice, apparently, the matter was arranged through a kind of broker or intermediary (known in England as 'chopchirche'). It was almost a business transaction and for everyone concerned a perfectly normal start on an ecclesiastical career.

[1] The right of the Glarus *Gemeinde* to choose a priest was asserted by J. M. Schuler, *Geschichte des Landes Glarus* (Zürich, 1836), 139, on inadequate evidence. Stumpf 2, II, 187 clearly implies a local choice. Zwingli's 'supplication' to Julius II (4 September 1506) is printed in ZSK 51 (1957), 34-5.

2

Parish priest: Glarus and Einsiedeln

For ten years, 1506–1516, Zwingli was parish priest of the little town of Glarus.[1] Most Swiss towns were no larger than some English or French villages; and Glarus, although the capital of an independent state (*Ort*), was simply a small rural market town of less than 2000 inhabitants. If it was fortunate to have attracted the services of a master of arts from Basle, Zwingli was at least equally fortunate to secure such a living when only 23 and without pastoral experience. Many of his contemporaries waited much longer before obtaining a cure of souls like this with a house and a guaranteed income.

Family influence, after the habit of the age, had much to do with it. The same uncle, Bartholomew, who had been responsible for much of his nephew's education, and was rural dean at Weesen, as such was able to put forward a name in the proper quarters. It is also not unlikely that the suggestion was supported by Zwingli's former tutor, Gregory Bünzli, who was also influential in the neighbourhood. Further, an arrangement had to be made with a well-known citizen of Zurich, Heinrich Göldli,[2] who was one of the many pluralists of the day and who had to be compensated for loss of his expectancy to the benefice.

The incoming minister had hardly started the study of theology at the university, and may well not have intended to continue it. This, however, was quite usual – the universities habitually themselves sent lists of recommended students to Rome, expecting graduates from the faculty of arts to be provided with benefices. It was not until the Council of Trent, sixty years later, paid attention to the problem of clergy-training, that the

[1] There is little to add to the monograph of G. Heer, *Ulrich Zwingli als Pfarrer von Glarus* (Zürich, 1884).
[2] Heinrich Göldli (or Göldlin), a natural son of one of the canons of the Great Minster, was a canon of Embrach and parish priest of Baden, and held the offices of equerry, chamberlain and attendant to the Pope. His services to Rome had been rewarded by the grant of eight 'reservations', benefices which were at his disposition if falling vacant in an 'odd' month. Glarus happened to fall into this category, and Zwingli agreed to pay Göldli 10 gulden annually for the renunciation of his rights. This may have been dangerously close to simony. Z VII, 479 n. 4; Farner I, 243, 247. O. Vasella, *Die Wahl Zwinglis als Leutpriester von Glarus*. ZSK 51 (1957), 27–35.

seminary system came into operation. As a university student, Zwingli had, along with the others, received a formal token snip of the hair which made him a clerk, *clericus*. This, however, did not mean admission even to the minor orders of doorkeeper, exorcist, reader and acolyte which preceded ordination as subdeacon, then deacon and priest. Any bishop, but only a bishop, could confer the sacrament of Orders; it was, indeed, one of the chief episcopal prerogatives and was often performed by a suffragan bishop after the payment of the appropriate fees to the bishop's Official. All the necessary ceremonies could be completed in one day, but the common practice was for the three Ember days after Holy Cross Day (14 September) to be used. This, apparently, was applied in Zwingli's case.[1]

There is no suggestion that Zwingli regarded his ordination as priest, with all the spiritual authority and power that this implied, as anything more than a routine requirement. The teaching of the church had been known to him all his life; he was doing as his friends and relations had done, and even the intense moment of his first mass, at Wildhaus, on 29 September, seems to have aroused no special emotions. His first sermon was preached at Rapperswil. He knew what he was doing, just as later he knew equally well what he was criticising. For ten years he was a normal parish priest – saying mass every day, reading the services from the Breviary, hearing confessions, baptising, marrying, burying, taking the reserved sacrament to the sick while pious observers knelt and crossed themselves, taking part in processions, administering extreme unction to the dying. In all this, the young man had the help of three or four assistants, older presumably than himself. It was all quite nice, smug and unexceptional.

Glarus[2] was a place of some political importance. It was the capital of a state which had been accepted into the Confederation in 1352 on somewhat subordinate terms to Zurich and the three original 'Forest Cantons', but by 1456 it was fully integrated, taking precedence immediately after Zug.[3] There could not be a more typically Swiss assignment for a young man. There were relics[4] of St Fridolin and St Hilary in the parish church to be exhibited, there were boys to be taught to read, and there were

---

[1] If so, he was some four months short of the canonical age of 23. No record of his ordination, almost certainly at Constance, has been preserved.

[2] For an early enthusiastic and uncritical assessment see J. H. Tschudi, *Beschreibung des Lobl. Orths und Lands Glarus* (Zürich, 1714). J. Winteler, *Geschichte des Landes Glarus*, 2 Bde. (Glarus, 1952, 1954) I, 204–341.

[3] It also shared in the administration of the Mandated Territories (*eidgenössische Vogteien*), a matter of some importance later. Staehelin I, 44.

[4] There was an altar with an indulgence for prayers said before it; there were a few other relics and church bells newly cast from the bronze of Burgundian cannon captured in 1466. Koehler *Zwingli*, 29.

sermons to be preached, this in itself being a somewhat unusual activity for a parish priest. Although a state capital, Glarus could hardly have been more rural in habits and outlook. Cattle were the chief source of livelihood and of exchange, so it was as well that the new pastor was himself a countryman.

Glarus was a fighting state. It had helped to secure independence by sending the largest contingent to resist the Habsburg forces at Näfels (9 April 1388), and its inhabitants well understood that security implied vigilance and armed defence, and also that successful warfare was profitable. In the main street of the little town that was the young priest's new home there were strong, rough, violent men accustomed to bloodshed and to settling arguments with edged weapons; there were lots of children and some loose women, plenty of noise and smells, and hardly anyone who could read or write.

The new priest was determined to take his work seriously. While at Basle, he had already directed his thoughts towards the Bible, and now, markedly under the influence of the renowned and much-admired Erasmus, he was coming to appreciate for the first time the purity and simplicity of the Gospel narrative. His parishioners, including the inhabitants of three quite distant villages, were his spiritual children for whom he was answerable to God. Early in his incumbency, he arranged for some regular instruction in Latin to be available in Glarus by forming a small grammar school there.[1] There were already a few boys who had learnt their letters, and for these he arranged tuition in elementary Latin, probably by a chantry priest who charged fees for his services. Zwingli himself shared in this teaching, but with a heavy programme of private study added to his normal parish duties, which he did not neglect, he obviously could only devote limited time to it. He also prepared a few boys, such as Aegidius Tschudi, for the university.[2]

These years at Glarus were ones of deliberate and effective reading and reflection, in some respects the most fruitful part of his life, since he had, and made good use of, ample time and opportunity to devote himself to his books. In view of later events, it is worth noting that when the income from the indulgence-endowed relics in his Church allowed it, he forwarded the construction in 1510 of a special chapel for their suitable exposition. It is from the Glarus residence that we have the first letter[3] to

---

[1] G. Heer, 'Geschichte des höheren Schulwesens im Kanton Glarus' in JHVG 20 (1883), 1-49.
[2] Aegidius (Gilg) Tschudi (1505-72), who always remained a Catholic, became one of the first historians of the Confederation. Another member of the family and possible pupil, Valentin Tschudi (1499-1555), later also priest in Glarus, was highly appreciative of Zwingli's activity and example. H. Trümpy, *Glarner Studenten im Zeitalter des Humanismus* JHVG 55 (1952), 273-84. [3] Z VII, 1-4.

him that chance has preserved, written from Cologne on 13 July 1510 by Heinrich Loriti (Glarean). Among sixteenth century scholars letter-writing was very much a conscious form of linguistic exercise. Letters were written with a view, if not to publication in the modern sense, at least to wide circulation. They were a recognised way of demonstrating literary style as well as conveying information. They followed, rather carefully, certain conventions of presentation and can seldom be read as if they were entirely private and objective communications, as is shown by many references to additional, possibly even contradictory, information to be supplied by the messenger. Thus, conscious artificiality and serious gaps diminish the otherwise overriding interest of the letters. When, later, they deal less with literature and more with religion and politics, these limitations become more serious. The prince of sixteenth-century letter-writers was Erasmus, to whom the well-turned phrase came so easily and so naturally and who outrageously flattered his rich and powerful potential patrons in his letters while keeping careful copies of what he wrote. Zwingli did not, apparently, go as far as this, with the result that most of his own communications are lost: we have, as it were, many 'in' letters, without the replies.

In some ways this first surviving letter of 1510 tells us a good deal. Heinrich Loriti was then 22, four years Zwingli's junior. He was to live to be over seventy and was to remain a Catholic and an exile from the homeland that gave him his name, Henry of Glarus. For him already in 1510 Zwingli is *humanissimus*, devoted to letters, and their contact is about books. Troubles in Venice, he reports, make Ptolemy's works unobtainable in Cologne where he was studying. There are, however, some maps available, to which Portuguese discoveries have made significant additions. The writer is conscious of the desirability of knowing Greek, for which the grammar of Chrysoloras was still the standard text and almost the only one available. A pilgrimage to the ancient basilica and to the tomb of the unsaintly St Charles the Great at Aachen, in which Zwingli took part, is taken for granted as a natural exercise for a young man. Finally, he announces his desire to exchange Cologne beer for Basle water (and wine), proceeding to explain elaborately that the Cologne university course was 'modern', based on Duns Scotus, full of word-spinning and futile mockery. He preferred the 'old way' of Basle. With the letter, he sent a copy of some lyrics that he had written. He refers, like so many of his contemporaries, to Pico della Mirandola who was to influence his later thought, and indicates in passing that he does not wish to become Zwingli's immediate neighbour as parish priest of Mollis.[1]

A great many letters are like this, the writer dashing irrelevantly from

[1] Z VII, 1–4.

one literary topic to another, and they show us what the young men of the day were thinking about. 'Humanissime' – every indication is that during the years 1506 to 1510 any moment that could be spared from routine parish business was devoted by Zwingli to intense study, to reading and commenting upon such books as could be purchased for him in Basle or Germany. The Latin classics came first – Cicero, Virgil, Livy, Caesar, Pliny, Aulus Gellius, Valerius Maximus,[1] for certain. Like Erasmus and Colet, he admired and used the writings of Lactantius, the 'Christian Cicero', whom he regarded almost as a Father of the church and whose views on providence formed a basis for his later thought about predestination.[2] Zwingli had a young man's passion for buying books, which it was now possible to do, and he later defended his retention from 1515 of a papal pension[3] on the somewhat weak grounds that he used it for this purpose. Book-buying went on, and there was now time for deep study which was to be denied him later – the quiet years at Glarus and Einsiedeln were invaluable to one with so retentive a memory. After his death, most of his books were acquired from his widow for the Great Minster library, and a number, complete with his own marginal annotations, have never left Zurich. Koehler listed and analysed all that could be found of these books in an invaluable monograph,[4] but there were many more. Later in life, two thirds of what he kept were theological, but at Glarus the proportion was much more in favour of the Latin classics.

There was, almost inevitably, the newest edition of St Augustine's *City of God* printed at Basle in 1515 by Petri,[5] much annotated by Zwingli; there were the works of Jerome and Origen, Cyril of Alexandria, Gregory of Nazianzen and Chrysostom among the Fathers, all mixed with the Satires of Juvenal, Laurentius Valla's translation of Homer, the writings of Pico della Mirandola, Plutarch's Lives, the Quodlibeta of Duns Scotus and, significantly, practically everything published by Erasmus.[6] There was the early and unsatisfactory *Lexicon Graecum* of Suidas, and Reuchlin's *Rudimenta Hebraica*. Making every allowance for the conventions of the age, the nature and content of these books indicate an exceptionally studious and active mind. Peculiarly interesting is the book now in the Cantonal Library of Aarau, the Vulgate, printed apparently in 1479, and given by Zwingli to Hans Fries. There are many *marginalia*, but their attribution is uncertain. It is, however, a cause for reflection that the man

[1] He relied very closely on this writer for his knowledge of Roman history.
[2] ZWA XIII, 375–89. [3] See below, 76.
[4] This appeared, not easily accessible, in 1921 – Koehler, *Bibliothek*, 84 NblW (1921). For the marginalia, ZKG 40 (1922), 41–73, Bd. 42 (1923), 49–76, Bd. 45 (1926), 243–76.
[5] Eight volumes of the 1506 (Basle) edition of the writings of St Augustine were given him by John Froben. Below 64.
[6] J. Rogge, *Zwingli und Erasmus. Die Friedensgedanken des jungen Zwingli* (Stuttgart, 1962), 27–8.

who in later life was so often to proclaim with assurance that his teaching was not only exclusively Bible-based but easily deduced from the Bible, was himself diligently studying the Bible and the Fathers for some ten years without showing any public signs of repudiation of the traditional church interpretation thereof.

Apart from routine duties, the Glarus–Einsiedeln incumbency is almost entirely one of continuous humanist study. His correspondence is almost exclusively literary, and the fashionable exchanges with such scholars as Glarean, Vadian, William Nesen, Peter and Aegidius Tschudi, Peter Falck, Conrad Grebel and Erasmus himself, indicate where his interests lay. These fragmentary survivals of what must already have been quite a considerable correspondence are concerned mainly with poetry, Latin pronunciation, Aristotle, the study of Greek, and there are also some references to the University of Vienna. Wide reading and care for Latin style resulted in the acceptance of the young priest into the little learned group of northern humanists. He also took care to build up his knowledge of Greek which, while unusual,[1] was not as good as that of Erasmus who was himself no great Greek scholar. Then came the study of Hebrew, laying the foundations of his knowledge of that language which he was later to develop considerably.

What began as part of the emulation of fashionable youth, the desire and determination to be associated with the current interest in classical antiquities and linguistic elegance, became merged with biblical studies. Zwingli undoubtedly had linguistic ability and was conscious of his tri-lingual attainments. The gift of tongues was that of the Holy Spirit, and when, in later life, he pondered on the story of Pentecost, his easy ascendancy over many of his opponents in knowledge of Greek and Hebrew strengthened his conviction that he was among the elect.

There was thus a certain serene normality about the thirty years of his life which preceded fame and notoriety. The country-bred youth from the Toggenburg with his strong local accent, graduate, priest, scholar, humanist, interested in letters, in his countrymen, in his parishioners, thought deeply about his reading, his duties and the state of the church in the light of his increasingly intensive study of the Bible. There was a good deal to think about, the more so if he considered, as he did, the history and background of his own people. Where was the seat of government? What held his society together? The government of which the Emperor Maximilian was the head counted for little: such laws as there were rested on local traditions and customs, supplemented by federal agreements and enforced by councils, local administrators and officers, able to secure peace

---

[1] In 1519 he could be said to be 'Latinae linguae doctissimus, Graecae non indoctus...semigreculus'. Z VII, 141, 226.

and safety for person and property by the use, where necessary, of armed force. It was while Zwingli was at Glarus that the Swiss Confederation came to consist of the thirteen independent cooperating units that lasted until 1798. Appenzell was admitted as a full independent member (*ein vollberechtigte Ort*) on 17 December 1513,[1] in spite of the fact that it was surrounded on all sides by the lands of the Prince Abbot of St Gall. No one at the time could have perceived that this was the end of an era of expansion for the Confederation, least of all the parish priest of Glarus.

In 1513 Zwingli returned to his parsonage after direct involvement in war and politics in circumstances which powerfully affected alike his future career and his convictions. No thoughtful inhabitant of central Switzerland could be indifferent, at the opening of the sixteenth century, to the fate of northern Italy. Savoy, Milan and Venice provided markets, sources of supply and opportunities for trade to their northern neighbours. The claim of Louis XII of France to be the lawful ruler of Milan was disputed by the Sforza dynasty of dukes, who were actually in possession, and by the Emperor as overlord. The neighbouring dukes of Savoy asserted authority over considerable areas of the Vaud which Berne regarded as its own and was soon to secure by war. The episcopal city of Geneva occupied a key-position in this rivalry; it could not stand alone, but with the alliance and help of Berne and the neutrality of France it might, and ultimately did, become independent.

In the east, Venice, needing security for its northern line of communication, had become involved in 1509 in hostilities with the States of the Church, that aggressive central Italian group of principalities, duchies and cities over which the Pope was temporal autocrat. To the north lay Rhaetia, the home of the Grey Leagues (*Graubünden*) of independent peasants allied with the Swiss Confederation and with uncertain frontiers. Similarly, no one was very clear about the line of demarcation between the numerous communities of Valais and the duchy of Milan. At the same time, Uri, Schwyz and Unterwalden were anxious to control the southern route, which meant the conquest or submission of the Maggia and Ticino valleys and the occupation of the northern shores of Lakes Maggiore, Lugano and Como. In this exercise, undertaken aggressively to secure the indispensable north–south trade route, the central states had learnt that much of the north Italian plain was at their mercy. Berne had obtained security by the overthrow of Charles the Rash and was poised for aggression. Charles' son-in-law, Maximilian, had suffered a humiliating defeat in the Swabian war and was certainly not anxious to renew the combat, the more so since Basle had entered the Confederation in 1501.

---

[1] Nabholz/Kläui, 90–5; R. Fischer, W. Schläpfer, F. Stark, *Appenzeller Geschichte* (Urnäsch, 1964) I, 300.

Military success indeed had nearly proved disastrous to the Swiss themselves, for the states had almost come to blows over the allocation of the gains of war, but this had been averted in time by the influence of the astonishing, or at least charismatic, character of Niklaus von der Flüe.[1] In 1510, then, when Zwingli had been four years in Glarus, Switzerland had, to use modern terminology, become a Great Power, unconquerable at home and able to wage successful war against any neighbour. There was no disciplined force in the world to equal a Swiss army. Given anything like equal numbers, victory was almost assured by its impenetrable squares of pikemen whose ranks could not be broken by cavalry charges and whose collective discipline was matched by individual bravery; by the devastation that could be caused by the fearful halberds and axes of men who came to kill relentlessly and not to take prisoners; and by the marksmanship of the crossbowmen.

Self defence had involved compulsory military service in each self-governing unit; security had demanded and obtained cooperation, first and foremost in preventing invasion of the homeland. In fifteenth and sixteenth century conditions, defence and aggression were neither distinguished nor distinguishable, and men from Glarus had learnt, as the English had discovered in the fourteenth century, that warfare paid handsome dividends, at any rate in the short run. There was little outlet for either industry or ability in the central states. Lumbering, while laborious, was scarcely profitable, for western Europe was well supplied with timber, and almost the only other means of livelihood in the countryside was cattle rearing. Far too little grain or grapes could be cultivated to satisfy even the frugal needs of growing families. A little spinning and weaving went on in a very few centres such as Zurich and St Gall, and there were tolls to be obtained from merchants in transit and some small profit in the carriage of goods. But it was all quite insufficient; life was extremely hard, and the peasant was usually miserably poor.

This poverty was emphasised by the existence of wealthy neighbours. The France of Louis XII was on its way to becoming the richest of European countries; while north Italy, in Guicciardini's words, 'not only abounded in inhabitants, merchandise and riches but she was distinguished by the magnificence of many princes, by the splendour of many noble and beautiful cities, by the presence of the papacy and the majesty of the church...she shone by her industry and her arts, she deservedly enjoyed among all peoples a distinguished reputation and renown'.[2] There was obviously there much that was to be had for the taking, as the French had

[1] R. Durrer, *Bruder Klaus. Die ältesten Quellen über den seligen Nikolaus von Flüe, sein Leben und seinen Einfluss*, 2 Bde. (Sarnen, 1917–1921).
[2] F. Guicciardini, *La Storia d'Italia* (ed. A. Gherardi) 4 vols. (Florence, 1919) I, 94.

already demonstrated. The men who returned from Morat and Nancy laden with booty whose value they had not realised soon learnt that it was possible in one short campaign to bring back enough to be rich for life. If there was no excuse by way of self defence for an incursion into Franche Comté or Ticino, there were tempting offers from kings and nobles anxious for bodyguards and permanent military striking forces. The Italian princes had long since hired soldiers, but from 1500 the French were the best paymasters. Ever since the demonstration of Swiss toughness at St Jakob an der Birs in 1448, French governments had recognised the military potentialities of their neighbours. There had been Swiss volunteers with the French army led by Charles VIII into Italy in 1494–5 where their exploits were noted with full appreciation, so much so that when Louis XII decided in 1499 to advance his claims to the Duchy of Milan and to depose Ludovico il Moro, his agents hired some 10,000 Swiss adventurers to support the French side. Maximilian had followed suit, so that, at the siege of Novara in April 1500 Swiss faced Swiss. They were unwilling to fight as they had promised. Hence Milan passed into French occupation and the Sforza ruler was sent to Loches a prisoner. It was not a creditable episode.

The Inner States took advantage of the situation to occupy the key position of Bellinzona and much of the territory around Lake Maggiore. This corporate occupation by the Inner States of the Blenio valley with Lugano and Locarno was accepted by Louis XII at Arona in 1503.[1] It was valuable territory, but the cost in Swiss blood had been so high that there was some agreement at a Diet[2] in July 1503 that foreign service and foreign bribery were objectionable and were to be avoided. This was not, however, practical politics. The Swiss balance of payments could be maintained only by an export policy of armed men some of whom inevitably would never return, but those who did brought to their homes and villages the means of a life a little above, and sometimes appreciably above, subsistence level. All this was specially true of central Switzerland. The men of Uri, Schwyz, Unterwalden, Lucerne, Zug and Glarus were willing volunteers because their families needed the gold they could bring, or send, home. The inhabitants of walled cities where a secure market concentrated trade, where government offices attracted taxation, where necessary household and farm articles could be fabricated for gain and where the rare luxury could secure a high price, scarcely understood that the hill men must move or perish.

A great deal depended upon the attitude of the authorities for there was

---

[1] EA 3, ii, 746–9, 1305–14.
[2] Of the twelve states together with Appenzell and the city of St Gall. EA 3 ii. 1314–1316 – the so-called *Pensionenbrief* or *Badener Verkommnis*.

little difficulty in inducing men to fight. Warfare was to be expected and soldiers did not so much volunteer for service as individuals as willingly allow themselves to be drafted by their natural superiors. Hence the locally elected or semi-hereditary governors could produce small companies of well-armed trained fighters, and they soon learnt to ask a good price for their services and a commission as well. The intense local solidarity of the village communities, communes or *Gemeinden*, made local acquiescence easy. In face of strong local feeling the Confederation as a whole was powerless.

Among the princes anxious to buy soldiers was, inevitably, the Pope. The Borgias had made the States of the Church into a coherent and cohesive dominion[1] ready when opportunity offered to extend its boundaries. The Pope for whom Zwingli prayed devoutly in the parish church of Glarus was Julius II (1503-13), the tough old warrior who enjoyed every minute of political intrigue and delighted in the use of armed force. Erasmus, the pacifist, disliked both the man and his policies, criticising him bitterly in the anonymous *Julius Exclusus* for his militancy.[2] He was the Pope whom Sir Thomas More had in mind when he warned Henry VIII: 'The Pope...is a prince as you are, and in league with all other Christian princes',[3] and Julius II was just this all his life. All his efforts had been devoted to the successful consolidation of the States of the Church; he was at least as much at home on the battlefield and in camp as he was in St Peter's or Consistory. In particular, he had led armed opposition to Venice, securing Faenza, Rimini and Ravenna, as well as maintaining a hold on Bologna.

The League of Cambrai (1508) which had facilitated this was not made to last, and if French domination in Italy was to be avoided the Pope must find further support elsewhere. The Emperor Maximilian, who had tried in vain to secure either territory or papal coronation in Italy, was entirely unreliable and could be ignored. In 1509 the Swiss arrangement with France, dating from 1474 and renewed in 1499, allowing for recruitment of mercenaries, lapsed. The situation in Italy was thus extremely fluid. The Swiss were ideally situated to help the papacy, and there were long discussions about relationships with the Holy See. Julius II's policy now was to weaken the northern states of Italy and reduce French influence there. This suited the expansionist interests of the central Swiss states admirably. Papal pay was good, mercenary warfare in Italy consisted much more in manoeuvring than in fighting, and simple piety might be allied to personal profit.

[1] The process has been well described by M. E. Mallett, *The Borgias* (London, 1969).
[2] *The Julius Exclusus of Erasmus* trans. P. Pascal, ed. J. K. Sqwards (Indiana University Press, 1968).
[3] *The Lyfe of Sir Thomas Moore...by William Roper* ed. E. V. Hitchcock (London: Early English Text Society, 1935), 68.

The Pope, too, had a splendid recruiting sergeant in Matthias Schiner,[1] Bishop of Sion from 1499, who was made Cardinal in 1511. This ambitious prelate, who may have hoped to make his bishopric into an independent principality, and who was 'papabile', feared and disliked the French and worked for their expulsion from north Italy.

In 1507 Louis XII had, in accordance with the existing Franco-Swiss treaty of alliance, hired Swiss soldiers who were used against Genoa, an action resented by the Emperor Maximilian and unpopular in Switzerland. The French king had found his allies both unruly and extortionate, while Bellinzona, which he regarded as his rightful possession, had been forcibly occupied by Uri and Schwyz and had had to be left to them. In place of the French alliance, Schiner succeeded in negotiating a five-year Papal–Swiss agreement on 14 March 1510[2] confirmed by a Diet at Lucerne in October. In addition to providing a bodyguard for the person of the Pope,[3] the Swiss agreed, with safeguards, to produce 6,000 men for the papal armies and to enter into no alliance hostile to the papacy. The pay was good, there were spiritual advantages and high expectations. Although the promise was merely to protect the papal states in the event of an attack, a dispute with the Duke of Ferrara was represented as just this, and thus it was hoped to bring in the new ally in an attempt to expel the common French enemy from Italian soil.[4]

Little came of this incursion in 1510: the Chiasso expedition, as it was called, was almost a farce; the Milanese defences were too strong, and a disappointed force returned at the end of the year. In 1511, however, having lost control of Bologna, the Pope succeeded in arranging the 'Holy League' with Spain, Venice and Henry VIII of England for the defence of the States of the Church, and hostilities were renewed. At the same time, the murder of two envoys from Schwyz and Fribourg near Lugano aroused local passions against the French and, in fact, many more than the stipulated 6,000 men were willing to aid the League.[5] But again the Pope

---

[1] Less correctly written Schinner. Born c. 1470, a nephew of Nicholas Schiner, bishop of Sion, who made him his Vicar General, he became bishop in 1499 and died on 1 October 1522. Büchi, *Schiner*; Büchi, *Korrespondenzen* (QSG) with useful notes.

[2] Büchi, *Schiner* I, 177; R. Durrer, *Die Schweizergarde in Rom und die Schweizer in päpstlichen Diensten* I. Teil (Lucerne, 1927), 48. Büchi, *Korrespondenzen* I, 90; P. M. Krieg, *Die Schweizergarde in Rom* (Lucerne, 1960); EA 3, ii, 481–3, 515–16, 1333–8 (Beilage 16).

[3] This body, with uniforms said to have been designed by Michelangelo, was largely disbanded in 1970.

[4] E. Gagliardi, *Der Anteil der Schweizer an den italienischen Kriegen 1494–1516*. Bd. I, *1494–1509* (Zürich, 1919).

J. S. C. Bridge, *A history of France from the death of Louis XI* IV, *1508–1514* (Oxford, 1929), esp. 59–60. C. Kohler, *Les Suisses dans les guerres d'Italie de 1506 à 1512*, Publications de la société d'Histoire et d'Archéologie de Genève. Mémoires et Documents. XXIV (Geneva/Paris, 1896), 151–7.

[5] This was to cause trouble later. The papal stipulations had been precise about numbers and there was no case for additional payment. All the soldiers naturally expected to be rewarded,

was disappointed. The Swiss contingents, able to preserve admirable discipline on a field of battle, were little more than a turbulent mob on the march. They had hardly any guns or horses, it was an intensely cold winter, and when it became apparent at Castiglione and Gallarate that Milan was to be effectively defended, they again turned back.[1] Como, Chiasso and Ponte Tresa provided plentiful plunder and some disgraceful excesses on the homeward journey, to the intense resentment of the suffering Italian peasants. None the less, in May 1512, 18,000 or more Swiss volunteers streamed through the Münstertal to Verona, undeterred by the knowledge that on Easter day, 18 April, a French army under Gaston de Foix had defeated the papal forces at Ravenna.[2] Once again 'the Cardinal' had by the combined appeal of spiritual benefits, a symbolic golden sword, cash down and promises of loot, achieved his aims.[3] Maximilian Sforza appeared to claim his rightful duchy, and with imperial, Venetian and Spanish cooperation for once reasonably well timed, the invaders swooped on 14 June on the French defending force at Pavia, swept it away, and went on to enter Milan, while the remnants of the opposing force under La Palice left northern Italy.[4]

Thus in 1512 the Swiss Confederation, *de facto* ruler of the Milanese,[5] was manifestly a power to be reckoned with. The twelve victorious *Orte* (for Appenzell had not yet been admitted to their number) took over the administration of Locarno, Lugano, Mendrisio, Balerna and Domodossola; and the Graubünden extended themselves southwards in harmony to include Bormio, Chiavenna, Tre Pievi and the Valtelline.[6] It was a highly profitable as well as a successful enterprise.

and complained when they were not. Maximilian, who had supported the League, noted the greed of the Swiss: 'communities to whom faith and loyalty are unknown' (Bridge, *History of France* IV, 70 n. 1, citing Le Glay, *Correspondance de l'empereur Maximilien I*^{er} *et de Marguerite d'Autriche* (Paris, 1839) I, 326–7. Cf. *Lettres du Roy Louis XII* (4 vols. Brussels, 1712) III, 98: 'Car nous les trouvons comme les malvais villains que plus les prie on et donne de bonnes parolles, et plus sont rudes, fiers, pervers et mauldis et pour ces causes...' (25 Nov. 1511).   [1] Kohler, *Les Suisses*, 263–80; Durrer, *Schweizergarde*, 64–6.
[2] Zwingli in a letter to Vadian asserted that Hannibal's victory at Cannae had not caused greater alarm and despondency in Rome and Italy than had the news of Ravenna in 1512. Z I, 32; VII, 21–2. Cf. Kohler, *Les Suisses*, 324–7; Durrer, *Schweizergarde*, 121–6.
[3] For this and the ceremonial cap and banners see Durrer, *Schweizergarde*, 103–8. The sword and cap went to Zurich as *Vorort*, and the keys of Milan were received by Bürgermeister Felix Schmid: G. Stucki, *Zürichs Stellung in der Eidgenossenschaft vor der Reformation* (Aarau, 1970), 68. Schiner was 'the Cardinal' for the Swiss as Wolsey was for the English – or as the Duke of Cumberland in the eighteenth century or the Duke of Wellington in the nineteenth was 'the Duke'.
[4] Kohler, *Les Suisses* 376–82; Durrer, *Schweizergarde* 144–6. In spite of assertions to the contrary, there is no direct evidence that Zwingli was personally present at this campaign. Z I, 24–8; Koehler *Zwingli*, 36; *Gedächtnis* c. 193–4; Bullinger, *Ref.* I, 8; Farner II, 94.
[5] Büchi, *Schiner* I, 42.
[6] A. Gasser, *Die territoriale Entwicklung der Schweizerischen Eidgenossenschaft, 1291–1797* (Aarau, 1932) 144–51.

The Pavia expedition, although permanently changing the southern frontier of Switzerland, had been almost too successful. A Confederation originally defensive only, now had possessions and commitments in the south as well as in the north. Yet there was neither the experience nor the administrative ability available to do more than conquer and occupy: the great city of Milan and its satellites could not have been effectively controlled by Alpine communities and uncooperative Swiss city states. The prize was too large to be held, although what remained as mandated territory proved in the long run to be an important factor in holding together a people soon to be hopelessly divided by religion.

The rapid departure of the French armies was temporary only. Julius II died on 21 February 1513, and in the following May a fresh French army, now supported by the Venetians as allies, moved into Lombardy and reoccupied Milan. Once again a Swiss contingent, this time a relatively small one, some 4,000 strong, took up a stand at Novara to stem the French tide. There, on 6 June, this reinforced contingent was decisively and vigorously victorious against French cavalry supported by German Landsknechte.[1] The international situation might be confused; there was a new Medici Pope,[2] Leo X (1513–21), and there was soon to be a new French king, Francis I, but at the moment the Swiss seemed to hold the balance of power on the continent by their manifest military strength. Novara had added to their repute. The French were again expelled, and the loot and contributions levied by the Swiss were considerable. Once again war had paid off.

To all this Glarus had contributed its quota of men, whose banner depicted the risen Christ,[3] and through them Zwingli obtained first-hand acquaintance with Italian and papal politics as well as with mercenary service. At first, his normal duties as parish priest, humanist classical studies and increasing attention to the Bible were sufficient occupation. It is also clear that he considered it his duty to take part alongside the armed men of his state in a campaign to which they had been invited by the Holy Father for the defence of the lands of Mother Church. Hence in June 1513 he acted as chaplain or 'field preacher', learning at first hand exactly what these military expeditions meant in practice. Immensely proud of his people, he thought of central Switzerland as a near-paradise, where free men, united by memories of successful resistance to Habsburg aggression, lived in countrified simplicity. This, however, did not correspond to the harsh facts of a campaign in which hired men were fighting papal battles on Italian soil for monetary gain. He had in fact already (1510)

[1] E. Gagliardi, *Novara und Dijon* (Zürich, 1907) 148–66, 335–9.
[2] His representative in Switzerland was Ennio Filonardi (created Cardinal in 1536) who henceforth intervened continuously in Swiss affairs. He was well known in Zurich and understood the situation there. J. C. Wirz, *Ennio Filonardi der letzte Nuntius in Zürich* (Zürich, 1894). [3] Staehelin I, 65.

commented on the situation in the 'Story of the Ox', a kind of *Animal Farm*, his first serious discourse on politics and war characteristically written in elegant Latin verse.

In this narrative,[1] the ox, a noble, simple animal, lived in happy simplicity in a peaceful meadow in the company of his faithful dog Lycisca. Then, through the fence, came trouble-makers – cats. There were other animals in and around this meadow who suffered from the attentions of a predatory lion. These decided to look to brother Ox for some protection and support, using the cunning leopard as their spokesman and the cats as professional advocates. He was, they said, so noble and so strong that if only he would intervene in the jungle outside his meadow he could impose his own terms and restore peace and tranquillity. And in spite of warning barks from the dog, he agreed, easily convinced by feline argument that what he did was on behalf of simple justice and right. The leopard rejoiced in the success of his scheme, hostile animals were driven away and the leopard lived in luxury.

Seeing this, the greedy lion himself stooped to seek the friendship of brother Ox, who, in all simplicity, was ready enough. Then the cats came; they assured him that the lion was dangerous, unreliable and treacherous, all of which the ox accepted and so rejected the leonine advances. Thus the leopard saw his chance: secure in this support, he could take action against his rival in deceit, the fox. Together they rampaged in the fox's territories, reducing him to such a state of alarm that he approached the shepherd, whose hen roost he had previously robbed, with an offer to make proper restitution. And so the shepherd, in spite of deceptions he had experienced in the past, protected the fox from leopard and lion and asked the ox, very persistently, to support him.

All this led to a renewed and confused struggle, the ox leaving the side of the leopard, while some goats entered the territory to take what they might. And in the end, the ox found himself isolated and alone. He was no longer safe: his earlier simple freedom had been corrupted by bribes, gifts and inducements: to it, now, relying only on his own courage, he must return.

It was a very transparent, simple story. The ox, obviously, was the good-natured bucolic Swiss, deceived into friendship with the French leopard and his partisans, the cats. The lion was the Habsburg monarch, Venice was the fox, the goats were any other interested parties. The whole story clearly implied that involvement with the French had been a mistake, and that even the good shepherd, the Pope, had been not without ulterior motives. Let the gallant Swiss people be content with their

---

[1] *Das Fabelgedicht vom Ochsen* Z I (10)–22 with the Latin version on alternate pages. The original is StAZ. I.3.I (2) but is not in Zwingli's own hand.

secure home-land and eschew entangling alliances and extraneous temptations.

However simplified, it showed that a young scholarly catholic priest was thinking about politics, international affairs and the proper role of his countrymen amid the French, imperial and papal triangle. Ideally the Swiss occupied a walled garden; others should leave them alone to cultivate their garden to the best advantage, and they, in turn, would keep within their garden wall and not interfere with their neighbours. Animals and crops would provide them with a livelihood, and the simple hard work of the fields would breed a hardy, virtuous people. It was a fantasy, but a fantasy tinged as it were with incipient patriotism and nationalism. Emphatically German, yet equally emphatically not subject to the jurisdiction of the Empire, the Swiss peasant, managing his own affairs locally by agreement, was different from, and much better off than, his central German counterpart who was constantly and successfully exploited by landowners, princes and knights. The most unpopular features of European serfdom were largely absent from this intensively traditionalist society. There was little need for money, and gold corrupted those who had it. If only men were content to stay at home, there was God-provided provision for all. Coming of well-to-do farmer stock, never having known severe poverty, Zwingli hardly realised that the soil could not support an increasing population, and that in fact they might have to go outside their garden wall for some essentials.

The Pope, it should be noted, is the good shepherd. If the shepherd is attacked by wicked men, the righteous will come to his help. Nowhere in this little moral story is there any suggestion of a disposition to dispute papal claims. The hierarchy of the church is as much taken for granted as is the structure of western society. Zwingli was, at the time of these his earliest writings, a far more conscientious priest than his admired friend and hero, Erasmus,[1] to whom Glarean had introduced him in April 1515. It was probably immediately after the return of the Pavia expedition that Zwingli wrote a short account of the way his compatriots had set about driving the French from Lombardy, all in somewhat embellished Latin for the benefit of his more learned friends.[2] The gathering at Chur, the choice of leaders, the presents brought by the Cardinal, the junction with the Venetians, the ever more precipitous retirement by the French before these fearless young enthusiasts who stripped to swim rivers carrying their deadly halberds, the entry into Pavia, all led to the triumphant conclusion

[1] Z v, 721–2 n. 5.

[2] Z I 23 (30)–37 'De gestis inter Gallos et Helvetios...relatio' cast in the form of an appendix to a letter to Vadian. It was first printed in 1611 and may have been written in 1512. It was hurriedly written, and there are some obvious geographical errors. The 'three hours' (p. 37) allotted for composition may be as fictitious as the three days Erasmus had needed to construct a tiny poem for Prince Henry of England in 1499. Allen I, 6.

'so was all Italy free'.[1] Never behindhand with words, the Pope rewarded his supporters by the Bull *Etsi Romani pontifices* with the title 'Defenders of the liberty of the church'.[2] Later in life, but perhaps with recollections of hearing mass said according to the Ambrosian rite in Milan Cathedral while on this tour, Zwingli made controversial use of the liturgical variations that he noted were acceptable there. It is all admittedly a little conjectural, but about his solid local patriotism and the acceptance of Catholic usages there need be no doubt.

Later still, almost certainly in 1516, Zwingli returned to his animal satire theme in the two hundred or so lines called 'The Labyrinth'.[3] This relates how Theseus, the hero, with the help of Ariadne's skein of thread, finds his way through the labyrinth to the giant man-eating Minotaur, whom he fearlessly slays. On the way he boldly encounters the one-eyed lion, the crowned eagle, the cock, the winged lion, the bear with a ring through its nose, and the ox. The labyrinth reflects the quite extraordinarily entangled international affairs as seen from Glarus. Of the animals, the one-eyed lion represents the short-sighted Leo X, the crowned eagle is the emperor, the cock symbolises the French, the winged lion Venice, while the bear and the ox are the Swiss people. Not many possible readers could have heard of Minos, Theseus, Ariadne and their attendants, or follow the implications of an argument that action without reason is like being without a guide in a labyrinth in which we may wander lost for ever. God alone can save us from ourselves and an evil world and from our wicked desires to quarrel and fight with our neighbours. To this, men are all too readily incited by the wilful selfishness of princes, but peace is far more valuable and should be maintained.

The victory at Novara had been followed up by a Swiss invasion of the Duchy of Burgundy which had taken them to the walls of Dijon in September 1513. There they consented to be bought off at a high price – 400,000 crowns together with the renunciation of French claims in Italy – an agreement made by the French general La Trémoille but later repudiated by his monarch.

There was a good deal of dissatisfaction expressed in Berne and else-

---

[1] Z I, 36. 'Ita omnis Italia...liberata.' Perhaps 'liberated' might express the implications even better.
[2] 'Defensores ecclesiasticae libertatis', W. Oechsli, *Quellenbuch zur Schweizergeschichte* (Zürich, 1901), 348 EA. 3, 2, 632–3. Above 33.
[3] Z I 39 (53)–60. The date 1516 explains the allusions, particularly since they fit in with Johannes Adelphius, *Ludus Novus* published in 1515, where a woodcut illustrates the confident cockerel (France), the crowned eagle (the emperor), the winged lion of St Mark (Venice), the Swiss ox, much as in the earlier poem. If, as Egli argues (Z I, 43–50), the bear means Berne, where French influence was powerful, while the ox refers to central and eastern Switzerland less anxious to forward French aggression and consequently dividing the country so that Swiss were actually serving in opposing armies, the allusions fall into place.

where at this outcome: there was likewise a feeling that a few leading families had indeed been enriched, but the ordinary soldier had gained little. The French then proceeded to come to terms with Henry VIII of England in June 1514, and Louis XII was preparing to reassert his rights in the Milanese when he died on the last day of this year, to be succeeded by Francis I.

The French attempts to secure exclusive Swiss support failed largely because of resistance from Zurich.[1] The Confederates stood by their allies, Maximilian Sforza, the Emperor Maximilian, the Pope and Ferdinand of Spain, but the tempting French offers were not forgotten. In May 1515 a French army was in Alessandria and an attack on Berne was anticipated. Morat, Grandson and Neuchâtel were hurriedly garrisoned, while some 10,000 soldiers from central Switzerland went to defend Milan.

They were not welcomed by the local inhabitants, and there was division of opinion about their objective. The Bernese leader, Albrecht vom Stein, wanted to meet the French invaders at the frontier, but the men of Schwyz and Glarus refused to agree. When the French forces crossed the Col d'Argentière in strength with some hired Swiss soldiers in their ranks, it was seen that neither Spanish nor papal support was in sight. The western contingents from Berne, Biel, Solothurn and Fribourg thereupon fell back towards Domodossola. At Rivoli in August discontent and disorder were apparent, and at Novara valuable guns were left behind. Finally, at Gallarate on 8 September, in return for pensions and a large sum in cash, their leaders agreed to abandon Milan and Genoa.[2]

It was thus left to the men from central and eastern Switzerland, including Basle, Schaffhausen and a force from Zurich under Bürgermeister Röist, to hold the line. Zwingli was with his parishioners at Monza where, in the market place near the present Palazzo Arengario, he preached on steadfastness and their duty to support the Pope.[3] Thence the now much diminished Swiss army marched towards Milan. Outside the city at Marignano[4] they faced Francis I on 13–14 September. The French had superior numbers, perhaps 60,000 men, with excellent cavalry and artillery: for twenty hours there was confused murderous hand-to-hand fighting, but the Swiss pikemen could not capture the artillery that did such slaughter, and when a Venetian force came to join the French, there was nothing for it but to retreat 'torn, maimed, wounded, with their banners in tatters, singing funeral dirges instead of songs of triumph'.[5] Over 10,000 Swiss lay dead on the field. It was not as obvious then as it was

[1] EA 3, ii, 849, 863, 872, 879.   [2] EA 3, ii, 902–4, 907–13.
[3] ZWA I, 387–92; Z VII, 540 n. 1.
[4] G. Thürer, *Die Wende von Marignano* (Zürich, 1965).
[5] Allen II, 149. 'Rediere domum aliquanto pauciores quam exierant, laceri, mutili, saucii, signis dissectis; proinde pro epiniciis celebrant parentalia.'

later that the Swiss Confederation had ceased to be a great military power because, manifestly, if the Swiss forces had remained intact that September, a French retreat or defeat would have been certain. But they were not united, and their discipline on the march, as distinct from the battlefield, left much to be desired. The young army chaplain came away with two convictions reinforced – the first, that mercenary service, the sale of flesh and blood for gold, was immoral; the second, that Swiss unity was an indispensable prerequisite for future achievement. It is a sad fact that Swiss soldiers continued to be hired by foreign powers until the nineteenth century, and that the Zwinglian Reformation split the country so profoundly that only the religious indifference of the twentieth century closed the gap.

At the time of Marignano, Zwingli was himself, like many others,[1] a papal pensioner and a supporter of Cardinal Schiner, but this meant little. It was, however, distasteful for him to perceive a political drift away from alliance with Rome and in favour of one with France. Back in Glarus in the autumn of 1515, he reflected deeply, perhaps for the first time, on the religious and human problems of his day. His faith in God and the Christian revelation grew in intensity as reading and experience brought further reflection. His acceptance of the creeds was never in doubt, but now his mind turned even more to exploration of their full meaning and implications.

At Glarus he began to realise that he, like most other clerics, had been accustomed to pay far too much attention to externals and to Bible commentaries instead of to the text itself; logic and verbal dexterity he had learnt at Vienna and Basle, and he knew his 'Sentences' and the jargon of the Thomists. He also knew, and delighted to imitate, the tortuous wordplay of some of the humanists and the delicate subtlety of men like Pico della Mirandola. Hellenistic Greek he was beginning to master, and in 1516 he was one of the first to secure that *Novum Instrumentum* which was the fruit of Erasmus' painful months in Cambridge. It was rushed out by Froben of Basle in March, and Zwingli rejoiced to be able to visit its editor there before the year was ended.[2]

Having the new original text before him, he determined not to accept traditional interpretations but to concentrate upon the meaning of the words themselves. How new this was and how courageous, our literate and incredulous age can appreciate only with difficulty. It is indeed almost impossible to recapture the thrill of this fine folio volume. Here was the very word of God in the original tongue and something he could use and reverence; no wonder he copied out most of the Epistles of St Paul or that

---

[1] They included Johannes Manz, Felix Frei, Heinrich Utinger, Erhard Weiss and Anshelm Graf. ZSKG 50 (1956), 362.

[2] A. Rich, *Die Anfänge der Theologie Huldrych Zwinglis* (Zürich, 1949), 17–18; Z v, 721–2 n 5.

he soon knew much of the great tome almost by heart. Literate in an illiterate age, humanist-trained and now at home with Greek script, certain that the key to eternal bliss lay in these crisp pages, the young man turned to Jesus as never before. It was this New Testament, added to study of St Augustine's treatise on the Fourth Gospel,[1] that opened his eyes and impelled him to fill his sermons with the new-found glad tidings.

The wider significance of this publication, including its influence on Luther, has been much debated, but for Zwingli it was exactly what he needed. He could appreciate the Latinity of the Erasmian commentary, he exulted in the fact that his own knowledge of Greek enabled him to value the discussion of words such as ecclesia, presbyter, poenitentiam agite, and to recognise that Bishop, Pastor, Apostle, were names of offices of service and not of authority. In the introduction he could read that Christ, eternal wisdom, alone could teach with authority and was the sole mediator for salvation. The Vulgate he knew already and extremely well, but here was the real thing, the divine word exactly as the Holy Spirit had guided the pens of the Evangelists. From Erasmus, too, he had already learnt to turn more positively and directly to Christ. Erasmus had long indicated, with that slightly insufferably superior urbanity that was his least attractive characteristic, reservations about the reverence popularly paid to the popular saints. Why go on a pilgrimage to a particular shrine?[2] How could a particular image be thought to possess wonder-working powers? From these considerations he moved to more profound topics. What was meant by an almighty and everlasting God? What was implied by man's free will? After 1516 a somewhat worried priest faced parishioners who trusted that his formulae were all-sufficient, and that their role was passive acceptance of prescribed duties and dogma. He shared his anxieties with correspondents like Vadian, Myconius and Wimpfeling who were similarly interested and concerned. The satire, gentle sarcasm and aloofness that came from the pen of Erasmus were less than he needed: his hope was that Rome would lead a return to the practices and teaching of the Apostles.

Rather slowly he was becoming convinced that nothing could be hoped for from the Pope, but his only positive move was to arrange to be transferred on 14 April 1516[3] to Einsiedeln, some fifteen rather inaccessible miles to the west, as stipendiary priest (*Leutpriester*).[4]

---

[1] *In Ioannis Evangelium tractatus*. MPL 35, 1379–1976.

[2] The Colloquy 'A Pilgrimage for Religion's sake', cast in dialogue form, with its transparent references to Walsingham, Norfolk, was extremely popular. C. R. Thompson (trans.) *The Colloquies of Erasmus* (Chicago, 1965) 285–312.

[3] Z I, 50, VII, 44 n. 3; Egli *4*, I, 16–19. He took up his duties on 26 November.

[4] There is no satisfactory rendering of *Leutpriester*. Professor G. R. Elton *Reformation Europe, 1517–1559* (London 1963), 66 rightly says, 'usually and rather inanely translated literally as "people's priest"', and suggests 'common preacher'. This, indeed, is what Zwingli later made of the office in Zurich, but the duties were not primarily those of preaching so much as

That Rome was satisfied enough was apparent when Zwingli was appointed a papal chaplain in 1518.[1] After Marignano, the Pope was on the losing side, was unable to pay for expensive professional soldiers and came to terms with Francis I at Bologna, making some remarkable concessions to the French monarch. Another striking outcome of the battle was the 'Perpetual Peace' (*Ewige Richtung*) with France of 29 November 1516. After long negotiations, first a bare majority of the states, and finally the whole thirteen, agreed not to attack, or to be partner to any attack on, France or French possessions.[2] A large sum, a million crowns in all, was paid by way of compensation for losses on earlier expeditions and for the castles of Lugano and Locarno (Bellinzona remaining Swiss).[3] Most significant of all, in return for pensions all round, the French king was permitted to recruit mercenaries for service with the French army, a practice that lasted until the French Revolution.

To this arrangement and its implications Zwingli was resolutely opposed. By it independence was exchanged for foreign gold and Swiss young men were taken from the land which nurtured them. To a Toggenburger the whole westernising policy of Berne and its allies was unwelcome and undesirable, and he expressed his opposition freely. This meant that he was in open disagreement with the policy-makers of Glarus and, since he could not change their minds, he would be better away. The move to Einsiedeln was thus welcome to both sides, the more so in that Zwingli did not cease to be rector at Glarus. Instead, in December 1518 he secured the services of Valentin Tschudi as his vicar at a wage, to do what was necessary – a perfectly normal arrangement commonly adopted by monasteries. At Einsiedeln it was his duty to minister to the spiritual needs of the small number of farmers, servants and tradesmen who gathered round the Benedictine abbey reputedly founded by Meinrad of Sulgen in the ninth century and richly endowed by the Emperors Otto I and Henry I. By 1516 lackadaisical abbots like Gerald of Hohensaxe and Conrad of Hohenrech-

---

the 'cure of souls', including baptising, marrying, burying, giving extreme unction to the dying, hearing confessions and saying mass. The *Leutpriester* was not, however, the parish priest: he did not receive the tithes or all the oblations and customary payments. 'Public preacher' or 'lecturer' equally do not convey the impression of the pastoral duties expected. At Einsiedeln Zwingli had to promise obedience to the abbot, was entitled to (free) meals in the refectory and received a stipend of 20 gulden annually together with certain customary fees and oblations. Horses and personal servants were also freely available.

[1] The diploma, delivered to him by the papal legate, Antonio Pucci, at Einsiedeln in September 1518, a month after Luther had been summoned to Rome, described Zwingli as 'virtutibus clarens et meritis sicut experiencia et fame laudabilis testimonio commendaris, illam in domini nostri pape et apostolice sedis conspectu gratiam meruisti'. The office of acolyte-chaplain (*acolitus capellanus*) had ritual duties attached to it only if the recipient was in Rome, which Zwingli never was. Farner, *Zwingli* II, 272; Egli *4*, I, 19–21; Z VII, 95–6.

[2] G. Stucki, *Zürichs Stellung in der Eidgenossenschaft vor der Reformation* (Aarau, 1970), 96–8.

[3] EA 3, ii, 1019–21, 1406–15.

berg had reduced the 'hermit monks' of the convent to a mere handful of mildly sceptical, nobly born Religious with a shrewd businessman, Diebold (Theobald) of Hohengeroldseck as administrator and manager.[1] It was, and long remained, one of the pilgrimage centres of the western world, a local Canterbury, Compostella or Loreto, if not Rome, with indulgences that rivalled those of St Gall or Mariazell.

Miraculous healing powers were popularly attributed to the image of the 'black Virgin' at Einsiedeln,[2] which may have helped to convince Zwingli that simple and ignorant people worshipped the object which they saw in the shrine. At this time he saw no objection to pilgrimages, and had even personally accompanied a party to Aachen in 1517. At Einsiedeln, Zwingli, now an experienced priest of over thirty, was at the height of his intellectual powers. The duties were light but were taken seriously, and the numerous pilgrims from eastern Switzerland found no difficulty in understanding his sermons. Many visitors came home to report that the preacher was saying new things and introducing passages from the Bible, and particularly of the New Testament, into his discourses.[3] They also noted that here was someone who advocated less reliance on prescribed prayers and formulae, less attention to conventional acts of piety, less materialism, less care about personal physical welfare – instead he made a passionate appeal for a direct approach to God the Father through God the Son. It was not what they expected to hear at a popular shrine, but there was no mistaking the intense earnestness of the preacher.

His range of knowledge, too, was remarkable.[4] He had by now mastered

---

[1] Diebold, monk from 1499, administrator 1513-1525, was a patron of learning and immediately responsible for Zwingli's transfer. To him Zwingli later dedicated his treatise on the Canon of the mass (see p. 151). After 1525 he lived in Zurich, married Agnes Hochholzer in 1530, and was killed at Kappel in 1531. Egli 4, 1, 16; Z VII, 48 n. 3, 609-10; J. B. Müller, *Diebold von Geroldseck*, hg. v. O. Ringholz, *Mittheilungen des Historischen Vereins des Kantons Schwyz*, 7 (Einsiedeln, Waldshut, 1890). For a time the whole convent consisted of the abbot, who was non-resident, and the administrator. R. Tschudi, *Das Kloster Einsiedeln unter den Aebten Ludwig II. Blarer und Joachim Eichhorn, 1526-1569* (Einsiedeln, 1946) 9-10; Müller, 7, 9. While in Einsiedeln Zwingli became acquainted with Johann (Hans) Oechsli, later minister of Burg vor Stein am Rhein (see below, p. 145) and Franz Zink (c. 1480-1530). This latter supporter, who assisted in the administration at Einsiedeln, was also minister at Freienbach and was concerned with the arrangements for Zwingli's papal pension. He took part in the Second Disputation at Zurich in 1523, acting as deacon, married in 1527, was present at the Berne disputation in 1528, preached the Zwinglian gospel at Wil and Zurzach and died 31 January 1530. Z VII, 467.

[2] Ringholz 38.

[3] Looking back in January 1524 Zwingli spoke of the days when he had given himself entirely to Bible-study. 'Ich...mich hůb gantz an die heyligen gschrifft lassen.' Z I, 379. Among his hearers was Caspar Hedio (above, 19 n. 5) of St Theodore, Basle, who was greatly impressed. Z VII, 213; Ringholz, 587; ZSK XIII (1919), 129-33.

[4] 'Versare diurna non cessat Grecorum Latinorumque et philosophos et theologos, qui quidem pertinax labor estus illos impudentes vel mitigat, si non extinguit.' Z VII, 111. He also corresponded with the Italian Greek scholar Paul Bombasius, diplomat and cardinal, formerly a lecturer at Bologna. Z VII, 75.

the Greek language as well as any man north of the Alps – More, Vadian, Budaeus, even Erasmus. From the Greek New Testament, and from Tertullian, Jerome and Lactantius, he was drawn to the study of the Greek Fathers, Origen, Cyril of Alexandria and Chrysostom in particular, and he noticed that the earlier they wrote the less their teaching seemed to support current doctrine, especially about purgatory.

Erasmus remained a source of admiration and imitation. These years brought him the *Enchiridion militis Christiani* (the Knight's pocket dagger or flick-knife) (1503), a satire which was also a summary of Christian humanism,[1] together with the indispensable *Adagia* (1508) and the amusing *Praise of Folly* (1511). There were also the *Paraphrases of the New Testament* from 1517 which were immensely welcomed and built into much of Zwingli's later thought. He began to read and annotate the Greek Fathers, and wider knowledge of their language and ways of thought accompanied growing distrust of the logicalities of the medieval Schoolmen. He discovered how readily the ancients made use of allegory and he became almost fascinated by figures of speech. Tropes, alloeosis, ellipsis, metathesis, aposiopesis, hyperbole, prolepsis, synecdoche, and the rest – all the tiresome lists of the language text-books – were at his fingers' ends.[2] Because he could identify them all, he tended to allude to them a little too readily, with, sometimes, a touch of rather patronisingly conscious superiority.

He read widely in Jerome, Tertullian, Lactantius, Lucian, Suetonius, Varro, with Ovid's *Metamorphoses* and the *Epistolae Obscurorum Virorum* as entertainment.[3] At the same time he actively continued his study of Hebrew. Started off again possibly by the writings of his youthful hero, Pico della Mirandola, anxious to be on the side of the angels (and of Erasmus) in the Reuchlin–Pfefferkorn controversy, his copy of Reuchlin's *Rudimenta Hebraica* (1506) shows how diligently he was applying himself to this tongue.[4] Relatively few clergy of the early sixteenth century knew Hebrew. One of the achievements of the Christian (or even of the northern) Renaissance was the raising of the study of Hebrew to its highest level. This was the language of Moses and the Prophets; in some sense it was God's own language, and was supposed to be the origin of others. With its mastery Zwingli's confidence grew steadily. Some of the best Christian Hebraists of his day, Capito[5] or Pellican for example, were among his early correspondents. Zwingli had, what Erasmus lacked, an appreciation of poetry, which later enabled him to apply his knowledge of Pindar to an appreciation of the Psalms. His circle of correspondents widened – Froben

---

[1] Z VII, 192.   [2] There are convenient lists with definitions in Z XIII, 839–54.
[3] Z VII, 42, 43, 47, 48.   [4] Z XIV, 878 and notes; Koehler, *Bibliothek*, 32.
[5] Wolfgang Fabricius Köpfel (Capito) 1478–1541, later Reformer in Strassburg. J. W. Baum, *Capito und Butzer Strassburgs Reformatoren* (Elberfeld, 1860).

and Amerbach at Basle, Beatus Rhenanus at Strassburg, Nesen, Glarean, Fabri, Peter Falck, exchanged with him letters which were also literary exercises. He also come into contact with the writings of John Eck,[1] whose skill as a controversialist he was later to know only too well and whose real abilities have been overlaid by Lutheran abuse and by the false supposition that because a man is a controversialist he is little of a scholar.

It was while Zwingli was at Einsiedeln that the notorious John Tetzel was using all the arts of the peripatetic cheapjack to sell indulgences at Jüterbog, which was the occasion of the issuing of Luther's 95 theses of 31 October 1517 and all that followed from this. While Zwingli accepted, as he still did, the fact of purgatory and the authority of the Pope, he also understood the implications of the nominal safeguards of contrition and confession built into the indulgence theory and was not directly interested in this particular issue. Like other 'benefits' that came from Rome with a price-label attached, the indulgence could be, and was, abused. In the diocese of Constance the special indulgence for contributors to the building of St Peter's, Rome, was being expansively advertised by Bernhardin Sanson.[2] Zwingli liked neither the man nor his wares nor his manner of producing them, and perhaps helped to exclude him from Einsiedeln.[3] In this indeed he was reflecting what a good many other clerics were thinking and saying, so that his attack on Sanson was as acceptable as it was moderate.[4] The question of indulgences was still an open one, and authoritative definition would be part of that early internal church cleansing for which he still hoped. In that same October he received an invitation to come much nearer to Constance, to Winterthur in the Mandated Territory of Thurgau, to be preacher or lecturer at the city church and headmaster of the boys' school. He declined.[5]

The patronal festival at Einsiedeln commemorating the legendary consecration of the church there by an angel always attracted numerous visitors, many of whom came from Zurich. By these Zwingli's sermons were heard with marked approval, and the possibilities of attracting him to Zurich were canvassed, particularly by Myconius and Bürgermeister Marx Röist. He had visited the Limmat city frequently, knew its leading intellectuals, and knew also that its streets and alleys were notorious for

[1] The handwriting of the marginal notes to his copy of Eck's *Chrysopassus* (Augsburg, 1514) make it practically certain after Usteri's investigations (Usteri, *Initia*) that he was first acquainted with Eck's writings while at Einsiedeln.

[2] L. R. Schmidlin, *Bernhardin Sanson als Ablassprediger in der Schweiz 1518–19* (Solothurn, 1898). The spelling 'Sampson', frequently met with, is incorrect.

[3] Ringholz, 590.

[4] The contrast with Germany is remarkable. The Zurich council readily prohibited this indulgence-preaching in its territory, and later both the Diet of the Confederation and the Bishop of Constance complained of Sanson's activities, whereupon he was quietly recalled to Rome.   [5] Z VII, 68–71.

violence and immorality and that there was corruption in high places among the councillors, who had profited corporately by the gains made by Hans Waldmann at the expense of his life.

If Zurich was no better than it might have been, neither, so some people said, was this preacher that so much was being heard of. It was notorious, said the gossips, that he had corrupted a young girl or had an affair with a nun. They were all alike, these celibate Seculars. It was not regarded at the time as a very serious charge (although if a nun had been involved it would have been technically incest), and twentieth-century readers are perhaps a little less shocked than were some a century ago. When he was confronted with the charge, Zwingli, in very involved language, frankly admitted that he had yielded to the advances of a common prostitute. Regret, remorse, repentance followed rapidly, and this in no superficial sense: his shame, sorrow and feeling of guilt almost overwhelmed him. The candid admission[1] and the statement of the circumstances satisfied the relatively small number of those who cared, and the episode was over-looked and forgotten save by a few who were later to seize eagerly upon anything that would discredit the reformer. The latter he was not yet, but he had become by November 1518 too well known as preacher, writer and correspondent for him not to be considered favourably for a preaching appointment when this became vacant. His opposition to the French alliance, to pensions and to mercenary service was acceptable to the Zurich politicians, and a well-known humanist scholar could be useful as well as suitably placed in a leading city. John Manz, provost of the Great Minster, died on 24 October 1518. Canon Felix Frei was chosen in his place and the Leutpriester Erhart Battmann became a Canon.[2] On 11 December 1518 the chapter of the Great Minster at Zurich, by 17 votes to 7, appointed Zwingli foundation preacher[3] with parochial responsi-bilities. It was as if a young English country parson was attached to St Paul's Cathedral and invited to preach regularly at St Paul's Cross. The choice had not been unanimous. There was an alternative candidate, Laurence Mär or Mör, a Swabian, described as a gasbag (*fumus*) and reputedly the father of eight children, but then and later active in the

---

[1] The letter, of 5 December 1518, 'apologia', to Canon Henry Utinger, who was commissioned to report on the matter to the Chapter, is written, deliberately, in somewhat obscure Latin. Z VII, 110–13; Ringholz, 594; Koehler, *Buch*, 40–4. It has perhaps received too much atten-tion. Schulthess resisted the temptation to suppress the letter from the first collected edition of Zwingli's works, saying, 'Protestantism stands for truth in all circumstances.'

[2] Z VII, 102 n. 2.

[3] Leutpriester, 'stipendiary priest', see above 5 n 2. Preaching was not an essential part of his duties: it was a voluntary addition to the regular and punctual saying of mass and caring for the revenues of the Great Minster. Technically the cure of souls rested with the Provost, to whom Zwingli was vicar or deputy. On 26 December 1518 he formally resigned his cure of souls in Glarus and Einsiedeln. Bullinger, *Ref.* I, 11; Stachelin I, 132.

pulpit. It is clear that careful enquiries were made and that the appointment was a considered and deliberate one. Zwingli had explained his own conduct frankly and reasonably, and his views on public policy were acceptable. On 27 December he moved permanently to Zurich, a resident alien in an influential position.

3

The Zurich ministry, 1519–1522

The word Zürich[1] (*Tigurinum*) had a double meaning at the opening of the sixteenth century. There was the city, exactly defined by its walls and defences; and there was the countryside with boundaries only marginally different from those of the twentieth century canton. Together they made up the *Ort*, state or canton, a highly developed political organism with a long tradition behind it. The inhabitants spoke their own Swiss-German dialect, not at all easily understood by a pure-bred German from Saxony or Hanover, different also linguistically from the usages of Basle, Berne and Lucerne.

There had been a Roman settlement where the Limmat flowed from the lake. Charlemagne was a legendary founder, patron and visitor; and his grandson, Lewis the German, set up and lavishly endowed a monastery[2] for Benedictine nuns in 853. This was intended from its beginning to be a place of refuge for religious-minded aristocrats; and the abbess – the first one was the king's own daughter, Hildegard – ruled the little cluster of buildings which expanded steadily round the cloister. The convent owned much land, and the abbess had rights of jurisdiction[3] over the tenants living thereon and also over the incipient market town. The church, known as *das Fraumünster*,[4] several times rebuilt, was served by seven canons, who, with the nuns, constituted the chapter; and by chantry priests and preachers in the usual style of a collegiate church. Initially, the abbess had the right to mint coins and to collect tolls on goods coming in

[1] Zurich is the accepted English spelling. From the large literature dealing with its history it is possible to select J. C. Bluntschli, *Staats- und Rechtsgeschichte der Stadt und Landschaft Zürich* 2. Teile (Zürich, 1856). K. Dändliker, *Geschichte der Stadt und des Kantons Zürich.* 3 Bde. (Zürich, 1908–12). A. Largiadèr, *Geschichte von Stadt und Landschaft Zürich.* 2 Bde. (Erlenbach–Zürich, 1945). An annual survey of current literature appears in ZT.
[2] Foundation charter in Bluntschli (1. Beilage) I, 487–8. See also G. v. Wyss, *Geschichte der Abtei Zürich*, MAGZ 8 (1951–8); J. R. Rahn, *Das Fraumünster in Zürich*, MAGZ 25 (1900–14) 1–36. For the extent of the endowment, Map 14, *Historischer Atlas der Schweiz.*
[3] Not extending to life and limb (*Blutgericht*). Bluntschli I, 134.
[4] The use of the word *Fraumünster* (or *Frauenmünster*) for the nunnery church seems to date only from the early fourteenth century. S. Vögelin, *Das alte Zürich* 2 Bde. (Zürich, 1879, 1888) I, 501.

and out;[1] her patronage was usually influential at the imperial court and at first was much sought after. Like St Alban's in England, the town grew up round the monastery, but it early secured substantial independence of it.

The principal parish church was built in what became the business and industrial quarter west of the river. It was collegiate from its earliest Carolingian days, with a school for training future clerics attached to it; and, early known as the Great Minster (*das Chorherrenstift am Grossmünster*), it dominated the religious lives of the citizens.

The town was at first little more than a place of refuge from Hungarian marauders in the tenth century, but, in the eleventh, expansion was possible. A market, walls and a mint soon appeared. The whole of the adjacent territory fell within the domains of the Counts of Zähringen (1096–1218) and then of Ulrich of Kiburg, followed by Rudolf of Habsburg. Zurich succeeded in establishing its status as a free imperial city in 1218, thus becoming 'immediate'. Hence the citizens owed a double allegiance, to the abbess as landlord and to the Emperor[2] who was represented by a deputy or vicar (*Vogt*) who met the small community in the Lindenhof. The abbess worked through her agent or *Schultheiss* whose authority ultimately devolved upon the city council. In October 1291, only two months after the conventional inauguration of the original Confederation, Zurich was a corporate entity able to make an alliance with Uri and Schwyz.[3] It was to be of some importance that Zurich developed into a city while Berne and Freiburg-im-Breisgau were created ones. As elsewhere, nobles from the countryside soon sought to build houses within the city walls, and the more prosperous city dwellers owned or had interests in land outside. Parentage and place of birth were all-important, and memories of ancestry were long. It could all too easily have become a narrow aristocratic city of lords and dependants, but it did not.

This was in large measure because there were thriving markets and sufficiently skilled craftsmen numerous and wealthy enough to make their voices heard – particularly the weavers of silk and cloth, supported by the leather-workers and smiths. These strongly objected to full citizenship being limited to members of families owning real property within the city precincts, living on rents and dues and allied to the few large wholesale traders who dealt in commodities in bulk. In 1336, reflecting in some ways the unrest that characterised the Europe of the mid fourteenth century, the craftsmen, led by Rudolf Brun,[4] effected a violent and rapid revolution which made Zurich into a gild-city, *Zunftstadt*, a fact of importance for

---

[1] The later *Stadtzölle*. Bluntschli I, 129.
[2] O. Redlich, *Rudolf von Habsburg* (Innsbruck, 1903) 107–12.
[3] Largiadèr, I, 86; Bluntschli, 341.
[4] A. Largiadèr, *Bürgermeister Rudolf Brun und die Zürcher Revolution von 1336*, MAGZ 31 (Zürich, 1936).

Zwingli later. The organisation of the artisans into thirteen (later, twelve) associations or gilds was now recognised[1] as equal in political authority with the patricians and capitalists who had hitherto dominated affairs through their own powerful group, the Constaffel.[2] Brun, as first Bürgermeister for life, became almost dictator, and was the real creator of the state as it existed until the end of the eighteenth century. It now had a constitution, '*der erste geschworene Brief*' (1336), and a perpetual alliance (*ein ewiges Bündnis*)[3] with the central states (Uri, Schwyz, Unterwalden and Lucerne) sealed in May 1351, accompanied by territorial expansion along both sides of the lake, pointing the way to further advances later. After an unsuccessful war with Schwyz and Glarus over the Toggenburg inheritance from 1436 to 1444, by a policy of steady purchase and acquisition, Zurich came to be master of a territorial state[4] second only to Berne in size and more productive in men and revenue. All this was very piecemeal, and the nature of the jurisdiction exercised by the Zurich council over the component parts of its territory varied from area to area according to the constitution of the previous authority and the terms of the takeover. The form of government was complicated enough and, as in most other medieval cities, rested in part on local custom. It was to be of decisive importance in the spread of the Reformation. The common use of the word Zurich to mean either the area enclosed by the city walls or the whole district over which its rulers had authority is a convenient one. It corresponds to the facts of the sixteenth century: it was a city state, the city was the state. The city was, as it were, the mainspring. Yet the real strength of Zurich lay in its countryside, whence came men for the armed forces, goods, services and money raised by rents, dues and taxes. All citizens were not equal – very far from it. There were ranks and grades, sorts and conditions within the city[5] and, equally, in the countryside. Men knew their

---

[1] Largiadèr I, 133; Bluntschli I, 331f; Zeller-Werdmüller, I, 72 n. 2, 101-15, expanded in ZT (1898) 108-31. *Zunft* is not easy to translate. 'Association' is a little too amorphous; 'city company', perhaps the closest parallel, does not fit a group of working artisans, and 'trade union' is scarcely applicable to vintners or grocers. 'Gild' is a neutral and acceptable English equivalent. [2] See below 54.

[3] A. Largiadèr, *Zürichs ewiger Bund mit den Waldstätten vom 1. Mai 1351* (Zürich, 1951).

[4] E. Gagliardi, *Hans Waldmann und die Eidgenossenschaft des 15. Jahrhunderts* (Basle, 1912); also *Dokumente zur Geschichte des Bürgermeisters Hans Waldmann*, 2 Bde QSG (Basle, 1911, 1913). Important accessions were Kiburg (1452), Stammheim (1464) and Winterthur (1467). See Map 45 (by Paul Kläui) in *Historischer Atlas*.

[5] The obvious class groupings were nobles (knights – *die Ritterschaft*), clergy (*der Klerus*) and citizens (*die Bürger*). There were also residents (*die Hintersassen, die Einsassen, die Einwohnern*) and strangers (*Fremdesvolk*) (Bluntschli I, 143). The simple fact of residence within the city boundaries did not make a citizen nor did it prevent some citizens from habitually living outside the walls. Nobles and clergy apart, citizenship was relatively easy to obtain in the fifteenth century: for the newcomer the necessary requirements were five years residence within the city walls, payment of taxes and membership of a gild. These were not specially difficult for a man of substance to secure.

status because it was that of their fathers: it was as difficult as elsewhere in Europe to escape from the state of life into which you were born save, as Hans Waldmann demonstrated most effectively, by successful military service. When, however, he seemed to be making himself dictator, he was hurriedly put to death (6 April 1489).

The outline framework of the government was simple and apparent, however complex in detail. Authority rested with the council – the 'mighty, powerful, honourable and wise lords, Bürgermeister and councillors'[1] – which appears in the twelfth century and expands in the thirteenth. It became an assembly of some two hundred elected and changing individuals, elected – chosen is perhaps the better word since 'elected' easily implies voting and selection, which hardly ever took place – by the organised craftsmen. There is an analogy with the City of London with its Common Council elected by the wards and its Lord Mayor and sheriffs elected by the Common Council and Liverymen of the City Companies meeting in the Guildhall. For Zurich there were the corresponding Bürgermeister, Zunftmeister, Zunftbrüder and a Rathaus. If we think of the council as a sovereign body of about two hundred and of the effective electorate as at most two thousand strong we shall not be far wrong. Further, since there was strong tradition of variation and alteration in the chosen representatives, most qualified artisans had a fair chance of appearing on the governing body and knew how the government functioned.[2] The twelve companies or gilds were formed by the retail shop-keepers, tailors, vintners, bakers, weavers,[3] smiths, tanners, butchers, shoemakers, carpenters, fishermen and gardeners, each with sub-divisions and each with its hall – 'zur Schmiden', 'zur Meisen', 'zum Saffran' and the rest, some of which have survived or been revived as restaurants and headquarters of social clubs. The thirteenth company was careful to retain a different title – *Gesellschaft* – an association of all those with accepted pretensions to nobility, whose meeting place was 'zum Ruden'. Before Brun's day, the 'Constables',[4] *die Gesellschaft zur Constaffel*, formed a

---

[1] 'ersamen strengen vessten fürsichtigen wyssen burgermeister und rätt zů Zürich.' Z VII, 469.

[2] Bluntschli I 332–3, II, 16–19; Largiadèr I, 184–5, 265–8; H. Morf, *Zunftverfassung und Obrigkeit in Zürich von Waldmann bis Zwingli* MAGZ 45 (Zürich, 1969); L. Weisz, *Verfassung und Stände des alten Zürich* (Zürich, 1938); H. Nabholz und W. Schnyder, *Quellen zur Zürcher Zunftgeschichte 13. Jahrhundert bis 1798* 2 Bde. (Zürich, 1936) print all the essential documents. P. Guyer, *Verfassungszustände der Stadt Zürich im 16., 17. und 18. Jahrhundert unter der Einwirkung der sozialen Umschichtung der Bevölkerung* (Zürich, 1943); Max Huber, *Die Verfassung des alten Zürich*, in *Vermischte Schriften* Bd. 1. *Heimat und Tradition* (Zürich, 1947) 173–87, is rather slight.

[3] Originally the wool weavers and the linen weavers (and dealers) formed separate gilds.

[4] The 'Constables' by word analogy included all the knights and those of noble family, together with citizens who lived solely upon the rents of their estates, the wholesale merchants, the cloth merchants, money-changers, bankers, goldsmiths and dealers in salt. The nobles and knights had usually obtained, or were descendants of those who had obtained, patents from

kind of House of Lords, with considerable powers. Even when their privileges had been largely surrendered, they retained precedence, social esteem and a tradition of leadership. The 'Constables' had the right to carry the city colours, but each company likewise had its own colours. Each company elected its own master (*der Zunftmeister*) twice annually, these masters representing their crafts on the council and leading the company's contingent of soldiers. In addition, each company chose a special committee of six[1] (*Sechser*), also twice a year, who acted as its executive and as conciliators in disputes and miscellaneous business. All this emerged in the sixteenth century from the successive modifications of the constitution known as the 'sworn documents'.[2] The governing body, the council,[3] consisted of two parts, large and small. The great or large council was made up of 162 members (*die Bürger*), twelve (*die Zwölfer*) from each company, with eighteen (*die Achtzehner*) from the 'Constables' – *die Constaffelherren*. The small council (strictly the two small councils, *die Kleine Räte*) had twenty-four masters and immediate past masters of the companies (*die Ratsherren der Zünfte*), Zurich born and resident, together with twenty-four representatives of companies and 'constables'. These latter in practice consisted of four direct nominees of the 'constables', with two more nominated by the whole council from among the eighteen (*die Achtzehner*), twelve chosen by the council from the companies, and six more (*die Ratsherren freier Wahl*) elected without any limitation. The two Bürgermeister for the year were *ipso facto* members.

The small (or inner) council, meeting on Monday, Wednesday, Thursday and Saturday, every member being also on the full council, was a kind of cabinet or executive committee responsible for the day-to-day administration of justice and carrying out the policy of the larger body. The great council was responsible for the budget, the money being entrusted to a treasurer (*der Seckelmeister*).[4] Foreign affairs, alliances, treaties, peace and war, the appointment of ambassadors, criminal justice, coinage, admission to citizenship, the acquisition and sale of territory, taxation and the choice of all officers from the Bürgermeister downwards, were likewise matters for the great council, whose direct significance increased steadily in the sixteenth century.

the Emperor, for whom the sale of such titles and privileges was lucrative. They wore armour and enjoyed the prefix *von*: it is curious how much interest there is in heraldry, coat-armour and family descent in 'democratic' Switzerland.

[1] Bluntschli I, 332; Nabholz u. Schnyder, *Quellen* 64 (no. 45).

[2] 1335–6 der erste geschworene Brief, 1373 der zweite, 1393 (26 July) der dritte, 1489 (25 May) der vierte, 1498 (20 January) der fünfte, each in some measure enhancing the authority of the council at the expense of the Bürgermeister and of the *Gemeinden* alike. Bluntschli I, 343–50.

[3] 'Bürgermeister, Rät und der Grossrat, so man nennt die Zweihundert der Stadt Zürich.'

[4] H. Hüssy, *Das Finanzwesen der Stadt Zürich im Zeitalter der Reformation* (Zürich Diss., Affoltern a.A., 1946), 27; Largiadèr I, 272–3.

There was a Town Clerk (*Stadtschreiber*)[1] with a deputy (*Unterschreiber*) and a small office or chancery; both the great and the small council quite frequently appointed *ad hoc* committees for particular purposes. One of these was a more or less permanent standing committee known as the Privy or Secret (*heimliche*) council, whose powers and influence have been supposed to be much greater than in fact they were.[2] The Bürgermeister was chairman of both councils, but his authority was limited by the election of a second or co-Bürgermeister, each in practice officiating for six months between the feast of St John the Baptist (24 June) and that of St John the Evangelist (27 December). Council changes were made at the same time, so that there was a Christmas council (*Natalrat*) and a Baptist council (*Baptistalrat*). These dates were to be of some importance in the progress of the Zwinglian Reformation.

Thus the council, although sovereign, was far from static; as new members came in in the second half of the year, policy might change. There is seldom any suggestion of voting or formal divisions since the assembly was small enough for its decision – 'common mind' – to be clear to the Bürgermeister who announced it. Attendance at council meetings obviously involved absence from a man's place of employment and, with nearly all members being *de facto* self employed and many finding it quite difficult to survive without constant attention to their own business, membership of the council was not often actively sought. Inevitably the richer, more substantial citizens, some of whom derived additional revenue from the ownership of property in the countryside, tended to be re-elected. As we should expect, the same names frequently recur in the lists of council members. If an influential person, and still more an influential family, could be won over to a cause, its chances of success were enormously enhanced. Grebel, Bindner, Thumysen, Escher, Lavater, Röist, Röubli, Wyss, Schmid, Fischer, Engelhard, Göldli, Edlibach, are names most frequently met with. Among the nobles, the families of Bonstetten, Bubenberg, Landenberg, Gachnang, were still powerful but steadily becoming less so.[3] In spite of the elaborate arrangements for election and rotation, public affairs were for long periods in fact dominated by a relatively small group of leaders of the greater companies, Constaffel, Meisen, Saffran, most of all. It was they, for example, who had brought Waldmann's brief and benevolent dictatorship to an end, and it was their support which was decisive for the Reformation.[4]

---

[1] Zeller-Werdmüller, vi.
[2] E. Fabian, 'Zwingli und der Geheime Rat, 1523–1531' in *Gottesreich und Menschenreich, Ernst Staehelin zum 80. Geburtstag* (Basle, 1969) 149–95. See below 390–1.
[3] Largiadèr, I, 279. Intermarriage between the leading families was extremely common.
[4] L. v. Muralt, *Stadtgemeinde und Reformation in der Schweiz*, ZSG x (1930), 349–84.

Although the city population[1] proper was less than 6,000, there were ten times that number in the dependencies of the countryside. The area (*Landschaft*) controlled by the council included the *innere Vogteien*,[2] the home counties, as it were, around the lake, and the country districts (*Landvogteien*) of Kiburg, Grüningen, Eglisau, Greifensee, Andelfingen, Regensberg, Knonau, Wädenswil, with certain shared rights of jurisdiction in Thurgau and Baden. They were controlled by Governors (*Vögte*)[3] and these lucrative offices were coveted. *Justicia est magnum emolumentum* – the profits of civil and criminal jurisdiction, added to the payments and taxes extracted from the country people, were considerable. These officials had power and dignity and were responsible for local defence, which might be expensive but could also be profitable. Between city and country there were the inevitable differences, but normally the councillors were skilful enough to recognise this and never strained the patience or loyalty of the farmers too far. The precise extent of the jurisdiction exercised on behalf of the council varied in accordance with the agreements by which the different areas had been taken over, and with local customs. In general, however, the council had complete authority, including the execution, or pardon, of criminals.[4] The coinage, for which the city had been fully responsible since 1425, was maintained at a consistent standard of purity, and was thus a stabilising element.[5]

Like all other states, Zurich relied for its security upon the army.[6] Military service was taken for granted; to be a citizen was also to be armed, and self protection was assumed. For all practical purposes there was a compulsory citizen army even if some of the obligatory parades and duties were not always popular. The Swiss reputation at the opening of the sixteenth century was that of a people of warriors and, certainly, warfare was almost endemic. There were few mounted men; a Swiss army fought on foot, relying on the weight of an orderly advance of men armed with long spears, halberds, swords and battle axes. Cohesion, discipline and

---

[1] Largiadèr I, 268 estimates 4,500, as does Gagliardi, *Waldmann* LVIII. Egli (Z VII, 245 n. 14) 5,000–7,000; Koehler, *Zwingli*, 45, favours 7,000; P. Kläui, *Zürich, Geschichte der Stadt und des Bezirks* (Zollikon, 1948), 62 gives 'rund 4,500'; P. Guyer, *Verfassungszustände*, 79 n. 1 is curiously precise – 4,615–5,540; L.v. Muralt, *Zürich im Schweizerbund* (Zürich, 1951), 47, has 4,600–5,500, followed by M. Haas, *Huldrych Zwingli und seine Zeit* (Zürich, 1969), 66; W. Schnyder, *Die Bevölkerung der Stadt und Landschaft Zürich vom 14. bis 17. Jahrhundert* (Zürich, 1925), *Handbuch* I, 427 gives 7,000 'auf höchstens'.
[2] Or *Obervogteien*. There were twenty of these. Dändliker II, 246.
[3] A common rendering is 'bailiffs' – they were local officers combining the duties of Lord Lieutenant and Sheriff with the administrative responsibilities of estate agents. The *Landvögte* in practice exercised their authority through local subordinates, *Untervögte*. Bluntschli I, 222–36, 395–400.   [4] Bluntschli I, 403–5; Dändliker, II, 237.
[5] Largiadèr I, 276.
[6] Die Feuerwerker-Gesellschaft (Artillerie-Kollegium) in Zurich has published a Neujahrsblatt annually since 1806, often splendidly illustrated, dealing with every aspect of the military history of Zurich.

determination gave a local force, where every man knew his fellow, remarkable fighting power. Marksmanship with the crossbow was assiduously cultivated and highly esteemed; shooting matches which were occasions of rivalry and competition were also social gatherings and provided an opportunity for mobilisation and training. The Zurich forces, whether civic, from within the walls, or rural, from the subject populations, were organised by 'banners', groups centreing on the standard-bearer with a commander and officers. Each gild in the city produced its own following, the 'constables' having traditional and unchallenged precedence in command. There was a civic armoury where spears and halberds were stored, and after 1477 there was a small train of artillery with specialists able to use it. There was no 'standing' army and no question that policy was decided by the civilians, the council. Only when war was imminent was an experienced officer chosen to command the whole available force, and he retired when the campaign was over. There were, however, plenty of such hardened warriors since from the mid-fifteenth century onwards mercenary service, especially in Italy, was continuous. Neither officers nor men were paid; they expected to be fed by the localities in their own state and to live off the country outside it. The purpose of warfare was loot – portable valuables for the men, territory for the state. All this implied constant vigilance. Within walled towns the walls were maintained and guarded. In Zurich, specially selected groups from seven sections of the city were responsible for guarding portions of the walls,[1] and this provided a nucleus for defence from attack if required.

The soldiers were also artisans or farmers. There were no barracks or 'full-time' regiments, but there were always sufficient men with experience in warfare. Zurich had sent a contingent of 1,500 men to the help of Berne at Morat in 1476, and similar numbers to the Swabian war and to Italy. In case of necessity, this could be greatly increased and Zurich could put into the field a powerful force of at least 15,000 men, greater than that of any other state except Berne, and less unruly than the detachments of some other constituents of the Federation.[2]

A flourishing trading centre holding the key to the main north–south trading route along which flowed supplies of salt, corn and wine, a busy manufacturing community, although its woollen and linen-weaving had

---

[1] There were seventeen towers and seven gates, and the fortifications were well maintained in the early seventeenth century. The seven sections or 'watches' were Oberdorf, Lindentor, Neumarkt, Niederdorf, Münsterhof, Kornhaus, Rennweg. Largiadèr I, 91.

[2] H. Escher, *Das schweizerische Fussvolk im 15. und im Anfang des 16. Jahrhunderts*, Nbl. der Feuerwerker-Gesellschaft in Zürich (Zürich, 1905–7). F. Rieter, *Von der militärischen Tradition Zürichs*, 139. Nbl. der F-G. (Zürich, 1948). J. Häne, *Militärisches aus dem Alten Zürichkrieg: Zur Entwicklungsgeschichte der Infanterie* (Zürich, 1928), 22, 143–4 estimates the effectives as 20,000, and enumerates 12,338 in 1529.

declined since the fourteenth century,[1] the city of Zurich also had considerable ecclesiastical importance. The enormous province of Mainz embraced most of the Confederation, the Archbishop of Besançon claiming the rest. There were three dioceses,[2] of which Constance was the largest, and within it Zurich was the greatest city. Berne was at the extreme western point of the diocese, the river Aar marking the line of demarcation. Within Zurich there were seven principal churches, fancifully compared with the seven churches of Rome[3] – the Great Minster, the Fraumünster, St Peter's, the new river church built on piles over the water, and the churches of the Augustinians, Franciscans and Dominicans.

There was also a small group of Beguines (later Dominican nuns) in the cloister of St Verena in the Brungasse near the Dominican church; while across the river and technically outside the city there was the large Dominican nunnery of Oetenbach with, not far away to the east across the Sihl, the Cistercian nunnery of Selnau (Seldenau) and Austin Canons at St Martin in the Zürichberg. There were monasteries at Embrach, Kappel, Rüti, Töss, Heiligenberg (near Winterthur) and Beerenberg near Wülflingen. In addition, the Order of the Hospitallers owned considerable property in the state and maintained three commanderies (*Komtureien*) at Bubikon, Wädenswil and Küssnacht.[4] All this was about the normal complement for a state of the size of Zurich; and it meant that friars, monks, nuns and priests[5] were extremely familiar figures, much seen in the streets, and church bells calling to worship were much heard.

The Great Minster was a splendid and renowned collegiate church founded in the eighth century, dedicated to Saints Felix and Regula (and, as a kind of afterthought, to St Exuperantius) and endowed with considerable real property in Meilen, Höngg, Schwamendingen and elsewhere. Before 1525 its Provost exercised important police rights in the neighbouring villages of Fluntern, Rieden, Rüschlikon and Rüfers.[6] This large parish, with, as its population grew, valuable oblations, provided occupation, opportunity and emoluments for the secular canons, who lived close to the church, following initially the Rule of St Chrodegang of

---

[1] This decline had been responsible for the reduction of the number of gilds or companies from thirteen to twelve in 1440. Largiadèr I, 269.

[2] Basle, Lausanne, Constance. The sees of Chur and Sion were outside the old Confederation; some parts of the south were ecclesiastically in the dioceses of Como and Milan.

[3] In 1514 Leo X agreed that pilgrimages to the seven churches of Zurich should confer the same advantages on pilgrims as did those to the seven churches in Rome. Largiadèr I, 287; J. C. Wirz, *Ennio Filonardi* (Zürich, 1894), 30–1.

[4] A. Nüscheler, *Die Gotteshäuser der Schweiz* (4. Hefte, Zürich, 1864–73), 438–73 enumerating 23 houses, some very small, within reach of the centre of Zurich. There were 60 nuns at Oetenbach in 1310 and over 30 in 1470. Cf. P. Kläui u. E. Imhof, *Atlas zur Geschichte des Kantons Zürich* (Zürich, 1951).

[5] There were at least 200 priests within the city walls. Schnyder, *Bevölkerung*, 67–70.

[6] Bluntschli I, 395.

Metz. When, somewhat surprisingly, Charlemagne had become a canon-ised saint in 1165, his effigy appeared on the Provost's seal[1] and the inevit-able relics were exhibited to the faithful. By the mid thirteenth century the body corporate consisted of a Provost and twenty-four canons,[2] each now with his own prebend and house, frequently of noble birth and with no duties save to take part in the elaborate choral services of the Minster, which, in turn, might be done by deputy. There was a treasurer, chancellor, precentor, *Scholasticus* and *Plebanus*, the latter, with three assistants, being primarily responsible for the spiritual welfare of the parishioners.

They were privileged people:[3] a canon vacating his office could nomin-ate his successor, so that expectants were always there waiting and hoping for the promotion or death of an incumbent. Since 1417 the canons had been obliged to reside, and in 1479 Pope Sixtus IV had agreed that if a canon died during the papal (or odd) months the city council might choose his replacement.[4] An open sale of the next turn would be invalid as being simony, but there are strong suggestions that value was sometimes received for a nomination and that this was widely tolerated. On the whole the Provosts were worthy of their calling: they had included a count of Toggen-burg, two came from the renowned Manesse family, one was a son of Bürgermeister Brun, and many were of noble birth, but by the sixteenth century a decline was apparent. Matthew Nithart (1440–66), for example, was also a Canon of Freising and had a benefice in Ulm, so that he left much of the Zurich business to his administrator (*custos*), Werner von Waldenburg, greatly to the indignation of the learned Canon Felix Hem-merli,[5] who, a little smugly and self-righteously, commented freely on the ignorance and loose conduct of his fellows. Following Werner von Walden-burg came Heinrich Nithart, who in the common fifteenth century tradi-tion also held canonries at Constance, Speier and Strassburg. Jakob von Cham (1473–94) and Johannes Mantz (1494–1513) were natives of Zurich, acceptable partly because they welcomed the alliance with the papacy and forwarded the recruiting campaign of Cardinal Schiner which Zwingli had recently found so distasteful. All these wealthy ecclesiastics, exempt from

[1] Largiadèr I, 103–4.
[2] They were classified as eight priests, eight deacons and eight sub-deacons, not, of course, implying that all were not in major orders. There were also thirty-two chaplains who could deputise when required. Largiadèr I, 104, 105; Jaques Figi, *Die innere Reorganisation des Grossmünsterstiftes in Zürich von 1519 bis 1531* (Zürich, 1951), Zürcher Beiträge zur Ge-schichtswissenschaft Bd. 9, 9. Cf. E. Egli, *Die Zürcherische Kirchenpolitik von Waldmann bis Zwingli*, JSG XXI, 13–14.
[3] The priests and chaplains were called Bürger, but they were not full citizens: they were specially protected persons, *Schutzgenossen*. Bluntschli I, 393–4.
[4] Largiadèr I, 281.
[5] P. Bänziger, *Beiträge zur Geschichte der Spätscholastik und des Frühhumanismus in der Schweiz*, Schweizer Studien zur Geschichtswissenschaft, 4 (Zürich, 1945), 52, 53. B. Reber, *Felix Hemmerlin von Zürich* (Zürich, 1846), 157–65.

state taxation, from military service and from any civic duties, responsibilities or jurisdiction, were an obvious target for criticism.[1] The nuns across the Limmat in the Fraumünster had fallen steadily from the condition in which their abbess had at one time been almost owner and ruler of the community. Invariably daughters of high-born nobles or patricians, they seem to have treated the cloister as a highly exclusive hotel or nursing home. The finances were grossly mismanaged, little attempt was made to enforce and maintain inherited privileges in the face of a growing, powerful and potentially hostile city, and their numbers dwindled. The council appointed an administrator of the property who easily became its protector and director. Property-rights, tolls, coinage, control of weights, measures and market-dues had been alienated one by one.[2] By Zwingli's time state control over what had once been a superior corporation was complete, so that when the end came in 1524 the one surviving Lady passed simply into gracious and adequately compensated retirement without fuss or bother.[3]

Attached to both the Great Minster and the Fraumünster were chaplains and chantry priests, together with two small grammar schools wherein a few selected boys, paying fees, were taught Latin to what might be described as 'university standard'.[4] These were, obviously, potential future clerics; they had been through the song-school, they sang anthems and responses in the increasingly elaborate services, they went in annual procession to the Lindenhof and were often to be seen, in surplice and with lighted candle, accompanying the priest carrying the reserved host through the streets to the sick.

In addition to the churches, monasteries and chantries, there were three hospitals, a word that has so much changed in meaning and connotation as to be highly misleading without a gloss. A medieval hospital[5] was a place where selected infirm persons resorted for rest together with care and attention which was primarily spiritual. The first duty of the hospital master and his staff – there were some fifty of these attached to the main

[1] Anti-clericalism was no new thing: Zurich had welcomed Arnold of Brescia and his teaching in 1139. Clerics were obliged to take an oath of fealty to the city and state and were forbidden to appeal to any external authority except in purely spiritual matters. In 1506 the Bishop of Constance accepted that the Zurich Council had jurisdiction over felonious priests within its borders. Bluntschli, 125-6, 393-4. J. M. Steffen-Zehnder, *Das Verhältnis von Staat und Kirche im Spätmittelalterlichen Zürich* (Diss. Zürich, Immensee (Schwyz) 1935).
[2] Bluntschli 379-82.
[3] The last abbess (1481-96) was Katharina von Zimmern of a renowned Swabian noble family who executed the final deed of transfer on 30 November 1524 (Egli *1*, 265 (No. 595)), married Eberhard von Rischach (Reischach) of Schaffhausen a little later, and died in 1529 or 1530. Z VIII, 203 n. 1.
[4] Largiadèr I, 287.
[5] R. M. Clay, *The Mediaeval Hospitals of England* (London, 1909); B. Milt, *Geschichte des Zürcher Spitals*, in *Zürcher Spitalgeschichte* (Zürich, 1951) I, 11-26.

Zurich hospital – was prayer; if there was healing, it was not the result of medical knowledge, drugs, surgery or nursing. A hospital, therefore, from a secular point of view, could be something of a parasite; the many priests of Zurich were reinforced by those serving the hospital chapel which was situated between the Dominican cloister and the river. In addition, there were larger houses for lepers, so called, isolation hospitals for those with seriously contagious skin diseases – St James on the Sihl and St Maurice on the north road.[1] The clerical community was thus large and wealthy, but for long it had been becoming less and less independent of the state government.

In any sizeable and compact community there always appear a few outstanding individuals who provide unity, direction, purpose, policy and leadership. Such men had never been lacking in Zurich, whose people were notorious for their easy ductility, volatility and intelligence. Everyone there knew and admired figures like Marx Röist, Bürgermeister between 1505 and 1523; Felix Frei, Provost of the Great Minster and chairman of the Chapter; the Grebels,[2] Ritter Peter Grebel and his brother James (Jakob), executed in 1526 for supporting foreign recruiting and accepting a pension from foreign agents, and James's son Conrad, a brilliant student, Zwingli's intellectual peer and his most serious antagonist. Gerold and Hans Edlibach were wealthy, stable and conservative.

This Zurich city population had many of the characteristics of a village society, intimate, gossiping, subject to the vicissitudes of plague and external danger, almost as closely crowded together as passengers on board ship. Everyone was class conscious and status conscious; the most obvious line of distinction was between Zurich-born propertied citizens whose ancestry everyone knew and to whom office came almost as a birthright, and the strangers who came to the city to seek their fortunes and who were assimilated reluctantly and slowly. For the leading citizens, there were opportunities and duties, districts to be governed, castles to be garrisoned, church and monastic foundations to be supervised, men to be coerced and money to be collected.

Outside the city, the basic unit was the *Gemeinde*, the rural village community and usually also a parish with its church and priest. Originally, it had normally been formed by small groups of families cohering for protection against dangerous wild beasts and for the cooperation essential to communal grazing and farming. It was the smallest group with which corporate feeling could be connected, and there was an obvious measure of similarity between these communities which made common treatment, within the framework of customary law, possible. With larger places,

[1] Largiadèr 1, 289.
[2] K. Keller-Escher, *Die Familie Grebel* (Frauenfeld, 1886); Wirz, 382.

country towns like Winterthur, Elgg, Bülach, Eglisau and Rheinau, or fortified positions (*Vorburgen*) like Regensberg, Glanzenberg, Grüningen, Greifensee and Maschwanden, relations were different.[1] Where there were walls and a market and usually a local constitution, it would be almost like bargaining between equals, with the Zurich Council almost invariably able to enforce its own policies but acting with circumspection and reasonableness. The fundamental divisions remained between nobles, knights, ecclesiastics and townsmen on one side, and the cultivators of the soil, some free, some almost serfs, burdened with obligations of service and of payment, collectively designated peasants[2] (*Bauern*).

The peasant was no slave. He, or his farm, was indeed often burdened with heavy obligations; there were many inescapable customary payments, tolls and dues; he must take an oath of obedience to his masters; he was obliged to undertake military service if called upon and he was subject to some legal disabilities compared with the city dwellers, but he was far less at the mercy of the arbitrary whims and fancies of an individual overlord than many of his fellows in Germany. A common policy for the state was supplied by the Council, and local law, custom, precedents and the corporate wishes of the inhabitants were always given serious consideration.

The councillors of Zurich thus had to exercise knowledge, tact, firmness and persuasion in dealing with their subjects, and this was done with considerable skill. It is on the whole remarkable that with very small legal and chancery departments things went so smoothly. Thus, in 1519, Zwingli came to a city in which the art of government was effectively and efficiently practised.

Zurich was accepted as *Vorort*, the first among the thirteen dissimilar cooperating units that made up the Confederation.[3] Its own external or foreign policy was dictated by geography, tradition and events. The Zurchers were highly conscious of their German connections; the Rhine whither they had strained to reach in the north was not so much a barrier as a magnet or meeting place. It was with the inhabitants of the Black Forest, Baden, Württemberg, Swabia and upper Bavaria, that commercial and personal relations were closest, although there was growing suspicion

---

[1] Dändliker I, 310–12; Winterthur was easily the most important. H. Kläui, *Geschichte von Oberwinterthur in Mittelalter* (Winterthur, 1968–9), Nbl. der Stadtbibliothek Winterthur, 299. Bluntschli, 183–5.

[2] Cf. F. Martini, *Das Bauerntum im deutschen Schriftum von den Anfängen bis zum 16. Jahrhundert* (Halle, 1944) 240–301.

[3] Lucerne had occupied this position before c. 1480. G. Stucki, *Zürichs Stellung in der Eidgenossenschaft vor der Reformation* (Aarau, 1970), 11–13. The Diet of the Confederation and its allies usually assembled eight times a year, frequently in the Zurich Rathaus – 161 meetings have been counted between 1500 and 1520. Staehelin I, 122.

and dislike for the rulers of the Habsburg lands around and beyond them. At the same time, their neighbours of Zug, Lucerne, Glarus, St Gall abbey and city, Appenzell, Schwyz and Uri, were never forgotten, and it was with them that a series of compacts and understandings had been made for security, trade and joint advantage, which were valued by all the components.[1] Zurich's interests were thus predominantly German, eastern and in a sense imperial, while the need to keep open the route towards Italy was always apparent. These principles controlled policy; Zurich could never, in fact, act entirely in isolation whether in matters of religion or of politics.

There was one other inescapable consideration. Seventy difficult miles to the south-west lay Berne. Neither the Switzerland of the sixteenth century nor the course of the Reformation there can be comprehended without taking into careful account the position of the city and state so often playfully designated 'the bear'. Berne adhered to the Reformation slowly but decisively – how this came about will be described later. Basle, the largest city in the Confederation, was reluctant to break directly with the Papacy in spite of the long residence there of Erasmus, the teaching of Oecolampadius and the close connection with Strassburg and Lutheran Germany. The lead came from Zurich, and from Zurich only, because of the abilities, persistence and convictions of Zwingli.

On Saturday, 1 January 1519, the thirty-five year old priest announced in his first sermon in the Great Minster that on the following Sunday he would begin a series of discourses on the Gospel according to St Matthew, ignoring the customary limitations and divisions known as pericopes, expounding instead the complete plain text without any accretions of scholastic interpretation.[2] Preaching the pure Gospel was an indispensable element of the Reformation and it therefore used to be said that Reform in Zurich began there and then.

It was not as simple as that. Exactly what was said in these sermons we shall never know, for Zwingli did not write them out and it was only a good deal later that diligent disciples, Megander and Leo Jud in particular, began to record their recollections of what he had said.[3] Certainly he was introducing a new and thoroughly Erasmian concept of Bible-ap-

---

[1] E.g. 1 May 1351, alliance of Zurich, Lucerne, Uri, Schwyz, Unterwalden; 4 June 1352, alliance of Zurich, Schwyz, Uri, Unterwalden, Glarus; 7 October 1370, renewed alliance of Zurich, Lucerne, Zug, Uri, Schwyz, Unterwalden. (*Pfaffenbrief*) 23 May 1477, alliance of Zurich, Berne, Lucerne, Fribourg and Solothurn; 22 December 1481, renewed non-aggression agreement of Unterwalden, Glarus, Berne, Uri, Schwyz, Lucerne, Zug and Zurich (*Stanser Verkommnis*).

[2] Bullinger, *Ref.* I, 12; Z VII, 106. At Einsiedeln he had confined his exposition to the said pericopes (Staehelin I, 135); Luther had at first observed a similar limitation.

[3] Mörikofer I, 57. In any case Leo Jud knew of the early sermons only by hearsay since he did not come to Zurich until the end of 1522. ZWA VII, 486.

proach[1] and exegesis, but this was to be expected from an advanced humanist-minded thinker of his age.

Even more than Luther, Zwingli valued preaching very highly and was indefatigable in the pulpit. The sermons now consisted in the first place of reading the whole Bible text methodically but not chronologically. The start was with the genealogy of Jesus Christ (Matthew 1. 1–17), known to the middle ages best from the Jesse windows in some great churches, then to the whole of St Matthew, the Acts of the Apostles, the epistles to Timothy, Galatians and of Peter, so to all the New Testament except the Apocalypse, and finally the books of the Old Testament in apparently arbitrary order.[2] He began with simple, didactic Bible lessons, moving to more difficult subjects only after his hearers, to whom the Bible was almost unknown and most of whom were unable to read it, had had adequate instruction. His chief objective in preaching was to repeat the word of God unabbreviated and unadulterated, clearly setting out the Law and the Prophets, vehemently calling his hearers to repentance and, with the gentleness of a shepherd, guiding the community to salvation. The actions of the preacher should correspond to his words, and he must be prepared, if necessary, to accept a martyr's fate.

That his sermons were adapted to his hearers, full of plain speaking and homely illustrations, preaching such as had not been heard before in Zurich, is certain enough. There were no gimmicks, no rhetoric, no violent gestures or theatrical denunciations, but simple conviction combined with humour, allusions to current affairs and local personalities and happenings, all set out with rare simplicity, clarity and honesty. The delivery was quiet, but later experience enabled him to fill a large church with his voice. Offenders high or low, monks and recipiants of foreign pensions in particular, were attacked vigorously; sometimes it was even possible to identify the individual to whom reference was made,[3] and when occasion called for it, he was outspoken in his denunciation of the opponents of the Gospel.

These included those, bishops and others, who tried to prohibit vernacular translations of the Bible. It is easy to exaggerate, as it is difficult to assess accurately, the extent and importance of Bible reading at the opening of the sixteenth century. That there had been much interest in the Bible, sometimes connected with the educational work of the Brethren of the

---

[1] Koehler, 'Zwingli als Theologe' *Gedächtnis* c. 41 shows that his doctrine was still Catholic. Erasmus had very similar influence on some English preachers. J. K. McConica, *English Humanists and Reformation politics under Henry VIII and Edward VI* (Oxford, 1965), 15–38, 114–20.

[2] Z I, 133 and n. 2; Wyss 9, 67, 92.

[3] Farner *3*, 116–29 shows how political matters became increasingly the theme of such sermons as were reported.

Common Life, and also an accompaniment of increasing literacy, is certain. The literature that came from the early printing presses was largely theological in nature. The new Bible-based preaching was as welcome as it was unusual: instead of stories from the legends of the saints, anecdotes, or commonplaces about the seven deadly sins, the people now heard the plain text with unusual words explained and difficult passages compared with similar or analogous ones which might make them clearer. Above all, there was no appeal to tradition; long-accepted belief or practice, the ruling of Pope or council or canon law were not to prevail against, or even to be used in amplification of, the words of holy scripture. To the Zurich artisans it was all new, exciting and challenging.

Vernacular Bibles were far from unknown before the appearance of the first edition of Luther's translation of the New Testament at Wittenberg in September 1522, which was reprinted by Adam Petri in Basle in December of that year. Other editions and reprints followed[1] and were eagerly purchased.

In addition to his sermons, the newly appointed priest said mass, heard confessions, took his place in processions and highly ritualistic services in an image-packed church, dressing and speaking like his colleagues. He was, however, fast becoming completely scripture-dominated. This was not the result of sudden revelation or conversion: there was no Lutheran 'tower-experience': there was not even Calvin's decisive moment of choice. A good deal of attention has been given, not very profitably, to the attempt to define the precise moment when Zwingli became evangelical. That he was an orthodox Catholic priest at least until the end of 1518 is reasonably certain; that he was no longer so by 1522 is also clear. There is no clean dividing line.[2] His own testimony is in a letter of 29 December 1521 to Berchtold Haller, in which he insisted that it was five years since he started to work on the Gospels. The chronology thus fits in admirably with Zwingli's mastery of sufficient Greek to enable him to compare the text of the Greek New Testament (1516) with the Vulgate and to study intensively the divine word in the original.[3] We can readily accept the statement that

---

[1] The earliest printed German Bible appeared in 1483, and by 1522 eighteen German versions of the Bible had already been available. See below 128 n. 4.

[2] Koehler, *Zwingli* 70–5; G. W. Locher, *Die Theologie Huldrych Zwinglis im Lichte seiner Christologie*: 1 *Die Gotteslehre* (Zürich, 1952), 54; A. Rich, *Die Anfänge der Theologie Huldrych Zwinglis* (Zürich, 1949), 93–5; H. W. Pipkin, *The Nature and development of the Zwinglian Reformation to August 1524* (Hartford (diss.) 1968): copy in StaZ.

[3] Z I, 256 n. 4; ZWA VIII, 504–5, 512–19; J. F. Goeters, *Zwinglis Werdegang als Erasmianer* (Witten, 1969) 268–71 (*Reformation und Humanismus. Robert Stupperich zum 65. Geburtstag*) 255–71. It is a pity that later events unnecessarily caused the historical question of the originality of Zwingli's contribution to the Reformation to be involved with the unfortunate controversy with Luther. The tendency of modern scholarship, especially since Joseph Lorz, has been in the direction of making Reformation history less personal and stressing con-

he had not directly come into contact with, let alone read carefully, Luther's early works. None the less, the critical approach, deriving among others from Valla, was becoming part of the tissue and fabric of the age, and a widely disseminated Bible must have been revolutionary in any case. Many a modern Marxist became so before reading *Das Kapital* or even the *Communist Manifesto* of 1847; so, too, there were Lutherans who had not read the three Reformation treatises. Luther himself confessed to having reached Hussite conclusions before he read Hus' book *On the Church*. Zwingli was frequently accused of being a follower of Wyclif, not one word of whose writings he can have read.

The historian is wedded to records, to the written and printed word. Unrecorded conversations can only be guessed at, and in the sixteenth century an enormous amount depended upon word-of-mouth communication. In this way after 1517 a good deal of what was happening in Saxony could quite well have been known in a pilgrimage-centre like Einsiedeln without being recorded. The absence of evidence of the existence of a printed Lutheran text does not necessarily mean that some part of the content of these writings was entirely unknown. In this connection, some rather speculative deductions have been drawn from the marginalia in Zwingli's books, particularly those in his earlier handwriting.[1] It has, for example, been argued that before 1519 he had already worked out his later pneumatology from 2 Peter 1. 21.[2] That the Bible was the direct word of God, the revelation of Him who was Truth itself, he never doubted, but there was nothing specially new about this – it was a commonplace assumption of the Fathers and the scholastic theologians. What was new for him was the growing realisation that traditional, conventional and even authoritarian interpretation must be subject to individual conviction based on careful study. He had early transcribed a good deal of the Pauline epistles and, with a trained and retentive memory, could reproduce long passages as well as convenient texts, verbatim. All this was to be of great value in the public disputations in which he was involved and in the controversial writing which had to be produced rapidly.

Like his contemporaries, he submitted himself wholly and willingly to the tyranny of the Book.[3] Then, and much later, there was no questioning the canon of the scriptures, which included, but with considerably

---

tinuity rather than personal innovation. After the Council of Trent, it was too easy to represent the Roman Catholic Church as a huge monolith, which it was not in 1519. In this year Zwingli's thought was emphatically Erasmian. It was Erasmus who was forced by events (and a temperamental determination to keep out of trouble) to avoid identification with heresy and to break, one by one, with Hutten, Luther and Zwingli.

[1] These investigations were started by Usteri, *Initia*.
[2] F. Schmidt-Clausing, *Zwingli* (Berlin, 1965), 41.
[3] C. Nagel, *Zwingli's Stellung zur Schrift* (Freiburg/Leipzig, 1896).

diminished authority for him, the Apocrypha. Just as for Luther the general Epistle of James was 'an epistle of straw', so, for Zwingli, quite early, the Apocalypse was somehow suspect. Even this qualification was made slowly. What was wonderful to him and his generation was that they had before their eyes the original Greek, and Hebrew, texts. The very words directly inspired by the Holy Spirit[1] were there for them to read, and the printing-press made possible an exactness unknown previously. It was in 1516 that this great treasure had been delivered into Zwingli's hands, and early 1519 allows exactly the right length of time for assimilation and cogitation. Further, during the immediate pre-Zurich years, he had read and re-read all that he could of the Fathers, Jerome, Ambrose, Augustine and, in place of the usual Gregory, Origen. Here again it is the disciple of Erasmus that appears. From the Basle presses, overseen by Erasmus and with his introduction and comments, each of these had come or was to come.[2] The study of Patristics was indeed still in its infancy, texts were uncertain and deductions from them disputable. While Zwingli perused them eagerly, he applied his full critical faculties to them; they provided useful supplementary ammunition, but not much more.

The Zurich Zentralbibliothek guards Zwingli's own copies of them all except, probably, the Ambrose, which bears no mark of his ownership, although he quotes from this unconvincing author often enough. The great folios of *Augustini Opera*, delivered to him with Froben's compliments as a gift, bear a large number of annotations which reveal the diligent reader, but the books were in his possession all his life and St Augustine was too much the most popular of the Fathers to be specially decisive at this stage. In his edition of Jerome (Basle, Froben, 1516) which was to be re-used by Pellican and still again by Bullinger, Zwingli a little self-consciously writes his name in Greek characters.[3] The introductions by Erasmus were obviously valued, as were also the Jeromean comments on the Prophets, notably Jeremiah. Erasmus had a special affection for Jerome and was particularly attracted to Jerome's *Letters*, while both he and Zwingli could not fail to note that Jerome himself had suffered some persecution because of his efforts to secure a satisfactory Bible text.[4] We think, and rightly, of

---

[1] That 'all scripture is given by inspiration of God', II Timothy 3.16 (which appears in the New English Bible as 'every inspired scripture has its use for teaching the truth and refuting error') was basic to Zwingli as to Luther. This in turn depended upon the acceptance of Christ as the centre and purpose of all revelation. Through him both old and new Testaments proclaimed the word of God. Zwingli's religious thought never ceased to be dominated by the Incarnation.

[2] Amerbach had printed at Basle the works of Ambrose in 1492, Augustine in 1506, and called in Erasmus to help with Jerome in 1514. Ambrose was re-edited by Erasmus in 1527, Augustine in 1528. P. S. Allen, *Erasmus, Lectures and wayfaring sketches* (Oxford, 1934) 47–55.

[3] Koehler, *Bibliothek* 19 (No. 150).

[4] P. S. Allen, *Erasmus, Lectures and wayfaring sketches* (Oxford, 1934), 72.

Zwingli as the independent commentator on the Bible and even as a critic of the Vulgate text, but the solid learning and sensible as well as sensitive thought of Jerome were never entirely forgotten by him and were specially prominent in his mind in these early Zurich days.

His edition of Origen was that printed at Paris in 1512,[1] and again his annotations, and his later commendation of this Father to Myconius,[2] indicate appreciative study. Anyone who has tried to use, or even to move about, these great folio volumes, will realise that their assimilation and annotation occupied many studious hours. Later in life, Zwingli frequently had to read and write at high speed under pressure, and it was then that he was grateful for solid foundations that he had been able to lay in his early thirties. Zwingli must have brought with him to Zurich one of the best libraries possessed at the time by a simple secular priest, and his books he esteemed all his life.[3] Many threads were now being drawn together in 1519–20 – memories of rather barren university scholasticism with no desire on his part to return to Aristotle, Peter Lombard, Aquinas, Scotus and the rest, yet he knew them well and was therefore suitably equipped to meet his opponents in verbal-logical Latin discussions, each knowing that the other side was well trained in the formalities of logical thought. Over and beyond this was the almost fashionable humanist, ready to produce the telling sentence, the well-turned epigram and the apt quotation; able to read and write in Greek, knowing his Plato, poets and playwrights, rejoicing, in common with Erasmus and More, in the light satire and subtle wit of Lucian. Solid learning, classical outlook, parochial and pastoral duties being fulfilled and under control, Italy visited at least twice, Swiss military service shared and evaluated, his name known at Rome, the *Leutpriester* of the Great Minster had much to offer outside the pulpit as well as from it.

Bold and even corrosive as some of this preaching was, it was already, as it always remained, basically and fundamentally Christ-centred.[4] The Cross, and all that it meant, was never absent: the tidings were of eternal salvation. There was no word or sentence of the three creeds, that of the Apostles to which he believed each of the Twelve had contributed a clause, that of Nicaea and that attributed to Athanasius with its uncompromising

---

[1] Koehler, *Bibliothek*, 30 (No. 250). [2] Z VII, 287–91.
[3] Koehler, *Bibliothek*, 3–32. This was exceptional; it was noted as something unexpected of his predecessor, Hemmerli, that he had a good library. Zwingli may have known that Johannes Heynlin von Stein (de Lapide) (1430–96) gave 283 volumes to the Carthusians of Basle. J. Rosen, *Die Universität Basel im Staatshaushalt 1460 bis 1535,* BasZG 72 (1972), 207.
[4] A. Rich, *Zwinglis Weg zur Reformation*, ZWA VIII, 511–35 esp. 523–32; Z VII, 341–5. The second point for discussion at the first Zurich disputation emphasised this. 'The essence of the Gospel is this that our Lord Christ Jesus, the very son of God, brought us tidings of the will of his heavenly Father and by his sinlessness saved us from death and reconciled us to God.' Z I, 458; Z II, 27.

definition of the Trinity, which he did not fully accept and proclaim. He was no more 'modernist' than was Luther, Cranmer, or Calvin. Angels, Satan, the virgin birth, the biblical miracles and Christ's physical ascension were the certainties to him that they were to all save Jews and infidels. Deep as was the division that his later teaching was to bring, he was at one with his opponents about the basic articles of the Christian faith.

It was the message of salvation as set forth by Christ's own words in the Gospels that this cheerful, sanguine, short-sighted priest was now starting to deliver. The 'establishment' was clearly a little taken aback. The elderly Canon Conrad Hofmann, who had helped to bring about Zwingli's election and supported his attacks on mercenary service and the hierarchy, found the sermons not entirely to his taste. There were too many attacks on notorious sinners, too much exposure of evils sometimes best not proclaimed from the pulpit, and all this spoken too quickly. Zwingli should not think himself wiser or more learned than everyone else and should show greater respect for authority, whether of the church, the government or the traditional and accepted writers of antiquity. More care should be given to examination of the new teachings of Luther, exaggeration should be avoided and not everything which could be said or written for the clergy in Latin was necessarily suitable for ignorant laymen. A little less violence, a little more respect for the Virgin Mary, the rosary and prayers to saints would be appreciated, while attacks on purgatory and excommunication, and unreliable views on infant baptism should be abandoned.[1]

Other canons supported Hofmann, but Zwingli was not to be stopped.[2] He insisted that he was no innovator, that he was following the teaching of the early church as found in the Bible, and that it was his duty to expound this teaching to the artisans of Zurich in words that they could understand. It was indeed the matter rather than the manner of his discourses that was popular, combined with manifest sincerity and charisma. The great age of the sermon was just opening: it was to be the most powerful instrument of the coming century. The word was power.

There were, however, other things beside sermons to think about. The new minister must ride frequently to Wytikon and Zollikon, he must know his parishioners, baptise, administer extreme unction, say mass, hear confessions, urge his penitents to make offerings to the fabric of the church and see to it that his assistants were usefully and suitably employed. At the end of his first month, he was being asked questions, as he had been before, about the indulgences which Sanson[3] was offering at the

---

[1] Egli *I* 59–65 (No. 213); Z II, 683 n. 8.
[2] O. Vasella, *Huldrych Zwingli und seine Gegner*, ZSK 56 (1962), 281–300.
[3] Z VII, 115 n. 4, 183–4; Bullinger, *Ref.* I, 13–18. See above 44 n. 2.

city gate, coming from Constance and calling for money. His answers were naturally, hostile. Without directly condemning the whole theory behind the offer, he insisted that people were not properly informed about the conditions of the indulgence which they did not understand or perform and were being induced to part with their money on what amounted to false pretences.[1] This was nearly two years after Luther's 'Ninety-five theses', and by now the topic had received wide publicity and had become for Germany much more than a doctrinal dispute. The Bishop of Constance let it be known through his Official that he did not support Sanson, who in any case was taking money out of his diocese. The Zurich council refused him entry to the city, as did Bremgarten, and everywhere the whole business was thrust into the background.[2] At Rome the authorities were anxious that the fire that had been started at Wittenberg should not spread to Switzerland. The papacy was the ally of the Confederation and a generous employer; Zwingli himself had not attacked the Pope and was still on friendly terms with Fabri,[3] the bishop's adviser. Sanson was recalled and the affair seemed at an end.

It had, however, meant that the problem of authority within the church would receive renewed attention; Luther's writings were now being widely circulated, and Zwingli welcomed them. Further south, these tendencies and the treatment of Sanson had not passed unnoticed. Word came from Myconius[4] of rising concern at Lucerne.[5] This place was, and long remained, the heart of Catholic Switzerland, the principal bastion of the papacy within the Confederation. It was also at the very core of this latter, the natural meeting point for the original Confederates, Uri, Schwyz and Unterwalden which, with Zug, later acted together as the 'Five *Orte*'. It was their largest town and well situated for communication by water. The inhabitants were almost entirely employed in agriculture or pastoral activities, usually poor, ignorant and limited in outlook. Much of the land was barren mountain and utterly unattractive – there were no tourists then – grain, iron, salt and wine, all had to be imported; life was exceedingly hard. What this bred was a tough, unyielding and conserva-

---

[1] T. von Liebenau, *Zur Geschichte der Ablassprediger in der Schweiz*, BasZG II (Basle, 1903), 78–80.

[2] EA 3, 2, 1141.

[3] As late as 18 October 1520, Zwingli and Fabri were in amiable correspondence with one another. See below 209–310.

[4] Z VII, 317. 'Evomunt contra Zinglium non quidem vera male interpretantes, sed omnino pervertentes.'

[5] P. X. Weber, *Der Kanton Luzern vom eidgenössischen Bund bis zum Ende des 15. Jahrhunderts. Geschichte des Kantons Luzern von der Urzeit bis zum Jahre 1500* (Lucerne, 1932) III. Teil, 627–866. S. Grüter, *Geschichte des Kantons Luzern im 16. und 17. Jahrhundert* (Lucerne, 1945) 50–2. W. Brändly, *Geschichte des Protestantismus in Stadt und Land Luzern* (Lucerne, 1956), 91. (LuzernGeschichte und Kultur hg. v. J. Schmid, II. Staats-und Kirchengeschichte. Kirchengeschichte Bd. 4.)

tive peasantry clinging devotedly to the past and jealously disliking and despising the more fortunate dwellers of the plain. Lucerne itself, although a walled city, shared the prejudices and convictions of the country people and reflected the age-long dislike of the food producer for the food consumer. The very poverty and barrenness of the land made the area especially susceptible to outside inducements, above all to foreign pensions to the leading citizens. A little gold went a very long way, and the leaders of the communities were willing enough to see young men, whom it was difficult to employ or to feed, go off as mercenaries. That this had papal approval made it all the better, and if it also kept the path to Italy open this too was advantageous.

Hence northern criticism of papal indulgences and foreign pensions were much resented there. Suspicions of heterodoxy, even heresy, were roused when news came that another highly controversial matter was being ventilated in the Zurich pulpit. The assiduous study of the New Testament, particularly the Acts of the Apostles, had caused the preacher to examine with special care the nature and institutions of the primitive church. This led to diligent consideration of the now controversial subject of clerical celibacy and clerical morality. Before long he concluded that clerical celibacy rested on no adequate biblical basis, the new touchstone by which he was now testing everything, and, although he had little sense of history, he was also aware that before the eleventh century many priests could, and did, marry.[1]

On the themes both of indulgences and clerical marriage there was still room for manoeuvre. Canon law on these subjects might be amended by papal decree, by a General Council or even by favourable interpretation; a great deal more and clearer definition was needed, much of which was to be supplied by the Council of Trent for another generation; but, while much was still fluid, discussion should proceed. One of the popular convictions of the day was that a suitable way of reaching conclusions was by a public verbal exchange of views. The universities had long since encouraged the formulation of questions for debate, discussion and settlement by the application of the agreed logical rules of the schools. It was but to take this a stage further to believe that wider conclusions could be reached by similar methods. In addition, the printing-press made written controversy inevitable, indeed interminable. Question and answer, challenge and response, the flat assertion, the written dialogue, the open letter, were all being employed. There were no laws of libel or of copyright, and at the same time the printed word had all the fascination of a new invention and also the authoritative implications of scholarship for the unlettered. Zwingli certainly hoped that Rome itself might be influenced by

---

[1] See below 78-80.

the force of argument in writing and public discussion. There was much that needed elucidation.

However, the new *Leutpriester* had completed only some six or seven months of duty[1] before he came near to relinquishing his post for ever. In August 1519, Zurich received its visitation of the plague.[2] Such outbreaks were common enough in the sixteenth century, but they were serious enough also. Complete ignorance of the nature of the transmission of disease, and the close crowding together of people in uncleansable narrow lanes with animals wandering about freely, made infection unavoidable. At this visitation at least one in four died;[3] there can hardly have been a house in Zurich without at least one corpse to be buried. Such a time was obviously dangerous for a priest whose duty it was to fortify the dying with the last consolations of religion. All who could afford it left the city, and it is to Zwingli's credit that in duty bound[4] he returned to his post. In September he caught the disease and nearly died.[5] It is well to remember that if this illness had proved fatal to him, as it did to his brother Andrew,[6] his name would have remained almost unknown except to diligent historians of south German humanism. It is also curious that he may have owed his survival to the skilled attentions of the papal legate's personal physician who was sent to him at Zurich. Quite certainly Zwingli knew that he had been at death's door, and like many another man, he was never entirely the same after so serious an illness. How he prepared himself for death he described later in a German hymn or poem[7] in three parts, each of four stanzas, giving expression to his feelings at the onset, at the height of the fever, and during convalescence. In few, but moving, words, he commits himself entirely to God's mercy

[1] In July 1519 he had obtained leave of absence to visit Pfäfers (near the present-day Rhine frontier of St Gall but then in the county of Sargans) for a 'cure' and had to be hurriedly summoned home. It is a little curious that he had already thus intermitted his sermons and pastoral work so soon after his appointment.

[2] Bullinger, *Ref.* I, 28.

[3] Koehler, *Zwingli*, 76, estimated one in three; Egli, Z I, 62, between one in two and one in four.

[4] Koehler, *Buch*, 68.   [5] Z VII, 200 n. 2; Z I, 62.

[6] Z VII, 211 n. 1.

[7] This single page of verse, frequently reprinted, being almost the earliest of Zwingli's known writings, has been subjected to minute analysis. There are several references in letters to a lost treatise or tract written by him in the autumn of 1519 entitled *Dialogus pestis*: possibly the *Pestlied* was an arrangement of the essentials of this, set to music to be sung as a kind of psalm. In favour of this is the well-known fact that Zwingli was exceptionally musically gifted even for that age; against it, that he would be unlikely to put his thoughts just in this form. It is all made more complicated by the existence of a later version, perhaps a semi-independent composition, owned and used by Bullinger with an even later recension (1551) attributed to Theodore Beza. Farner II, 360–73, and the authorities cited on p. 477 especially A. Walther, *Zwinglis Pestlied*, in Neue Kirchliche Zeitschrift (Erlangen/Leipzig, 1901) XII. Jg., 813–27; A. Bouvier, *Henri Bullinger, Réformateur et conseiller oecuménique* (Neuchâtel, 1940) 269–71, 514–16; J. Schweizer, *Reformierte Abendmahlsgestaltung in der*

Thy purpose fulfil:
nothing can be too severe for me.
I am but thy vessel
to be made whole or broken in pieces.[1]

Restored by God's will, he is ready for anything that the world has to bring

With thy help,
without which I can do nothing
I will gladly endure the knocks
and noise of this world
as the price of health.[2]

There was no appeal to the saints or the Virgin Mary, no vow, no suggestion of reliance on the church; his grave illness had brought him into direct contact with eternity.[3] By God's mercy he had been granted life, and this life was now to be lived for God's purposes only. He was a man with a mission. At the end of 1519 he felt, what he had not done at its beginning, an intense sense of purpose, complete self-confidence, arising from the assurance that God would use him and direct his steps and thoughts to His chosen ends. It carried with it that strengthening of faith that could remove mountains, a certainty of aim which overcame doubt and brought with it invaluable self-assurance and optimism.[4] Later in life he was to think of himself as a prophet, knowing that words came to him from above, sure that his opponents were at best mistaken, at worst wickedly and vainly opposing God's chosen instrument. This *Pestlied* thanksgiving was rightly compared to a psalm, and there was thenceforth something of King David about his ways and action. During his illness and recovery some notable events took place in Germany.

Schau Zwinglis (Basle, 1954), 54–5; A. Rich, *Die Anfänge der Theologie Huldrych Zwinglis* (Zürich, 1949), 104–19. Perhaps too much has been read into 75 lines of poetry!

[1] Z I. 67   Thů, wie du wilt;
                          mich nüt befilt.
                          Din haf bin ich.
                          Mach gantz ald brich.

[2] Z I. 69   So wil ich doch
                          den trutz und boch
                          in diser wält
                          tragen frölich umb widergelt
                          mit hilffe din,
                          on den nüt mag vollkummen sin.

[3] ZWA v, 323.

[4] By 31 December 1519 he was writing enthusiastically to the gloomy Myconius: 'We are not alone; in Zurich there are more than 2000 relatively enlightened people.' Z VII, 245.

On 28 June 1519 the young Charles was elected Holy Roman Emperor and was crowned at Aachen on 23 October 1520, between which dates, as was to be of significance for Zurich later, Duke Ulrich of Württemberg was forced to leave his duchy. Martin Luther, distinguished university professor and Augustinian friar, had written the too-notorious 95 theses in October 1517, and within twelve months these, and their author, had received wide publicity so that a charge of heresy had to be faced. Refusing to retract when asked to do so by Cardinal Cajetan, at Leipzig in July 1519, he rejected Pope and Council alike and was excommunicated on 15 June 1520.[1] By then he had written the three celebrated treatises – *To the Christian Nobility of the German Nation*, *On the Babylonish Captivity of the Church* and *On the Freedom of a Christian*. These, with his other works, were soon in print and sold widely. In April 1521 he made his celebrated appearance before the Emperor at Worms, and in May, outlaw and heretic, he went underground temporarily at the Wartburg.

Few topics have been more discussed than the impact of Luther upon Zwingli in 1520 and 1521, and necessarily without certain conclusion. What can be said with a degree of certainty is that it was Erasmus' thought to which Zwingli owed most in these early years. However, as from 1519 onwards, more of Luther's writings were available in Basle, copies reached Zwingli, and in 1521 he was considering them carefully.[2] By then, too, the term 'Lutheran' was already being applied indiscriminately to anyone who was critical of the hierarchy or of accepted doctrine, and Zwingli came within this category. To support a heretic, to be *fautor*, was to be in danger of the stake to which heretics were consigned unless there was hurried and adequate recantation. The ban of the Empire did indeed mean very little in practice unless, as in the case of Ulrich of Württemberg, powerful interested parties were prepared to maintain it by armed force, but it could have appreciable legal inconveniences. There might well be occasion when individually or corporately Zurich citizens needed to approach one of the imperial courts, and to find themselves excluded as supporters of Luther would not be good enough. Zurich was an imperial city and unwilling to risk any curtailment of its legal rights. The Pope, too, still owed Zurich money for military services rendered but not paid for, and there was no intention of gratuitously offering the papacy an opportunity to repudiate its obligations.

Zwingli came to Zurich at the moment when the controversy about

---

[1] The effective excommunication was on 3 January 1521 by the Bull *Decet Romanum Pontificem*. E. G. Rupp and B. Drewery, *Martin Luther* (London, 1970) 62–7.

[2] Z VII, 365–6, 461; ZWA III, 162–80; Koehler, *Zwingli*, 60–1. In May 1521 in England Wolsey presided at the first of the futile burnings of Lutheran literature there, which advertised its existence and also showed the tendencies of some of the more reflective elements of English society. A. G. Dickens, *The English Reformation* (London, 1964), 68f.

mercenary service was at its height. The Zurich tradition had been to support Pope and Emperor as against France, whereas the other Swiss cantons were orientated towards France, drawn in large measure by the interest of Berne. The Popes were extremely anxious and careful to maintain close contact with Zurich as a source of manpower. Through a series of nuncios, particularly Ennio Filonardi, efforts were consistently made to keep up the supply of soldiers. Whether, if the expeditions of 1510 and 1511 had been more successful, if papal promises of cash payments had been promptly honoured and if Zwingli's eloquence had been less singularly compelling, the result might not have been different, cannot be answered. What is certain is that the early preaching of reform was tolerated by Rome in Zurich because its military support was needed. Although in fact no more such help was forthcoming, it was to the advantage of the papacy that in May 1521 Zurich refused to join the other twelve states in an alliance with France.

All these factors militated against the acceptance of Lutheranism, the more so as after 1521 any hopes of its reconciliation with Rome vanished. The citizens of Zurich were not likely to be willing to be accounted followers of a German heretic instead of their own minister. The decision, in any case, would lie with the council. Luther was safe and able to continue writing and preaching because he had the support of his prince, the powerful and almost autocratic Elector of Saxony. Zwingli had to carry with him two hundred leading citizens, unwilling to risk reputation and possibly livelihood without sound reason and conviction, a large body of experienced men who could be relied upon to act circumspectly and rather slowly. The sermons of a stranger, however compelling, would hardly suffice.

Zwingli's appeal was to the Bible, and here he was at one with Luther; *Schriftprinzip*, the text of Holy Writ, was paramount. He also accepted, having reached the same conclusion independently, 'justification by faith', solifidism. Many pages have been written on the Lutheran discovery or exposition of Romans I. 17, *Justus ex fide vivit*, a text to which Zwingli alludes infrequently. Instead, and with ever increasing emphasis, he was preaching that faith was the first of the virtues and must take precedence of all else, that without the certain conviction of redemption through Christ, a conviction that could come only by the grace of God through the Holy Spirit, a man could not be a true Christian. To those to whom this supreme revelation had been vouchsafed all else, in greater or less degree, might be added. They, and they alone, could understand rightly the divine message. To them was shown the meaning of the scriptures, and if this conflicted with practice, tradition or even, but here again with certain qualifications, with reason, these must give way. The books of the Bible formed a coherent whole, entirely reconcilable, unalterable and comprehensible through faith by any adult. The partial revelation of the Old Testament was completed in the New Testament, the Law of Moses was merged into and submerged by the Law of Christ. This in one sense was commonplace and universally acceptable; in another sense it meant the rejection of the traditions of the ages, canon law and papal authority. Human interpretations – *menschensatz* is Zwingli's favourite word – must give way to the certainty of the pure Bible text. Personal actions, however strenuous, virtuous and good, were of no avail without faith.

Some time in 1520[1] the council was sufficiently impressed to require all priests to preach the Gospels and Epistles in accordance with the pure texts of the two testaments, avoiding human additions and explanations. 'Innovations', however, were to be avoided also, and there is little evidence that the decree meant anything more than a kind of vote of confidence in Zwingli as an acceptable preacher.

Two years of steady expository activity were rewarded for Zwingli on 29 April 1521. On that date he was elected to a canonry in the Great Minster vacated by Dr Heinrich Engelhard[2] who had been persuaded to exchange this for a similar position in the Fraumünster. This was the outcome of some considerable negotiation and was an indication that many of the canons were now sympathetic to the new teaching. It meant also that Zwingli, by becoming a canon, became also, for the first time, a full citizen of Zurich. He continued to act as public preacher with two assistants, Georg Staehelin and Heinrich Lüthi; he now had a house, a horse, a secure if modest income (seventy gulden) and a base for further operations.[3] It gave him greater authority and he was proud of it. 'I am in this city of Zurich bishop and pastor, the cure of souls has been laid upon me; I have taken an oath to this effect which the monks have not done.'[4] His influence was manifestly growing, but it is worth emphasising that as Luther was leaving Worms for the Wartburg, Zwingli was accepting the position, and taking the requisite oaths, of one within the Roman hierarchy and part of the governing body of a great collegiate church.

---

[1] The exact date is uncertain, and the source is Bullinger, *Ref.* I, 32 – 'all gemeinlich, und fry die heyligen Evangelia...vnd rächter göttlicher geschrifft beider testamenth, predigen söllind...Was aber Nüwerungen vnd von menschen erfunden sachen vnd Satzungen syend, dess söllind sy geschwigen.' ZWA II, 166–72, 208–14.

[2] Z I, 144–5 n. 3; VII, 113 n. 7, 475; Wyss, 17; Egli *1*, 897 (No. 164 *b*); Egli *4*, I, 22–4.

[3] Mörikofer I, 94–5; Staehelin I, 193.   [4] Wyss 19.

4

The first rift

In January 1522 Zwingli had been preaching the gospel in Zurich for three years. He had a considerable following, but he was manifestly feeling that the services and routine of the seven churches went on much as before and that the work of evangelisation was laborious. He also now knew that effective action required the positive support of the Council, to which, as Canon and citizen, he now had easier access.

Ash Wednesday fell on 5 March in 1522, and shortly after that day an event occurred which involved Zwingli in the public assertion, and then defence, of one application of the Bible message which he had expounded and to which he had given intensive study. It came over a minor matter, one of the most adiaphorous of the adiaphora, the rule of fasting during Lent. It also happened in association with one of Zwingli's earliest supporters and admirers, the printer Christopher Froschauer, for it was in his house that trouble over this started. His press,[1] operating in the shadow of the Dominican cloister, had been in existence for several years, and from it had come the usual books of piety and elementary instruction that characterised the early days of printing. He specialised in cheap, handy octavo volumes, and was quick to use illustrations provided on occasion by Holbein, Cranach, Graf or Dürer. Compared with Basle or Venice, the establishment was insignificant, yet without it much of Zwingli's work would have been impossible.

It was in the parlour of Froschauer's house that a small company

---

[1] Froschauer was a Bavarian who was made a full citizen of Zurich in 1519. He had been preceded as a printer by Peter and Hans Hager and Hans Rüegger – the earliest indication of his press is in 1518. P. Leemann-van Elck, *Zur Zürcher Druckgeschichte* (Berne, 1934), 60. F. J. Schiffmann, *Der Dominikaner Albertus Albo Lapide und die Anfänge des Buchdrucks in der Stadt Zürich* (ZT 1899), 100–30. J. Staedtke, *Christoph Froschauer, der Begründer des Zürcher Buchwesens* (Zürich, 1964). J. Staedtke, *Anfänge und erste Blütezeit des Zürcher Buchdrucks* (Zürich, 1965). P. Leemann-van Elck, *Der Zürcher Drucker Christoph Froschauer* (Festschrift der Schweizer Bibliophilen Gesellschaft, 1931). P. Leemann-van Elck, *Die Offizin Froschauer. Zürichs berühmte Druckerei im 16. Jahrhundert. Ein Beitrag zur Geschichte der Buchdruckerkunst anlässlich der Halbjahrtausendfeier ihrer Erfindung.* MAGZ Bd. 33 H. 2 1939–1943 (Zürich, 1940). G. R. Potter, *Zwingli and his publisher, The Library Chronicle* (Philadelphia, 1974) XL. 108–17.

met[1] early in the Lenten season of 1522. There part of a simple evening meal consisted of some form of sausage. Zwingli was among those present but did not eat any of this although most of the rest of the company did so, but he also raised no objection. They all knew that they were offending against the law and custom of the church and that this law and custom would be, if necessary, upheld by the authority of the Zurich council, as in fact it was on 9 April.[2] It would have been easy to have escaped any serious consequences. It could have been explained as an accident or a mistake; it could have been admitted as sinfully wrong and absolution sought and obtained; it might even have received retrospective dispensation from the bishop or his Official. This could have been granted on the grounds which were in fact rather feebly advanced as an afterthought, that the printers were engaged upon heavy manual labour, which indeed they were, and that special pressure of work on an edition of the Epistles of St Paul for the Frankfurt book fair called for nutritious food. Monks and friars, like those in the neighbouring cloister, were required by their Rule to abstain from butcher's meat altogether, but it had long since been accepted that the Rule could be modified for the sick in the Infirmary who needed special nourishment, and this had become a notorious loop-hole for evasion. There would be no difficulty, particularly if a little money passed as a token of regret and as a fee of recompense for drafting any necessary documents, about overlooking the whole matter. Instead, Zwingli not only condoned the action but made it a public issue in his sermon of 23 March, which was enlarged on 16 April into a short pamphlet, printed by the same Froschauer firm, on the right to choose freely what to eat (*Von Erkiesen und Freiheit der Speisen*).[3]

By April 1522 Zwingli had sorted a good many things out for himself. He had ceased to be primarily a humanist and a scholar; he had parted company with his revered master, Erasmus, because he was now making the

---

[1] Egli, *1*, 72–6 (Nos. 233–5); Bullinger, *Ref.* 1, 69–70; Farner, *Zwingli* III, 237–52. Reports varied about the number of people present and participating: Leo Jud, Heinrich Aberli, Bartlime Pur seem certain; Georg Binder, Hans Utinger, Hans Hottinger, Wolf Ininger, Lorenz Hochrütiner, Hans Ochsenfuss are probables. Goeters, *Vorgeschichte*, 239–81.

[2] Egli *1* 77 (no. 237); Mörikofer I, 97. Froschauer was fined a small sum. Things were not improved by the news that there had been a minor riot in Basle caused by someone deliberately eating pork in Lent; Z VII, 509. Froschauer claimed that he had been unable to afford fish and that a vegetarian diet was inadequate.

[3] Z I, 74 (88)–136. A formal complaint had been made to the Bishop of Constance about Zwingli's sermon. The complainants were thereupon fined by the council for taking the matter outside the jurisdiction of Zurich, and the defendants were allowed to justify their action. This they did, but before the council had given a ruling the Bishop of Constance intervened to call the clergy of the city together to hear a communication requiring their obedience on this issue. Intervention by the council was therefore unavoidable in order to prevent episcopal dictation within the city walls. After some discussion, Zwingli was allowed to state his case, which he then developed into this treatise. Z VII, 515–16 n. 6. It is almost certain that he made use of Luther's *Von der Freiheit eines Christenmenschen*.

reborn Christ ('Christus renascens') into a guide for thought and action in a way that Erasmus could not, and he was cutting himself loose from Rome.

Already towards the end of 1520, he had formally declined to receive further instalments of his Papal pension.[1] At Glarus and Einsiedeln, he had satisfied his conscience about accepting money from this quarter by using it for the purpose of buying books on the principle *pecunia non olet*. At Zurich, however, he was adequately recompensed as Canon and preacher, so that this reasoning no longer applied. Further, Bible study and self-examination, intensified by illness, made him unable to accept papal claims; the pope in his view was shrinking to one bishop – albeit of Rome – among many, and a number of traditional episcopal prerogatives were being challenged.

From the pulpit his evangelical sermons continued to be heard, to the growing embarrassment of some of his fellow-Canons, Hofmann in particular, and there were even demands for his resignation or removal if he did not come more into line with the others. Instead, he was pushing things even further by his words about fasting. It was a deliberate and critical decision. He could assuredly have secured a well-paid sinecure in return for inaction, and he could have devoted his time and talents to the humanist studies in which he delighted. From Rome came, with calculated secrecy, some significant advances. As late as January 1523 there was a formal letter from Pope Adrian VI, itself an indication of approval, and the nuncio, Ennio Filonardi, hinted that a cardinal's hat might be the reward for compliance.[2] So far he was, it is worth repeating, like Erasmus, outwardly an orthodox Catholic priest, saying mass, hearing confessions, taking part in all the ceremonial routine of the Great Minster. He had already learnt to hasten slowly.[3]

Like many others, he was dissatisfied about a number of particular issues such as indulgences and fasting, which he wanted clarifying in the light of scripture. In the justificatory tract *Von Erkiesen und Freiheit der Speisen* (*Of choice and freedom in the matter of food*) he explained that he had never spoken against abstention from meat-eating during Lent or on Fridays:[4] he had spoken of freedom in Christ, and this had been inter-

---

[1] Farner, II. 414 regards this as a decisive stage in the course of Zwinglian Reformation. Wyss 17; Z I. 396; Z II, 314.

[2] Z VIII, 13–14 and notes; Farner III, 319. Myconius asserted that Zwingli was offered 'omnia certe praeter sedem papalem'. For a more sceptical view G. Müller, *Die römische Kurie und die Reformation, 1523–34* QFRG 38 (Gütersloh, 1969), 14 n. 29. A similar suggestion of a bishopric had reached Luther in 1518. J. Mackinnon, *Luther and the Reformation* (London, 1928) II, 102; WA 4.1, 274 and 277 n. 28.

[3] 'by going slow', he wrote to Jud in May 1522, 'we achieve our ends' – 'faciendum enim interdum, quod minime velis, ut, quod maxime velis, aliquando sequatur'. Z VII, 520.

[4] Together with the Ember days, Rogation days and the vigils of saints days. F. Schmidt-Clausing in *Die Religion in Geschichte und Gegenwart*, Bd. II (Tübingen, 1958), coll. 883, 884; Z I, 99 n. 2.

preted by some as implying that they need not abstain from meat since this was not required by the Bible. It was this opinion, rather than the action taken, that Zwingli sought to justify. The ceremonial laws of the Old Testament have been superseded by the Gospel, which is not one of works but of faith and love. The freedom brought to humanity by the New Testament was something invaluable and inalienable. Food was a necessity of life more important than gold (as Midas discovered), and the principle that the Sabbath was made for man, not man for the Sabbath, must be applied to fasting likewise. This must be optional, not obligatory. In attempting to oblige all to fast at specified times, Canon Law and the spiritual authorities have acted *ultra vires*. Many local regulations such as abstention from milk, butter, cheese (as derived from beasts) or eggs, have been relatively recently · made, and dispensations or exemptions have been freely sold. If it had been sinful to take milk or eggs on fast-days, why had it taken the authorities fourteen centuries to discover the fact? If it was not sinful, as it was not, then the requirement was made only for the money to be obtained by securing exemption.

Freedom, it is insisted, must be combined with love; those who fast must be respected and not interfered with; the motive, not the action, matters, and of the motive it may be impossible to judge. The Bible teaching, above all the example of St Peter (Acts 10. 10–16) and the divine permission to eat freely, together with St Paul's exposition to the Corinthians (I Cor. 6. 12–14), left Zwingli confident that his opinion was right.

Having demonstrated that fasting was a human rather than a divine command, and urging that it is, in any case, like working on saints' days (but not on Sundays), a matter of indifference, having expressed his willingto be corrected from the Bible if wrong, insisting throughout on charity in judging others, the more so if they have yet to come to know God's word fully, he returns at the end to the freedom of the individual to choose in this particular instance. The bishops have exceeded their rightful powers and have fleeced their flocks rather than fed them.

The treatise itself, like many to follow, was hurried and at the same time reasonably cautious. He was well aware that feelings could easily be roused, and he was anxious to avoid tumult and disorder. The bishop directly concerned was the good-natured native of Zurich, Hugo of Hohenlandenberg, Bishop of Constance,[2] who soon made it clear that he was not prepared to go any of the way with the new demands. On 24 May 1522, the Zurich council was invited in a letter from the bishop to maintain a stand for peace and unity within the church. This letter, and a similar one to the

[1] Z I, 109–10 for details.
[2] A. Willburger, *Die Konstanzer Bischöfe Hugo von Landenberg, Balthasar Merklin, Johann von Lupfen (1496–1537) und die Glaubensspaltung* (Münster i.W., 1917).

Chapter of the Great Minster,[1] was in fact written by the bishop's Official, Dr Johann Fabri (or Faber) of Leutkirch who had at first been attracted to Zwingli both as a humanist and as a preacher, but had recently visited Rome and returned to act as advocate and pamphleteer on behalf of the papacy. The question of fasting during Lent raised, obviously, the whole general issue of ecclesiastical authority. To flout the bishop was to flout the Pope and thus the authority of the church, unless, as Zwingli vainly hoped, the bishop gave way.

Before the relatively minor matter of eating meat during Lent had been considered, a much more serious topic was raised by the Zurich evangelicals: the question of clerical celibacy.

The incompatibility of the priesthood with the married state had a very long history behind it.[2] Although the ministers of the early church had included many married men, a preference for the single state early manifested itself. Monasticism helped this tendency, as did papal pronouncements. But married clergy, although officially disapproved and where possible disregarded, were common enough before the twelfth century (Ailred of Rievaulx, like many other notable clerics, had a long clerical ancestry). After 1100, however, the combination of high esteem for asceticism with the efforts of the Hildebrandine reformers and the necessity of preventing ecclesiastical benefices becoming hereditary, was decisive. Matrimony and the priesthood were made incompatible. It does not need any very extensive knowledge of medieval literature to make it clear that society then was 'permissive' enough. Chastity was sufficiently rare to be regarded as of itself almost a qualification for sanctity. Opportunities for sexual indulgence were notoriously numerous and taken for granted. University towns, the breeding grounds of future clerics, were overrun with loose women; in tiny Zurich itself everyone knew where to find a brothel. The fact that Zwingli's own admitted lapse did not prevent his selection for his notable position in Zurich speaks for itself, as does also, for example, a similar admitted act by Sir Thomas More.[3]

For all practical purposes much of northern Switzerland had a married clergy.[4] Legally this was impossible; the priest and his concubine could

---

[1] Z I, 190. The small council was prepared to support the bishop, but the great council ('the two hundred') insisted that Zwingli should be heard.

[2] The literature is considerable – over a thousand treatises are reported. It was conveniently and unsympathetically summarised a century ago by H. C. Lea, *History of Sacerdotal Celibacy in the Christian Church* (Philadelphia, 1867; 3rd edition, 2 vols. Philadelphia and London, 1907). M. Thurian, *Marriage and celibacy* (London, 1959); W. Bertrams, *Der Zölibät des Priesters*[2] (Würzburg, 1962) and an article, *Célibat*, by Leclerc in *Dictionnaire d'archéologie chrétienne et de liturgie* (with bibliography) II, coll. 2802–32 (Paris, 1910).

[3] P. S. Allen, *The Age of Erasmus* (Oxford, 1914), 205.

[4] Zeller-Werdmüller I, 16 n. 1. 'Offene Concubinatsverhältnisse der Geistlichen waren während des ganzen Mittelalters die Regel, wie zahllose Urkunden beweisen.'

not be man and wife, for canon law had forbidden such matrimony for centuries. Yet in the dioceses of Constance and Chur the existence of such unions was almost officially recognised. The bishop's officers collected a kind of protection money from clergy with families, and in return for regular payments made no attempt to bring any action in the episcopal court. It was even encouraged by allowing the children of priests to inherit property by will as if they were legitimate. The income to the bishop was appreciable. In Zwingli's own diocese there were said to be 1,500 children of priests, for each of whom the bishop's Fiscal (agent) received four (later five) gulden.[1] While there could not be any canonically recognised union in much of Switzerland, the status of the 'priest's whore' was a respectable one. It was, none the less, a manifestly unsatisfactory compromise. Luther came out explicitly in favour of clerical marriage in his *Address to the Christian Nobility of the German Nation* of June 1520, saying no more indeed than many had done before, but saying it with firmer emphasis.[2] Such a message was obviously not acceptable to Rome, to the Bishop of Constance or to the Canons of the Great Minster, but Zwingli had already reached a similar conclusion. The difference was that what Luther proclaimed from the house tops was put forward in Zurich at first cautiously and hypothetically. Zwingli usually had a good sense of timing, and in this important matter he held his fire until it could be directed to the best effect. By 1520 he was convinced that clerical celibacy rested on no adequate biblical basis.

Some of his early marginalia indicate a certain preoccupation with the Gospel and Pauline teaching about matrimony, the latter very much reinforced by the writings of St Augustine. His own lapse was a constant burden and reproach to him, while he knew perfectly well how often many of his fellow priests found outlets in visits to the 'baths', while others, to everyone's knowledge, lived with their housekeepers and often raised families.

Some time early in 1522 Zwingli secretly married a lady of higher social rank than himself, Anna Reinhart, widow of Hans Meyer von Knonau.[3]

---

[1] O. Vasella, *Reform und Reformation in der Schweiz* (Münster, 1958) 28; Z I, 225. The fine was nominally as penance for 'Nicolaitism' (from Acts 6. 5, Rev. 2. 6–7, 15). Z I, 225 n. 6; R. Durrer, *Die Schweizergarde im Rom* (Lucerne, 1927), 317 n. 8.

[2] J. Mackinnon, *Luther and the Reformation* II, 240; WA I, 6., 440–1; H. C. Lea, *History of Sacerdotal Celibacy in the Christian Church*[3] (London, 1907), 41; L. von Muralt, *Zürichs Beitrag zur Weltgeschichte im Zeitalter der Reformation* ZT 1945 (Zürich, 1944), 61–85. H. Denifle, *Luther und Luthertum in der ersten Entwickelung quellenmässig dargestellt*. 2 Bde. (Mainz 1904–9. Also trans. J. Paquier, *Luther et le luthéranisme*, 4 tomes, Paris, 1910–13) especially the introduction.

[3] Anna Reinhart was the daughter of the keeper of the inn *zum Rössli* in Zurich. Exactly Zwingli's age, she had made a love-marriage with Hans Meyer von Knonau (died 1517) against the wish of the latter's father. There were three children of this marriage – Margaret, who in 1527 married Anton Wirz (killed at Kappel, 1531) and secondly Hans Escher vom

This could not be kept hidden, and was one of the reasons that brought about a petition to the Bishop of Constance on 2 July 1522[1] signed by him and ten other priests. The other signatories were Balthasar Trachsel,[2] Georg Staehelin,[3] Werner Steiner,[4] Simon Stumpf,[5] Erasmus Schmid,[6] Jodocus (Jost) Kilchmeyer,[7] Huldrych Pfister,[8] Kaspar Grossmann,[9] Johann Schmid[10] and Leo Jud. This serious appeal, which had the qualified support of Erasmus, was promptly rejected at Constance and was also sent, in modified and more popular form, in German, to the wider lay public of the Confederation.[11] This was a deliberate bid for popular support enhanced by praise for his countrymen and an assurance that a married priesthood would not mean that church endowments would be used for the benefit of the families of the recipients.

This little printed pamphlet starts with a charmingly simple introduction to the Gospel message, the preaching of which was now said to be almost entirely neglected. Instead, the emphasis was on routine attendance at mass, insistence upon payment of tithes and oblations, the pushing of indulgences, the enhancement of the authority of the Pope, and the multiplication of saints and their shrines. To call preaching the Word heretical,

Luchs; Gerold, to whom Zwingli was to dedicate his treatise on Education, *Quo pacto* etc. in 1523 (below 217–18 and n. 2), and who likewise perished at Kappel; and Agatha, who married Hans Balthasar Keller. At 38, Anna agreed in the early part of 1522 to be Zwingli's wife, and their cohabitation was well known, e.g. to Glarean in Basle, Myconius in Lucerne and Berchtold Haller in Berne. It was not until 2 April 1524 that he 'went to church' – i.e. publicly recognised marriage with her. This was three months before the birth of their first child, and was followed by a lawsuit about Frau Reinhart's property. Staehelin I, 224; Z IV, 407 n.; Wyss 33; Koehler, *Zwingli* 87; ZWA III, 197–221, 229–45; Durrer, *Schweizergarde* 317 n. 8.

[1] Z I, 188 (197)–210. *Supplicatio ad Hugonem episcopum Constantiensem*, written in Latin for limited circulation.   [2] Dean of the collegiate church of Arth, married in 1521.
[3] From Schwyz, also known as Calybeus.
[4] Of Zug, son of the Ammann, and widely travelled. He later settled in Zurich and helped Bullinger.
[5] A former monk from Franconia, and friend of Beatus Rhenanus, who had become incumbent of Höngg on the resignation of his uncle Nicolaus Petri. There was opposition from the Abbot of Wettingen and a lawsuit.
[6] Erasmus Schmid (Fabricius) c. 1492–1546 graduated M.A. at Freiburg in 1514, taught at Sion, was beneficed at Stein a. R., and from 1521 was canon of the Great Minster and a devoted adherent of Zwingli. He took part in the first Zurich disputation, was dismissed for his part in the Ittingen affair, became well known in Zurich for his scholarship, and died as minister at Reichenweier (Alsace). Z I, 139; Z VII, 84 n. 1; ZSKG 50 (1936) 360–6.
[7] Canon of Lucerne. He tried, but failed, to reform Rapperswil.
[8] Or Pistoris, from Uster.   [9] Megander.
[10] Faber, one of the canons of the Great Minster.
[11] Z I, 210 (214)–248. *Eine freundliche Bitte und Ermahnung an die Eidgenossen*, 13 July 1522. Its only obvious effect outside Zurich was to stiffen the opposition. Myconius, for example, who was known to be one of Zwingli's friends and disciples, was dismissed from his position as schoolmaster in Lucerne, and was with considerable difficulty provided for in Zurich. There were to be many similar rather pathetic figures during the next ten years. Vasella, *Reform und Reformation*, 63 n. 165 pertinently asks why the appeal was both to bishop and confederation.

Hussite or Lutheran, was utterly unfair. 'We truly have nothing in common with Luther or anyone else who might harm Christian peace and doctrine.'[1]

The personal preference for the single state shown by St Paul was no divine command; on the contrary, the 'bishops' of the early church were married men. A young priest, hearing confessions and in close contact with girls and young married women, could well be a 'dangerous animal'. Give him a wife, children and a home, and his passions will be cooled. This simple observation is followed rather incongruously by a haphazard appeal to early church history, including the Synod of Gangra (c. 345), the Council of Toledo (400) and references to St Hilary, St Augustine and Pope Nicholas I (858-67). The state of matrimony was a highly honourable one; it was monstrous that the children of priests should be despised and rejected, unable to learn a decent trade or become a gild member if boys, unacceptable as suitable wives if girls. The Swiss were born in one honourable Confederation; they suffered together and they fought together; could they not together defend Bible teaching against the misinterpretation of the Pope and the hierarchy? The petitioners asked only for recognition, not for special privileges for wives, nor that benefices should descend from father to son. Clerical marriage should be openly avowed and recognised, and society would be the better for it. Preachers of the Gospel should be protected against Pope, bishops or their agents.

It was an eloquent and well-written appeal.[2] Within Zurich itself, support was gathering. The nomination of Leo Jud as stipendiary priest at St Peter's on 1 June 1522 was one sign of the time. Another was the acceptance of Zwingli's claim to preach in his own way.[3]

Outside Zurich, opposition was mounting. To meet this, Zwingli published, on 23 August 1522, his first major statement of faith, *Apologeticus Archeteles*[4] intended for all his countrymen, 'who are not the same as Germans'.[5] The very title is significant, an apology in the commonly used sense of defence, and this was to be 'once and for all'.[6] It was written in Latin and completed exactly three months after the note from the Bishop of Constance to the Chapter of the Great Minster to which it was the

---

[1] Z I, 224. 'Wir warlich nüt gmeins habend weder mit dem Luter noch mit dheinem andren, das christenlicher ler und rüw ützit schaden mög, ja gar dhein gemeinsamy.'
[2] Erasmus himself wrote in favourable but guarded terms, and many letters refer to the minor sensation that it caused. Allen v, 46; Z I, 192–3; Staehelin I, 229–31; Goeters, *Vorgeschichte*, 250.   [3] Koehler *Zwingli*, 81; Egli *I*, 107 (no. 301); Z I, 257.
[4] Z I, 249 (256)–384.
[5] Z I, 270: 'et Helvetii inter Germanos non censeantur'.
[6] 'Archeteles' is one of the composite Greek-derived nouns which early sixteenth-century humanists, following Erasmus' example in *Enchiridion militis* or More's in *Utopia*, loved to invent: in this case ἡ ἀρχή 'beginning', τὸ τέλος 'end'. Zwingli could seldom resist the temptation to advertise his knowledge of Greek.

reply.[1] As such, it was gratuitous. Zwingli had not been mentioned by name in the episcopal letter, and any reply to the Bishop should have come from the Chapter as a whole. Yet he knew quite well that his preaching had started the trouble and that his defence of meat-eating in Lent had been a challenge. He was also well aware that the bishop personally had not the scholarship needed for a learned discussion and that his real enemies in Constance were the suffragan bishop, Melchior Fattli(n), and the active Official, John Fabri. Moreover, the matters raised by the bishop were of public concern, and his communication could not be regarded as private episcopal advice to the governing body of the collegiate church. Zwingli's task was to defend the preaching of the Gospel in Zurich and to demonstrate to his fellow-countrymen that no heresy was taught there.[2] Every device – indignation, irony, logical argument, scriptural citation, history, law, even classical analogy – was used in this treatise. Indignation at the opening: there in Zurich they lived in the utmost quiet and repose, and the council had encouraged evangelical preaching as against the anecdotes and irrelevances of the Mendicants.[3] The apology opens with a tribute to the new-won freedom to expound the Gospel, which they were determined not to lose or abandon. The true pastors, who may be simple people, must defend themselves against false prophets, ravening wolves, guided merely by human reason and tradition. In season and out of season, the Gospel must be heard against even those who enjoy high office, authority, power, wealth, honours and glory. Christ's teaching is for the spiritually minded, not for the learned exclusively – woe to those who call evil good, good evil,

---

[1] The episcopal communication, grandly described as 'paraenesis' (Z I, 263–9), had been received on 24 May 1522. In it the bishop had warned the canons against the wolf already in the fold, an oblique reference to Luther whose excommunication by Leo X (*Exsurge, Domine*, 15 June 1520) had been confirmed on 3 January 1521 (*Decet Romanum*). The Diet of Worms (8 May 1521) had added imperial condemnation of the new doctrines whose promulgation was forbidden in the Empire, including Zurich. The bishop emphasised that innovations and alterations in the traditional church services were to be avoided. Cf. [Sebastian Meyer] *Ernstliche Ermahnung Hugo von Landenbergs, Bischofs zu Konstanz, zu Frieden und christlicher Einigkeit, mit schöner Auslegung und Erklärung*, hg. v. K. Schottenloher. Bd. IV, Heft 5 of *Flugschriften aus den ersten Jahren der Reformation* hg. v. O. Clemen, 277–8 (Leipzig, 1911).

[2] At the Lucerne meeting of the Diet (EA 4, 1a, 194) 27 May 1522, complaints of presumptuous preaching causing division and error among Christians were plainly directed at Zurich.

[3] This action by the council had the result of a challenge by the Franciscan friar, Francis Lambert of Avignon, who also defended image veneration at a debate in Zurich on 21 July 1522 in the presence of Bürgermeister Marx Röist, two Company Masters, Hans Ochsner and Heinrich Walder, and the Town Clerk, Kaspar Frei. The three Regular Orders had been represented, as had the Canons of the Great Minster and the three stipendiary ministers, Heinrich Engelhard from the Fraumünster, Rudolf Röschli from St Peter's and Zwingli from the Great Minster. Zwingli's energetic claim to be the principal exponent for Zurich 'ich bin in diser statt Zürich bischof und pfarrer' was accepted, and in future Bible-preaching only, and not the teaching of Duns Scotus and Aquinas, was to be encouraged. Z I, 257–8 n. 3, 337; VII, 532; Wyss 17–18 and notes; Bullinger, *Ref.* I, 77–8; Goeters, *Vorgeschichte*, 246.

light darkness, darkness light, bitter sweet and sweet bitter.[1] Let the opponents cease to put their sanctions before the grace of God, selling dispensations that should be free, terrorising tender consciences, driving men to desperation, demanding chastity where Christ allowed freedom, and living in most unapostolic luxury.

The bishop would have it that the new errors were worse than the old ones, as if 'that countrified Zwingli'[2] was worse than Sabellius who had taught tritheism, Arius who made Christ less than the Father, Manichaeus who claimed that there are two Gods – good and evil – and Marcion who believed that Christ was never fully human. 'I shall not cease from aiming to restore the ancient unity of the Church, and I will prove that I am neither a leader of faction nor a heretic.' It is the opinions of his critics which are breeding sedition, tumult, war, enmity and all that is evil.

He reminded his readers that for four years (1519–22), for the edification of his fellow countrymen, he had set forth the plain Gospel message: 'We planted, Matthew, Luke, Paul and Peter watered, and God gave wonderful increase.'[3] In so far as his bishop was a true bishop, all had been done in agreement and harmony with him.

Basing his preaching exclusively on the Gospels, Zwingli called men to repentance and to generosity toward the poor. To the best of his ability, human, man-made doctrines had been rejected, false prophets denounced, traditions accepted only when in harmony with the divine word. Without any vainglorious belief that the spirit of God was upon him, he none the less believed that he was the instrument for the delivery of God's word. After this vigorous defence he went on to reply to the bishop's insistence that the Gospel implied the existence of a united church behind it. Was the Bible not there at the time of Arius, or of Pope Liberius (352–66) himself an Arian, or Anastasius II (496–8), under all of whom the Christian church was manifestly divided? Nor was it good enough for his opponents to shelter under the Augustinian aphorism 'I would not believe the Gospel unless the church had approved it.'[4] But where was the church when, only nine years after the Resurrection, Matthew wrote his narrative? The gospels were there before St Augustine wrote, independent of him and of the church. The church received the message at the hands of the four evangelists and no approval was needed.

He then passed to some familiar assertions. The rock, so much appealed to, could refer to Christ just as easily as to St Peter, and therefore it would seem to be impious sacrilege to call the Roman pontiff supreme and chief

---

[1] Cf. Isaiah 5. 20.   [2] 'rusticus iste Zuinglius': Z I, 283.   [3] Z I, 285.

[4] Z I, 293. Strictly 'Ego vero euangelio non crederem, nisi me catholicae ecclesiae commoveret auctoritas.' (Contra Manichaei epistolam quam vocant fundamenti. *Corpus scriptorum ecclesiasticorum Latinorum* (Vindobonae [Vienna] 1891) xxv, 197.) MPL, 42. c. 176.

priest, universal bishop. Bishops waging war, dazzling men with the splendour of their equipage and furniture, collecting money on any and every pretext, were a sad sight. As for Fabri himself, he should cease to obstruct the rebirth of Christianity[1] – he and his friends were like unto the pseudo-apostles who taught human satisfaction instead of the redeeming blood of Christ, seeking ever for honours and reward – *pecuniam omnino habere oportet.*

Even General Councils could err, for councils had disagreed with one another, one allowing clerical marriage and another forbidding it, whereas the scriptures could not be wrong, and from the scriptures not the letter that kills but the spirit that gives life (2 Corinthians 3. 6). From this basis of *sola scriptura*, Zwingli urged the elimination of a great deal of the sacerdotalism, antiquarianism and ritualism that had accreted to worship. The Christian community (*respublica Christiana*) had been at its best in the earliest days when ceremonies hardly existed, as contrasted with the German and Swiss cities where pseudo-bishops must needs anoint the walls of the churches with water, salt and ashes, as if bells could not ring without the application of holy water or altars be used without being first rubbed with consecrated oil.

He then appealed to the anti-clericalism seldom far below the surface in the medieval city. He contrasted priests with laity, the learned ones with the illiterate, the key-holders with those with empty purses, the idle Religious with the sweating workers, the debauched and adulterers with faithful husbands, the tax-exempt men of leisure with those who paid rates and taxes, the peacefully sleeping clergy not liable to watch and ward duties with those whose vigilance saved the city from danger while religion refused to allow the others to lift a finger in its defence. They thought they were always in the right, that they alone steered by the pole star, *cynosura*, that majority opinion was with them.

In one of the many parentheses, Zwingli showed a thoroughly sixteenth century distaste for democracy or majority rule. Everything of value had been the work of minorities – the early apostles had been but a handful among a mass of unbelievers, no philosopher of repute would be so crazy as to prefer the judgement of the ignorant many to that of the understanding few, nor could any such majority rule apply today. This is the more interesting because in later life and in different circumstances Zwingli was to appeal to a majority vote in a community on a religious matter as decisive.[2] He would also not accept compulsory conversion – *compelle intrare* meant 'try hard to persuade them to come in', not 'bring them in by force'.[3] But here again, when Zurich was to become an entirely

---

[1] 'renascenti Christianismo' Z I, 301; 'herbescentem Christum' Z I, 307. See above 75–6.
[2] See below 348, 373.   [3] Z I, 316; Luke 14. 23.

evangelical city, the inhabitants had no option but to conform or go away. It was wrong for the Abbot of St Gall to force his faith upon his tenants and subjects, for they must be free to choose; but Zurich state subjects were certainly not free to choose to follow the errors of the Anabaptists.

However much *Apologeticus Archeteles* may have been thought of as a 'once and for all' final statement, it was in fact nothing of the sort: it marked a stage, and a very transitional stage, in Zwingli's thought. Few things are more misleading in his case than to attribute a defined body of doctrine to him at a particular point in time and label it Zwinglian. Even more than with Luther and Calvin was it true that, standing firm indeed upon the basic principle of the infallibility and certainty of the Bible, his ideas grew and changed. Much that seemed simple in 1522 was recognised as needing explanation, modification, adjustment and even abandonment later. In this sense Zwingli may have been one of the most progressive and adaptable of the Reformers.

He insisted that neither individually, nor even in General Council assembled, could bishops be entrusted with the interpretation of the Bible. Many bishops were scarcely literate; and scholarship, in any case, was not enough. The layman might know more than the priest; the divine truths were often revealed to the simple minded and hidden from the professional theologians,[1] a conviction that was to cause difficulties long after Zwingli's time.

From inspiration he passed to prayer. The early sixteenth century saw in some respects the culmination of the medieval conviction of the need for, and the efficacy of, ceaseless supplication to heaven. In addition to being individual, prayer could also be corporate and vicarious, which was a reason for the endowment and support of many houses of religion and the employment of innumerable chantry priests. In this treatise, the value of prayer to the saints is, revealingly, not considered; but attention is directed to the need for a man personally to beseech for divine mercy and forgiveness. This came of grace and divine favour, by no means of right or certain due; and, while we must pray all the time, the goodness of God and not any merit acquired by words alone allowed us to hope for favour. The section ends with an appeal for humility.

Finally, Zwingli once again appealed to the fact that his teaching had been accepted in Zurich with enthusiasm. Order was now better maintained there than in any other Swiss city;[2] dissension had largely ceased,

---

[1] Z I, 322: '...indoctissimi quique, modo pii sint, scripturam iuxta mentem dei quam simplicissime capiant'. The biblical truism was again to be qualified later when Zwingli's opponents appealed against his own teaching to their 'inner light', cf. Z I, 382.

[2] Z I, 325: 'in alio Helvetiorum pago'.

peace and happiness were apparent. If the Bishop of Constance could but bring himself to abandon 'human traditions', dreams and worthless superstition, he could count on the enthusiastic friendship and support of Zwingli and his friends.

Apologeticus Architeles was certainly a good start if not an end. It was vigorous, challenging and clear. It asserted scriptural authority as plainly as ever Luther did. It showed the way to future doctrinal development; yet it was sufficiently cautious, open-minded and reasonable to provide a basis for further discussions could these but have been possible. No answer, of course, was vouchsafed, but the position had been stated in print for all to read, which many did with approval. It was, however, although relatively hastily composed, a scholarly and controversial statement, from a priest to his superior and suitably 'veiled in the obscurity of a learned language.'[1] Two weeks after its publication, he was repeating and simplifying much of it in the vernacular for those who could not read Latin. In this case, it was the nuns of Oetenbach, it being a safe assumption at the opening of the sixteenth century that a nun could not read or understand the Latin of the services she said and sang with monotonous regularity.[2]

The ladies at Oetenbach, the very site of which can now be traced only with great difficulty, were of the Dominican order,[3] some sixty of them in a large building with considerable endowments. Some of the most respected city families were represented there,[4] aloof, cut off, their spiritual needs catered for by the friars of their own Order of Preachers, Zwingli's most active opponents. These needs included sermons which, coming from the Dominican friars, were entirely conventional and traditional and not, as the Bürgermeister and council required, based on 'the holy Gospels, St Paul and the prophets, casting aside Duns Scotus and Aquinas'.[5] The friars refused to alter their style in favour of direct evangelical exposition such as Zwingli offered, and this caused comment and a demand that secular preachers should be allowed access to the nunnery pulpit.

Echoes of what was being said outside could not fail to reach the cloister, and one result of Zwinglian preaching was internal discord, so that the council had to intervene in December 1522 to require the ladies to live

---

[1] It included a poem by Grebel (Z I, 327) which marked almost the end of Grebel's friendship.
[2] E. Power, *Medieval English Nunneries* (Cambridge, 1922) 246–55; A. Hamilton Thompson, *Visitations of Religious Houses in the Diocese of Lincoln*, II (Horncastle, 1918) I, 49, 91; *Visitations in the diocese of Lincoln 1517–1531* II (Hereford, 1944), 90.
[3] H. Zeller-Werdmüller u. J. Bächtold, 'Die Stiftung des Klosters Oetenbach und das Leben der seligen Schwestern daselbst,' in ZT (1889), 213–76.
[4] E.g. Agatha Grebel, sister of Junker Jakob Grebel, was among those who left the convent in 1523. Egli *I*,132 (no. 367).   [5] Z I, 329.

peaceably together until the following spring. Each nun was to be free to choose her own confessor, and in March 1523 evangelical pressure was stepped up by the nomination by the council of Leo Jud as priest-in-charge, the Dominicans being excluded from the pulpit.[1] After this, a number of the younger Religious left to get married, and, in effect, the nunnery was dissolved.

It was for the edification of these religious ladies, while still together and possibly bewildered by pulpit instruction cutting across their uncertain residual convictions, that Zwingli wrote, in September 1522, a short introduction to Bible study: *Von Klarheit und Gewissheit des Wortes Gottes*[2] (The clarity and certainty of the Bible). It was an exposition and assertion in the first place of the irresistible power of the Word and secondly of its essential lucidity. The Holy Spirit unfailingly reveals the meaning of the Bible to those who truly seek to know God's message as opposed to those who merely expect their opinions to be confirmed by the Bible text.[3] It was likewise one of the many statements of his basic position that he was to write, and also, as almost always, it included a statement of the nature of God and of the essentials of the Christian faith. Immortality was assumed; therefore, all people desire salvation, which means an eternal life with God for the soul, which is so much more than the body with which it is fused in this earthly life.

God showed his omnipotence in the creation of the universe and mankind; when, after the Fall, death and daily toil became the common lot, God continued to reveal himself in the Old Testament prophets and in some of the great figures of the ancient world. God's promises were sure, Christ came to rule the world, showed the power of the word by miracles, and revealed God, timeless and eternal. The Incarnation, resurrection, the sending of the Holy Spirit, and a careful and orthodox account of the Trinity in Unity, are included. This leads on to a section on the certainty and strength of God's word. God's promises in the Bible will be fulfilled. Zwingli then faces the obvious difficulty that, in fact, through the scriptures God speaks often in parables and apparent uncertainties. This is true on the surface, but by careful study, attention, faith and recognition of the limitations of the human intellect, full understanding is possible. This comes by God's grace; those who are spiritually healthy and well have the faith accorded to Noah, Abraham, Moses and the prophets; those who are sick try to twist God's word to suit their own inclinations and self-will.

[1] Egli *1*, 122, 123, 131-2 (Nos. 346, 348, 366). See below 143.
[2] Z I, 328 (338)–384. It was translated into English by Sinonoys (see below, 391 n. 1). 'A booke which is intituled De claritate verbi Dei', y^t is to say of the playnelynesse or lyghtsomnes of gods word. That booke I have already träslated into English & is called a short pathway to come to thee ryghte understäding of Gods word.' No example seems to have survived.
[3] Z I, 382.

To the understanding enlightened by God his word is abundantly clear. The 'schoolmaster' who must teach them is Christ – not the Doctors of the church, or the Fathers, or the Pope, or the classroom, or church councils. Human additions to God's word whether by bishops or others are unnecessary and must be rejected. God reveals himself through his Spirit, in obedience to whom comes all knowledge and understanding.

In this way, too, will come proper understanding of the meaning of the Bible, hitherto little known and overlaid with traditional human interpretations which must be abandoned. The fact that majority opinion sometimes favoured some particular application of the scriptures was of little or no significance; Christ stood alone against the High Priest and his supporters; the apostles were a tiny group, with city people as well as country people against them; if there were ten disbelievers to one believer, this did not alter the fact that the latter was right.

Not only the majority might err, so too might (and did) the scholars. Philosophy[1] was not sufficient guide; *theologica scholastica* was merely human light which paled before the light of God: learned men were as liable to mistakes as others were, the disciples had been taught by Jesus and not by the men of learning; God reveals the truth to those who pray, and faith will follow. Again and again this splendid confidence that others, like the preacher himself, can and must replace speculative deductions by divine certainty, comes to the fore. In matters on which the Bible thus considered spoke clearly there could be no question of submission to human authority; on all other matters the secular government must be obeyed.[2]

From this note of obedient humility to ascertained scriptural teaching in a sermon which, if delivered as printed, must have left the hearers bewildered by its variety and depth, Zwingli turned to a piece of revealing self-defence which is also in part autobiographical. It is a little curious that having written a treatise which rejected the concept of the nun as the virgin dedicated to God, he turns, in September 1522, to a lyrical defence of the perpetual virginity of the mother of Christ.[3] His uncle John was still Abbot of the Monastery of Fischingen, a Benedictine house half way to St Gall, and at least one of his sisters had 'entered religion'.

It was to these relatives that Zwingli now vindicated himself, well

---

[1] By a curious linguistic quirk, Zwingli uses exactly this word and spelling but with a narrower meaning than in English. Z I, 378.

[2] From this principle so early established, Zwingli never departed. In Zurich, the government based its laws and administration (to Zwingli's satisfaction) upon Holy Writ. Obedience to it, therefore, was entirely proper. Only in this sense was there a Zurich 'theocracy'. R. C. Walton, *Zwingli's Theocracy* (Toronto, 1967) 49, 218. L. von Muralt, *Zum Problem der Theokratie bei Zwingli*, in Discordia Concors II (Basle, 1968) 387–90.

[3] 'Von der ewig reinen Magd Maria' Z I, 385 (391)–428.

knowing that his opponents were spreading stories of his greed, licence and heterodoxy. Specifically, among other things, it was widely alleged then and later that he had maintained that the Virgin Mary was a light woman, a trollop (*ein andre trüll*).[1]

Having so warmly urged the exclusive authority of the scriptures, Zwingli had, without resource to 'tradition', to explain the texts in Matthew and Mark[2] from which it could be deduced that Mary married Joseph and that they had other children. This false opinion, Zwingli explained, had been put forward long since by Helvidius; there were other ways of interpreting the texts;[3] without a nominal husband Mary might have been stoned to death; as it was, she was included in the well-born family of David. To deny that Mary remained *inviolata* before, during and after the birth of her son, was to doubt the omnipotence of God; a virgin birth was foretold by Isaiah, and it was right and profitable to repeat the angelic greeting – not prayer – 'Hail Mary'.[4] From Mary we can learn humility, unswerving constancy of faith in her son when all others had deserted him,[5] simplicity, faith and hope. God esteemed Mary above all creatures, including the saints and the angels – it was her purity, innocence and invincible faith that mankind must follow. Prayer, however, must be from the heart and to God alone; God is not to be approached through any creature but through Christ alone. The Virgin was an example, not a mediator. To say 'Hail Mary' was praiseworthy, but no number of *Aves*, no amount of indulgences attached to them, no mechanical telling of the beads would of itself be of avail. Such good works had been put up for sale all too freely and easily, so much so that, with a collecting box or alms dish near the object of indulgence, men were freely enquiring the cost of sin. Heaven and hell were thus offered for money like horses, pigs and cattle.

About himself Zwingli told his family in sorrow and in self-exculpation that men were saying[6] that he had fathered three children, had been found

---

[1] Z I, 404–5, 488.   [2] Matthew 1. 24; 13. 55–6; Mark 6. 3.
[3] Z I, 422 'brothers', for example, can mean 'friends'.
[4] Z I, 407.
[5] Z I, 421. It is somewhat remarkable to find Zwingli referring to St Anselm's ninth homily (MPL 158, c. 644–9), 'Stabat autem iuxta crucem Jesu mater eius' (John 19. 25 Vulg.), embroidering on the theme as 'foolish' (*närrisch*) because it assumed that the ladies at the cross were weeping and mourning. Zwingli was somewhat ambivalent on this subject. Constantly as he insisted upon the certainty of the perpetual virginity of the mother of God he accepted neither her Immaculate Conception nor her Assumption. K. Federer, *Zwingli und die Marienverehrung*, ZSKG 45 (1951) 13–26.
[6] This gossip was repeated in Chur by the wealthy Jakob Stapfer, formerly master of one of the Zurich companies. He had supported the sending of military assistance to Ulrich of Württemberg in 1519. 'Jakob Stapfer, früher Zunftmeister, hatte kurz vorher in Chur behauptet, Zwingli sei Vater von drei Kindern, er treibe sich Nachts auf den Strassen umher, er beziehe nicht nur vom Papst sondern auch von Frankreich eine Pension, er habe in einer Predigt

wandering in the streets at night and that he was in the pay both of the Pope and of the King of France. For such reports he cared little – 'the more my name is abused among men, the better it is with God'. Being human, he was sinful, but he had never taught what was untrue. He had long since renounced his papal pension and he had refused attractive benefices at Basle and Chur. He had demonstrated God's mercy and righteousness from the Bible, to be obtained by grace and faith, contrary to the teaching of those who have exalted good works, have set themselves up as judges of sin, assessing their magnitude and the punishment they involve, assessing this in terms of hard cash, which, when collected, they spend on fair ladies and elaborate dwelling-places. It was all this that he opposed, for Christ was the man of poverty and suffering in whom all are brothers. Those who would overcome the world must first learn to overcome themselves. It was a remarkable exculpation: of its effect on his family we shall never know.

While he was seeing this personal statement through the press, the Medici Pope, Leo X, whose political actions Zwingli had observed with increasing distaste for nine years, was replaced by the Dutch-born Adrian VI. This admirable idealist was well aware of the successes and popularity of Luther; impressed also by the defeat of the French at Bicocca[1] on 27 April 1522, he turned hopefully to the Imperial Diet summoned by the Council of Regency to meet at Nuremberg before the end of the year.[2] It was only moderately well attended; the Emperor was represented by his brother the Archduke Ferdinand, the Pope sent Cardinal Francesco Chieregati as his nuncio.[3] This envoy had a private interview with Ferdinand on 28 September 1522, reports of which were soon spread abroad. The papal policy was now one of peace: if Francis I, Henry VIII and Charles V could be reconciled, there might be good hopes of a reform in Christendom, among the clergy especially, and peace could well mean that more money and men were available against the infidels.[4] It was, however, the Pope insisted, also necessary to eliminate all that was opposed

---

gesagt, "*Ave Maria* sei so viel as *Gott grüss dich Gretlin usw.*". Z I, 405 n. 2. Cf. Z VII, 576. Such attacks went on all his life. In January 1528 he was accused of stealing 20 gulden. Strickler, I, 588–9 (Nos. 1885a, b).

[1] Zurich was not represented at Bicocca, where her contingent might well have altered the fortunes of the day. The other Swiss states remained true to the French alliance, but their men, who had not been paid, returned home as soon as the outcome of the battle was apparent.

[2] O. R. Redlich, *Der Reichstag von Nürnberg 1522–23* (Leipzig, 1887, reprinted Göttingen, 1963). The internal situation in Germany was relatively favourable. The danger from the knights had been ended by the deaths of Franz von Sickingen and Ulrich von Hutten. The latter, whom Zwingli always admired, 'the distinguished protector of religion and German freedom', died a bankrupt refugee at Ufenau in 1523. Z I, 431, VIII, 128; see below 127–8.

[3] L. Pastor, *Geschichte der Päpste* IV, 2 (Freiburg, 1907), 88–92; E.T. IX (London, 1923) 127–37.

[4] Rhodes fell after a long siege on 21 December 1522, the Grand Master of the Order of St John, Villiers de l'Isle-Adam, being obliged to retire to Malta.

to God and the love of one's neighbour, and this included the heretical teaching of Martin Luther and his adherents, among whom Zwingli was now generally counted.

Zwingli, constantly in touch with south German affairs, reacted rapidly and almost violently to the tidings. What was being prepared at Nuremberg could be to the advantage neither of the Gospel nor of German freedom. There was no serious hope that the Pope could eliminate the manifest abuses of the clergy, while the suppression of Luther and his doctrines would have serious political as well as religious repercussions.

These ideas Zwingli set out in a paper, written with great humility for the consideration of the German Diet.[1] There is no evidence that it ever reached Nuremberg, where it certainly had no influence; perhaps what we have is only a draft of a more elaborate memorandum that was never written or presented. It contains a remarkable appreciation of Luther, 'undeniably devout and learned',[2] for if he is lost, who is safe? The writer, however, was concerned with the cause of the Bible, since all who sincerely preach the Gospel are classed as Lutherans. He warns the Germans that an agreement between the Emperor and the King of France will result not in an army being sent against the Turks but in the suppression of Luther's adherents at home. If this were to happen, Rome would control more than the Germanic Kingdom, the whole of Christendom[3] would be subject to it.

If Pope Adrian were really concerned about the welfare of the *respublica Christiana*, he would take steps to ensure the pure preaching of the reborn Christ and the restoration of discipline rather than attempt merely to reduce the number of cardinals, an institution whose value could be challenged.

Further, Zwingli adds, there was a persistent rumour that Erasmus, the most pious and innocent of men, whose only weakness was his reasonableness and moderation, was to be declared a heretic, primarily because of his edition of the New Testament. This would be monstrous, but from the new Pope Zwingli had little hope. In this he was justified by the event, because before 1523 was out Adrian VI was dead and another Medici, Clement VII, reigned disastrously in his stead.

Disappointed by the cold shoulder from Germany, Zwingli turned to his own Zurich, where the fruits of four years of persistent expositions of the New Testament text in the vernacular were becoming apparent. Zurich was still to all outward appearance a Catholic city. The Christmas

---

[1] 'Suggestio deliberandi super propositione Hadriani pontificis Romani Neroberg̨e facta.' Z I, 434–41.
[2] Z I, 440. 'Vir sine controversia pius et doctus.'
[3] Z I, 439. 'Obtinuit Roma non iam totius Germanįe regnum, sed orbis Christiani monarchiam...'

of 1522 was celebrated with the usual ritual; mass was said in all the churches, friars and secular priests moved in their customary processions, the Canons of the Great Minster functioned normally. In fact, however, Zwingli had many adherents among clergy and influential laity alike. It was apparent that no remedy was to come from Constance or from Rome, that the rules about fasting were not to be relaxed, clergy were not to be allowed to marry, the monastic life continued to be esteemed as the best and the precepts of the Gospel were not to be enforced in such institutions. This was not good enough and the time was ripe for a show-down.

Without it there would be danger of civil commotion. The preacher in the church of the Augustinian friars across the river was preaching something very different, conservative, conventional, defensive and scholastic. He had been wilfully interrupted[1] by Leo Jud, stones had been thrown and disorder with difficulty averted. The advanced thinkers needed explicit public support, official encouragement and a clear mandate to continue. If the Bishop of Constance would not allow free exposition and discussion of the new way of approach, another method of expressing it must be found. This meant the panacea of the age, a public debate.

The issues were becoming clear. The rulers of Zurich were aware that they had among them a humanist, second only to Erasmus in Switzerland, a university graduate thoroughly versed in the outmoded scholastic philosophy of the age, a priest with much parochial experience, versed in politics, passionately patriotic. For at least six years he had been studying the Bible in its original Greek and Hebrew, applying to the text his own considerable linguistic and exegetical abilities. He, if any one, could refute publicly the charges that were being freely made that Zurich was the home of heretics, followers of the excommunicated Luther.

Indulgences, the celibacy of the clergy, the obligation to abstain from meat-eating at certain times, the validity of perpetual monastic vows, all these had recently been challenged in sermons and in writing. It was quite a formidable indictment, especially when added to it was a relatively new controversy, 'image-worship'.[2] Representations of the Virgin and the saints were extremely common all over Europe. The poorest country church contained pictures painted on the walls or on canvas, stained glass with stories of the legends of saints, and statues of them in wood or stone, in great variety, sometimes of real artistic merit, sometimes crude suggestive representations. All these had multiplied in the fifteenth century. Such 'images' were constantly said to be 'the Bible of the poor', encouraging

---

[1] Staehelin I, 259; L. Weisz, *Leo Jud, Ulrich Zwinglis Kampfgenosse 1482–1542* (Zürich, 1942), 39. An action which, when taken later by Anabaptists, was roundly condemned. C. Pestalozzi, *Leo Judä* (Elberfeld (1860), 17; Egli *1*, 136 (No. 373).

[2] H. v. Campenhausen, *Die Bilderfrage in der Reformation*, ZKG 68 (1957), 96–128.

devotion and instructing the ignorant; but what these ignorant illiterate people made of them we cannot know, because they could hardly express their thoughts in speech, let alone in writing.

There was indeed a general conviction that the whole great company of the saints, depicted so strikingly as individuals, could, and did, plead before the Almighty on behalf of those on earth. In the hour of danger or anxiety, to call upon a saint might be to secure instant help or relief. A man looking into his church, as he ought to do, on his way to work in the fields, would probably gaze upon a picture of a great giant St Christopher staggering under the weight of the little Christ whom he carried over the river. This was thought to act as a kind of insurance ticket, and for that day the man was safe from harm or accident. Popular thought, encouraged by anecdotes introduced into many a sermon, was permeated with expectation of the direct intervention in human affairs of the saints in heaven.

To distinguish between the concrete and the abstract was not always easy, especially for untrained minds familiar only with animate and inanimate objects. That the relics of the saints worked miracles was almost a matter of faith. It was almost equally easy to believe that the image, the representation, especially if it were of some antiquity, could do likewise. To pray to the saint, in some sense to worship the saint, and so likewise his or her image, was an easy and natural transition. Every priest knew, or ought to have known, that worship was due to God alone (and possibly in less degree to the Virgin Mary), but that to all others, even St Peter himself, veneration, but not worship, was called for.[1] There were different words which could be paraded at the appropriate moment – *latria* and *dulia*, the one for God, the other for creatures.

In practice, however, the shrines of popular saints were crowded with those saying their prayers to them; Zwingli had seen a great deal of this when he was closely connected with the wonder-working shrine of the Virgin at Einsiedeln, and he preached, walked in procession and said his services every day in the Great Minster amidst a profusion of these representations.

'You shall not make a carved image for yourself, nor the likeness of anything in the heavens above, or on the earth below, or in the waters under the earth. You shall not bow down to them or worship them...' The word of God, re-emphasised in the New Testament, could hardly be clearer than that; the practice of many ordinary people was in contradiction to it, and official explanations might not be convincing. Much of the earlier

---

[1] This was elaborated in the *Auslegen und Gründe der Schlussreden* (Z II, 191) and more fully in *Eine Antwort, Valentin Compar gegeben*, Z IV, 84–128. 'Hyperdulia' was the special honour reserved for the Virgin Mary.

satire of Erasmus (particularly in the *Colloquies*) which the young Zwingli had lapped up, had been directed against pilgrimages, relics and images. By the end of 1523, but how long before it is impossible to be sure, study of the whole Bible and of the relationship of the new to the old law had convinced Zwingli that images and pictures of the holy men and women of the past were more than objects of common abuse. They were impious and so must be removed. They hindered the direct access of the individual soul to God; they were at best vain distractions, at worst they encouraged idolatry. Money offered at the shrine of an image would be much better given to the poor.

Elimination of images from the churches was a serious matter. The clergy were not likely to do this spontaneously, but neglect to take action meant that what were coming to be regarded as superstitious objects would remain. The temptation then would be for young enthusiasts to take matters into their own hands, and this some would do very willingly. Destruction was easy and, in a measure, pleasurable. To make a bonfire of pictures and wooden superstitious objects, to smash glass and hew down stone monuments could be fun. Youth did not need much encouragement to vandalism; let the young wreckers loose and they would gleefully make a job of it if they knew there were no proceedings to follow.

Violence was very near the surface in sixteenth century society, where excitement was often lacking. A Christian government, indeed any government, could not tolerate disorderly conduct or damage to churches and their contents. If men had been mistakenly taught, if the divine word did condemn images, if iconoclasm was desirable, it should be carried out under supervision and by authority, not by indiscriminate smashing by youths who could all too easily become gangs of hooligans. If what the bishop ruled about fasting, indulgences, vows and clerical marriage was to be overruled by an appeal to a higher tribunal, that of the scriptures, so too must the matter of the images.

This was, in fact, soon to become one of the characteristic features of the Reformation in Switzerland. It could hardly be represented as an insignificant matter, and, added to the other points already in dispute, it would mark an open breach with Rome if hostile action were to be tolerated or encouraged by the civil authority. The mere presence or absence of the images might perhaps be regarded as a matter of taste or choice, although reformers from the days of St Bernard and the early Cistercians had complained of the danger of distracting attention in church from true personal worship, prayer and contemplation. It was also true that, provided the distinction between veneration and worship was clearly made and understood, the more obvious objections were met; where the true spirit of the teaching of the church was operative there was no bowing down and worshipping.

Then, however, there could be little use for or need of physical representations. Many of these were crude, many unintelligible, many frankly undesirable. For unknown, dubious, or unworthy martyrs and confessors of long ago to have attributed to them miracles which far surpassed anything related of Christ and the apostles in the New Testament was both excessive and liable to rouse sceptical disbelief. Unless the memorials were removed, those who saw them might accept the most imaginative of legends and easily be distracted from Bible reading, prayer and worship.

Zwingli concluded that to pray to, or invoke, the saints was useless. There was no biblical testimony in favour of this practice. It was not the custom of the primitive church and it was repugnant to reason, for God to be approached through a creature. With these thoughts abroad, the government of Zurich at the end of 1522 had much cause for anxiety. The opposition must be taken seriously. The bishop of the diocese, leading figures in the Great Minster and a majority of the delegates who attended Diets of the Confederation seemed to regard them as Lutherans, heretics and outlaws. There were threats of violence to be considered as well. Matters must be publicly brought to a head; Zwingli must state his opinions clearly in writing, and a decision must be reached about religious practices hitherto taken for granted, but definitely within the wide control of the government. The latter could not refuse to accept responsibility.

A particular case helped to bring matters to a head. It had long been accepted that jurisdiction over members of a state (*Ort*) lay with its government alone and external interference was not to be tolerated. Among those who were proposing to give practical attention to the new recommendations from the Great Minster pulpit was Hans Urban Wyss, who from 1520 had been minister of Fislisbach.[1] He had all too faithfully echoed and paraphrased to his own congregation what he had heard and come to believe, and, in particular, had declared against intercessions to the Virgin Mary. Fislisbach was just south of Baden, whither Zurich's authority did not extend exclusively. A Federal Diet met at Baden on 24–25 November 1522 and complaints about the new preaching were made to it.[2] The minister was arrested, accused of heterodoxy and handed over to the Bishop of Constance, at whose orders he was strictly imprisoned in the

---

[1] Wyss was a native of Eglisau and therefore a subject of Zurich and in August 1523 became an assistant preacher at Winterthur.

[2] Not for the first time. The matter was raised again on 15 December, when the Diet resolved that preaching innovations – neuen lehre – should be prohibited. Zurich and Basle were asked to forbid the printing of 'sölicher nüwen buechlin'. EA, 4, 1a, 247–50, 255, 348, 489.

near-by Gottlieben Castle, where John Hus had been incarcerated before him. After over seven months of incarceration, torture and examination, he recanted and was allowed to return to his duties,[1] but by then Zurich had taken a decisive step towards religious independence.

[1] The case aroused remarkable interest all over northern Switzerland. Z I, 501 n. 9; Z VII, 623 n. 7; Z VIII, 34–7. Bullinger, *Ref.* I, 80. The recantation was dictated by Fabri.

5

The road to independence

All over Europe in the sixteenth century we come across public debates, disputations, altercations, dialogues and confrontations. The universities had long since tended to claim that controversial issues properly posed could be, and should be, settled by the application of the principles of logical reasoning. At Paris, Oxford, or Vienna, it was by sustaining a thesis successfully in public argument that the bachelor of arts could enter the society of masters and doctors. It was, indeed, accepted that orthodoxy must prevail, that a proposition could be philosophically sound but theologically false, any possibly heretical conclusion being disavowed beforehand. This apart, however, the superior argument prevailed, and the opponent gave way. Even in the law courts, there was in a sense the same appeal to the public argument, in so far as a jury presented its verdict on the facts put before it. Pico della Mirandola had offered to debate any one of 900 propositions with any or all comers, and it has often been pointed out that there was nothing exceptional about the presentation of Luther's ninety-five theses. Uncertainties could be resolved by reason, and reason meant the rules of logic worked out by long generations of scholastic philosophers. This could, and sometimes did, degenerate into mere verbal subtleties and argument about words from the substance of which all meaning had departed. Beyond them, however, lay the assumption that the dogmas of the church were apart and irrefutable. This could mean in practice that the Pope, the maker and interpreter of Canon Law, had the last and decisive word. Suppose, however, that Pope and councils could be mistaken, then the only appeal was to Holy Writ. This, in effect, had been implicit in some of Erasmus' writings, and quite explicit in Luther's thought by 1521. Since there were still a number of disputed and debatable matters, like flesh-eating in Lent or clerical marriage, these, now that the Bible for the first time was readily available in the original tongues, could, it was thought, be settled by question, answer, rational exposition and conclusion. To approach this tribunal had been increasingly Zwingli's intent from 1519 onwards. By the end of 1522, he had won over a sufficient following among influential people to be able to urge upon his rulers its

97

adoption as a working principle. Zurich had been challenged to prove its orthodoxy. Let this challenge be accepted: the word of God could not fail as a court of appeal, for in it was truth. So far from Zurich practice or preaching being wrong, the opposite was the case – it was their opponents who had departed from the teaching of Christ and the apostles, and had fallen into human error and misapprehension. All this should be argued publicly and exhaustively. The new council that came into office towards the end of 1522 adopted, after careful and serious debate, just this position. They would meet their critics in open debate, and the whole dispute could be settled thus 'according to the truth of Holy Writ' – and in the German language.[1]

These were highly important provisions. The Bible in German had only recently become accessible to the literate minority, and there was no vernacular text that was acceptable to Rome. Everything turned upon who was to interpret the Bible, and the claim from Constance that this should be the responsibility of those who understood its technicalities was difficult to resist. Such discussions had previously been university affairs.

Secondly, the debate was to be in German. In so far as the matters under discussion were theological, which was the case to a considerable degree, the German of north Switzerland was not the best of instruments for this. Theological discussions had almost invariably been in Latin and by trained disputants; a debate in a local language with laymen to decide about matters in which they had no training was very different.

The Zurich Council had long ago accepted responsibility for the maintenance of the true Christian faith within their dominions. The councillors, land owners, administrators, business men, successful craftsmen, now wanted to know what it was all about and decide on a course of action after a public discussion. They had been criticised in the Diet of the Confederation, and so all represented there would be most gladly heard in Zurich; other city states, Basle, Berne, Schaffhausen, should send their best clerics and laymen; above all, the Bishop of Constance should attend, suitably accompanied, and answer for his church. Nor did Zurich intend it to be all purely defensive; their leading scholar should set out his case in traditional form in propositions, conclusions, articles or theses.[2] The

---

[1] 'mit warhaffter göttlicher geschrifft in thütscher zungen und sprach anzögend' (Z 1, 467) Stumpf 2, 1, 174.

[2] Z 1, 458–65. Also, translated, in C. S. Meyer, *Luther's and Zwingli's Propositions for Debate* (Leyden, 1963) 35–51; A. C. Cochrane, *Reformed Confessions of the 16th century* (Philadelphia, 1966), 36–44; *Ulrich Zwingli (1484–1531) selected works*, ed. S. M. Jackson, introduction by E. Peters (Philadelphia, 1972), 111–17.

Koehler, *Zwingli* 93, rightly insists that there is no analogy with Luther's 95 theses composed in completely different circumstances. The *Schlussreden* were indeed hurriedly composed for a particular occasion and were not carefully thought out, but they were, nevertheless, an outline of an all-embracing programme of religious reform for Switzerland and beyond.

agenda was to be a discussion of these 67 *Schlussreden*, as they were called, under civic guidance in the Town Hall (*Rathaus*)[1] on 29 January 1523.

The answers to the invitation, or challenge, which was sent out on 3 January, were disappointing. All the responsible clergy within the jurisdiction of Zurich were called in, and nearly all obeyed the order. But practically all the constituent members of the Federal Diet, whose earlier strictures had invited a reply, refused to consider representation. So, too, more surprisingly, did Basle, seat of a bishop and a university where Johannes Oecolampadius (Hans Huszgen) had come in 1522 and was pursuing a course parallel to Zwingli's own. He feared lest a public disputation might become a public demonstration. The refusal was also partly due to inter-state jealousy; if there was to be a general doctrinal discussion, Basle, where old men could recall the days of an oecumenical council, should be the venue.[2] The Bishop of Constance certainly did not in any case intend to be present in person to argue with his inferiors, nor, indeed, were bishops of the early sixteenth century expected to be theologians or debaters. There could be no real debate in any case; it was from their bishop that his flock could receive directions and, if necessary, explanations. However, the invitation could not be ignored altogether; it was arranged that the diocese should be represented by observers who would attend on the bishop's behalf 'not to argue, but simply to listen, to give advice and to act as arbitrators'.

The bishop was, in fact, in something of a dilemma.[3] To ignore the invitation altogether was to abandon any hope of leading a reform movement with some of whose objectives he sympathised. Although he later indicated that he regarded the whole business as unworthy of his notice, that it was a mere 'tinkers' convention' (*Kesslertag*), a gathering of vagabonds, hippies and layabouts, in fact the matter was given careful consideration at Constance, and Fabri's presence was no accident. The disparaging remarks from the bishop were inevitably reported in Zurich and aroused resentment which was exploited by the anti-clericals.

The gathering was on the whole well stage-managed, apart from the failure to produce the agenda until just before the meeting started. It was fair comment for Fabri to complain that the 67 theses, some of far-reaching importance, were being circulated only on the day before discussions started, hot and wet from Froschauer's press.[4] Major issues, usually reserved for councils, bishops and universities, were to be publicly debated

---

[1] Not, of course, the existing building, which dates from the late seventeenth century, but an earlier Gothic structure on the same site.

[2] Z I, 445; Z VIII, 12, 29.

[3] B. Moeller, *Zwinglis Disputationen. Studien zu den Anfängen der Kirchenbildung und des Synodalwesens im Protestantismus*. ZRG 56 (1970), 278.

[4] Z I, 548–9 n. 5; Egli *I*, 199–204 (No. 484).

without any chance of their formulation being studied beforehand. It was not intended to be sharp practice, but it could be so represented, and the hurry was unnecessary. Possibly the otherwise inexcusable delay was deliberate: the episcopal delegation might well have refused to attend had they seen the theses beforehand.

The Zurich disputation was what might later be described as a public inquiry: it was arranged by the government, whose duty it was to ensure that proper preaching and teaching was available for its subjects. This had long been accepted, and it was now peculiarly important that the pulpits, the equivalents of press, public advertisement, radio and television, should be under control.

Although discussion and debate were envisaged, the outcome was largely prejudged because of the terms of reference. From the Bible there was no appeal; so that, any practice or teaching based solely on prescription however long, on councils however oecumenical and venerable, must be rejected. Thus, the council was in fact undertaking in 1523 what Henry VIII did eleven years later, to assert its supremacy in matters of religion.

At the centre of the 600 interested parties who crowded into the hall on a January morning,[1] was Zwingli with a group of friends and supporters and the folio volumes of the Greek New Testament, the Hebrew Old Testament and the Latin Vulgate, open before him. This was, in itself, impressive enough. Long years of study and a powerful memory meant that he could appeal instantly to the text or passage that supported his contention, and there was almost no one who could challenge his rendering of the Greek and Hebrew into Swiss German, which they all spoke. He also surpassed his possible opponents and critics in his understanding of the many different forms of speech to be found among the prose and poetry of the Divine Word. He was on his own ground, and the chairman, Bürgermeister Marx Röist,[2] was his ally.

It is astonishing that this specially convened council meeting which was to decide what was and what was not scriptural, and was to sit in judgement upon the papacy, tradition and ancient institutions and usages, did not take the simple precaution of keeping proper minutes of the proceedings and recording the evidence upon which its decisions were based. The days of shorthand reporting were not yet, but there were notaries public in Zurich whose official testimony could be of international evidential value, yet they were not used. There were no official minutes or *acta*, partly

---

[1] Z I, 483.
[2] A man of distinguished and wealthy family, now nearly 70 (1454–1524), who had fought and had been knighted at Morat by René of Lorraine and Hans Waldmann and had been a member of the council almost continuously for 30 years. For a short time he was captain of the papal bodyguard at Rome (1518). Wirz, 482; ADB XXIX, 405–6; Z I, 483 n. 2; Wyss, 13 n. 2.

because in theory the council was simply receiving verbal evidence,[1] but this left room for disputes and recriminations later.

The public inquiry soon became a public demonstration rather than a full, fair and free discussion. It was manifestly impossible in one day, before a large tribunal of busy men taken from their normal occupations, themselves mostly illiterate and in any case without any kind of theological training, to set out the whole case. Even allowing that the words of the Bible were alone to be decisive, almost any one of the great themes raised needed far more time and knowledge than were available there.

Zwingli's opponents were not only ill-represented, but they also put their case very badly. There were, in fact, four representatives of the bishop of the diocese there, who consistently and explicitly insisted that they were present only as observers and reporters and were not prepared to deal with any of the matters to be raised in any official capacity.[2] Matters as deep and far-reaching as those raised now could properly be discussed only at a

---

[1] The first Zurich disputation deserves, from its intrinsic importance, fuller study. A. Baur, *Die erste Züricher Disputation am 29. Januar 1523* (Halle, 1883), was a pioneer piece of work whose conclusions are also embodied in the same writer's *Zwinglis Theologie*. The material is collected, with introductions, in Z I, 442 (479)–569 (esp. 483 n. 1) and is adequate. The essential facts are not in doubt.

The independent narrative of Erhard Hegenwald, *Handlung der Versamlung* etc. (Zürich, 1523) has perhaps been given too great prominence; the various reprints, however, suggest that it coloured local opinion. ZWA XIII, 559–560 n. 14. Fabri issued his own account (*Wahrliche Unterrichtung*) of the meeting, nominally for the benefit of Archduke Ferdinand of Austria and the administration at Innsbruck (cf. J. G. Mayer in *Katholische Schweizer-Blätter* (Lucerne, 1895), 51–65, 183–95), and another version exists. There is also the unreliable but not insignificant satire *Das Gyrenrupfen*, composed by seven of the younger and less responsible auditors (J. Baechtold, *Geschichte der Deutschen Literatur in der Schweiz: Anmerkungen* (Frauenfeld, 1892), 135) and accounts by Bullinger, *Ref.* I, 84–90, 97–107, and Salat, 42–53.

[2] The four delegates from Constance were Ritter Fritz Jakob von Anwyl, an undistinguished knight, comptroller of the bishop's household, who was later to accept the Reformation; Domherr Georg Vergenhaus, an equally undistinguished Canon of Constance cathedral; Dr Martin Blansch or Plank, a second-rate theologian from Tübingen; and Dr Johann Fabri, the bishop's Official or vicar general. The only other 'outsiders' known to be present were Sebastian Hofmeister from Schaffhausen and Sebastian Meyer from Berne. Z I, 445.

Johannes Fabri, or Faber (the words are interchangeable but Fabri is more correct) (1478–1541) was an able man whose early career had some parallels with that of Zwingli. He was a humanist and an admirer of Erasmus, with whom, and with Zwingli, he exchanged friendly letters. A visit to Rome in 1521 convinced him of the dangers of the new Erasmian tendencies and he may also have perceived that the way to promotion was by active participation in the verbal and written polemics so much to the taste of his contemporaries. From then onwards he was Zwingli's indefatigable opponent, facile, unscrupulous, commonplace, elusive and well-versed in the standard text-books of orthodoxy. In 1530 he was made Bishop of Vienna, where he founded the trilingual college of St Nicholas, and in 1538 he was provost of Basle. Allen II, 189; I. Staub, *Dr. Johann Fabri (1518–23)* (Einsiedeln, 1911), 90–7, 121–3; L. Helbling, *Dr. Johann Fabri und die schweizerische Reformation* (Einsiedeln, 1932–3); A. Naegele, *Dr. Johann Fabri Generalvikar von Konstanz Malleus in haeresim Lutheranam* (1524) (Münster i. W. 2 Bde. 1941, 1952), Corpus Catholicorum, 23–6. The second part was completed, with valuable notes, by F. Heyer.

general council of bishops and doctors,[1] or an international Christian convention or possibly before a great university like Paris, Cologne or Louvain.[2] It was, they very reasonably pointed out, absurd that major controversies should be decided in a small city like Zurich when they concerned equally all France, Spain, Italy and Northern Europe. At the Diet of Nuremberg,[3] it was resolved, in February 1523, that a general council ('*ein frei cristlich concilium*') should be held in Germany to discuss just such matters, the first of the many proposals that were ultimately to lead to the Council of Trent.

These very reasonable objections were swept aside by Zwingli in a torrent of words. The fact that an abuse was of long standing did not make it less of an abuse; the Pope himself had agreed that custom gives way to truth.[4] The gathering at Zurich was a 'Christian Assembly' and, for that matter, a gathering of bishops,[5] perfectly competent to reach conclusions from the Gospel. This latter had been kept hidden all too long, but now it was available. 'God does not ask us what Popes, bishops and councils have ordered, or what is praiseworthy old custom, but how his will, his word and his commands are to be followed.' 'We have the infallible and impartial judge, Holy Writ, in Hebrew, Greek and Latin',[6] and there were competent theologians and canonists there too with, most important of all, hearts inspired by Christian faith.

One of the reasons publicly set out for the disputation was that Zwingli had been denounced in general terms as a traitor and a heretic,[7] and almost the first question put to the packed assembly was, 'Is there anyone here prepared to call Zwingli a heretic?' There was, explicably, no reply. One country clergyman merely remarked, 'If no one says anything against

---

[1] 'einer gantzen christlichen versamlung aller nation oder vor eim concilio der bischoffen unnd andrer gelerten, so man findt uff den hohen schůlen' Z I, 491.

[2] Z I, 493. The selection is not uninteresting. Paris was a very obvious choice, as was Cologne with its Dominican *studium*, and Aquinas, Albertus Magnus and Duns Scotus as past residents; but Louvain, which was less than a quarter of a century older than Basle, was less so. It had only recently come into prominence because Pope Adrian VI had graduated there and a *collegium trilingue* had been founded there in 1517. All three were rigidly orthodox, even reactionary. H. Rashdall, *The Universities of Europe in the Middle Ages* ed. F. M. Powicke and A. B. Emden (Oxford, 1936) II, 255–6, 266–8.

[3] RTA III, 746–7; H. Jedin, *Geschichte des Konzils von Trient*[2] Bd. I. (Freiburg, 1951), 169–70.

[4] Decretum Gratiani I. Dist. 8, cap. VI. *Corpus Iuris Canonici* (ed. Friedberg, Leipzig, 1897), 15. 'Revelatione ergo facta veritatis cedat consuetudo veritati.' However desirable some of the reforms suggested may have been, to speak of them as 'manifestly true' was a typical Zwinglian overstatement.

[5] Zwingli, basing his exegesis on the Greek New Testament, always insisted that a bishop was a simple 'overseer', a minister or clergyman – 'das ist uff gůt dütsch: ein pfarrer'. Cf. Z I, 231 (*Eine freundliche Bitte* etc.): 'alle pfarrer bischoff sind'. Z I, 495–6.

[6] Z I, 497, 498. Cf. ZWA XI, 479–98 for Zwingli's rejection of General Councils.

[7] Z I, 484 'von etlichen ein verfůrer, von den andern ein ketzer gscholten und hinderredt'. His accusers included the Mendicant Orders and Canon Hofmann. Egli *I*, 59–65 (No. 213).

Zwingli and no one contradicts him then he must be right and the bishop wrong.'[1]

To the issues raised from the 67 propositions, Fabri contented himself with his initial statement that he was not there to enter into any formal argument, but he put forward some commonplaces of orthodox apologetics. Heresies had constantly given trouble, and they reappeared in different forms – Novatian, Montanist, Sabellian, Ebionite, Marcionite, and, more recently, Beghards, Bohemian brethren, Wyclifites and Hussites. Was this the time and place to call into question practices that had seven hundred years prescription behind them? If there was no authority with bishops, cardinals, Popes and the monastic orders, if purgatory, the Blessed Virgin and St Peter were not to be accepted, where did authority reside? Was Zurich to set itself against the rest of the world? Unlike Zwingli, who made too much of his linguistic skill, he admitted that he knew no Hebrew and only a little Greek, while his Latin was adequate enough. In its way, this was a dignified and telling answer. 'I am no orator or poet.'[2] The spirit of God, he insisted, is not to be found in clever, smooth, eloquent words; quotations from the scriptures are more easily produced than the proper understanding and interpretation of them.

Fabri's intervention on the theme of clerical marriage was long remembered. After Zwingli had explained his position, Fabri insisted that there had been no married priest for 1,200 years, since the days of Tertullian (d. c. 220) and the Council of Nicaea (325). To this, one of the councillors present rejoindered, 'Maybe not, but they have been free to keep mistresses.'[3] The answer was an embarrassed silence.

There were other exchanges, but they were neither lengthy nor effective: some were brushed aside as 'sophistry', of which Zwingli said, 'I, too, used to be good at this'.[4] The first Zurich disputation was indeed a striking personal triumph for Zwingli, comparable only with his later spectacular victory at Berne in 1528. The debate was stage-managed, one-sided, and unfair to the Catholics, whose case had very largely gone by default. Fabri was determined not to enter into any serious discussion with his opponents, and there was no one else able or willing to uphold their cause.

Zwingli succeeded in establishing two major principles – that it was the duty of the government to control public worship and religious observances, and that the only preaching to be tolerated within its borders was

---

[1] Z I, 501–2.
[2] Z I, 511. Orator in the Ciceronian sense of eloquent and persuasive pleader, *poeta*, adept at humanist Latinity.
[3] Z I, 522. 'Aber hůren hatt mann wol erloubt.'
[4] Z I, 552: 'ich habs ouch wol vor zyten in der sophistery gelesen'.

such as was compatible with the text of the Bible.[1] The outcome of this first disputation was that the council agreed that Zwingli's sermons should continue and that all clergy within its jurisdiction should adopt the same exclusively evangelical approach. It was a notable achievement but it was not, and was not intended to be, a breach with Rome. Mass continued to be said in Latin as before. The Catholics could, and did, maintain that the Bible was the foundation of the Christian faith and that any departure from it might be heretical: it was all a question of interpretation. None the less, it implied the rejection of papal claims and thus was the first step on the road to a protestant Zurich.[2] Something of what the first disputation meant was seen when the sixty-seven propositions which had been before the assembly were generally available in print with Zwingli's commentary.[3] This was five months later and thus allowed for elaboration and answered Fabri's claim that the propositions were not founded on scripture. In this careful exposition, Zwingli's theological position is more clearly and concisely set out than anywhere else, except perhaps in the last confession of faith sent to Francis I of France in 1531.

On two major matters, there was to be serious deepening and modification later, namely on the subjects of baptism and the eucharist, and these themes can be more suitably described in conjunction with the Anabaptists and with Luther than within the framework of 1523. Basically, in the public debate, his opponents had denied both the truth and the biblical foundations of his assertions. They could now have the whole matter plainly set before them in German. The immediate recipients supposedly consisted of his former friends and parishioners in Glarus, but, as the Bishop of Constance and the Elector of Saxony were quick to recognise, it was addressed *urbi et orbi*, and it stated the results of a decade of consideration of the Bible message. It was intended to be highly practical; it took up every worthwhile issue that was under discussion at the time, and it was above all written for his 'admirable Confederates',[4] who, under Christian freedom,[5] are better off, and who can secure this freedom more peacefully, if they will, than any other Christian society in the world.

First and foremost, he insisted that it was necessary to establish the exclusive priority and superiority of the revealed word;[6] it was both erro-

---

[1] Z I, 447, 470–1, 547: 'was sy mitt dem heyligen euangelion unnd sunst rechter göttlicher geschrifft bewären mögen'. Egli *I*, 115 (No. 327).
[2] L. v. Muralt, *Die Reformation*, in *Historia Mundi* (Berne, 1957) Bd. VII, 73–4.
[3] The public debate closed on 29 January. Z I, 569. The commentary on the sixty-seven propositions was printed on 14 July 1523 by Froschauer. (*Auslegen und Gründe der Schlussreden*.) Z II, 11 (14)–457.   [4] 'einr loblichen Eydgnoschafft'. Z II, 19.
[5] This 'freedom' was duplex – freedom through Christ from the restrictive law of the Old Testament and freedom from man-made papal and ecclesiastical regulations and requirements. Koehler, *Zwingli*, 94–6.
[6] Z I, 458: 'uss grund der geschrifft, die theopneustos – das ist: vonn gott ingesprochen'.

neous and blasphemous to pretend that if no New Testament had survived, the church or councils could dictate the conditions which could secure eternal bliss, salvation, for humanity. The conclusions were not intended as a general apologetic for the Christian faith. The existence of God (in whom alone is perfect truth and perfect goodness, eternal, the creator of the universe, revealing himself to man in time through his son), the immortality of the soul and human fallibility, are taken for granted. His exposition thus was not addressed to those who, like Jews and infidels, are hardened in perfidy and disbelief.

The true only son of God, Christ, guiltless man, the exemplar of divine love, died once and for all on the cross for humanity, thereby reconciling God and man and saving mankind from eternal death. Adam had chosen to disobey God who had created him, and had thus brought death, sin and suffering to the human race which could no longer of its own accord fulfil God's will in righteousness, truth and goodness. The book of Genesis is as basic to Zwinglian, and indeed to Reformation, theology as the Gospels. The fall of man happened in measurable past time exactly as narrated – it, and the creation, were no allegories or explanatory stories.

The Gospel was not the product of human reason; it was complete, it could not be overruled or added to, and through God's spirit it was entirely comprehensible to those with the gift of faith. Church, Pope, the Fathers, could neither interpret, improve, nor alter it. Through God's goodness, righteousness and mercy, through the death of the sinless Christ, salvation was available to all mankind. Grace indeed had some immediate as well as continuous applicability. No creature of his own accord could fulfil God's will, our nature not being such that we could not be moved by unworthy desires or anger. All believers knew the struggle of body[1] and soul, but where there was faith, God working through Christ, there was also love of God and the intent and ability to keep his commandments. Having told his readers in beautiful simplicity that, where the love of God is, there is also God's spirit, he goes on, almost to the point of bathos, to condemn as evidence of the opposite, pilgrimages, processions, lights, incense, noisy hymns,[2] vigils, vain repetitions, hired masses, mural

---

[1] The body, flesh, was both weak and corrupt. The concept of necessary human sin, frailty, weakness, sickness, was especially vivid for Zwingli – Präst, Mangel, Fehler, Gebrechen, Krankheit, he multiplies physiological indications to illustrate his point without ever precisely defining the extent and the nature of this inherent 'weakness'. That, however, it was something curable by truth and divine mercy he never doubted.

[2] The qualification *noisy* hymns (hülen) (Z II, 48) is interesting. Zwingli was intensely musical and loved harmony of sound. Church services in the fifteenth and early sixteenth centuries, with very primitive organs and with large numbers of untrained males singing out of tune at the tops of their voices, could easily become unedifying. When, as frequently depicted in early wood and metal cuts, dogs were present in church and cannot have failed to raise their voices as well, the effect must have been disastrous. Zwingli did not object to all hymn singing in church.

paintings and other decorations in churches, the purchase of prayers and indulgences and the running after relics in the streets.

This is followed by a denunciation of the vanity of gambling, buffoonery, bad language, immorality, drunkenness and expensive clerical vestments – better that the money were spent on the poor and needy, rent-reductions and better pay for the workers.

From this the argument returns to the Bible (with a plea for more teaching of Latin in order to understand it), to its insistence that Christ, and not the Pope, is the head of the Church. But what is 'the church'? The conclusions now set out were basic to much of Zwingli's thought. Manifestly there was the community of all true believers in Christ, united through the Spirit in one faith, universal, Catholic, known to God alone. But what of the visible church on earth? For this the primitive church of the apostles provided the model. Nothing in scripture called for a 'representative' church (*ecclesia representativa*), still less for a Roman church with any such claims. Instead, it was groups of Christians meeting together and living side by side locally as a community (*Gemeinde*) that constituted a church.[1]

It followed that no council or assembly of bishops could act or speak for the church; to call the Roman Church the universal church, or the Bishop of Rome universal head, was unacceptable, and from all this followed serious consequences, as the reader was warned. Their master must be the Bible alone, to which they must submit with humility. If the Fathers were found to disagree with the Bible, so much the worse for the Fathers: those who followed them in such disagreement were not included in the church of Christ. 'The Bible must be your master: you are not master of the Bible'[2] – the principle of *sola scriptura* could hardly be more plainly stated. Such exclusiveness was later to prove almost an embarrassment.[3]

The attack on the papacy, the hierarchy, canon law and the exclusive pretensions of the clergy attracted attention to the 67 articles but made them less theologically effective. They also intensified Catholic opposition; as the writer well knew, 'this little book will bring much disapproval'.[4] When he went on to compare the normal public services of the Great

---

[1] Z II, 56–8. The word church – 'kirck oder kilch...Kahal, ecclesia, concio' – sometimes used to describe a building, properly signified a meeting or assembly, 'ein versamlung, gemeinsame oder gemeind des volks...die besunderen zemenversamlungen, die wir pfarren oder kilch-hörinen nennend'. (Kirchgemeinde, Pfarrei, Versammlung der Genossen einer Kirchgemeinde.) The congregation of God's people which is at Corinth (I Cor. 1, 2) Zwingli calls 'Der gemeind, die in Corintho ist.' There is no adequate English equivalent of Gemeinde – village, manor, township, parish (whether civil or ecclesiastical) are too topographical, village community is too artificial. The Swiss Gemeinde, of the existence of which every government was highly conscious, included the whole local community, men, women and children, able to express opinions through a gathering of the adult males, all together part of the whole Christian church.

[2] Z II, 62: 'die gschrifft üwer meister ist, und ir nit meister über die gschrifft sind'.

[3] Yoder I, 21: See below 175.   [4] Z II, 64.

Minster with Jewish ceremonial, and the financial system of the medieval church with the burdens imposed on the Jews but condemned by Christ, the negative and destructive nature of this section was made a little too prominent.

Further, Zwingli now openly challenged the codified legislation of the church, the canon law as set out in the *Corpus Juris Canonici*. This consisted largely of papal pronouncements, relying for its validity upon papal enactment and promulgation, and was dependent upon the concept of the Pope as vicar of Christ. Zwingli's case was that canon law was valid only when, and in so far as, it agreed with God's word. In the event of a conflict, it was of no effect, and of the existence of a conflict ordinary people, guided by the Bible, must judge.

'People', however, meant in practice the organised community, the government. Thus, by implication, the authority of the Pope and councils was transferred to the state; it was by the government that laws relating to the church must be enforced if acceptable and abrogated where they were not compatible with the Bible, and of this the secular authorities were the judge. With them rested responsibility for enforcing the law. While urging submission to a Christian magistracy, the Swiss equivalent of the 'godly prince' elsewhere, Zwingli supplied the clear guidance which was just what the Zurich Council in Rathaus assembled wanted – this body had already secured most of the authority formerly exercised by the bishop; in the future they could assume that of the Pope as well, the more so in that the papal claim to rule as a temporal prince was now shown to be repugnant to Christ's instructions to his apostles.

New Testament theory: sixteenth century Swiss practice – it was relatively easy to emphasise the contrast, and no opportunity of doing this was omitted. Quite suddenly we move from appealing exposition of divine grace and love, and penetrating paraphrase of some profound biblical truths to strong denunciation of those who 'in this city' impede the propagation of the sweetness and comfort of the Bible.[1]

Salvation by faith is set out with some simplicity. Belief, then baptism, then salvation from God, all can understand this, but not all heed the warning of the Psalmist – *omnis homo mendax* – wherefore men twist the scripture to their own purposes, whereas only what is revealed by God is assuredly true, anything else is suspect. Human teaching, good works, our private efforts, however well meant, are valueless, vain, even deceptive; righteousness can be achieved only by God's mercy, by hope and faith.

---

[1] For editions of the Bible available see below 128 n. 4. It was assumed that all literates could secure a copy of the Bible, although this was relatively expensive. When the Pfarrer from Schlieren complained that he was too poor to be able to purchase a copy of the New Testament, Zwingli insisted that he could easily either borrow one or persuade a well-to-do layman to buy one for him. Z I, 564-5.

The alternative was damnation. Hence, obedience is better than sacrifice, provided that it is obedience to God and not to men. Inevitably the supersession of the 'law and prophets' by the new law of love and of the spirit requires explanation and exposition. The Gospel brought a new freedom; the spirit of God shows man what God requires. Cautiously and with appropriate qualifications[1] Zwingli urged simple reliance upon Christ and his teaching through the Spirit. Again and again, Zwingli, here and elsewhere, warns, indeed fulminates, against hypocrisy. He found it, or seemed to find it, at every turn – so much mechanical repetition, so much action, even payment without conviction behind it, seemed apparent. Sometimes it seemed almost an obsession: any action by his opponents and any argument by which it was supported could be swept majestically and magisterially aside with the word *Gleisnerei*, mere pretence.

Christ alone was High Priest, and any attempt or claim to assume the honour and the power that is his alone, any claim to be his representative, lieutenant, 'statthalter', was vain; any one displacing Christ was himself Antichrist. He who has the keys does not replace the giver of the keys, and the keys were not for Peter alone but for all the disciples together. Others, St Paul especially, fed the sheep just as much as St Peter did. The drift of all this was obvious enough. Papal claims to supremacy were as clearly rejected as they had been three years previously by Luther in *To the Christian Nobility of the German Nation*. None the less, throughout the section dealing with the Pope, there is a certain caution, reticence and avoidance of direct vituperation rather unusual at the time.

Much twentieth century scholarship has demonstrated the antiquity and the profundity of papal claims; for some purposes the Pope was God upon earth.[2] Measures and men had long since depended on him: the law of the church, canon law, derived much of its validity and most of its accepted interpretation from papal authority, while the appointment to almost any benefice might be in his hands. Concordats, like that made with France at Bologna in 1516, might indeed mean that in practice this authority was delegated to monarch or government; but even so, what had been granted might be taken away. The Pope 'created' his cardinals; archbishops, bishops and heads of religious orders were papal nominees. Without the Pope the catholic church of the west ceased to function according to pattern and plan. Manifestly, it is the breach with the papacy which marks the acceptance of the Reformation in Saxony, England,

---

[1] 'Weliche sich nun mit aller zůversicht an'n herren Christum Jesum lassend...' Z II, 81. 'Darumb můssend wir zů aller zyt durch den einigen, gerechten, unschuldigen Jesus Christum zů got kummen.' Z II, 478.

[2] W. Ullmann, *Medieval Papalism* (London, 1949), especially 118, states the papal case. See also the same author's *The Growth of Papal Government in the Middle Ages* (3rd ed., London, 1970) and G. Barraclough, *The Medieval Papacy* (London, 1968).

Scotland, the Scandinavian countries. Wherever there was a coherent government, an obvious test of orthodoxy was its treatment of and by the papacy. By implication the Zurich council in its approval of the evangelism of 1523 had also broken with the papacy, but this was not realised then, or even a good deal later.

From papal authority, Zwingli goes on to deal with the mass. The basic antiquity of this service is now accepted as being much greater than earlier ages knew; but, equally, it is recognised that the liturgy, and the accompanying thought about the nature of the eucharist, had evolved slowly with almost continuous change. For many purposes the fourth Lateran Council of 1215 provided a simple starting point; transubstantiation was then clearly stated, communion in one kind and the necessity of individual auricular confession were made obligatory upon all the faithful. Of these developments, that of communion in one kind, the wine being for the priest only, was, of itself, intrinsically a matter of 'indifference' or of practice. It was the Hussites who had made so much of this matter that it assumed a significance out of proportion to the subject. Zwingli was well aware of this, and, although finding it 'surprising' that the cup was withheld,[1] it was to a clear statement of more fundamental issues that he now turned.

He was now convinced that Christ's offering of himself for sinful humanity was complete, once-and-for-all, final, and that there was no need for, and indeed no possibility of, the repetition of this sacrifice. It was the treatment of the mass as a sacrifice, a repetition of Christ's suffering on the cross, which was totally unacceptable to him. Christ's action was unique, never to be repeated; whereas for the devout Catholic, the priest, holding in his hands the body of Christ, enacted once again the offering made at Calvary. Quite apart from any question of transubstantiation, there was here a clear divergence of thought about this central theme of church worship, which could not be closed and was almost bound to widen.

Zwingli, like many others of his time, was fascinated by words; he was humanist enough to know that the meaning of many common Latin words had changed considerably since classical times, and yet he was unwilling to accept the interpretation of another age. *Sacrificare, sacrificium,* could not be the same as 'offer', 'offering', just as *sacramentum* meant for the humanist a solemn oath of allegiance like that taken by the soldier on entering military service, and was illegitimately used to mean a holy mystery.[2] This constant harping upon semantics or etymology is a little wearisome because it so often seems to lead nowhere and because some-

---

[1] While he was beneficed in Glarus, Zwingli had been shown an 'obsequial' or service book from Mollis not more than two hundred years old, apparently containing clear evidence that communion in both kinds had been available there even to children. Z II, 133-4.
[2] Z II, 118, 120; see p. 290 n. 3 below.

times the derivations are either demonstrably wrong or irrelevant. If sacrament, *sacramentum*, meant an oath, then confirmation, ordination and extreme unction were not sacraments; if *sacramentum* was to be expanded into *sacrae rei signum*, a sign of a holy thing, then the elements, the bread and the wine, became this. If they were signs, they must be signs of something, and therefore could not be a sacrifice. It would be far better not to use the word sacrament at all: 'Wir Tütschen bedörffend dess worts sacrament nit.'[1]

There was indeed occasional polemic in this section, but there was also much simple Christian pastoral advice. Man in this life is never free from the cross, from the suffering which is the common lot of humanity. To live an acceptable life, a man must bear tribulation, sickness and pain with humility. Following Christ involves sweat and toil, renouncing the devil who offers honour and renown, submitting patiently to God's will. 'If you would sacrifice anything to God, sacrifice your pride.'[2] All this, and much more in this treatise, may be the commonplaces of the moralist but are not therefore insignificant.

The word 'testament' brought him back to the theme of 'sacrifice' and remembrance. Unlike Luther, he would gladly avoid using this noun which had such explicit legal implications of inheritance of property, preferring his favourite word, remembrance, *Wiedergedächtnis*. By now (July 1523), Zwingli had thought out a great deal, although he had not reached such finality as he ever attained about what it is convenient to label the 'doctrine of the real presence'. He was not yet, as he put it, prepared to argue with the *theologi*.

Leaving this major matter on one side for later consideration, some other topics were raised and disposed of in this commentary with some decisiveness. The five traditional sacraments beside baptism and the Last Supper were easily put into a different category. Extreme unction was a degenerate and unnecessary extension of the apostolic practice of the friendly visit to the sick and the speaking of words of faith.[3] The accompaniments had become childishly ornamental, the anointing oil being insignificant in comparison with the words that went with it. Confirmation received rather fuller treatment. It was a friendly action expressive of what had already happened, a public recognition by those coming to the age of discretion of the obligations assumed at baptism. For baptism and the eucharist there was the fullest biblical authority, and Zwingli's treatment of these in the *Schlussreden* was soon to require further elaboration.[4]

[1] Z II, 125.   [2] Z II, 130.   [3] As described in James 5. 14.
[4] See below, chaps. VII, XIII. In baptism it was not the water but the faith that the baptised person showed in salvation through Christ that washed away sin. He writes in terms of adult comprehension; the difficulties surrounding the applicability of this principle to the baptism of infants were passed over in silence. Similarly at this stage he seems to have accepted the

All this was manifestly so closely allied to what Luther was writing and saying that Zwingli, not for the last time, had to assert his own independence. He insisted that he had already started preaching directly from the Bible at Glarus and Einsiedeln in 1516, as Diebold von Geroldseck could testify, before Luther's name had been known in the neighbourhood. When three years later he came to Zurich, 'I set forth...how I would, if God willed, preach the Gospel written by Matthew without human additions or controversial comment...No one here knew anything about Luther except that something had been published by him about indulgences.'[1] This, Zwingli insisted, gave him little help since his attention had been drawn to abuses of indulgences by Thomas Wittenbach,[2] his admired teacher at Basle. 'Luther's book on the Lord's Prayer[3] was published after I had spoken on Matthew' and then he found himself taken for its author. 'Why did the Roman cardinal and representatives who were staying at that time in our city of Zurich begin to hate and want to ensnare me, not making me out to be a Lutheran until they knew that Luther was a heretic?...I began to preach before ever I heard Luther's name, and to that end I began to learn Greek ten years ago in order that I might know the teachings of Christ from the original sources...The Papists say, "You must be Lutheran, you preach just as Luther writes." I answer, "I preach just as Paul writes, why not call me a Pauline?"... Luther, as I think, is a mighty upholder of God who has closely studied the Bible and that with greater seriousness than has been done on this earth for a thousand years...no one has been like him for the manly immoveable courage with which he has attacked the Pope.' None the less, 'I will not bear Luther's name for I have read little of his teaching and have often intentionally refrained from reading his books...I will have no name but that of my captain, Christ, whose soldier I am...yet I value Luther as highly as anyone alive.'[4]

possibility that the unbeliever was in some spiritual sense brought into contact with the body of Christ at the communion, a position he was later to abandon. The exposition of Article XVIII (especially Z II, 142–3) is not as clear on this point as it was later when he had to maintain that for the complete disbeliever there was no presence of Christ at all at a service of which he was not really a participant.

[1] I.e. 'Ein Sermon von Ablass und Gnade' (WA I, 243–6) which appeared in 1518.
[2] Z VIII, 84 n. 1. Wackernagel, Basel III, 320. He became the Reformer of Biel.
[3] *Auslegung deutsch des Vaterunsers für die einfältigen Laien. 1519.* WA II, 81–130. Translated in *Luther's Works*, ed. M. O. Dietrich (Philadelphia, 1969) 42. 19–81.
 The first reference to Luther in the Zwingli correspondence was in December 1518 (Z VII, 123), and after that Zwingli read Luther's writings when he found occasion. At first he seems to have regarded Luther as a fellow-humanist opposed to the barren scholasticism of the universities (Koehler, *Zwingli*, 60–2).
 It is likely that Zwingli's friends were more anxious to send him Luther's writings than he was to receive them.
[4] Z II, 146–50. Zwingli's claim to independence of Luther was justified, and is, with qualifications, now generally accepted. He was interested and concerned to emphasise this, just as

From this generous tribute he returns to the mass as a sacrifice, repeating his own insistence upon the uniqueness of Christ's passion. The contrary opinion had been maintained because it was profitable: later, when saying mass for the living seemed sufficiently profitable, they included masses for the dead. These, and the teaching about purgatory that went with them, were, however, worthless.

The question of purgatory was, presumably deliberately, only lightly[1] touched on, but that of prayers to the saints was argued in some detail. A mediator or arbitrator must be one acceptable to both parties, able to understand both. Moses, the type of Christ, had uniquely mediated between Israel and God: for the Christian only Christ could do this, having revealed on earth his father's will, given a sure promise of divine grace, and saved the souls of men from death. Christ was both God and man; as God alone, mediation would be self-contradictory, for the one God could not mediate with himself; but having taken human nature upon him, he was the sole possible approach. A creature, a saint, even the Blessed Virgin herself, could not be a mediator because humanity was subject to human weakness, unable to fulfil the law, the eternal and unalterable will of God, without the grace brought by Christ's sacrifice. The will of God and that of Christ were identically and necessarily the same since there was but one God. Through Christ, in the name of Christ, God, asked in Christ's name and needing no other mediator, gives all to man. At this stage, 1523, this question of the intercession of the saints dominated Zwingli's thought. He admitted that he had formerly himself offered the usual prayers until convinced from the scriptures that prayers to the saints were idolatrous. To the demonstration of this from the Bible he devoted some fifty pages, discussing the meanings of sanctity, returning to the theme of faith, the ineffectiveness of good works, the essentially evil nature of mankind, 'where there is faith there is also the spirit of God and where this is, good works will be also'.[2]

And it must be an active faith. For there were, he insisted, living Christians who were foolish enough to believe that they had but to secure by prayer the support of a patron saint in order to be sure of salvation, thus thinking themselves free to make war, gamble, blaspheme, rob, burn and commit adultery with impunity. With an image of St Sebastian in his hat, a man accounted himself safe against accidents and the plague; a daily greeting to St Christopher guaranteed him against sudden death that day. They put

---

Luther was convinced of the opposite. Like Luther, Zwingli was powerfully influenced by his study of St Augustine, as his marginal notes and his lectures on the Psalms demonstrate. Similarly, he was much affected, particularly in his reliance on the Bible and his Christology, by Erasmus. Koehler was, however, manifestly right to insist that 'the Reformation' begins with Luther. Koehler, *Zwingli*, 62–81; L. Febvre, *Au cœur religieux du XVIe. siècle*² (Paris, 1968) 12–13.   [1] See below, 205, 339.   [2] Z II, 185.

an image of St Barbara got up like a prostitute on an altar for protection; they danced to St Sebastian on his festival and felt secure.[1] The Spaniards pray to St James for victory, the French to St Michael,[2] as if the saints in heaven would fight one another. How can the saints, whose property it is to be freed from human feelings of sorrow, need, anxiety and weakness, be concerned or affected by human needs? They can but repeat human prayers to God, to whom they are already known, they cannot pray for what they know will not be granted, the appeal to their intercessions is a diminution, rejection or refusal of the saving passion of Christ.

There were, Zwingli admitted, a few passages in the Bible which needed consideration in relation to the saints. A passage in the book of Baruch (3. 4) could easily be swept aside with the diminished authority attributed to the Apocrypha, a mere cuckoo's egg laid among Holy Writ, the one hundred and fiftieth psalm[3] was not relevant, the passages in the Apocalypse[4] were rather more puzzling but could be considered as alluding to a communication rather than to a prayer or request. In any case, the author of the Apocalypse could not have been St John the Evangelist, and its authority was dubious. Nor could the authority of St Jerome be acceptable as an interpreter in the whole matter, since, as Erasmus also demonstrated, he was mistaken here. As to the appeal to Vigilantius,[5] this is so worthless that he is better called Dormitantius, the Sleeper, than Vigilantius, the Watchman.

Reliance upon the miracles worked by saints was equally irrelevant. Where these were genuine, they were the result of the grace of God and not of any merit of the 'martyrs': in any case, false Christs and false prophets could work miracles, and had done so. The saints know of us men only what God chooses to reveal to them, and of this the Bible gives no clear testimony.

Zwingli gave much thought to the meaning of prayer: its very nature precluded the intervention of the saints, since Christ's teaching was that prayer was for the living only, the reaching out and the contact of the spirit with God.[6] It came from the heart, and many words were unnecessary.

---

[1] Z II, 187–8. [2] Z II, 197.

[3] 'Laudate dominum in sanctis eius' (Vulg.) Ps. CL – the English prayer book version 'O praise God in his holiness' indicates Zwingli's interpretation. The New English Bible has 'Praise God in his holy place.' Few things are more illuminating as showing the difference between sixteenth century and modern thought about the Bible than the treatment of the Psalms. For Zwingli, as for Luther, the whole of the Old Testament directly foreshadowed the New Testament.

[4] Rev. 5. 7; 8. 3 'the prayers of all saints', 'de orationibus sanctorum omnium' (Vulg.). Z II, 208–11, cf. above, 64.

[5] Vigilantius was a priest from the south of France who attacked the cult of the relics of martyrs (c. A.D. 400) and was opposed by St Jerome. Z I, 535 n. 1.

[6] From St Augustine *De Tempore* V. Part II (MPL. 39). 'Quid est autem oratio nisi adscensio animae de terrestribus ad coelestia, inquisitio supernorum, invisibilium desiderium.'

Much later, when Zurich had its own liturgy and form of prayer, a feature of it was to be quite long intervals of silence which must have made it something like a later Quaker assembly. Silent prayer was little cultivated previously: Zwingli's appeal at this early stage for the individual reaching out of the heart in communion with the eternal was something almost original. Erasmus had indeed said something of the same sort in an oft-quoted Preface, but that the ploughman and the blacksmith should pray while at work was itself a new concept.

From an eloquent repetition that Christ must be the only mediator, the only source of righteousness for whom, through whom and from whom good works alone are of any worth, Zwingli moves to the well-worn theme of the contrast between the poverty of Christ on earth and the flaunting wealth of contemporary prelates and priests. It was the devil's working which brought it about that men made themselves rich in the name of God. 'Religion gave birth to riches and the daughter devoured the mother'.[1] Two falsehoods have forwarded this trend – the one that St Peter was the vicar of Christ' the other that of the Donation of Constantine, 'a lie as clear as daylight'. Hence, instead of being overseers and preachers, bishops have become swaggering squires (*gotsjunckheren*), offenders, warmongers, usurers, cheats, traitors and deserters: 'if I kept quiet the very rocks would cry out against me'.[2] Their works are built on mere fairy tales, their laws on vain imagination, as in the case of fasting during Lent. How can it matter whether you satisfy your hunger with veal or with fish? This freedom he would extend to ensure greater productivity. Saints days, turned into days of compulsory idleness, were often unnecessary and even injurious. Instead, after attending a short service, a man should return to his work. Sunday was indeed for rest from toil, but apart from Sunday there was a case for only four holidays a year – Christmas day and St Stephen's day (25 and 26 Dec), the Annunciation (25 March) and St John the Baptist (24 June) – these to remember the faith of the prophets, and St Peter and St Paul (29 June) for the sake of the apostles and evangelists.

There was relatively little discussion at the first Zurich disputation or in the *Schlussreden* about the place of images in churches and the reverence paid to them. A question had, however, been asked early in the proceedings about the torture and imprisonment of Hans Urban Wyss of Fislisbach for opposing prayers to the Virgin Mary, and the whole subject was soon to come to the fore.

Zwingli was no opponent of the arts.[3] He tried to prevent the destruction of painted windows, to which no reverence could be paid. His best

---

[1] Z II, 242.
[2] Z II, 243; Luke 19. 40.
[3] Ch. Garside, Jnr., *Zwingli and the Arts* (New Haven, 1966) Z III, 906, IV, 84.

known differentiation was between a statue of St Charlemagne which, honoured inside the Great Minster, was objectionable, but high up on the tower, where it remains undisturbed, it could do no harm.[1] There was, he consistently maintained, nothing wrong with a picture or image as such: it was the honour or worship paid to it that mattered. No one worshipped the stone monkeys in the Fischmarkt or the gilded weather-cocks. But in practice the existence of images in churches led to worship of them, and so they must be eliminated.[2] Even the crucifix was unacceptable. Christ, indeed, was to be worshipped, but in his divine nature, and this could not be depicted, while his human nature, which might thus be, was not to be adored. Nothing should be allowed to distract attention from the worship of God.

It is characteristic of Zwingli's common sense that the elimination of the many holy days was accompanied by a popular recognition that certain traditional and accepted breaks in the daily routine were needed. To concede them was illogical[3] perhaps, but advisable. Unconditional statements of principle combined with willingness to make temporary or necessary concessions to human weakness or existing conditions was always part of the Zwinglian approach. Thus, while opposed to special clerical vestments and preferring the minister to appear in ordinary lay, but markedly sober, dress,[4] Zwingli was prepared to offer that wide freedom of choice for which he himself frequently strove. What was specially loathsome to him was pretence – hypocrisy, the repetition of meaningless phrases, the assertion that in no way corresponded to the deed, the reliance upon external signs – these were the clearest testimony to the absence of godly purpose.

If there was no need for special distinctive clerical garments, still less was there any useful place in Christian society for the orders of monks, canons and friars, or for the title of 'Father' which was so usual. The orders had become associations for the collection of money, their individual vows of poverty were transcended by their corporate wealth, they obeyed neither God nor the state, they were exclusive, aloof and unaware of the needs of those who should have benefited most by their ministrations. The triple monastic vow of poverty, chastity and obedience, like clerical celibacy, was impracticable, undesirable and constantly evaded. The brief discussion in the *Schlussreden* is based more on the inadequacy and uselessness of the actual lives of monks and friars than on any serious attempt to show cause why contemplative orders, following the Rule, should be unacceptable.

[1] Z IV, 95–6.   [2] Z IV, 106.
[3] Most illogical, and equally most natural of all, was the later decision by the Council to recognise the feast of SS. Regula and Felix as a public holiday. Egli *1*, 453 (No. 946).
[4] Z II, 252 with a note about later practice in Zurich.

For a young man to take the monastic vow of chastity was to tempt God; it had no biblical sanction but could very easily be the irresponsible act of a youth promising what he might be unable to perform, relying on a strength and capacity which might be denied to him. Whereas adultery was plainly forbidden by divine decree, marriage was lawful alike by human, natural or God's law, the latter because only what God has forbidden is sinful. We cannot promise to God what we have not got, and if the gift of chastity has not been vouchsafed, matrimony is the right and proper alternative.

If, as was now becoming likely, Zurich was to break with the Roman Catholic church, denying its claim to be Christ's body, consideration had to be given to the membership of what was to be recognised and accepted in its stead. That there could not be more than one true church was axiomatic to all: for certain purposes decisions must be made on behalf of the church, decisions which had formerly come from Rome. In particular, baptism being accepted as (*inter alia*) the token of admission, there must be some means of eliminating the publicly unrepentant disbeliever or sinner from among the visible community of church attenders. There was incontrovertible scriptural authority for this, and men had long since been accustomed to diocesan excommunication by the bishop or the major excommunication by the Pope. Now they were offered something at once more primitive and more subtle. No one individual, article 31 insisted, could deprive another individual of membership of the visible church; only the whole church could do this. For working purposes in dealing with a notorious evil-liver the church was the community in which he lived, and this body was guided by its pastor, whose special duty it was to watch over his flock. The offender, accused of some obvious wickedness such as assault, rape, adultery, blasphemy in public, slander, drunkenness, lying, or even neglect of duty (*müssiggon*), must first be warned privately by the minister; then, if failing to amend, he must be named to the community[1] along with credible witnesses. Only then, after further enquiry, and when the offences were both established and notorious, might the ban be applied. Rightly and charitably used it was valuable and necessary.

All this, it was explained, was very different from current practice when debt or underpayment of tithe and minor offences were visited with the maximum penalty, and this for the sake of the money that could be extracted for absolution. Characteristically, when there had been war in 1499 between the Swabians and the Swiss, partly provoked by gross slander

[1] Z II, 281: 'ein iede besundre gmeind, die wir kilchhörinen nennend'. Cf. Z II, 58: 'die besunderen zemenversamlungen, die wir pfarren oder kilchhörinen nennend'. The definition was more useful for destructive opposition tactics in 1523 than valuable later when baptist-dominated communities could appeal in vain to this concept as saving them from the domination of the Zwinglian state church. R. C. Walton, *Zwingli's Theocracy* (Toronto, 1967), 170 ff.

against the latter,[1] the bishops had done nothing to stop it when excommunication of the offenders would have done much good. Instead, they had used the opportunity to add where possible to the elaborate and complicated contributions that were exacted from the faithful. It was a fundamental condition of the Confederation that an inhabitant ought not to be brought before a foreign judge. Ought this not to apply to the Bishop of Constance? This obviously raised complex problems of lawful jurisdiction which were to be considered more fully later.

It also, in fact, raised the question of the proper relationship of church and state, a matter which Zwingli introduces a little abruptly by expressing objection to the practice by which money or goods captured in war, or taken in circumstances which made restitution to the original owner impossible or impracticable, were handed over to monasteries or applied to church building. Such property in his view should be applied to the relief of the poor. This was obviously a matter for the civil authorities, the government, to whose duties and obligations he devotes several pages. Obviously no complete exposition of the nature of government was, or could be, attempted within the framework of these conclusions. The immediate purpose was to demonstrate the excessive powers claimed by the spirituality. Civil government (*die Obrichkeit, der weltlich Gewalt*) rested upon divine authority explicitly assured by Christ himself, whereas the claims of Pope and bishops to exercise power were without biblical sanction. There was, naturally, no thought of any divorce between religion and ethics or any notion that the clergy should be 'kept out of politics'. The whole attitude of the age was opposed to any such distinction.

The clergy were there to feed their flocks, to seek to persuade men, by humility, friendliness and good behaviour, to follow the example of Christ in charity, simplicity and service. One of the purposes of the debate of January 1523 was to convince the Council that a change of direction in religious policy would actually increase its authority. Provided that a lawfully constituted government had not degenerated into tyranny[2] (which was not defined), it must be obeyed and need not fear to uphold the teaching of the gospel. If, indeed, everyone was truly righteous there would be no need for laws to be enforced, but mankind was not in fact like this. Outside paradise there were bound to be evil doers who needed the restraining hand of the police.[3]

Christ himself had willingly submitted to be enrolled by and taxed by

---

[1] Z II, 282–3 and notes. H. Sigrist, *Reichsreform und Schwabenkrieg. Ein Beitrag zur Geschichte der Entwicklung des Gegensatzes zwischen der Eidgenossenschaft und dem Reich* (Aarau, 1947), 114–41.

[2] 'so verr sy nit tyrannen sind', Z II, 304.

[3] Z II, 305. 'Gäbind aber alle menschen got, das sy im schuldig sind, so dörffte man gheines fürsten noch obren, ja, wir wärind nie uss dem Paradys kummen.'

the government of his day, whereas the clergy were now claiming un-justifiable exemptions from taxation. Clerical immunities and exemptions had no biblical sanction and should be relinquished voluntarily. For example, clerics should not act as judges, since their work was preaching and teaching, not the administration of justice. Instead of demanding power they should seek to serve, to obey and to pray for those in authority. Like Zwingli himself they should preach peace and repentance among Christians.

From the eleventh century, at least, it had been a commonplace that the 'two swords' of Luke 22. 38 referred to spiritual and secular jurisdiction of which the Church (i.e. the hierarchy) retained the former while per-mitting the lay power to exercise the latter. This interpretation Zwingli now challenged. The two swords referred to the Old and New Testament respectively. The Pope, like Peter, should put up his sword and cease to encourage wars in Italy or even take the lead in expeditions against the Turks. Insisting that he had always earnestly preached peace in Zurich,[1] Zwingli now switched the argument to current affairs. Cardinal Schiner had recently been actively recruiting soldiers for service with the papal armies, calling for a speedy response before opposition could be whipped up from the pulpit.[2] As a result, some 6,000 men, more than was asked, had left Zurich for Piacenza, supposedly for use against the Turks. The French forces in Italy under Lautrec had been singularly unsuccessful against Charles V in spite of the alliance of the King of France with the Swiss Confederates (except Zurich) of May 1521.[3] The Zurich contingent was used to help in the successful defence of Milan[4] against the French, who were forced to retire. The soldiers, however, soon found that the re-wards promised were not forthcoming, and trouble over this lasted a long while. In January 1522 all foreign mercenary service, including that with papal forces, was prohibited in Zurich.[5] The Turkish menace indeed re-mained a reality. Rhodes had fallen to the armies of Suleiman I just before Christmas 1522, and Pope Adrian VI renewed the too-familiar appeal for a crusade under his leadership. He would act as a mediator between Charles V and Francis I to unite the west in a combined effort against the advancing infidel. The authorities in Zurich were well aware that heretics could receive equally hostile treatment and that an alliance aimed at the Turks could be diverted against themselves.

[1] Z II, 313.
[2] Z II, 315: 'Man mûss mit der sach ylen, ee das der pfaff widrumb an der cantzel weere.'
[3] E. Wüthrich, *Die Vereinigung zwischen Franz I und 12 eidgen. Orten und deren Zugewandten vom Jahre 1521* (Zürich, 1911), 133-52.
[4] Bullinger, *Ref.* I, 53f. W. Gisi, 'Der Antheil der Eidgenossen an der europäischen Politik 1517-21' in *Archiv für schweizerische Geschichte* 17 (1871), 63-132.
[5] Egli *1*, 66-7 (No. 215). Private pensions were formally forbidden on 15 November 1522. Egli *1*, 103-5 (No. 293).

While on this theme Zwingli took the opportunity to interpolate an explanation of his acceptance and renunciation of a papal pension. 'For three years I earnestly preached the gospel of Christ, whereupon the papal cardinals, bishops and legates often tried to entice me away by promises of friendship, by prayers and threats, by inducements of great gifts and benefices, to none of which I yielded, save for a pension of 50 gulden which they paid me annually – they wanted to give me 100 gulden which I refused. In 1517 I renounced this but for three years they would not accept this as decisive until I gave written notice in 1520. I acknowledge my sin.'[1]

He now insisted quite explicitly that the attempt to merge spiritual with temporal authority was to produce a monster, a sea-serpent, *merwunder*.[2] Instead, all the clergy, including the Pope, should be subject to properly constituted civil authority. The Pope himself should accept this and as a sign renounce the name of vicar of Christ. The magistrates had every right to impose the death penalty for public offences against the public interest, for the removal of a diseased member might be necessary for the health of the whole. Private individuals had no right to kill, for individuals should forgive their enemies at all times; even collective killing for money in mercenary warfare was group manslaughter. Mistakes, of course, might be made, for magistrates were sinners like other men. Their justice, essential for the cohesion of society, was only a shadow of true justice, for they could judge of public actions only and therein they did their duty as God's officers.

For this – and Zwingli thinks of government in terms of the maintenance of law and order, the public peace, in the first instance – they were entitled to be paid, and the necessary money must be found by taxation. Christ had accepted the principle of lawful taxation, and exemptions from it were unreasonable and unnecessary. The wealth and flaunting extravagance of many ecclesiastics, from the Pope downwards, who paid little or nothing, were deplorable.

The one exception allowed to complete obedience to a duly appointed government was 'so far as they do not order what is contrary to God'.[3] From this principle Zwingli never wavered: if you were certain that a government order was contrary to God's word then disobedience was necessary, even if this carried the death penalty. In the days of the early church, many Christians suffered martyrdom, and the Christian faith benefited thereby. Similarly, it might be necessary to resist a papist prince

---

[1] Z I, 396; Z II, 314, 317; Z VII, 95–6. See above 26 and 76. Caspar Wirz, *Akten über die diplomatischen Beziehungen der römischen Curie zu der Schweiz 1512–1552*, QSG XVI (Basle, 1895), 135, 173.　　[2] Rev. 13. 1.
[3] Z II, 323. Acts 5. 30: 'We must obey God rather than men' was the constantly-repeated proof-text in this regard.

who tried to prevent the preaching of the Gospel: in such a case blood and life should be willingly offered. Where Nero, Domitian and Maximian had failed, a sixteenth-century prince was not likely to succeed. They would be called Lutherans, heretics, little boys (*büben*), revolutionaries,[1] but with God on their side they were sure to triumph in the end.

Such confidence was best left so expressed. However, if the government, the prince, was to be in complete sovereign and exclusive control of human beings and their actions, some guidance about resistance was necessary. Some twenty pages rather indicated that Zwingli was aware of the problem than provided any complete answer. He never produced a coherent political theory of his own, nor did he think it was within the province of a minister of religion to do so. He was, however, more politically-minded than Luther, and was prepared to face the problem of the 'ungodly prince', the tyrant who abused his authority, connived at manifest iniquity and failed to punish notorious evil-doers. Tyrannicide,[2] so much discussed in the previous century, he refused to consider. For the private individual the command 'Thou shalt not kill' was inescapable; those in authority alone had rights of life and death. To them obedience, service and financial support were due, and from them good administration in accordance with sound Christian principles was to be expected.

These expectations, however, were all too frequently disappointed. 'Tyrants', unfortunately, were 'as numerous as fleas in August', misgoverning, extorting, oppressing.[3] Their minds were all too often set on war, their extravagance was notorious, they encouraged monopolists, were surrounded by usurers, advised by flatterers and yes-men, treating their subjects all too often as worse than cattle.

How could such rulers be eliminated so that the people did not suffer for their misdeeds? Violence was ruled out:[4] murder, assassination, civil war and rebellion were acts of the ungodly: it was ultimately for God to act. However, if a ruler were elected by the people, he might be deposed by the common action of those who chose him;[5] similarly, if a select few had the right to nominate to high office, they should require their unrighteous nominee to resign. Again, it might be possible to treat a recalcitrant ruler

---

[1] Bundtschüher – the Bundschuh or laced boot or clog of the agricultural worker was used as a symbol of discontent and conspiracy. It became later the badge of the insurgent German peasants. N. Cohn, *The pursuit of the millennium* (London, 1962), 250–1.

[2] The murder of the Duke of Orleans in 1407 at the admitted instigation of the Duke of Burgundy led to long debates on this matter at the Council of Constance. The result, to which Gerson contributed a treatise, was the rather half-hearted condemnation of Jean Petit's *Justificatio Ducis Burgundiae*.   [3] Z II, 338–42.   [4] Z II, 333, 344.

[5] Possibly Zwingli was influenced by acquaintance with *Defensor Pacis*, the 'Editio Princeps' of which had appeared at Basle in 1522 with its striking attack on ecclesiastical authority and its provisions for the 'correction' of the legislator. C. W. Previté-Orton, *The Defensor Pacis of Marsilius of Padua* (Cambridge, 1928), 96–9.

as a child or an idiot, but basically Zwingli has no solution to offer. Universal opposition, a kind of general strike, would necessarily be effective, but was hardly likely to be attainable in practice. Particular rebellions there must not be. The tyrant might well have to be endured for his life time, the punishment for our sins, in the certainty that in his own time God would come into his own.[1] Above all, the sign of a government acceptable to God was that it allowed and encouraged the preaching of the Gospel, which could not be to its disadvantage.[2] Tyrants disliked God-fearing people, preferring to rule over the ignorant. Where, on the other hand, God's word was clearly preached, the righteous were encouraged and protected, good laws upheld by public opinion were effective, and the government was strong and efficient.[3] This, mercifully, was the case in Zurich, better administered than any other state of the Confederation. The best and strongest government was that which was in harmony with God. As with the Jews, prosperity followed upon keeping God's commandments, however continuously difficult and requiring constant vigilance and effort this might be. In the end, Christ's cause must triumph, however many guns the opponents might produce.[4]

From this persuasive and somewhat simple digression into politics in the wider sense, Zwingli turned to some general considerations upon the kind of public worship he envisaged in the light of his proposals. He had earlier set out his views on prayer.[5] Quiet, even solitude, might be helpful; the intoning of the psalms in Latin (which only one in a hundred understands) had nothing to recommend it, for their poetry needed to be read, and explained, carefully. Noise and gesture hinder thought and have no effect upon God. For all these reasons, supplemented by a renewed attack upon hired singers and paid prayers, the conclusion is repeated that silent inward prayer is most acceptable, that common prayer at home or in church, unpaid and spontaneous, is needful, and attendance at the sermon, the exposition of God's word, the highest duty of the pious Christian. In 1523, this was an aspiration for the future, but much of it was rapidly to be translated into practice. For the benefit of the Zurich councillors and for security later, Zwingli urged caution and reasonable circumspection. The community must not be rushed into change, the majority must not be offended, the weak must be helped to strength and the weaknesses accepted until they are better and more fully instructed, even about such matters as fasting and clerical marriage. Briefly, but more emphatically than previously, the extreme Petrine claims were again demolished, the familiar

---

[1] J. Kreutzer, *Zwinglis Lehre von der Obrigkeit* (Stuttgart, 1909), 81–9. H. Schmid, *Zwinglis Lehre von der göttlichen und menschlichen Gerechtigkeit* (Zürich, 1959), 234–6.

[2] Z II, 331, 342. [3] Z II, 330, see below 399 and n 4.

[4] Z II, 347. [5] See above, 113 and n 6.

texts of the rock and the keys, binding and loosing, were disposed of as having no narrow, limited application to an individual but referring to Christ's disciples and their lawful successors, all true believers. Thus sins were forgiven by God alone, the sinner who has repented and has shown signs of amendment receives an assurance from the priest of his state. This, and no more than this, lay within the priest's capacity, and to call such an opinion heretical was to call St Jerome, most revered of the Fathers, a heretic too. The keys, likewise, delivered not only to Peter but to all believers, referred to the duty to preach the plain words of the Gospel, disbelief in which carries damnation. All this confident, repetitive, but also somewhat superficial exegesis of some central New Testament themes was followed by a rejection of compulsory auricular confession further supported by a reasoned appeal to history. He was conscious that the element of compulsion had only 300 years behind it compared with the uncertain freedom of 1,200 years preceding the Fourth Lateran Council, but the time factor was less prominent than the current abuse of the confessional for money-raising purposes and even personal advantage. As for 'cases reserved', these, like much else, were invented out of greed and were repugnant to the spirit of freedom and to Christ's promises. At the same time, Zwingli refuses to discuss, as something unfathomable, the sin against the Holy Spirit[1] to which both previously and since so much speculation had been, and was to be, devoted. It is, of course, only obligatory auricular confession that was rejected. Those whose faith was uncertain could benefit by consultation with, or confession to, their spiritual leader. At least equally striking, and more explicit and unconditional, was the rejection of the teaching of the church on purgatory. In this instance, since some scriptural authority could be adduced on the other side, and the whole appeal of the public debate of 1523 was to the Bible, the matter had to be set out a little more fully. It was relatively easy, given the climate of thought of the age and the very general nature of the New Testament passages to which appeal was made,[2] to put forward a scriptural disavowal. There were indeed a few words of Judas Maccabaeus (2 Mac. 12. 38–46) upon which much had been built, but the interpretation would be suspect even if *Liber Machabaeorum* were in the canon of scripture, which it was not. It was of no more evidential value than the history of Josephus, the pretensions of

---

[1] Matthew 12. 31. The obviously unforgivable sin was disbelief, the denial of God – any further speculation was like blind men talking about colours. Z II, 409, 414–15.

[2] The texts were Matt. 5. 26: 'You will not be let out till you have paid the last farthing' ('das letzt Örtlin' in the text used by Zwingli, and in Vulg., 'non exies inde, donec reddas novissimum quadrantem') and I Cor. 3. 10–16, esp. 15–16: 'he will escape with his life, as one might from a fire' (in Vulg., 'ipse autem salvus erit, sic tamen quasi per ignem'). In this passage St Paul was in fact urging on his readers the simple Gospel as opposed to the elaboration of the philosophers. Zwingli insisted that the 'prison' referred to could not be shown to be used of a future state.

Hildebrand or the fables of the notorious John of Mandeville. The Christian revelation was simple: there was heaven and hell, nothing more.[1] For an intermediate stage there was neither evidence nor need; salvation through Christ was by God's grace and mercy; could man come to God through purgatory there was no need for the life and death of Jesus. What the judgement upon the departed may be is known to God alone; very little knowledge about the future state has been vouchsafed to us in the Bible, and for this very reason we ought not to seek for further enlightenment about matters to which the human intellect was not able to provide an answer. Zwingli, too, would have no speculation about the 'sleep of the soul', psychopannychism, which was so much to exercise the thought of some of his contemporaries.[2] In heaven there was no measurement of time, and sleep was for the body not the soul. It was a vigorous and useful assertion of the limits of scriptural authority.[3] It also had far-reaching implications – no purgatory, no indulgences. Masses offered, even prayers said, for the souls of the departed, paid for by relatives and others, were worthless, and the money involved could be put to better use.

The same insistence upon the need for positive scriptural evidence was applied to the claims of the priesthood. Current Catholic doctrine taught that ordination conferred upon the recipient a 'character', an 'indelible stigma', a special status derived from the episcopal laying on of hands, the token of an 'apostolic succession'. Round this ancient tradition a great body of deduction and practice had grown up. Zwingli gladly accepted the need for the physical contact by hand, for this was apostolic and acceptable. It was, however, no more than a sign or token of the gift of the Holy Spirit by God alone and not brought through apostle or bishop. Priesthood was an office, a function, not a status, honour or dignity. Anyone who truly and regularly carries out Christ's commands is God's agent, the shepherd or watcher over the salvation of souls, the honoured announcer of God's word. It is the doing this that makes a man a priest, elder, senior or presbyter – proclaiming the word of God, teaching, visiting the sick, helping and feeding the poor, studying, translating and expounding the Greek and Hebrew of the Bible. If this was not done, you were no longer an officer any more than the Bürgermeister who had ceased to carry out his duties was continued in office. True priests should indeed be given respect and maintenance; those who preach the Gospel should live by the

[1] Z II, 425.
[2] For the significance of this doctrine of a watchful awareness of the righteous soul between physical death and the resurrection of the body to which Calvin was attracted see Williams, xxvi, 580–98.
[3] The modern world finds it hard to realise that particular words in the *Song of Songs* 5. 2, 'Ego dormio et cor meum vigilat' – 'I sleep but my heart is awake' – were seriously taken into account in this controversy. Z II, 431.

Gospel, receiving lodging, meat and drink at the hands of the faithful. For this, and no more, there was adequate scriptural authority. As usual, however, Zwingli could not leave it at that, but must proceed to attack current abuses. The fact that there were prelates who deprived simple parsons of a moderate livelihood while growing fat on tithes and compulsory offerings[1] did not alter the general obligation upon the Christian community to support their own minister. After the outburst comes the note of caution: there was no call for expropriation of present office-holders; further abuses should be prevented and present occupants allowed to enjoy their privileges and revenues for their life time only. On the death of the holder, the endowments should be distributed 'in Christian charity' by the civil authorities, thus placating the demands of ordinary people for immediate action and securing the peace and quiet needed for the expansion of the word of God.[2]

One serious challenge had to be faced. Opponents of such reforms appealed to a General Council which should meet these insistent criticisms and ensure improvement by agreement. This raised the whole question of what sort of a council, by whom summoned and with what measure of acceptability for its decrees. A mere gathering of prelates, tinkering with and misconstruing God's word, was unacceptable: there had been a council at Basle[3] whose promised reforms had not been implemented. If indeed a council were to be fully representative of all Christians from the humblest upwards, unanimous in its decisions and not concerning itself with secular matters, it would indeed be acceptable. But for all essential matters God's word was clear enough, and tradition could not stand in its way. This brought up again the question of the mass. It was now assumed to be apparent from the Bible that the mass was not a sacrifice and therefore that all the elaborate superstructure built upon this mistaken notion, the property left by wills for its maintenance, should be swept away and church property be administered by the government for the benefit of the community. In this there must be no self help and no violence against the enemies of God's word. 'All who take the sword die by the sword'.[4] God does not need human weapons for the triumph of his word, and private individuals must await events, suffering persecution patiently if necessary without resorting to violence. The only qualification allowable was that God's enemies, unable to refute the truth but hindering God's teaching by conspiracy, rebellion and abuse, should be restrained and silenced by public authority, after they had been given an opportunity of stating their

---

[1] Among those enumerated are mass fees, confession fees, consecration fees, public collections, exequies, funeral services, anniversaries, commemorations and offerings. Z II, 443.
[2] Z II, 444–6. [3] 23 July 1431 to 16 May 1443.
[4] Z II, 308. Matthew 26. 52. Seven years later Luther was to repeat these very words on receiving news of Zwingli's death in battle.

case and had, in turn, been instructed in the scriptures. The axe is laid at the foot of the tree. The light is coming; lies, hypocrisy and the vain prophecies of astrologers[1] will give way before it.

As a kind of appendix to this splendidly confident appeal, in his last article (67), Zwingli offered to open further discussions explaining his position about usury, tithes, unbaptised children and the ceremony of confirmation. Very briefly he indicated that no disturbance of the status quo was contemplated, contracts already entered into must be kept and ministers could be assured that they would not be reduced to beggary. He had no doubt that children dying unbaptised, at any rate if born of Christian parents, could not be assumed to be damned and should be given Christian burial. Over and above all, he submitted his views to God's word, God-inspired scripture, of which man could not be the judge.

The *Schlussreden* of 1523 outlined every aspect of Zwingli's now firm convictions. Much was to be more fully developed later, most obviously his views on the eucharist and on infant baptism, but Zurich now had the aims and purpose of one who from that time could be called the 'reformer' clearly set forth for all the world to read. After the Zurich disputation and the publication of the 67 articles, there could hardly be any doubt about Zwinglian heterodoxy. The Pope and the mass, the pillars of the church of Rome, had been openly attacked and disavowed, and this, at any rate by implication, was upheld by the Zurich Council. It is indeed true that the assumption of the debate was that it was the hierarchy that had departed from the Bible and thus had fallen into error and that what was wrong could be amended.

The age would not have understood any such term as 'Swiss Reformation'. There was but one Christian faith as there was but one living and true God, whose nature and purpose were revealed for all time in the Bible. It was now possible to understand and interpret this aright, which was what was being done and what was of universal application. The Church of God was simply a federation of many communities of which Zurich was one which had perceived what was needed. The others had lamentably fallen into error which the light of the Gospel would disperse. There was no thought of comprehension or toleration yet, because there could be but one true and right view. It was not until many years after 1523 that any other line of thought became acceptable.

[1] Z II, 454; Sabbata, 136. Reliance upon astrology was widespread, then and later. There was a general belief that an unusual conjunction of planets in 1524 betokened heavy rain and perhaps a world flood. Collimitius (George Dannstetter) was able to calm local anxieties. ZWA I, 276–8.

6

From argument to action

Revolutions are notoriously difficult to date with acceptable accuracy. 14 July 1789, for France, or 6 November 1917, in Russia, are commemorated by public holidays but hardly mark more than particular events. So, too, with the religious revolt of the sixteenth century enthusiastically dated by German protestants from 31 October 1517, or, less enthusiastically, by Anglicans from 1534 – in every case the precise moment of change is alike disputable or meaningless.

This applies also to Zurich. In this case, no one now thinks of 1 January 1519, as anything more than a token date. Perhaps the most convenient event in the various Swiss communities to mark a decisive turning point in religious allegiance is the rejection of the Roman mass. After that had happened, their inhabitants, deprived of the mass, could not be regarded by Catholics as other than heretics. Zurich abandoned the mass on 13 April 1525, thus completing a cycle of events which was set in motion by the First Disputation of January 1523. Zwingli was never excommunicated by name, as Luther was, although from 1523 onwards Zwinglians were liable to be treated as Lutherans by their Catholic neighbours, who had no doubt that they were heretics to be burnt alive if circumstances permitted. Prior to 1524 at least, while the gap between Zurich and Rome was widening, it was not unbridgeable. Abstention from meat during Lent, and even marriage of the clergy, were debatable issues, like indulgences. Evangelical preaching could be made acceptable – the friars had always claimed to be offering just that – while the divine inspiration of the Bible was unchallenged. In 1523 and 1524 Zurich still accounted itself a Catholic city state in communion with Rome, while questioning prerogatives claimed by Pope and bishop, and criticising certain aspects of current thought and practice. A very small withdrawal, a little less public criticism from the pulpit, a renewed rejection of Luther's teaching, would have re-established normality. Zwingli had only to follow the lead of Erasmus, stop writing in German and haranguing illiterate artisans, and eliminate bitterness from his attacks on the hierarchy, to be left alone.

Instead of this, opposition was allowed to intensify. The papacy reluctantly realised that no more mercenary soldiers were to be hired from this important northern source of supply, and ceased to suggest accommodation. The central peasant states added religious antagonism to existing political and economic rivalry and hoped to use the federal bond for their own ends.

Apart from the relatively minor trouble over meat-eating in Lent, three even more controversial matters had been raised – clerical marriage, the retention of representations of saints in churches, and the status, indeed the continued existence, of the Regular orders. The outcome was the 'cleansing' of the churches, the elimination of the altars, the closing of the monasteries and finally the suppression of the mass. All this happened in 1523–5 with manifest general approval but also not without active and vocal opposition. In many places pictures and statues were spontaneously removed by zealous individuals, lights extinguished, glass windows smashed, 'superstitious objects' burnt. The secularisation of the monasteries was facilitated by their willing desertion by many of their members. All this, the Catholics believed, was the effect of an accessible vernacular Bible and the sermons in the Great Minster.

The exclusive appeal to the text of the Bible provided powerful ammunition for those who wanted to go much further, and in particular to those who were insisting upon examining the principle and practice of child baptism. To these, and to their use of Zwingli's identification of the church with the local community as a claim to set up separated groups with complete freedom of preaching and worship, attention must be given later. The only universal agreement was that the essentials of the Christian faith were impregnable. To attack the Incarnation, resurrection, ascension and the last judgement would be blasphemy, and all were agreed that this was intolerable. The notion of any public toleration for agnostics or atheists was entirely alien to the century.[1]

Immediately, however, if beliefs and practices based only on tradition were to be dropped, if sacerdotalism was to be replaced by congregationalism, if processions, lights, organs, choral services, vestments, masses for the dead, were to be replaced by something simpler, a great deal remained to be done. 1523 saw the first clearing of the trail and 1524 the certainty of a breach.

It was in this year (1523) that the Duke of Bourbon, Constable of France, deserted Francis I, that Frederick of Schleswig-Holstein displaced Christian II on the Danish throne (thus allowing Gustav Vasa to become King of Sweden), and that the Knights' War miserably fizzled out in Germany, leaving Ulrich von Hutten to be attacked by Erasmus but

[1] Cf. L. Febvre, *Le Problème de l'incroyance au XVIe siècle, la religion de Rabelais*, coll. L'évolution de l'Humanité (Paris, 1942).

given hospitality by Zwingli on the Lake of Zurich.[1] Throughout both 1523 and 1524 the European scene was dominated by the rivalry of Charles V and Francis I, symbolised by the renewed efforts of the latter to maintain his position in Milan and by the growing menace of the Turkish advance. These were the conditions which allowed Zurich to act with the confident independence which ultimately led to a third, presbyterian, force in the Christian world.

The public debate which ended in the late afternoon of 29 January 1523, had been held in order that the Zurich council should be fully informed about Bible teaching, so as to be able to exercise what had long been regarded as its rightful authority in matters appertaining to public worship within its jurisdiction. The immediate outcome was a ruling that Zwingli could and should continue his sermons and that others should preach only what could be supported by the Gospels and Holy Writ.[2]

Obligatory preaching from the biblical text obviously assumed that every preacher possessed or had access to a copy of the Bible and could read it.[3] If Erasmus' New Testament and Paraphrases were too erudite and expensive for some country parsons, the situation was remedied by a German translation of St Paul's Epistles and the Paraphrases by Leo Jud in 1521, although the whole Bible was not available in Swiss-German until 1529.[4]

[1] The remains of Ulrich von Hutten were buried in the church of Ufenau (Inseln Au) and were identified in 1965. He died on 29 August 1523 aged 35. Zwingli, writing to Boniface Wolfhart on 11 October 1523, said, 'he had no books and no furniture except his pen', although others speak of a 'few printed books'. The relations of Zwingli and von Hutten have been studied by H. G. Keller, *Hutten und Zwingli* (Aarau, 1952). They are hardly mentioned in the English account of him by H. Holborn, *Ulrich von Hutten* (Göttingen, 1968) which adds very little to the narrative by the same writer in 1929. Z VIII, 127.

[2] See above 104 n. Egli *1*, 115 (No. 327): 'Es söllent ouch all andere ire lütpriester...anders nüt fürnemen nach predigen, dann was si mit dem heiligen Evangelion und sust (mit) rechter göttlicher geschrift bewären mögen...' ZWA XIII, 567.

[3] See above, p. 107 n.

[4] Even so, the complete Zwinglian or Zurich Bible preceded the Lutheran. Luther's own translation of the New Testament was completed in February 1522 and was available in September from the press of Adam Petri at Basle. Between 1522 and 1524 at least twelve editions of the New Testament and a number of translations of various parts of the Old Testament appeared. In 1524 Froschauer twice printed Luther's New Testament ('*Das gantz | Nüw Testament recht | grüntlich vertüscht*'), and there was a third edition in 1525 with interesting linguistic variants. Various books of the Old Testament followed, and the Zurich translation of the whole Bible, mainly the result of the 'Prophezei' (below 221-4) was ready in 1529. A small octavo 'pocket' edition followed in 1530 from the Froschauer press and a fine folio illustrated edition in 1531 – *Biblia bey der Allt vnd Newen Testamëts Teutsch* (P. Schöfern, Worms). The whole Lutheran Bible first came from H. Lufft, Wittenberg, in 1534.

The various editions of the many vernacular Bibles have been diligently studied. J. J. Mezger, *Geschichte der deutschen Bibelübersetzungen in der schweizerisch-reformierten Kirche* (Basle, 1876). T. H. Darlow and H. F. Moule, *Historical catalogue of the printed editions of Holy Scripture in the library of the British and Foreign Bible Society* vol. II. *Polyglots and languages*

While the parsons from Zurich were considering how to obey their instructions and, without training, start to expound the pure Bible to rustic audiences, personal attacks, often to be repeated, were being made on Zwingli publicly in Diets at Baden, Berne and elsewhere.[1] He was said to have called his compatriots 'bloodsellers and cannibals',[2] he had condoned adultery and was the father of illegitimate children, he was the Antichrist of the Great Minster, a pensioner of a foreign power and a heretic whom the governors (*Landvögte*) of Baden and Frauenfeld had instructions to arrest if he entered their territory.[3] He had now become public enemy number one of the Christian faith, of the authority of the church, of the *status quo* in Switzerland and of the economic welfare of his country. At any rate he had achieved notoriety.

Violent language of this sort was a commonplace of the age. Even kings and magnates, the scholarly Henry VIII or the saintly Thomas More, said such things about intellectual or ideological opponents who were out of their reach, and to the personal charges Zwingli did not answer. But to the Diet of the Confederation meeting at Berne in July 1523 he wrote strongly defending his orthodoxy,[4] appealing to his public defence of the Virgin Mary. He admitted, indeed, that he had attacked the acceptance of pensions and corrupting gifts from foreign powers, but this was because of his care for the good name of his country. Their forefathers had lived simple, God-fearing lives and had flourished exceedingly because of it; the expensive magnificence which he now found conspicuously flaunted by private individuals he considered utterly demoralising. He appealed (in vain) to the Diet to scotch such rumours, to bring, if they could, some explicit charge against him 'before my lords of Zurich, since I am a citizen-canon, born in the Toggenburg,[5] native of Schwyz and Glarus'. There was to be no reconciliation of such varied opinions about him in his lifetime or for long after.

For the area within the jurisdiction of Zurich evangelical preaching was both secure and fashionable after 1523, although in the countryside, where few ministers had any adequate knowledge of the Bible, there were some

other than English (London, 1911). A. Fluri, *Luthers Uebersetzung des Neuen Testaments und ihre Nachdrucke in Basel und Zürich 1522–1531* (Schweizerische evangel. Schulblatt, 57, Berne, 1922). J. C. Gasser, *Vierhundert Jahre Zwingli-Bibel* (Zurich, 1924). W. Hadorn, *Die deutsche Bibel in der Schweiz* (Leipzig, 1925) 9–60. P. Leeman-van Elck, 'Die Offizin Froschauer', MAGZ. 30 (Zürich, 1940) 55–70. *Die Bibelsammlung im Grossmünster zu Zürich* (Zürich, 1945). *Cambridge History of the Bible*, II ed. S. L. Greenslade (Cambridge, 1963), 94–174.

[1] EA 4, 1a, 351, 377, 405; Egli *1* 254 (587), 264 (593).
[2] EA 4, 1a, 295, 378 'Die Eidgenossen verkaufen das christliche Blut und essen das christliche Fleisch...Blutverkäufer oder Blutfresser.'
[3] Z VII, 621, 643; Z VIII 108–9; Farner III, 321. See above p. 89–90.
[4] Z I, 570 (574)–579. '*Entschuldigung etlicher Zwingli unwahrlich zugelegter Artikel, an die Tagsatzung zu Bern*' (3 July 1523). Cf. VIII, 101–3.
[5] Z I, 578; Z VIII, 206–11 for Zwingli's attachment to Toggenburg.

manifestations of discontent. There were those who simply accepted the situation as it had always been and wanted no change, caring little for the Bible or its preachers. Others heard the biblical message with excitement. A necessary corollary to the *Schriftprinzip* was that simple people could, by divine grace and faith, understand the inner meaning of the scriptures, as well as the most learned of scholars. Faith, indeed, must come first and was indispensable. It did not come as a result of Bible reading but was strengthened and assured thereby.

Inevitably there were some who pushed this teaching to what they regarded as its logical conclusions. Confident in their faith, believing themselves to be among those able to expound the new biblical evangelism, they were anxious to force the pace. Attention soon began to be directly focused on the visible representations of the saints that filled the churches. This subject, which was in the background at the January disputation, was now actively advanced. In September 1523 Leo Jud was publicly calling for the removal of the 'idols'[1] and found almost embarrassing support. In the Fraumünster,[2] in St Peter's,[3] at Höngg and elsewhere,[4] there were demonstrations and damage. The leading case, however, was that of the crucifix of Stadelhofen. There, just outside the city walls, and on private property, the local miller had erected at his own expense a great wooden crucifix which was much revered by the local inhabitants. It was also an obvious target for two evangelical extremists, Klaus Hottinger and Hans Ockenfuss, who incited[5] some enthusiasts to pull it down by violence. The owner naturally sought legal protection and a remedy against the trespassers. He was on all the stronger ground in that, whatever objection there might be to the reverence paid to portrayals of dubious or locally admired minor 'saints', the representation of Christ was obviously in a special category. It is scarcely surprising that the Small Council, Zurich's standing executive, showed little sympathy for the attackers, who were placed under restraint in the Wellenberg gaol. This caused immense excitement, and the matter was referred on 29 September 1523 to a commission consisting of the Bürgermeister, eight leading councillors and the three *Leutpriester*, Zwingli, Jud and Engelhard, whose views had already been clearly ex-

---

[1] Egli *1*, 160–1 (no. 416).

[2] Here the leaders were Lorenz Hochrütiner and Wolfgang Ininger who smashed lamps burning before shrines and splashed the floor with holy water in mockery. They were arrested, and released on bail; but Hochrütiner, from St Gall but also a Bürger of Zurich, was later imprisoned. Egli *1*, 159 (no. 415); Goeters, *Vorgeschichte*, 261; Sabbata, 96; ZWA XI, 225.

[3] Lorenz Meyer was prominently concerned here. Egli *1*, 158–61 (nos. 414, 415, 416); Sabbata, 95.

[4] Thomas Platter burnt a wooden image of St John while church bells were ringing. *Lebensbeschreibung*, hg. A. Hartmann (Basle, 1944), 61–2.

[5] Mörikofer I, 192; Z II, 665.

pressed.[1] Their suggestion, which was adopted on 15 October, was that the accused should be released on bail until the whole matter had been officially dealt with after another public debate.[2]

This was not to be confined to the one topic of images, but was also to be extended to consider the doctrine of the mass. It was not intended that this should be an exclusively local affair; it was to be a general Swiss gathering from all the states and their allies. As on the earlier occasion, the Bishops of Constance, Chur and Basle, and the University of Basle, were invited directly, together with all ecclesiastics and officials on Zurich territory.[3] The decisions, of course, were to be based on 'the divine scriptures of the Old and New Testament'.[4]

The bishops emphatically repeated their refusal of the previous January to send representatives,[5] as did once again the University of Basle and all the states of the Confederation except Schaffhausen.[6] Even so, up to 900 men, 350 of them in holy orders, crammed themselves into the hall on 26–28 October.[7] From the city of St Gall came Zwingli's friend and correspondent, Vadian; Christopher Schappeler (Sertorius) came from Memmingen and Johannes Zwick from Riedlingen.

The second Zurich disputation was almost an *ad hoc*, exploratory affair rather than one intended, like the first, to give direct advice to the council. Zwingli dominated the proceedings even more than at the beginning of the year, and everything went as planned, although the almost complete lack of serious opposition left him at less than his best. Except for Conrad Hof-

[1] Egli *1*, 167 (no. 424); Z VIII, 124.
[2] After the disputation, Hottinger was banished from Zurich for two years (Egli *1*, 178 No. 442) and, in fact, never returned, being apprehended as a heretic near Baden and put to death at Lucerne on 26 March 1524, thereby becoming 'the first evangelical martyr in Switzerland' (Egli *3*, 256; EA 4, 1a, 384). Ockenfuss paid a fine and gave trouble later. Hochrütiner, a third principal, was ignominiously expelled, and returned to St Gall. Zwingli regarded his punishment as unnecessarily harsh. Z VIII, 130; Goeters, *Vorgeschichte*, 272.
[3] Z II, 666, 678.
[4] 'uss der göttlichen geschrift des alten und nüwen testaments' Egli *1*, 171 (No. 430).
[5] The Bishop of Constance was reported to have sent a spy to report on the proceedings. Z II, 736 and note 10.
[6] Its delegate was Sebastian Hofmeister (1476–1533), a Franciscan, D.D. of the University of Paris, who had come to Zurich in 1520, was convinced by Zwingli's doctrine which he tried to teach in Constance and Lucerne, whence he was expelled, and returned to evangelise Schaffhausen. J. Wipf, *Sebastian Hofmeister, der Reformator Schaffhausens*, Beiträge zur vaterländischen Geschichte, Heft 9 (Schaffhausen, 1918) 1–62. St Gall accepted: Berne and Solothurn sent friendly apologies.
[7] They were packed so close that they had to stand for prayer, there not being room to kneel. Farner III, 435. The proceedings were honestly reported by Ludwig Hätzer and Georg Binder as *Acta oder geschicht, wie es uff dem gespräch den 26. 27. u. 28. winmonats in der christenlichen statt Zürich ergangen ist.* Z II, 664 (671)–803. Bullinger later wrote a more selective account. *Ref.* I, 129–34. R. C. Walton, *Zwingli's Theocracy* (Toronto, 1967) 185–6; Bergsten, *Hubmaier* 116–17. ZSK 48 (1954), 184–5; Ch. Garside, *Zwingli and the Arts* (New Haven 1966) 129–45.

mann,[1] who had himself complained of the excesses of the hierarchy and opposed mercenary service, the defenders of tradition were conspicuously and deliberately absent. There was, however, a vocal 'left wing', led by Grebel, Hubmaier and Stumpf, who wanted action to come much faster and more spontaneously.[2]

On the first main topic, images, there was singularly little informed discussion. Their only serious protagonist was Heinrich Lüti from Winterthur, whose arguments from tradition and the Bible[3] were readily answered by Jud and Commander Schmid.[4] The latter took the opportunity to attack the contention that all papal ordinances were irrefrangible.[5] The assembly was readily persuaded that images were specifically condemned in the Old Testament, and should be removed forthwith. However welcome this was to the radicals, especially Grebel and Hubmaier, Zwingli, with his chief supporters, was prepared only for a gradual phasing out of traditional but undesirable practices. There was general agreement that their bishop had failed to act as leader and shepherd and that the duty of guiding and educating the people devolved upon the government.

The discussions about the mass turned mainly upon the meaning of sacrifice, Martin Steinlin of Schaffhausen[6] alone coming forward in its defence on the basis both of the Bible and of long tradition. His opponents insisted that at the mass, forgiveness, grace and mercy were requested and received by the faithful; there was no repetition of Christ's sacrifice. The corollary was that masses could not be said effectively for the souls of the faithful departed, thus rejecting the accepted teaching about purgatory. Scripture supported the claim that the communion should be in both kinds, bread and wine, for laity and clergy alike. There was also some inconclusive discussion of the use of unleavened bread in the eucharist, the mixing of water with the wine, placing the wafer in the recipient's mouth, and celebrating mass on mornings only.[7] The mode of reception Zwingli was willing enough to leave to the individual parishes, but he was opposed to the wearing of vestments and called for a vernacular rather than a Latin

---

[1] He left Zurich in 1524, was replaced by Ceporinus and died at Bremgarten in 1525. Z VIII, 168 n. 1. T. Pestalozzi, *Die Gegner Zwinglis am Grossmünsterstift in Zürich* (Zürich, 1918) 37–60.

[2] Z II, 687, 741–7. See below 177–185.

[3] Z II, 693–9.

[4] Konrad Schmid (c. 1476–1531), M.A. of Basle, priest at Seengen (Aargau), was Komtur (Commander) of the house of the order of St John of Jerusalem at Küsnacht near Zurich. He had been won to the evangelical cause by Zwingli in 1520 and remained his consistent supporter, preaching at Lucerne and Einsiedeln, presiding at the Berne disputation in 1528, and was killed at Kappel, 1531. S. Vögelin, 'Konrad Schmid Comtur zu Küsnacht', ZT 1862, 175–208; C. Dändliker, 'Comthur Schmid von Küsnacht, ein Lebensbild aus der Reformationszeit, ZT 1897, 1–41.

[5] Z II, 697: 'Alles, das der bapst ordnet, macht und insetzt, das ist recht und mag nit fälen.'

[6] Z II, 684.   [7] Z II, 789–92.

service. Hubmaier, who was one of the ten doctors present and sat close to Zwingli (who referred to him as his 'dear brother'), also, along with Jud, wanted a German eucharist service and communion in both kinds.[1]

The second disputation, like the first, was a triumph for Zwingli before a large audience. It was, however, more a demonstration than an exchange of views, a propaganda exercise rather than a debate, and in any case without any effective authority. The outcome was, immediately, disappointing to those who had hoped for some conclusions to be enforced forthwith. Mass continued to be said in Latin and communion remained in one kind, and, while it was agreed that private individuals might remove particular images quietly, and congregations could do likewise, in fact most of them remained in their places. A commission of fourteen[2] was appointed to study the conclusions and their possible implications. Zwingli had in fact further used the opportunity to expound his views on the nature of the evangelical duties of a minister of religion.[3] Citizens and clergy now knew what freedom of evangelical preaching implied. In order to help the preachers, Zwingli again set out his own ideas in writing in a *Short Christian Introduction* which he had printed in November 1523, primarily for distribution among the ministers who had been required by the government to preach the Gospel.[4] By the light of the Gospel and inspired by love, men could recognise sin; and by grace and through faith in Christ, they could avoid its consequences. The law showed the way to righteousness, but its mere observance did not make a man either good or righteous. Deeds, actions, works, were themselves of no avail, but they were indications of a state of acceptability: it was utterly wrong to teach that, because our works do not save us, but the grace of God alone does so, it followed that we might sin with impunity. The emphasis was on salvation by faith, and everything in the *Christian Introduction* was still reconcilable with the looser definitions of the pre-Tridentine Church on this matter.

The necessary validity of the demands of the Mosaic Law and the Prophets came to an end when John the Baptist opened a new era: the ceremonial, the sacrifices, the Temple-observances of the Old Testament, all types foreshadowing Christ, now gave way to the law of love. Freed

---

[1] Bergsten, 113; Bullinger, *Ref.* I, 130–2.
[2] Including Schmid, Joner, Brennwald, Jud, Engelhart and Zwingli. Z II, 667.
[3] See below, 135–6.
[4] *Eine kurze christliche Einleitung* Z II, 626 (628)–663. The enumeration is interesting – 'prelates, abbots, deans, stipendiary priests, rectors, clerics and exponents of God's word' – 'Prelaten, äpten, dechant, lütpriestern, seelsorgeren, pfarrern und des götlichen wortes verkündern in unsern stetten'. Z II, 628.
     The treatise was accompanied by an order (Mandat) from the Zurich Council for distribution, and thus had official approval.

from the obligations of the ceremonial law, assured through Christ alone of freedom from the punishment and intolerable burden of our sins, we must show this freedom by humility, patience, peace, care for the salvation of others, and self-effacement.

There were some who talked of killing priests, drowning nuns, burning monks, in their zeal for righteousness without humility. Self-willed, egotistical, quarrelsome, opposed to all men, they cared only for themselves, aspiring to riches and power, bringing disunion with them.[1] This was an early allusion to the small number of revolutionary recalcitrants who were soon to be brought together as 'Anabaptists', and was a sign of future anxieties.

On the immediate practical level the fact that the canon law of the church of Rome was no longer acceptable was not to be taken to imply that tithe, rent-charges, rent or interest need not be paid: on the contrary, civil contracts must be properly honoured. What the government declared to be a debt or obligation must be accepted, obedience being the first duty of a citizen. It was for the government to decide about the disposition of superfluous property of the covetous and exhibitionist clergy, where practicable, for the benefit of the poor. Again and again the *Christian Introduction* insisted on the duty of the government to make decisions, and on the subjects to obey. Images should be removed without disorder, after quiet instruction about their worthlessness. Even after a repetition of the denunciation of the treatment of the mass as a sacrifice, of the denial of the cup to the laity and of the abuse of the ceremony as a means for making money, the writer accepted, until the government decided otherwise, that the mass priests must be allowed to go about their work undisturbed. Zwingli did not advocate either quietism or passive obedience, but Zurich was now on its way to becoming a model Christian polity, and for this he was well prepared to wait and work.[2] He also accepted that there should be initially a kind of standstill on the image issue – reliquaries were not to be placed on the altars, statues and pictures were to be covered over where practicable until further order was given, but they were not to be forcibly removed by private individuals. The Latin mass continued to be said, so that where the chantry priests continued to fulfil their contracts no impediment was to be placed in their way until some regulation was issued by the council. It was in fact fairly obvious that this must soon come and what form it would be likely to take; many priests simply abstained from their former duties with impunity. Such negation was not good enough, and Zwingli, along with

[1] Z II, 650–2.
[2] A good deal of rather unnecessary discussion has been devoted to the precise moment when a decisive break was made. E.g. H. J. Hillerbrand, *Zwingli's Reformation turning-point*, Bibliothèque d'humanisme et Renaissance 31 (1969), 39–46; MQR 32 (1958) 108, 128–40; 45 (1968) 45–56.

Wolfgang Joner[1] and Commander Schmid, toured the parishes of the city and its immediate neighbourhood[2] to offer explanations and advice. In particular, there was a general demand that Zwingli's own statement or sermon made at the opening of the second public debate should be available for all, and, with the conventional reluctance of the busy scholar who would prefer further study to writing articles, the sermon was put into print as *The Shepherd*.[3] This was an ingenious combination of advice and exhortation, defence and attack. By setting out what the true pastor, the ideal shepherd, the efficient bishop, should do, and contrasting this with the actions of the false hirelings, a great deal could be said.

The little tract was dedicated, at Vadian's suggestion, to Jacob Schurtanner ('Ceraunelateus'), by whose ministrations from Teufen, Appenzell,[4] the smallest and newest of the cantons, 'in faith last but not least', was receiving the Gospel, evidence of the rapid progress of the new ideas eastwards. Following the Bible, the only sure guide, the ideal minister will renounce self completely so as to be entirely and merely God's agent. He should set an example to his people in his own life, in the sobriety of his dress, in his upbringing of his own children. Covetousness, greed and hypocrisy were to be avoided, hypocrisy being the special characteristic of the followers of the Pope.[5]

Most of all, he must teach and preach, for preaching is the sign of the true pastor, and for this he needed knowledge in order, with God's guidance, to understand the Scriptures. Obedient to good government, he must also preach qualified resistance to those who impeded the progress of God's word or who overburden their subjects with taxes. There was a wealth of Old Testament encouragement for the prophet to speak in no uncertain terms to the ungodly ruler. The times were hard, inflation all too prevalent, the world was wicked.[6] Yet faith and love must assuredly prevail

---

[1] Joner (Rüppli), abbot of the Cistercian monastery of Kappel, was an early supporter of the Zwinglian reform. When the abbey was taken over by Zurich, he became headmaster of the school there, with the former prior, Peter Simmler, as his assistant. He died at Kappel on 11 October 1531.

[2] Mörikofer I, 199; Staehelin I, 348; Farner III, 453. Joner went to the Albis area, Schmid to the Grüningen district (the lake communities), Zwingli to Schaffhausen and the north.

[3] *Der Hirt* Z III, 1 (5)–68 (March 1524).

[4] Egli 3, 358–9; Z VIII, 131.

[5] Z III, 23. 'Here I do call papistes al the sorte of thē that are called spirituall, or the clergye, thē beyng excepted, which preache purely and sincerely the word of God.' This is from the translation into English published as *The ymage of bothe Pastoures, sethe forth by that mooste famouse clerck, Huldrych Zuinglius, and now trāslated out of Latin into Englische by John Wernon Sinonoys...Cum privilegio 1550.* STC 26142, 26143. Copy in Zurich Zentralbibliothek ZW, 25 c.

[6] Z III, 29. 'Die gantz welt ligt in bossheit, und er soll sy aber nit beschelten.' 'Behold, ȳ whole world doth lye buried in the stinking puddel of synne, & is all togeather drowned in vyces' (in the English transation). At the same time, Zwingli proclaimed that the word of God was spread abroad now as never before.

with divine help in the end. The preacher should go as far as example and persuasion could, but no further: men were not to be compelled to believe.[1]

From the true shepherd, Zwingli turned, with perhaps some gusto, and at much greater length, to the false variety, most obviously characterised by pride, pomp, extravagance of dress and manifestations of wealth. He first welcomed the way in which the monasteries were being deserted by monks and nuns as manifest evidence of the success of Gospel-preaching.[2] Then, from monasteries, he turned again to his definition of the church, the congregation, known to God alone, of all who truly believe in Christ and secondarily the local community of worshippers. The church of Rome ('if they believe in Christ there') was but one church among many, like the church of Appenzell or that of the Corinthians.[3] Hence it followed that Rome could not impose conditions on other communities of equal stature with itself. It was a bold claim but one scarcely relevant to an account of the duties of a minister of religion, and one which was not to be maintained in his own state. Zurich, in many cases, was not prepared to allow any such independence to the *Gemeinden* under its own jurisdiction. Then quite abruptly the theme moves back to the individual pastor. By his sermons rather than by his works he should be judged; mere public prayer, psalm-singing, 'pypinge, lulling, belowinge and roaring', masses paid for by endowments, indulgences[4] given for money, manifest falsehoods in his sermons, were signs of the worthless incumbent.

Wherever necessary the minister should marry, yet avoid the temptation to enrich himself or his family, being ready to suffer, never causing trouble or warfare. After a fling at the Pope, who has been erected into a kind of God,[5] Zwingli ends on a note of warning against any attempt to eliminate unworthy preachers by individual action. If their doctrine was wrong, it should not be heard; and if the whole congregation (*Kilchhöre*) was unanimous in its condemnation, then the pastor should leave, but action must be taken by proper public authority, and until this came people must wait patiently for God to intervene. The last advice to the hireling priests was that they spare those poor oppressed people who were hungry for God's

---

[1] Z III, 38. 'Christus nit wil, mit gwalt ieman zů dem glouben bezwungen werden.' They could, however, be prevented from listening to false doctrine. This, like other aspects of Zwingli's thought and practice, was to be developed more fully under pressure of later events.

[2] At the same time, Zwingli asserted that without monasteries evangelical preaching made easier and more rapid headway. Z III, 46. 'Wo in einem volck wenig klöstren sind, da wirt dem wort Christi wenig widerfochten.' He appears to have overlooked the fact that in the neighbouring state of Zug, as in Uri, there were very few monastic establishments yet the allegiance of its people to Rome was unshakable.

[3] Z III, 48. The English version reads, 'after the same maner, we cal the churche of London, the same congregatyon, that is in London.'

[4] Z III, 52: 'das der ablas nüt anderst denn ein erloubnus aller lastren xin ist', a categorical and (if unqualified) unfair definition.

[5] Z III, 62: 'Aber die Bäpstler habend iren abgott, den bapst, ein irdischen gott genennet.'

word. Thus, ceasing to rely upon temporal princes, they might yet repent in time.

It was not, for all its good advice, an eirenicon, and some of its recommendations were in fact already embodied in a document sent by the Town Clerk of Zurich to the Swiss Diet assembled at Lucerne in the first week of April, 1524.[1] This gathering, whose members were by no means well disposed to clerical pretensions, received what the council of Zurich had applied for in vain, a deputation from the Bishops of Constance, Basle and Lausanne, within whose jurisdiction the whole of the then Confederation was. They complained of the steady and increasing alienation of growing numbers from the teachings of the Church, and asked for support from the secular arm, particularly over action to be taken against recalcitrant priests. That no effective answer was given or action taken may have been in part due to the stinging note received from Zurich[2] and in fact written by Zwingli. This time he did not conceal his hostility.

What had been set forth in Zurich was no innovation but a return to the teaching of Christ and the Apostles from which they would not be divorced and which they hoped the Confederates would allow to be proclaimed freely. The insolence and arrogant pretensions of the prelates were intolerable; they disliked the obedience which the Gospel bade them give to the civil governments;[3] they have gathered riches and power at the expense of the poor, speaking as if they constituted the church of Christ, sometimes talking of a General Council, but too busy with war to allow its summons; they sell for money spiritual services which should be given freely; they have made profitable their invention of purgatory and their witholding the chalice from the laity; they have forbidden priests to marry in order to benefit by the concubine-tax. The Bishop of Constance had declined invitations to appear at Zurich, departing, with his fellows, from his duty to uphold the word of God and entrusting the statement of their case to such defenders as Eck, Fabri, Cochlaeus, Caspar Schatzgeyer and King Henry VIII of England.[4] Instead of acting as shepherds, they have become ravening wolves, dividing the Confederation, continuing to deceive the Swiss people as they had so notoriously done in 1499.[5] If, in addition to allowing the Gospel to be preached freely, the Confederates should also follow the example of Zurich in forbidding mercenary service, so much the better. There was no mistaking the earnestness of the appeal, but, so

---

[1] EA 4, 1a, 398–406; Z III, 69 (76)–85.
[2] The fact that it was printed and sold was later made a cause of offence. Egli *3*, 262.
[3] 'Die weltlichen wol regierenden obergheit.' Z III, 76.
[4] Z III, 81–3.
[5] During the Swabian War, the Swiss victory at Schwaderloo (11 April 1499) had been followed up by a victorious advance which had been checked by opposition from the castle of Gottlieben of which the Bishop of Constance was overlord.

far as any action was concerned, it fell on deaf ears. Zurich must continue the struggle alone.

There, early in 1524, a number of incidents indicated the way things were going. Candlemas (2 February) was not celebrated with a choral service and solemn consecration of lamps and candles,[1] processions of robed clergy with lights and crucifix round the outside of the churches ceased, worshippers did not go with palms and relics on Palm Sunday to the Lindenhof,[2] there was no creeping to the cross on Good Friday, the altar-pictures (triptychs for the most part) covered or closed in Lent remained so.[3] These were indications of the direction in which public thinking was more and more moving, and these opinions spread rapidly. One outcome of the religious position taken up by Zurich in 1523 was to leave an enduring impress on the whole country. The group of Inner States – Uri, Schwyz, Unterwalden, Lucerne and Zug – agreed to arrange for common action after consultation in a local assembly or Diet, the first of which met at Beckenried on 8 April 1524.[4] This was but one of many examples of local cooperation for particular purposes. Out of this meeting, however, grew the regular Catholic conventions or Diets which became influential in the administration of central Switzerland. After 1524 the Five States (*die fünf Orte*) formed a permanent group within the Confederation.

Immediately it was resolved to ascertain which other states would support them in their resolve to 'suppress, punish, pursue and root out to the utmost of their power the pernicious, erroneous, Lutheran, Zwinglian and Hussite doctrine'.[5] They were assured that all the Confederates except Zurich and Schaffhausen were willing to insist upon fasting during Lent, celibacy of the clergy, and the exclusion of 'Lutheran' teaching and practices. Attention, however, was diverted from religion to foreign affairs. A French army, under Bonnivet, weakened by the desertion of the Duke of Bourbon, had entered north Italy in the summer of 1523, and every state of the Confederation except Zurich had supplied Francis I with soldiers.[6] None the less the French siege of Milan had been a failure, the general was incompetent, the Venetian alliance was not renewed, the renowned Chevalier Bayard was killed, and the whole expedition an inglorious defeat. Although not many Swiss lives had been lost, it had been a highly unsatisfactory business, retreating in the snow with very little plunder to be obtained from poor and hostile Italian peasants, while even the pay promised by France was not forthcoming.

[1] Z III, 92.   [2] Egli 3, 264.   [3] Mörikofer I, 200.   [4] See below, 209 n. 6.
[5] EA 4, 1a, 410–11; Egli 3, 257, 262; W. Oechsli, *Die Anfänge des Glaubenskonflikts zwischen Zürich und den Eidgenossen 1521–1524* (Winterthur, 1883), 15.
[6] Some 6,000 men in all, in accordance with the Paix perpétuelle of Fribourg, 29 Nov. 1516 (EA 3, ii, 1406–15) and the alliance (*Vereinigung*) of 5 May 1521 (EA 4, 1a, 1491–1500).

This growing discontent seemed a suitable opportunity for another Zwinglian attack on the whole policy involved. In May 1524 there appeared an anonymous pamphlet[1] by an 'absent patriot', the authorship of which was at once and rightly attributed to the Zurich preacher. Once again he put forward the familiar argument that the acceptance of foreign money for military service had brought corruption, division and greed in return for loss of lives. Their forefathers had lived in freedom and security and had proudly refused to have foreign masters, but now their successors were selling obedience for lucre. Some lost their lives, leaving their relatives destitute; some lost the land which they had mortgaged to equip themselves for battle; while those who prospered returned to flaunt their wealth and ape the nobles, demoralised themselves and demoralising others, contributing, it was believed, to the price-rise which was being felt everywhere. Farms had been deserted and productive land left uncultivated, in the shameless endeavour to get rich by bloodshed. How much better if they gained a livelihood as their forefathers had done, from the produce of the land. Work was a most valuable discipline, good, even divine,[2] and they should not neglect it. As to complaints about the new teaching,[3] *die nüwen leer,* being erroneous and unable to survive, the opposite is true. They should ignore those who say 'that is heretical, Lutheran', but they should seek the honour of God and the good of their neighbours, abandon greed and selfishness, and allow the word of God to be preached freely. It was an eloquent appeal to Swiss patriotism but it met with little response.

Meanwhile, in and around the city of Zurich, men were demanding to know when some final official action was to be taken about the images so plainly denounced by their spiritual guide and leader. This was the more urgent because, in fact, an episcopal defence of the images (on the conventional lines that no reverence was paid to the objects but that these were there in order to help to lift men's thoughts to the eternal and invisible values which they illustrated) was on its way from Constance.[4] As late as May 1524, in a seven-point mandate issued by the council forbidding dancing except at public weddings, noise at night, street singing, indiscriminate shooting by youths, excessive drinking, fanciful clothes, there was, mixed in with this thoroughly medieval paternalism, a stern injunction to 'men and women, young and old, seculars and clergy', to do nothing about images until the council gave its orders.[5]

---

[1] *Eine treue und ernstliche Vermahnung an die Eidgenossen,* Z III, 97 (103)–113.

[2] Z III, 106. 'Und ist doch die arbeyt so ein gůt, götlich ding'. Cf. R. H. Tawney, *Religion and the Rise of Capitalism* (London, 1926) (Pelican Books reprint, 1938, 217) 'Labour...is a spiritual end, for in it alone can the soul find health, and it must be continued as an ethical duty long after it has ceased to be a material necessity.'

[3] Z III, 110; EA 4, 1a, 225. The reformers consistently maintained that not they, but their opponents, were innovators.   [4] Staehelin I, 376.   [5] Egli *I*, 230–1 (No. 530).

Consideration needed also to be given to the form, purport' and meaning of the mass, but this much larger issue was very properly kept separate. By the end of May 1524, Zwingli had reiterated with growing distinctness his demands. Charitably and without bitterness the images should be removed from the church buildings. Where they were known to be the property of the fabricator or donor, these should be given eight days notice to remove them, after which the images should be put outside by the verger or sacrist. Where the owners were the whole community or congregation, this should decide, by a majority if necessary,[1] whether the images should remain or be removed. If they were allowed to remain, no candles or incense should be burnt before them or reverence shown, and no new ones should be made. The crucifix, as signifying the humanity of Christ, was acceptable,[2] and in any case personal interference with it should be punished.

This was moderate and practicable enough, and on 15 June[3] 1524 the council ordered, with exactly Zwingli's conditions and exceptions, the images to be removed forthwith:[4] any endowments attached to their maintenance were to be used for the benefit of the poor, who were themselves in God's image.[5] It was apparent that this was another challenge to the Bishop of Constance, who, after long delays, had stated his case,[6] insisting upon his determination to avoid if in any way possible, a breach with 'das vorderste Ort' of the Confederation, whose great Collegiate Church was second only to the Bishop's own Cathedral within his large diocese. 'We cannot sufficiently marvel', the City Fathers wrote to the Pope, 'that your holiness suspects us of belonging to the Lutheran sect whereas in fact we have suffered nothing to be preached save the pure word of God and nothing that cannot be defended from the Old and New Testament. Where we can be shown to be wrong we will most gladly abandon it.'[7]

---

[1] 'an gmeynen kilchgnossen oder dem merteil ston'. Z III, 116.

[2] 'An invisible God cannot be depicted.' Z III, 226. Mörikofer I, 230. Zwingli rather reluctantly parted with the crucifix from his own room. He claimed that personally he found works of art, fine pictures and carving exceptionally agreeable: he was of course opposed to any superstitious or even formal reverence paid to them.

[3] Staehelin I, 376–7; Egli *1*, 234–7 (nos. 543, 546); Bullinger, *Ref.* I, 173–4. By chance this was the feast of St Vitus, himself the recipient of many hoary legends (St Vitus' dance) and frequently depicted. It also saw the appearance of a comet. Wyss, 39–40.

[4] The city of Zurich and the countryside were, as usual, treated separately. Removal was to be by authority and in orderly fashion.

[5] Egli *1*, 237 (No. 546) – the order is well set out and of interest. It is translated in C. Garside, *Zwingli and the Arts* (New Haven, 1966).

[6] 'Christenliche vnnderrichtung des Hochwirdigen Fürsten vnd Herren, Herren Hugo, Bischoffen zů Costantz, die Bildtnüssen vnd das opffer der Messz betreffend, Burgermeister vnd Rhat zu Zurch vff den ersten tag Junij diss vierundtzweintzigsten jars vbersendt.' This answer, presumably written by Fabri, in fifty pages of manuscript, was not received in Zurich until the beginning of June 1524; it was examined carefully by an ecclesiastical commission (9 ministers and 8 councillors) and then read to the council. Farner III, 483; Egli *3*, 271.

[7] Egli *1*, 247 (No. 570).

The parallel between idols, images and other representations was then set out at length; tradition, Fathers, the Third Council of Constantinople (680), were easily put out of consideration – a gathering that does not follow the Bible is not a church of Christ, Christ did not order images as aids to devotion, the argument from antiquity is 'foolish', Popes and councils have differed from one another, the miracles supposed to have been worked by images are irrelevant, teaching should be by words, not by pictures, for only the word can penetrate the heart. The council had removed the images because they had impeded access to God and because they had been abused. The money that had been attracted to them would in future help the poor.[1] It was the now familiar story.

Direct action had started at Zollikon[2] on Whit Sunday, 15 May 1524, when a gang pulled down the high altar and broke up the images in the church. The church committee of fourteen Zurich councillors and advisers met on the following day[3] to consider Zwingli's recommendations. Finally on 15 June the council ordered[4] that in every commune which, after proper instruction, wished, by a majority, the images to be removed, this should be done forthwith, exception being made of the crucifix. If the commune wished to retain its images, these were not to be honoured and candles were not to be burnt before them.

In the city of Zurich itself, official action followed, and for two weeks individuals were taking their own images to their private houses, after which, carpenters, smiths, stonemasons and locksmiths descended in orderly gangs on the churches and forcibly removed the pictures and statues.[5] Some of these were known to be valuable, particularly those from the comparatively new Wasserkirche, and there was real concern at their loss; but, in general, there was thorough satisfaction. There were some fine bonfires[6] of the carved wooden representations, and the stone ones were broken up. The bones found in the reliquaries were buried in the churchyards.[7] When the workmen had finished, white clean walls looked

---

[1] H. v. Campenhausen, *Die Bilderfrage in der Reformation*, ZKG 68 (1957) 98–128.
[2] Mörikofer I, 227; Z III, 114–15. Zollikon was an entirely separate village – it was not until the nineteenth century that it began to be included in the Zurich conurbation.
[3] 16 May, Whit Monday, when, until this year, there had been a general pilgrimage to Einsiedeln which was now intermitted. Wyss 52 n. 1.
[4] Egli *I*, 236, 237 (Nos. 544, 546).
[5] The deaths on 13 and 15 June of Felix Schmid and Marx Röist, who had been opposed to removal of the images, made the transition easier. There was no violence, no looting and no public disturbance – it was a kind of public slum clearance operation from 20 June to 2 July.
[6] Possibly also of some small organs. It would be interesting to know which of the seven churches (apart from the Great Minster) had an organ and what became of it.
[7] This took place towards the end of June 1524. The suggestion by P. S. Allen (Allen v, 547 n.) that the date 'des 20 Juny' (20 June) given by Bullinger (*Ref.* I, 175) for the official removal of images was a mistake for 2° July, is ingenious but unlikely. Wyss, 42–3, esp. 40 n. 5; Farner III, 487 and notes. Staehelin I, 377 speaks of an 'image war' of two weeks, from 2 to 17 July

down on such little seating as private initiative left in the naves; the stalls of the canons in the choir remained, often in mutilated form. It was a striking public demonstration of the implications of the Zwinglian teaching.

It was also in fact a declaration of open revolt: after Whitsun 1524 compromise was almost impossible: notice had now been served on the Bishop of Constance (and consequently on Rome) that the greatest Swiss state had left the fold. The door had been closed: it was ultimately to be bolted and barred by the abolition of the mass, although this was deferred until Easter of the following year so that the ground could be fully prepared.

One result of the iconoclasm in Zurich was that Lucerne, Schwyz, Uri, Unterwalden, Zug and Fribourg formally refused to meet its representatives in Diet in Zurich or elsewhere.[1] They were, however, unable to carry with them Berne, Basle, Solothurn and Glarus, and the Confederation was not dissolved.[2] Berne was already insisting that questions of religious observances were not matters that concerned the Confederation, where internal harmony and secular cooperation should prevail. Basle, Berne and Solothurn, while maintaining their catholic orthodoxy, were prepared to countenance evangelical preaching,[3] and Schaffhausen and Appenzell sided openly with Zurich, as did the city of St Gall and much of Thurgau. Berne, anxious in any case to retain the allegiance of its own conservative and somewhat recalcitrant subjects in the eastern Oberland, was determined to restrain its neighbours from direct or violent action for as long as possible.

There was likewise little danger in 1524–5 of external intervention: imperial and French forces were preparing for the confrontation in the Milanese which was to lead to the capture of Francis I: Clement VII was more than fully occupied in upholding the precarious independence of the States of the Church (for which he constantly needed Swiss military support and the funds to hire it), and in Germany the rumblings of the coming Peasants' Revolt were becoming louder.

All this caused some nervous apprehension. The danger to every sixteenth century government was local separatism: the subordinate units, whether nobles or localities, must not be allowed to take the law into their own hands: hence the firm control by the administration of the cleansing of the churches in Zurich territory. Among the obvious possible foci of resistance, there remained the recalcitrant monasteries. Zwingli, like Luther, stood for the freedom of the Religious to emancipate themselves from their monastic vows, and this most of those living within the jurisdiction of Zurich proceeded to do. Many of the younger nuns married, most of

[1] EA 4, 1a, 457–8.   [2] Staehelin I, 387.   [3] Egli 3, 263, 309.

the friars and monks obtained employment, many of them as ministers of religion or as teachers; those who wished to remain cloistered were allowed to do so, but no more novices were to be received and the monastic properties were to be administered for the future by government-appointed agents on behalf of the poor.

On these terms the dissolution of the monasteries in the city of Zurich proved relatively simple. Augustinians, Franciscans and Dominicans were for the most part won over by persuasion. On 3 December 1524 all the monks and friars of Zurich who had not left the cloister already were brought together at the Franciscan friary, while the houses of the Dominicans and Augustinians came under state administration. There they were told that the younger members could learn a trade or, if suitably equipped, pursue Bible-study, while the old ones would be allowed to enjoy their revenues but not to recruit new members and would cease to wear the monastic habit.[1] The same principles applied to the nuns, whose 'dowries' would be returned to them. The Dominican nuns of Oetenbach[2] proved a little more recalcitrant. They were subjected unwillingly to a good deal of preaching, cajoling and near bullying by Leo Jud, who had been made responsible for their spiritual ministrations in 1523 as part of his duties at St Peter's.[3] When he mounted the pulpit, he was threatened with a knife by Hans Walder, after which the Dominican Fathers were forbidden access to the conventual buildings.[4] Permission to leave the cloister was given by the council in June;[5] those who left (e.g. to marry or become nurses in the hospital) were not allowed to return, no novices were to be received, and those who were permitted to remain were provided with work and required to attend sermons and abandon their habits.[6] The submission of the few ladies of the Fraumünster has already been described; their cloister became a schoolroom and lecture room, and their church a place for sermons to those living on its side of the Limmat. The monasteries outside the city, Rüti, Kappel, Embrach and Töss, accepted their fate with resignation or even alacrity.

Adjoining Zurich was Thurgau. This Habsburg territory, formerly held

[1] Bullinger, *Ref.* I, 228–9; Wyss, 56; Z III, 505–6; Egli *I*, 265 (No. 597, 598); *Gerold Edlibach's Chronik* hg. v. J. M. Usteri (Zürich, 1847), 272. (MAGZ IV). Begging was forbidden, and a kind of soup-kitchen for the poor was set up in the Dominican cloisters.
[2] Oetenbach was technically outside the city. Many were unwilling to follow the example of their Prioress, Küngolt von Landenberg, who, suitably pensioned, gave up the veil on 24 November 1524. H. Zeller-Werdmüller, *Die Stiftung des Klosters Oetenbach*, ZT 1889, 213–76.
[3] Wyss, 21.   [4] Egli *I*, 120 (No. 345), 122, 123 (Nos. 346, 348), 131 (No. 366).
[5] Egli *I*, 131–2 (No. 366).
[6] Egli *I*, 279–81 (No. 630). They were joined by some nuns from the Grimmenturm and the ancient Cistercian foundation at Selnau. By 1535 only one representative remained of what had been a characteristic social group in the state. Wyss 37, 38, 59 and n. 4; Z III, 385–6 and notes. Bullinger, *Ref.* I, 110 is unreliable, in spite of the fact he later married one of the nuns.

from the lords of Kiburg, had been conquered in 1460 by Confederate forces acting in self-defence, and retained initially as a guarantee against further attacks. It was the largest of the Mandated Territories (*gemeine Herrschaften*) and its administration was the joint responsibility of the ten occupying powers. In practice the individual states took it in turn to nominate local governors for two years; these were responsible for civil and criminal jurisdiction, defence of the castles and the collection of the customary dues and taxes.

The new evangelical preaching found willing hearers in Frauenfeld, Winterthur, Diessenhofen, Bischofszell and Stein am Rhein.[1] People like Erasmus Schmid (Fabricius), canon of the Great Minster, and Hans (Johann Ulrich) Oechsli from Einsiedeln actively spread the doctrine that the Bible, and not the hierarchy, was infallible and irresistible. The practical results of this evangelical teaching were soon apparent. Zurich, from whence it came, accompanied by attacks on images and on the cloisters, was only one of the ruling powers. In the Federal Diet, a gathering of representatives of sovereign powers, there was an overwhelming Catholic majority which was not prepared to tolerate, let alone facilitate, this evangelisation. The Diet itself, however, had no direct responsibilities there and could act only through the particular state responsible at the time for administration. The local governor had wide discretionary powers, but how far these extended to religion was not clear. Local authority was often shared with monasteries, ecclesiastics and nobles, while some districts, such as Frauenfeld and Diessenhofen, looked to all the occupying powers for guidance and control. In Thurgau there were monasteries at Fischingen (well known to Zwingli because of family connections there), Tänikon, Tobel, Griesenberg, Kalchrain, Münsterlingen, Steckborn and Ittingen. These were also considerable landowners and were natural centres of resistance to teaching which threatened them with elimination. Further, if Thurgau could be 'reformed', thus accepting the leadership of Zurich in religious matters, it might well come under its control politically. Such an outcome would bring an important accession of strength and wealth, and would alter the balance of power within the Confederation.[2] This, however, would not suit the interests of Berne and it would deprive the other protecting states of opportunities for enrichment.

All these considerations had to be taken into account. Zwingli's supporters now publicly advocated freedom of Gospel preaching, the freedom

[1] The process is well described in Knittel 1.
[2] Provided it was Thurgau only that was to be reformed, this might not be too serious, but it could not stop there. It had been generally assumed that Thurgau was a sphere of special interest to Zurich. Mörikofer 1, 234.

of the local community to choose its own form of worship and to cast off the jurisdiction of the Bishop of Constance. From many Thurgau *Gemeinden* came vigorous complaints of the episcopal courts at Constance, especially of the high fees, intolerable delays and the use of excommunication for the collection of small debts. Religious and secular obedience, they now maintained, should be kept separate – a notion unacceptable to the age, and impracticable. Nor could any government (in this case the occupying powers working through agents) tolerate violent self-help by subjects: discontent was far too near the surface and far too dangerous for that.

All over northern Switzerland, the question of local responsibility for law and order was a complicated one. This was particularly the case in relation to the town of Stein am Rhein which had come in 1484 within the territory and jurisdiction of Zurich. In the neighbouring countryside and in the extension of the town across the river, Burg bei Stein, it was only jurisdiction over minor offences (*niederen Gerichte*) which rested with Zurich, responsibility for serious offences involving life and limb (*obere Gerichtsbarkeit, Blutgericht, Blutbann, Hochgericht*) remaining with the Protecting Powers of Thurgau. The effective local administrative officer was the governor (*Landvogt*) residing at Frauenfeld.

A similar dual jurisdiction existed a few miles away at Stammheim.[1] There Zurich was represented by an assistant governor (*Untervogt*), Hans Wirth, who was also lay administrator of St Anne's Chapel, where his son, another Hans, was Chaplain.[2]

On 17 June 1524, following the lead from Zurich, the Stammheim community agreed to 'cleanse' their church of images, pictures and ornaments, which was done on Midsummer day in spite of a little opposition.[3] The movement spread rapidly to neighbouring places, Waltalingen, Nussbaumen and, instigated by another enthusiast, Zwingli's friend Hans Oechsli, to Burg and Eschenz.

The governor[4] properly reported all this to his masters meeting at

[1] Strictly there were two communities, Oberstammheim, where there was a small ancient church dedicated to St Gall, and Unterstammheim, where the presentation to a newly-built church lay with the abbot of St Gall. There was also nearby the popular pilgrimage chapel of St Anne. Egli *3*, 272.

[2] A second son, Adrian, was also ordained and had been an assistant at the Zurich Great Minster, and all three were faithful supporters of Zwingli. The reorganisation of this latter foundation left Adrian redundant, and he returned home to Stammheim with a letter of introduction from Zwingli, eager to preach. The elderly incumbent of the parish church, Dean Adam Moser, a strong traditionalist, refused to accept him, but pressure from the parishioners secured him a hearing. He attacked the Roman mass, pilgrimages and the veneration of images in his sermons, and also married an ex-nun from Winterthur.

[3] Egli *3*, 274; Farner III, 493–4; Z III, 512–13; A. Farner, *Geschichte der Kirchgemeinde Stammheim und Umgebung* (Zürich, 1911), 134. A graphic description of the whole proceedings follows, 142–74.

[4] Joseph Amberg from Schwyz who had abandoned earlier evangelical convictions. Bullinger, *Ref.* I, 180–1.

Baden. There, complaints against Zurich were already under discussion.[1] The attack on images and the mass, attempts to prevent the reservation of the sacrament, cases of individuals dying unconfessed and without the viaticum, were causing the Catholic-committed states[2] to repeat the demand for the expulsion of Zurich from the Confederation. In the midst of argument, excitement[3] and deferment, the Diet determined to exercise all the authority it could in Thurgau, and through its agent, the governor, take proceedings against those responsible for iconoclasm.

This involved a challenge to Zurich, which was determined to secure freedom for the preaching of the Gospel in the Mandated Territories and to protect its rights and those of its subjects. Locally this was connected with an existing agreement between Stammheim and Stein that in the event of danger of fire or of any attempt to interfere with the preaching of the Gospel, mutual assistance summoned by ringing the church bells should be available.

On 4 July, Hans Wirth senior[4] was on his way home from Stein when he received a warning that the Governor's officers were waiting to arrest him at St Anne's Chapel. A messenger brought the news to Stein and Stammheim, the bells pealed, men appeared in arms, and the bailiffs moved away without making any arrest. The Governor again reported the incident to the Diet at Zug, complaining that he had been impeded in the execution of his duty.[5] Hence Zurich was again invited to refrain from countenancing religious innovations in territory over which it had joint control. Zwingli refused to recommend any compliance – the state must protect its subjects, and it was the duty of ministers of the Gospel to preach the scriptures whatever the opposition. Both sides sent observers to watch the situation.

The governor now (12 July) received explicit instructions to punish those guilty of heretical teaching, and specifically to arrest Hans Oechsli who by now was almost notorious as a trouble maker.[6] This time there was no mistake, and on the night of 17 July the minister was arrested in his home in Burg, partly because of his own negligence.[7] The scuffle attending his apprehension was heard at nearby Stein and the castle of Hohenklingen. Again the bells rang, men came together, but too late and

---

[1] EA 4, 1a, 444–50.   [2] Lucerne, Uri, Schwyz, Unterwalden, Zug and Fribourg.
[3] How exciting things were can be seen from the adventures of Vadian, who had to flee for his life from Zug and escaped trial as a heretic only by adroitness and good fortune. Sabbata 117–18; Näf, Vadian II, 201–2.
[4] Egli 3, 280.   [5] EA 4, 1a, 454.
[6] Egli 3, 277; EA 4, 1a, 460, 462–3, 588–9, 593. Johannes (or Hans) Oechsli (c. 1485–1536), known as Bovillus, came from Einsiedeln to Eschenz and Burg in 1508. He actively promoted the 'cleansing' of his church and was very popular. He moved later to Elgg, Zurich, Weesen and finally to Bülach where he was highly respected. Z IX, 106.
[7] Farner III, 495–6; Staehelin I, 391; Knittel I, 73.

in insufficient numbers to intervene, while Oechsli was hurried off to Frauenfeld where Zurich could claim no jurisdiction.

By the early morning of 18 July, at least 3,000 men had gathered on the banks of the Thur, the men of Stein under the Bürgermeister, Konrad Steffan, and the indefatigable Erasmus Schmid, those of Stammheim under Wirth jnr., those of Nussbaumen under Untervogt Rütimann. They demanded the release of their pastor, which the Governor, safe behind the walls of Frauenfeld, refused even to discuss. The crowd, hot, thwarted and discontented, halted their march at Ittingen, five miles from Stein, where there was a Carthusian monastery. This was a Catholic stronghold where two monks, Valentine and Alexius, had recently been disciplined for asking advice of Zwingli about how to leave their house. The prior,[1] Peter Thaler, who was known to be a friend of the Governor, refused to give food and drink to the insurgents, spoke darkly of divine punishment and told them to go home. The result was that the mob broke into the monastery, stole the keys from the prior, took food and drink, and then, thoroughly out of hand, looted, smashed windows, pictures and church ornaments, defaced and tore up books and documents, drove off cattle, drained the fish pond, and finally set fire[2] to the monastic buildings. Hans Wirth and his two sons from outside the monastery vainly tried to restrain the mob which was urged on by Erasmus Schmid. For a moment it seemed as if there might be bloodshed when the governor's supporters arrived in some numbers, but the rioters went home and a force of some 4,000 from Zurich prevented any further disorder. The connection with the recent peasant violence in south Germany was not overlooked, and a potentially dangerous rising was nipped in the bud.

The consequences were however of the utmost significance. For Zurich this proved the point of no return. Zwingli's original challenges to the bishop over fasting and clerical celibacy had grown to a denial of episcopal, and then of papal, authority in religious matters. The government had supported Bible preaching and iconoclasm, had taken over the monasteries, allowed its clergy to marry, and had accepted the exclusive authority of Holy Writ in religious affairs. For all this Zurich was being ostracised by its fellow Swiss states. Zurich was fully capable of defending itself, and its government was well aware of the fact that there were still

---

[1] He was supported by the administrator (*Schaffner*) Iodocus Hesch, who had 'entered religion' late in life, after marriage, was a good scholar who corresponded with Luther (whom he much respected) and Zwingli (see the interesting letter Z VIII, 158–65). He resisted all efforts to convert him, maintaining the Catholic cause with passionate conviction and great sincerity, abstaining entirely from the personal abuse that was so common. Mörikofer I, 237–41, Staehelin I, 359–61.

[2] The fire was said to have been started by a man whose child had been killed by a boar belonging to the Prior which he had refused to remove or restrain. Staehelin I, 391; Knittel, 79.

many orthodox catholics within its frontiers who disliked the changes, retained earlier observances and heard mass where possible. The Ittingen incident led to provocative retaliation from the Catholic side. The Diet, somewhat surprisingly supported in this by the titular Abbot of Kappel,[1] requested Zurich to punish the rioters since they came from Stammheim and were subject to its jurisdiction.[2] Four known leaders of the rioters were thereupon imprisoned[3] and examined, and proceedings were opened against seven more; iconoclasm might be condoned, but looting and burning could not. There the matter could well have rested, but the leaders of the Catholic states would not hear of it. They insisted at Baden that sacrilege and heresy were involved, that the prisoners were therefore guilty of felony (*malefizisch*, an uncertain term) and that their punishment was a matter for the whole Confederation. The legal situation was, in fact, extremely complex, and there was much discussion and bargaining in early August. Finally, after long debate, and against Zwingli's advice,[4] the council reluctantly handed over four of the six accused, on 19 August 1524, to the Federal officers, on condition that they were to be punished as rioters and not for their beliefs or religious practices. No notice was taken of this, and three of the accused were condemned to death as heretics, iconoclasts and rioters.[5] The Catholics had forced a showdown,[6] and Zurich took up the challenge.

The Ittingen riot and its fatal consequences has a significance out of all proportion to the particular episode. In addition to nice questions of local jurisdiction, politics and religion were deeply involved. Politically, Zurich had received a setback; its wishes had been ignored, it had not been able to protect its supporters, and its influence in Thurgau had been diminished. The Reformation seemed in real danger. The consistent claim from Zurich that the removal of images from the churches was in accordance with the Bible was emphatically rejected, and those who followed Zwingli's

---

[1] Wolfgang Joner.   [2] EA 4, 1a, 465.

[3] Hans Wirth sen. (*Untervogt*), Adrian and Hans Wirth jun. and Burkhart Rütimann of Nussbaumen. Farner III, 496–7. E. Schmid and Konrad Steffan managed to get away to safety in Constance.

[4] Z III, 527–8; Bullinger, *Ref.* I, 187–8.

[5] They were subjected to lengthy questioning under torture, and confessed to heresy, but consistently maintained that their beliefs were derived from independent Bible-study and that Zwingli was not responsible for them. Adrian Wirth and Oechsli were acquitted, but the Hans Wirths, father and son, and Rütiman were executed on 28 September. They met their fate cheerfully and, as so often, affected many by their heroism and impressive piety in their last moments. O. Vasella in E. Iserloh u. K. Repgen, *Reformata Reformanda* (Münster i.W., 1965) I, 379–80.

[6] After long negotiations compensation was paid at Ittingen for the damage done; a silver cross was restored, and the monastery was unwillingly rebuilt by compulsory local labour. Orthodox Catholic priests replaced the 'heretics', and everywhere in northern Switzerland from Basle to St Gall felt the Catholic backlash. W. Oechsli, *Die Anfänge des Glaubenskonfliktes*, 33–4.

teaching were executed as heretics. It was no longer possible, after July 1524, to think in terms of any compromise on religion within the Confederation. It is partly for this reason that in his observations on the Ittingen affair Zwingli reopened in the widest terms the question of the mass.[1]

Public Christian worship in the middle ages centred on the mass. Mass was said in most churches every day, and good Christians were present frequently, certainly on Sundays and the many saints' days. The service, or liturgy, had a long and complicated history, far longer and far less simple than Zwingli, who had little sense of history, realised. The celebration of the holy eucharist was thought of as the primary duty of the priesthood; only a properly ordained priest could do this. That the service was in Latin, that it followed an almost invariable pattern, that the congregation was expected to play a passive part, the ordinary man seldom communicating more than the statutory once a year, and then receiving the bread only, that the priest performed a miracle in that with the words of consecration he held the body and blood of Christ in his hands, all this had become commonplace long before the sixteenth century.

The mass, for the middle ages, was above all a sacrifice, an 'unbloody' one, at which Christ was offered ceaselessly many times daily for the sins of the world. This Zwingli, as a Catholic priest, had accepted, and for more than ten years he had assisted at the normal services and followed the prescribed liturgical forms. With growing intensity of Bible study, doubts arose, first about the restriction of the cup to the celebrant alone, then about the nature of the 'sacrifice', and finally about the validity of the accepted doctrine of transubstantiation.

Zwingli first gave some attention to the connection between the mass and the meaning of Christ's death upon the cross when the matter was raised almost incidentally at the first Zurich disputation of January 1523. The argument then had been concerned primarily with masses for the departed and with the concept of the mass as a constantly renewed sacrifice. There had been the inevitable discussion about the meaning and use of the words *sacramentum, testamentum, missa*. Christ, the unique High Priest,[2] had once and for all offered himself as the full, perfect and completely sufficient sacrifice for the sins of mankind. Zwingli now reiterated

---

[1] Z III, 533–8.
[2] Hebrews 6. 20: 'Jesus, having become a high priest for ever in the succession of Melchisedek'. Psalm 110. 4, Genesis 14. 18. Sixteenth century biblical exegesis interpreted the whole of the Old Testament as anticipating the New Testament. The sacrifices of the Old Testament are treated as promises and tokens of the one sacrifice by which Christ saved the human race. Any connection between the word 'missa' and 'sacrifice' has long since been abandoned. J. A. Jungmann, *Missarum solemnia; eine genetische Erklärung der römischen Messe*[3] (Freiburg, 1952) I, 225–33; *Religion in Geschichte und Gegenwart*[3] IV, 885–93.

his view that the mass cannot be a sacrifice; is man to sacrifice Christ again and spare himself? The mass was not a sacrifice, even an 'unbloody' one, but a memorial or remembrance of Christ's death on the cross. The implications of all this were applied in the first place to advocate communion in both kinds for the laity and then to call for the elimination of the chantry priests. The restoration of the cup to the laity had scriptural support and was clearly not heresy. The restriction of distribution to the wafer only was a relatively recent innovation and inadequately explained away by the teaching that the whole of Christ's body and blood was contained in each particle of the whole and the cup denied because of the possibility of spilling.[1] The doctrine of purgatory and of the 'treasury of merits' was likewise relatively new and unacceptable.

As late as June 1523 Zwingli was prepared to accept the orthodox teaching about transubstantiation as defined at the Fourth Lateran Council (1215).[2] Further reflection and the attacks of his opponents led him towards a position in regard to the eucharist which he could reconcile with his own realist philosophical training while rejecting the implications of the viaticum and the reserved sacrament. Names, he said, like consecration, benediction, transubstantiation, did not worry him. 'I know that if I act and teach as Christ has bidden that I do right, and relying upon his word, may be free from sin, whatever name you like to use.'[3]

The first direct evidence of an essential change of view appears on 15 June 1523, when he wrote to his former tutor at Basle, Thomas Wittenbach,[4] now married and living in Biel, that he rejected transubstantiation. 'Just as you can dip someone a thousand times in the water of baptism but if he has no faith it is in vain, so too, I think, the bread and wine remain unchanged to the unbeliever.'[5] It is possible to make too much of one

---

[1] Zwingli knew from his visits to Lombardy that the Ambrosian rite differed from the standard pattern.

[2] Koehler, *Z & L* I, 21–2. This indispensable commentary on every detail and aspect of Zwingli's sacramental teaching lacks the author's revision of the second volume. It also has to be read in conjunction with Baur, *Zwinglis Theologie*, of which it is frequently critical. This does not mean that there is not much useful information in Baur's volumes.

[3] *Z* II, 157. This rejection of 'names' may reflect the 'realist' claim: 'nos imus ad res, de terminis non curamus'.   [4] *Z* VIII, 84–9.

[5] 'Ego haud aliter hic panem et vinum esse puto, quam aqua est in baptismo, in qua frustra millies etiam ablues eum, qui non credit.' This long and important letter was not intended to be a full discussion of the subject but an indication of the way Zwingli's thoughts were moving. He does however indicate clearly that it is the faith of the recipient that is effective and alone matters. It is unprofitable to enquire how it works for the believer: 'quicquid hic agitur, divina virtute fieri, modum autem nobis penitus ignotum, quo deus illabatur animę, neque curiosos esse in hac re oportere, quam soli fideles sentiant.' It is apparent that it was the problem of the veneration paid to objects, to images and statues, which was the urgent issue at the moment. This forced a consideration of the veneration of the reserved sacrament, and hurriedly and without any full argument Zwingli comes out against this practice. For him the believer received the body and blood of Christ at the time of reception, but there was no *opus operatum* irrespective of any faith, and the bread, after consecration and apart from the

private letter,[1] but the trend of thought was unmistakable, and the letter itself would have satisfied most Inquisitors that its contents were heretical. The matter was constantly in his thoughts for the rest of that year.[2]

Soon after writing this letter he was called upon to give some practical advice about the form of service which might be suitable for those who were no longer prepared to use the whole text of the standard mass book. Leo Jud had already introduced a modified baptismal service in German in Zurich,[3] and enquiries or requests for something similar for the mass were coming in. To help them and to answer criticism of those who were omitting parts of the mass, Zwingli wrote in four days (19–23 August) a Latin essay, *Epichiresis*,[4] one of those Greek words so singularly acceptable to the age, on the Canon of the mass. This he now sent, or dedicated, to Diebold of Hohengeroldseck, administrator of Einsiedeln. Basing his knowledge apparently on Platina's *History of the Popes*,[5] Zwingli tried the historical approach and outlined what he thought had been the development of the liturgy under Popes Alexander I (121–32), Gregory I (590–604), Leo II (682–3) and Sergius (687–701), indicating (incorrectly, it is to be feared) that it was all of less antiquity than commonly believed. He renewed his objections to the word *missa* and insisted that *eucharistia* had no direct biblical sanction. It was easy for the humanist to show on grounds of style alone that the Canon could not be of the time of the primitive church and that the words of consecration were not directly scriptural.[6] The service, also, he insisted, contained too many irrelevant prayers for Pope, saints and monarchs.[7] The words of the Canon he analysed sentence by sentence with a certain display of etymological learning, considering derivations, grammar, style and logical construction. The conclusion again was for a complete and direct rejection of the possibility of a repetition of Christ's sacrifice.

---

commemorative act of the Last Supper, remained plain bread and could not be adored without idolatry. Farner III, 417, goes too far in his deductions from this one letter that Zwingli had already destroyed all his bridges behind him.   [1] Köhler, *Z & L* I, 23, 28–9.
[2] Zwingli's views were set out with increasing emphasis and detail in: (i) *Auslegen und Gründe der Schlussreden* (July 1523), Z II, 111–57; ZH III, 143–202; (ii) *De canone missae epichiresis* (August 1523), Z II, 552 (556)–608; (iii) *Eine kurze christliche Einleitung* (November 1523), Z II, 626 (628)–663; (iv) *Ratschläge betreffend Messe und Bilder* (December 1523) Z II, 804 (808)–815.
[3] Z II, 553; Wyss, 36–7 n. 3; F. Schmidt-Clausing, *Zwingli als Liturgiker* (Göttingen/Berlin, 1952). Ulrich Äberlin (or Buebli) was the first child to be christened in the Great Minster in German. Bullinger, *Ref.* I, 112.
[4] Z II, 552 (556)–607. For a translation into German with useful notes see F. Schmidt-Clausing, *Zwinglis Kanonversuch eingeleitet…und kommentiert* (Frankfurt a. M., 1969). The urgency was because printed copies were needed for the Frankfurt fair in September.
[5] Bartolommeo Platina, who was Vatican librarian until his death in 1481, wrote *Opus de vitis ac gestis summorum pontificum* and *Liber de vita Christi ac omnium pontificum*. L. A. Muratori, *Rerum Italicarum scriptores* III, pt. I, ed. G. Gaida (Città di Castello, 1913–32).
[6] Z II, 558–9.   [7] Z II, 559, 573; Farner III. 415.

A considerable section of the treatise is concerned (relying on a controversial quotation from Origen)[1] with the argument that because a prayer for the dead was included in the Canon, therefore purgatory must exist. Zwingli insisted that this was, at best, a human conjecture. It was the invention of the *theologastri*: the New Testament admitted the existence of heaven and hell only, and this should be sufficient. The destiny of the souls of the departed is unknown to us, and we must be content to have it so.

Vestments, later to be emphatically rejected, Zwingli at this time was willing to tolerate as matters of indifference. They might be allowed to have some symbolical significance, although their elaboration and expensive ornamentation seemed unnecessary. This seems to have caused comment, and in a kind of postscript written three months later[2] he agreed that their use was undesirable but might be tolerated for those unwilling to renounce them. Similarly, he had been willing to maintain a number of the traditional prayers and even a certain amount of Latin, but more and more he was moving towards greater simplification.[3] Singing, for the time, he accepted, again with the reservation that the words should be exactly those of the Bible, and even this concession he was later to withdraw altogether.

In many respects these are two interesting little tracts.[4] Zwingli recognised the need for some standard form of service and the importance of the words used in it. The Canon of the mass was the central portion of the service including the consecration of the host. Hence to many it was even better known than the Bible. Judged by modern standards, Zwingli's critical analysis is thin and superficial, but it must have been impressive to the often ill-educated Swiss clergy, and it marks a further stage in the writer's reliance upon scripture alone.

From August 1523 onwards controversy about the mass continued, until the matter was settled for Zurich by the abolition of its celebration according to the Roman rite in April 1525. All the well-known theologians – including Luther, Erasmus, Karlstadt, Oecolampadius and Bucer – were involved in discussions, one outcome of which at one time seemed likely to be a kind of parity-compromise in Zurich in which some churches retained the old form of service and some modified it. This indeed existed throughout 1524, with the mass-priests becoming increasingly anxious about the permanent security of their employment. In the sixteenth century, however, no state that was to be strong – and Zurich certainly needed to be so in view of the gathering opposition – could afford a

[1] Z II, 593–4 and n. 2.   [2] Z II, 617 (620)–625 *De canone missae libelli apologia.*
[3] Farner III, 423–4.
[4] F. Schmidt-Clausing, *Zwingli als Liturgiker* (Göttingen, 1952), *Zwinglis Kanonversuch* (Frankfurt a.M., 1969) and *Zwinglis liturgische Formulare* (Frankfurt a.M., 1970), has demonstrated that Zwingli continued to be interested in liturgy to the end of his life.

religious two-party system. The government – which, in Zurich, meant the majority of the council – must decide the religion for the state. It was not until January 1525 that Zwingli's supporters, led by Diethelm Röist and Heinrich Walder, had a majority there, and there was for long after that a considerable number of Catholic sympathisers occupying important positions.[1] Prominent among these was Joachim am Grüt, Unterstadt-schreiber or Deputy Town Clerk, an unobtrusive conservative administrator who did everything that an official could do to prevent religious change. He was probably jealous of Zwingli's talents and influence; he knew everyone who mattered, and he understood the realities of power. He had been sent to Rome by the council to negotiate with the Pope, Clement VII, about the payment of arrears of wages owing to mercenary soldiers, and although he was unsuccessful in this he returned a totally convinced defender of the Roman church.[2]

Other active and dedicated defenders of the Catholic church were not lacking either, equally willing to state their case in print. By their restless activity and by their anxiety to fasten the epithet of Lutheran heretic on to their opponent, they helped to clarify Zwingli's thought in a more radical direction. Two such antagonists made themselves prominent in 1524, Emser and Eck, men of very different character and background, neither especially well equipped for his self-imposed task but both competent and self-confident. The first of these, Jerome Emser (1478–1527), had been a student at the University of Basle,[3] which he had to leave, somewhat under a cloud, having insulted a don, Gregory Bünzli. He had also while there been a notorious supporter of the Swabians in their hostility to their Swiss neighbours and he now, a quarter of a century later, gave vent to similar feelings in a pamphlet, *A defence of the Canon of the mass against Ulrich Zwingli*.[4] In this there was little serious argument, merely statements that his opponent, who had set himself up against the saints of the Catholic church (*universa ecclesia sanctorum*) was a shameless and self-

[1] The valuable study of Jacob has applied the 'Namier technique' to an analysis of the leading citizens of Zurich, and emphasises, what Koehler first pointed out, the weight of opposition to the Reformation.

[2] am Grüt, who returned to Zurich with a letter from Clement VII (Egli *1*, 221–2 (No. 505)), remained in close contact with the conservative Constaffel. He is a somewhat shadowy figure; there seems not to be any useful recent monograph. There are other examples of visitors to Renaissance Rome (e.g. Fabri) who, unlike Luther, returned strengthened in their faith. Koehler, *Z & L* I, 156.

[3] B.A. 1497, M.A. 1499. He was often known as 'Ibex' because of his persistent use of the family coat-of-arms which included this device. Wackernagel, *Matrikel* I, 249–50. A. H. Hartmann, *Die Amerbachkorrespondenz* (Basle, 1942) I, 113; Wackernagel *Basel III*, 15, 137; K. A. Strand, *Reformation Bibles in the crossfire* (Ann Arbor, Mich., 1961) 21–8.

[4] *Canonis missae contra Huldricū Zuingliū Defensio...MDXXIIII.* This little 32 page quarto, printed at Dresden, 1524, came to Zwingli's notice only because a traveller from St Gall, Georg Vadian, happened to see it at the Leipzig fair and brought a copy home with him. *Z III*, 230.

contradictory juggler or actor, as over-rated as Karlstadt or Luther and equally heretical.

In his reply[1] Zwingli repudiated any appeal to historical continuity; the Bible was the sole authority to be recognised, since through it the Holy Spirit guided the communities of true believers who formed the particular churches which together made up the one church.[2] The earlier arguments against merits, the repeated mass sacrifice, the mediation of individual saints, the existence of purgatory, were restated. It was all set out in the excellent Latin of which Zwingli could be a master when he allowed himself scope and opportunity. On the question of purgatory, Emser had quoted in his support John Fisher, Bishop of Rochester, but Zwingli had never heard of him.[3] The paragraphs dealing with the mass were brief and biblical; the writer had not read Emser's refutation of Luther, and the marginal note 'Eucharistia cibus spiritualis est' sufficiently summarises the passage. Setting such thoughts on paper and answering challenging questions was a sure way to building up an independent body of doctrine, and Zwingli's answer to his other opponent of 1524, John Eck, did just this.

Eck was a more serious opponent than Emser, a finer scholar and by 1524 almost a professional controversialist. He had initially been attracted in the Erasmian direction, and had obtained some distinction at the University of Ingolstadt as a humanist,[4] but after a visit to Rome he became renowned for the verbal dexterity of his conflicts with Luther. In 1523 he first turned his attention to Switzerland, and, after the second Nuremberg Diet of January 1524 where there had been renewed talk of a national church council[5] preceded by provincial councils, his interest increased. In the light of this discussion, and with the encouragement of Archduke Ferdinand of Austria, Campeggio, the papal legate, and a number of South German bishops, Eck addressed himself to the Swiss Diet at Baden[6] (August 1524) with an attack on Zwingli's 67 theses, claiming to have

[1] *Adversus Hieronymum Emserum antibolon.* Z III, 230 (241)–87. Further study may have convinced Zwingli that the Roman mass had a longer continuous history than he had supposed, and that an appeal to antiquity might not help his case very much.

[2] Z III, 257. 'Hęc est illa ecclesia, quę errare non potest, quod sibi pontifices tam falso quam impudenter arrogant.'

[3] Z III, 276–7. 'Sed ad Roffensem quendam remittis, quem an homo sit, an fortasse deus aliquis, ignoramus.' It was through Oecolampadius that Fisher's writings became known in Switzerland. See G. R. Potter, 'The initial impact of the Swiss Reformers on England', *Discordia Concors*, II (Basle, 1968) 391–400.

[4] His treatise, *Chrysopassus*, had been one of the books read by Zwingli at Glarus in 1514. Zwingli's copy, with numerous marginal annotations, survives. Koehler, *Bibliothek*, 13. The standard biography of Eck (1486–1543) is still T. Wiedemann, *Dr. Johann Eck. Eine Monographie* (Regensburg, 1865). Cf. *Gedächtnis*, 274–5; *Neue Deutsche Biographie* IV, 273–5.

[5] H. Jedin, *Geschichte des Konzils von Trient*[2] (Freiburg, 1951) I, 171; S. Skalweit, *Reich und Reformation* (Berlin, 1967), 169, 173.

[6] EA 4, 1a, 473; Z III, 290.

found errors and misunderstanding amounting to Lutheranism and therefore manifest heresy. He suggested that he should confront Zwingli before a committee appointed by the Diet which would judge the validity of the case, and by whose decisions Zwingli should be bound. The latter's immediate reaction was one of indignation and anger: Eck, he insisted, was a mere impudent self-seeker, frustrated at not having been made a bishop, and a man of notoriously evil life.[1]

His opponent had attacked Swiss interests in the matter of the papal bodyguard, and had dabbled in magic. He was ready enough to meet him in argument, but at Zurich, and with the Bible, not the Pope, as the supreme judge. The suggestion that the meeting should be at Baden was entirely unacceptable. If Eck refused to come to Zurich where he would be perfectly safe, why should Zwingli thrust himself into the power of the six states which had already prohibited the reading of his works in their territories, had burnt him in effigy and had already decided that his teaching was heretical? For them, the Pope was the sole interpreter of the Word of God, and he knew already what this would mean. There was indeed to be a religious debate at Baden, but this was not to be for another year, by which time the Zurich Council had declared its intentions much more clearly.

While the argument with Eck was being continued by Sebastian Hofmeister of Schaffhausen, Zwingli turned his attention a little more closely to the problem of the eucharist. He had already, in article 18 of the 67 theses, rejected the Roman view of the mass as a sacrifice, but had given no clear indication of his constructive thought about the eucharist. Partly, he had not yet reached a firm conclusion, partly he was anxious not to lead others before they were ready to be led, but in the light of the situation in 1524 the need for a decision as to whether the mass should be prohibited or allowed to continue in Zurich was becoming urgent. To allow it was more difficult after Eck's attack and after Zwingli's criticisms. Zwingli indeed was convinced that Luther's 'consubstantiation' interpretation of the eucharist was not acceptable, and there were now increasingly good reasons why he should make his own position plain. He was not a Lutheran; of that he was certain. How then did he stand in relation to other contemporaries who were all engaged on the same problem?

Andrew of Bodenstein (c. 1480–1541),[2] known as Karlstadt from his birth place, had, like Luther, studied at Erfurt, and while quite young had become Archdeacon and Professor of Theology at Wittenberg. At first he supported Luther, opposing Eck at Leipzig in 1519, preaching reform in

[1] Z VIII, 216–18.
[2] The standard biography is H. Barge, *Andreas Bodenstein von Karlstadt*, 2 Bde. (Leipzig, 1905), cf. E. Hertzsch, *Karlstadt und seine Bedeutung für das Luthertum* (Gotha, 1932).

Wittenberg while Luther was in the Wartburg translating the Bible. He married in 1522, renouncing his Archdeaconry, and was obliged to leave Wittenberg when Luther denounced him as a sectary. He went off, dressed as a simple layman, to preach a personalised form of the Gospel to the common people. He also inaugurated a simple vernacular communion service without elevation or vestments and with all sharing the bread and wine.[1] In November 1524, five treatises on the eucharist came from Karlstadt's pen and the printing presses of Basle[2] – the printers got into trouble for distributing them – which were eagerly seized upon by the more enthusiastic of Zwingli's supporters or rivals.

It was apparent that Karlstadt, somewhat crudely, was putting forward a view of the eucharist so similar to Zwingli's (and Oecolampadius') that unless some clear guidance was forthcoming Zurich might move in an unwelcome direction.[3] Hence, on 16 November 1524, Zwingli set out his position more clearly than ever before in an open letter to Matthew Alber.[4] Matthew Alber was minister at Reutlingen, one of the south German cities more within Zurich's orbit than that of Wittenberg, and was supported by a slightly more explicitly Lutheran colleague, Konrad Hermann,[5] with whom Zwingli had already had some dealings.

The open letter was, in fact, a curious literary device; although Matthew Alber was a real person, the letter was neither actually sent to him nor intended for him.[6] It was not printed until March 1525, by which time it had been copied a good many times and had been circulated widely in manuscript.

In November 1524, advanced thinkers in Zurich, perhaps following Hubmaier,[7] were demanding an evangelical form of the Last Supper such as Karlstadt had distributed in Wittenberg until Luther had driven him out. This could easily have led to civil commotion and in turn have imperilled the whole reforming enterprise. The opponents were only too anxious to show that Zurich was 'going Lutheran' or 'going Anabaptist', and much of Zwingli's effort was directed to showing that it was not doing so.[8]

---

[1] He had celebrated thus in Wittenberg on Christmas Day 1521 in Luther's absence. He wandered round south Germany, earning a living by manual labour, until Zwingli secured a place for him as deacon at the Zurich hospital and then as minister at Altstetten. In 1534 he joined Myconius as Professor at Basle. Wackernagel, *Matrikel* II, 7.

[2] Allen V, 596.   [3] Koehler *Z. & L.* I, 68–9; Baur II, 293–306; see below, 293 n. 4.

[4] Z III, 335–54. Staehelin I, 417. Koehler *Z & L* I, 72–4; see below 293 n. 6.

[5] A former Franciscan who later adopted Zwingli's eucharistic teaching and used his liturgical forms at Esslingen.

[6] M. Brecht, 'Hat Zwingli seinen Brief an Matthäus Alber über das Abendmahl abgesandt?', ARG 58 (1967) 100–2.   [7] Bergsten, 214ff; Baur II, 293–306.

[8] W. Walther, *Zur Wertung der deutschen Reformation* (Leipzig, 1908), 211–56, answered by W. Koehler, 'Die Schweizer Taktik gegen Luther im Sakramentsstreit', ZWA II (1912), 356–62.

By then he had repeatedly rejected the Roman mass: he now had to produce something, some corpus of teaching, that was not Lutheran and yet was biblical and suitable for a form of worship which could be approved by the government. The Latin mass was still being said in the Great Minster, although any priest who wished (as many did) could abstain. Time was becoming short. If he circulated his views to those who could understand the problem, he might gain sufficient adherents without upsetting the public. It was all part of Zwinglian-Fabian tactics not to advance too fast or too far: the open letter was a very skilful performance.

The key text to his present and future argument was John 6. 63, *spiritus est qui vivificat; caro non prodest quidquam.*[1] The Word was infallible: hence the attention paid to certain combinations of words in the Bible. There now began a kind of evangelical card game between Luther and Zwingli with texts for cards, each trying to trump the opponent's ace. The Letter to Alber was the first hand in the game.

God, His risen Son and the Holy Spirit, one eternal God, was a spirit. This was commonplace Christian orthodoxy; only in the emphasis that Zwingli laid upon it was he 'spiritualist'. Christ was the bread of life, the living bread, and just as human food fed the human body so the spiritual food fed mind and soul. In this sense to eat Christ was to believe in him and vice versa; spiritual eating was not the same as physical consumption. Faith alone gives spiritual life, and therefore when Christ spoke of eating he spoke of believing: *edere est credere.*[2] Salvation lay through Christ, not through the consumption of material bread and wine – 'What else is it to be a Christian but to believe that Christ, the son of God, suffered for us?'[3]

And so the argument, which was to rage long after Zwingli's death, turned on the simple words of institution spoken at the Last Supper. There, Zwingli now insisted, the operative word was the verb, *is*; and *is* was used in the sense of *signifies. Edere, credere; est, significat* – the basic Zwinglian minimum was now for the first time plainly stated in this Latin epistle. Parallel passages could be adduced from the Bible[4] and the early Fathers.[5] Similarly, the cup or chalice and the wine therein signified the testament, the remembrance of the shedding of the life-giving blood of Christ. Manifestly it followed that the consumption of the elements had nothing to do with the forgiveness of sins; it was the symbol or sign that

---

[1] Vulgate 64. 'The spirit alone gives life; the flesh is of no avail.' This 'proof text' reappears endlessly.

[2] This was one of the many Latin jingles which became so popular – 'Quid hic Christus per "edere", nempe "credere" intelligat'. Z III, 341.

[3] 'Quid est aliud Christianum esse, quam credere Christum dei filium pro se passum esse?' Z III, 342. This fundamental conviction was shared by all sides.

[4] As they were, constantly repeated: Foxe's 'Acts and Monuments' is full of them.

[5] Especially Tertullian, one of Zwingli's favourite writers, 'a man of wonderful piety, most singular linguistic ability and amazing eloquence' Z III, 346.

it was through Christ's death that, for true believers, their sins had been forgiven.[1]

The letter to Alber marks a further stage in the development of Zwingli's thought: in the sixty-seven theses he had rejected the notion of the mass as a sacrifice, but his words were at any rate not entirely irreconcilable with acceptance of transubstantiation.[2] The letter to Wittenbach implied that he had abandoned this doctrine after June 1523 and thenceforward he was opposed to the reservation of the sacrament since it was the action (*usus*) alone that mattered.[3] Hence, likewise, the notion of a miraculous or semi-magical *opus operatum* was unacceptable. Influenced by Erasmus, Luther, Rode, Hoen and Karlstadt, he made it clear by November 1524 that he regarded both the Catholic and the Lutheran sacramental positions as untenable.[4]

Everything was involved – both the conviction that heresy imperilled the soul and that its promulgation could be followed by loss of faith upon which salvation depended. Only those who rejected immortality, and they were very few, and silent at that, could be indifferent to these discussions. There were indeed abstractions included which have occupied the human mind across the ages, the implications of appearance and reality, the name and the thing, mind and matter, the particular and the universal. Argument raged over the meaning and nature of presence, substance and reality among men fully acquainted with formal logic and philosophical terms, knowing what induction and proof could imply. Inevitably, therefore, the disputes turned on the meaning of words, but to see in this mere verbal fencing, discussion for discussion's sake, is completely to misapprehend the age. They were desperately in earnest, since upon a right judgement of the meaning of Christ's death on the cross and his words at the Last Supper eternal life depended.

Inherited traditions and human and personal factors were inevitably present as well: Scotist opposed Thomist, the nominalist-trained theologian yielded no ground to the realist, school fought school, and whole communities were easily involved. The war of words, behind which lay convictions for which men and women willingly died, was to continue and

---

[1] Z III, 351. 'Symbolum eorum esse, qui firmiter Christi morte exhaustum et deletum esse peccatum credunt et gratias agunt.'
[2] Koehler *Z & L* I, 20.   [3] Koehler, *Z & L* I, 22.
[4] There has perhaps been too much of a tendency to search out 'influences': what C. W. Dugmore said of the English Reformers – 'as if they had no theological training, no knowledge of the Schoolmen or of the Fathers, and were utterly incapable of thinking for themselves' (*The Mass and the English Reformers* (London, 1958), vii) can be applied to Zwingli in relation to other writers. For a fuller discussion see below p. 292–3; Koehler *Z & L*, I, 26ff; A. Peters, *Realpräsenz, Luthers Zeugnis von Christi Gegenwart im Abendmahl* (*Arbeiten zur Geschichte und Theologie des Luthertums*, Bd. 5, Berlin, 1960); C. C. Richardson, *Zwingli and Cranmer on the Eucharist* (Evanston Ill., 1949).

to become intensified. The leaders lacked neither self-assurance nor a certain natural human vanity, but they honestly believed that truth was on their side and that truth must prevail. Zwingli, like many others, knew that he was right and that his cause would triumph. It was therefore worth fighting for; if wars seemed to turn upon struggles about the eucharist it was because this seemed to them at least as important as freedom, liberty, self-government or democracy did to later generations. In Zurich, at any rate, the word of God, now available to all in an open Bible, should prevail. How it was to be interpreted was not as simple as it seemed, and it was soon apparent that other leaders beside Zwingli were to seek and to find different meanings in the word of God.

7

The radical challenge

Throughout 1524 and well into 1525 the antagonism in Zurich between those unwilling to face the consequences of an open breach with Rome and traditional beliefs, and those who were convinced that this was now unavoidable, grew in intensity. The council had indeed accepted the principle that the Bible was the sole authority by which religious affairs should be conducted, but the practical implications of this were realised rather slowly. The councillors collectively were not afraid of responsibility, but they were conscious of it. If the Bishop of Constance was to be ignored, the mass abolished and Zurich to be different from other communities in worship and belief, they must know why. Not unreasonably, it took many months for Zwingli's teaching to be assimilated and accepted.

For all Zwingli's caution, the transition to an evangelical community was neither easy nor peaceful. Those who had been, or feared to be, dispossessed – monks, friars, chantry priests, with their servants, suppliers and attendants – formed a discontented group which had friends among the aristocrats who disliked the authority of the gilds, and the simple conservatives who remained Catholic at heart.[1]

At the other end of the scale were the enthusiasts, who had long felt that things were not moving fast enough. They had heard Zwingli's sermons, they had read the Bible, and they knew something of what was being taught at Wittenberg. They were men in a hurry. They were also prepared to act when occasion arose, which, in turn, might lead to disturbance. This both the council and Zwingli were anxious to avoid: Zurich must remain a peaceful and well-ordered community. In fact there had been manifestations of discontent for some time, and it was because of this that, in December 1524, Zwingli submitted to his masters an analysis of current discontents which showed remarkable acumen and insight. In *The Trouble-makers*[2] he professed to be writing for the Christian Church or community

[1] The analysis of the situation by N. Birnbaum, *The Zwinglian Reformation in Zurich*, in *Past and Present*, no. 15 (1959), 27–47, and in *Archives de Sociologie des Religions* 4, 1959 (No. 8) 15–30 is not convincing. The Kämbel gild, which actively supported change, was numerous and vocal, if socially unimportant. E. G. Rupp, *Protestant Catholicity* (London, 1960), 12 goes too far in detraction.   [2] Z III, 355 (374)–469, *Wer Ursach gebe zu Aufruhr usw.*

of Mülhausen,[1] but this was a transparent fiction: it was Zurich that was under examination. There were, the writer believed, four groups of 'false brethren' among the newly enfranchised Christians – anti-clericals, selfish opportunists, greedy self-seekers and misguided sectaries. In addition, there were the exhibitionist prelates and monks who cared only for their privileges. Some of his own adherents were merely negative opponents of the hierarchy, those who were always ready to join in any movement directed against the clergy in general and the papacy in particular. It was resentment, dislike and suspicion of Rome that made them enemies of the Roman faith, but nothing more. Willing to help to overthrow, they had nothing constructive to offer; envy, hatred and malice were an insufficient foundation for a truly Christian society. To some extent they had hitherto been restrained by the coercive power of the Catholic church; now, released from this, their frowardness, misconduct and even violence were all the more apparent. They discredited their adherents rather than otherwise; judged by their actions, their talk of faith was meaningless.[2]

They were joined by many more unworthy supporters who welcomed a new-found opportunity to do as they pleased. When told that there was no scriptural justification for enforced Lenten fasting, they used this as permission for unrestrained gluttony and drunkenness. If Lent need not be marked by sobriety in clothing, some women would all the more parade their peacock finery at all times. There were likewise monks and nuns who were persuaded that they could ignore their vows, but who, wanting the best of both worlds, treated their cloister as a residential club, from which, dressed as they liked, they could go in and out at will.[3]

These were minor aberrations: a good deal more serious were the efforts that were being made by some to use the new teaching as a method of evading or refusing lawful customary payments. Two particular matters were being brought forward and required serious consideration – the payment of tithe, and interest on loans. In one sense these provide examples of attempts to have it both ways, since the medieval church which insisted on the regular payment of tithe also refused to countenance usury or interest. Both issues raised nice points of biblical exegesis and public policy, and in regard to both Zwingli combined shrewd common sense

---

[1] This Alsatian city and surrounding country entered into a 'perpetual alliance' with the thirteen states of the Confederation in January 1515. For many purposes it counted as part of the Confederation, but Catholic opposition prevented its acceptance with any higher status than that of ally (*Zugewandte*), and as such the connection slowly weakened as French interest in, and pressure on, Alsace, grew. H. Baur, *Rottweil und Mülhausen* (Zürich, 1932); Oechsli 2, 62, 88–91, 115, 366–7.   [2] Z III, 355–8, 380–3.

[3] Including visits to 'the baths' at Baden and elsewhere, which were notorious for debauchery. These complaints, Zwingli agreed, did not apply to Zurich – there, the former monks were either preachers, teachers, or engaged in some handicraft, while the nuns who remained unmarried worked industriously at Selnau or Oetenbach. Z III, 385–6.

with a certain over-simplification of the legal and practical implications. In the end, but with limitations, both were accepted.

Tithe was basically a rural problem, directly affecting the country dweller, and it was one with which the country-bred Toggenburger was well acquainted. The clergy of the primitive church[1] had been supported by the voluntary offerings of the laity, and this had become regularised into a compulsory levy of one tenth of the produce of the land, including the animals thereon, and of the profits of labour. Round the assessing and collection of tithe an economic machinery had been erected which was elaborate and effective. Antiquity, canon law,[2] current practice and commercial convention accepted tithes as reasonable. Most of the monasteries, indeed, continued to flourish because they drew the greater or rectorial tithe from their churches, paying a vicar to perform the parochial duties.[3]

What relation did this bear to the new regime? If neither tradition nor canon law[4] was binding on Christians, then the question of tithe had to be considered in relation to scriptural pronouncements. Tithes had indeed some considerable warranty in the Old Testament,[5] but this had been superseded by the New Testament, in which no explicit authority for the compulsory payment of tithe could be found. Discussion about this was widespread and went far beyond Switzerland.[6] As early as 1520 Zwingli had been obliged to consider the question of the tithes payable to the Great Minster.[7] In March of that year he had read the observations of Gabriel Biel and Conrad Summenhart on the subject[8] and concluded, but discreetly kept his comments in Latin only, that tithe was not necessarily payable by divine law. The implications of *sola scriptura* and of the Zwinglian sermons of 1522 and 1523 might thus be that there was no scriptural or moral obligation to pay tithe, and that this was one of the

[1] L. Vischer, 'Die Zehntenforderung in der alten Kirche' ZKG 70 (1959), 201–17.

[2] Especially *Decretal. Gregor. IX.* lib. III tit. xxx *De Decimis.* Z III, 392–4 and notes, 455 n. 24.

[3] Z III, 397–8. G. Constable, *Monastic tithes, from their origins to the twelfth century* (Cambridge, 1964) is well documented for the early history. For later development G. G. Coulton, *Five Centuries of Religion*, III (Cambridge, 1936) 149–56, 179–97, 225–6, and *The Medieval Village* (Cambridge, 1925) 289–98, remain useful.

[4] Z II, 298–346 (esp. 325–33) and L. v. Muralt's valuable introduction (1–49) to *Huldrych Zwingli, Von göttlicher und menschlicher Gerechtigkeit, Sozialpolitische Schriften für die Gegenwart* ausgewählt und eingeleitet von Leonhard von Muralt und Oskar Farner (Zürich, 1934).

[5] Gen. 28. 22: 'And of all that thou givest me, I will without fail allot a tenth part to thee.' Lev. 27. 30; Num. 18. 21, 24; Mal. 3. 10.

[6] The matter was debated in many places in south Germany. In Thuringia, for example, Jakob Strauss denounced tithe in 1524 and was implicitly supported by the court chaplain, Wolfgang Stein, who was anxious to proclaim that the rules of the Old Testament were no longer binding on Christians. J. Rogge, *Der Beitrag des Predigers Jakob Strauss zur frühen Reformationsgeschichte* (Berlin, 1957), with facsimiles. [7] Z VII, 272.

[8] *Tractatus de potestate et utilitate monetarum. Tractatulus bipartitus de decimis: defensiuus opinionis theologorū aduersus cōiter canonistas de quotta decimarum si debita sit iure diuino vel humano.* Hain, *Repertorium Bibliographicum* (Tübingen, 1838) 3188, 15177. Z VII, 279.

extortions practised by the clergy for their own enrichment. Such teaching would be welcomed by the average farmer, who would most gladly withhold his tithes, especially in a bad season. In 1523 and 1524 some parishes, instigated possibly by Simon Stumpf of Höngg, actually tried to refuse tithe payments and had to be coerced by the Zurich government into acceptance of liability.[1] Zwingli now introduced some important modifications and qualifications into his teaching. He insisted that the original purpose of tithe, paid by a man to the church in which he was baptised, was for the maintenance of the building with its ministers and for the support of the poor, and was therefore a good one.[2] It was later abuses, introduced by greedy Popes and prelates, that had caused difficulties. The evolution by which tithes had become money payments and therefore instruments of commerce, was deplorable: it could be explained only by foolishness, and formed a just punishment for the sins of those involved. None the less, bargains had been struck and contracts entered into: 'we have willed the tithes on to ourselves'.[3] Thus tithes, and charges directly deriving from tithes, had become normal debts and obligations recognised and accepted by authority and therefore they must be paid like any other obligation. To repudiate them would strike at the contractual basis of normal business: non-payment would lead to violence, which the government could not tolerate.

The fact that original intentions had been abused could not be allowed to invalidate arrangements that had been freely entered into by the community. There was in fact, Zwingli insisted, no reason to suppose that the poor would benefit in any way if payment of tithe ceased. Nor was communism compatible with human society since the Fall:[4] 'thou shalt not steal' clearly implies the existence and recognition of individual possessions and, by extension, of authority which can define and protect them. All this is no sphere in which the individual can take the law into his own hands or act according to the imagined dictates of his own conscience.

Zwingli was prepared if necessary to deal fairly drastically with the tithe problem. The tithe payments used for the maintenance of monasteries would not be needed as the monks perished of inanition. The 'small' tithes on fruit, roots and other vegetables he was prepared to see remitted

---

[1] Z III, 363. Witikon, Marthalen, Benken, Wildisbühl, Truttikon, were involved. Egli *1*, 246 (no. 568). In 1523 Zollikon, Riesbach, Fällanden, Hirslanden, Unterstrass and Witikon complained to the Zurich council against payment to the Provost and Chapter of the Great Minster. Goeters, *Vorgeschichte* 256–7.

[2] Z III, 394.

[3] 'Also sind wir in der zehendenschuld nit one unser schuld. Wir habend (das ist: unsere vordren) alle mit einandern daryn verwilliget.' Z III, 399; cf. II, 512–15.

[4] Z III, 402: 'das uns gott die zämengeschütten gemeinschafft nit gebüt', which the Latin translation expands into 'promiscuam illam, quam Catabaptistae somniant, rerum et bonorum omnium communionem'. Sabbata, 142; see below 176.

altogether, while the proceeds of the 'greater' tithe should be used for their proper purpose, the maintenance of church services and the relief of the poor. All this, however, must be done according to due process of law: no one could refuse to pay what was lawfully due from him. It was for a Christian administration to see to it that payments, including tithe, were for the public advantage, and this, with qualifications, was what happened in Zurich.

With an expanding Swiss economy combined with fresh consideration of any conventional ethical ideas, the question of interest on loans was bound to come under consideration. This was not a simple matter. In theory all loans were interest free, but a number of ingenious ways had been found of evading the requirement 'lend, hoping for nothing again' (Luke 6. 35) by invoking risk, possible loss or altered circumstances as excuses for allowing 'barren metal' to 'breed'. Interest was contrary alike to canon law and the Bible, and had recently (1517) been condemned by the fifth Lateran Council,[1] but the prohibitions were constantly and knowingly evaded.[2] What had become commercially indispensable had somehow to be made acceptable. There was, indeed, no easy way round the plain words of the Bible, and there were men like Stumpf and Lüthi who were preaching that mortgages, rent-charges and similar compulsory dues, were unchristian and need not be paid. Zwingli, who first considered the problem in 1523,[3] returned to it more than once. The earth belonged to God, and sinful man cultivated it to his own selfish advantage. In any properly Christian society, all debts would be readily paid and all loans would be interest free. But human society was not Christian in the sense that men were ruled by man-made, not God-given, laws. A Christian must keep his pledged word, contracts must be honoured, government regulations observed and the peace kept. Refusal to pay rent or mortgage could not be justified. At the same time, Zwingli would have no one live

---

[1] Reinforcing the definition by the Fourth Lateran Council (1215) of usury as 'quando videlicet ex usu rei quae non germinat, nullo labore, nullo sumptu, nullo ve periculo lucrum foetusque conquiri studetur'. Hardouin, *Conciliorum collectio maxima* (Paris, 1715) IX, 1773.

[2] Usury was considered by Aquinas and many medieval writers; Angelus de Clavasio, for example, in the widely read *Summa Angelica de casibus conscientiae* devoted 39 closely printed columns to this subject. General studies include F. X. Funk, *Geschichte des kirchlichen Zinsverbotes* (Tübingen, 1876) 1–53; W. Cunningham, *Christian opinion on usury* (Edinburgh, 1884); B. W. Dempsey, *Interest and usury* (Washington D.C., 1943); E. Ramp, *Das Zinsproblem. Eine historische Untersuchung*, QGSP 4 (Zürich, 1949); H. Barge, *Luther und der Frühkapitalismus*, SVR 168 (Gütersloh, 1951) which is less valuable than its title suggests; G. W. Locher, *Der Eigentumsbegriff als Problem evangelischer Theologie*[2] (Zürich, 1954); J. T. Noonan, *The scholastic analysis of usury* (Cambridge, Mass., 1957); O. Capitani, *Sulla questione dell' usura nel medio evo. Bolletino dell' Istituto storico italiano per il Medio Evo* (Roma, 1958); B. Nelson, *The idea of Usury*[2] (Chicago, 1969); *Cambridge Economic History of Europe* III (Cambridge, 1963) 564–70. The pioneer work of W. J. Ashley, *Introduction to English Economic History and Theory* (London, 1909) I, ii, 397–421 demonstrated the more obvious methods of customary evasion. [3] Z II, 516–21.

without working for a livelihood, no rentiers, no pensioners, and the tiller of the soil would receive the proper reward for his labour. If he had borrowed money to purchase or stock his land and had knowingly promised to pay for the use of borrowed capital, such a promise must be kept. This was a purely secular matter; if the proper official decided that such a debt had been incurred, it must be discharged, and this was in accordance with Bible teaching.[1] Zwingli was prepared for elaborate, and probably unworkable, arrangements by which payments might be made in kind and be adjusted to the harvest, and he also believed it was possible to prohibit the raising of further loans and to pay off those already incurred by a kind of sinking fund.[2] This again was not worked out in any detail and was not applied. Gross and grasping gains were abhorrent:[3] the shameless usurer must expect appropriate treatment at the Day of Judgement. As a compromise, Zwingli was prepared to accept interest payments of 5% as tolerable, and this became an arrangement that was enforced by the government.[4] Divine justice was different from human justice, and the state ordering of interest payments must be accepted even if it was unbiblical. To show how and why this was so required some ingenuity which Zwingli provided, to the indignation of the radicals, but to the peace and security of Zurich. For those who cheated as money-changers,[5] false coiners and those who made fortunes by creating monopolies or manipulating tolls and dues he had nothing good to say.

These references to economics and morality were not worked out in any detail, and from them Zwingli turned to attack those whom he indicated as the real disturbers of public order. These are the prelates, the great bishops and abbots who have scandalously neglected their duties of leadership, teaching and preaching, in order to involve themselves in secular affairs and to secure worldly advantage and personal possessions at any cost. Their God is Mammon, they charge for services that should be given freely, their misconduct, drunkenness and deception are as notorious and shameless as their pride and magnificence. Not a penny of their great wealth is shared with the poor; rather, by keeping in the background, they are the real trouble makers, preventing the spread of the

---

[1] Z III, 391: 'gottes wort umb die zytlichen güter lasst die richter diser welt urteylen'.
[2] Ramp 74–6. [3] Z III, 392.
[4] This *Zinsmandat* (9 October 1529) was probably written by Zwingli. With reservations, Luther, Eck and several cities were prepared to tolerate interest at 5%. Egli *1*, 681–4 (No. 1612), 699–701 (No. 1652); Funk 42; Z II, 518–19, 521; Yoder 2, 89; H. Schmid, *Zwinglis Lehre der göttlichen und menschlichen Gerechtigkeit* (Zürich, 1959); A. Farner, *Die Lehre von Kirche und Staat bei Zwingli* (Tübingen, 1930), 60; K. Rischar, *Johann Eck auf dem Reichstag zu Augsburg 1530* (Münster i.W., 1968), 4.
[5] Z III, 433 n. 14. The bewildering differences of sixteenth century Swiss and south German currencies made for fraud. H. Altherr, *Das Münzwesen der Schweiz bis zum Jahre 1798* (Berne, 1910).

Gospel, using monks and priests to oppose the true Christians, turning, if they are abbots, their houses into lodgings for great nobles while the poor freeze and starve outside. The Popes themselves are chief among these greedy extortioners; dispensations have been used to make money, the existence of purgatory has been invented for the purpose of gaining from payments for indulgences, and innumerable charges have been supplemented by the gifts and offerings of the faithful. At the same time, excommunication has become intolerable: men have been put to death as heretics because they have eaten a little meat at forbidden seasons,[1] and clergy have been forbidden to marry while being allowed to live in systematic concubinage on the payment of money. Preaching the Gospel has been attacked as heretical and those who do this indiscriminately labelled 'Lutherans'; in Germany in particular gold has been drained away with an occasional reference to a future General Council to appease their victims.[2] Much of this had already been said in a different context and was acceptable enough to the Zurich Council as an analysis of some obvious features of a disturbed polity.

Zwingli also referred to the new threat to social and religious harmony at home – the extremist evangelicals, self-confident, highly critical of others, lacking in charity, opposing the established civil government, quarrelsome, envious, back-biting hypocrites.[3] To the baptism of children they were utterly opposed, and by their constant discussions at every street corner and their open-air preaching, the Gospel was in danger of being brought into disrepute. It was an indication of the existence of a religious left-wing in Zurich that was long to trouble church and state.

The conclusion to this disconnected December manifesto was that the effective intervention of the civil power must be firmly and widely applied. The government had a paternal and inescapable duty to bring the advantages of godly administration to its subjects with patience, care and love.[4] The prelates must be prevented from opposition and harmful intervention since their whole influence made for disorder[5] rather than public tranquillity. No new monastic professions should be made, so that as the ageing Religious died, the property of the monasteries could be applied to the benefit of the community and especially of the poor. The tithe payments to the monasteries should be similarly distributed and care should be taken that new interest or other charges on their property did not arise. The old order had meant that the word of the Pope had displaced that of God, and this must be reversed. Finally, Zwingli assumes the mantle of

---

[1] The reference was to the condemnation as heretics of Siegmund the stone cutter (surgeon) at Ensisheim (February 1523) and Klaus Hottingen at Lucerne in March 1524. Z III, 443 n. 7. See above 131 n. 2.   [2] Z III, 428–44.   [3] Z III, 403–12.
[4] Z III, 459.   [5] 'Nun ist das gantz bapstůmb ein missordnung.' Z III, 462.

the prophet – unconsciously echoing Geiler of Kaysersberg thirty years previously, he concluded, 'It is bound to collapse' – '*Das muss brechen*'.[1] Zwingli now had to meet probably the most serious and significant challenge of all, that of the independents, of whom those known then and later as Anabaptists were the spearhead.[2] Mistakenly, but genuinely, these radicals were regarded and represented as social revolutionaries whose teaching would overthrow society and religion alike. The immediate controversy centred on infant baptism, but behind it lay a view of world Christianity that was new, permanent and challenging. Before the days of Constantine, the Christian church had consisted of a small persecuted minority of believers with all the strength and coherence of an underground movement. The maintenance of unity of belief and practice after Christianity had become the state religion of the Mediterranean world had not been easy, but had been substantially accomplished after the four General Councils of Nicaea, Constantinople, Ephesus and Chalcedon. Educated men thereafter thought in terms of one Roman Empire, with one religion, long after east and west were going their separate ways. The gap indeed between Rome and Constantinople slowly widened into schism, but schism it remained – the divergence was hardly different in kind from that between Rome and Avignon (1372–1417), and, indeed, after the Council of Florence (1439), some of the cracks had been papered over. The desire for unity was always present. Wyclif, Hus, Luther, Zwingli, Calvin and Cranmer were agreed in maintaining that there was but one Catholic church whose creed was the same and should be known to all. Their model was that of the primitive church of the days of the Apostles; it was from this that Rome, the Popes and the hierarchy had manifestly

[1] Z III, 469; cf. L. Dacheux, *Jean Geiler de Kaysersberg* (Strasbourg, 1876), 498; E. J. D. Douglass, *Justification in late medieval preaching: a study of John Geiler of Kaisersberg, Studies in Medieval and Reformation thought*, ed. H. A. Oberman, I (Leiden, 1966).

[2] The Anabaptist literature is considerable – for detail see H. J. Hillerbrand, *A bibliography of Anabaptism 1520–1630* (Institute of Mennonite Studies, Elkhart, Ind. 1962). Also in *Quellen zur Geschichte der Täufer* x. Bd. (Gütersloh, 1962) QFRG xxx. ME, ML, and Clasen, have useful bibliographies. E. Troeltsch, *Die Soziallehren der christlichen Kirchen und Gruppen* (Tübingen, 1912, translated as *Social teaching of the Christian churches*, London, 1931); Max Weber, *Gesammelte Aufsätze zur Religionssoziologie*, Bd. I, *Die protestantischen Sekten und der Geist des Kapitalismus* (Tübingen, 1921); E. A. Payne, *The Anabaptists of the sixteenth century* (London, 1949); G. F. Hershberger (ed.), *The Recovery of the Anabaptist Vision* (Scottdale, Pa., 1957); F. H. Littell, *The Anabaptist view of the church. A study in the origins of sectarian Protestantism* (Boston, 1958) (To be used with caution); P. J. Klassen, *The economics of Anabaptism 1525–1560* (The Hague, 1964); H. J. Goetz, *Innere und Äussere Ordnung in der Theologie Thomas Müntzers*. Studies in the history of Christian thought, II. (Leiden, 1967). Specifically for Switzerland: W. Koehler, 'Das Täufertum in der neueren kirchenhistorischen Forschung', ARG 37. (1940) 93–107, 38. (1941) 349–64, 40. (1943) 246–70, 41. (1948) 164–83. 53. (1962) 152–180. O. Vasella, 'Zur Geschichte der Täuferbewegung in der Schweiz', ZSK 48. (1954) 179–86; M. Haas, 'Täufertum und Revolution', *Festgabe L. v. Muralt* (Zürich, 1970) 286–95. Cf. *Zur Geschichte des schweizerischen Täufertums*, NZZ 7 Nov. 1971 no. 519. Muralt/Schmid; Muralt, *Glaube*; Blanke *1, 2, 3*; Yoder *1, 2*.

departed and so had led men away from Christ. The Reformers always insisted that they were neither innovators nor heretics; they were seeking to reestablish the visible congregation of Christians upon the right foundations and principles. There was, and there could be, only one church of Christ on earth.

For Zwingli, as for almost everyone of his day, the visible church must be coexistent with the whole local community, the people, who must live and worship in harmony. Now, however, new groups were appearing, for whom the church consisted of the few only, those who truly believed and lived rightly. These Radicals were also biblicists, strict adherents to the letter of the Bible; some, 'spiritualists', placed much greater emphasis on the direct personal inspiration of individuals by the Holy Spirit than did others, but contemporaries like Luther (and some modern writers) saw no need to differentiate between the various sectaries (*Schwärmer*).[1] Their work lay through local congregations of voluntary members who regarded themselves as altogether set apart from the secular state. For them the one true church of God was made up of convinced believers only. In so far as this applied to the 'invisible' church, whose members were known to God alone, there was no difference with the Zwinglian view. But when it came to identifying the adherents to the visible church on earth, there was a real divergence of opinion. There, was, indeed, no sure way of distinguishing between the true believers and the hypocrites, the nominal adherents whose probity might be challenged but could not necessarily be disproved. But, the opponents insisted, tests could be applied covering both conduct and belief, and those who did not reach the standard expected should be named and expelled. This was a new distinction. For Catholic, Lutheran and Zwinglian, the visible church embraced all professing Christians and thus, with insignificant exceptions, the whole community. The new alternative was groups of believers who constantly scrutinised their own membership, eliminated the unworthy, and worshipped, prayed and associated in separate and usually small voluntary communities or churches. This, so obvious and acceptable to the twentieth century, was then a new, revolutionary and often abhorrent suggestion. It has been only within the last fifty years that the sectarian movement which Zurich faced from 1524 onwards has received sympathetic and understanding consideration.

To a considerable degree, this has been the result of American study and enthusiasm. Mennonites, Amishes, Hutterites, Schwenckfeldians, form prosperous communities in the New World, with an active interest in their own roots and origins. The result of fuller knowledge has been greater sympathy, while literary achievements like the completion of the

---

[1] Their sub-divisions are discussed by G. H. Williams and A. M. Mergal, *Spiritual and Anabaptist Writers* (London, 1957) 20–4, 28–35.

Mennonite Encyclopedia, or the daunting *Corpus Schwenckfeldianorum* have provided a body of readily accessible information which has made greater understanding possible. No historian nowadays can write off the 'spiritual' movement with the prejudice and ignorance that were predominant before 1930. There is indeed almost a danger that the pendulum swings too far the other way. Not all the 'spiritualists' were the simpleminded, injured innocents that they have been represented: some were plainly selfish, obstinate and stupid.

There is at the outset a problem of nomenclature. What were these new sectaries to be called? Zwingli preferred to speak of them as catabaptists or anti-baptists; they themselves rejected the title Anabaptists because for them there was only one baptism and that for adults only. In practice, apart from a few Jews, every one in western Europe had been baptised soon after birth, so that any later baptism was technically *re*-baptism, hence the name 'Anabaptist'. The adherents of the new movement insisted that infant baptism was no baptism at all; consequently their enemies quite unfairly labelled them enemies of baptism, which they were not. Yet to speak of them as 'Baptists', without qualification, is to introduce confusion, since the Baptist churches of a later age have a long and varied ancestry and in most cases are not conscious of any continuity with the 'Swiss brethren'.[1] 'Anabaptist', it is true, has suffered from memories of the excesses of Jan Matthys and John of Leiden, and the communism and polygamy in Münster, but this can be discounted, and 'Anabaptist' be used as a historically neutral term for a phenomenon of the age.

The ritual ceremony of baptism universally used in Zurich until 1523, and continuing to be used until 1526, was an elaborate affair. In addition to the sprinkling with water by the priest, and the pronunciation of the biblical formula, the child was anointed with the chrism that a bishop alone could consecrate, with accompaniments of salt, spittle, blowing, signs of the cross and exorcism. These accompaniments Zwingli found increasingly unpalatable, but he was willing to accept them until a simpler service was inaugurated.[2] The biblical command was clear, and dipping in or sprinkling with water was universal, but for Zwingli, as for his opponents on this matter, the water was a sign and not a vehicle of divine grace; it was a testimony to what had already happened. First and fore-

---

[1] This may be the most satisfactory terminology, although not contemporary. They called themselves 'brothers' and 'sisters'. ARG 37 (1940), 242–3; Williams, 120. Of the four main groups, the Swiss brethren, the Hutterites of Moravia, the Melchiorites of Münster and the Mennonites, Zwingli was concerned only with the first.

[2] This was produced by Leo Jud in German, and first used in the Great Minster in August 1523, following closely Luther's first *Taufbüchlein* (WA, 1.12, 38, 42–8). It was modified in 1525 and later. Z IV, 680–3, 707–13. F. Schmidt-Clausing, *Zwinglis liturgische Formulare* (Frankfurt a.M., 1970) 11–17.

most there must be assured faith bringing with it true repentance, followed by an avowal or confession of sin, promise of amendment and an inward conviction of forgiveness or absolution. The sprinkling or immersion was a token only, entirely subordinate to faith, inner conviction or feeling.

The difficulty of applying this doctrine to new-born babes was obvious, and it was round this that controversy gathered. It thus secured far too much prominence, whereas in fact it was subordinate to the belief in a 'gathered' church of groups of true believers. It was their opponents who made so much of their rejection of infant baptism and their insistence on an adult ceremony which they claimed to be the only one with biblical warranty. Perhaps it was, no doubt unconsciously, intended to divert attention from the thoroughly biblical nature of their teaching and from the simplicity and purity of their lives. They were seldom able to state their case clearly and without interruption, although they were usually voluble enough when given the opportunity. They were all in varying degrees biblicists, 'spiritualists'[1] and individualists; although there was general harmony in their thinking, there was no prescribed creed or accepted conformity of practice. For them the inner light, the word from within, the self-assurance of personal revelation, was decisive. It took precedence even over the texts of the Bible, coming likewise direct from God. This inner certainty brought strength. They knew they were of the Elect, and often welcomed persecution. They would join themselves only with like-minded enthusiasts in small, but visible, groups. They expected to be misunderstood and submitted meekly and humbly to injustice and suffering: indeed suffering was for many almost a necessary concomitant of a state of grace; martyrdom came easily to them.

For Luther and Melanchthon all their non-Catholic opponents from Karlstadt onwards, were fanatics (*Schwärmgeister*),[2] including, of course, the Zwinglians. Zwingli regarded his own Swiss opponents in a very similar light, so that they were subjected to the full force of Lutheran and Zwinglian polemic as well as consistent and active Catholic opposition. All this, in turn, served to enhance their own uncompromising intransigence, of which the more remarkable demonstrations came after Zwingli's death and outside Switzerland.

The Anabaptist problem is indeed a complex one. For the modern world the existence of separate 'churches' or groups of Christians believing,

[1] They relied too demonstrably upon the inspiration of the Holy Spirit for this description not to apply, but the word is differently defined by the theologians and is not used here in any technical sense. There could be, and were, 'spiritualists' who were not concerned about adult baptism.

[2] Luther opened fire on them with *Ein Brief an die Christen zu Strassburg wider den Schwärmergeist* (1524), WA 1.15, 380–97, followed in 1525 by *Wider die himmlischen Propheten, von den Bildern und Sakrament*, WA 1.18. 62–125, 134–214.

associating and worshipping independently is regarded almost as an obvious human right, equally applicable to those of any faith or of none. The notion of uniformity of religion or compulsory attendance at church is as difficult for us to comprehend as compulsory attendance at school would have been for the sixteenth century. A community without a common ideology was at the mercy of one which was united. Christendom itself, a small part of the then known world, was in serious danger from the infidel Turk, and its unity had already been broken by Luther. If this was now to be splintered still further by other recalcitrants, the outlook was dark. Internal religious differences practically meant civil war, and this in turn imperilled the very existence of the state. There was the utmost unwillingness to admit that there could be more than one path to salvation; those who took the wrong one were not only on the way to eternal damnation themselves but were also leading others thither. This was intolerable.

Zwingli's new opponents were dangerous for three reasons. First, they were deliberately and consciously disruptive. For Catholics, Lutherans and Zwinglians there was but one comprehensive body of the faithful, one church. For the Anabaptists this was unacceptable: it was the few who were the church, meeting together in separate independent units, selective and exclusive. Luther blamed the incomplete acceptance of his teaching as much on the misguided enthusiasts and fanatics who went their own ways as on the Papists who failed to recognise their errors. Zwingli was convinced that it was anarchist opposition within his own camp that impeded Swiss unity under the reformed banner. Secondly, these opponents turned his own weapon against him. They accepted *sola scriptura*, the theme of the Great Minster sermons since 1519, and insisted that they were simply carrying his own teaching to its logical conclusions. Thirdly, and perhaps most dangerously of all, they were exclusive politically as well as religiously. They refused to accept the normal obligations of citizenship, they claimed to be above the law and wanted to form tiny self-governing states within states, and as such they could no more be accepted than could the early Mormons in the United States of America.

Complete separation of church and state was not practicable anywhere in Europe before 1550. If this was what the radicals wanted (and it may be doubted whether any of them considered its implications), they could not have succeeded, for the time was not yet ripe. They came too soon for success to be possible.[1] In Zurich, as elsewhere, the condition of success for the reformers was that they should carry the government with them. If, and only if, the rulers, regarded as representing the whole community, were behind them, could they hope for success. The Catholic states stood

---

[1] Blanke 379; F. Schmidt-Clausing, *Zwingli und die Kindertaufe*, Berliner Kirchen-Briefe no. 6 October 1962.

for religious aggression, and it was only by reformed communities that were united in religion and capable of self-defence, in which they might need every man available, that freedom could be maintained. In so far as the Anabaptists hindered this, they in fact forwarded the cause of the Counter-Reformation.

When the Swiss Anabaptists claimed that their teaching derived from that of Zwingli,[1] they were thinking primarily of the appeal to the text of the Bible, and the New Testament in particular. They, too, submitted themselves completely to the tyranny of the Book. There was truth itself, absolute, the word of God, inspired by the Holy Spirit, unmistakable to those who would read it right. It was also the Bible of the Middle Ages and much more, since it was independent of interpretation by Popes, councils, canon lawyers or university doctors. In one sense both Zwingli[2] and the radicals were uncritical about the Bible in that they made no attempt to go behind the received Hebrew and Greek texts to original manuscripts, and were not concerned that alternative readings were possible – quite the contrary, there was but one text.

This, however, was in Greek and Hebrew, and Zwingli readily admitted that translation was exceptionally difficult, but it was also feasible. There could not be two possible interpretations, and he who had found the right answer knew, through the Holy Spirit, that it was so. Thus *Schriftprinzip* was infallible provided it was upheld by linguistic knowledge, industrious study and prayer. It was not indeed like twentieth century 'fundamentalism' (an unhelpful word) since it implied a great deal of ratiocination. Simple facts were of course taken as certain; the historical narrative of creation, the garden of Eden, the flood, the age of the patriarchs, the Old Testament miracles, were accepted without difficulty, or possibly even thought. All this was common to Lutherans, Zwinglians, Anabaptists and, with appropriate modifications, to the Catholics themselves. It explains, in fact, the demand for Bible reading and the necessity for sermons and exposition. Following Erasmus, it was hoped that the Bible in translation would be in the hands of all, but the illiterate farmer could not compare biblical passages and thus could be woefully misled unless guided by his pastor.

Much of the Old Testament and parts of the New Testament were written in poetical language which in its turn required training to understand and offered scope for argument and difference of opinion. But with thought, prayer and discussion, conclusions could be reached, and right ones too. Individuals received special enlightenment by divine intervention: Zwingli never doubted that the grace of understanding could be

[1] Zwingli admitted that 'they came from among us but were not of us' (1 John 2. 19). Bender, *Grebel* 81–3; Yoder *1*, 31, 33; Z IV, 208, VI i, 47; MQR xxxvii (1963), 142–61.
[2] C. Nagel, *Zwinglis Stellung zur Schrift* (Freiburg, 1896).

vouchsafed to very simple people, but that this had been the case would be demonstrated by the correspondence of their inward conviction with conclusions reached by those who arrived at certainty by ordered study. This may be where the divergence between Zwingli and the Anabaptists began. Both accepted the received text, and both agreed that tradition, the hierarchy and any human authorities, however ancient or eminent, must give way to the Word. The power of the Gospel, *vis Evangelii*, inspired both and caused each to lay great stress on the need for preaching. Yet for all his reverence for the sacred text, Zwingli, partly because of the Anabaptist challenge, applied his critical mind to its contents. He recognised that the Bible was not a handbook of ancient history. Historical events could be set down wrongly because they concerned the temporal only, and it was indispensable to differentiate between the temporal and the eternal in the Bible. The letter of the Gospels no less than the letter of the law could be misleading without considering the divine message as a whole. He himself could choose between the Gospel of St John, which was like unto the sun, and the Apocalypse, in which he found little comfort.

At the same time, he consistently maintained that the meaning of the Bible was perfectly clear if read by the guidance of the Holy Spirit in faith and love. This, he insisted, was just what his opponents did not do; their ignorance, malice, passion and contentiousness were evidence that they did not approach the Bible in the right way. Every factor – time, place, person, figures of speech – had to be taken into account; the word of the Bible was indeed authoritative, but authoritative only when properly understood.[1] Zwingli profoundly believed that he, by God's grace, understood it aright, while his opponents did not. Luther, Zwingli and the sectaries started from the same premises and came to different conclusions, and in the end the critical study of the Bible benefited from this.

Perhaps the Swiss brethren did a service to the Reformers by their narrow and uncompromising bibliolatry in that they forced Zwingli to modify his own earlier simple views. The combination of the publication of the Greek text of the New Testament when Greek was becoming a fashionable study, and the multiplication of vernacular translations of the Bible by the printing press, meant that a considerable number of people had relatively easy access to the infallible word. Who was to say what the inspired words meant in the 1520s – the Pope, bishops, ministers of religion, separate communities, governments, or any individual who believed himself to have received inward guidance? It was on this rock that the Reformed ship foundered and the crew took to lifeboats. The Catholics

[1] Z II, 76, 449; III, 319, 633, 670–1.

resisted placing the Bible in the hands of the masses as long as possible and solved, or partly solved, the problem of interpretation in their own authoritarian way, but this satisfied only those who accepted the primacy of Rome.

It was because access to a vernacular New Testament was possible after 1522 that a number of advanced thinkers then drew certain conclusions of their own of which the undesirability of infant baptism was the most publicised but not the most important. Like Luther, but much more so, they detached themselves from the government, politics and administration of the state.[1] They recognised its existence as an institution maintaining law and order, regulating merely human affairs, with which they were not concerned.[2] Their concern was with a new Christian society, a minority entering upon a new life of religion, a community needing no restraint that was not self-imposed, no laws but those of the Bible, and no machinery for their enforcement.[3] They were not anarchists, although they could be made to seem so. The kingdom of heaven and earth was close at hand here and now. Much more than Luther, who himself preached a certain aloofness from secular affairs, they were convinced that they were 'living in the last age of the world, on the very edge of time'.[4] They combined a sense of urgency with conviction, and were infuriated by Zwingli's caution, patience and waiting.

As part of their general policy of non-cooperation with the government of the day, they, like the later Quakers, with whom there are other parallels, declined to take an oath.[5] This was indeed a serious matter in the sixteenth century. The oath was an essential constituent of the cement that held a largely illiterate society together; it was the equivalent of the 'signature' or 'mark' of the modern world. Perjury, with its assumed certainty of divine punishment, supported by heavy temporal penalties, was abhorred. Without the public oath, indispensable in any court of justice, a great deal of the ordinary daily administration of public affairs would break down.[6] Zwingli had no doubt that an oath for the glory of God and neighbourly love was lawful. In the universities, the oath was in many respects the equivalent of the modern examination. It was the basis or normal accompaniment of every formal contract. The Swiss Confederation itself was traditionally dated from the famous oath-taking of 1291, and

---

[1] Luther thought that intervention by ministers of religion in secular affairs should be limited only to matters of the conscience, a qualification capable of considerable extension.

[2] Muralt *Glaube*, 45; Blanke *3*, 83; Klassen, 172–3.

[3] Z IV, 172 'das kein oberkeit sin sölle'.

[4] Muralt *Glaube*, 14; E. G. Rupp *The Righteousness of God* (London, 1953), 10. It was a little less true of Switzerland than of Germany.

[5] Relying on Matthew 5. 34, James 5. 12. Z VI, i, 154–5.

[6] Zwingli put this neatly in 1527. Z VI i, 144. 'Iusiurandum autem tolle – iam omnem ordinem solvisti.' Cf. v, 97–8, VI i, 229–31.

after 1481 quinquennial meetings to renew the Federal bond were regarded as indispensable.[1]

Similar difficulties arose when the Bible command 'thou shalt not kill' was strictly and literally applied. It meant that the Anabaptists refused to undertake military service of any kind.[2] This was of very great significance in sixteenth century Switzerland. There was no paid standing army, and for that matter no regular police force either. Every man looked to his own defence and was expected to appear armed when called upon by the government, ordained clergy alone being exempt. The soldier was the guarantor of public order and corporate independence; every one knew that any relaxation of military preparedness would mean domination from outside. The walls of the city must be guarded according to a set pattern. There was a state armoury and cannon provided from public funds, and regular cross-bow practice and competitive shooting matches were encouraged. Every male was liable to military service; fighting and warfare were normal and expected masculine duties for which boys were trained from an early age. For a man to refuse military service was, in effect, to renounce citizenship: it could easily be represented as leaving to others an indispensable duty, and was thus resented.

Similarly, any attempts to avoid payment of tithes or interest as well as to escape normal civic responsibilities were greatly disliked. Among the reasons for the unpopularity of the Catholic hierarchy had been their claim to be judged only in their own law courts and by their own law, together with exemption from taxation. In a sense this was just what the radicals wanted also. Not only was their code of law the Bible, a position with which Zwingli could sympathise, but for them also it was not a complete and final revelation but rather a source of inspiration and guidance. The Holy Spirit could, and did, bring the meaning of the Word to the hearts of the true believers, and so guided they could not be wrong. It was an exaggeration of what Zwingli himself had said,[3] with entirely unacceptable overtones. If a new revelation was granted, earlier opinions and promises could be repudiated: 'We stood still', they said, 'until God bade us do otherwise'.

Their church was one of true believers only, whereas for Zwingli the visible church on earth contained believers and unbelievers, convinced and indifferents, wheat and tares, side by side.[4] The elect were without sin

[1] W. E. Rappard, *Du renouvellement des pactes confédéraux* (Zürich, 1944), 64.
[2] H. S. Bender, 'The Pacifism of the sixteenth century Anabaptists' MQR xxx (1956), 5–18. J. M. Stayer, *Anabaptists and the Sword* (Lawrence, Kansas, 1973) 73–90.
[3] Z 1, 558, 559. 'Der geist gottes uss der geschryfft urteilt selbst... Ich verston die geschrifft nit anders, dann wie sy sich selbst durch den geist gottes usslegt; bdarff keins menschlichen urteils.' Cf. Z II, 784, 799. Zwingli also pointed out that 'Geist' was used by them not only as an argument against their opponents but also to cover up a great deal of internal bitterness, rivalry and disagreement. [4] Z III, 255.

7-2

and it was therefore indispensable to expel the sinner from their midst. Hence the Anabaptists brought back excommunication, the ban, and used it readily. Any who failed to live according to the Gospel and to their literal interpretation of it must be expelled from the gathered exclusive suffering church of the believers. They laid great stress on this, but its practical application was not always edifying. Logic, scholarship, letters, the world of the intellect, they repudiated utterly; like Luther,[1] but much more so, they condemned recourse to reason.

They were often reproached with communism because, within their own closed circle they were prepared to share possessions in imitation of the primitive church where they had 'all things in common' (Acts 2. 44; 4. 32). It was, however, more the expression of a principle than a way of life; they respected the property of others and conformed to the external standards of the day in this respect as in many others.[2] That worldly goods should be used or shared for the common benefit was acceptable to Erasmus, Melanchthon and Zwingli[3] alike, but this was far removed from general communism. There were indeed, after Zwingli's time and outside Switzerland, more explicitly communist groups, but with them we are not here concerned. It was events in Zurich which first drew attention to the question of adult or believers' baptism and its implications.

In Zurich it was possible in 1522 for thoughtful literates, clergy and laity, to discuss among themselves the newest ideas; they knew of Karlstadt's differences with Luther, Zwingli's *Schlussreden*, and above all had the recently released text of the New Testament. One group of such met in the Rennweg at the house of Klaus Hottinger, the enthusiast who, along with Hans Ockenfuss, had landed himself in trouble over the Stadelhofen crucifix. They included a cripple on crutches, Andreas Castelberger from the Graubünden who had been employed as a colporteur between Glarus, Einsiedeln and Basle and who now read and commented on the Epistle to the Romans with marked independence of thought. His Bible class included several intelligent laymen such as Heinrich Aberli, Lorenz Hochrütiner and Bartlime Pur, who were to be vocal enough later.[4]

---

[1] Luther subordinated reason to faith only where scriptural evidence was plain. He always remained a university professor intensely concerned with education who was almost as much a rationalist as Zwingli and who interpreted *sola scriptura* much more liberally than his 'left-wing' opponents.

[2] P. T. Klassen, *The economics of Anabaptism 1525–60* (The Hague, 1964), 28–32; Bender, *Grebel*, 254 n. 9. Echoes of the controversy remained in Art. 38 of the Anglican thirty-nine articles (1562): 'The riches and goods of Christians are not common, as touching the right, title, and possession of the same, as certain Anabaptists do falsely boast.'

[3] Z VI i, 85: 'En tibi, ut publica velint esse omnia! Perditi homines mediocrium bona communia volunt esse, sua vero, si quae habent, nulltaenus; si nulla habent, sic communia faciunt omnia: laborem partiuntur aliis, ipsi, ne nihil faciant, ocium colunt, deinde in commune edunt.'

[4] Egli *1*, 276–8 (No. 623); Goeters, *Vorgeschichte*, 254–5.

Another convinced biblicist was Simon Stumpf,[1] the ex-monk from south Germany, parish priest of Höngg. One of Zwingli's earliest supporters and one of the first priests to marry, he had protested against payment of tithe to his patron, the Abbot of Wettingen, and had supported the plea for the abolition of the mass at the second Zurich disputation. He now began to preach in somewhat vague fashion that only those who knew themselves to be free from sin formed a true Christian brotherhood from which others should be excluded. He was supported by Felix Mantz,[2] a scholarly priest, son of a canon of the Great Minster.

They were joined before 1522 by the most attractive and influential of all the young Zurich radicals, Conrad Grebel.[3] Son of a renowned patrician family, educated like Zwingli at Vienna and Basle, he had been brought up in an atmosphere of luxury and refinement, became a humanist admirer of Erasmus and was a close friend of Vadian, to whom his sister was married. In 1522–3 he actively supported Zwingli in Zurich, but support turned to opposition before the year was out, and he was soon to be found among Zwingli's ablest and most bitter critics. After the Zurich disputations, particularly the second,[4] at which he had supported Zwingli, he was deeply disappointed. Nothing, it seemed, was to be done; mass was still allowed to be said, and the council had not undertaken the 'cleansing' of the churches, so urgently necessary. Zwingli had thus come to be numbered among the false prophets after having set his earlier followers

---

[1] His dishonesty and his violent sermons, including the advocacy of the elimination of all Catholic priests, brought about his imprisonment and his expulsion from Zurich territory on 23 December 1523. He was flogged at Lucerne in March 1524, reappeared in Zurich in 1527 and moved thence to Ulm. He was the most persistent of those who complained of Zwingli's 'go-slow' tactics. Egli *1*, 114, 178, 179, 190, 540 (Nos. 326, 341, 446, 463, 1167); Z VI i, 33 n. 3; VII, 195 n. 1; VIII, 133 n. 2; Wyss 24, 28 n. 2; ZWA IV, 321–9.

[2] c. 1500–1527. He learnt Hebrew, as did Zwingli, from Andrew Böschenstein and early joined Grebel in extreme biblicism and then opposed child baptism actively. He drew up a protest to the Zurich council on behalf of his fellow Anabaptists towards the end of 1524 (this is usually but wrongly attributed to Grebel. Bender, *Grebel* 129–30; but see ZWA IX, 139 and Muralt/Schmid 23–8, no. 16). He was imprisoned in February 1525 along with Blaurock, was released on payment of costs, but again imprisoned, and renewed his debate with Zwingli in March. He managed to escape to Chur but was sent back to Zurich on 18 July 1525, and was imprisoned there 18 July–7 October. By then his teaching was regarded by the government as socially and politically subversive; he was again in prison from 8 November 1525 to 21 March 1526, and finally from 13 December 1526 to his death on 5 January 1527. He had become violently opposed to Zwingli in 1525 under the influence of Blaurock; he was given every opportunity to state his case: juridically and by all contemporary standards his execution was justified, however mistaken. Muralt/Schmid 47, 73, 93, 217; Clasen, *Anabaptism*, 172, MQR 36 (1962) 76–87. The biography by Krajewski is sympathetic but slight.

[3] 1497–1526. Bender, *Grebel* is a favourable, almost enthusiastic account, which needs some correction. K. Keller-Escher, *Die Familie Grebel* (Frauenfeld, 1884), 54–8; Z VII, 62 n. 1; Z II, 692 n. 8; Wyss, 14 n. 1. MQR 26 (1952), 126–30.

[4] Goeters, *Vorgeschichte*, 278; Yoder *1*, 23.

on the right path.[1] The breach, for Grebel, was complete by December 1523, when in a letter to Vadian he wrote of his former friend and mentor : 'anyone who thinks, believes or says that Zwingli is performing his duty as a pastor, believes and says what is ungodly'.[2] He was associated with yet another critic in a hurry, William Röubli,[3] the incumbent at Wytikon with pastoral duties at Zollikon, both then villages five miles from Zurich and dependencies upon the Great Minster to which tithe was paid. He was the first priest in Switzerland to be publicly married and perhaps the first to preach in the pulpit against infant baptism. Exactly when and how controversy about this particular matter came to overshadow others in Zurich cannot be traced with complete chronological exactitude. Among Zwingli's early adherents was the scholar and priest Ludwig Hätzer (c. 1500–1529).[4] This young man eagerly supported the new trends, was particularly active in the opposition to images in the churches, and contributed to literature attacking them. He was prominent at the second Zurich disputation in October 1523, of which he wrote an account. Soon after it he declared his conviction that infant baptism could not be upheld from the Bible, and thus was unable to remain in Zurich. At Basle he translated some of Oecolampadius' writings into German; he moved to Strassburg and preached and wrote in Augsburg, where he had a small separatist congregation of supporters and was suspected of Unitarianism. On 4 February 1529 he was executed in Constance on a charge, for which there was only rather scanty evidence, of bigamy or adultery.[5] There were others like him, literate scholars, who continued the struggle.

Zwingli's attention was early drawn to the urgency of the Baptist claims

[1] Goeters, Vorgeschichte, 278; Yoder 1, 23.
[2] Vad. Br. III, 50 (no. 374). 'Qui Zinlium ex officio pastoris agere putat, credit vel dicit, impie putat, credit et dicit. Williams, 96 'Zwingli, the herald of the Word, has cast down the Word, has trodden it underfoot, and has brought it into captivity.'
[3] c. 1484–1559. Röubli or Reublin (with other variants) is a somewhat elusive figure. Little is certain about his early career except that he was a priest from Rottenburg (on the Neckar) and was in Basle in 1521. There he eagerly adopted Zwingli's teaching and was removed from St Alban's because of his preaching against fasting and the veneration of relics. His marriage in April 1523 to Adelheit Leeman of Hirslanden was the subject of much comment. He was imprisoned in Zurich in 1524 and expelled in 1525. He then moved to Waldshut, Strassburg, Reutlingen, Austerlitz and other places in south Germany. Possibly he was reconciled to the Catholic church before his death. Z II, 462; VII, 509 n. 6; IX, 210 n. 3; ML III, 477–81; ME IV, 304–7; Wyss, 20, 25; Yoder 1, 54; Wackernagel, Basel, III, 329; Goeters, Vorgeschichte, 247, 255–6; Goeters Ludwig Hätzer (c. 1500 bis 1529) Spiritualist und Antitrinitarier (Karlsruhe, 1955, also in QFRG Bd. 25), 31–2, 49.
[4] Goeters Hätzer (esp. 46–54) is reliable and corrects F. L. Weis, The life and teachings of Ludwig Hetzer (Dorchester, Mass., 1930); ME II, 621–6; MQR XX. (1955), 251–62, XXXIV. (1960), 20–36; ZKG 70 (1959), 218–30, 344–5; Rupp, Patterns of Reformation (London, 1969), 24; Bergsten, 161. Zwingli recommended his writings; Z II, 654, 668, VIII, 200. E. M. Wilbur, A History of Unitarianism (Cambridge, Mass., 1946), 30–1; ZWA XIII, 580–90.
[5] H. C. Rublack, Die Einführung der Reformation in Konstanz (Gütersloh, 1971), 168–71. H. Buck, Die Anfänge der Konstanzer Reformationsprozesse (Tübingen, 1964), 305–21.

by his friend Balthasar Hubmaier (c. 1480–1528), known from his birth-place at Friedberg (near Augsburg) as Pacimontanus.[1] A gifted youth, he had made his way to the University of Freiburg, where he was helped by Eck, earned money by grammar school teaching at Schaffhausen, and was brought by Eck to Ingolstadt, where he proceeded D.D. in 1512 and was made professor of theology. A Catholic priest and a humanist, he obtained a church appointment at Regensburg in 1516, where his anti-Semitic sermons made him notorious. The mob burnt the synagogue, and a chapel was built in its place, complete with a much-frequented miracle-working statue of the Madonna, whose cult the young priest actively en-couraged. In 1521 he became parish priest at Waldshut, which brought him into contact with the humanist group at Basle, and so with Beatus Rhenanus, Oecolampadius, Vadian and Zwingli. His later career is characteristic of many others. He early accepted the reformed teaching, visited Zwingli at Zurich, took a prominent part in the second disputation of 26–8 October 1523,[2] and came into contact with Grebel. Waldshut, whither he returned, was administered by the Austrian government at Ensisheim, and was in many respects a key position. Its location on the Rhine and close to the Aar made it valuable for both Berne and Zurich. There Hubmaier was concerned to secure not only freedom for the Gospel, but also, if possible, emancipation of the city from imperial domination; and in the spring of 1524 it looked as if he would succeed. He published eighteen theses closely following the Zwinglian model, denouncing the obligatory Lenten fast, supporting the marriage of priests, and rejecting the mass as a sacrifice along with the Catholic teaching on purgatory.[3] In all this he secured sufficient support from the council of Waldshut to ensure that he was not handed over to the officers of the Bishop of Con-stance to stand trial as a heretic.

Stühlingen, where the German Peasants' War started, was too close to Waldshut for Hubmaier not to become involved, and it was even alleged that he was responsible for the famous twelve demands.[4] He had ceased to be a close follower and admirer of Zwingli, and had become acquainted with Karlstadt, Hätzer and Müntzer. He now openly agreed with those who rejected child baptism and told Oecolampadius so, moved thereto,

[1] Z IV, 577–83. Bergsten is admirable; *Balthasar Hubmaier Schriften*, hg. v. G. Westin u. T. Bergsten (Gütersloh, 1962) QFRG XXIX. Older works include J. Loserth, *Doktor Balthasar Hubmaier und die Anfänge der Wiedertaufe in Mähren* (Brünn, 1893); H. C. Vedder, *Balthasar Hübmaier. The leader of the Anabaptists* (New York/London, 1905); C. D. Sachsse, *D. Balthasar Hübmaier als Theolog* (Berlin, 1914); W. Mau, *Balthasar Hubmaier* (Berlin, 1912); J. H. Yoder, 'Balthasar Hubmaier and the beginnings of Swiss Anabaptism, MQR 33 (1959) 5–17 (derived in part from Yoder 2). Cf. MQR 45 (1971), 123–44.
[2] Z II, 716–62, 786–8. See above, 131–3.   [3] Hubmaier, *Schriften*, 71–4.
[4] See below, 201 n. 1.

he insisted, by the teaching of Christ, by truth and his own conscience.[1] On Easter Sunday 1525 he allowed himself to be baptised, along with some sixty others, by the indefatigable Röubli.[2] Waldshut, however, was no longer safe after Zurich volunteers had been withdrawn, and he was forced to leave, going to Basle and then to Zurich. He was not present at the debate of 6–8 November but was discussing baptism with Jud, Myconius and Hofmeister in December. He preached Anabaptism from the Fraumünster pulpit, was imprisoned and perhaps tortured in the Wellenberg, publicly recanted some of his beliefs and was expelled. Back at Augsburg he taught Latin and Greek and met Hans Denck,[3] but was forced to leave in 1526, and set up a 'church' or congregation at Nicolsburg (Mikulov) in Moravia. In 1528 he was apprehended by Austrian agents, taken to Vienna and burnt as a heretic on 10 March.[4]

Hubmaier was a significant figure chiefly because of his writings which attracted the hostile attention of Zwingli, Oecolampadius and Fabri. He was an Anabaptist in so far as he never doubted that faith must precede baptism which was meaningless without it, but in every other respect his opinions were moderately reconcilable with those of the Reformers, in general if not in particular. He was not prepared to reject civil authority as so many Anabaptists did, and it is not entirely fair to class him with them. If he had lived he might have formed a group of Hubmaierians, and his name was sufficiently weighty to receive condemnation along with Luther and Zwingli by the Council of Trent. He is one of the most sympathetic and human figures among a sometimes unreasonable group, and there is a touch of Cranmer about him.

It was not until 1524 that the discussions about baptism became matters of public interest and concern in Zurich. Zwingli had secured freedom for Gospel preaching and a measure of agreement about fasting, images and

[1] Staehelin, *Briefe* I, 341–3; *Das theologische Lebenswerk Johannes Oekolampads* (Leipzig, 1939), 378–9.

[2] Muralt/Schmid, 391–2 (no. 404).

[3] Hans Denck (c. 1500–27) was a Bavarian who studied at Ingolstadt (B.A. 1519) and Basle, became proof-reader for Cratander and Curio, then headmaster of St Sebald's school, Nuremberg until 1525. In 1526 he became an Anabaptist and was in touch with Müntzer. Then he moved to Augsburg, St Gall, Strassburg, Worms (where he collaborated with Hätzer in translating the Old Testament Prophets) and finally to Basle, where he died. He has been described as the 'abbot of the Anabaptists', but there is much that is uncertain about his movements and his teaching, and it is unsafe to count him as more than a fringe adherent to the Anabaptist movement. ZKG XII (1890), 452–93; *Hans Denck, Schriften*, hg. v. G. Baring u. W. Fellmann; QFRG XXIV (Gütersloh, 1955, 1956, 1960); F. L. Weis, *The life, teachings and works of Johannes Denck* (Strassburg, 1924); ML I, 401–3; MQR 31 (1957), 227–59, 46 (1972) 245, 47 (1973), 327–38; Muralt/Fast, 403 n. 5; Z VIII, 303 n. 22.

[4] For his writings see below p. 192. Kessler inserted a striking appreciation in Sabbata, 106–7, 284. Näf *Vadian*, II, 184; *Vad. Br.*, 240 (No. 92); Z VIII, 470; MQR, 31 (1957) 227–59, 33 (1959) 12–17; Williams 140–1; Yoder I 79–89, 173; *Briefwechsel des Beatus Rhenanus* hg. v. A. Horawitz u. K. Hartfelder (Leipzig, 1886), 263 (No. 192).

the mass – all this after public discussion and with the approval of the authorities. After Christmas 1523 the activists, now led by Grebel, were calling for something which would clearly demonstrate that positive action should soon follow. How their disappointment was linked to separatism and how Zwingli spared no effort to show that they were utterly mistaken is a curiously involved story.[1] Possibly it was the preaching of Röubli that was responsible for starting off direct trouble. In August 1524 two farmers, Hans Huber and Rudolf Maler, from his parish of Wytikon,[2] refused to bring their infants to church for baptism.[3] It was this action that posed a problem for the authorities.[4] Attendance at church was expected of all citizens; the unbaptised could not be admitted, and this could be extended to the parents of unbaptised children for whom they were responsible. It was an act of defiance, and soon there were others who copied it. Further instances of neglect of baptism were reported from Zollikon, involving Max Bosshart, Rüdi Thomann, Leonhard Bleuler and others,[5] some of well-known families. Whether or not baptism was essential for salvation, these farmers were defying authority, as was made apparent on 11 August when the council issued an order that any unbaptised children should be brought for baptism forthwith.[6] Discussions had in fact been taking place between Zwingli, Jud, Engelhard and Myconius on one side, and Grebel, Brötli and Castelberger on the other, from October onwards,[7] so that direct action cannot have been entirely surprising. Provocative acts occurred, like the interruption of sermons,[8] or the breaking of the font in Zollikon church. The offenders and their supporters were summoned to the Rathaus on 12 January and required to attend a public discussion of baptism there on 17 January. This, the first of its kind, duly took place: Zwingli dominated the proceedings and dealt effectively with points raised from the Scriptures by Mantz, Röubli, Castelberger, Blaurock,[9] Brötli,

[1] Above 167 n. 2. Blanke *1, 2* and *3*; E. Egli, *Die Zürcher Wiedertäufer zur Reformationszeit* (Zürich, 1878) has worn well and can still be consulted with profit. Egli realised that Bullinger's account printed in March 1560 was more propaganda than history as the full title indicates – *Der Widertöufferen vrsprung* etc. Bullinger also wrote 'von dem vnuerschampte fräfel, ergerlichem verwyrren, vnnd vnwarhafftem leeren, der selbsgesandten Widertöuffern' (Zürich, 1531). H. Fast, *Heinrich Bullinger und die Täufer: ein Beitrag zur Historiographie und Theologie im 16. Jahrhundert* (Weierhof, Pfalz, 1959); C. Bergmann, 'Die Täuferbewegung im Kanton Zürich bis 1660', QSRG 2, 1–22 (Leipzig, 1916); W. Koehler, *Die Zürcher Täufer* (Ludwigshafen, 1925); ZWA VI, 65–85; Goeters, *Vorgeschichte*, 239–81.
[2] P. Guyer, *Die Bevölkerung Zollikons im Mittelalter und in der Neuzeit* (Zürich, 1946), 37–9; Bender *Grebel* 124.   [3] Muralt/Schmid, 10 (no. 11).
[4] And indirectly led to Zwingli's *Wer Ursache gebe zu Aufruhr* in December. See above, 117–21.
[5] Blanke *1*, 29–30; Muralt/Schmid, 38–40 (Nos. 29–31).
[6] 'Alssdann ettlich verirtter meinung redend, man sölle die jungen kind nit touffen, biss die zuo iren tagen kommen'. Muralt/Schmid 11 (No. 12); Egli *1*, 270 (No. 618).
[7] Z VIII, 261–2; Bender, *Grebel* 128.
[8] Jacob Hottinger interrupted a sermon by Megander on 12 January 1525. Muralt/Schmid 33 (No. 23). Blaurock was equally violent.   [9] *Handbuch*, 459.

Hätzer and Grebel, although the latter claimed with some justice that he and his friends were denied full scope for discussion.[1] Their very volubility told against them, and the temper of the meeting was somewhat hostile. The outcome was that Zwingli was adjudged to have answered all objections effectively, and next day, 18 January, came orders that all unbaptised children must be brought for baptism within the next eight days under penalty of expulsion from Zurich. Unauthorised preaching or illicit gatherings for worship must cease, and the font in Zollikon church was to be repaired and restored to its place.[2]

It was in the light of this decision that a small group of dissenters gathered on 21 January at a house in the Neugasse owned by Felix Mantz's mother, to consider their next move.[3] Prominent among those present were Grebel and the blue-coated Blaurock.[4] The party joined together in prayer, after which Blaurock stood up and called upon Grebel, the leader of the group, to baptise him. This Grebel did, and then Blaurock baptised fifteen others.[5] This, 'the first adult baptism' on record, was not total immersion, but a substantial wetting on a January day. There was likely

[1] Bender, *Grebel* 129.

[2] Muralt/Schmid 35–6 (No. 26); Z IV, 162.

[3] Krajewski, 38, 75–7; G. F. Herschberger, *The Recovery of the Baptist Vision*[2] (Scottdale, Pa., 1962) 61. Blanke, *2*, 76, MQR XXVII (1953), 17, and XXXI (1957) 220 rather too precise and definite. The narrative is in part drawn from *Die älteste Chronik der Hutterischen Brüder. Ein Sprachdenkmal aus frühneuhochdeutscher Zeit* hg. v. A. J. F. Zieglschmid (Ithaca, N.Y., 1943), a late and suspect (esp. p. 47) source which was too readily accepted by Blanke and G. H. Williams. The editor's notes are valuable.

[4] Georg (Jörg) vom Haus Jakob (also Cajakob and other variants, c. 1492–1529), known as Blaurock from the coloured coat which he almost always wore, was a married ex-priest of good peasant family from Bonaduz (near Chur, Graubünden). In 1524 he came to Zurich, where he soon became the most prominent and outspoken of the Anabaptists. At Zollikon he tried unsuccessfully to force his way into the pulpit with the words 'du bist nit, sunder ich (bin) gesandt, ze predigen' (Egli *1*, 285 (No. 636)), and later managed to do so at Hinwil. He may have been present at the first Anabaptist debate before the Zurich council in January 1525, and was so persistent in his preaching that at the end of March the Council ordered his repatriation together with that of his wife. On the whole, he preferred preaching in villages to preaching in towns, and wandered from place to place between Chur, Hinwil and Schaffhausen, baptising adults all the time. He returned to Zurich and was imprisoned in the Wellenberg on 18 November 1525. After his release he persisted in haunting the Zurich streets and preaching. In January 1527 he was in prison, flogged at the Niederdorf Gate, once more expelled, and threatened with drowning if he returned. He then moved into the Tyrol, where he made many converts, appeared at Berne in January 1528 and at Basle in February 1529, and in April 1529 he was active in Appenzell. Soon afterwards he was captured by imperial agents at Klausen near Innsbruck, tortured and burnt as a heretic on 6 September. He was a huge man with sparkling eyes and jet black hair, much the most picturesque of the 'three Anabaptist martyrs', Grebel, Mantz, Blaurock. Z IV, 168–9, 288 n. 11; Wyss, 78 n. 2; ML I, 227–34; ME I, 354–9; O. Vasella, 'Von den Anfängen der bündnerischen Täuferbewegung (Jörg Blaurock), ZSG XIX (1939), 165–84 shows the close connection of the Bundner Anabaptists with Zurich. J. A. Moore, *Der starke Jörg* (Kassel, 1955) is a brief popular account.

[5] Yoder *1*, 41; Bender, *Grebel*, 137; Blanke *1*, 21–2; Z VI i, 40 n. 1; (for dates) Williams, 122.

enough a sense of urgency as well as of deliberate defiance.[1] For, at the same time, as Grebel must have known from his friends, Bürgermeister Röist[2] and the council were making an order, requiring Grebel and Mantz to abstain from further propaganda; while their associates, who were not citizens of Zurich, Röubli, now described as 'der pfaff' of Witikon, Brötli[3] of Zollikon, Hätzer and Castelberger, were required to leave Zurich territory within eight days.[4] It was a usual, but serious sentence, there was no obvious place of refuge and they must become men on the run.

On the next day, 22 January, Hans Oggenfuss, tailor of the then village of Stadelhofen, was hurrying with a new suit of clothes to Röubli. On his way, at the fountain or well (*Brunnen*) of Hirslanden, he met Brötli whom he knew as a former priest and an educated man, together with Fridli Schumacher. There he acted as witness to the baptism of the latter.[5]

Shortly afterwards, probably on the following day,[6] Grebel was present at another gathering, in Jacob Hottinger's house in Zollikon.[7] There he read from the New Testament and preached on the Last Supper and on baptism, following this by cutting up a small bread roll and distributing it with some local wine, each recipient promising henceforward to lead a Christian life.[8] This simple service was a further act of defiance, since no decision about the mass had yet been made.

[1] For Williams, 119, this was the critical moment: 'The first gathered church of sectarian "Protestantism" came into being precisely at that moment when a former priest in the home of a university-educated prophet of the new order received baptism on confession of sin from the hand of a layman, and when all present defended their action on the ground that the Christian conscience was no more beholden to the reforming magistrates and their divines than to priests and prelates.' This is rather extravagant, but it was clear after the first debate that they must try to form a separated community. Goeters, *Haetzer*, 53; Hershberger, 61.

[2] Egli *1*, 278 No. 624; Muralt/Schmid 34–6, Nos. 24–6.

[3] Johannes Brötli came, like Blaurock, from Graubünden, was at St Gall, at Basle in 1515, at Quarten in 1521, married in 1523, and was assistant preacher at Zollikon in 1524. After his expulsion from Zurich, he moved to Hallau, where he was burnt as a heretic in 1529. J. A. Moore, 'Johannes Brötli', *Baptist Quarterly* 15 (1953), 29–34; ML I, 275; ME I, 439.

[4] Muralt/Schmid, 35–6 (No. 26) (misprinted 1521). Castelberger ('Andreas auf den Stülzen') was allowed a temporary respite because of illness. Egli *1*, 279 (No. 629); Muralt/Schmid, 37 (No. 28).

[5] Egli *1*, 283 (No. 636); Williams, 123; Muralt/Schmid, 41–2 (No. 31) with a cautionary note; MQR xxvii (1953), 17–18.

[6] The details are derived from testimony taken on 7 February 1525 from a number of prisoners in the Wellenberg. These are on separate sheets of paper collected at E I. 7. 1 in StaZ, but the order and chronology are uncertain.

[7] Where Brötli was assistant minister and claimed to be the only rightful preacher. Blanke *1* (E.T.), 23; Blanke *3*, 77; Bender, *Grebel*, 136–8 and note 7.

[8] The exact chronology is again uncertain, and too much has been read into imperfect reports. Krajewski, 91; Bergsten, 313–14; Muralt/Schmid, 37–43 (Nos. 29, 31, 32); Yoder 2, 109, 110 (no. 36). It is straining the evidence to see in this spontaneous action 'the moment when the "Free Churches" were born and a new type of religious organisation created'. John C. Wenger, *Even unto death* (Richmond, Va., 1961), German text, *Die dritte Reformation* (Kassel, 1961) 19–20. Bender, *Grebel*, 264, argues that Hottinger was baptised in his own house on 5 February and that Grebel was not present.

There was another meeting in farmer Thomann's house in Zollikon, perhaps on 25 January, with Bosshart, Röubli, Jacob Hottinger, Brötli, another Thomann, Bruggbach (or Brubach), Mantz and Blaurock all present and assuredly not by accident.[1] In a markedly revivalist atmosphere combining fervour with conscious alarm at their own temerity Bruggbach and Hottinger were baptised, and a simple communion service followed, when Blaurock rose to say: 'He who believes that God has redeemed him through his death and rose-coloured blood, let him come and eat with me of the bread and drink with me of the wine.' Thomann was perturbed and did not participate; Bosshart was not baptised until the following day when Blaurock accepted his repentance as sufficient to warrant baptism.[2] For the whole of the week of 22–9 January there were similar incidents involving Brennwald, Schad, Roggenacker, Breitinger, Oggenfuss, Schuhmacher and Bleuler, and there was a report that eighty adults were baptised in Zollikon in three weeks.[3]

The requirement that all babies must be baptised was repeated on 1 February, and some who had failed to comply were arrested but allowed to return home only on a very large bail of 1,000 gulden.[4] Mantz and Blaurock were held in the Wellenberg prison, and 25 others were lodged in the former Augustinian monastery.[5] They were interviewed by Zwingli, Jud and Megander, and there was renewed disagreement about the nature of the baptism performed by the Apostles. Zwingli reported to the council the existence of a separate independent group administering baptism and communion.[6] In February and March there were several meetings for discussion; partly with the larger group, partly with Blaurock and Mantz separately. These, particularly that or those on 16 March and 20 March, are sometimes described as the second baptismal disputation,[7] but apart from the fact that really exact information is not easy to come by, they were different from the earlier debates of 1523. They were not in any sense 'public', they were not called by the Zurich Council (although held under its authority), no visitors from outside were invited, and there was no supposedly impartial chairman. The arguments ranged over the whole field of the sinless church, community of goods, the ban, tithes, interest, government, the workings of the spirit, all matters to which Zwingli was

---

[1] Geiser, 143. [2] Blanke, *1*, 25–9.
[3] Yoder, *1*, 47–8; Geiser, 143. Blanke, *1*, 41 counts 35, but (*1*, 54) speaks of 'at least eighty' baptisms in the week of March 8–15.
[4] Muralt, *Glaube*, 22. They paid costs and took an oath to keep the peace. The early Anabaptist converts or sympathisers were seldom really poor. P. Peachey, *Die soziale Herkunft der Schweizer Täufer in der Reformationszeit* (Weierhof, Pfalz, 1954); MQR xxviii (1954), 102–27.
[5] Muralt/Schmid, 47 (no. 37); Egli *1*, 282–6 (Nos. 636, 637); Blanke *1*, 43.
[6] Z IV, 162–3; Krajewski, 89–91.
[7] Williams, 126; Krajewski, 89–97; Koehler, *Zwingli*, 144.

to recur and all without positive conclusions.[1] Blaurock was his more than usual violent self and poured scorn on Zwingli personally; adult baptism was indispensable, anyone neglecting it remained a heathen, a conclusion scarcely likely to be acceptable to Zurich councillors. Even so, the worst that happened was that some were fined, others warned, and a few re-imprisoned and perhaps allowed to escape. Mantz was bound over and obliged to pay costs, Blaurock as a foreigner was expelled with ignominy; Grebel, Röubli and Brötli went into Thurgau or the neighbourhood of Schaffhausen where they had some success. Hans Hottinger, the night watchman who had been voluble in his accusations,[2] was dismissed from his post, and some who refused to come into line were expelled.

In spite of these indications of official disapproval and the threatened penalties, the new teaching spread with remarkable rapidity during the early months of 1525: adherents appeared in Grüningen, Waldshut, the Klettgau, Appenzell, St Gall, Schaffhausen, Basle, Berne, Chur, Constance and a number of Swabian towns. When a small group in Zurich drew attention to themselves by parading with ropes round their waists and willow rods in their hands, crying, 'Woe, woe to thee, Zurich', calling Zwingli 'The old dragon' and proclaiming that only forty days remained for repentance,[3] more positive measures were seen to be needed. It was no more possible for Zurich to ignore such men than it would be for a modern government to accept refusal to pay taxes, or an army commander to countenance disobedience to orders. It was a challenge which Zwingli had to face more than once. Blaurock was at least equally positive. His opponents were worse than the Pope, Zwingli was the real Antichrist, falsifying the words of the Bible to suit himself, a thief, a murderer, a heretic. Zwingli's answer was to insist that Blaurock, who was unable to read the Bible in Latin, let alone in the original tongues, was merely a crazy visionary. It was unfair to dismiss the enthusiast thus, just as Luther was equally unreasonable in dealing with the much abler Karlstadt.

The third and last, but the only one properly so called, of the debates on the subject of baptism took place in the Great Minster from Monday to Wednesday, 6–8 November.[4] Hubmaier, to his disappointment, was prevented from attending,[5] but Mantz, Grebel and Blaurock were eloquent for the cause. They were confronted by Zwingli, Jud and Megander as

---

[1] Z IV, 164–6.
[2] Muralt/Schmid, 57 (No. 47); Egli *1*, 291 (No. 655). He had stated that Zwingli had previously preached that children should not be baptised, a gross misrepresentation, and maintained that in asserting that God had called children to the font he had lied 'like a scoundrel, a coward and a heretic'.
[3] Rev. 12. 3. Blanke *1*, 68f; Bergsten 323; Z VI i, 43; Clasen, 119; Egli *1*, 352 (No. 748).
[4] Bullinger, *Ref.* I, 294–8; Stumpf *1*, 1, 284.   [5] Bergsten, 344–5; Sabbata, 150, 190.

disputants, with Vadian, Conrad Schmid and Joner as supporters. There was no serious exchange of views, for each side had by now taken up a position from which it could not be moved, and the meetings degenerated into uproar, each shouting abuse at the other.[1] Zwingli, with what Grebel described to his brother-in-law Vadian as devilish cunning,[2] put forward three propositions for debate – that Christian children were God's children, that baptism replaced circumcision, and that second baptism was unbiblical. Since both sides insisted that there could not be a second baptism, it is not surprising that orderly argument ceased. The only episode that caught notice was a rather heavy-handed piece of humour. 'Zwingli, I adjure you by the true and living God, tell me but one truth', called out one rustic. 'That I will', was the answer. 'You are the worst specimen of a trouble-making, discontented farmer that we've got in the neighbourhood.'[3] There was general applause, and the whole matter was left, as was intended, to the discretion of the council. After this no compromise was possible.

The councillors were now satisfied and soon dealt more severely with wild men who shouted in the streets, 'Zion, Zion, freedom for Jerusalem'. When Hubmaier arrived, he was arrested,[4] broke down under questioning by Jud, Hofmeister, Myconius and Zwingli, four formidable inquisitors, admitted his errors, then recovered his nerve and went back on his promises. He was re-arrested, tortured, again agreed to recant and preach the Bible in Zwinglian fashion only, and was allowed to leave for Constance. Here he renewed his attacks on Zwingli before moving, ill, hunted and poverty-stricken, into the kingdom of Bohemia, from whence he went to his death.[5] Other dissenters were lodged in the Wellenberg prison for an indefinite time, refused visits by friends and given only bread and water. Those, like Michael Sattler, who were not natives, were expelled.[6] Grebel, Mantz and Blaurock re-appeared in March 1526 to renew their attacks on Zwingli as a 'false prophet'[7] and to repeat their demands for separatist worship. Threats were clearly as useless as arguments with these shameless, disorderly, self-advertising agitators, who were again taken into custody, where they could rest for all the council cared.[8] Continued dis-

[1] Egli, *Zürcher Wiedertäufer*, 47; Krajewski, 119–20; Yoder *1*, 73–9. [2] Geiser, 134.
[3] Bullinger, *Der Widertöufferen Vrsprung* (Zürich, 1560), 11; Egli, *Zürcher Wiedertäufer*, 47. Fast, *Heinrich Bullinger und die Täufer* (Weierhof, 1959), 115; Muralt/Fast, 612–13.
[4] Muralt/Schmid, 159/160 (No. 157).   [5] See above p. 180 and n. 4.
[6] 'so lang und vil Gott ein benüegen hat und mine Herren guot bedunkt' Egli *1*, 406 (No. 863). Egli *1*, 444–5 (No. 934).
[7] Z VIII, 542.
[8] 'Man wolle sie also im thurm ersterben und fulen lassen.' Egli *1*, 444 (No. 934); Egli, *Zürcher Wiedertäufer*, 55; Bender, *Grebel*, 156; Bergsten, 390–1; Muralt/Schmid, 159–60. Much is made of this sentence – they were in fact soon outside: apparently a window was left open and a supporter threw them a rope.

obedience to government orders and manifestations of sedition and religious mania could not be tolerated any longer. On 7 March 1526 came the notorious mandate that 'henceforth in our city, territory and neighbourhood, no man, woman, or maiden shall rebaptise another; whoever shall do so shall be arrested by authority and after proper judgement shall without appeal[1] be put to death by drowning.' This was ordered to be read in the three principal churches on Sundays, and to be publicly exhibited and announced by the local government authorities.[2]

This order has frequently been quoted as an example of the singular intolerance of the age, which indeed it is. Zwingli, technically, had nothing to do with it, but there is nowhere any indication that he disapproved.[3] The death penalty in all countries in the sixteenth century was inevitably used as almost the only ultimate sanction available. There was little respect for human life as such. Compared with the criminal justice of France or England, or with the torture of suspected heretics by the Inquisition, or the burning of Protestants in Catholic states (and vice versa), the punishment was mild, and was, in fact, inflicted only four times in all. The Anabaptists tended to rejoice in martyrdom[4] and to neglect opportunities to leave quietly when these were offered.

The situation in 1526 was not a happy one. Zurich was isolated, and the Catholics were gathering for the final overthrow of the heretics at Baden. There had been trouble with recalcitrants in the countryside, especially the Grüningen district, and it was necessary that the government should assert its authority. On 5 January 1527 a small boat carrying Felix Mantz put out from the left bank of the Limmat in sight of the Zurich Rathaus. He had taken a solemn oath to leave Zurich territory and not to baptise any more, but he had deliberately returned in spite of warning and continued the practice, thus becoming an avowed perjurer and a notorious disturber of the peace. Now, in the presence of witnesses, who marvelled at his constancy, his hands were tied and he was lowered into the clear

---

[1] 'on alle gnad ertrencken lassen'. Often translated 'without mercy', rather unfairly.
[2] Egli *1*, 445 (No. 936) cf. 444–5 (Nos. 934, 935, 936, 937). Muralt/Schmid, 180–1 (no. 172).
  'Alss dann unser herrenn bürgermeister, rat und der gross rat, so man nempt die tzweihundert der statt Zürich, sich ein gůt zythart mit sonderm ernst geflyssen, die verfürten, irrigen wydertöffer von iro irsall abzestellen etc., so aber iro ettlich alss verstopfft wyder iro eyd, glüpt und zůsagungen beharret und gmeinem regiment und oberkeit zů nachteil und zerstörung gmeins nutzes und rechten cristenlichen wesens ungehorsam erschinen, sind ir ettlich, männer, frowen und tochtern, in unser herrenn schwäre straff und gfengnuss gelegt. Und ist daruff der genanten unser herrenn ernstlich gepott, geheiss und warnung, dass weder in ir stat, land und gepietten hinfür niemants, männer, frowen noch dochtern, denn andern wyderumm touffen sölle. Dann wer also wyter den andern touffte, zu dem wurdent unser herrenn gryffen und nach iro jetz erkantter urtel on alle gnad ertrencken lassen. Darnach wisse sich menglich zů verhütten und dass im selbs zů sinem tod niemants ursach gebe.'
[3] Yoder *2*, 141; Bender, *Grebel* 269 n. 91.
[4] Cf. Muralt/Schmid, 78–9 (No. 70)

water by a rope and left to drown.[1] He died willingly and impressively; his death was perhaps more important than his life. His property was confiscated for the state. He was thus the first Baptist martyr;[2] three others followed later,[3] after which any other notorious adherents fled or were expelled, and there was then peace in Zurich. Melanchthon indicated his approval, and letters of warning against Blaurock, Denck and Hätzer went to Berne, Basle, Augsburg, Constance, St Gall and Appenzell.[4]

All this had obliged Zwingli to consider carefully baptismal doctrine and the claims of his opponents. The subject of baptism, bristling with difficulties and contradictions, was both theological and practical. Abstractions such as sin, faith and grace were very much involved, as well as the simple physical action of sprinkling with, or dipping in, water. It is true that the visible act of baptism was not the chief matter in the controversy with the Anabaptists and that the meaning of the church, the operation of the Holy Spirit, relations of church and state, civil disobedience and the right to worship freely were also involved, but it was round the act of baptism that the dispute centred. Traditionally baptism was a sacrament, a means of grace, indispensable for release from original sin inherent in man since the fall of Adam. In some ways popular thought was crude; an infant must be brought into contact with water and the baptismal formula pronounced. There was an element of magic about it – the child who died soon after the words were spoken was, as most believed, assured of eternal salvation, while if the words and action were lacking to his twin brother, there was the contrary presumption. The one was a member of the church outside which there was no salvation, the other was not. Hence the urgent instructions to midwives upon how to act in an emergency; hence the invariably early presentation at the font.

This view of a sacrament – *opus operatum* – Zwingli early rejected; water could not wash away sin and was not indispensable, and the trinitarian formula might vary; baptism could be in the name of Christ alone.[5] God saved whom he would irrespective of words and actions, and the souls of virtuous heathen who had lived before – and by implication after – the

[1] Before his death he wrote a pathetic but unrepentant letter to his brethren, and a well known hymn. Egli *1*, 529–30 (No. 1109); Bullinger, *Ref.*, I, 381–2; Muralt/Schmid 218–21 (No. 201, 902) 224–6 (No. 204). The precise place is indicated in S. Vögelin, *Das alte Zürich* (Zürich, 1878) I, 475.   [2] Williams, 146; Rupp, *Patterns of Reformation*, 353.
[3] Jacob Falk of Gossau, Heini Reimann of Grüninger Amt (1528) and Konrad Winkler of Wasserberg (1530).
[4] ZWA VI (1934), 65–85, an article by von Muralt criticising (with many misprints indicating imperfect knowledge of English) articles by J. Horsch in MQR, summarised in *Goschen College Record, Review supplement* XXVII. (1926), 1–14. Cf. MQR XLIII, 98.
[5] Z III, 771–3 and notes; Z IV, 268. Zwingli acutely pointed out that the formula used by the Greek church differed from that of the west but was fully as comprehensive: 'in the name of' was the equivalent of 'by the grace or power of'. As in the discussion of the mass, he insisted that words, and above all particular words, were powerless.

birth of Christ might reach heaven. The dying thief on the cross had not been baptised, nor had Joseph of Arimathea, Nicodemus, Gamaliel, nor again many a confessor in the days of the Roman Empire.[1] Fire for the martyrs might take the place of water.

Zwingli insisted that baptism, like circumcision by which it was fore-shadowed, was a sign, a simple form of action which was of itself certainly not necessary for salvation. There was also a spiritual or internal baptism, given by God in man's heart, presuming and requiring faith. Not only did baptism not wash away sins, but its recipient was not then or later sinless; Christ alone was this. It was an indication that an obligation to live a Christian life had been accepted by, or on behalf of, the recipient.[2] Baptism was thus a public assurance that children would receive a Christian educa-tion, and an initiation ceremony to show their future allegiance. Luther seemed to accept the view that baptism eliminated original sin, whereas Zwingli, for whom the 'weakness' of original sin was inherent in all adults, insisted that believing Christians, being made free from the effects of original sin by the crucifixion, had their children baptised as an assurance that they shared this advantage and belonged to the whole community of those who had received this grace. A new Christian life was begun. Children were just as much members of the church, inheritors of the kingdom of God, as their parents.

Baptism had ample, almost too ample, biblical support. The question, however, now arose that if, as Zwingli maintained,[3] baptism was dependent on faith and meaningless without it, how could infants have faith? More-over, if baptism followed faith, it was of minor account. On one point he was quite consistent: nothing was effected by the sprinkling with or dipping in water.[4] A physical object whether water or bread or wine did not of itself bring anything with it. As such, it could not even strengthen faith.[5] On this point, however, Zwingli shifted his ground and admitted that his second thoughts were not the same as his first ones. He found an addi-tional powerful argument in favour of child baptism – election. Some were predestined to salvation. Among infants no human being could possibly know those whom God had chosen, and so to deny baptism to any one of these would be to assume knowledge which did not, and could not, exist. Therefore all children of Christian parents could and should be baptised. At the same time Zwingli, like his opponents, was sure that there could be only one baptism: repetition was meaningless. But they, of course, argued that only the ceremony that followed assured faith could be true baptism.

---

[1] Z IV, 223–4; Yoder 2, 18. Judas and Simon Magus, disbelievers, had been baptised.
[2] Z IV, 199–201, 229–31. [3] Z IV, 191. [4] Z II, 143.
[5] Yoder 2, 94 argues that Zwingli's later position was the opposite of his earlier one. This is true only in so far as reliance was to be placed exclusively on the text of the Bible. For the later Zwingli, faith might follow baptism, and this his opponents denied.

To extract infant baptism from the New Testament, particularly from the Acts of the Apostles, required all the ingenuity that Zwingli possessed. His main scriptural arguments were based on the fact that the baptism of John preceded that of Christ, that baptism replaced circumcision and that the apostles had baptised children (Acts 16, 15, 33, 1 Cor. 1, 16, Romans 4. 11, Col. 2. 12). This exegesis was denied by his opponents with some reason. He also argued[1] that where the New Testament gave no clear guidance, the Old Testament must be called in where the analogy was clear. That this was so in regard to circumcision as the parallel to baptism he did not doubt, and much of his thought derives from this. There was the general command to the apostles to baptise all people (Matt. 28. 19) and, since the baptism of children was nowhere forbidden, it was concluded that they were included. Again, even if the record stated or implied that the apostles baptised adults, this did not necessarily mean that they had not baptised children as well, without its being so stated. Nor, even if they baptised adults only, did it follow that children should not be allowed this privilege. *Sola scriptura*, as Zwingli often pointed out, did not mean that everything was written down. Much obviously was not. There is no statement, for example, that the apostles themselves or the Virgin Mary were baptised. Reasonable and manifest deductions it was the duty of the Christian, and especially of the Christian minister of religion, to make. It was his opponents who used the Bible unfairly with their clamour of *Gschrift, Gschrift*, setting themselves up as lords of the Scriptures because the spirit brought them certainty.

In addition to numerous letters, sermons and parts of other writings,[2] Zwingli produced no less than four major statements of his views on this urgent issue – *Von der Taufe, von der Wiedertaufe und von der Kindertaufe* (27 May 1525),[3] *Antwort über Balthasar Hubmaiers Taufbüchlein* (5 November 1525),[4] *Gutachten betreffend Taufe* (1526)[5] and *In Catabaptistarum strophas elenchus* (31 July 1527),[6] the latter intended to be the *coup de grâce* against malicious opponents who had already rendered themselves liable to the death penalty.

Zwingli's earliest comprehensive treatise on the subject[7] was written for Vadian in May 1525 to help to combat Baptist claims in St Gall, where active Baptist propaganda had been remarkably successful. In it the author again readily admitted that he himself had at one time thought that baptism

---

[1] Z III, 409.
[2] Especially *Wer Ursache gebe zu Aufruhr usw.* Z III, 374–469 (Dec. 1524) and *Von dem Predigtamt* Z IV, 369(382)–433 (30 June 1525).
[3] Z IV, 188 (206)–337; Z VIII, 331; ZH *II*, 5‑155; Baur II 79–112.
[4] Z IV, 577 (585)–642; Baur II, 141–175.   [5] Z V, 448 (451)–452.
[6] Z VI, i 1 (21)–196.
[7] *Von der Taufe, von der Wiedertaufe und von der Kindertaufe*; Näf, *Vadian* II, 231.

should, or at any rate might, be deferred until years of discretion but had changed his opinion after closer study.[1] He pointed out that the Anabaptists tended to make as much of a simple ceremony as their opposites, the catholic priests, had done. They were persuading themselves that the act of baptism washed away sin and that they were henceforward without sin, a gross perversion of the truth. They were also, he insisted, reintroducing salvation by works under a smoke-screen of humility and sanctity. Further, and this in fact was of deeper significance although a distortion of the position of a 'separated church', they regarded themselves after adult baptism as constituting the real Church of Christ: only they were true Christians, a position also comparable with that of Rome and the followers of the Pope. They were equally arrogant – any one who ventured to disagree with them was wrong, ignorant and ungodly.[2] Blaurock, in particular, was distinguished by his audacity and determination to create a disturbance wherever he went.

So much emphasis had already been placed upon the supreme and exclusive authority of the Bible, the essential feature of Reformed teaching, discussion and debate, that Zwingli was forced to find biblical grounds for upholding infant baptism. Apart from the analogy of circumcision – and he was well aware that analogies had to be used with great caution if he was not to play into the hands of his catholic opponents – the New Testament gave slight guidance. The Anabaptists were pushing Zwingli's own treatment of the Bible as expounded by him in January 1523 to its logical conclusions.[3] While consistently rejecting the doctrine that the hierarchy had become the repository of tradition ranking *pari passu* with the Bible, he was obliged to resort to some rather negative arguments from silence and to some wide generalisations based on incidental remarks. Thus 'then those who accepted his word were baptised' (Acts 2. 41) applied, in context, to adults; but adults, he insisted, included children. Or when (Acts 16. 15) it was recorded that Lydia 'was baptised, and her household with her', household, he insisted,[4] included the children, an argument reinforced by reference to I Cor. 1. 16, 10. 2, 16. 15, and by the confident assertion that

---

[1] Zwingli agreed that child baptism was neither expressly forbidden nor commanded in the New Testament. Z III, 409. Z IV, 228–9 n. 21.

[2] Like most of their contemporaries, they did not spare their opponents personally. Zwingli's sermons were 'unspiritual', he was a loose-liver, an adulterer and worse. He was a mouthpiece of officialdom who had himself upheld transubstantiation and communion in one kind. 'We all seriously misbehaved in this regard', was his answer, 'until God brought it about that the deceiving ungodly mass has been entirely excluded from among us without any disturbance, God be praised for ever and ever.' Z IV, 165; 322–3.

[3] C. Nagel, *Zwinglis Stellung zur Schrift* (Freiburg, 1896) evades this criticism. The Anabaptists were consistent biblicists, while Zwingli was prepared to modify his earlier rigidity. Yoder 2, 94 n. 46. It was Grebel's chief complaint that Zwingli had departed from his earlier reliance on the Bible, and Blaurock objected that he twisted and falsified the Bible worse than the Pope. Egli *1*, 289, 443. See below, 399 n. 5.   [4] Z IV, 312–13.

the Old Testament words for parents included the children. Similar controversial deductions were drawn from the rebaptism of Apollos (Acts 19. 1–7). To Swiss country pastors and Zurich councillors Zwingli's knowledge of Greek and Hebrew was decisive, but in fact some of his confident assertions rested on superficial or erroneous etymology. Zwingli never fully understood his opponents' position in relation to the Bible text.[1] While making full use of individual texts when they served his purpose, he none the less could not agree that the whole of God's commands were written into the New Testament. *Gschrifft, Gschrifft*,[2] he insisted, was not of itself good enough unless reinforced by further biblical support or by clear plain reason.

In July 1525 Hubmaier, who had perhaps been in contact with Thomas Müntzer, restated his case in a small widely-read pamphlet (*Taufbüchlein*).[3] In a disarming prefatory letter to the Zurich council he referred to Zwingli as his 'dear brother' and insisted that his own desire was to find out the truth, and this from the Bible: if he were proved wrong from Scripture he would at once recant. He repudiated the suggestion that his supporters were in any respects sectaries, and insisted that they would willingly obey the orders of the civil government provided these were not against God. He rejected the word 'Anabaptist' since, he urged, child baptism was no baptism, John the Baptist had never baptised children, and the biblical sequence, preaching, repentance, faith and then baptism, must be followed.

Zwingli proceeded to answer him point by point,[4] and since Hubmaier's case was basically both moderate and cogent[5] (for he genuinely wanted a friendly exchange of opinion), he had to resort to grammatical quibbles and personal detraction to satisfy his readers. It did not help greatly to be told that sectaries were acting illegally because they opposed the government, or that they would not submit to the judgement of the Church when, in this instance, the voice of 'the church' was that of the Zurich Council, or even that Hubmaier was copying the Catholics in declaring baptism necessary for salvation. Baptism, Zwingli repeated yet again, was simply a token of membership of the Christian community, a public advertisement, an initiation and an acceptance (by deputy in the case of infants) of the obligations of the followers of Christ. It was none the less obligatory by governmental decree. Hubmaier discarded God's provi-

---

[1] Yoder *1*, 163; Yoder *2*, 37–8.
[2] Z IV, 604, 618.
[3] *Von dem Christlichen Tauff der gläubigen* (Strassburg). Hubmaier, *Schriften*, 118–63; Baur II, 137–40 with the dating corrected by Z IV, 580. Cf. Bender, *Grebel*, 188, 273, 294–6; Williams, 146.
[4] *Antwort über Balthasar Hubmaiers Taufbüchlein*, Z IV, 577 (585)–641.
[5] It is well analysed in R. S. Armour, *Anabaptist Baptism* (Scottdale, Pa. 1966) 27–56.

dence and human reason alike: he proclaimed 'external baptism is of no avail', but failed to explain how true inward baptism could be bestowed. Faith, the essential, involved the whole of the covenant that the human race had with Almighty God, not the assertion of the inward conviction of the individual. Were those, like Nicodemus, Joseph of Arimathea or Gamaliel, who had been in heaven for 1500 years, now to be chased out because they had not fulfilled the fictions and inventions of one whose knowledge of biblical languages was imperfect, who himself had not searched the scriptures (for Christ's words unquestionably referred to the Old Testament) and who added to his impudent lying the false assertion that grown men should submit to immersion because they could not know whether they had been baptised or not?[1] The answer was effective and avoided none of Hubmaier's assertions, but it was rough, peremptory and unnecessarily personal.

There is no direct evidence that either Hubmaier's pamphlet or Zwingli's answer had any wide circulation, but it is certain that the separatist church movement gained many adherents in 1526. They were numerous enough to meet in a convention at Schleitheim on 24 February 1527 and to produce for the first time an outline confession of faith[2] (*Brüderlich Vereinigung*). It set out in seven general articles the now familiar claims – the right to choose their own pastors, to exclude sinners from their purified society, unspotted from the world, to decline to testify on oath, to refuse civil or military service, needing no secular government, or resort to force. They baptised only adults, administered a simplified Lord's supper and reverted, as they claimed, exactly to the ways of the church of the apostles.

There was also in circulation at the same time a version of the Schleitheim confession in print written in the Zurich dialect, all copies of which have disappeared. It was this anonymous 'libellus' *Von der Kindertaufe*

---

[1] It was partly because of this assertion by his opponents that Zwingli persuaded the council in May 1526 to order that registers of baptisms should be compiled and preserved by recognised ministers. Similarly, with the repudiation of the jurisdiction of the Catholic church courts, marriages needed to be registered to establish the legitimacy of children for inheritance purposes. These arrangements were copied at Basle in 1529. P. Roth, *Durchbruch und Festsetzung der Reformation in Basel* (Basle, 1942), 61. Thomas Cromwell's action in 1538 in England inaugurating the 'parish registers' may well have been influenced by the Zurich example. Z IV, 617–18; Egli *1*, 466 (No. 982); Bullinger, *Ref.* I, 381; see below 216 n. 1.

[2] The text was printed by Koehler in *Flugschriften aus den ersten Jahren der Reformation* 2. Bd., 3 Heft, 279–337 (Leipzig, 1908) with a good introduction, and again by Jenny, *Das Schleitheimer Täuferbekenntnis* (Thayngen, 1951) with a commentary. Muralt/Fast 26–35. J. C. Wenger provided a convenient but not very satisfactory translation in MQR 19 (1945) 243–53 (Schleitheim am Randen, Randen being a local place-name descriptive of the area between Klettgau and Hegau, appears rather curiously as ' Schleitheim on the border'). There is a version in W. L. Lumpkin, *Baptist Confessions of faith* (Chicago, 1959) and by J. H. Yoder, *The Legacy of Michael Sattler* (Scottdale, Pa., 1973). Cf. ARG 37 (1940) 242–9; MQR 41 (1967) 187–99.

which Zwingli set out to refute.[1] This he may have done the more willingly because he believed Grebel, who had died at Maienfeld in 1526, to have been the author. The result was the long and in part technical Latin treatise *In catabaptistarum strophas elenchus*, a guide to the tricks of the Anabaptists.[2] Like much else, it was hastily composed, but it was also intended as Zwingli's final word on the subject. His opponents, he indicates at the outset, are themselves impervious to argument, emissaries of Satan sowing tares in the Christian field, a perpetual menace to settled government, law and order. When their errors are demonstrated from the pages of Scripture, they deny its validity compared with their own inner light; they are moved by every wind of novelty; their appearance of peculiar sanctity, renunciation of the world and their devotion to good works are on the surface only. In truth, their thoughts and actions are evil, as examples prove,[3] and while

[1] The authorship has been much disputed, although it is of minor significance. Baur (ZKG 10 (1899), 331–5) attributed it partly or entirely to Hubmaier. Usteri (ZKG 11 (1890), 162–4), Staehelin I, 528 and Koehler (Z VI i, 4–5, 101 n. 1) favoured Grebel, as did Bender, *Grebel*, 186–91 and 273 n. 30a. The lines quoted by Koehler in *Mennonitische Geschichtsblätter* 3 (1938), 11–12 from an exchange of letters between Bullinger and Myconius of 2 and 9 June 1536 are not conclusive. Hans Strickler argues persuasively for Michael Sattler in *Mennonitische Geschichtsblätter* 21 (1964), 15–18, followed by Muralt, *Glaube* 24 and G. H. Williams, *Spiritual and Anabaptist writers* (London, 1957) 31, Blanke ARG 37 (1940) 242–9 and Bergsten 48 n. 86. Michael Sattler, who came from the Black Forest, had been a monk at St Peter's, Freiburg, and was a considerable scholar. He had accepted Lutheran teaching and had married before coming to Zurich, where he proclaimed himself an Anabaptist and gathered groups of followers in the neighbouring woods. Deeply religious and now entirely committed, he was expelled in November 1525 (Egli *1*, 406 (No. 863) and moved to Strassburg. Unable to secure approval there, he joined forces with Röubli to evangelise in Württemberg, fell into Austrian hands, was tortured and burnt as a heretic at Rottenburg (Neckar) on 21 May 1527. Williams, 186. Koehler regarded him as one of the noblest and most profoundly religious of the Anabaptist circle. *Flugschriften*, Bd. 2, Heft 3 (Leipzig, 1908), 295.

[2] Z VI i, 1 (21)–196. Both *elenchus* implying refutation, and *strophas*, contrivances, were rare non-classical words derived from Greek. Their introduction made it apparent that Zwingli was writing for scholars and anxious to show himself as a humanist. There is a convenient German version (abbreviated) in *Ulrich Zwingli eine Auswahl* (Zürich, 1918) 678–709, and an English translation by H. Preble and G. W. Wilmore in *Ulrich Zwingli selected works* ed. S. M. Jackson, reprinted with introduction by E. Peters (Philadelphia, 1972), 123–258, part of a never-completed plan for the publication of translations of all Zwingli's major works.

[3] Again and again Zwingli refers to the fratricide of St Gall. A certain Thomas Schugger or Schinker beheaded his brother on 8 February 1526 in unpleasant circumstances and explained that he had a 'call' to do so. It was, in fact, manifestly a case of mental aberration, but it was good enough for argument. Muralt/Fast 410 (No. 488), 571–2. 'The will of God is fulfilled' – 'I bring you tidings of the day of the Lord', he told Vadian, Bürgermeister of St Gall, proudly. Z VI i, 92–5 and notes; Näf, *Vadian* II, 235–6; Sabbata, 160–2. As late as 1527 ('Abschid der Stette Zürich Bern vnnd sant Gallen / von wegen der wider-teüffer ausgegangen, iij') it was still brought into prominence, evidence of continued interest. Joachim v. Watt, *Deutsche Historische Schriften* hg. v. E. Götzinger (St Gallen, 1877) II, 407–8.

There was a man who committed adultery at Weesen and brazened it out, arguing that even if he did commit adultery he did not sin, 'for those who are in our church cannot sin'. Z VI i, 193. Zwingli in fact most unfairly made the most of an occasional lapse – all modern investigators rightly stress the 'suffering' rather than the militant side of the movement. Clasen, *Anabaptism*, 127–9; Peachey, *Soziale Herkunft*, 76–8.

they willingly deceive others, they are inconstant themselves. They speak of their rejection of the Old Testament, failing to appreciate that this was 'the scriptures' for the Apostles, their causing baptism to be followed by a communion celebration was a mere superstitious gimmick by which the ignorant common people, always anxious to rush after some novelty, were deluded. Anxious for separatism they arrogate to themselves the right to eliminate those whom they judge unworthy, in spite of the fact that this lies within the sphere of the whole community (*Gemeinde*) only. Their sect, Zwingli insisted, was outside the Church; they should therefore be called pseudo-baptists or Anti-baptists or, as some prefer, Anabaptists.[1] In spite of their repudiation of the term 'Anabaptist', it stuck, and that it did so and became a term of opprobrium, was in no small measure the result of this widely read treatise.

To add fuel to the flames of indignation, Zwingli drew attention to their attacks on the social and convivial meetings of the gilds and societies in their halls and club rooms, *honestissime* as these are well known to be. He also said that while they condemned the popular pilgrimages to Loreto, Aachen and Altötting, they themselves met by night in woods and forests and did not confine these surreptitious gatherings to the male sex.

They condemned citizenship although Roman citizenship was invaluable to St Paul, who was proud of it. They objected to treaties because these are sworn to, on oath. They never carried offensive weapons as ordinary people did, and they thus extended the divine injunction not to resist evil to secular governments to whom it was not addressed.

'I protest with all my might', Zwingli continued, 'against the notion that Christians have no need for authority.' The true perfect Christian would not indeed ever need to have recourse to a magistrate, but such perfection is not in fact to be found among mortals: no more than the monks are the sectaries *in statu perfectionis*. It does not follow that because Christ refused to be a judge, that men should do likewise – divine and human justice are very different matters. A good judge indeed could do more for the public peace than all these sectaries, greedy for power and for the property of others. Hypocrisy, backbiting, lying, harming others, discord, perfidy, the terminology of Satan – these were their weapons. And they would abolish the solemn oath, in their ignorance misinterpreting their Bible as usual. None the less, Zwingli needs some ten pages to convince himself and his readers that an oath, never blaspheming God's name, could rightly be demanded and conscientiously taken.[2]

[1] Z vi i, 114–15 and n. 3; see above 169 and n. 1.
[2] Z vi i, 155. 'Iusiurandum non arbitror exigi debere aut citra conscientię molestiam exigi posse, quam tum, cum aut humana obtestatio omnis cessat aut proximi salus, graviter periclitatur, atque super hęc omnia, cum in nulla re, quam iuraturi sumus, nomen dei blasphematur.'

In the final section of the *Elenchus* Zwingli becomes a little more constructive.[1] He again expounds his view that baptism was a sign of the renewal for all peoples of God's covenant with Abraham, and thus a token of admission to the Christian community and hence to citizenship.[2] There were not two Gods, one of the Old Testament, one of the New; for God is one, unchangeable and eternal, with his son Jesus Christ likewise in unity everlasting. Since his coming on earth, the shadows have gone, the light of the Gospel can illumine all; grace depends on faith, not deeds. Circumcision, the sign of the covenant, was for boys; yet girls were equally within the covenant, and for the 'Catabaptists' to maintain that the children of Abraham were the children of God whereas ours were not, was merely wicked. The disputes among the Apostles about the abrogation of circumcision was itself a clear implication that they baptised their children, and later writers who could have known, Origen and Augustine, were of the same opinion.

More briefly, in facing those of a 'gathered' rather than the universal Church, Zwingli had to deal with the claim that they were of the elect, which led him to consider the nature and implications of election,[3] a theme to which he several times returned, and which he admitted involved difficulties. Salvation comes by faith, and faith is the divine gift bestowed by God at his will, freely given. Divine deliberation, choice, destination, the call, the gift of faith and with it the certainty of salvation – this is the order. He who believes is undoubtedly saved, chosen before conception, doing good works because he is of the chosen, assured of this by the inner witness of his spirit. Of these, some die as infants, and they too are of the elect. Baptism is for all, the eucharist for those who understand the nature of their faith, preaching for those few who are sent by authority.[4] Preaching, faith, baptism or circumcision were all subordinate to election, which is sure and which is freely bestowed by God in his inscrutable wisdom.

He also took the opportunity to deal with the insistence by his opponents on the sleep or dormancy of the soul, psychopannychism, until the day of the resurrection. This notion, later also to be combated by Calvin, may have been revived by the fertile brain of Karlstadt and was known to both Luther and Grebel. Zwingli brushed the belief on one side by insisting that Hebrew, having no word for sleep, used dying in its place.[5] In this, in

---

[1] It has been called a semi-official statement of Zurich theology. ZKG 10 (1889), 341.

[2] Williams, 194, somewhat extravagantly speaks of it as 'the covenantal seal of civic-religious membership in the new Alpine Israel, the Swiss Confederation, of which Zurich might be considered the foremost tribe'.

[3] See below 324–5 and Z VI i, 172–8.

[4] Z VI i, 183. The dispatch of preachers and the laying on of hands as a divine direction is hardly ever mentioned by Zwingli. Ordination was no sacrament; the absence of clear Bible guidance was sufficient warranty for this statement.

[5] Z VI i, 189–90.

fact, he was wrong, but there were very few who could argue with him on the matter. On the discussions on the immortality of the soul, he was as orthodox in approach as was the fifth Lateran Council[1] (1512–15). It was also necessary to touch on the question of the 'celestial flesh of Christ' and the doctrine of an inward feeding upon it.[2] Some maintained that Christ, being the eternal son of God, was not wholly born of his mother, thus reviving echoes of ancient controversies. That some of his opponents may have advanced such views was for Zwingli, whose orthodoxy on this point was never in doubt, but further evidence that they lacked scriptural support, and that they fell into error because they were convinced that the Spirit taught them to interpret as they pleased.

The whole lengthy and elaborate refutation, lacking summary or conclusion, repeats a good deal of what has been said before. It undermined the Anabaptist appeal to adult experience and secure faith by an insistence upon the predestinating of the elect in Christ by God's will before the foundation of the world. This was to carry the argument a good deal further and to anticipate some later Calvinist and Puritan theology. Although Zurich was satisfied, the Anabaptist movement gained momentum elsewhere and had a long development before it. After 1527 the concept of a 'gathered' or 'suffering' church was not proclaimed publicly in Zurich and the focus of attention moved northwards into Germany, where other events were to attract Zwingli's interest.

[1] Williams, 106; C. J. Hefele, *Histoire des Conciles*, ed. H. Leclerq (Paris, 1917) VIII, 339–548.
[2] Williams, 107–8, 325–8. There were two versions current – that Christ was from the beginning one Person in one Nature that became visible or corporeal in his mother, or that, at a moment in time, begotten and not created, he had a human nature from Mary as well as a divine nature.

197

8

Peasants, opposition, education

One problem that arises from any study of the early Anabaptists in Switzerland is that of their connection with the Peasants' War in Germany. Its nature and extent, if it existed at all, is exiguous, uncertain and controversial, yet it cannot be entirely dismissed, since some of Zwingli's teaching is reflected, albeit vaguely and dubiously, in the disturbances of 1525.

The Swiss peasant was, like his fellows all over Europe, the true backbone of society. Upon his labours in the field everything else depended; it was the local farmer and the local harvest that kept men alive. To some extent he was idealised while also being exploited by his superiors and laughed at by literate townsmen for his supposed credulity, ignorance and obstinate conservatism. William Tell was the perfect peasant: honest, upright, God-fearing, industrious, patriotic, freedom-loving and brave. Zwingli, who did not fail to draw attention to his own rustic upbringing, constantly paid tribute to the tillers of the soil.

They were, in fact, a depressed majority. Although serfdom in its more objectionable forms was light in Switzerland, the burdens of service and of payment in kind exacted from the peasant were considerable. There were dues for grinding his corn, for marrying his daughter, for entering on his inheritance; his best beast was the property of his master when he died, and there were customary payments at every turn. In addition, the church not only exacted a fee for all services from baptism to burial, but derived much of its income from the tithe of the peasants' crops and animals.

Peasants had always tried to evade payment of tithe, and now that the scriptural validity of this began to be called in question, the country folk were peculiarly interested.[1] Zwingli was possibly sorry that he had so soon become involved with the problem of tithe, or that he had agreed that there was no scriptural justification for turning a payment which had originally been a voluntary one into an exaction enforced by customary and canon law. He now faced a difficult decision. On the one hand, he

---

[1] R. J. Böppli, *Die Zehntablösung in der Schweiz, speziell im Kanton Zürich* (Zürich, 1914), 32ff. See above, 161–4.

must uphold the established political and social order, which suited him very well, and this included heavy economic pressure on the country people. On the other hand, he could hardly uphold customary payments simply on the ground of immemorial tradition. In the religious sphere, where tradition had been against him and his appeal had been to the Bible, this was not helpful in the matter of tithe. Hence he was now obliged to differentiate between moral and legal obligations, and between ecclesiastical tradition and secular customary rights. With the legal requirement that tithe should be paid, he was satisfied; it was sufficient that the government ordered and enforced it upon its subjects whose duty it was to obey and pay.

As early as August 1523, there had been refusals to pay tithe of hay to the Dean of the Great Minster, but this was apparently simply a piece of local resentment which had many parallels elsewhere.[1] Recalcitrance, encouraged by evangelical preaching, spread to the Grüningen district, where there were threats to the well-endowed Premonstratensian monastery of Rüti and to the house of the Order of St John of Jerusalem at Bubikon, followed by some looting.[2] A little later, in the same area, the peasants were demanding the right to choose their own ministers, the end of serfdom and the discontinuance of a number of customary payments, including tithe.[3] Others desired to choose their own preacher and to support him by voluntary offerings, a demand which fitted in alike with the separate church called for by the Anabaptists and with similar demands from north of the Rhine.

It is not entirely accidental that Grebel, Mantz, Blaurock and their friends were setting forth their original and disruptive doctrines at the same time as social grievances were coming to a head in several parts of central Europe. There was, indeed, almost certainly no direct connection between Anabaptism and the German Peasants' War, but they coincided too closely in time for them to be entirely separated.[4] If American research may be thought to have put the early days of the independent church of the Baptists into truer perspective, the treatment of the peasants in both Germany and Switzerland has received equally stimulating and sympathetic treatment at the hands of the Marxist historians.[5] For them it

---

1 Simon Stumpf preached at Affoltern that the small tithe need not be paid. Egli *1*, 93 (No. 267), 143 (nos. 391, 392).
2 H. Nabholz, *Zur Frage nach den Ursachen des Bauernkrieges, 1525. Gedächtnisschrift für Georg v. Below* (Stuttgart, 1928), 244. Goeters, *Vorgeschichte*, 246.
3 A. Largiadèr, *Untersuchungen zur zürcherischen Landeshoheit* (Zürich, 1921), 35–7.
4 The older histories of Switzerland, e.g. K. Dändliker, *Geschichte der Schweiz*[3] (Zürich, 1901), 529–32, connected the movements too closely. Bergsten, *Hubmaier*, 21 n. 45; Clasen, 152–7. ARG 37 (1940), 105.
5 The standard account of the Bauernkrieg is Gunther Franz, *Der deutsche Bauernkrieg*[7] Bd. I, Darstellung, Bd. II, Akten (Darmstadt, 1965, 1968). F. Engels, *Der deutsche Bauernkrieg*

is the class struggle that matters, and the Peasants' War was undoubtedly this among other things. It was also part of the economic transformation that was everywhere leading to the forming of larger units and more consolidated holdings with both owners and tenants anxious to retain such traditional rights and obligations as were advantageous to them. There was a long tradition of egalitarianism. 'When Adam delved and Eve span, Who was then a gentleman?' had been heard in England in 1381, and the dissemination of the Bible could not fail to provide further support for claims for personal freedom and improved conditions.

Agrarian discontent, long endemic in south Germany, had previously shown itself in the Bundschuch demonstrations and had been further roused by the egalitarian preaching of Karlstadt and Thomas Müntzer.[1] A simple strike on the estates of Count Sigismund of Lupfen spread before the end of 1524 to a general revolt for peasant independence. Grebel, Castelberger, Mantz and others may have been in communication with Müntzer in September 1524, but it hardly amounted to more than an enquiry about biblical and liturgical matters and a message of goodwill.[2] It is less important than the obvious appeal of both peasants and Anabaptists to Luther's principle of *sola scriptura*. Prominent, however, among the notorious Twelve Articles was the second which, while accepting the great tithe of corn, ended 'the small tithe we will not give, be it either to spiritual or to temporal lord...for we esteem this tithe for an improper

(1850 and Berlin, 1951) and *Marx/Engels Werke* Bd. 7 (Berlin, 1960) perhaps inspired M. M. Smirin (Russian, trans. Hans Nichtweiss (?Hanna Köditz)) *Die Volksreformation des Thomas Münzer und der grosse Bauernkrieg* (Berlin, 1952), a serious if politically motivated study. E. Belfort Bax, *The peasants war in Germany 1525-1526* (London, 1899) is antiquated but convenient for a translation of the twelve demands. N. Cohn, *The pursuit of the millennium* (London, 1957) 251-83, with bibliography, is stimulating, as is Gordon Rupp, *Patterns of Reformation* (London, 1969) 157-250.

[1] c. 1490-1525. He studied at Leipzig, Frankfurt (Oder) and Mainz, was ordained priest, early accepted Lutheran teaching, developed advanced views as minister at Zwickau, Prague, Allstedt and Mühlhausen (Saxony). His mystical theology and sincere biblicism have been increasingly appreciated since the publication of his writings. He supported the German peasants and was cruelly executed when captured. A large literature has accumulated round him and shows no sign of lessening. Ranke, *Deutsche Geschichte im Zeitalter der Reformation*, ed. Joachimson (Munich, 1925) II, 141-70 was the first to show his significance. O. H. Brandt, *Thomas Müntzer, sein Leben und seine Schriften* (Jena, 1933) is the standard biography with T. Müntzer, *Schriften und Briefe. Kritische Gesamtausgabe...von* P. Kirn hg. v. G. Franz, QFRG 33 (Gütersloh, 1968). H.-J. Goertz, *Innere und Aussere Ordnung in der Theologie Thomas Müntzers* (Leiden, 1967), *Studies in the History of Christian Thought* II; ARG 54 (1963) 145-79; Rupp, *Patterns of Reformation*, 157-353; MQR 43 (1969) 142-52; ME III, 785-9; A. Meusel, *Thomas Müntzer und seiner Zeit* (Berlin, 1952).

[2] Muralt/Schmid, 13-21 (no. 14); Bender, *Grebel*, 110-19, 171-83, 282-7; G. H. Williams, *Spiritual and Anabaptist writers* (London, 1957), 73-85; W. Rauschenbusch, 'The Zurich Anabaptists and Thomas Müntzer', *American Journal of Theology* 9 (1905) 91-106. The letter was certainly drafted, and a copy exists, but it may never have been sent, or, perhaps, never received. Rupp, *Patterns*, 322, 345-6; MQR 47 (1973), 153.

tithe of man's devising'.[1] They also demanded freedom of hunting, fishing, wood gathering, and the reduction or abolition of servile incidents, tenures and status – 'We do find in scripture that we are free and will be free.'

The revolt could easily spread south towards Zurich, and the appeal to the Bible had to be taken into account, but the Swiss peasant[2] was more favourably situated than his German counterpart, and there was no love lost between Swabia and northern Switzerland. The early success of the Swabian peasants alarmed the states of the Confederation, especially when Waldshut declared in their favour, Freiburg and some other cities were compelled to do likewise and infiltrating parties appeared in Thurgau and the Rheintal. The danger was discussed at several Diets in April and May[3] at which it was agreed to hold the line of the Rhine, and Basle and Solothurn manned their walls and closed their gates. Hence, although there were stirrings of discontent in the Bernese Emmental, Aargau, Thurgau, Appenzell, St Gall, Solothurn, Basle and Schaffhausen, these were in a sufficiently low key to be brought under control almost without bloodshed. The obligations of servile tenure in northern Switzerland were not particularly onerous and were in process of alleviation; the superficial attraction to the social egalitarianism of the Baptists and their associates soon wore off in the light of actual experience. All the same the situation was delicate. Obviously the less the peasants had to pay in tithe, rent or mortgage-interest, the better pleased they would be. Their life interests were usually narrow and local; they could not see beyond their own valley and tended to resent government 'interference'. Like other people, they wanted protection and justice without having to pay for it. To this extent, they sympathised with the German movement; but whereas in Germany the fruits of victory went to the princes and nobles, in Switzerland these

[1] For the text of the Twelve Articles, G. Franz, *Quellen zur Geschichte des Bauernkrieges* (Munich, 1963), 174–9. Hubmaier was early suspected as the author of these, and Fabri, for interested reasons, openly accused him of being so. He certainly approved of the contents, but their origin must remain uncertain. Schappeler (now the favourite), Lotzer and Fuchssteiner have also been named. Bergsten 281–6; Z VIII, 322 n.; Smirin (trans.), 33; A. Stern, *Die Streitfrage über den Ursprung des Artikelbriefs und der zwölf Artikel der Bauern. Forschungen zur deutschen Geschichte* 12 (Göttingen, 1872) 494–5; F. L. v. Baumann, *Die zwölf Artikel der oberschwäbischen Bauern, 1525* (Kempten, 1896) 129–36, ARG 36 (1936) 193–213; A. E. J. Hollaender, 'Articles of Almayne': *Studies presented to Sir Hilary Jenkinson* (London, 1957) 164–77; ZKG 85 (1974) *passim*.
[2] The word 'peasant', which it is impracticable to avoid using, is not entirely satisfactory in the Swiss context. The south German *Bauer* or farmer was usually concerned mainly with arable, tilling the soil. His Swiss counterpart was more likely to be engaged in pastoral work approximating somewhat to a cowboy or rancher. V. Lötscher, *Der deutsche Bauernkrieg in der Darstellung und im Urteil der zeitgenössischen Schweizer* (Basle, 1943); O. Vasella, *Bauerntum und Reformation in der Eidgenossenschaft. Historisches Jahrbuch* 76 (1957) 59; F. Martini, *Das Bauerntum im deutschen Schrifttum* (Halle, 1944), 294–9, 302–28 (for events in northern Switzerland). [3] EA 4, 1a, 625, 629, 648–9; Staehelin I, 496.

classes were far less influential and any revolt must be against traditional and constituted authority. Hence Zwingli's constant insistence upon the Christian duty of obedience as well as upon the sanctity of contract. Even if there was something that seemed morally wrong[1] about a legal transaction it must still be performed.

In the hard spring of 1525 the peasants of the Grüningen district and those of the former county of Kiburg were calling for the abolition of serfdom, poll taxes, 'heriots' and lesser tithes.[2] None the less there was no serious trouble. When four thousand peasants gathered at Töss[3] they were pacified by promises of investigation[4] of their grievances from Bürgermeister Walder and Rudolf Lavater, the local governor, seconded by very generous entertainment from the local nunnery. The nuns may have been stimulated to this by news that the monastery of St Blasien in the Schwarzwald had recently been looted. These eastern complainants received a fuller answer from the Zurich Council at the end of May based upon Zwingli's advice.[5] It was conciliatory but also basically conservative and skilfully drafted. The government would investigate and remedy real grievances as had been done in the past; law and justice had prevailed, and improvements had been introduced. Rent, tithe, interest, resting upon known contractual obligations must be paid; there was in fact very little serfdom and this had biblical sanction – Abraham, Isaac and Jacob had possessed serfs, and the institution was tolerated by St Paul. The implication, from which Zwingli would not have dissented, was that the illiterate field-worker was not competent to criticise his superiors and that it was his first duty to do what he was told.[6]

Obedient subjects should recognise how real and considerable were the improvements in their position that had resulted from the actions of their governors; no other administration would, or could, do as much, and mere greed from the recipients was no sign of affection for the Gospel.

There were other demonstrations, as one near Cloten in June, but the

---

[1] 'etwas wider gott ist'. Z III, 388. O. Dreske, *Zwingli und das Naturrecht* (Halle a.d.S., 1911) 59. See above 119–120.

[2] H. Nabholz, *Die Bauernbewegung in der Ostschweiz 1524–5* (Bulach, 1898) 56–7. There was even talk there of paying back to Zurich the money for which the area had been pledged (raising the money by taking over the monasteries of Rüti and Bubikon) and then making the area independent. Stumpf 2 1; Bullinger, *Ref.* 1, 266; Egli *1*, 315–17 (Nos. 696, 699, 701).

[3] E. Beurle, *Der politische Kampf um die religiöse Einheit der Eidgenossenschaft. Ein Beitrag zu Zwinglis Staatspolitik* (Linz, 1920) 97–100.   [4] Bullinger, *Ref.* 1, 277–9.

[5] Z IV, 338 (346)–60, esp. 346–7: 'Ratschläge der Leutpriester auf die Beschwerden der Grafschaft Kyburg und Genossen und Erstes Gutachen betreffend Zehnten'.

[6] Z IV, 355: 'Dann wo ghein obergheit ist, da ist nútz denn ein uffrûr. Wo nit ghorsame ist, da ist nútz anders weder ein mördery.' Cf. Egli *1*, 336–7 (No. 726). This represented Zwingli's practical conclusion. The subject is clearly discussed in J. Kreutzer, *Zwinglis Lehre von der Obrigkeit* (Stuttgart, 1909, reprinted Amsterdam, 1965) and H. Schmid, *Zwinglis Lehre von der göttlichen und menschlichen Gerechtigkeit* (Zürich, 1959).

potential rioters likewise returned home peacefully. How much this was the result of reason and moderation, and how much because of news of decisive defeats of German peasants at Frankenhausen and Sindelfingen and of Alsatian insurgents at Zabern in May 1525 cannot be estimated. Men learnt, too, that Luther had urged the princes to severity in the most notorious of his pamphlets[1] whereas the attitude of the Swiss authorities was wisely moderate. The complainants were in fact eminently reasonable, even humble and respectful. They had listened to the preachers of the Gospel sent from Zurich, and had accepted the principle of the Bible as the sole guide to faith and conduct. At first it seemed as if they might obtain, by agreement, some amelioration of the smaller tithes and the abolition of personal serfdom which in any case was extremely mild. There was also a suggestion, which Zwingli favoured, that part of the revenue from church property should be applied to the benefit of the poor.[2] The government of Zurich, he insisted, had dealt fairly and equitably with its subjects, from whom obedience was due – agitators who urged the non-payment of tithe or rent made for anarchy. If the farmers remained recalcitrant they would show little gratitude for the spread of the Gospel and the mildness of their masters. Contracts must be kept and customary payments continue.[3]

In August 1525 when it was apparent that no uprising was now likely, Zwingli reviewed the whole subject of tithes for the benefit of the council.[4] He outlined the historical and the Old Testament background, and admitted that the matter was a question of economics and of politics, upon which the New Testament gave only general guidance. Both the ministers of the church and the poor needed support and maintenance; and lawful, peaceable possession should not be disturbed. It was all very sensible and suited those who were content with the status quo. After 1525, in Zurich-controlled territory at least, the agitation for tithe-abolition died down as more urgent matters came to the fore.

In fact not very much was done to improve conditions except for some minor adjustments in tax payments and some local improvements in conditions of service. Zwingli, unlike Luther, consistently urged that peasants should be treated with humanity and moderation,[5] and this was accepted; the ministers were told to care for the oppressed as well as to preach; ground rents should be reduced in years of bad harvests, and debtors might receive some assistance. Public welfare, law and order after the rough pattern of the age were secure once more (as was also the case in Berne), and to this Zwingli had contributed appreciably.

---

[1] *Ermahnung zum Frieden auf die zwölf Artikel der Bauernschaft in Schwaben. Wider die räuberischen und mörderischen Rotten der Bauern*, WA 18, 291–334; 357–61.   [2] Z IV, 339–41.
[3] Z IV, 344, 353–9.   [4] Z IV, 530 (536)–545.   [5] Nabholz, *Bauernbewegung* 50–4.

It was in the light of all this, and while the countryside was slowly returning to normality, that Zwingli completed a treatise on the church which was also a personal confession of faith[1] for the edification of Francis I, although this monarch, held in ignominious captivity in Madrid, had some other matters to consider beside theological controversy. This treatise *On the True and the False Religion*, at which Zwingli toiled night and day for over three months, sending it to the printers in March 1525, indicated to all his theological position. False religion, that of Rome, was superstition as opposed to a just and true faith derived from the Bible. The one true, eternal, almighty God, creator of the universe and beyond human comprehension, the highest good, wisdom and perfection, has revealed his nature in the Scriptures. Such imperfect knowledge as was vouchsafed to the heathen or to abstract thinkers was inadequate and imperfect.

Man, God's creation on earth in his own image, fell from grace because of his self-love, and remained inherently weak, sinful and incapable of obedience to God's will. In the constant conflict of body and soul, flesh and spirit, the unrighteousness of man always prevailed. Hence the need for the Incarnation and the assurance of salvation to the true believers henceforward no longer under the power and inevitability of sin and death. Faith, the divine gift, was the supreme necessity without which all else was in vain. By the grace of God alone, through Christ's sacrifice, there is hope of salvation for sinful man.

From this basis the treatise becomes a kind of running commentary on current Christian doctrine and practice. The divinity and the humanity of Christ were assumed, along with the perpetual virginity of Mary and complete acceptance of all the biblical miracles. Consideration of grace, mercy and prayer is followed by a discussion of repentance, absolution, and then of the primacy of St Peter, which is denied. The church, the assembly of Christian people, must not be identified with either the hierarchy or with any particular self-constituted group. Throughout, the appeal to the text of the Bible is persistent, some pages consisting almost of strings of texts with occasional discussions of particular key words like 'keys', 'rock' and 'bind'.

The section on the sacraments,[2] recognising two only – baptism and the eucharist – objecting mildly to the use of a Roman military term for an experience based on faith, is at once too short and dogmatic for a sustained argument and too involved for a simple explanation such as the nature of the treatise would seem to demand. There was but one baptism, that of both John and Christ, having no positive effect as an action but remaining a

---

[1] Z III, 590(628)–911. *De vera et falsa religione commentarius*, printed by Froschauer, 1525. A translation into German by F. Blanke is in ZH 9 and 10 with useful additional notes.
[2] Z III, 604–12, 757–824.

sign of an obligation to lead a new life. The writer recognised that the necessity for child baptism could not be directly proved from scripture except by analogy with circumcision or by implication. To this he was to return in other writings; in early 1525 it was sufficient to call its opponents faction-ridden, quarrelsome and cantankerous.

Similarly in the discussion of the institution words of the Last Supper he develops a little further his earlier explanation in article 18 of the *Schlussreden*. It is not sufficient to assert that in faith, which comes neither from human wisdom nor by human choice, we believe in the bodily and sensible presence of Christ's flesh,[1] for faith and sense-perception are different. When Christ said 'is' he meant 'signifies', a symbolical explanation which is both scriptural and intelligible. This he was later to expound again and again, with much elaboration. The mass as a sacrifice was utterly unacceptable and the numerous mass priests, it followed, should be more usefully employed and not replaced when they died. Monastic vows are neither binding nor acceptable and the monasteries themselves are superfluous. Salvation by works is rejected, and merits and free will are subordinated to providence. Predestination, a theme to be developed more fully later, is reasserted. Purgatory is denounced (with further reference to *Adversus Hieronymum Emserum antibolon*) as unscriptural and a money-making invention;[2] the Pope is Antichrist;[3] the worship of images is no matter for indifference, and their removal from Zurich had been accomplished in quietness without any trace of disorder.[4]

The French monarch could be reassured (and this was a prime purpose of the treatise) that to follow the Gospel was not to promote civil disobedience. In this regard the Zwinglian requirements were the precise opposite of those of the Radical reformers. The latter had explicitly declined to be involved in public affairs, whether national or local, whereas in fact, Zwingli insisted, the best Christians made the best officials. The happiest and most successful states are those in which true religion reigns. Church and state must equally support impartial justice, the former through the law of reciprocal love, the latter by regulating in the interest of the whole the tendency of the individual to consider only his own advantage. Such a sentiment, which harmonised with the theory of the French monarchy, could appeal equally to an oligarchy, such as that which controlled Berne.

A Godless government, Zwingli continued, is almost necessarily tyrannical, whereas a God-fearing autocrat becomes *ipso facto* a just ruler rightly commanding the obedience of his subjects. Zwingli would have

---

[1] Z III, 786. 'Fide credimus corpoream sensibilemque carnem Christi hic adesse. Fide creduntur res a sensu remotissimae...Disparata igitur sunt: credere et sentire.'
[2] Z III, 855-7.   [3] Z III, 894.   [4] Z III, 901-6.

found little to quarrel with in the Tudor concept of the Godly Prince restraining vice and encouraging the righteous – he would have been well content with an Edward VI fulfilling the promise of his youth, or with Elizabeth I had she heeded a little more the words of the preachers. Swiss governmental traditions expected the enforcement of ecclesiastical decrees by the state, and stressed the responsibility of the secular rulers of the community for the conduct and morals, as well as for the peace and quiet, of the citizens. Even an unbelieving magistrate – for any government is better than no government – is to be obeyed so long as the Christian faith is not impeded. Or, again, slavery, which still existed in pockets in Europe in Zwingli's day, was not necessarily incompatible with Christianity (an opinion shared by George Washington). Zwingli likewise rejected the medieval appeal to the 'two swords', ecclesiastical and civil. On the contrary, there should rightfully be but one, and this, being human, must be that of the civil administration. Only the children of darkness feared authority which was properly constituted and necessarily exercised even within an all-God-obeying community, since others would be included who came from without and who needed restraint. Where, as in Zurich, the governors were chosen by electors, experience and ability were to be expected from them as well as truth and uprightness. Under such leaders the ordering of the worship, as well as the conduct, of the citizens was safe. It was from Zurich and not from France that the good example was to come. The three hundred pages of this treatise cannot be summarised in a few paragraphs: for Koehler[1] it was the first and only systematic exposition of Zwingli's theology. Baur devoted over eighty pages to his estimate of it,[2] and Wernle was equally enthusiastic.[3] The treatise ends with a reminder that the Papacy had drawn men away from the right worship of God and that they must return to the true religion of faith, justice, innocence and mercy.

The Anabaptist problem remained with Zwingli to the end. In almost his last composition, the confession of faith to Francis I, *Fidei expositio*, he wrote: 'This plague of Anabaptism intrudes itself above all mostly where the pure teaching of Christ has started to grow. So much the more easily, King, can you perceive that it was sent by the devil to spoil the good seed by sowing weeds. We have seen that cities and towns which had started to take the Gospel seriously, after they had become infected by this plague remained like a state that was unable to attend to divine or human business because of the disturbance'.[4] Zwingli stressed what had been achieved because attacks on his state, as well as upon himself, were becoming increasingly menacing. Manifestly at the opening of 1525 Zurich could no longer be regarded as a Catholic state. The authority of Pope and

[1] Z III, 593.   [2] Baur I, 380–461.   [3] Wernle, 143–245.   [4] S IV, 66.

bishop had been openly flouted, the Lenten fast ignored, images and pictures broken, the clergy encouraged to marry, monasteries and nunneries emptied and their property taken over by the government.

The preacher who had brought this about, who had denounced mercenary service and Anabaptist pacifism, had also published his rejection of transubstantiation, of the hierarchy and of canon law. At the same time he insisted on maintaining and even exaggerating his independence of Luther. His followers were not Lutherans. Reluctantly perhaps, but with growing conviction, the Zurich council had accepted the consequences of this. Monks and clergy were treated as ordinary citizens, not as a caste apart. The authority of the Bishop of Constance and his courts was no longer acceptable, and this meant that the state, already administering church revenues, must assume responsibility for contracts, wills, personal relationships and other matters falling within the scope of the canon law. Of these, matrimonial causes were of high importance. With the Scriptures as the only guide-post, there was unlikely to be any major change; but firm decisions, involving legitimacy and the descent of property, must be taken about what constituted a valid marriage, and if and when it could be dissolved.

The government must also control public worship. It had already inhibited the radicals from baptising and preaching freely: it must now come to grips with the decisive issue of the mass. Consideration had already been given to church services. After the Zurich disputations of 1523, followed by further attacks on the mass as a sacrifice, a number of priests simply omitted the Canon of the mass from the service, but kept the remainder, and that in Latin, to the disgust of some of the more advanced citizens, who absented themselves conspicuously from supposedly obligatory services. Zwingli had indeed suggested, as early as August 1523, some minor but significant liturgical alterations. It was utterly characteristic of him that he wrote these out as *De canone missae epichiresis*,[1] using this unusual and rather fanciful Greek word, meaning project or suggestion, to put forward a number of rather small and technical modifications in the traditional form of words. The 'project' was not well received; the traditionalists condemned any alteration and perceived that he had shifted the emphasis from the act of consecration to the reception of the elements by the worshippers, while the more advanced thinkers, especially among the young priests, called for something much more drastic, some simple vernacular prayers to take the place of the daily mass.

As the conviction grew that Zwingli's eucharistic teaching was completely incompatible with any of the forms of the Roman mass, increasing

---

[1] Z II, 552(556)–608; F. Schmidt-Clausing, *Zwinglis liturgische Formulare*, 22–7. See above, 151 n 4 G. J. Cuming, *A History of Anglican Liturgy* (London, 1969) 35–6.

numbers of priests neglected this altogether for sermons, Bible-readings and extemporary prayers. This, however, was manifestly unacceptable since the communion service was an indispensable part of the reformed teaching, and when, in the early spring of 1525, it was apparent that there was hardly a priest willing to say the accepted Latin mass, further action was needed, the more so since the Anabaptists had already been offering for some time a radically simplified celebration of the Last Supper. On Tuesday in Holy Week (11 April), therefore, Zwingli, Jud, Engelhard, Megander and Myconius appeared as a deputation before the council and formally asked for the cessation of the 'idolatrous' mass and its replacement by an evangelical communion service, supporting this with the now familiar Zwinglian interpretation of the words of consecration. There was at once opposition from Joachim am Grüt, and the Council referred the matter to a committee of four to report on the following morning. Their recommendation was that the mass should be abolished, and by a narrow majority this was agreed.[1] It was a decisive vote, although this might not have been immediately apparent. Mass was openly said for the last time on 12 April and the break with Rome was complete.

On the following day, Maundy Thursday, a large congregation assembled in the Great Minster.[2] A table was placed between the nave and the choir; on it were wooden platters with plain bread rolls, and a jug of wine. Thus the altar with its implications of a sacrifice was eliminated and the practice of communion in both kinds accepted. There was no singing: there was a prayer or collect, the reading of passages from the Bible, a short explanatory sermon and the recitation of the *Gloria in Excelsis* and the Nicene Creed by men and women, verse by verse alternately. After a prayer for forgiveness of sins, an invitation and admonition, all said the Lord's Prayer, which was in German, as was the whole of the service.[3]

The biblical words of consecration were then read and the ministers in simple dark clothes or gowns distributed the bread and wine to the congregation in silence. Some broke a piece of bread themselves, others opened their mouths to receive it, and then the wine, from the ministers. The service ended with the 113th (Vulgate 112) psalm, 'Praise the Lord, you that are his servants'[4] and a blessing.

It was short, simple, comprehensible, with pauses for silent prayer, all

---

[1] Egli *1*, 306 (No. 684).
[2] *Gerold Edlibach's Chronik*...hg. v. J. M. Usteri, MAGZ 4. (1847), 273.
[3] *Aktion oder Brauch des Nachtmals. Gedächtnis oder Danksagung Christi wie sie auf Ostern zu Zürich begonnen wird im Jahr, als man zählte, 1525.* Z IV, 1(13)–24; J. Schweizer, *Reformierte Abendmahlsgestaltung in der Schau Zwinglis* (Basle, n.d. (1954)); F. Schmidt-Clausing, *Zwinglis liturgische Formulare*, 28–39.
[4] Wyss, 62; Staehelin I, 444–5; F. Schmidt-Clausing, *Zwingli als Liturgiker* (Göttingen, 1952), 128–43; Z IV, 6–8, 17–24.

to indicate the working of the Spirit through the Word. Young people were present on Thursday, their parents on Friday and the elderly on Easter Sunday, divided, as was the custom, by sex. Such communion services, with later modifications, settled to four celebrations annually, at Christmas, Easter, Whitsun and the Zurich local festival on 11 September, the feast of SS. Felix and Regula. It was all a little experimental, and minor changes followed, but the decisive step had been taken. The Roman mass was proscribed, a good Catholic thereafter had to cross the border for it, unless he could find a priest willing to risk the penalties of defiance. There was now no doubt that, for Catholics, Zurich was a 'heretical' state, and this meant a further breakaway from other states of the Confederation.

The threat of this had been continuous throughout 1524.[1] Eleven states on 20 April 1524 had already agreed at Lucerne to have no association (*Gesellschaft*) with heretics,[2] and on 28 June representatives of Zurich, Schaffhausen and Appenzell were excluded from a meeting of the Swiss Diet, in spite of protests from Berne, Glarus, Basle and Solothurn.[3] In January, February, April, June, July,[4] October and November, hostilities had been openly discussed by the Diet, although there was no precedent or legal justification for Federal proceedings against heresy or for an unprovoked attack on a member state.

If Zurich could be induced to attack another state, this could be an excuse for coercion, but its council was far too wise to do that.[5] The Gospel was making its own way on its merits and, in fact, it was the opponents who had belligerent intentions, not Zurich. These opponents were, basically, the five inner states,[6] who hoped to bring in others by suggesting that an attack on Rapperswil was imminent or that Zurich was in alliance with subversive elements in eastern Switzerland and north of the Rhine. Eck was to be their emissary and publicity officer, and his appeal of August 1524 to the Swiss Catholics brought a crushing rejoinder from Zwingli.[7]

---

[1] Z III, 539–41. [2] EA 4, 1a, 412.
[3] W. Oechsli, *Die Anfänge des Glaubenkonfliktes zwischen Zürich und den Eidgenossen, 1521–24* (Winterthur, 1883), 17.
[4] EA 4, 1a, 360–1, 373, 375–6, 455–7. On 16 July 1524, the representatives of the V Orte with Fribourg gave notice that they would refuse to be associated with Zurich in common meetings unless 'Lutheran' teaching was abandoned. See below p. 250 notes 2, 3, 4.   [5] Z III, 541.
[6] See below 398–9. The five states had agreed at Beckenried on 8 April 1524 to stand by 'the old, true, right, Christian faith and to root out this Lutheran, Zwinglian, Hussite erroneous and dangerous teaching from our territories and dominions'. EA 4, 1a, 410–11; H. Dommann,*Das Gemeinschaftsbewusstsein der V Orte in der Alten Eidgenossenschaft. Der Geschichtsfreund* 96 (1943) 152–55; Z VI ii, 337 n. 6. S. Skalweit, *Reich und Reformation* (Berlin, 1967) 219, following Oechsli, *Gedächtnis* c. 130, speaks of the gathering as a Sonderbund – 'Sie schlossen sich schon 1524 in einem Sonderbund zusammen'. L. v. Muralt in *Handbuch* 468 insisted: 'Die Vereinbarung zu Beckenried...gründete aber keinen "Sonderbund" in Stile des 19. Jahrhunderts'. Little wonder 'Sonderbund', 'U.D.I.' is hardly translatable into English. Fribourg sometimes acted with these '*V Orte*' as an independent group (*Gedächtnis* c. 124) but its connection with Berne restrained it a good deal.   [7] Z III, 305–12.

There had also been a suggestion of an Austrian attack on Zurich on the basis of the agreement reached at a Diet at Frauenfeld (October 1524) for the handing over of 'Lutherans' by either side for punishment as heretics. There were secret discussions with the Habsburg officials at Waldshut, but no serious help was likely to be forthcoming from that quarter, and in any case a Habsburg alliance involving possible admission of dormant Habsburg claims to territory was not likely to be popular. On 28 January 1525 the committed catholic states (excluding Basle, Schaffhausen, Appenzell, Zurich, Graubünden and St Gall, city and monastery) had agreed on what they meant by the Catholic faith and its protection.[1] There is a slight flavour of the Counter-Reformation about their definition. Clergy for example should reside in their parishes or sees, concubinage should be forbidden and benefice-hunting discouraged, all of which, if enforced earlier, might have deferred the Reformation. There were also recommendations to improve the economic position of the peasants.

The situation was, or at any rate seemed to be, tense. It was common knowledge in Zurich that messages were passing between the Catholic states and that Zurich was practically isolated. The only terms on which this might be reversed and leadership in the Confederation regained were that evangelical preaching must cease, as must the printing and circulation of Zwinglian and Lutheran writings, soldiers must be provided for papal and other armies, and policy in general brought into line with Lucerne and its neighbours. This would mean acceptance once more of the spiritual authority of the Bishop of Constance and his unpopular courts, abandonment of the successful expansionist policy in eastern Switzerland and south Germany, full restoration of the mass, and either burning heretics or else handing them over to episcopal officers. It would mean the repudiation of Zwingli, the removal of his friends, the repeal of the order for biblical teaching and the end of all that had so far been accomplished. For such capitulation council and people alike were certainly not prepared.

Out of this state of affairs there perhaps emerged one of the strangest and most controversial documents in the whole Zwinglian Odyssey. Some time, possibly towards the end of 1524, but much more likely in 1525–6, Zwingli produced his written opinion[2] about what should be done in the event of war. Zwingli was no pacifist. His experiences in the Italian wars, culminating in the slaughter of Marignano, had indeed convinced him of

---

[1] EA 4, 1a, 572–80, sometimes called *Glaubenskonkordat*. JSG 14 (1889) 261ff.

[2] Z III, 539(551)–583. *Plan zu einem Feldzug*. Zwingli's authorship is reasonably certain and the date in Z was ascribed to July 1524 to 4 January 1525, hence its treatment here. Vasella showed convincingly that the date of composition must be placed in 1526. ZSG 20 (1940), 54ff. *Ulrich Zwingli und Michael Gaismair, der Tiroler Bauernführer*, ZSG 24 (1944), 388–413. Farner IV, 235–6. Hauswirth, *Philipp*, 76.

the wickedness of wanton aggression and of hiring men to be killed. Erasmus had persuaded him intellectually that war was to be abhorred and that the spectacle of Christians fighting one another was deplorable. This did not mean, however, that evil men should not be resisted or that hostile forces should not be repelled. On the contrary, a man's duty was to take up arms in defence of the independence and integrity of his country and even of his own property.[1] In a perfect Christian society peace would necessarily reign, but in the imperfect world in which they lived violence was to be expected and guarded against. Like others of his age, Zwingli had been trained in the use of arms from his youth, and he expected others to be so too. If the government summoned its subjects to war they must follow, and Zwingli, as he demonstrated in 1529 and 1531, would be with them. In 1525 it was abundantly clear that if the liberties of Zurich were to be preserved and the right to preach the Gospel maintained, bloodshed might be inevitable. There were good biblical precedents, especially in the Old Testament, for taking the sword in defence of God's kingdom.

Zwingli's *Plan* was an overall survey of the international situation as seen from Zurich. The Catholic cause relied for military support upon the house of Habsburg. Fortunately it was apparent that the Emperor Charles V need not be feared immediately since he was far too occupied with his detestable intrigues elsewhere, for which God would punish him in due season. The now hostile Austrian administration, however, should be reminded that Zurich had more than once been helpful in the past, especially in enabling the Archduke to occupy Württemberg in 1519[2] and in opposing the French in Milan. If the Emperor chose to aid the opposition, he might himself be removed by joint Swiss action. Francis I of France should be made use of, if possible, to divert their opponents by demonstrating that the intrigues of the Inner Five with the Habsburgs could not but be to the disadvantage of the French; Zurich's refusal to accept French pay and the French alliance could be explained away; Swiss civil war could not be of advantage to the French, whose king might wish to avoid further warfare. Enquiry should further be made as to the intentions of the Duke of Savoy,[3] who was thought to be more than fully engaged nearer home.

The document then goes on to consider in some detail the precise situation within the Confederation, its subjects, allies and neighbours and what it all meant in terms of military and diplomatic logistics. Berne and Basle, both well disposed to the Reformation although both still tolerating the

---

[1] W. Koehler, *Ulrich Zwingli und der Krieg. Die christliche Welt*, 29 (1915) 675–82. J. Rogge, *Zwingli and Erasmus* (Stuttgart, 1962) 37, 43.
[2] See below, 300–1. After contact with Philip of Hesse, Zwingli was to take a different view about Württemberg and to work for the restoration of Duke Ulrich.
[3] Charles III, 1504–53.

mass and officially Catholic, could be counted on for support – if there was to be any mediation, they would be useful, and they would carry with them Glarus, Appenzell and Solothurn. Neutrality would not be good enough. Schaffhausen presented a certain difficulty. This little northern state was showing no special anxiety either to imitate or to cooperate with Zurich, but from it, although the hated 'idols' had not yet been cast forth from its churches,[1] at least neutrality was expected. If this was not the case, then the bridge of boats across the Rhine should be broken in a night attack. The friendship between Zurich and the city of St Gall must be re-affirmed and intensified, the city should be encouraged to occupy the buildings and ground of the great monastery and assume jurisdiction over its tenants. The abbot might have to be evicted. Appenzell should occupy Rorschach, and Wil should come under the joint control of the inhabitants of Toggenburg and the people of God's house from the south. These latter, parts of the Graubünden or Grey Leagues, a little Switzerland within Switzerland, could be expected to put pressure on their immediate northern neighbours, including Sargans, and to neutralise the valleys of the Adige, the Inn, the Wall and western Tyrol. Church property would also be secularised. Valais was apparently inflexibly Catholic, but a much divided area which might well be made harmless by encouraging local conflicts.

The inhabitants of Zwingli's native Toggenburg were to be pressurised into exchanging their alliance (*Landrecht*) with Schwyz (while retaining that with Glarus) for co-citizenship (*Burgrecht*) with Zurich. If all this and some complementary schemes came to fruition, the whole of eastern Switzerland, Thurgau in its most extended sense, could be brought under Zurich's control, while any counter-measures from south or west could be guarded against by diplomatic pressure or by threats of forcible action against Rapperswil,[2] Weesen, Gaster and Einsiedeln. Baden and Aargau might be coerced by threats into inactivity. With all this secure, help would be more than likely from Strassburg, Lindau and Constance, bridgeheads against Austria. Diessenhofen and Kaiserstuhl were to be threatened with fire and annihilation if they failed to close their bridges to imperial troops. Basle was to be allowed to become master of Rheinfelden as part of the price of support.

---

[1] Sebastian Hofmeister (Oeconomus) (1476–1533) had preached in favour of evangelical reform with some success, and the state had taken over the Benedictine monastery of All Saints much as Zurich had the Fraumünster. But the excesses of the Anabaptists and fear of the peasants caused a reaction; Hofmeister was forced to leave in 1525 and iconoclasm was forbidden. Z III, 560. Schaffhausen was, in fact, much closer to Zurich than Zwingli seemed to realise. Egli 3, 1, 116–18; J. Wipf, *Reformationsgeschichte der Stadt und Landschaft Schaffhausen* (Zürich, 1929), 154–5, 201–18, 286–9.
[2] Rapperswil had been a free imperial city, and after 1464 was independent, protected by Uri, Schwyz, Unterwalden and Glarus.

The writer was, in fact, advocating immediate aggression in defence of the Reformed faith and at the same time putting forward an ambitious political plan which could make evangelical Zurich the dominant unit in the Swiss Confederation. He also recognised that a high public morale was needed, backed up by proper military preparedness. Sixteenth-century propaganda came from the pulpit. Prayers for success should be said in the churches, and preachers should make it clear that a war against those who denied, thwarted or frustrated the word of God, was just and even necessary. Only thus could the precious inheritance of the open Bible be defended.

In addition to trusting in God, they must keep their powder dry. Military victory required organisation, and how this was to be secured was set out in a detail that matched the analysis of the political situation. The choice of the General in command (*der Hauptmann*) was of first importance, and next to this his deputy (*der Pannerherr*), a member of the council, with a chain of command down to the appointment of company commanders of detachments of 1,500 men.[1] The General must possess the confidence of his men; he must be weather wise, know the ground, be ready for night operations by moonlight, not attack unless position, wind and sun made him reasonably certain of success, and above all realise the importance of speed. Unselfish, self-reliant, silent, God-fearing, conscious that the enterprise is undertaken solely for the protection of evangelical convictions, he will welcome the support of his chaplains to console, encourage and strengthen the morale of his men.

The best and most modern weapons were to be supplied, above all the guns[2] which now already provided invaluable support for the pikemen. There were to be provisions with these latter for two or three days so that there was no need for foraging or looting before battle. There must be proper observation of weather conditions, adequate precautions against surprise by constant watch and patrol, no dispersal of forces, certainty that every man in uniform knew the horn or trumpet signals and was prepared to meet or to undertake ambushes, feints, skirmishes and surprises. It was all so utterly cool and practical that it is hard to realise that it was written in the golden age of bastard chivalry when such counsels would have been ignored at the courts of France or Burgundy.

Modern commentators, without overlooking the fact that Zwingli was drawing in part on his knowledge of Roman military treatises, have been unanimous in their praise of his keen discernment and wide knowledge of tactics and strategy, combined with acute political perceptiveness. It is

---

[1] Z III, 553–5. Cf. Locher, 65–8.
[2] He enumerates Hakenbüchsen (arquebus), Gabelbüchsen (stand-guns), Handbüchsen (crossbows), Streitbüchsen and Halbschlangen (light field cannon).

indeed remarkable that he could turn his mind so rapidly from theology to politics and from politics to military tactics. There is, however, also a decided touch of the armchair strategist about it all, the advice is all a little too good, the outcome too optimistically assessed, too little account taken of the element of chance or even that opposing commanders were likely to be equally well aware of such maxims. It was also a remarkable exercise to be undertaken by a theologian, preacher and minister of religion. Aggression was not directly commended, but the inference that attack might be the best form of defence had serious implications. It involved, indeed, cool calculation on a local civil war, Swiss killing Swiss in the name of religion. 'The pious state of Zürich prefers to lose city, possessions, land, equipment, bodies and lives rather than depart from what it knows to be the truth'.[1]

There was in fact no war: the elaborate combined operations envisaged were quite beyond the communication capacities of the day, nor would local rivalries and suspicions have been laid aside as easily as was imagined. The little treatise provides an admirable basis for commentary upon prevailing conditions, but it is just as well that it remained a scheme which was not put into operation.

After Easter 1525 the Zurich community was spiritually largely isolated. Celebration of mass had been made illegal, and there could now be no doubt that the government and people were no longer Catholic and would be treated as heretics by their neighbours. At the same time they strenuously insisted that they were neither Lutherans nor Anabaptist sectaries. They were simply reverting to the practices of the early Christian church from which Rome had departed and which the others did not properly understand. It was this conviction that they were on the right path and their rivals were in error that inspired confidence. Political conditions enabled them to 'go it alone', and this they proceeded to do. The government had already taken over, or had accepted, full responsibility for all church property. It had been for some time de facto patron of the benefices within its territory, and it had closed the monasteries, applied their revenues to religious and educational purposes and had provided for their inmates.

There was, however, one sphere in which the authority of the church and the exclusive applicability of canon law had, so far, been accepted – that of matrimony. Marriage was a sacrament and irrevocable: all matrimonial causes had been taken for decision to the court of the Bishop of Constance and beyond this, if funds allowed, on appeal to Rome. Complaints of delay, obstruction and expense at all stages were frequent. Now that the break with Rome was open and manifest, who was to decide what

[1] Z III, 551.

constituted a lawful marriage, and whether children were the heirs to their parents' property or *spurii*, nobody's offspring?[1] In a society in which family relationships were all-important, it was necessary to decide speedily and authoritatively what were the permitted degrees of marriage, by whom and under what conditions the marriage ceremony was to be performed. In modern times these are the affair of the state and of the 'law of the land': in the sixteenth century they had been the province of the law of the church, the Pope's law which Zwingli had repudiated.

The suggestion that he now put forward, which, after consideration by a committee, was adopted as a temporary measure on 10 May 1525[2] (and like many temporary measures lasted a very long while), was that a local matrimonial tribunal should be set up to hear and decide all causes brought before it. There were to be six 'Divorce Court Judges' (*Eherichtern*), two being beneficed clergy, two laymen from the small council and two from the great council, one of whom was to be chairman (*Obmann*), this office changing every two months. They were to appoint a clerk and have a seal for affixing to decrees.[3] If necessary, they were to meet on Mondays and Thursdays, the Bürgermeister being authorised to appoint a substitute in the event of any judge or the clerk (*notarius, amtliche Schreiber*) being ill. They had power to call witnesses (at least 2) under oath and to collect costs.[4] An appeal from the tribunal would lie to the great council, beyond which there was now no other authority and which had thus displaced the church in this important sphere.

At the same time the council laid down certain principles in a kind of matrimonial statute. The prohibited degrees were those set out in Leviticus 18. 7–18; the minimum age for marriage was 14 for a girl, 16 for a boy; the consent of the parents was necessary for either party under the age of 19;[5] notice of intent to marry had to be given, and the ceremony was to take place in church in the presence of two witnesses. A register of

[1] Or questions such as what was to happen if one of the parties was unable to consummate the marriage or was a manifest and hopeless imbecile?

[2] Z IV, 176–87; Egli *1*, 326–9 (No. 711); K. Kilchenmann, *Die Organisation des zürcherischen Ehegerichts*, 11ff – a useful, but mainly legal, commentary. Oechsli, 3, *Gedächtnis*, c. 119f.

[3] The first members were Heinrich Engelhard of the Fraumünster and Leo Jud of St Peter's (ministers), Junker Felix Schwend and Gild Master Thomann Sprüngli (small council), Hans Haab and Ulrich Funk (great council). Heinrich Utinger was named as clerk and Pelagius Kaltschmid as usher. Z IV, 183 n. 6.

[4] Koehler, *Zürcher Ehegericht und Genfer Konsistorium* Bd. 1: *Das Zürcher Ehegericht und seine Auswirkung in der deutschen Schweiz zur Zeit Zwinglis*, QSRG VII (x der ganzen Sammlung) (Leipzig, 1932) 55, 68–72. (Bd. II (Leipzig, 1942) is not concerned with Zurich). The Ordinance is translated in *Selected works of Huldrych Zwingli* (Philadelphia, 1901, reprinted 1972) 118–22. For the text, Z IV, 182–7.

[5] It was assumed in the case of a girl that this would normally be required – one notice spoke of 'any one so neglectful as not to get her daughter married before 19'. Z IV, 184.

marriages was to be kept.[1] A bachelor could be obliged to marry a girl who was with child by him unless her parents objected.[2]

In case of manifest or notorious adultery, divorce[3] was obligatory, the guilty party to be excluded from church services by the minister and severely punished by the state. Prostitutes were similarly dealt with. There were to be no dispensations for marriage within forbidden degrees; impotence extending over a year nullified the marriage; the tribunal was to act at its discretion in cases of lunacy, incurable disease, malicious and prolonged desertion and cruelty amounting to danger to life. The new matrimonial courts worked well enough to become a model copied by St Gall, Berne, Basle, Schaffhausen, some south German cities and by Geneva (and Scotland) as the Consistory. They were not popular, since they involved a good deal of external supervision of domestic life and left many at the mercy of suspicion and gossip. But that they were also an improvement upon what had gone before and that they tended to raise and simplify matrimonial status was undeniable.

If the Reformation meant that the Zurich government became responsible for matrimonial matters, it also needed to pay some attention to public education, in so far as this phrase can be used of a century when everywhere only a small number of selected boys received any sort of regular schooling. In the past, teaching had been mainly in the hands of ecclesiastics, the civil authorities being scarcely involved, although benefactions were often received from well-to-do laymen. Most people, especially in the country, were unable to read or write and had no formal education of any kind. However, Zurich, like other cities, had its schools. Attached to the Great Minster and to the Fraumünster, as to practically every other large collegiate church of the time, were grammar schools where the elements of Latin were taught to a small number of boys who would hope to become sufficiently literate to seek a career in the church, medicine or law. Chantry priests provided most of the instruction along traditional lines, and beyond this little is known of the establishment.[4]

[1] Egli *1*, 466 (No. 982), 30 May 1526.

[2] The obligatory marriage decree had later to be rescinded because of abuse by interested parties. In June 1526 the Court received authority to punish prostitutes and close houses of ill fame which existed in Zurich as elsewhere. Once again the civil government extended its concern with the private lives of its citizens, and Zurich was the better for it. Kilchenmann, 39–41; Koehler, *Ehegericht*, 142; Egli *1*, 451–3 (No. 944).

[3] Marriage was not a sacrament in the eyes of the Reformers: it was a divinely ordained institution involving a contract which could be broken if the conditions were not fulfilled. What is remarkable about the Zurich action is the speed and efficiency with which the new (and essential) machinery was set up. It was a good example of the way in which a city-state could act.

[4] U. Ernst, *Geschichte des Zürcherischen Schulwesens bis gegen das Ende des sechzehnten Jahrhunderts* (Winterthur, 1879) 19–37; R. Staehelin, *Der Einfluss Zwinglis auf Schule und Unterricht* (Basle, 1889); W. Gut, *Zwingli als Erzieher*, ZWA VI, 289–306.

Their future needed thought. Zwingli was one of the best known scholars in Switzerland, and an appeal would almost inevitably be made to him, as it was to Erasmus. He had himself taught Latin to schoolboys while a student at Basle, and had prepared pupils for the university at Glarus. This task he obviously could not now add to his many other duties at Zurich, while he eagerly continued his own studies in the company of a few like-minded clerics in a literary group, a Zurich *sodalitas*, like the many such that his old teacher, Conrad Celtes, had set going.

In 1522 he had been joined by the red-haired Ceporinus (Jakob Wiesen-danger of Dynhard near Winterthur) who had studied Greek at Vienna and Hebrew under Reuchlin himself at Ingolstadt.[1] At Zwingli's sugges-tion he was made a canon of the Great Minster (in spite of the fact that he married a former Dominican nun) in order that he might teach Greek and Hebrew. Together they represented the new humanist learning based on a study of classical authors and attention to niceties of style and phrase. Both, too, were keen students of the Bible, the Greek text of the New Testament made available by Erasmus, and the Hebrew of the Old Testament as well.

Bible-inspired sermons and exclusively biblical religious teaching im-plied a wide diffusion of the Bible and therefore also of many able to read it, and to read it aloud to their neighbours. Hence the welcome for the new art of printing which enabled copies to be multiplied relatively cheaply and en-sured that the same text, and even the same pages, were available for all. For the first time, original texts, both of the Bible and of other standard authors, were available for all who could use them. If this great invention was to be suitably exploited, increasing numbers must be able to read. In order that they could understand what they read in the Bible, an educated clergy was necessary, able to preach the Word from the pulpit. For this, aptitude for languages, itself a sign of divine grace, was needed; and so, since ability to read Latin provided the key to all further knowledge in the sixteenth century, the sooner this was acquired the better. The breach with Rome meant a greater need for home-produced scholars.

Zwingli's own ideas on education had been set out for a wider public in the curious treatise *Quo pacto ingenui adolescentes formandi sint* dated 1 August 1523.[2] This was presented as what was called a 'bath gift'

---

[1] He had, at the age of twenty, produced an elementary Greek grammar *Compendium Gram-maticae Graecae* published by Curio at Basle in 1522 and dedicated to Zwingli which con-tinued to be used for over a century. In addition to correcting proofs for Cratander, he also edited in Greek *Dionysii orbis descriptio, Arati astronomicon* and *Procli sphaera*, a commentary on Hesiod's *Works and Days*, and the Hebrew grammar of Rabbi Moses Kimchi. Egli *4*, II, 145–60; Wyss, 4 n. 1; Z II, 536 n. 1; Z VII, 353 n. 3, 651 n. 2.

[2] Z II, 526 (536)–551. The first translation or paraphrase into German was made by Ceporinus (Augsburg, 1524) and another, possibly by Zwingli himself, was printed by Froschauer in 1526. 'Wie man die jugendt in guoten sitten und christenlicher zucht uferziehen und leeren

217

to his stepson, Gerold Meyer von Knonau,[1] a youth of fourteen who had just returned from a 'cure' at the notorious thermal springs at Baden. Judged by almost any standard, this tract is a disappointing exercise. There is the usual parade of classical allusions to Pericles, Nero, Seneca, Ennius and Scipio Africanus (which were appropriately omitted in the later German version), and a brief excursus about the nature of God, good and evil, the fall of Adam and hope in Christ through the Gospel. There is some rather obvious paternal advice to a 'teenager' – to abstain from over-eating and excessive drinking, avoid expensive and elaborate clothes, shun the gambling table (cards and dice), play serious games like chess with opponents of at least equal ability, be helpful to neighbours, choose a good wife and be faithful to her, and uphold truth and honesty at all times. Needless to add, the youth did not follow these admonitions.[2] To Polonius-like platitudes are added semi-contradictions; eloquence and verbal facility are desirable accomplishments, but at the same time silence was often golden and the words of the teacher must be heeded and not interrupted. In addition to Latin and Greek, the boy must know some mathematics,[3] and with mathematics was bracketed music, a theoretical subject in the schools, but too much time must not be devoted to this. Military training must be included, since any man may be called upon to defend his Fatherland. All schoolboys, including intending ministers of religion, should in any case learn a trade or craft (*Handwerck*) for the benefit of the community and for the avoidance of pernicious idleness. Games were encouraged only when they were in some way instructional or served to keep the body in good health – running, jumping, fencing and throwing stones or rocks were suitable for the young Swiss, but not wrestling, and swimming only in great moderation. A study of history, meaning of course the history of classical Greek and Rome, was a

sölle, etliche kurze underwysung, durch Huldrychen Zwinglin beschriben. Getruckt zuo Zürich, by Christoffel Froschouer, M.D.XXVI Jar.' Z v, 427–9. There is an edition (made for the four hundredth anniversary of Zwingli's birth) and a translation by Koehler, *Auswahl aus Zwinglis Schriften* (Zürich, 1918) 367–78, and by E. G. Rüsch, *Huldrych Zwingli an den jungen Mann. Zwinglis Erziehungsschrift aus dem Jahre 1523* (Zürich, 1957). E. Egli, *Mr. Ulrich Zwingli's Lehrbüchlein, Lateinisch und Deutsch mit einer Beigab* (Zürich, 1884). It bears comparison with Erasmus, *Declamatio de pueris statim ac liberaliter instituendis, 1529* (ed. J.-C. Margolin, Geneva, 1966) and *De ratione studii, 1511*. W. H. Woodward, *Desiderius Erasmus concerning the aim and method of education* (Cambridge, 1904).

[1] Z IV, 407 n. 1. Zwingli had not yet publicly acknowledged his marriage to the boy's mother, Anna Reinhart (See above, 79 n. 3.) Gerold, born 1509, married in 1525 to Küngolt Dietschi, was a promising if wayward scholar and a pupil of Glarean. He died, aged 22, at the battle of Kappel.

[2] O. Rückert, *Ulrich Zwinglis Ideen zur Erziehung und Bildung im Zusammenhang mit seinen reformatorischen Tendenzen* (Gotha, 1900), 4.

[3] Z v, 441. 'Die kunst des ussmässens, rächnens und der zal (under die man ouch die musick zellet)'.

kind of desirable but dispensable adjunct. The art of conversation should be encouraged, but truthfulness was requisite at all times, moderation and the avoidance of violence were indispensable.

The purpose of education was preparation not for life but for the hereafter. Faith was the first pre-requisite for a Christian and this was the gift of the Holy Spirit, announced in Christ's words and expounded by the preachers. A pure heart and knowledge of the Bible must come with it, and for the latter a knowledge of languages was unavoidable. You learned letters primarily so as to be able to read the Bible in the original tongues. Greek was therefore more valuable than Latin, but good Latin must be acquired first[1] because much information was available through it alone. Through it youth could be brought to the 'sources',[2] to the Greek of the New Testament and of the eastern Fathers who expounded Christ's teaching better than did the Latins, and finally to the Hebrew of the Old Testament, a language only to be acquired with a good deal of toil and specially valuable because the Greek of the New Testament is so saturated with Hebraisms as not to be fully intelligible without this language as well. All this requires time – Christ, who was already learned in the scriptures at the age of twelve, was thirty before he started to preach.

Neither in this treatise nor anywhere else is there any suggestion that girls, as well as boys, should be taught languages. All that the Renaissance offered for female education was ignored; silence becomes a woman most. There were indeed 'learned daughters' in the primitive church who praised God in psalms and hymns, but this was enough – from the notion of a female preacher Zwingli, like nearly all his contemporaries, recoiled.[3]

Zwingli was clearly not interested in education in the modern, or even in the Renaissance, sense of the word. There is no suggestion anywhere that the almost total lack of public facilities for general education should be remedied or that public money should be made available for it. It is significant that Zwinglian Zurich never developed a university or even a notably cultivated civic society. That most of the population, young and old, would be illiterate was taken for granted. What mattered was belief; there must be enough adults who were able to read the Bible to others, and there must be an adequate supply of preachers who would and could continuously expound the Christian message from Holy Writ. Education, in fact, was needed to secure an ample supply of parsons.[4] Religion, theology

---

[1] Avoiding however the Latin texts, unspecified, which encouraged impudence (petulantia), aggressiveness, domineering, deceit and vanity. Z II, 543.

[2] Z V, 437. 'Desshalb sol man den jüngling zů den brunnen wysen (Ad fontes igitur hic noster mittendus est).'

[3] Z II, 543; Rückert, *Erziehung*, 88–91.

[4] K. Spillmann, in ZWA II (1962) 427–48, shows that Zwingli's sole purpose was to train preachers: he had no direct interest in education.

and politics dominated Zwingli's life and thought, and his educational influence in Zurich led to what can only be described as over-specialisation in theology.

A civic mandate of 29 September 1523[1] had ordered a reform of the abuses of the Great Minster, a reduction of its staff,[2] redistribution of duties and revenues, and with it an overhaul of the system of instruction connected with the foundation. All this, particularly the reorganisation of the finances, took some time; some of the money was diverted to local defence measures in the light of the threatening attitude of the southern states, and there was the usual reluctance to devote much 'public' money to education. There was, apparently, also a personal reason for the delay. The canon responsible for the Grossmünster Grammar school (*scholasticus*) was Dr John Niessli, who continued the traditional course[3] until his death on 3 April 1525. The council then at once named Zwingli Principal (*Schulherr*) and with his customary energy he promptly set about giving institutional form to the mandate of September 1523, a matter further facilitated by the death of Canon Conrad Hofmann, whose distrust of popular education and conservative opposition to Zwingli had been another delaying force.

Zwingli now put his educational ideas into operation, with long-lasting effects. The chief purpose of a school being religious instruction meant that the schools at the Great Minster (*schola Carolina*), the Fraumünster (*schola abbatissana*) and St Peter's were designed primarily as seminaries of the preachers and divines that a Christian community must have. He therefore divided the former minster school into two parts – a grammar school for boys and a theological college for the training of ministers. For both institutions he formed a kind of board of governors of four,[4] with himself as chairman.

Additional accommodation for the school was taken from the Great Minster buildings, two new classrooms were provided, and a staff of four,[5] which was generous for the age, was authorised. There was to be a Head-master (*ludimagister*) and his assistant (usher, or *provisor*). There were also two subordinates (*collaboratores, attendentes, curatores*), who were respon-

---

[1] 'ein christenlich ansehen und ordnung'. Egli *1*, 168–71 (No. 426); Bullinger, *Ref.* I, 115–19; Z II, 528, 609; Z IV, 398 n. 5.

[2] There were 24 canons and 32 chaplains. Dismissal was not suggested, but as one of the latter died he was not replaced. J. Figi, *Die innere Reorganisation des Grossmünsterstiftes in Zürich von 1519 bis 1531* (Zürich: Affoltern, 1951).

[3] Johann Heinrich Hottinger, *Schola Tigurinorum Carolina* (Tiguri [Zurich], 1664) 191–218 gives some interesting details about the earlier school.

[4] The others were Canon Heinrich Schwarzmurer, Rudolf Thumysen and Ulrich Trinkler. Z IV, 368; Wyss, 57 n. 2, 107 n. 6.

[5] The number of canons serving the Great Minster was further reduced from 24 to 18 to make this provision possible. Schmid-Clausing, *Zwingli*, 59.

sible for the provision of the necessary equipment, which in the sixteenth century was minimal, and for discipline. This tantalising glimpse is almost all we have; it was a grammar school like others, primarily for the purpose of teaching elementary Latin from the usual text books of grammar – Donatus, Alexander of Villa Dei and the rest – together with a little Greek. There was also instruction in simple 'numeracy', music, and in the rules of logic and composition – the traditional trivium and quadrivium. The stipends of the teachers, derived from the endowments of suppressed prebends at the Minster, were low.[1] Collin was also a rope-maker, Musculus a weaver, Kessler a saddler, while Leo Jud's wife supplemented the family income by spinning. The ages of the pupils, who were expected to pay some fees, were between seven and fourteen or fifteen. Books were few, learning was largely by verbal repetition and lessons may have been for four or five hours daily. The example of Zurich was copied on a smaller scale at Kappel, Rüti, Winterthur and Stein, but the provision was never extensive.[2]

The theological college was far more original. It was known, from the exercises in public speaking or preaching which were its central themes, as the *Prophezei*.[3] Part of each day except Friday and Sunday was to be devoted to detailed Bible study. On these occasions the young men, a dozen or so boys of sixteen joined by at least an equal number of ministers, mostly former priests from the city, were to be exposed to 'public lectures' to be given in successive periods[4] in Latin, Greek and Hebrew. In the case of the two latter languages this can only have meant in practice grammar and translation, using the New and Old Testaments as text books, followed by some simple exposition in German. Practically everybody present, for example, would know the Latin Psalms by heart and hence could be brought into direct contact with the Hebrew version, and equally they had been made well acquainted with long passages of the Vulgate New Testament which could be compared with Erasmus' translation and then with the original Greek. The polymath who was to be responsible for the day-to-day working of this ambitious programme was Ceporinus, who was a competent Hebraist. He was paid from the proceeds of the prebend vacated by Hofmann, and gave his inaugural lecture on 19 June 1525.[5] Both he and his hearers soon found the strain of all this too great; no

---

[1] ZWA XI (1962), 432–3, 443–7.
[2] Ernst, *Geschichte des zürcherischen Schulwesens*, 64–5, 74–81.
[3] Z IV, 398 n. 5; Z XIII, 289–90; Bullinger, *Ref.* I, 289–91; Sabbata I, 203–4; Wyss, 66–7; Farner III, 551–60.
[4] There were to be two lectures, one in the morning, 7 a.m.–8 a.m. in the Minster during the summer; 8 a.m.–9 a.m. in the Canons' Common Room (*Chorherrenstube*) during the winter; and one in the afternoon, 3 p.m.–4 p.m. in the Fraumünster. Z IV, 660, 666.
[5] Z IV, 362–3, 365, 367; Ernst, *Schulwesens*, 56; Bullinger, *Ref.* I, 290.

ordinary person even then could hope to follow three such lectures con-
secutively, and to move straight from one to the other was beyond even
Ceporinus' powers.[1] Hence it was soon agreed that Ceporinus should
instruct in Greek one day and in Hebrew on the following day, while
Zwingli was to undertake the Latin lecture himself. The Septuagint,
which Zwingli esteemed highly, was constantly available for comparison
and comment: in practice the lectures or classes in the Great Minster were
almost exclusively concerned with the Old Testament.[2]

When instructed themselves, the 'prophets' were to be regarded as in
some way superior to the ordinary minister (*Pfarrer*), who looked to them
for instruction and advice – a good deal of deference was expected to be
paid to them because of their linguistic abilities, even if, ultimately, the
community must judge whether their inspiration came from God. No one
denied that there were learned doctors among the papists and, too, like
Hubmaier, Mantz and Grebel, among the Anabaptists. Zwingli recognised
the problem presented by the agreed teaching that truths might be revealed
to simple people that were hidden from men of learning, but that did not
mean that ignorance of itself conveyed assurance of divine guidance – the
evangelists themselves, after all, were learned men.

The significance of the 'Prophezei', an arrangement suited to Zurich in
the 1530s but comprehensible only with difficulty to a secularised world,
has tended to be overlooked. From it came preachers, teachers and missionaries, saturated with knowledge of the Bible. From it, too, came the
Zwinglian commentaries on many of the books of the Old Testament
which have now been carefully edited. What is most apparent is the great
attention paid to words; it was not only that the exact meaning must be
discovered, but also derivations and implications from derivations. It was
all rather primitive; the sixteenth century did not have the linguistic
equipment of the seventeenth, let alone of later centuries, and many of the
discussions could seem barren or misguided. If it was entirely biblical, it
was also genuinely critical. Day after day and for a full two hours on end,
a small group of earnest men was bestowing concentrated attention upon
some of the difficult passages of the Law and the Prophets. It was an admirable training in that it involved the closest attention to the meaning of
the words of the original text and constant comparison of one passage with
another. It could however easily degenerate into rather speculative philology or insoluble questions of metaphorical interpretation.

[1] He died about 20 December 1525 and was replaced by Pellican for Hebrew and Collin for
Greek. Egli 4 II, 5–32, 145–55; Wyss, 4 n. 1. Jud, Grossmann, Ammann and (later) Bibliander were also brought in.
[2] Bullinger in a small way had presided over a similar arrangement for theological lectures at
Kappel in 1523–5.

From it all emerged the Zurich Bible.[1] Zwingli was directly responsible for the versions of Isaiah, Jeremiah and Lamentations, but he was the driving force behind the whole undertaking. He personally paid special attention to the Septuagint, partly, perhaps, because his largely self-taught Hebrew was never quite first class.[2] Hebrew, however, was indispensable, and its poetical imagery appealed to him as much as the derivations of the words and the allegory of much of the text. For him translation and exposition were inseparable; there was mysticism as well as accurate rendering about the Bible lessons of the theological school to whose aims and purpose he contributed so powerfully.

The 'Prophezei' went from strength to strength.[3] It was copied in Strassburg and Basle and has its parallels in Puritan England and Scotland. Some of the recruits for the school lived in Zwingli's own large house and provided both income and domestic worries for his wife; like Luther, Zwingli was seldom alone for a meal, and it was at meal times that he was available to help them with their studies or inspire them with his personality. The growing activity of the Zurich press indicated increasing literacy; again and again refugee ministers from Catholic territory were provided with teaching employment and with congregations. The lectures in the Great Minster continued uninterrupted, even while Zwingli was away at Marburg, until 1531. They ensured the adequate supply of talent, which the Zwinglian ministry needed.

As the institution developed, a distinction was very properly made between theological lectures (*Prophezei*) and sermons, although the one might provide ammunition for the other. In some cases, quite clearly, the discussions which had gone on among the language-instructed clergy and students were relayed to the people in German, no doubt with explanation and amplification. The lectures were held in the choir, the sermons were preached from the pulpit in the nave of the Great Minster. The sixteenth century had a passion for sermons not easily comprehended by a later age – daily sermons, at which attendance was almost obligatory, were heard by large numbers in the Great Minster, Fraumünster (three days a week) and St Peter's. The sermon in this way replaced the mass, and the preacher displaced the priest. As an institution the *Prophezei* produced the 'prophet' who had a higher status and greater responsibilities within the Christian community than the simple evangelist or preacher. He could, because of his specialised knowledge, expound and interpret the scriptures authoritatively; it was to him that the village parson should turn for advice

---

[1] L. Weisz, *Leo Jud, Ulrich Zwinglis Kampfgenosse 1482–1542* (Zürich, 1942) 46–7, 56–7. See above, 128 n 4.
[2] ZWA I, 153–8; Z III, 138–9 n. 6; Z XIV, 878–81. Zwingli indignantly repudiated the suggestion that he had learnt Hebrew from a learned Jew in Winterthur.
[3] Sabbata 380; Wyss, 66, 67.

and guidance. Luther himself constantly insisted that the 'doctor' had an important place in the church, and this notion was given even greater emphasis by the office of the Zurich 'prophet'.[1]

It was, moreover, the duty of the prophet to warn as well as to instruct.[2] He must watch over those for whom he was responsible, call sinners to repentance and publicly denounce the wicked, the hard-hearted and the Godless or impious.

This required fearlessness and firmness; if the government overlooked evil, the prophet must point it out and that in no uncertain terms and without regard to persons. The times were evil, but the existence of the 'prophets' was a sign of divine approval. It was the duty of the prophet, if need be, to intervene in politics, for only thus might a truly Christian community be formed. Zwingli spoke with the authority of a Jeremiah, but with hope and assurance. *Christianismus renascens*.[3] Unlike his opponents, Lutherans and Anabaptists, he never spoke as if he anticipated an early Second Advent. On the contrary, a new world was being formed. The future might be bright, the prophet might be heeded, Zurich might become the instrument to win the Swiss people to Christ and thence outward to the bounds of Christendom. The *Prophezei* was the power-house for all this, and those early morning Bible classes were calls to action as well as to reflection.

These measures were, in a sense, Zurich's substitute for a university,[4] as was also in some degree true of Strassburg and Geneva. In general the sixteenth century universities had come to be regarded as clerical, conservative, scholastic and obscurantist institutions, opponents of the Reformation, with Wittenberg as an obvious exception. The drop in student numbers after the 1520s was, in some places, quite remarkable. Conventionally the foundation of a university required an imperial or papal decree, and Zurich was not likely to apply to either Emperor or Pope. The University of Basle, after an interval of internal reconstruction, continued to provide for Swiss needs. In Zurich higher education remained restricted. Zwingli's conviction that biblical studies were supremely important meant that his educational legacy was, in effect, almost illiberal. High-quality Sunday schools and a kind of extended theological college with special facilities for the study of Latin, Greek and Hebrew, were all that was needed.

[1] F. Büsser, '*De prophetae officio*', in *Festgabe Leonhard von Muralt* (Zürich, 1970), 245–57.
[2] S. Rother, *Die religiösen und geistigen Grundlagen der Politik Huldrych Zwinglis* (Erlangen, 1956) 63–72.
[3] Z VIII, 200 '*Clarum ergo est, quod omnino mundum instaurari, et per verbum, inquam, instaurari oportet.*' Z XIII, 299; Z XIV, 269.
[4] H. Nabholz, *Die Universität Zurich, 1833–1933* (Zürich, 1935), 4–8; E. Gagliardi , H. Nabholz u. J. Strohl, *Die Universität Zürich, 1833–1933, und ihre Vorläufer* (Zürich, 1938).

9

Reform and reaction 1524–6

The remarkable rapidity with which 'the Reformation' was spreading in the years 1524, 1525 and 1526 was perturbing to the Catholics. This was also true, as Campeggio found to his undisguised alarm,[1] of the great cities of south Germany, themselves so closely allied to their Swiss neighbours. If the Catholics did not close their ranks and defend what was left to them, there might be nothing left to defend. Pope and Emperor must find some basis for cooperation, perhaps in a free national council, perhaps in local anti-Lutheran alliances. The bishops of Austria, Bavaria and Württemberg, for example, must concert measures for the repression of heresy, and the well disposed among the princes must cooperate. A preliminary step towards this had been taken at Regensburg (28 June–8 July 1524), where Ferdinand of Austria, the Dukes of Bavaria, and Campeggio had discussed the situation with a number of south German bishops. At this 'convention' Eck and Fabri were the moving forces, and measures to improve the moral and intellectual conditions of the clergy were agreed. An active campaign against heresy was mounted[2] and assurances of Imperial cooperation were readily forthcoming.

It was a characteristic challenge-and-response situation which had important repercussions in both Germany and Switzerland – in Germany where a number of princes and cities explicitly disassociated themselves from the Regensburg resolutions, and south of the Rhine where the idea of summoning a similar Swiss convention was actively canvassed by Eck. The Bishop of Constance was ready to join forces with Catholic well-wishers in Zurich and with the now aggressively orthodox central states. The defeat of the German peasants with its repercussions in the diocese of Constance, the strengthening of the Habsburgs after the battle of Pavia, iconoclasm, the Anabaptists and the explicit rejection of

---

[1] Ranke, *Ref.*, 120, Bd. II, 95, 105ff., 120; H. Jedin, *Geschichte des Konzils von Trient* [2] Bd. I (Freiburg, 1951), 171–2; A. G. Dickens, *The German nation and Martin Luther* (London, 1974), 180–97, 218–19.

[2] An approved German version of the Bible and an answer to Melanchthon's *Loci Communes* were also promised. Catholic students were to be discouraged from attending the University of Wittenberg. Ranke, *Ref.* II, 121–4.

transubstantiation by Zwingli and Oecolampadius, all reinforced the call for action.

The prohibition of the mass in Zurich after Easter 1525, the clarification of Zwingli's own views of the Eucharist, their proliferation verbally and in writing, added weight to the opposition. An evangelical revolution in north-eastern Switzerland had in fact now been inaugurated, accompanied, and in part brought about, by public discussions in which the Catholics had either not been represented at all or only very inadequately. All through 1525, therefore, these latter were preparing for a public showdown or counterblast in a public debate, carefully stage-managed to secure the maximum publicity. This was the more urgent because little help came, or could come, from the Rome of Clement VII, and also because upon the outcome of such a meeting might depend the future allegiance of Berne and Basle. The Zwinglian disease, it began to be apparent, was not to be cured by locally administered medicine: it might have to be left to complete isolation.

This ostracism of Zurich, however, could mean the end of the Swiss Confederation as it had existed for the last two centuries. Loose as this Commonwealth was, it had common traditions, a common language and a common religion. Without religious solidarity it was everywhere accepted that a political community could not cohere. The Catholics insisted increasingly on the value of unity if only because a federal military force must not be divided against itself over religion. Hence the renewed warnings to Zurich of exclusion from the Diet, hence the pressure to allow the celebration of the mass at least for those who wished to attend, hence the suggestion in September 1525, which came to nothing, that six central states[1] together with Glarus should mediate an arrangement. A more serious effort was made in November 1525 when the five central states combined with Fribourg and Solothurn to put pressure on Berne to request that, as a very minimum, some opportunity, if only in some private chapel, might make it possible for a Catholic to hear mass in Zurich. Yet, in spite of the fact that a deputation of leading Bernese patricians headed by Sebastian von Diesbach came to press the case, they could not change the determination of the council to continue to go its own way independently of Rome.

There had been political as well as religious motives for this. The breach with the papacy, so far as Zurich was concerned, had taken place already. Moreover, the opposition to mercenary service which Zwingli championed so strongly was specially applicable to Rome, since the papal

---

[1] Fribourg, Uri, Schwyz, Unterwalden, Lucerne, Zug. Z IV, 648, 655: 'die sechss alten und ietz siben ort'. Solothurn made up a seventh opposed to Zurich, but consistently refused to adopt an intransigent attitude.

armies consisted necessarily of hired mercenaries and Zurich had contributed its share in the past, support which was still urgently needed. But the situation was altered by the opposition from the pulpit, and Zwingli's arguments were reinforced by practical considerations. A contingent from Zurich had taken part in the Piacenza expedition of 1521, but only a small part of the considerable sum of money due as wages had been repaid by the one honest Pope of the decade, Adrian VI, and this only after persistent and prolonged evasions by Cardinal Schiner, Ennio Filonardi, Antonio Pucci and Caspar Röist. A renewed protest in 1523 had been put off with renewed promises,[1] Pucci this time pleading papal poverty. It was further indicated from the Vatican that it was the duty of the citizens of Zurich to cherish, venerate, defend and protect their dearest beloved mother, the Roman Church, and eliminate the nefarious Lutheran heresy. Papal money was scarcely likely to be paid to heretics.

A further embassy from Zurich to Rome[2] in July 1524 was equally unsuccessful and brought back only complaints of their 'new faith and changes in church services', to which the council indignantly replied by repudiating any attachment to Lutheranism and insisting that everything that had been done had been entirely in conformity with Bible teaching.[3] The futile negotiations continued for the whole of the year with growing exacerbation. Am Grüt was sent again to Rome in October 1525 to collect the debt; while there, he showed his personal hostility to Zwingli, thus encouraging the curial officials to renew their accusations of heresy and to promise payment only on condition that Zurich returned to the Catholic faith.[4] There was a suggestion from Rome that a discussion of doctrinal differences might take place at Lausanne or Geneva, or better still, in Rome itself, a proposal which was promptly countered by Zurich's insistence that it should be in Zurich itself and nowhere else. The council again repeated that they were true Catholics, keeping only to Christ's words, believing the Creeds, repudiating heresy. In any case the men had been sent on the Piacenza expedition (to which Zwingli had been personally opposed) without any religious strings attached and had fulfilled their contract and so were entitled to payment, failing which, reprisals might be necessary.

Zwingli had a good case against am Grüt, who had opposed him on the Eucharist issue and over tithes; am Grüt, he insisted, was unreliable, could

---

[1] Egli *1*, 129: No. 357 'apud quem nil aliud nisi verba invenimus'. See above, 118.
[2] The composition is interesting: Jacob Werdmüller, financier (Leo Weisz, *Die Werdmüller, Schicksale eines alten Zürcher Geschlechtes*. 3 Bde. (Zurich, 1949) 16–59), Jacob Grebel (executed 30 October 1526), Schultheiss Hans Effinger, and the crypto-Catholic Joachim am Grüt, the ablest and most consistent of the defenders of the old régime. They were all to a greater or less degree Zwingli's opponents.
[3] Egli *1*, 247 (No. 570).   [4] Z IV, 722–5. Koehler, *Z & L* I, 156.

not be trusted to present Zurich's case fairly and should be recalled with all his documentation if he failed to apply for an audience with the Pope and to bring back the 15,000 gulden. The outcome of all this considerable exchange of words – and it will be noted that Zwingli was still not excommunicated (except *ipso facto* as a 'Lutheran' which he was not) nor was Zurich placed under an interdict – was that am Grüt died in Rome in 1526 recalcitrant to the last, no attempt was made to repay the debt, but a tenuous political connection between Rome and Zurich continued to be maintained: as late as 1533, nearly two years after Zwingli's death, Enio Filonardi, as papal legate, was still trying, in vain, to recruit military support in Zurich.[1]

The repeated suggestion of a public religious discussion embracing the whole of Switzerland was now vigorously taken up by the central states. They had already forbidden, wherever possible, Lutheran preaching, and had burnt Lutheran books. After the Ittingen affair and the popular disturbances that accompanied the Peasants' War, complaints against Zurich increased. The reply, of course, was that the preaching in Zurich was biblical, not Lutheran, and that, far from disturbances being rife among the common people as a result of 'Hussite levity', the state was peaceful and well governed. Even so, the Bishop of Constance, who had kept himself largely aloof from the earlier disputes, was now convinced that direct action was necessary.

All this was intensified by the activities of the irrepressible, competent and aggressive Dr John Eck of Ingolstadt, who now came to the fore ready to challenge Zwingli as he earlier had Luther. Eck was perhaps anxious for self-advertisement; he eagerly seized on Zwingli's denial of transubstantiation as manifest evidence that he and his followers 'hated the light and were wandering in the dark'.[2] The matter seems to have been brought to his attention by am Grüt, and he also knew that Oecolampadius at Basle was writing along lines that were closely parallel,[3] if not identical, with those of Zwingli. He further recognised that the Zwinglian position with regard to the Eucharist was not reconcilable with that of Luther, but was closer to the teaching of some of the Anabaptists. Eck, therefore, now sought to widen the gap between Lutheran and Zwinglian, bringing Lutheranism closer to pre-Tridentine Catholicism, classifying Zwingli with Anabaptists and sectaries and explicitly charging Zwingli and Oecolampadius in December 1525 with heresy.

Thus both Rome and the Confederation were ready for, and even asking

---

[1] Z IV, 727.   [2] Z IV, 746.
[3] He had read and commented unfavourably on Oecolampadius' *Über die wahre Erklärung der Worte des Herrn: das ist mein Leib...(de genuina verborum Domini)* (Basel, 1525). J. J. Herzog, *Das Leben Johannis Oekolampads, und die Reformation der Kirche zu Basel* (Basle, 1843) I, 322ff.

for, a public debate which should closely follow the pattern laid down by the Zurich Council in 1523. This could not easily be rejected. There were, however, many questions which needed to be answered before it could come to pass. Where was the discussion to take place? In what language? What, precisely, were to be the topics discussed or the 'terms of reference'? Who might attend? What was to be the order of speaking? Who was to preside and what were the chairman's powers of closure? How were resolutions to be put and how to be decided? Were 'votes' to be taken and if so how? What record was to be kept and by whom? To all intents and purposes what was proposed was 'a Swiss General Council', almost an international conference, and of these there was singularly little experience in western Europe. There was, however, one advantage – that most of those likely to attend were thoroughly experienced in, and competent at, public debate. Those who had been to a university had grown up in an atmosphere of endless disputations; in an age when written examinations were unknown, it was triumph in the 'schools' of the university that spelt success. Every graduate knew the rules of logic and knew how conclusions were reached which were regarded as 'irrefutable'. What, however, was certain was that the disputants could not agree to accept the overriding authority of canon law or of the Pope. Who, then could judge? Zwingli had his well known answer – Holy Writ, which it was assumed was sufficient. This manifestly was not acceptable to the Catholics, and without agreement upon the judge the exercise was almost necessarily bound to fail. Eck, however, was determined that it should take place. After a good deal of inconclusive skirmishing in the last months of 1525, in which Fabri, as Official of the Bishop of Constance, took part, and of which the Austrian authorities in south Germany were kept fully apprised, it was agreed[1] that a special Diet of the Confederation should meet on 1 February 1526 to decide all the questions about a meeting which was to settle the chief matters in dispute.

Both Zwingli and Eck were very much in earnest. The Zurich Council constantly pressed for the discussion to take place in their own city[2] where adequate faciles were available and where safe conduct and good treatment for Eck and his friends could be assured. Eck at first insisted that he was willing to argue verbally or in writing with anyone anywhere, but when it came to a decision he declined to go to Zurich. Fabri, more cautious, was on principle not prepared to discuss doctrine with laymen at all[3] and, in fact, he rather early recedes into the background. He did, however, throw all his influence against a meeting in Zurich which, in any case, was never likely to be accepted by the other Swiss states. Zwingli

---

[1] At a Diet at Lucerne 18 Jan. 1526. EA 4, 1a, 828-9. Muralt, *Baden*, 49.
[2] Muralt, *Baden*, 56. [3] Helbling, *Fabri*, 48.

naturally denounced this as a deliberate insult to the *Vorort*, as a cunning ruse to make sure that his followers did not obtain a fair hearing and as an effort on Eck's part to destroy the unity and endanger the freedom of the Confederation. There were long discussions about possible meeting-places – Basle, Berne, Schaffhausen, Constance, St Gall, even somewhere in Valais,[1] were canvassed, but of these only Basle and Berne were within the Confederation, all were agreed that Berne was not acceptable and Basle made it clear that it would prefer not to be chosen. In fact the Catholics had already decided on Baden, while for Zwingli and his friends only Zurich was acceptable. Since there was no preliminary agreement on either the place for the trial or the judge and jury, the concept of an all-Swiss religious confrontation was doomed from the outset.

The central states were first and foremost out for Zwingli's blood; if they could succeed in removing the arch-heretic they could hope to turn the tide of reform in their own land. There might well be promises to him of a bodyguard or a safe conduct,[2] but faith need not be kept with heretics, and Hus had been burnt at Constance in spite of a guarantee of safety from the Emperor Sigismund himself. More recently there had been serious fears for Luther's safety at and immediately after the Diet of Worms, while nearer home Klaus Hottinger and the Wirths, father and son, had been put to death in March and September respectively (1524) in spite of the fact that the Confederation had no jurisdiction in religious matters. Eck intended to restate the catholic position on transubstantiation, the mass as sacrifice, the honour due to the Virgin Mary and the saints, and the doctrine of purgatory. Then having demonstrated to a sympathetic audience that Zwingli was a worse heretic than Luther, he hoped to have him carried off for immediate burning.

In January 1526 the Zurich council set out its case in a formal com-munication to Eck.[3] For over a year Zwingli had been prepared to answer personally the errors and misrepresentations of his opponents, and he had produced his own rejoinder to Eck in writing.[4] As things were, the government was not prepared to give Zwingli any leave of absence or per-mission to dispute outside its own territories, while guaranteeing a free safe-conduct to anyone who would meet him in his adopted city.

This notification had not the slightest effect on the other side. After the acceptance of Baden as the agreed place for the public debate, two months of meetings[5] and negotiations followed, Basle and Zurich being again rejected as meeting places. On 20 March Baden was finally named by a

[1] Z IV, 748; Muralt, *Baden*, 65, 67.   [2] Muralt, *Baden*, 86.
[3] Z IV, 755–63. A copy with minor variants is in the British Library, 3908 cc. 42.
[4] Z III, 305–21.
[5] 3 Feb. 1526 at Baden, 27 Feb. 1526 at Einsiedeln, 20 March at Lucerne. EA 4, 1 a, 838ff, 855ff, 866–7.

majority of the representatives of the *Orte* as the meeting place,[1] all the Swiss states and their associates[2] were to be invited to send delegates, as were the Universities of Tübingen and Freiburg and the Bishops of Constance, Basle, Lausanne, Sion and Chur. Eck and Fabri were known to be the nominees of the Bishop of Constance, and the persons most concerned. The invitation[3] came, as was intended, directly to Zurich, where, on 31 March 1526, the council appointed a committee of eight[4] to draft a reply and sent its refusal to the Diet at Einsiedeln in April.[5]

In the first place they asserted that after the Zurich public debates of January and November 1523 no additional gathering was necessary.[6] Well knowing that this was an unacceptable *ex parte* assertion and knowing too that efforts[7] to get the Baden gathering postponed had failed, Zwingli renewed his assertion that the proposed Baden debate would be no fair, free and open discussion but that he would be pleading before a tribunal consisting of his known opponents who had never shown any intention or desire to listen to any other side of the case.

In this he was almost entirely right. The Baden debate was never intended to be, what its Zurich predecessors very largely had been and some of its successors were to be, a plain statement of a case with reasonably full opportunity for the presentation of the opposing point of view. No public discussion or confrontation has ever, probably, entirely satisfied all parties since, where vital issues are at stake, neither side is likely to feel that its case has been fully and effectually presented. Nor could any judge or arbitrator be entirely impartial or competent. Accustomed as the sixteenth century was to academic discussions and the rules of logic, 'clear reason' ('*die klaren Warheyt*', the phrase used) could mean that the clarity was all too easily apparent to one side only. Further, in the case of the truths of religion this method was not acceptable: God's purpose and intention were not to be subject to the syllogisms of the schools. For the Catholics, the church, which in practice could mean the Pope, was the supreme arbiter; for the Protestants, the word of God to be found in the Greek and Hebrew texts of the Bible must be decisive, and the Confederates could not set their collective judgement above God's word. Zwingli also set out this familiar argument in his 'friendly letter to the

[1] EA. 4, 1a, 867.
[2] *Zugewandte* – Valais, Graubünden, Mülhausen, Biel, Rottweil and the city and abbey of St Gall.
[3] Muralt, *Baden*, 59.
[4] Egli *1*, 454 (No. 947); Z v, 2–3.
[5] The invitation made it clear that no genuine discussion was intended – the Baden meeting was thought of from the outset as a forum on which to stage a public condemnation of Zwingli and his dangerous heresies. Muralt, *Baden*, 60.
[6] EA 4, 1a, 878.
[7] By Berne, Basle, Solothurn, Zug and Unterwalden. Z v, 2.

Confederates'[1] which was adopted as Zurich's official reply. For him and his supporters no individual or human judge could override Scripture wherein difficult, obscure or controversial passages were to be interpreted by clear ones. In addition to this manifestly inadmissible precondition, he insisted that the meeting must be in a 'free' city,[2] which Baden certainly was not since it was under the legal jurisdiction and practical control of the Inner States,[3] where he had already been declared a heretic whom they would burn if caught, as they had already burnt his books and his effigy. Further, he insisted that the matters to be discussed must be agreed beforehand and no alterations or additions allowed. There must also be full and adequate safe-conducts for all participants, with special security precautions for named individuals. The May Diet at Einsiedeln did indeed attempt to meet this point by promising a special guard of twenty to thirty men for Zwingli, but this was really inadequate. Finally, in his address to the Confederates, Zwingli appealed strongly to Swiss local patriotism. The managers at Baden would be Eck and Fabri, strangers, former opponents of the Swiss, whereas he himself was a born member of the Confederation on whose behalf he had suffered much.[4]

This was one aspect of his appeal. While it was being written, Zwingli learnt of a letter (*Sandbrief*) supposedly sent to him by Fabri, never in fact delivered,[5] but an example of the 'open letter' so often resorted to for publicity purposes. He at once realised that it had a double intention, to discredit him with the Confederation as a whole and to entice him away from the security of Zurich. In his reply he noted Fabri's efforts to divide him from Luther, a vain hope in the overall picture when they both had basically the same faith derived from Christ[6] and the same rejection of the papacy. What had been done in Zurich was not the setting up or formation of a separate church but the firm establishment there of the one church of Christ;[7] images and pictures had been removed in orderly fashion, there had been no incitements to popular discord, even the recalcitrant Ana-

---

[1] 'Ein früntliche geschrift an gemein Eydgnossen der 12 orten unnd zûgwandten, die disputation gen Baden...betreffende.' Z v, 1(10)–27; Muralt, *Baden*, 66.

[2] Constance, Schaffhausen, St Gall, Basle, Berne, as well as Zurich, came under this description.

[3] Since 1415 the county of Baden had been a Mandated Territory, or common bailiwick (*Gemeine Vogtei*) ruled collectively by Berne, Glarus, Lucerne, Uri, Schwyz, Unterwalden, Zug and Zurich, each in turn appointing a governor for two years. The rights of jurisdiction were complex. J. I. Höchle, *Geschichte der Reformation und Gegenreformation in der Stadt und Grafschaft Baden bis 1535* (Zürich, 1907), 10–17.

[4] Z v, 27, 104: 'der ein gborner Eydgnoss bin'. Cf. L. v. Muralt, *Zwinglis Reformation in der Eidgenossenschaft*, ZWA XIII (1969), 19–33. The whole appeal is redolent of a Swiss patriotism quite unusual at the time. Zwingli was always deeply conscious of the federal ties that should have united his countrymen, and he now made the most of his Toggenburg origins of which he was proud. Strictly speaking, of course, he was not a native of one of the thirteen Federated states.

[5] Muralt, *Baden*, 66; Z v, 35.   [6] Z v. 37, 70; Muralt, *Baden*, 73.   [7] Z v, 46–7.

baptists had been very moderately treated,[1] and within the city of Zurich education[2] was forwarded and the poor were admirably cared for in a community where public morality had markedly improved. As to the statement that all twelve of the Federated States had called for a meeting at Baden, this had been the result of a deceitful intrigue, and neither Berne, Basle, Solothurn, Unterwalden nor Zug had been in favour of it.[3] He went on to insist that in all his teaching there was nothing un-Christian, nothing unbiblical, nothing contradictory, even if the claims of the papacy were unacceptable. All this he was prepared to defend in person and in writing; if any of his books were shown to be erroneous, he would gladly burn them – but not at Baden, where people gathered to 'take the waters': 'it's wet there and the books wouldn't burn well'. The choice of Baden was an obvious trick; there would be no free debate there, anyone who spoke against the Pope would be imperilled at once, safe-conduct or no safe-conduct; only Rome would hope to gain. Once again he pleaded for a fair hearing in Zurich, Berne or St Gall.

Turning from Fabri's 'open letter', on 10 May 1526[4] Zwingli renewed his appeal, based on peace and patriotism, to the representatives of the Confederation. Again he defended his own probity, desiring friendship rooted in honesty, reason and affection. Although he was Swiss-born, one of those whom Eck had defamed at Rome as cowherds or worse (*kughyer*), his writings were suppressed while those of Eck were widely circulated. Any impartial person would recognise the moderation and the desire for peace that his writings showed. If, for security, he came to Baden with a great company of armed men, it would be highly inappropriate, he had no intention of coming to an insignificant place of entertainment, although any large strong city would be acceptable.

This was directed to the Swiss representatives: within the same week, on 15 May 1526, he was writing to Fabri once again, reminding him of his bishop's failure in the past to be represented when invited to the two Zurich debates, showing the strong self-confidence in his own cause which was never wanting when he was under attack, accusing his opponent of cowardice, greed, insincerity and intimidation. 'I speak the truth and you tell lies':[5] rather than face the Bible, Fabri, like his friends Eck and Emser, did nothing but retreat. Moved by greed, anxious to divide a

---

[1] Compared, that is, with the burning for heresy which faced them in any Catholic state. The imprisonment of some in the Wellenberg prison had been precautionary and had not been recommended by Zwingli.   [2] Z v, 37.   [3] Z v, 45, 65.

[4] Z v, 95(99)–108. Muralt, *Baden*, 83–4. Bullinger, *Ref.* I, 540–2, writing much later tried to show that the date 10 May 1526 had special significance because on that day Hans Hüglin of Lindau had been executed for heresy after a trial at Meersburg. This was a mistake for 1527 as v. Muralt, *Baden*, 153 following Egli, ZWA II, 381–2, shows.

[5] Z v, 135; Strickler, *Actensammlung*, I, 468–70 (No. 1439) for Fabri's answer.

peaceful community, Fabri was stupid, ignorant and an oppressor. When it came to personal abuse there was little to choose between the two antagonists.

When, just before the Baden Conference opened on 16 May, a safe-conduct arrived for Zwingli and his friends,[1] it was rejected as inadequate, as had been expected. The principle had long since been established that no citizen could be brought to trial outside his own state. The Federal Diet had no jurisdiction in matters of faith, and on legal, as well as political, grounds, Zurich's position was impregnable.

If Fabri and Eck may be regarded as counsel for the prosecution, their clerk or junior was the Franciscan from Lucerne, Thomas Murner. This ambitious friar had established a small printing press there, and in print and from the pulpit had been virulent in his coarse denunciations of Zwingli and his followers.[2] He now prepared the case for his superiors, sifted and arranged the evidence, collected testimony to attacks on church property, suppression of monasteries, marriage of nuns, rejection of ecclesiastical jurisdiction, iconoclasm, interference with the text of the Vulgate, as well as details of the challenge to the mass which was known to be the chief topic of discussion. It was this same Thomas Murner who was also to provide his own account of what happened in a narrative that he printed at Lucerne almost a year later.[3]

The proceedings at Baden were skilfully managed by Eck and Fabri, with Eck consistently holding on to the lead and arranging the business to bring the maximum discredit to the Zurich cause. The Diet of the Confederation[4] was already in session when Eck and Fabri arrived on 18 May, accompanied by an impressive military and ecclesiastical escort. There were also nominees of the Bishops of Constance, Basle, Lausanne and Chur (but not Sion), and of the Abbots of St Gall and Engelberg. In all, some 118 priests, including a number from south Germany, crowded into the little pleasure resort as direct participants, of whom 87 could be counted upon to support Eck.

The opposition in Zwingli's absence, was reluctantly, but far from inadequately, led by Oecolampadius from Basle. It is doubtful whether a better man could have been found, although this 'Hans Husschin' was less forceful in debate than Zwingli would have been. Basle was still a catholic

---

[1] Muralt, *Baden*, 85–6; Z v, 155–8; EA 4, 1a, 896–7.
[2] Muralt, *Baden*, 75–7. Some of his satires are in ZB Zurich, RE, 198.
[3] Muralt, *Baden*, 92–3.
[4] The Diet opened on 14 May. Representatives of all 13 *Orte* were present, together with delegates from Mülhausen and the Abbot and City of St Gall. Valais and the Graubünden had been invited, but declined to appear. Zurich sent Rudolf Thumisen and Hans Bleuler, Berne sent Caspar von Mülinen, and Lucerne sent Hans Hug, a bitter opponent of the reformers. EA. 4, 1a, 890ff. Muralt, *Baden*, 95–6.

city, and Oecolampadius, while basically in agreement with his friend Zwingli, was certainly not his mouthpiece or agent. His own views on the eucharist, for example, which he had set out at some length, harmonised with the Zwinglian viewpoint but were not identical with it.[1] Gentle and retiring, he was none the less determined and devoted to the cause for which he risked his life amid a throng of hostile, petulant and noisy opponents. 'Would that that tall fair man had been on our side', one of the latter remarked,[2] and, in fact, he held his own admirably. That he could do little was clear from the outset. As soon as mass had been sung at 5 a.m. on 19 May, procedure was discussed, or, more accurately, dictated by Fabri and Eck. Oecolampadius' submission that the text of the Bible was decisive in the event of disagreement, was brushed aside, and he was given no adequate opportunity to state his case.

There were to be four alternate chairmen or presidents[3] only one of whom, Dr Ludwig Bär of Basle, was not completely committed to the Catholic cause. There were to be four notaries to record the course of the speeches, and careful precautions were taken to see that no other notes were made and that no independent report of the proceedings was sent to any printers. These initial arrangements underlined the fact that the gathering at Baden was a Catholic demonstration rather than a public enquiry. Each day's meeting opened with the celebration of mass, but evangelical sermons were prohibited. The Catholic case was presented under pre-arranged headings, and the expression of contrary opinions treated as offensive, provocative and evidence of heresy. For the period of the debate the participants were prisoners in Baden, strictly prohibited from communicating in writing with their friends outside. Zurich was but fourteen miles off, and Zwingli was impatient for news and ready with exhortation and advice. The walls and gates of Baden were carefully guarded by fifty men against spies and emissaries, but the hundreds of additional visitors had to be fed, and every morning at daybreak countrymen and women would be admitted with fresh milk, eggs, butter, chickens and other supplies. Among these was Zwingli's friend and admirer Thomas Platter.[4] This young man managed not only to get inside the walls but also to hear, or hear of, a good deal that was said, which he reported to Zwingli. Letters

---

[1] J. J. Herzog, *Das Leben Johannis Oekolampads und die Reformation der Kirche zu Basel*, 2 Bde. (Basle, 1843), is admirable for its date, but almost is entirely superseded by E. Staehelin, *Briefe*, and *Das theologische Lebenswerk Johannes Oekolampads* (Leipzig, 1939) (QFRG XXI). G. Rupp, *Patterns of Reformation* (London, 1969), 3–46.
[2] Mörikofer, II, 35.
[3] Barnabas, Abbot of Engelberg, Jakob Stapfer (St Gall), Hans Honneger (Bremgarten), Ludwig Bär (Basle). (For the latter, Z VII, 321–2.)
[4] Muralt, *Baden*, 120; *Thomas Platter Lebensbeschreibung* hg. A. Hartmann, (Basle, 1944), 74. O. Farner, *Die grosse Wende in Zürich* (Zürich, 1941) 55–6. Zwingli also received information from Hieronymus Zimmermann (or Wälschen) of Winterthur. Knittel, 130.

235

thus went to and fro and Zwingli was able to exchange notes with Oeco-lampadius and to send his supporters some help and advice.

Eck had drawn up a list of seven propositions[1] for discussion aimed at the destruction of his opponents under the general headings of transub-stantiation, the mass as a sacrifice, mediation of the Virgin Mary and the saints, images, purgatory, original sin and the efficacy of infant baptism, the regular stock-in-trade of the hardened controversialist. It was to these carefully drafted propositions that Oecolampadius and his few supporters were required to speak; even so, they were given no facilities, and faced frequent interruptions intended to divert attention from the remarks of certain fair-minded Catholics to the effect that the opposing case was well stated. The presidents always allowed Eck the final word; he had advisers and books of reference constantly at hand and delighted in shouting down opposition, punctuating his overbearing insolence with coarse humour. To this he added the occasional appeal to Swiss sentiment: they were united in admiration of a glorious and entirely orthodox past, while division marked the ranks of their opponents. Luther, the arch-heretic, taught differently from Zwingli, the Anabaptists were anathema to both, Oecolampadius's own eucharistic teaching was not precisely that of Zwingli.

From Catholic Berne, characteristically a little late, came a party which included Peter Kunz and Berchtold Haller.[2] This latter trusted emissary, who had been a canon at the Berne minster but was no great scholar, had read the Bible carefully, had been accounted a 'Lutheran', and now sup-ported Oecolampadius. His rather ineffective interventions were conse-quently received with contumely and disdain which was resented in Berne. On the main eucharistic issue nothing new was heard; Eck could triumph over an absent opponent the more easily in that it was ruled that silence implied consent, and most were content to be unheard.

On one theme, that of justification, Oecolampadius had upheld the Zwinglian and Lutheran view that if man could attain salvation by his own efforts ('works') then Christ had died in vain. This provoked an exchange of texts, authorities, assertions and counter-arguments, but to little effect. When, on 8 June, a final count was made, Eck's original propositions were agreed by 84 supporters, with 24 opponents and 8 abstentions. What was noted with glee by the Catholics was that all four Lutherans present,[3] two from Mühlhausen, supported Eck. From this moment, Koehler rightly maintained, the Lutheran cause was lost in Switzerland, and the suspicion,

---

[1] EA 4, 1a, 927; Muralt, *Baden*, 100–1; Bullinger, *Ref.* I, 351.
[2] Z VIII, 691; Feller, II, 142–3. See below, 249 n. 3.
[3] Matthias Kessler, Benedikt Burgauer, Johannes Glotherus, Augustinus Krömer (or Kramer). Muralt, *Baden*, 119.

later heightened by Melanchthon, that there could be a Lutheran 'sell out' to Rome, was born. Neither the theological arguments of Oecolampadius, nor letters from Zwingli, had any serious effect. The Reformers' case rested upon their conviction that they were opposed only to papal innovations and were otherwise entirely orthodox. They also pointed out that the security of the Confederation was threatened by the now avowed papal–imperial alliance, but Eck and Fabri had no difficulty in securing support. When the last of the delegates took horse for their homes, the final attempt at a peaceful settlement had failed. In the light of the decision, the suppression of Zwingli's writings was again demanded,[1] together with the prohibition in every state of Lutheran preaching.[2] A final, official text of the whole debate was to be circulated.[3] There never was, in fact, an agreed account or minutes of this colloquy. Four secretaries or scribes had been appointed to take notes of the speeches and to compile an agreed version[4] in four copies of what was said, to be deposited with the governor (*Landvogt*) of Baden, who would then be responsible for a transcript which was to be circulated to all states as the accepted version. To the four official reporters the Schultheiss of Lucerne added a fifth, Hans Huber,[5] town clerk of the city of Lucerne, thus ensuring a Catholic majority among the reporters and the prevalence of the Catholic 'line' in the event of a dispute. Even so, when the minutes were available in print[6] the authenticity of this account was at once challenged. A request from Berne, Basle and Zurich for a sight of the original notes of the official reporters was refused,[7] thus enabling Zwingli to maintain that a full narrative of the debate would prove the validity of his case.

After the disputation, each state had, then, to decide on a course of action, since, whatever deference might be paid to the conclusions of an all-clerical assembly, they lacked any binding power. The politicians had to have the final word, and it soon became apparent that the sovereign components of Federation would each move its own way. Berne soon made

[1] EA 4, 1a, 914.
[2] EA 4, 1a, 922–37.
[3] It took almost a year, until May 1527, for the minutes to be printed and circulated, and even then in an unacceptable version. E. Staehelin, *Zwei private Publikationen über die Badener Disputation und ihre Autoren*, ZKG xxxvii (Gotha, 1918), 378–405; Muralt, *Baden*, 92, 131–2.
[4] Z v, 310.
[5] Muralt, *Baden*, 125; ZWA v, 41–6.
[6] As *Die Disputacion vor den xij Orten einer loblichen Eidtgnoschafft…MCCCCC und xxvi… vollendet* (Lucerne, 1527).
[7] Feller II, 147–8; Muralt, *Baden*, 131. Writing in July 1526 to the Confederates, Zwingli insisted that Murner was 'cooking' the evidence in Lucerne – 'Alle ding in Murners henden und gwalt sind, der aber trucken möcht, was er wölt oder die imm so wol vertruwend.' Z v, 315; Z vii, 708; Muralt, *Baden*, 131; T. Murner. *Caussa Heluetica orthodoxae fidei. Disputatio Heluetiorum in Baden…* (Lucerne, 1528).

clear its intention to act independently. Nine states[1] were prepared to come into line, and adopted the resolutions, so far as applicable to them, of the Regensburg Convention,[2] thus accepting the Edict of Worms (1521) as operative in part of Switzerland: Zwingli as a heretic like Wyclif and Hus and as a Lutheran adherent (which he was not) was *ipso facto* excommunicated and an outlaw in their eyes.[3]

Zwingli realised that at Baden the ranks of his opponents had been closed and that Zurich was still more isolated when the nine[3] states again threatened to refuse to join it in taking the common oath of allegiance to the Confederation.[4] Few things better illustrate the inextricable entanglement of religion and politics than this episode. The Baden colloquy had been a public discussion about church dogma carried on by a selected group of committed ecclesiastics, yet it immeditaely led to political action. The nine states (among which, Glarus was soon to revise its opinions) agreed to treat the inhabitants of Zurich as outcasts, but they were only minor states. Basle, Schaffhausen, and above all Berne, had yet to declare themselves. In Basle, Erasmus, who had refused an invitation to be present at the discussions,[5] found the current of popular opinion running against him and against the patrician families with whom he loved to associate. Oecolampadius returned to his preaching and writing with enhanced prestige, and the Rhine city became more alienated than ever from its bishop and one-time overlord. It was not Lutheran, nor Zwinglian yet, but it was not Catholic either.[6] Schaffhausen[7] had close economic and political ties with Zurich, and was well content that the Gospel should continue to be preached and the monasteries remain closed – Sebastian Hofmeister had put church affairs there safely on the Zwinglian path three years previously. Berne was still Catholic, but was moving towards the reformation that was urged by Haller, and in its own time and at its own pace was to arrange its own decisive public debate. There remained the complex of legal rights in the Mandated Territories, over which some nominal cooperation was indispensable, and of the varying alliances, some almost amounting to protectorates, all of which helped to prevent clear-cut division. There was, too, the ever-present tradition of Habsburg hostility. The

---

[1] Uri, Schwyz, Unterwalden, Lucerne, Zug, Solothurn, Fribourg, Appenzell, Glarus.
[2] Muralt, *Baden*, 136–7; EA 4, 1a, 935–7; see above p. 225.
[3] Koehler, *Z & L* I, 337; *Zwingli*, 166–7.
[4] Rappard, *Du renouvellement*, 53–6.
[5] Allen VI, 337–42 (correcting the date by Koehler, *Z & L* I, 146). Allen (338) mistakenly supposed that Zwingli was present at Baden.
[6] P. Roth, *Durchbruch und Festsetzung der Reformation in Basel* (Basle, 1942) (Basler Beiträge zur Geschichtswissenschaft Bd. 8), 8–10; *Die Reformation in Basel*, 1. Teil, *Die Vorbereitungsjahre (1525–8)*, Basler Nbl. 114 (Basle, 1936), 38, 46, 49.
[7] J. Wipf, *Reformationsgeschichte der Stadt und Landschaft Schaffhausen* (Zürich, 1929); ZWA V, 11–41.

Archduke Ferdinand, brother of the Emperor, had not accepted as permanent the loss of his family possessions south of the Rhine, and Switzerland was not to be internationally recognised as anything more than a German league within the Holy Roman Empire until 1648.

The Catholic triumph at Baden brought these considerations sharply to the fore. Berne with its French-orientated policy, with its need to secure the obedience of its frequently recalcitrant rural subjects, and with its determination that Aargau should remain under its *de facto* control, was forced to take a hard look at the implications of May and June 1526. Just as Basle upheld its leading preacher Oecolampadius, so Berne was not prepared to withdraw support from Berchtold Haller or even take action against the inspired cartoonist and rhymster, Niklaus Manuel.[1] Berne, likewise, could not accept the isolation of its mighty neighbour Zurich; and Berne, Zurich, Basle, Schaffhausen, together had valuable resources and strong positions. Just as the Colloquy of Baden did little more than proclaim the unity of the committed Catholic states, so the meeting of the Swiss Diet at Baden that same week reinforced the determination of the individual states to maintain their independent state rights. There was no majority vote which could commit others, the representatives reporting to their respective governments, each of which was free to choose its path. The patricians of Berne strengthened their defences and reconsidered their interests, while the Council at Zurich rejoiced that Zwingli had remained at home. He now became more vocal than ever, for he was near the apex of his influence there. The Catholics had little cause to be jubilant over their success, such as it was. They had, in fact, slammed the door on further discussion, had wrecked the cause of unity within the Confederation, and had demonstrated their dependence on external support. Eck had indeed carried everything to his own satisfaction, but he was an alien and disliked by many even of his own followers, whereas the reputation of his antagonist, Oecolampadius, was much enhanced. Baden forced the pace, but to the ultimate disadvantage of the victors.

Was Zwingli right to absent himself from Baden? Technically and juridically, yes – there was no need for him to attend and the Zurich government explicitly forbade it. His presence could have made little difference to the outcome and, at best, he must have suffered personal humiliation. The whole machinery of the disputation was constructed to crush and thwart him; he was to be declared a heretic and to suffer the fate of one.

None the less, morally, he had run away. If he had perished in the flames at Baden as a Confessor, in spite of the protection of a solemn safe-conduct, his influence might have been magnified tenfold, not diminished

[1] K. Guggisberg, *Bernische Kirchengeschichte* (Berne, 1958), 57–9, 71–5.

9-2

as it was to be by the dubious politics of the next five years. Zurich would have been the stronger for such a martyr: his doctrine was safe there, his disciples could maintain the cause, and his example would have convinced many more. Speculation is unprofitable, but so, too, are some of the arguments adduced in favour of the action he took. More reasonably, he might have maintained that providence directed his footsteps away from Baden in 1526 and to the field of Kappel in 1531. Humanly speaking, however, he neglected the opportunity to use his great abilities to state his case before a hostile audience, and seemed to lack the courage needed to meet Eck and the Catholic supporters and to face the consequences of his convictions.[1]

Koehler rightly regarded the remaining five years of Zwingli's life as a fatal compromise with the world of politics. If his teaching was to survive, it must have not only continued government support, but his government must have backing from outside – from the favourably inclined Swiss cities, from St Gall and Constance and thence from Württemberg and south Germany. Religious freedom in Switzerland could merge into the Protestant–Catholic struggle for the control of western Europe. If the evangelical cause was not to suffer from the Catholic triumph at Baden, some decisive counter-measures were required. First of all it was necessary for the distinction between Lutherans and Zwinglians to be more clearly and sharply defined. This meant reopening and elaborating the differences about the eucharist, showing, if possible, that the Lutheran teaching was dangerously close to that of Rome. Secondly, the sectaries had to be scattered and their plea for a separated church or series of churches rendered untenable, both in Zurich territory and beyond it. Thirdly, Zurich must now intervene actively to help the evangelicals in eastern Switzerland and take up the problem of monastic foundations there which included its relations with the city and the abbey of St Gall. The two other important governments impinging upon Zurich territory were Basle and Berne; at the time of the Baden colloquy, they were still officially Catholic; Erasmus was defending the Catholic cause against Luther from his house in Basle, and there, as in Berne, the powerful and respected patricians on their smaller councils were unwilling to depart from the faith of their forefathers. This situation was not to last much longer.

Constant attention also needed to be paid to the south German cities, where the cause of the Gospel had made such an encouraging progress in

---

[1] It is interesting to note that Heinrich Hug of Villingen, who recorded Swiss events with some interest, merely noted Zwingli's wilful absence. 'Aber der Zwingle, pfarer zù Zurich, wolt nit ge Baden'. He describes Zwingli's end with great coolness – 'keczersen bredicanten, genempt der Zwyngle...do fand man den Zwingle, den bredycanten, der alle kecery hatt geübt, der hatt ain grùn klaid an und zock under dem huffen wie ain ander kriegsman'. *Heinrich Hugs Villinger Chronik von 1495 bis 1533*, hg. v. C. Roder (Tübingen, 1883), 156, 198, 200.

Reform and reaction

Constance, Isny, Memmingen, Ravensburg, Biberach, Ulm, and as far north as Esslingen. The Austrian-Habsburg administrators had indeed succeeded in retaining southern Alsace, including Waldshut and Rheinfelden, for Rome, but the great imperial Rhine city of Strassburg,[1] with close trading and political relations with the Swiss, had already rejected papal authority without finding the whole of Lutheran teaching acceptable. Much might turn upon the form of worship finally adopted there, and this seemed likely to depend upon the impact made by Bucer.[2] If, as was easily possible, Strassburg, Mülhausen, Rottweil and Constance were to become closer allies, almost constituent parts of the Confederation, its strength would be greatly enhanced. That they never did so was a measure of the success first of the Counter Reformation and then of Louis XIV.

Above all, everything depended upon Zurich, which must remain secure for the faith. Even if he had wished it, Zwingli could not have avoided close involvement in internal and external politics, and this, in turn, meant personalities. Luther, safe under the protection of an autocratic German Elector, could, in his later years, very largely leave politics alone and concentrate on his ministry and writings; his attitude of detachment from secular affairs, for which he could find New Testament support and precedents, came easily to a born Saxon. There were good reasons to urge in its favour and, in Wittenberg at any rate, it was both sensible and simple. Such an approach, however, was not practicable for Zwingli; his 'Prince' was 'die Obrigkeit', the Government, the 212 pieces that made up his kaleidoscopic Great Council. Without its support his cause was lost, and therefore he felt obliged to concern himself more and more with public affairs. The Colloquy of Baden was a manifest setback from which he must recover, and this soon. His strength within the city of Zurich lay in the support he received from the leaders and rank and file of the gilds or companies who were in effective control of affairs and for whom, as for so many early-sixteenth-century city dwellers, religion, being right with God, was all-important.

The former patricians of the Constaffel were mostly traditionalists, and there was a considerable group among and around them (of whom Am Grüt had been representative) who were both satisfied with, and prepared to revert to, the conditions of 1519. There was Catholic reaction under the

---

[1] J. Adam, *Evangelische Kirchengeschichte der Stadt Strassburg bis zur französischen Revolution.* (Strassburg, 1922) 1–43. W. Andreas, *Strassburg an der Wende vom Mittelalter zur Neuzeit* (Elsass-Lothringisches Jahrbuch, 13 (Frankfurt a.M. 1934). R. Reuss, 'La Réforme à Strasbourg 1525–1530, 1530–1536' (Bulletin de la société de l'histoire du Protestantisme Français 67 (1918), 249–80, 68 (1919) 257–75). A. Baum, *Magistrat und Reformation in Strassburg bis 1529* (Strassburg, 1887).

[2] Bucer is how he came to be known in Cambridge from the Latinised form of Butzer which is nowadays preferred by some writers.

surface, and it was indispensable to keep it there, and this meant no compromise. It must be made abundantly clear that Zurich was even further apart from Rome than was Wittenberg. This involved a resumption of the eucharistic controversy. It also meant raising again the issue of gifts, retainers and pensions from foreign powers, the more so since many of those who were suspected of receiving gifts from foreign powers were also opponents of evangelism. All through the summer of 1526 the ministers were raising their voices in the pulpit, calling again for denunciation and punishment of the pensioners. Names began to circulate – there was Heinrich Rahn, who everyone knew had taken money from Ulrich, pretender to the Duchy of Württemberg,[1] while Heinrich Rubli, Ludwig Tschudi, Cornel Schulthess, Hans Peter Wellenberg, Hans Escher, all well-known names of famous local families, were all reported to be in the pay of the King of France, whose call for an all-Swiss alliance had been emphatically rejected by Zurich, and of Pope Clement VII who had refused to pay his lawful debts and was now identified by the reformers with anti-Christ. The most significant name among them, possibly, was that of Junker Jakob Grebel whose son was a leading figure among the Reformation Radicals.[2] The old man (he was 66) had, it was asserted, already pocketed 4,000 crowns and was asking the papal agent, William Falconer, (Guillelmus de Falconibus) for more.

From the pulpits the matter was taken up in the council chamber: these and similar allegations led to a committee of enquiry[3] on 22 September 1526, which found sufficient evidence of flame as well as smoke to ask for and obtain the appointment of a formal court or tribunal of 11[4] to receive explicit evidence. Zwingli and any others who had information were invited to supply actual names, dates and figures to justify their allegations. These were produced, some necessarily based on hearsay, which, however, was good enough for the age, which relied much on verbal reports, and there was sufficient direct evidence to substantiate a number of charges and to cause the tribunal to fear something worse.

Three of the many suspects were committed for further investigation, Hans Escher and Heinrich Leu being confined in the Wellenberg,[5] Grebel being detained more honourably in the Rathaus. Proceedings against him

---

[1] Z v, 409; Wyss, 66. See below 380–1.   [2] Z v, 402–12.

[3] Z v, 403. The four members were Seckelmeister Jakob Werdmüller, Konrad Gull, Hans Schneeberger, M. Jeckli. Egli *1*, 489 no. 1042.

[4] Z VIII, 779–80. Heinrich Walder, Diethelm Röist, Rudolf Thumysen, Hans Ochsner, Jakob Werdmüller, Hans Jäggli (Jäckli) ('bonus et incorruptus'), Ulrich Kambli, Thomas Sprüngli, Konrad Gull, Hans Schneeberger, Rudolf Binder – the hard core of Zurich businessmen and experienced politicians. For the individuals see H. G. Wirz, *Zürcher Familienschicksale im Zeitalter Zwinglis*, ZWA VI (1938), 537–574 and G. Gerig, *Reisläufer und Pensionenherren in Zürich 1519–1532* (Zurich, 1947).

[5] They were soon released on bail. Leu was a well known artist.

were continued; after torture, the white-haired old man was found guilty of pension-taking and treason, and on 30 October 1526 he was executed. It was entirely a decision by the council, with which Zwingli technically and administratively had no concern;[1] but had he suggested mercy the knight's life would assuredly have been saved. It is significant that his influence grew and that his two leading opponents were removed, as indeed they would have been in most other countries, on grounds which were not more than dubiously adequate. The safety of the state in the case of the father, the purity of the Gospel in the case of the son; in each case Zwingli seems to have looked with blinkered eyes upon what happened. The Grebel family was powerful in Zurich, and by his action Zwingli had demonstrated once again the extent of his influence and his opposition to the patricians. He had secured, as it were, a vote of confidence and further evidence that the government was behind his preaching. It meant also that he was becoming more closely involved in politics, and he failed to make the appeal for mercy which would better have become the minister of God. At a price, the way was now clear for the expansion and extension of his teaching over the whole of northern Switzerland and beyond. In particular, he must turn his attention to events in Berne and in St Gall.

[1] For a review of the evidence see L. Schelbert, 'Jacob Grebel's Trial Revised', ARG 60 (1969), 32–64.

243

10

Berne intervenes

The Catholic triumph at the disputation of Baden, however transitory, was a setback for all that Zwingli stood for. The forces of opposition had united against him in public discussions from which Zurich had been excluded. An answer there must be, likewise in a public forum, as well as in print, and this happened in January 1528, when the Swiss reformers came into their own. This, it is to be noted, was in Berne, the capital of the largest state in Switzerland.

Sixty miles of relatively difficult country separated Berne from Zurich and brought a greater degree of detachment than is suggested by the distance. Their boundaries nowhere coincided since between them was thrust the tongue of the Freie Aemter, part of the Mandated Territories under joint inter-state control. The two states had indeed been Confederates since 1353, and their inhabitants were German speakers, but their dialects were very different and their traditions almost equally divergent. Zurich, with its mildly democratic constitution, was an ancient trading centre where transport, commerce and manufactures kept its citizens busy and reasonably prosperous. Berne was an artificially created borough whose affairs were managed in practice by a small number of leading families; it was a rustic place, little more than a convenient cattle market and centre of supplies for farmers from the countryside.[1]

Berne had been the most successfully aggressive of all Swiss city states and had secured notable gains in central Switzerland. From Brugg in the north east to Meiringen in the south east and Aigle in the south west, a great semi-circle of territories was ruled by Bernese councillors, and further advances were yet to come. After Zurich had been coerced, early in the fifteenth century, into abandoning the Austrian alliance and had been cheated out of the Toggenburg inheritance, Berne had taken the lead in, and had reaped most of the profit from, the overthrow of Charles of Burgundy. This carried with it intimate involvement in French and Savoyard politics, and this for a state that was powerful only conditionally.

[1] Thomas Murner described it 'utpote civitatem simplicem, rusticam, indoctam, sed pugnacem, bellicosam et potentem'. ZWA xiii, 400 n. 2.

Berne was poor. It had expanded piecemeal and its state rights were limited by custom, law and practicality. Almost a federation in itself, its considerable possessions called for skilled and tactful management.

The rulers of Berne had learnt to exercise a remarkable capacity for government. Orders were issued and enforced; several hundred villages and local communities looked to them for guidance which was received and paid for. There was, indeed, sometimes discontent but it was never really serious for, through their local officers, the government kept a firm and restraining, but also understanding, hand on its subjects. There was consultation and intelligent compliance as well as domination.

As became the governors of a mainly bucolic population, the citizens of Berne had a deserved reputation for slowness, by some misguidedly confused with stupidity.[1] They had, in fact, constantly to guard against being overwhelmed by a combination of Pope, Emperor, France and Savoy. Hence the alliance with France, cooperation with Zurich and the recognition that the Reformation enhanced Berne's power as against that of the church. Hence, too, the acceptance by its leading citizens of French money in return for service with French armies in causes that suited Berne's interests.

With ambivalent policies almost forced upon Bernese governments, it is hardly surprising that their measures were sometimes mistrusted by the other Swiss states, which neither appreciated Berne's difficulties nor sympathised with its western preoccupations. Savoyard claims had to be resisted but Savoy itself had to be protected from absorption by France or the Empire. Berne was interested to maintain a peaceful Swiss Confederation and this was not made easier by the warlike propensities of its subjects. Violence was commonplace, boys were brought up to expect to fight, and war, especially when profitable, was accounted glorious.

There was very little in any way exceptional about the religious life of Berne. Its bishop was far distant – at Constance for all of its territory east of the Aar, at Lausanne for the greater part of the remainder. There was no suggestion of heresy and very little of dissatisfaction; relations with Rome were normal and friendly. Relics were esteemed, pilgrimages were popular, indulgences were purchased and no one doubted that the saints could and did work miracles. There had been some relatively minor differences with the Bishop of Basle, and the clergy and their property were very much under state control, but all without friction. The principal church, St Vincent's, collegiate only since 1485, known as the Minster, was well supported and had all that a great Gothic building could offer in

---

[1] The Bernese were the Bavarians of Swiss history, with Zurich, smart, alert and intelligent, as a foil. 'Die berner beklagend, die Zürcher sien ze hitzig, so klagen die Zürcher, die Berner sien ze witzig.' Anshelm v, 362.

impressive ritual and splendid decoration. Its clergy, drawn mostly from local patrician families, were not notable either for learning or for piety, and there were occasional clashes over matters of jurisdiction. The 'inferior' secular clergy were at best undistinguished and at worst lazy and ignorant. For the most part they were rather ordinary men of the peasant class, able to read the services and administer the sacraments, not expected to preach and usually living with a permanent housekeeper known to, and accepted by, everyone. Badly paid in many instances, frequently working on their own farms, they were neither admired nor disliked, save when they claimed excessive privileges.

The Regulars were even less esteemed. The monks were, by all credible accounts, idle. They had property rights which were upheld by the government, but they were often corporately in debt and administered their possessions badly; they did little or nothing for the poor, and performed their own statutory services slackly or not at all.[1] The friars, more active because they were licensed beggars, confessors and preachers, were not popular.

The complacent piety of the citizens of Berne and the reputation of the Dominican Order were shaken in 1509 by the strange Jetzer affair.[2] Hans Jetzer was a tailor by trade who in 1506 joined the Dominican order in Berne. Plausible, handsome, vain and a considerable actor, he soon attracted a good deal of attention, particularly from women, by his sermons and conversation. Soon he began to tell of his dreams, experiences and visions. First St Barbara, and then the Blessed Virgin herself, appeared before him, weeping tears of blood, giving him a seal with five drops of blood and finally imprinting the stigmata on his hand. She even indicated that she did not support the Franciscans in their insistence upon her immaculate conception. Soon Jetzer was working miracles; the excitement became so great that the city called for a public investigation, with disastrous results. Under pressure and torture, the friars confessed to connivance at deliberate deception, and although Jetzer, as a stranger, was allowed to return to his native Zurzach, four friars were burnt, the reputation of the order in Berne was markedly lowered and a blow was struck at the credibility of miracles. It came at a time, too, when questions were

---

[1] There were friaries at Burgdorf, Zofingen and Königsfelden, a number of nunneries and some sixteen monasteries including Interlaken, Thorberg, Frienisberg, Rüeggisberg and Trub. The government of Berne regarded itself as the 'protector' or guardian of the monastic property, which made later occupation easy. Feller II, 87, 91–2; K. Guggisberg, *Bernische Kirchengeschichte* (Berne, 1958), 24–7.

[2] R. Steck, *Die Akten des Jetzerprozesses, nebst dem Defensorium* (Basle, 1904), QSG XXII; N. Paulus, *Ein Justizmord an vier Dominikanern begangen* (Frankfurt, 1897); R. Steck, *Der Berner Jetzerprozess (1507–9) in neuer Beleuchtung* (Berne, 1902); H. von Greyerz, *Der Jetzerprozess und die Humanisten*, Archiv des Historischen Vereins des Kantons Bern 31 (Berne, 1932); Z v, 703 n. 5.

being asked about both the theory and the practice of monasticism. Scepticism about local miracles was engendered and also some critical thoughts about the special attraction of the life of the Regulars. There was, however, little obvious anti-clericalism, and the older aristocratic families remained firmly attached to traditional beliefs as expounded by the beneficed clergy, particularly the prebendaries of St Vincent's. Gifts continued to be made to the churches for ornaments, services were reasonably well attended and indulgences were purchased without much comment. The chief supporters of the Catholic cause were the three original Confederate states, Uri, Schwyz and Unterwalden, which, along with Lucerne, were on Berne's eastern flank and were unswervingly Roman and papal in their spiritual allegiance. The government of France, Berne's ally, in spite of some Lutheran infiltration, remained consistently Catholic, as, to the south, did the Duke of Savoy, son-in-law of the Emperor Charles V. Berne had profited most from the collapse of Burgundy and had taken a leading part in promoting the 'perpetual' French alliance in 1515, but had been disappointed and frustrated at its outcome. Bernese soldiers, too, had lost their lives fighting for a France which was increasingly unsuccessful in north Italy, and the subsidies promised were frequently unpaid.

The Cardinal Bishop of Sion, Matthew Schiner, although personally disliked and suspected by many leading citizens, had readily recruited soldiers for the papal armies both in Berne and Fribourg, the neighbouring state whose fortunes were so closely linked with Berne that for many purposes they acted in concert. Fribourg, however, remained consistently Catholic. What makes the outcome of events in Berne[1] so significant is that the triumph of the Reformation there meant that Berne and Zurich acted together at a critical moment in the history of Switzerland. If Berne had remained Catholic when the Counter-Reformation came, Catholicism might have been imposed on the whole Confederation, with Zurich coerced into agreement. While Berne acted in harmony with Zurich, or at least maintained a benevolent neutrality, Zurich could feel secure, being strong enough to resist successfully any local attackers.

Zwingli had known Berne well during his youth when he had studied there. There were family connections also and he was in frequent correspondence with some of the more intellectual and enlightened of the priests. At the same time, he was not popular because of his opposition to

---

[1] Feller II is the indisputable guide. The documents are assembled in Steck & Tobler. Some additional material is printed in M. von Stürler, *Urkunden der Bernischen Kirchenreform* I, *1520–1528* (Berne, 1862), a singularly difficult book to use; E. Bloesch, *Geschichte der schweizerisch-reformierten Kirchen* I (Berne, 1898). (Bd. II, 1899 is concerned with events after Zwingli's death). A number of facsimiles are helpfully collected in A. Fluri, *Die Beziehungen Berns zu den Buchdruckern in Basel, Zürich und Genf 1476–1536* (Berne, 1913).

the French alliance and to mercenary service, and he hardly understood the permanent necessities that guided Berne's policy.[1] There was, however, very little sign of any direct impact of Reformation thought on Berne before 1523, and its government had refused to be represented at the Zurich religious debates of that year. Luther's writings had, however, circulated in Berne before Zwingli was known there, thus preparing the way for his teaching. In any case, opposition to the papacy was acceptable since the Pope was hostile to Berne's ally, the King of France. Zwingli had, however, some influential supporters living within its city walls. They were, indeed, like Francis Lambert, at first regarded as Lutheran adherents, which meant that the new doctrines were not directly linked with Zurich in the first instance.[2] Included among them were Zwingli's own former teacher, the would-be humanist, Heinrich Wölfflin, and the artist-orator Niklaus Manuel (Deutsch).[3] This latter, a sincere, if slightly disreputable, character, appealed to the low humour of the Gasse-dwellers and was notorious for his jeering verses about the clergy and for his parodies of the mystery plays[4] which were enacted at street corners. A painter by trade, he became almost an artist of repute whose delineation of that strangely popular subject, the Dance of Death,[5] round the Dominican cloisters was almost as well known as that in the Basle Dominican cemetery and the superb woodcuts by Hans Holbein the younger. Manuel's noisy exhibitionism was not entirely superficial; he was also a sincere Bible reader who by 1522 had become convinced that better ways of worship, prayer and religious association were needed. He also recognised that the way to bring this about must lie through city politics, and he acted accordingly with remarkable skill.

Among the grey-robed Franciscans was their *Lesemeister* or theological instructor, Sebastian Meyer,[6] learned and eloquent, who was entranced by the Bible text and determined to base his preaching upon it. There was also the Bavarian, Jörg Brunner, indefatigable in quoting texts against the hierarchy, and Valerius Anshelm, one of the many medical men of the age with an interest in humane letters, which developed into independent

[1] Feller II, 186.
[2] Feller II, 113f. As the ally of France (which Zurich was not), Berne was in opposition to the strongly Catholic Habsburg Emperor.
[3] Born c. 1484 of Italian extraction, he was connected with the painter known as the 'master with the carnation'. C. A. Beerli, *Le peintre poète Nicolas Manuel et l'évolution sociale de son temps, Travaux d' humanisme et Renaissance* III–IV (Geneva, 1953); Feller II, 79, 88, 97, 115–20, 171.
[4] The most notorious of these was performed at Shrove-tide 1523, satirising the Pope and the hierarchy with coarse and boisterous vulgarity. Text in J. Bächtold u. F. Vetter, *Bibliothek älterer Schriftwerke der deutschen Schweiz*, II, *Nicklaus Manuel* (Frauenfeld, 1878) 29–111; Buck/Fabian, 360.   [5] J. M. Clark, *The Dance of Death* (Glasgow, 1950) 71–5.
[6] Z I, 541 n. 2; VII, 611 n. 1; Vad. Br. III, 12, 113.

views on the nature of the church and the sacraments, and which were reflected in the selectivity of his important chronicle.[1] Nicklaus von Wattenwil, Provost of St Vincent's from 1523, whom many expected to be the next Bishop of Lausanne, and with him Lienhard Tremp, Warden of the Hospital, belonging to the powerful tailors' gild, publicly sympathised with the reforming party.[2] Most influential of all was the official Minster preacher or lecturer, Canon Berchtold Haller,[3] a little busybody of a man, restless and passionately determined to share with others his joy and hope in the new-found Bible. Without Haller as his friend and ally, Zwingli might never have had a real following in Berne – their correspondence is among the most revealing of the surviving letters. Not only did Haller help to ensure that Berne did not break off diplomatic relations with Zurich, but he was also present at the Baden disputation and demonstrated the confused and tendencious nature of the minutes when these were available.[4] It was the refusal of a certified copy of these minutes to the Council of Berne which led to Berne's refusal to be accounted an organising participant and was one of the chief factors in precipitating the Reformation in that city. Having heard the arguments of Oecolampadius at Baden, Haller refused, on his return, to say the Roman mass in the Minster and was, in consequence, later dismissed from his lucrative canonry but allowed to continue preaching.[5] This was acceptable because already on 15 June 1523 the council had issued a mandate known from the saints' day on which it was promulgated as the Mandate of St Vitus and St Modestus,[6] requiring that preaching should be based on the Bible only, but free of Lutheran or other error. This had been done, as was thought, to protect the church from attack.

The rulers of Berne were thoroughly pragmatic. With matters of piety and religion they were not concerned, but what was said in the pulpit could affect the state and must be safeguarded. Similarly, they were pre-

---

[1] Anshelm's wife was fined for using words discrediting the Virgin Mary, Anshelm's salary as medical officer was reduced by half in January 1524, as a result of which he left Berne for his native Rottweil (Feller II, 123). He returned in 1529.   [2] Feller II, 129.

[3] Berchtold Haller (c. 1492–1536) from Aldingen (Rottweil) graduated at Cologne in 1510, taught Latin as Wittenbach's assistant at Berne from 1513, and was one of the priests attached to the Minster. He was not a notable scholar, but he was entirely honest, expressed his feelings with conviction, and was popular in Berne. In later life he grew so fat that a door in the Chancel had to be widened for him. (Z VII, 484 n. 1; Z IX, 10; XI, 480 n. 6). Myconius introduced him to Zwingli, whose devoted disciple he soon became. M. Kirchhofer, *B. Haller oder die Reformation von Bern* (Zürich, 1828), 226. He is not be to confused with Johannes Haller, priest at Amsoldingen, the first priest in Bernese territory to marry, but allowed by the government to retain his benefice, canon law notwithstanding. He later moved to Zurich and was killed at Kappel in 1531. Z VIII, 442 n. 18.   [4] See above, 237 and n. 7.

[5] Feller II, 143–4.
[6] Steck & Tobler, 65–8 (No. 249); Feller II, 122. A facsimile in A. Fluri, *Schweizerisches Gutenbergmuseum* 14 (1928), 3–6 and E. Büchler, *Die Anfänge des Buchdrucks in der Schweiz*[2] (Berne, 1951), 103–4.

pared to decide whether clergy should be taxed, whether excommunications from Basle should be effective in their territory, or whether nuns might leave their Houses to be married. Zwingli recognised how the Mandate and the thinking behind it could help his cause and wrote *Von göttlicher und menschlicher Gerechtigkeit* in July to demonstrate that there was nothing subversive about his own biblical teaching.[1] Tithes, rent, interest, if approved by the government, must be paid; human laws are necessary because of the inherent wickedness of mankind. After Adam all men were selfish, and a human magistracy is necessary to keep their worst instincts in check. Human justice is a poor and inadequate substitute for divine righteousness but it must be accepted thankfully. A government serves God by suppressing disorder and bringing peace and security. Its laws must be obeyed, but the preaching of God's word must not be forbidden.

All this was music in the ears of the Bernese councillors. In 1524 their representatives at Federal Diets at Lucerne in April[2] and Zug in July[3] had heard agreed resolutions recommending the exclusion of 'heretical' participants (i.e. from Zurich, Schaffhausen and Appenzell) from future assemblies.[4] 'Heretical' in the first instance meant Lutheran, and Zwingli urgently and consistently maintained that he and his followers were not Lutherans, heretics or sectaries. His teaching was orthodox, deriving directly from the word of God interpreted by manifest reason. Even without reference to this argument, Berne was in any case unwilling to agree that any resolution of a majority of the states of the Confederation could be acceptable in matters of faith. This was not in the province of the Confederation and therefore any suggestion of the exclusion of Zurich on such grounds was rejected. It was as if to reinforce this principle that on 22 November 1524 a second order about religion[5] was made in Berne, again calling for purely biblical preaching but also upholding clerical celibacy, fasting and recourse to images.

Even so, in 1525 Zurich seemed quite alone.[6] If it were cast out from an all-Catholic Switzerland, Berne would obviously take its place as the leading state; but, politically, this would be unwelcome to the others because of Berne's western-orientated expansionist policy. Exclusion was also, in fact, exceedingly difficult to bring about. The Diet had no executive authority. It was a consultative body only, whose deliberations to

---

[1] Z II, 458(471)–525; see above, 117–121.
[2] EA 4, 1a, 412–13.   [3] EA 4, 1a, 453–4. See above, 209.
[4] Feller II, 126–7; Theodor de Quervain, *Kirchliche und soziale Zustände in Bern* (Berne, 1906).
[5] Steck & Tobler 155–6 (No. 510); Feller II, 129. The reading of Lutheran books, privately owned, was not forbidden.
[6] Koehler, *Zwingli und Bern* (Tübingen, 1928), 17; G. Stucki, *Zürichs Stellung in der Eidgenossenschaft vor der Reformation* (Aarau, 1970), 133–5.

become operative had to be ratified by each constituent government. Thus the formation of a new Bund of twelve states excluding Zurich was almost impossible and Berne was, in practice, able to veto the suggestion.

Berne's traditional inclination to caution was reinforced in 1525 by two notable events. The battles of Novara (30 April 1524) and Pavia (25 February 1525), and the capture of its ally, the King of France, meant an end to Italian expeditions, of which Berne had never fully approved. There was now no immediate danger from north Italy, and the policy of abstention from military adventures advocated by Zurich was seen to have paid off. The Peasants' War in the north was perturbing. Berne had a large peasant population and, although there was no serious trouble because of the skill and reasonableness of the government, still a watch had to be kept and external intervention avoided. On 7 April a third ordinance about religion[1] came from the Berne Council, retaining the seven sacraments but again emphasising its own responsibility for, and control of, church affairs. A week later came news that Zurich had prohibited the mass and this was received with marked indifference. It was Zurich's affair and Berne was not prepared to intervene.

In September the six fully committed Catholic states[2] together with Glarus formally requested the Zurich Council to re-establish the mass[3] and received no answer. Two months later, in association with Solothurn, the attempt was renewed and Berne was now urged to send its own delegation to Zurich.[4] And so on 29 November 1525, four leading Bernese councillors[5] appeared before the Zurich Bürgermeister and council in the Rathaus. There they urged that in the interests of all it should at least be made possible for a Catholic to hear mass openly somewhere in Zurich. They were sent away with a courteous reply that further deliberation was needed and that a written answer would follow soon. The drafting of this, a reasoned refusal, was entrusted to Zwingli himself.[6]

This reiterated the willingness of Zurich to be refuted from the Bible, quoted the now familiar texts (especially John 6. 63, 65) and set out the argument that the mass as a sacrifice was not what had been instituted by Christ but was a human invention, a mere source of clerical revenue, allowed by God to exist because of their past sins. To allow even one priest to say mass within their purified state was impossible, for it would introduce utterly unacceptable divisiveness. Differences about the mass, however, should not, it was urged, be allowed to affect cooperation between

---

[1] Steck & Tobler I, 190–5 (no. 610).
[2] Uri, Schwyz, Unterwalden, Lucerne, Zug and Fribourg. Berne was already regarded by them as of uncertain orthodoxy (Feller II, 132) and Solothurn tended to act as mediator.
[3] EA 4, 1a, 777.   [4] EA 4, 1a, 798.
[5] Sebastian von Diesbach, Anton von Erlach, Konrad Willading, Anton Bütschelbach; Z IV, 649; EA 4, 1a, 806.   [6] Z IV, 648(655)–60.

states in purely secular matters. What was now advocated was the acceptance of the principle of one state one faith, accompanied by recognition of another faith in a neighbouring state, *cuius regio eius religio* in fact, the compromise so painfully and unwillingly accepted for all Germany a generation later.

There was no reason, Zurich agreed, why men should not worship differently yet fight in a common defensive cause: 'belief should be free and no one (i.e. no state) should be obliged to accept another way of thought unless convinced thereto by biblical proof'.[1] If contingents of soldiers were serving together, one group could hear mass while another held an evangelical service, neither interfering with the other. Similarly, it was urged, Lutherans and Zwinglians (but not, by implication, Anabaptists) could cooperate for common ends. There was also a hint in the Zurich document that where, as in Thurgau, the responsible governments were of divergent creeds, local religious autonomy could be acceptable. The supreme need was for Swiss unity in face of threats from the Emperor, the King of France and some German princes. They were united in a common Christian faith as evidenced by their public instruments, most of which began, 'In the name of the Lord, Amen', and they all accepted the doctrine of the Trinity in Unity.

The appeal had no immediate effect, and Zurich's opponents were able to engineer the Baden disputation but were unable to prevent a steady advance of the new opinions in Basel, Schaffhausen and elsewhere. Haller had supported the Zwinglian case at Baden, and Berne moved a little nearer to reform after this assembly.[2] On Whit Monday, 21 May 1526, the Berne Council in a fresh order had again upheld Catholic services and also maintained evangelical preaching, thus bringing a further approximation to religious freedom for their subjects. The government also continued its rejection of the principle of necessary Federal religious unity based on majority agreement among the states, implying as it did the exclusion of Zurich and the forcible reimposition there of the Catholic faith which could only be brought about by war.

Another sign of the widening gap between the parties was apparent when the oath to uphold the Confederation, agreed by the *Stanser Verkommnis* (1481), ceased to be sworn. This had taken place with unfailing

---

[1] Z IV, 659: 'und glouben lassen, wie ein jeder vermeinte siner seel sälikeit ze sind, und desshalb mit niemant weder tzwytracht nach unwillen anfahen; dann der gloub fry, ouch niemant darzů anders dann mit dem waren gottlichen wort genöttiget sol werden'. Even with the important final qualification it is a remarkable statement of principle for 1525. Machiavelli, with a totally different approach, had reached similar conclusions ten years earlier, but the *Prince* (unpublished) cannot have been known in Zurich.

[2] Steck & Tobler, 314–15 (No. 892), 'dass jeder glouben mog was in gůt beduncke'. See above 236.

regularity every five years. When in 1525 the turn came round again, the Catholic seven[1] were not willing to be associated with Zurich and its supporters in this exercise. To this exclusion, however, Berne was opposed,[2] and since the evangelical states were unwilling to take an oath by Mary and the saints, after several meetings and adjournments it was tacitly accepted, after an imperfect conjuration in July 1526, that agreement was impossible. Hence the practice ceased until 1798 and then was renewed only momentarily.[3]

On 3 February 1527 there was a meeting of representatives from Zurich, Berne, Glarus, Basle, Schaffhausen and the city of St Gall to consider their relations with the Diet of the Confederation which, as Zwingli consistently maintained, could not interfere in matters of faith and conscience.[4] Berne, still technically Catholic, a little resented being hurried or pressurised into common action – it was fully competent to manage its own affairs in its own moderate and realistic way.

It was at the Easter elections to the Berne Council in 1527 that a sufficiently large number of evangelically inclined members were chosen for the Great Council and added to the Small Council for these bodies to have for the first time a distinctly 'reforming' slant.[5] More priests began to ask, and to receive, leave to marry their housekeepers, and the objections of certain of the gilds to masses for the repose of the souls of former members, in the efficacy of which they no longer believed, were upheld. Another (the fifth) order about religion of 27 May 1527 followed, renewing the insistence on evangelical preaching but still resisting innovations. For the rest, the councillors knew their public and acted with predictable ponderous dilatoriness. In July they began to make preparations for much closer control of the monasteries.[6] Nothing was done without consultation with the localities, some of which showed little enthusiasm for married priests; the gilds on the other hand were emphatic in their demand for a public religious debate. This was accepted by the council on 15 November[7] to take place on 6 January 1528, and invitations[8] went out two days later to all

---

[1] Lucerne, Uri, Schwyz, Unterwalden, Fribourg, Solothurn, Zug.

[2] Steck & Tobler, 258–9, 262 (Nos. 813, 814).

[3] Wyss, 71 n. 3; Rappard, *Renouvellement*, 51–79.

[4] Beurle, 119–23; EA 4, 1a, 1031–2, 1048, 1073; HZ 40 (1878), 127.

[5] Feller II, 149–50; Z IX, 103, including Haller's comments. Guggisberg, *Bernische Kirchengeschichte* 98–9; Anshelm V, 199–200. Ritter Niklaus von Mülinen, the leading Catholic supporter, lost his seat.   [6] Feller II, 152–3.

[7] Z VI i, 206. For the whole proceedings, VI i, 202–498; Z IX, 290–6, 304–10; Feller II, 155; T. de Quervain, *Gedenkschrift zur Vierhundertjahrfeier der Geschichte der Bernischen Kirchenreformation* I (Berne, 1928); W. Kochler, *Zwingli und Bern* (Tübingen, 1928); K. Linth, 'Der theologische Gehalt der Berner Disputation'. The latter portion of Anshelm and Bullinger, *Ref.* I, 395ff, give contemporary, but not invariably accurate, detail. Steck & Tobler, 517 (no. 1368).

[8] Steck & Tobler, 518–521 (No. 1371).

the states of the Confederation and their allies, to a number of south German cities, to the four bishops concerned, Sion, Constance, Basle and Lausanne, and to every beneficed priest within the Bernese territory. To these latter, some 300 or more, it was not so much an invitation as a government order – if they did not attend they would lose their benefices. The threat, accompanied with assurance of hospitality, was sufficient, but it is an interesting commentary upon the authority assumed by the council that it could have been uttered. Henry VIII of England or Francis I of France could hardly have issued such a decree in 1527.

The considerable and rather aristocratic Catholic party in Berne was now put on the defensive; they were informed that there was real doubt about what faith their government should uphold and that certain major issues needed to be decided by open debate. It was to be an officially sponsored discussion and argument, 'ein gemein gesprech und disputation'[1] on 6 January 1528, the feast of the Epiphany, and, fatal but essential condition, it was to be based on the pure text of the Bible (alein biblische gschrift)[2] without reference to any later interpretation or addition by the Fathers or anyone else. An agenda drawn up by Berchtold Haller and Franz Kolb accompanied the guarantee of safe conduct to all those invited.[3] The topics were by now very familiar ones. Berne had, as it were, caught up at last. Tradition, vows of chastity and the marriage of priests, purgatory, images, the intercession of the saints, the mass as a sacrifice, the eucharist, the meaning of the church and its head, were collected into the ten articles for public discussion, none of them by now in any way original.[4] These were to be discussed in the light of the Bible text, 'the clear pure word of God', after which the Council of Berne would decide on its course of action. The theses (Schlussreden) were written in German and translated into Latin (with modifications) by Zwingli, and a French version was also produced. There was no printing press available in Berne: hence the printing was undertaken by Froschauer in Zurich.

On 2 December 1527, the Bürgermeister of Zurich, Diethelm Röist, gave Zwingli formal leave to attend the Berne disputation, where he was also to be joined by Oecolampadius, from Basle. From that moment the Proceedings took on a new dimension; the Berne disputation was to be the protestant reply to the Catholic-engineered colloquy of Baden, and upon its deliberations would depend the decision of the Bernese government about the religious alignment of the state. The government would not act without popular approval, and everything done must bear public inspection.

[1] Or as Anshelm v, 219 put it: 'ein offen, fri, kristlich gegengespräch, disputation gnemt'.
[2] Anshelm, v, 221.   [3] Anshelm, v, 223-5.
[4] Z vi i, 207, translated in A. L. Cochrane, Reformed confessions of the 16th century (Philadelphia, 1966), 49-50.

Hence, every detail was planned with Bernese precision and punctiliousness. The presidency or chairmanship was to rotate among four respected figures from different states, and after much discussion the indefatigable Commander Schmid of Küssnacht, Conrad Schilling, Abbot of Gottstadt, Niklaus Brieffer of Basle (after the more illustrious Dr Oswald Bär had declined) and Vadian from St Gall were nominated. Information[1] from Zurich indicated that four[2] councillors had consulted with the three stipendiary ministers[3] about the policy to be followed.

For Zwingli the Berne disputation was very much the complement to Baden. He had been forbidden (and had declined) to attend this latter and now regarded Berne as the forum from which he could say the things that he had not been able to proclaim at Baden.[4] It was to be a public appearance, the outcome was immensely important for the future of the Gospel, and there was a certain conscious finality about it. The traditionalists were to be invited and given every opportunity to state their case. If, however, they were adjudged to have failed (on scriptural grounds), the toleration previously accorded to their teaching and practices would be withdrawn. The government would be responsible for the (not very great) expenses of its representatives, but not, obviously, of their opponents; and each of them would have a separate safe-conduct.

In the light of events at Baden, very great care was taken to ensure that the records or minutes of the Berne meeting were impeccable. Five secretaries were appointed, Peter Cyro, town clerk of Berne, Eberhard von Rümlang town clerk of Thun, Johannes Huber of Lucerne (who did not in fact attend), Georg Hertwig of Solothurn and Georg Schöni of Berne.[5] Books of reference were made available: the Greek New Testament in Erasmus's now well-known text, the Hebrew (but not the Septuagint) version of the Old Testament, the massive folios, mostly printed at Basle, of Augustine, Jerome, Tertullian, Iraeneus, Cyril and Chrysostom,[6] with good Hebrew scholars like Myconius and Hofmeister there in advance to see that the texts were in order. The church of the Franciscan friars was specially fitted out by the city architect with seating for the large numbers expected (perhaps 500 in all).[7] The participants were explicitly instructed to speak slowly so that their words could be taken down.

Certain setbacks were anticipated and were forthcoming: from the Imperial court at Speier (28 December 1527) came a declaration that the assembly was illegal, that they should wait for the forthcoming Diet of Regensburg[8] and that matters of doctrine should be discussed only at a

---

[1] Z VI i, 211–13, *Ratschlag der 4 Verordneten und 3 Leutpriester wegen der Disputation zu Bern.*
[2] Binder, Sprüngli, Uli Funk, Conrad Gull.   [3] Zwingli, Jud, Engelhard.
[4] As Haller put it, 'Er hat badet, du solt den bärentantz füren'. Z IX, 308.
[5] Z VI i, 246 n. i.   [6] Z IX, 314.   [7] Farner IV, 274.   [8] RTA VII i, 160–229.

future General Council.[1] This made little difference. The Catholic states, including Fribourg and, with reservations, Solothurn, not only condemned the whole proceedings but announced that delegates would be prevented from crossing their territories,[2] an action of dubious legality within the Confederation; but nearly all the other recipients of the invitation accepted. Zurich, St Gall, Basle and Schaffhausen were formally and adequately represented; Glarus sent Fridli Bruner and allowed any citizen to attend who wished to do so. The whole roll-call was an impressive one. Men rode in over the snow from St Gall, Biel, Strassburg, Ulm, Augsburg, Mülhausen, Nuremberg,[3] Geislingen, Memmingen, Lindau, Constance and Isny, but not from Rottweil. Oecolampadius, Bullinger, Bucer, Blarer, Capito, Pellican, Hofmeister, Haller, Bär, Commander Schmid, Megander and Collin were there to support Zwingli – it would have been hard even for Germany to have produced a similar galaxy of Protestant talent.

In contrast, the Catholic representation was minimal. The four bishops – Constance, Sion, Lausanne and Basle – were absent; The Bishop of Constance insisted that the church should be judge, for it had been there before the New Testament was written and had decided what books were and what were not, canonical. The Bishop of Lausanne set out but had a convenient accident on the way; there was, however, a small party present from Lausanne, all French speakers who remained silent observers throughout. To Zwingli's disappointment, Eck and Cochlaeus from Ingolstadt, who might have been worthy opponents, refused to attend[4] for some of the same reasons as had kept Zwingli away from Baden, and their case was left to the able apologist Konrad Träger (or Treyer) from Fribourg, weakly supported by Grat (Ulm), Buchstab (Zofingen), Maurer (Rapperswil), Huter (Appenzell) and one or two others quite unable to match either the biblical knowledge, the learning or the verbal dexterity of the other side. Eck, indeed, loved publicity, but not of the kind that he was likely to meet at Berne, and his absence was as intelligible as that of Zwingli at Baden.

Zwingli attended a fine New Year's Feast in the hall of the Skinners' Company (zum Schnecken) before setting off in style for the three day journey.[5] He, with the Bürgermeister and a band of faithful clergy, rode on horses; others, well able to walk a good thirty miles a day, went on foot. Accompanied by carts with provisions and protected by a contingent of

---

[1] Feller II, 158. Berne later said that the imperial answer had been received too late to allow the meeting to be called off.   [2] Z IX, 336-7 n. 10; Feller II, 156.

[3] Nuremberg as a Lutheran city sent Andreas Althamer, who maintained a position of opposition to Zwingli, particularly in the discussions on the eucharist. Anshelm V, 231-2.

[4] ZWA VI, 580-88; XIII, 283-5; Z IX, 325, 328.

[5] Farner IV, 268. At Mellingen there was a moment of hostility to Zwingli and a shot was fired, but the intruder was ejected.

men armed with crossbows, swords and halberds, they took the road via Mellingen and Lenzburg to the Bernese frontier at Aarau, where a Bernese escort of two hundred awaited the party. It was a demonstration, but it was also a precaution, as Zwingli had to cross territory which was under hostile control in the Freie Aemter, and had he been unguarded he could have been taken as a heretic. Berne was reached on 4 January 1528. Within the city of Berne, Zwingli declined official hospitality and stayed, in somewhat exaggerated simplicity, with Lienhard Tremp with whom there was some family connection.[1] The whole business was stage-managed with great care and skill, and in many ways it marks the highest point in Zwingli's career. His arguments and his presentation of the case were successful. By accepting the Zwinglian teaching Berne joined forces with Zurich, and in spite of all later disasters this was decisive. Berne might have copied its neighbours, Fribourg and Solothurn, and have remained Catholic, or, at best, uncommitted. A Catholic Berne would have meant an isolated Zurich, and Zwinglianism might have gone the way of Socinianism and become a minor sect. It was a Zwinglian Berne that saved Geneva from Catholic domination and thus made Calvin's work possible. In some ways the fate of French Huguenots, Dutch and Scots Presbyterians, and perhaps 'Free Churches' all over the world depended upon the outcome of a debate held in Berne in January 1528.

The disputation itself is unusually well documented: by a happy accident, some of Zwingli's own notes, written down while his opponents were speaking, have survived.[2] The four secretaries kept the record straight, and their published narrative,[3] unlike that of Baden, was prompt, full and fair. With great tactical skill, Zwingli kept himself in the background and let the two local ministers, Kolb and Haller, do most of the talking. At the same time he was always ready to suggest, to prompt and to intervene frequently with a telling phrase, embarrassing question, or logical definition.[4]

When the sessions opened in the nave of the Franciscan church with Vadian as President on 6 January 1528, the first topic to be faced was that

---

[1] Feller II, 159; Z II, 473-4. That Tremp was Zwingli's brother-in-law, as sometimes stated, is unlikely. ZWA IV (1928), 21-6.

[2] Interestingly, they were written in Latin – Zwingli thought in Latin rather than in German in such a context, further evidence of the powerful influence of his university training in disputation. Some discussions were in Latin because of the presence of French speakers. Z VI i, 215.

[3] 'Handlung oder Acta gehaltner Disputation zů Bernn in Uchtland', Zurich, Froschauer, 1528; A. Fluri, *Die Beziehungen Berns zu den Buchdruckern in Basel, Zürich und Genf, 1476–1536* (Berne, 1913), 35-6.

[4] As, for example, commenting on Mark 14. 24 ('This is my blood of the new testament'), 'a liquid cannot be the new testament, the blood of Christ is a liquid and therefore the blood of Christ cannot be the new testament. Hence it was the blood of Christ shed on the cross that was the pledge of the new testament.' Cf. Bullinger, *Ref.* I, 436; Z VI i, 350-1.

of the nature and authority of the church. The Catholics as usual argued that the church had decided which writings constituted the Canon of the scripture,[1] and that through the charge to Peter Christ had instituted the authority of the Pope and the hierarchy. Haller and Bucer joined to make the familiar case that the church was the body of Christ and Christ therefore its only head. Moreover, the church was the institutional expression of the humanity of Christ, who in his manhood paid the price of human salvation while in his Godhead he was necessarily also the origin and creator of all things.

When Alexius Grat, the Ulm Dominican from the Bernese monastery zur Insel, tried to defend the power of the keys, Zwingli, for almost the only time, brushed the case aside with a piece of Greek philology involving the accent on the Greek word εἰς which no doubt sounded very convincing to the simple parsons present but was in fact untenable.[2] Conrad Träger advanced the now familiar Catholic allegation that the divisions among the Protestants was evidence in itself of their inadmissibility as true members of Christ's one church; differences among Christians called for an adjudicator and this could but be the church, and this, for the speaker, meant the papacy. It was for him enough to trust the church in matters of belief: the will and intention to submit to the teaching of the Church, 'implicit faith' in the theological sense, was sufficient for salvation, while its absence was evidence of damnation.

Both Bucer and Zwingli sincerely believed that Träger could not only be refuted from the Bible but also was grossly wrong in supposing that it needed supplementation or that everything necessary for salvation was not to be found within its pages. If only men would recognise that the Bible contained no contradictions, that from its words through the guidance of the Holy Spirit all doctrine could be ascertained, the church could once more be united in simplicity and assurance. Christ in both his natures head of the church, the virginity of his mother an attested miracle, the doctrine of the Trinity unmistakable – these were certainties, while other matters such as the conduct of church services or external directions in church affairs could be left to the locally gathered community. There was a careful exposition[3] of the Zwinglian view of the eucharist.

---

[1] Zwingli excluded the 'Revelation of St John the Divine' which he, like Luther but unlike Bullinger, regarded as supplementary rather than authoritative and argued against the Johannine authorship. (Z VI i, 223, 395, 397, 401–2; Farner IV, 283). He was flatly contradicted by Gilg Maurer of Rapperswil, who insisted that it was part of the Bible equal to the rest. Zwingli was driven to the somewhat weak argument that the Holy Spirit taught true believers which biblical passages were authoritative and which not. He consistently denied the right of the hierarchy (or councils) to make such decisions, nor would he admit the full rights of private judgement claimed by the Baptists. See above 63, 173.

[2] Z VI i, 219, 254.

[3] For five days 14 to 19 January. Farner IV, 280; Koehler, Z & L I, 582–602.

Burgauer[1] from St Gall and Althamer[2] from Nuremberg presented the Lutheran case. They agreed to reject the Catholic doctrine of transubstantiation, Burgauer himself recognising that Zwingli spoke 'in good Christian fashion' – a sentiment which Luther would hardly have accepted. It was all to be repeated elsewhere, at Marburg in particular. Other decisions taken at the Berne disputation had significant immediate results. That the mass was not a sacrifice, that Christ offered himself but once and thereby completed the work of human salvation was urged by all the reformers and readily accepted by the participants.

There was a lively discussion on the subject of prayers to the saints as mediators. The saints, Zwingli insisted, did not die for us and do not intercede for us; it is we who are enjoined to be constant in prayer.[3] There was no scriptural evidence for saintly mediation, and neither pilgrimages nor the miracles worked at shrines were any evidence for the intervention or even for the heavenly presence of saints.

The relatively simple arguments against purgatory and the power of the priests to accelerate release therefrom, Zwingli gladly left to Haller. There was the usual dispute about the interpretation of texts, the nature of sin and the meaning of forgiveness, in which the orthodox case was put by Johann Buchstab, schoolmaster of Zofingen.[4] That those whose sins were forgiven went to heaven was conceded, but this depended not on human endeavours, actions or even suffering, but upon God's mercy and a whole faith. All are sinners; believers sin with shame and sorrow, disbelievers do so unashamedly, but that all this assumes an intermediate stage, where souls await not the day of judgement but release in finite time, is a figment of interested ecclesiastical imagination.

Still more briefly the honouring or worshipping of images and representations of the saints was refuted. The plain implications of the first commandment, the impossibility of depicting God the Father, were

---

[1] Benedict Burgauer (c. 1494–1576), formerly priest at Marbach, then at St Laurence, St Gall, was only semi-Lutheran. He had been present at the second Zurich disputation and now (1528) left St Gall for Schaffhausen. Schmid/Muralt 1; Muralt/Fast, 330; Egli *4*, I, 62–8; Z VIII, 323 n. I; Allen VII, 526.

[2] Andreas Althamer (c. 1500–64) was a faithful supporter of Luther and a severe critic of the Anabaptists.

[3] Occasionally we get a good glimpse of the cut and thrust of argument:
MURER: The intercession of the saints in heaven I demonstrate from Jeremiah 15. 1, 'Even if Moses and Samuel stood before me, I would not be moved to pity this people'. Here, plainly, the prophet Jeremiah speaks of the dead as being in heaven, for at the time of writing they were long since dead.
ZWINGLI: Were Moses and Samuel in heaven before the coming of Christ or not?
MURER: I say not.
ZWINGLI: Then your argument is of no avail.
Z VI i, 400. (According to medieval theology they were in the outer courts of hell, *limbus patrum*). [4] Z VI i, 286–7.

readily accepted as decisive. To leave images in the churches was like playing with fire; it was far better to avoid fire than to be burned by it. The last topic debated, that of the marriage of priests, provided Oecolampadius with an opportunity to exhibit his learning and his mild, yet devastating, logic. Since, admittedly, there were married apostles, bishops and priests in the primitive church, scripture seemed clearly on the side of the Reformers. There were indeed Nazarenes whose devotion had involved chastity, but this was when men were under the law and not, since Christ's advent, under God's grace. The contrary case was weakly presented, the argument being that priests in the earliest days were permitted to marry because of their earlier ignorance and lack of training, and that this had since been rectified. Just as, in civil law, a promise that is contrary to public policy will not be enforced by the courts, so too, Oecolampadius insisted (following Luther), a vow that was displeasing to God could be ignored. And on that note the assembly dispersed:[1] as at Zurich, it was for the council, the government, to act on the advice that it had itself called for.

The days of discussion in the Franciscan church were supplemented, as seemed so natural to that age, by a catena of sermons in the Minster. There, every other day at least, Zwingli, Sam,[2] Gassner,[3] Megander, Commander Schmid, Blaurer,[4] Bucer and Oecolampadius developed their themes from the pulpit uninterrupted[5] by questions and challenges in discourses which were also confessions of faith.

Zwingli used the opportunity to reinforce his orthodoxy by exposition of the Apostles' creed,[6] each sentence of which he believed, as most people did, to have been contributed by one of the Twelve. This gave him a renewed opportunity to expound to 'us Germans' what was implied in

[1] The formal closure came on 26 January. The French-speaking representatives of the Bishop of Lausanne were not allowed to speak in Latin, and no record of any intervention by them was made, although there was an exchange of words between them and Farel. They left on 11 January. Feller II, 159–60; Z V, 401 n. 2, 412. Eck, as might have been expected, rapidly produced a confutation of the whole proceedings including an attack on Zwingli's character and methods. Koehler, *Z & L* I, 597–600, 604. This was printed as *Verlegung der disputation zu Bern, mit grund götlicher geschrift: durch J. Eck an die christenliche Ordt der Eydgnosschaft*, an action of which Berne later complained. Z VI i, 140.

[2] Conrad Sam (1483–1533), Franciscan, studied at Tübingen and Freiburg, from 1526 Zwingli's constant supporter at Ulm. Z VIII, 632 n. 1.

[3] Thomas Gassner (d. 1548), a moderate supporter of Zwingli, preacher at Lindau from 1524, active also in St Gall, refusing to take sides in the eucharistic controversy.

[4] Ambrosius Blarer (Blaurer) 1492–1564, of Constance, M.A. Tübingen 1513, Prior of Alpirsbach, from 1525 reformer (with his brother Thomas) at Constance and its neighbourhood. Z VIII, 97 n. 1.

[5] A few Anabaptists who might have become vocal were imprisoned. ZWA v, 409–13. One Catholic priest who heard the sermons was so impressed that he announced his determination never to say mass again. Bullinger, *Ref.* I, 436.

[6] ZH II, 19–65; Z VI i, 443(450)–98.

belief in God, the highest good and perfectly wise and omnipotent, and in his providence (*Fürsichtigkeit*). This was followed by explanations of the Trinity in unity, the implications of 'almighty', the nature and wonder of creation, the meaning of eternity and the two natures of Jesus Christ, the only son of God. The virgin birth, with a renewed assertion of Zwingli's esteem for Mary, the crucifixion, resurrection, and ascension received brief and cautiously orthodox exposition. There was little attempt to do other than offer a concentrated theological lecture to his interested hearers. 'Sitting at the right hand of God' became the text for a long, if unoriginal, restatement of the preacher's eucharistic teaching. It involved some logic and some metaphysics, all directed to the insistence that the ascended Christ, in his humanity, remains in heaven until the day of judgement. This led to the conclusion that the body of the risen Christ in heaven could not be eaten in the communion; transubstantiation was demonstrably false and Luther's concept of Christ's 'ubiquity' was unacceptable. Neither the body of Christ nor the risen Christ is in the bread.[1] All this, he insisted, was the belief of the first Christians,[2] directly from the Bible and supported by the testimony of antiquity. He was not asking for any innovation. The sermon ended with an unexpectedly mild denunciation of the separation of the Baptists and their mistaken views on the sleep of the soul.

Zwingli's last public statement before he left was expressive of his approval of the elimination of images and altars from the Bernese churches and an appeal for unity and constancy. What had been begun must be carried through; a task left half completed were better not started. Perseverance must be based upon real conviction: it was useless to remove images from the buildings and yet not cast them forth from their own inward thoughts. Let there be no more bickering and arguing; a christian government had made its decision and should be obeyed. Through difficulties and persecution they had now won religious freedom as their fathers had won political freedom. On to this they must hold, sure of the ultimate victory of truth which would prevail in the end among their confederates as it had among themselves. It was Zwingli at his best. The disputation had lasted three weeks with full opportunity for free expression of views. If conclusions could be reached by debate there was ample and adequate opportunity for this – with the reservation of the initial limitation to the pure Bible text, which was in itself unacceptable to one side. Zwingli left Berne on 31 January, returning to Zurich via Lenzburg, since

---

[1] Z VI i, 469: 'der lychnam Christi wirt mit keiner gschrifft dargebracht'; 486: 'das weder das brot der lychnam Christi sye, noch im brot...'
[2] Z VI i, 487, 'Die uralten lerer der Christen' – to be found also in the writings of Ambrose and Jerome.

the more direct route through Bremgarten was blocked by Catholic armed forces.

The last days of January 1528 saw Zwingli rising to the height of his powers and influence. He had now worked out his own theology in detail and was ready to defend it and to extend it; he had the complete support of his own government and he had won the confidence of its greatest rival. The Catholics were in retreat and confusion; the papacy had not recovered from the weakness and shame of the sack of Rome and was confronted with the demands of the English king that he should be set free to give his realm the male heir that it needed. Lutheranism in central Germany was steadily gaining adherents, and Philip of Hesse, temporarily thwarted by the Pack episode, was emerging as a powerful statesman.

The acceptance of the Zwinglian Reformation by Berne was almost as significant as that by Zurich from whence it derived. The Berne disputation was a triumphant answer to the catholic victory at Baden and was to have even more decisive results. It saved the Reformation in Switzerland and perhaps in Europe, for German Lutheranism, left alone, could hardly have developed into an ecumenical faith. It was, moreover, Zwingli's church doctrine that won the day; it did not follow that Berne was prepared, or even able, to follow his political aims also. Bernese external policy was not changed, and from 1528 to 1531, while the partners were agreed on matters of worship and belief, their political and economic interests remained unchanged.

Zwingli's recommendations arising from the debate were adopted almost without alteration.[1] The articles that had been presented and debated were declared to be scriptural and therefore entirely acceptable, and the Bernese ministers were charged to say nothing that contradicted them. For the rest, Berne's patricians were nothing if not practical. The ministers would receive a short Order of Service (*Taufbüchlein*) which would tell them how to lead their congregations. The Roman mass was not to be said, and altars were to be destroyed, and any remaining images were to be removed forthwith.[2] The clergy were permitted, and even encouraged, to marry, the officials of the Minster were released from their oaths to the bishop (itself a singular assumption of power by a lay government but thoroughly in the Berne tradition), some church dues and taxes were

---

[1] *Anweisung für das Berner Reformationsmandat Jan. 27–31 1528.* Z VI i, 499(504)–8. The order itself – *das grosse Reformationsmandat* – was issued on 7 February. Steck & Tobler, 629–34 (no. 1513); Koehler, *Zwingli und Bern* (Tübingen, 1928), 21; L. v. Muralt, 'Zwingli als Begründer der reformierten Berner Kirche' (*Mélanges Charles Gilliard*, Lausanne, 1944), 325–30.

[2] Farner IV, 287; Feller II, 161–2; Anshelm V, 245; Z VI i, 493 n. 4, 499–508. Mass was said for the last time in St Vincent's church that day (Z IX, 354 n. 8) and the organ played, also for the last time, 'Judas, how you have betrayed your master'.

abrogated and others diverted to different ends, rural deans were required to watch over, instruct and report on the clergy, Heinrich Wölflin (Lupulus) was restored to his Canonry, and Sebastian Hofmeister (Oeconomus), Caspar Megander[1] (Grossmann) and John Rhellikan were called to Berne to introduce the teaching of Hebrew and Greek and to bring about an improvement in the low standard of education, particularly of the clergy. A *Chorgerichtsordnung*, also copied from Zurich, dealt with matrimonial problems. Monastic property was taken over by the state, pensions and mercenary services were prohibited; and lurid, but unenforceable, prohibitions were issued against immodest dress, blasphemy, swearing, gambling, excessive drinking and carrying offensive weapons. There were to be no unnecessary ejections of incumbents unless they were notoriously provocative and even then, submission might well bring compensation. The government of Berne proceeded with moderation, caution and great skill to secure the consent of their subjects. By careful collection of opinion, by explanation, conciliation, consultation and a certain amount of pressure, acquiescence, and often willing approval, were obtained. The monasteries, unable to recruit novices, slowly perished of inanition, but there were no forcible ejections.[2] Inevitably there was some uncertainty locally about what the new order implied, and as the implications became clearer there were signs of unrest in the still only partly assimilated Bernese Oberland.

The government of Berne, in accordance with established practice, consulted its subjects about the changes in 1528. All agreed with them except Frutigen, Obersimmental and Lenzburg.

The Benedictine monastery at Interlaken, where there were at one time 300 nuns, and 30 canons to say services in the church, was older than Berne itself and had been rich, powerful and self-governing. It was, however, almost a classical case of mismanagement: in spite of property and jurisdiction, debts mounted and Berne was able to offer both loans and protection. These were gratefully received, but little by little protection became control, essential to Berne if it was to be secure in the Oberland. Thus when the change-over came in March there was no resistance. The monastery had not been popular as a landlord, and the tenants not unnaturally hoped that with its elimination there would be benefits to themselves, but they soon learnt that dues and services were to remain unaltered and that they had gained nothing but a more efficient master. 'My lords of Berne', it was said, 'have become Lutherans for the sake of

---

[1] Z IX, 361 n. I.
[2] Those who had paid money, as was customary, on entry, might have it returned, and some monks who married were granted an allowance from monastic funds to set up house. Feller II, 164.

the loot to be obtained'.[1] Why should not the local communities take over monasteries themselves? Farther east, the peasants, whose grazing-lands brought them into direct contact with their neighbours in Lucerne and Unterwalden, were encouraged by these to resist. The disappearance of the mass was not understood; they still had to pay tithe as before, they had neither schools nor hospitals for which purposes some of the money had been diverted, above all they resented interference with established customs by a government which claimed to reverence antiquity while in fact tightening its control over them. In the Hasle district some hoped to remain Catholic and found a separate state of the Confederation. The mass was reintroduced into Frutigen, Obersimmental, Grindelwald, Meiringen and Oberhasle; reforming pastors were ejected,[2] orders from government officials disobeyed and lawful payment refused. These districts looked for support from their Catholic neighbours in Valais, Uri and Unterwalden.[3] At the end of September 1528 there was open rebellion accompanied by the occupation of Interlaken. On 28 October 800 men from Unterwalden had come over the Brünig and reached Brienz and Unterseen. To support the rebellious subjects of a neighbouring state against their lawful government was a manifest breach of the Federal pact, explicitly so re-defined in the *Stanser Verkommnis*.[4] A force from Berne was sent to the area, the Unterwaldner hurriedly returned home, the recalcitrant peasants accepted the change in religion and were readmitted to citizenship in November, before Fribourg and Solothurn could offer mediation. The main revolt had lasted only a few weeks, but its consequences were serious.[5] The rebels themselves were treated with characteristic mildness. The rulers of Berne were grateful for Zurich's immediate support, writing on 29 October, 'We have received to-day your welcome agreement to support us and this we shall never forget.'[6]

---

[1] Feller II, 168; Z IX, 411 n. 10.   [2] Anshelm v, 281.

[3] Moral support was promised in August at a meeting in Lucerne. EA 4 1a, 1368. Knowledge that Berne could count on support from Zurich was sufficient to prevent action. Oechsli *3*, c. 135; HZ 40 (1878) 140–2.

[4] After the event, the Unterwalden authorities, who had been promised help from Marx Sittich of Hohenems, which never came (Vasella 2, 80), hastened to disclaim responsibility with the usual assertion that the 'volunteers' had acted spontaneously. Berne was certainly right in maintaining that the movement of so large a force could and should have been checked and that the action was a manifest breach of Berne's sovereignty and of the *Stanser Verkommnis*. It was accepted by all parties that Lucerne, Schwyz and Zug were not involved.

[5] See below, 351–2. H. Specker, *Die Reformationswirren im Berner Oberland 1528: ihre Geschichte und ihre Folgen* (Fribourg, 1951) ZSKG Beiheft 9, with a useful map. An early account, very much from the Zurich angle, came from Oswald Myconius, *De Tumultu Bernensium intestino MDXXVIII. Commentarius* (J. Lauffer, *Historische und Critische Beyträge zur Historie der Eidgenossen* IV. Teil, Zürich, 1739, 1–163); Vasella *1*, 280–92; Feller II, 178–82; Tardent, 221–32.

[6] 'dess sol in die ewigkeit niemer vergessen werden'. Strickler I, 677 (No. 2134).

In Berne itself the noble idealism inspired by the sermons and prayers of January was giving way to calculations of self interest, and many of Zwingli's high hopes of active support were rebuffed. It was as much as Berne could do to stamp out revolt in the Oberland, which was to lead it into an unwanted struggle with Unterwalden. The Reformation in 1528 was indeed enforced throughout the wide Bernese territories, but at appreciable cost of manpower, money and energy.

As a result of the events of 1528, Berne had to reorientate some of its policy to suit its Zurich allies, but did so with growing caution, hesitation and even resentment. As soon as the Unterwalden business was more or less settled, Berne became less anxious to help Zurich. Its assistance to Zurich had been made necessary because of danger from the potential enemies around and the lack of support from Solothurn and Fribourg. The junction of Berne and Zurich meant for the first time that Zwingli's dream of an all-Protestant Switzerland had some possibility of fulfilment. Before the critical Berne conference, only Biel, Schaffhausen and St Gall supported Zurich. St Gall, however, was but an ally and not a Confederate, and in any case the city had no territory and hence no great influence, particularly while the Prince Abbot was active. Schaffhausen was a recent, distant and relatively minor member of the Confederation, whereas Berne was at its very centre.

At the end of 1528 Berne renewed its alliance for mutual protection and co-citizenship (*Burgrecht*) with Constance,[1] and since there was already a similar arrangement with Geneva,[2] the axis Constance, Zurich, Berne, Geneva, was highly significant, the more so in that Oecolampadius returned from the Berne conference greatly encouraged and confident that the evangelisation of Basle would soon become official. All sorts of possibilities were opening out. Berne, most secular minded of all the states, cautious, realist, thoroughly Swiss, consistently emphasised that the Confederation was one for military, economic and political protection and that religion was in no way its concern. It was for each state to make its own religious arrangements, the preaching of the Gospel should be allowed everywhere, and in cases where territory was held or controlled in common by several powers, each constituent community could choose freely its own form of worship. With this view Zwingli was prepared to concur only for political ends. His objective in 1528 was becoming clear: the protestant cities within and beyond the Confederation would join forces; together they would ensure the undisturbed preaching of the Gospel first in the Mandated Territories and then in the Catholic states

[1] Bender, *Ref.* 164.
[2] Cf. L. v. Muralt, *Berns westliche Politik zur Zeit der Reformation* reprinted in *Der Historiker und die Geschichte* (Zurich, 1960) 88–96.

themselves. The power of the Word was irresistible: before it the walls of ignorance and prejudice would fall and the Confederation would be united under Zurich–Berne leadership in the Protestant camp.

What he was not prepared to contemplate was the reverse side of the coin. Freedom to preach the Gospel in Catholic states did not mean that Catholic priests could be allowed to say mass in Reformed states, or a house of one of the Regular orders be opened therein. Freedom of conscience was not practical politics in the sixteenth century. Just as no Christian government could tolerate public expression of atheism, so it was not reasonable to expect differences of religious belief to be acceptable within a state. There was but one true Christian faith, and those who departed from it were wandering in error and darkness. At best they must be allowed to exist in the hope that they would see the light, just as Jews and infidels were to be unwillingly tolerated, but no more than this. The Roman mass was increasingly regarded as blasphemous idolatry by the Reformers and therefore could not be allowed to be celebrated in their dominions. Equally, for the Catholics, heresy was the worst of crimes, to be prevented from entering at all costs, to be rooted out by fire and sword when it was detected. The two concepts were irreconcilable, and the Bernese statesmen knew it.

After 1528 Zwingli aimed hopefully and fervently at the triumph of his reformation throughout the Swiss Confederation. This, however, he recognised, was not to be brought about by human power without external help, and it was to securing this that he now turned. He must support and encourage his adherents in Germany, particularly in cities like Constance and Strassburg, and he must join forces with the enemies of Rome wherever they were. He had increasingly become so openly and publicly opposed to the essential teaching and practice of the Catholic church that there could be no compromise with the papacy. If his followers were to be victorious, they must not be confused with the Lutherans, who seemed to be willing to come to terms with the Catholics on some vital principles. Zurich, he had always rightly insisted, had never been a Lutheran city nor had his teaching been Luther-inspired. His enemies were trying to use this historical fact to regain lost positions by securing Lutheran neutrality until the Zwinglians were crushed. Both the triumph and the maintenance of his cause were at stake in the active and partly successful attempts to encourage his followers and to find new allies.

Once Berne was with him, and Basle reasonably certain as well, full attention could be paid to potential adherents further afield – to Philip of Hesse and, immediately, to St Gall and to the Mandated Territories in eastern Switzerland where the Gospel had already made good progress amid difficulties.

11

Zurich and St Gall

Sixteenth-century Switzerland was not overburdened with monasteries, which, politically and socially, posed less of a problem there than elsewhere. Some of the greater houses, Engelberg, Dissentis, Reichenau, for example, were outside the Federation, while no city state of the Federation was seriously troubled by the existence of a great monastery within its walls. Schaffhausen had indeed the Benedictine house of All Saints with which to contend, and Zurich itself had at one time been almost an appanage to or dependent upon the Fraumünster, but by the fifteenth century, the governments almost everywhere had reduced the Regulars to a state of semi-dependence.

There was not a single monastery in Uri or Unterwalden and effectively none in Schwyz; therefore there was no local feeling against them, whereas Zurich had wealthy foundations within its territory, whence they received considerable revenues. Roughly speaking, where monasteries were numerous reform was welcomed; where they were few the opposite was the case. The difference between the 'possessionate' monks and nuns, professedly removed from the world, devoting their whole lives to the ordered services and internal routine of their houses, and the 'non-possessionate' friars, preaching and begging among the people, had ceased to be a reality in the sixteenth century. They were all 'Regulars', with rule and a habit; some, like the Premonstratensians and Augustinians, were endowed canons with extra-mural duties; others, like the members of the order of St John of Jerusalem, had few obligations. All, however, had taken the vows of obedience, chastity and poverty and were familiar figures among the clerical population. The men were, in practice, almost invariably in priests' orders.

Zwingli, unlike Luther, was a secular priest and was well aware of the rivalries of the past between Seculars and Regulars. At the same time, he knew what monasticism implied and its claims to be the highest and best Christian life. He had lived with the Dominicans in Berne, an uncle was a monk and at least one of his sisters continued to live in the cloister after accepting the new regime of sermons and vernacular services.

267

The monastic orders had been under attack before Zwingli came to Zurich; Erasmus had made his dislike of monasticism very apparent, primarily because the monks were so often the enemies of 'good letters', but also because they had so little to offer society from which they took so much. For Zwingli, monks and friars were the professional defenders of masses for the dead, of images, relics and indulgences, of clerical celibacy and papal supremacy. Preaching and Bible study were neglected by them. These Regulars were all obvious targets for a Zwinglian, as also for a Lutheran, attack. Once vows of celibacy, restrictions on diet, payments for masses, the mass itself as a sacrifice, were rejected as unbiblical, it became difficult, if not impossible, for the defenders of monasticism to find justification for the institution.

What, then, was to be done with the monks and nuns who were now represented as the hypocrites *par excellence*? There was no dramatic 'dissolution' of the monasteries in Protestant Switzerland, Regulars were not turned out from their homes into a hard and unaccustomed world, and there was hardly any wanton destruction of monastic churches and buildings. Provided men and women were free to leave at will, to marry, to cast off their habit, to earn a living with their hands or intellects, the Zwingli-guided administration of Zurich was well content to allow monasticism to perish of inanition.[1] It was agreed that no new monastic vows should be taken after 1524, and, in fact, the cloisters rapidly emptied. Their funds, which the Reformers had little difficulty in demonstrating had been often misapplied if not directly embezzled, were placed under the control of administrators appointed by the council and were reallocated for the benefit of the poor, for a limited amount of education and for the maintenance of the still numerous preachers and theologians.

Within the city walls of Zurich[2] and in its immediate vicinity, at Oetenbach, Selnau, Küssnacht, and at the practically deserted Cistercian house of Kappel, all this was relatively easily accomplished. Further afield, it was not so easy, as was discovered first at the Premonstratensian house of Rüti and then at Stein am Rhein. The happenings at Rüti are illustrative and instructive.[3] Here, as elsewhere, a great deal turned on the administrative head, the abbot.[4] Without his consent the corporate body could not act, while there was a great deal which he could do of his own authority both

---

[1] See above, 115, 127, 142–3.
[2] The Zurich monastic establishments are usefully listed in A. Nüscheler, *Die Gotteshäuser der Schweiz* III. 2 (Zürich, 1873), 438–73.
[3] Z IV, 520–4, supplemented by H. Zeller-Werdmüller, *Die Prämonstratenser-Abtei Rüti* (Zürich, 1897) (MAGZ XXIV) and an interesting article by P. Kläui, 'Kirche und Kloster Rüti' in *Zürcher Monats-Chronik* 141 (1945), 28–31.
[4] The word 'abbot' used of the head of each Benedictine and Carthusian house, but elsewhere limited, as with the Cluniacs, to certain houses only, had become in Switzerland practically a generic term displacing 'Prior' or 'Provost'.

legally, for every subordinate owed him implicit obedience, and in practice. At Rüti, Abbot Felix Clauser had at first rejected the orders from Zurich to eliminate images and pictures, to abandon the monastic habit, to introduce new forms of service, departing from tradition. He was not, however, ready for a collision with the government, the more so when the peasants of the neighbourhood at the beginning of 1525 were refusing to pay tithe and customary dues and services.[1] They not unnaturally hoped that a triumph of the Gospel would bring them greater freedom and lower taxation. When in February 1525 the abbot indicated that he was prepared to leave the premises, he very reasonably asked that administrators might be appointed to ensure that the monastic property rights were not infringed. While the Zurich officials were dealing with this request, on 22 or 23 April on a foggy night the abbot decamped with the seal, archives, cash, jewels and plate of his house to Rapperswil, which was outside Zurich's jurisdiction and where he had a confederate. As soon as he had gone, there was an attack on the monastic buildings and grounds by the local farmers. It was reported in Zurich that 1,200 rioters were moving across the fields, but the local governor, Berger of Grüningen, acting on peremptory orders from Zurich, dispersed the insurgents.

Instructions were then sought about the future of the monks of Rüti, now leaderless within their house, and about the disposal of their property and revenues. The council acted with considerable firmness. It was agreed that the abbot, having left, should not return; he had lost his authority, which devolved upon Hans Breitenmoser, who was sent to assist or direct operations. The monks might, if they wished, remain as before; there would be communal arrangements for meals and service, the infirmary attached to the monastery was to remain open, and each monk was to be allotted 30 gulden annually for his maintenance, but certain deductions were to be made from income accruing from distant benefices. As the monks died, the revenues allocated to them reverted to the Zurich council, but their personal property[2] went to their heirs. A careful inventory of all the remaining properties and chattels was arranged. Finally, in August, Zwingli wrote out his recommendations or requirements for the future.[3] First and foremost, instruction in the Bible. For an hour every morning each inmate was to read aloud, at a moderate pace, four or five chapters from the Old Testament, beginning with Genesis. This Bible reading was to be followed by a morning service including four psalms, the Lord's Prayer, the collect for the Sunday, Benedictus or Te Deum and the Kyrie.

---

[1] See above, 199.
[2] It is a measure of the general decline of the monastic ideal that this should exist, since individual poverty was nominally part of the rule.
[3] Z IV, 526–9. Their significance is that, with modifications, they were widely copied later.

After this service, a specially appointed teacher was to read for 45 minutes from the New Testament. There were to be Vespers in the evening consisting of a lesson from the New Testament, the psalms for the day, the Magnificat or Nunc Dimitis and a collect, a service curiously like the later Anglican 'Order for Evening Prayer daily throughout the Year'. Being Canons, all this might be said in Latin, but to make sure that this was properly understood, Wolfgang Kröwl (Chroil) was appointed to teach grammar if required, and external pupils were allowed to attend his classes. He was married, received the same stipend as the canons (30 gulden) with a house rent free, but he had to act as parish priest as well as part-time teacher. Effectively the monastery had come to an end and a further precedent was set for action elsewhere.

Rüti was directly under the control of the Zurich council. The situation in the walled city of Stein on the Rhine was more complicated.[1] This formerly free city had sought security in a defensive alliance with Zurich and Schaffhausen in 1459 which expanded in 1484 to protection. This meant that the Zurich council could, and was expected to, act as arbitrator in the increasing differences between the city and the wealthy Benedictine monastery of St George within its walls. The monastery had been founded by the sainted Emperor Henry II at the opening of the eleventh century, and the Holy Roman Emperors retained that nominal special relationship that everywhere appertained to founders' representatives. These rights of patronage by descent, purchase and agreement had devolved in the fourteenth century[2] upon the Austrian Habsburgs and were now claimed for the Archduke Ferdinand on behalf of the Emperor.

The city of Stein argued that any imperial rights had disappeared after the Swabian war and the peace of Basle (1499), and that Zurich (or was it the Swiss Confederation?) was the imperial substitute. The abbot in 1524 was the resourceful David von Winkelsheim, who had to face brethren, some of whom inclined to the new doctrines, a hostile city and the demand from Zurich that the monastic property should be placed under the control of a government-appointed administrator.[3]

Early in 1526 the Zurich Council was ready to treat the monastery at Stein in the same way as it had the Regulars within its own walls. Zwingli was twice consulted about the position, first in March and then in September 1526.[4] His first suggestions were that the monks (or canons) should preach the Gospel, that services should be of an evangelical type, Bible-reading should be encouraged, monks who wished to marry and leave the cloister should be free to do so, and that the revenues from the monastic

[1] See above, 145. [2] By the *Kauf- und Übernahmebrief* of 1359.
[3] Conrad Luchsinger, one of Zwingli's most convinced supporters, was appointed.
[4] Z IV, 764(769)–72; Z V, 397(399)–401.

property, administered by Zurich, should be applied for the benefit of the poor.

The abbot was not willing thus to relinquish his authority, his monks were divided, and Rhellican, the preacher and lecturer sent from Zurich to instruct them in languages, was not popular. The abbot was naturally anxious to retain his position as long as possible and also, in the event of the monastery reverting to the status of a collegiate church, to obtain as much compensation for himself as possible. To put himself in a stronger bargaining position, he moved to Rudolfzell, where Austrian support was available, and negotiated further.

Zwingli's second report was more emphatic. The protection of Zurich must be accepted, a good understanding with the town of Stein was recommended, no novices or new monks were to be brought in, divine services as demanded by the parishioners were to be of an evangelical pattern, the monastic treasures and jewels were to be placed at the disposal of the administration to be used for the poor, Abbot David's personal property, including silver plate, would be returned to him on condition that he agreed to these proposals. For this he was not prepared, nor would he accept arbitration; refusing any concessions, he died on 11 November 1526. The city of Stein then somewhat awkwardly accepted the new situation, and Zurich became de facto owner of the monastic property.[1]

All this affected Zurich in its dealings with the city and monastery of St Gall, where, however, conditions were different. There was no question of any rights of jurisdiction, the monastery was far more powerful, and in the end, after a hopeful start, Zwingli's policy received a notable setback which affected Swiss history long after his death.

Zwingli was very well acquainted with the great abbey of St Gall.[2] This famous foundation, in origin the result of Irish missionary activity in the sixth century, had become a wealthy Benedictine monastery with wide lands and a rich, if little used, library. Round the monastery, as at the English St Albans with which there are remarkable parallels, had grown up a walled town, whose industrious citizens had established a thriving linen trade and had largely succeeded in freeing themselves from dependence on their former overlord. There was thus a small but strongly civic-conscious

---

[1] F. Vetter, *Zwingli und Zürich in der Unterhandlung mit dem Abt von Stein im Jahre 1526.* Beiträge zur vaterländischen Geschichte 5 (Schaffhausen, 1884), 190–4, JSG 9 (1884) 301ff,
[2] Situated in an entirely German-speaking area, the place is best known as St Gallen. For its origins, F. Blanke, *Columban und Gallus. Urgeschichte des schweizerischen Christentums* (Zürich, 1940). J. M. Clark, *The abbey of St. Gall as a Centre of Literature & Art* (Cambridge, 1926) is the best study in English. *Historischer Atlas* Map 41 is helpful. The St Gall affair is well documented, *Sabbata* being particularly informative. Secondary studies of value are Näf, *Vadian*; Spillmann *1*; Spillmann *2*; Spillmann *3*; Müller; Knittel; Muralt, *Abtei*; W. Ehrenzeller, *St. Gallische Geschichte im Spätmittelalter und in der Reformationszeit* (2 Bde, St Gall, 1931, 1938).

community facing the monks and their abbot, a prince of the Holy Roman Empire. The abbey had fallen into some decay in the fifteenth century but had been reactivated after the election of Ulrich Rösch as guardian (*Pfleger*) in 1458 and as abbot in 1463.

After 1457 the city, with about 4,000 inhabitants, was accepted as a free imperial city (*Reichstadt*), and from then onwards the constant endeavour of the citizens was to free themselves from all monastic control and then to absorb the wide monastic possessions. These included much of the territory of the former hereditary Counts of Toggenburg, which the abbey had succeeded in acquiring in 1468 mainly by purchase.[1] In the first place, there was the ancient demesne (*alte Landschaft*), land in the immediate neighbourhood of St Gall, including Wil, Waldkirch and Rorschach, which had been owned and ruled by the monastery from time immemorial, to which had been added individual manors and jurisdictional rights secured sporadically across the ages. Over Toggenburg and an area on the upper Rhine known as Hof Kriessern, still more recently acquired, the monastic control was lighter and more remote.[2]

Both abbey and city were closely associated with the Confederation. Abbot Caspar von Landenberg had made a perpetual alliance (*ein ewige Burg-und Landrecht*)[3] with Lucerne, Schwyz, Glarus and Zurich on 17 August 1451; and on 13 June 1454 the citizens of St Gall were accepted as perpetual confederates (*ewiger Eidgenossen*) by Zurich, Berne, Lucerne, Schwyz, Zug and Glarus.[4] The abbot gained a promise of assistance in case of any revolt by the tenants and serfs of the countryside, and promised to help his allies in the event of war. The city went further, sacrificing any independent foreign policy and renouncing any alliance that was incompatible with those of its confederates but gaining guaranteed security. Protection for the abbey was obtained by the presence of a Protector (*Schirmhauptmann*) living in the abbey and appointed by the four protecting states for two years, each state nominating in turn.[5]

Representatives of both abbey and city were almost invariably summoned to the Diets of the Confederation, and they were usually included by name in Confederate treaties with outside powers.[6] The abbey of St Gall was easily first among the allies or associates (*Zugewandte*), but neither city nor abbot secured any higher status. This was partly because their rivalry had become so intense as to make common action impossible.

---

[1] T. Mayer (hg.), *Adel und Bauern im deutschen Staat des Mittelalters* (Leipzig, 1943), 140–1.
[2] Kägi, 19; G. Thürer, *St. Galler Geschichte* (St Gall, 1953) I, 266–70.
[3] EA 2. 255 (No. 387) Beilage 29, 864–6; Nabholz-Kläui, 52–6. It was renewed 9/11 June 1490. Spillmann *I*, 11.
[4] EA 2., 878–81; Nabholz-Käui, 56; Oechsli 2, 17; Thürer I, 286–91.
[5] By the *Hauptmannschaftsvertrag* 8 November 1479. Spillmann *I*, 12; Müller, 2; Oechsli 2, 54–5.   [6] Oechsli 2, 248–55.

In particular, the demand by the city in 1490 that the abbot should not alienate any monastic property without the consent of the city (which had itself originally been part of this property and remained an island in the midst of it) ended all chance of effective cooperation. The government of the city was of the familiar concentric pattern with Bürgermeister, small council of 24 and great council of 90, with the six gilds extremely influential if not dominant.[1] It was a prosperous community with a considerable export trade in linen.

Zwingli had a special personal connection with the city of St Gall that helps to explain events there. Joachim von Watt (1484–51) known as Vadian, was the son of a wealthy patrician of St Gall and one of a business family traditionally concerned with politics and interested in scholarship. He and Zwingli were contemporaries at the University of Vienna in 1500, and although Zwingli left after two years Vadian stayed the whole course (M.A. 1508 and Rector 1516). By March 1514 his public recognition by the Emperor Maximilian as a 'poet' (*poeta laureatus*) had established him as an exponent of *studia humanitatis*, the associate of Cuspinian, Collimitius, Tannstetter, and others who cultivated elegant latinity (*litterae politiores*).

Like many another humanist, he turned to the study of medicine, then regarded as an entirely theoretical discipline, and became M.D. in May 1517. He was also one of the first geographers, he learnt a little Greek, was relentless in parading his considerable erudition and fully conscious of the potentialities of the printing press. In 1518 Vadian returned to his native St Gall, where (after some months of travel, including Leipzig, Posen, Breslau, Krakau and Vienna), he married in October 1519, Martha, sister of Conrad Grebel who, like his father, was later to cause Zwingli so much trouble. He was soon city doctor, advised – from a safe distance – about taking precautions against the plague, and eagerly supported the few likeminded humanists with whom he came into contact. These included Myconius, who taught Latin in the city for a time, and Glarean, who shared his admiration for everything Swiss. Erasmus, indeed, gave him very little encouragement, and his own contributions to serious scholarship were a little superficial, while his family connections made politics a natural focus for his interests.

Politics in St Gall were inextricably involved with the long struggle of the city to free itself from the clutches of the monastery and to become powerful in its own right. In 1489 the tension between city and monastery was such that the scholarly Abbot Rösch (fl. 1463–91) had planned to move the convent to the peace and quiet of Rorschach. New buildings were started there, but, aided by men from Appenzell, the citizens of St Gall

---

[1] Thürer, 209–33; *Handbuch*, 556.

forcibly prevented their completion, and the abbot had to return to St Gall. The Protecting Powers on appeal sent men to his support, the city of St Gall had to pay damages, but the abbot had to renew the treaty of protection and his lands became in practice almost a Mandated Territory.[1]

Attention now moved to the whole concept of monasticism. Some of the citizens were ready to question whether the monk was the true Christian, renouncing the world, benefiting all humanity by his continuous service of prayer and by the masses offered daily in the great monastic church which towered above the city. Were not the monks the allies of the opponents of humanism? Vadian remained a layman and was no expert theologian; he had, however, the humanist's interest in a critical examination of the sources of knowledge, and he was early attracted by the writings of Luther. He also knew of the ferment in Zurich after 1519, but there is little to suggest any special interest in either Lutheran or Zwinglian teaching among the citizens of St Gall before 1522. Vadian himself had undertaken some critical Bible study in an effort to interpret the Apostles' Creed to his fellow-citizens. Without any crisis or personal conversion he found himself irresistibly drawn to the new teaching. This led him on to a study of the primitive church and of the *Acts of the Apostles*: he was discoursing to a small audience on the latter at the same time as the great Zurich debate was going on in January 1523. In October, indeed, he was a co-president at the second debate. From study of the Bible to acceptance of exclusive Bible infallibility was a considerable step, but Vadian took it, and slowly, at his own speed and in his own way, by the time he became Bürgermeister in 1526 he was a convinced Zwinglian.[2]

His influence, combined with the anti-monastic interests and sentiments of the leading traders of St Gall, brought about first toleration and then encouragement of evangelical preaching by Benedict Burgauer, Wolfgang Wetter, Dominic Zili and John Kessler in the city. On 4 April 1524 the council required the priests in the city church of St Lawrence to preach the Gospel 'clearly and plainly and in accordance with the text of the Bible.'[3] A little earlier, Sebastian Hofmeister and Leo Jud, returning from a rather fruitless Gospel-mission to Appenzell, had reinforced these tendencies[4] and in July 1524 the images in St Laurence were removed. The sermons were popular and increased in numbers. At the same time

[1] Spillmann 3, 62; Näf, *Vadian* I, 90–5; Müller, 3–6.
[2] This is discussed at some length by Näf II, 165–80, Spillmann I, 14–18, and C. Bonorand, *Vadians Weg vom Humanismus zur Reformation und seine Vorträge über die Apostelgeschichte (1523)* (Vadian-Studien 7 (St Gall, 1962)).
[3] Näf, *Vadian* II, 189, 195, Muralt/Fast, 339: 'dass hailig evangelium predigend, clar und luter, wie sy das mit der biblischen geschrifft erhalten mögen'. Cf. Sabbata, 112. The Bible text was to be expounded 'hell, clar und nach rechtem cristenlichen verstand, one inmischung menschlichs zusatz'. Spillmann 2, 40; Egli 3, 349.　　　[4] Müller, 22.

the city adopted, as Zurich had done, some elementary measures to relieve manifest poverty[1] while at the same time forbidding begging in the streets. These happenings all intensified the division between city and monastery, the more so since in July 1525 the abbot had secured an appreciable increase in his authority over his tenants.[2] There was also some considerable difficulty with the Anabaptists, who had been encouraged by the preaching of Lorenz Hochrütiner, a native of St Gall, Volimann, Grebel and Blaurock, and who were said to have some five hundred adherents.[3] Zwingli's treatise *Vom Tauf*,[4] dedicated to the St Gall council, may have helped the reaction against them,[5] and by the end of 1526 the agitation had largely died down. Similarly, there was a little disorder created by those who wanted the immediate removal of images and pictures from the city churches; these were placated by a cautious but effective 'cleansing' of them in December 1526. After the Baden conference, which the city council had prohibited Vadian from attending, and where the abbot's steward had been one of the chairmen, St Gall was threatened with exclusion from Federal Diets because of its evangelical tendencies.[6] The city council refused to yield to pressure, and although the mass was not officially abolished until 17 July 1528[7] it had already been replaced by an evangelical communion service and St Gall city had become a reformed enclave within a monastic state. The clear-cut division of the city of St Gall and the abbey of St Gall, which was an outcome of the Zwinglian reformation, was not apparent until after 1531, and is one of the lasting consequences of Zwingli's defeat and death. The city never succeeded in swallowing the abbey as Zurich swallowed the Fraumünster or even as Schaffhausen reduced the monastery of All Saints to insignificance. Although Bürgermeister Vadian was in physical possession of the abbey buildings in 1530 and the abbot exiled in his castle of Meersburg, the legal continuity of the convent was unbroken. Similarly, although the evangelical teaching was accepted by a large majority of the villages of the countryside, there never was a complete 'reformation' of both city and monastery. The abbot retained his position, the convent in the end re-entered into its possessions stronger than ever, and the city maintained its independence.

The evangelisation of St Gall in fact was secure only for as long as the

---

[1] Näf, *Vadian* II, 198–9.
[2] W. Müller, *Landsatzung und Landmandat der Fürstabtei St. Gallen*, MVG (St Gall, 1970) 19–31, 219–20. [3] Egli *I*, 377; E. Egli, *Die St. Galler Täufer* (Zürich, 1887) 45–7.
[4] See above, 190–1.
[5] When Zwingli's arguments were read in St Laurence's Church by Zili he was interrupted by Gabriel Giger declaring 'We want God's word, not Zwingli's.' Näf, *Vadian* II, 232; *Sabbata*, 145; Muralt/Fast, 388 n. 2, 389 n. 13.
[6] Näf, *Vadian* II, 248; EA 4, 1 a, 962–3, 1039. [7] Näf, *Vadian* II, 266–7; Müller 45.

city could be sure of protection against its monastery, the Austrian administration and threats from the Catholic Confederate states. For this the alliance with Zurich was invaluable, and with such support the city council could, and did, carry through the dissolution of the two nunneries of St Catharine and St Leonhard in November 1527.[1] What was really decisive, however, was the victory of the reformed teaching in Berne in January 1528, after which events happened quickly as political considerations came prominently to the fore.

For nearly a century the city had been the associate of Zurich, Berne, Lucerne, Zug and Glarus, but this combination was no longer effective after Berne had become evangelical. Local security was, moreover, still further assured when, on 3 November 1528, after considerable discussion, St Gall was received into the Christian Civic Union[2] with Zurich and Berne on an equal footing. This implied that the city had ceased to be an ally (*zugewandter Ort*) of the Confederation but was an equal partner of Zurich and Berne. It was also a city without territory, inside the lands of the abbey and thus unique in its position and problems.

The situation in present-day Switzerland of the two half-cantons of Appenzell Inner-Rhoden and Appenzell Ausser-Rhoden entirely surrounded by St Gall has no applicability to the sixteenth century. Appenzell[3] was indeed the smallest and most recent of the *Orte*, but its position as such was secure, whereas city and monastery of St Gall remained outside the Federation until 1798. To its north and south were the federally-held Mandated Territories, Thurgau, Uznach, Gaster, Sargans and Rheintal. Neither St Gall city nor the monastery had any share in the government of these districts, but a good deal turned on their future. If they became Protestant and therefore within Zurich's sphere of influence, and if a Protestant city of St Gall took over the rights of its great monastery thus becoming a powerful and wealthy state, the balance of power in north eastern Switzerland would be decisively altered. For the inhabitants of Thurgau it might mean that districts subject to the monastery where Bible reading and evangelical preaching had been discouraged[4] would in future be able to worship as they chose and be freed from obligations to perform military service or to pay suit to the ecclesiastical courts. In any case the combined military forces of Zurich, Schaffhausen, St Gall, Thur-

---

[1] Näf, *Vadian* II, 267–8; Müller, 45. The nuns mostly went to Bischofszell. Knittel I, 182; ZSKG 55 (1961), 214–15.
[2] See below, 352–3. EA 4, 1 a, 1433, 1526; Näf, *Vadian* II, 281; Spillmann *I*, 20; Z VI ii, 346.
[3] Appenzell, an *Ort* since 1513, was divided in religious allegiance after 1524, the inner portion (*die innerer Rhoden*) remaining Catholic. Appenzell could thus speak only with a divided voice, and limited its intervention in external affairs to mediation or neutrality. H. Dörig, *Ein Datierungsproblem in der Appenzeller Reformationsgeschichte. St. Galler Kultur und Geschichte* (Festgabe für Paul Staerkle 2) (St Gall, 1972) 106–16.
[4] Knittel I, 118–20.

gau, Rheintal, with, probably, Glarus and Appenzell, would be formidable and thus a powerful potential ally for the Zwinglian-minded cities of south Germany.

Hence the complexity of the situation. For the whole of north-eastern Switzerland to be dominated by Zurich would suit neither Berne nor the Catholics nor St Gall city. For the abbey to retain its authority would be greatly to the advantage of the Catholic states who would thus be able to maintain their communications with the Austrian Vorarlberg and so limit further Protestant expansion. If the city controlled the abbey lands when evangelised, it would be too powerful to suit the political ends of Zurich, which, as a protecting power, had rights over the abbey which might otherwise be lost. If the whole of the Mandated Territories remained evangelical this would be entirely to the disadvantage of the Catholics, who had a majority in the Diet of the Confederation. If Zurich were to control them and take over the secular jurisdiction of the abbot, it would benefit enormously and the city of St Gall would retire to its former relative insignificance.

Of the implications of this Zwingli was fully aware, but he was concerned primarily with its relevance to his preaching. Zurich was not anxious for the disappearance of the monastery of St Gall if this meant that the property and rights of the abbey would revert to the city, which could thus become an eastern rival. Rather, Zurich hoped to expand its influence by becoming *de facto* sole Protector of the abbey, administrator of its property and inheritor of its rights, all leading to thinly disguised aggrandizement. The city of St Gall would of course retain, perhaps even slightly increase, its autonomy, but nothing more.

Meanwhile within the city the tide was running strongly in favour of reform. The council was purged of Catholics in 1528. With Zwinglian services prevailing throughout the city since 1525, the mass abolished, images removed, the Bible opened, attention was naturally transferred to the abbey church. There, by order of the city council, a spectacular, but dubiously legal, cleansing took place on 23 February 1529.[1] All images of saints were removed and destroyed, and the great screen which, as usual in a monastic church, separated choir from nave, was pulled down. No one was injured, and the crosses, chalices, candlesticks and altar cloths were unharmed. Dominic Zili preached evangelical sermons from the pulpit, and Vadian, as Bürgermeister, occupied the monastic buildings in the name of the city.

---

[1] Sabbata, 311–12 (a vivid account); Müller, 57–61; Näf, *Vadian* II, 286–94; Z VI ii, 346. It was not done at the instigation of Zurich, as Strickler II (1879), 68 suggests. Spillmann 3, 67 n. 35. Vadian argued that the monastic church was not exclusively for the monks but a public building for all citizens and that therefore the city could rightly intervene. Z x, 40 n 1; *Vad. Br.* IV, 151–9.

All this was taking place in the spring of 1529 just at the moment when a confrontation between the reformed states and the Inner States, supported by Austria, seemed likely and even imminent. In this situation a good deal turned on the abbot, Franz Gaisberg (Geissberg), distantly related to Vadian, a man of upright character, charitable and active, but determined to maintain to the full the rights of his monastery. He had withdrawn in October 1528 along with the few choir monks who constituted the 'convent', to Rorschach, where he now lay dangerously ill in the castle. At the same time a number of communities on monastic territory, as Altstätten, Berg, Gossau, Bischofszell, Wil, Steinach, Steckborn, Arbon, Rorschach, and Waldkirch, were demanding evangelical ministers and services.[1] Thus, monastic St Gall, like Vadian's city, was rapidly becoming a Zwinglian outpost.

The abbot was not likely to accept elimination without a struggle. His position was guaranteed by his alliance with Zurich, Lucerne, Schwyz and Glarus, and of these Lucerne and Schwyz were strongly Catholic but Glarus, at first uncommitted, became evangelical and joined forces with Zurich. Their joint authority was, however, exercised by Jacob Frei[2] of Zurich. His appointment as Protector (*Schirmhauptmann*) had been properly made in November 1528 by Zurich, which thus had excellent opportunities for intervention. Up to that date the abbot had been able to rely upon the support of the Protector against his opponents. Now he could no longer expect such help in dealing with his tenants in spite of the fact that the Protector had instructions[3] to uphold the rights and income of the abbey. Frei early received orders from the energetic Bürgermeister Röist to take precautionary measures in case the abbot should die. In this event if the remaining monks could be persuaded not to elect a new abbot, without whom nothing could be done, they were to be guaranteed a good income for life, while Frei was to take over the administration of the

---

[1] The abbot was patron of these churches, whose parishioners wished to choose their own ministers. Spillmann I, 23. Waldkirch has a special interest in that its affairs were the subject of one of Zwingli's many memoranda (Z v, 759–62). The monastic tenants there had been trying to improve their political, legal and social rights as against the abbey for half a century (Knittel I, 116–18). Their economic demands were refused in 1525, and an appeal to biblical prededents led to an order from the abbot forbidding the purchase or owning of a vernacular Bible. Kägi, 36.

In 1527 the community called for the removal of images from their church, which of course the abbot, supported by Lucerne, Schwyz and Glarus, refused. They were able, however, with the good will of Zurich, to do just this in November 1528 and to welcome an evangelical preacher. After the battle of Kappel (1531) the commune was forcibly re-Catholicised by the Catholics.

[2] Jacob Frei (c. 1480–1531, killed on 24 October on the Gubel) had been appointed for two years from 25 November 1528. He was an active politician and a strong supporter of the Reformation. Spillmann *1*, 22. Jacob 156; Z x, 43 n. 2, 133 n. 1.

[3] Spillmann *1*, 29.

monastic territory in the name of the four protecting powers.[1] The Catholics were aware that something was in the wind and took such countermeasures as they could.

The abbot and his advisers were in touch with the Five Catholic States and with representatives of Ferdinand of Austria at Feldkirch.[2] They counted on aid from Marx Sittich of Hohenems and his brother-in-law the lord of Musso. This abortive intervention must be described elsewhere. It did not, in fact, directly affect St Gall, but the possibility, and even the likelihood, of an armed attack was seriously anticipated.

It was in the light of this situation that, early in 1529, Zwingli had felt obliged to urge his government to intervene. He now suggested[3] that the Zurich Council, of its own right or in conjunction with the city of St Gall, should at once enter into written communication with the abbot at Rorschach, who should be asked to receive a delegation from Zurich and St Gall. A further discussion of the matter with Berne should take place at Aarau. He urged that because of the progress already made by the reformed doctrines there should be an agreement by the eleven surviving monks of St Gall that on the death of their abbot they would not proceed to the election of a successor. The monks would then be free to marry and to obtain alternative employment, and they would receive generous pensions. The monastic tenants should be assured that the conditions of their tenure would be substantially improved.[4]

Vadian, as Bürgermeister of the city of St Gall, was far from happy with these proposals. If Zurich took over the jurisdiction of the abbot, his city might very soon find Zurich officials exercising authority within its walls, since the abbot still had admitted rights there, as well as over all the monastic territory. All this latter the city had plainly hoped would devolve upon its own Council when the monastery disappeared. Berne, equally, was not anxious to see the territories of its chief rival extending to the lake of Constance and perhaps beyond. The situation was obviously becoming critical. It was on 23 March 1529 that Abbot Gaisberg died from dropsy at Rorschach.[5] This should have been the occasion for the plans of both Zwingli and Vadian to take effect and for the monastery to fade away into oblivion. Unfortunately for them, however, Jacob Frei as Protector and secular administrator of the monastery was slow off the mark. The monks

---

[1] Spillmann *3*, 64, 66, 67; EA 4, 1 b, 59, 63; Strickler, II (1879) 29–30 (No. 46); Z VI ii, 348. Zwingli was not directly associated with this action, but agreed with the policy. Z X, 43.

[2] Z VI ii, 349–50; Spillmann *1*, 31. Ferdinand's election as King of the Romans following Charles V's coronation by the Pope was anticipated.

[3] Z VI ii, 354–60. Cf. EA 4, 1 b, 35–6. Zwingli could do no more than suggest – he was not a member of the council, which accepted full responsibility for action. Some of his suggestions were adopted, some ignored. (Spillmann *1*, 45–7.)

[4] Z VI ii, 347.

[5] *Sabbata* 314; Z VI ii, 350, 354 n. 5; X, 87–8; Müller, 93 n. 2.

of the convent – there were now effectively only five of them – had decided on their course of action. They kept the death a secret until they had got themselves safely on to neutral ground at Rapperswil. There, two days later, in a room in the Red Lion Inn, but with scrupulous care to observe the canonical requirements, they elected one of their number, Kilian German, as their new head.[1] This action, which Zwingli had been anxious to prevent, was a distinct political triumph for the Catholics, who hastened to recognise and promise support to the new prelate. He was well-connected, intelligent if not very learned, popular and approachable. He had many friends and few enemies.

From Zurich, followed by Glarus,[2] both protecting powers, came a shrill and emphatic note of protest inspired by Zwingli. The pretended election was invalid. The death of Abbot Franz had been concealed and the election had been made in secrecy where it should have been an open one: the protecting powers had not been informed,[3] as had always been the case in the past, and they had not given the customary *congé d'élire*. The election should properly take place at St Gall within the precinct wall of the monastery wherein the monks were required by their rule to remain.[4] Rapperswil was not an acceptable place for an election, at which the titular Abbot of Rüti had, irregularly, been present. The abbot-elect had not been presented to the protecting powers; he had sought, but had not received, confirmation of his election from Rome and was thus an 'invader' or 'intruder'. He had none the less entered immediately upon

---

[1] Müller, 93–4; Spillmann *1*, 33; Z X, 87; Z VI ii, 355; Näf, *Vadian* II, 298. He was also known as Köiffi, Köuffi and Germann.

[2] Zwingli was always concerned about the progress of his teaching in Glarus. The first clear signs of open discontent with the Catholic regime appeared in 1527. Early in 1528, following the Berne disputation, images were removed from the churches at Matt and Schanden, and in August there was general expectation in Zurich that Glarus would declare openly for reform. EA 4, 1a, 1380; J. Winteler, *Geschichte des Landes Glarus* (Glarus, 1952) I, 302ff; G. Heer, *Kirchengeschichte des Kantons Glarus* (Glarus, 1900) III, 69, 71; G. Heer, *Geschichte des Landes Glarus*[2] (Glarus, 1898) I, 317–22. An attempt to secure agreement at a *Landsgemeinde* in May 1528 was unsuccessful (Winteler I, 308; Z IX, 600), and the report which reached Zwingli in January 1529 of a majority for his supporters – 'Clarone vicit pars, que est ab euangelio. Deo gloria!' – was premature (Z X, 50; Winteler I, 312). The *Landsgemeinde* on 2 May 1529 by a majority accepted Zwinglian doctrine but allowed the Catholics freedom of worship (Winteler I, 313f). From 1529 to 1531 Glarus was ranged on the side of Zurich and was no longer an ally of the Catholics: this was what mattered in the critical dealings with the Abbot of St Gall. Haas, *Kappelerkrieg*, 100.

[3] Representatives from Lucerne and Schwyz were in Rapperswil, but Zurich and Glarus were given no information. Nothing in the original treaty of protection required that representatives of the protecting powers should be present at the election, and the precedents for the election of the previous abbots (1491, Giel von Glattbrugg and 1504, Franz Gaisberg) were not conclusive.

[4] For the requirement of 'stability' see Butler, *Regula Benedicti* (Freiburg i.B., 1912) XLVI; G. G. Coulton, *Five Centuries of Religion* I (Cambridge, 1923), 207–10, 280. It could scarcely be seriously appealed to in the conditions of the sixteenth century.

his office on 7 June, he had decamped in the fog with some monastic property (i.e. plate and service-books) to Steinach, Überlingen and Meersburg,[1] whence he tried to enforce the celebration of mass throughout the monastic territories (*Alte Landschaft*).

On technical points of law Zwingli was, in fact, standing on very dubious ground; canonically the election of Abbot Kilian was almost certainly valid.[2] There were, however, many other matters to be taken into consideration. His consistent argument from 1523 onwards had been that there was no biblical ground for the exercise of temporal authority by ecclesiastical persons. Spiritual and temporal jurisdictions were separate; the duties of the clergy were to advise and exhort.[3] He equally consistently maintained that the monastic life had no biblical support and the institution therefore could not be upheld by Zurich. The absentee abbot could not justify his position (*münchenstand*) from the Bible and thus any claims arising from it were invalid. Further, Kilian would obviously restore the mass throughout the monastic dominions if he could, and for the monastic income to be devoted to this undesirable purpose was entirely unacceptable. It was the duty of the protecting powers to ensure that the tenants benefited directly by their own funds.

An ingenious corollary from this was that the abbot's usurped or unwarranted jurisdiction devolved upon the four protecting powers. These were equally divided for and against – Lucerne and Schwyz opposing Zurich and Glarus. In such a deadlock Zurich, it was argued, had a moral casting vote as *Vorort*, which it obviously exercised in its own favour.[4] At best, Kilian might have been accepted as guardian of the monastic estates, administering the revenues to benefit the poor and to improve the conditions under which his tenants lived. Instead, he had deserted his post and had sought foreign help. He was a usurper and a thief, a traitor and a rebel.[5] He should be referred to only as 'Herr' Kilian Köiffi. The tenants had met together at Lömmenschwil (April 1529) and had declared that they would abide by God's word and recognise no abbot who was not approved by Zurich.[6] The Abbot of St Gall could find little comfort in the

---

[1] Z x, 165 n. 2. Lavater had arrived too late to prevent the flight.
[2] Muralt, *Abtei* 307–8. Zwingli was, in fact, well informed on the subject of canon law and probably recognised that the election could not be rejected on these grounds alone. Canon law, however, was man-made and was overridden by divine law (the Bible), from which the abbot could derive no support. F. Schmidt-Clausing, *Das Corpus Juris Canonici als reformatorisches Mittel Zwinglis*, ZKG 80 (1969), 14–21, esp. 16; Z vi ii, 683, 718–19.
[3] H. Schmid, *Zwinglis Lehre von der göttlichen und menschlichen Gerechtigkeit* (Zürich, 1959), 237–8; Z i, 462; 298–304; Spillmann *i*, 22; *3*, 68. See above, 117–118.
[4] Muralt, *Abtei*, 304, 308, 311–12; Oechsli 2, 249; Kägi, 49–51.
[5] Z vi i, 628–32; Spillmann *i*, 60–1, 63–4; Müller, 133.
[6] ZWA xiii (1969), 28; Sabbata, 315–16; Müller, 100. Zwingli had suggested that representatives from Zurich should attend the Lömmenschwil meeting, but no such action was taken.

outcome of the first Kappel war. In a series of well-informed notes or opinions[1] Zwingli demonstrated to his council that the abbot's position was unbiblical and unlawful: the monastic tenants were entitled to the protection of their rights and property that had been promised to them, and the preaching of the Gospel was not to be hindered. The abbot had no 'Herrschaftrechten' and in his lands the mass should be discouraged if not suppressed.

The abbot, none the less, was in a strong position. He was recognised by Lucerne and Schwyz as protecting powers and by all the Catholic states, he was supported by Austria and was a Prince of the Empire, entitled to attend its Diets,[2] and even Berne and Schaffhausen were cautiously prepared to negotiate with him.[3] He was physically safe at Meersburg. The Swiss Catholics insisted that Zurich and Glarus were irregularly interfering in the affairs of another state, thus acting contrary to the principles of the Confederation, and that, by negotiating with monastic tenants about the appointment of officials, they were supporting rebels, a point on which Berne was specially sensitive.

There was the further problem of the city of St Gall, a member of the Christian Civic Union and now thoroughly evangelised by Vadian. Zurich was very careful to maintain the distinction between abbey and city and to deal with each matter separately as an interested party. This was apparent when, at the end of August 1530, Zurich agreed that the city of St Gall was entitled to purchase for 14,000 gulden the site, buildings and some other possessions of the monastery.[4] Any monks who remained in residence were to be under constant surveillance. The monastic treasures were to be recovered for the city, information about them being extracted by torture if necessary. But there was no question of the city of St Gall being allowed to secure any control over the former monastic territories when these were evangelised. This would be contrary to the expansionist policy of Zurich,

---

[1] Z VI ii, 345–60, 372–81, 552–68, 611–32, 657–719. They were not all adopted by the Zurich Council. Spillmann *3*, 66. The most important is the 'Anbringen' of 8–9 January 1530. Cf. EA 4, 1 b, 506–9.

[2] He attended the Diet at Augsburg and, with support from Lucerne, appealed to the Emperor for help which was promised but did not materialise. Spillmann *3*, 72; Müller, 153–5; Spillmann *1*, 86.

[3] Müller, 143. The case was again stated at a Federal Diet at Baden in January 1530, but without effect on either side. EA 4, 1 b, 507–9.

[4] Vadian, *Diarium* III, 266 (in *Deutsche Historische Schriften* hg. E. Götzinger, St Gallen, 1879). For many other notices see pp. 227–528. EA 4, 1 b, 747–53; Z VI ii, 392; Vadian II, 305–12; Spillmann *1*, 101. From Zurich it was emphasized that the acquisition of site and buildings which had been in civic occupation since June 1529 was only reluctantly agreed to and that no rights of jurisdiction were conveyed with it. It is important not to over-estimate Zwingli's share in the vital St Gall negotiations. His advice was asked for and considered, but the council, and particularly the able Bürgermeister Röist, acted quite independently. Spillmann *1*, 77, 87. The abbot protested strongly against the city's action, and Berne never formally recognised the secularisation of the monastery.

whose forces, it was intended, should garrison for an indefinite period a religiously 'liberated' *alte Landschaft*. This was not to the liking of the city of St Gall, which saw itself excluded from this 'ancient demesne' where the abbot and Zurich were now conscious competitors for power. The triumph of the Reformation in Switzerland implied the elimination of the abbey. Zwingli was right to pursue his opponent relentlessly, for Kilian's courage and persistence greatly helped to strengthen Catholic morale. He visited Einsiedeln, then settled for a time in Wil, where he promised reductions in taxation and did everything in his power to please his tenants by generosity and concessions. Zwingli, for his part, recommended that Zurich should offer promises of reduced taxation accompanied by the exclusive encouragement of evangelical teaching.[1] When the monastery had disappeared, Rorschach, Rosenberg and Oberberg should be garrisoned and the inhabitants should be given a new constitution including an oath of allegiance to Zurich.

After the first Kappel war and the occupation of most of eastern Switzerland by Lavater in June 1529, the abbot hurried from Steinach to safety at Meersburg and never returned to St Gall territory.[2] The men of Rorschach took control of their own city. The tenants of the ancient demesne, however, who in September demanded substantial independence, including the right to choose their own Landamman with full legal authority to administer justice,[3] were disappointed. When representatives of the protecting powers (whose rights were consistently upheld) met in October at Wil, it was clear that no agreement between them was possible while Lucerne and Schwyz supported the abbot. The inhabitants wanted complete independence, which Zurich was not willing to grant; the Zurich policy really amounted to annexation. Zwingli's thoughts, it should be emphasised, were consistently on religion; freedom of preaching must be upheld at any cost throughout all the St Gall territories, especially his beloved Toggenburg. The eyes of the inhabitants had already been opened, they must not be closed again as assuredly they would be, forcibly, if the Catholics were allowed to regain control. After further discussion at a Diet at Baden in November,[4] the Zurich council decided to take over the administration of the area, which was of considerable military importance to it; and a commission was set up at Zurich to draft a constitution. Berne had reluctantly agreed to allow Zurich a free hand.

On his return from Marburg Zwingli had joined Bürgermeister Röist, Ochsner, Schwyzer, Cambli and Werdmüller in a kind of working-party[5] on the matter, which recommended that the existence of the abbot should

---

[1] Z vi ii, 359–60.   [2] Spillmann 2, 41; Müller, 119; Sabbata, 319.
[3] EA 4, 1b, 366–7 (StAZ A. 244. 2 No. 14).   [4] EA 4, 1b, 438.
[5] Z vi ii, 616 (StaZ.A.244.2 No. 17); Spillmann 3, 70.

be ignored and that the views of Glarus, if unfavourable, should be over-ridden. There was now no suggestion of granting the independence which the inhabitants called for.

Not all of this was acceptable to the Zurich council, which opened uni-lateral negotiations with the tenants at Wil[1] on 10 December. These negotiations were to be based on a draft constitution of fifteen articles, partly drawn up by Zwingli himself,[2] by which the powers of the local Landammann were transferred forthwith to Zurich. Instead of their own elected Landammann, authority was to be vested in the Protector (*Schirm-hauptmann*), still nominally acting on behalf of the four protecting powers but in practice an evangelical nominated by the Zurich Council. He was to be appointed for two years and assisted by an advisory council of twelve, four his own nominees and eight chosen by the twenty-nine com-munities of the countryside. This body in turn would appoint the local magistrates or administrative officers, with approval from Zurich, while the parishes (*Gemeinden*) would be free to choose their own ministers who, however, must be tested and certified as suitable and competent at Zurich, Constance or St Gall and would then obtain a certain security of tenure. Church property, valuables and vestments were to be taken over by the government, which collected tithe, rents and customary payments as before. These revenues would be applied through churchwardens (*Kirchenvorstehern*) for the support of the minister, the fabric of the church and the relief of the poor. Evangelical preaching[3] was to be enforced by the Protector in consultation with Zwingli. Berne, which had no authority in St Gall, wanted peace there, but accepted Zurich's argument that the abbot was subordinate to the Protecting Powers, which had come to mean Zurich; and Zurich, obliged to uphold God's word, was equally obliged to defend the monastic subjects from any attempt by the abbot to oppose the Bible or Bible-preaching.

There was little enthusiasm for this draft when presented locally. It was obvious enough that real independence or local self-government was to be denied.

The discontent of the monastic tenants was vocal enough for Zurich to send an ultimatum – if they did not cooperate, Zurich's protection would be withdrawn.[4] In Wil the government representatives had to seek refuge in the castle in face of a serious, if bloodless demonstration, but the dis-content died down. There was a meeting there for further discussion on New Year's Day 1530,[5] where a vague promise was given that obligations

---

[1] Where the appointment of Lorenz Appenzeller as Statthalter had been resisted by Lucerne and Schwyz. Müller, 165; Spillmann 3, 71.   [2] Z VI ii, 628–30 (StAZ.E.1.3.1 No. 57).
[3] 'dem göttlichen wort, ouch evangelischer leer und warheit günstig und nit zewider sige'. Müller, 183: EA 4, 1b, 1496. Cf. Z VI ii, 625.   [4] Müller, 169–78.
[5] Spillmann 1, 78; Vad. Br. IV, 195–7 (No. 588).

to the abbot would be fulfilled provided he justified his 'münchenstand' by the Bible, which, of course, he could not do. The constitution itself, after further discussions, was produced in its final form on 25 May.[1] Although some social and economic improvements were vaguely promised, in fact the tenants found that services and dues were required of them exactly as previously; only the church liturgy and sermons were altered. It was also an entirely unilateral arrangement. Schwyz and Lucerne, whose rights all along had been nominally safeguarded, recognised Abbot Kilian as the only lawful ruler and supported his efforts to maintain the mass and Catholic services. To appeals by the abbot to the Diet of the Confederation and to charges that the innovations were illegal, Zurich replied by appealing to the terms of the first peace of Kappel[2] and to the Zwinglian doctrine of the incompatibility of spiritual with temporal authority. The position of the abbot, it was asserted, was based on canon or papal law which was man-made and could not supersede divine law. The monastic tenants wanted and needed access to God's word, and in this they should be supported. To recognise the abbot would be to reject reform and return to popery, an argument with which Berne reluctantly agreed, refusing to recognise the abbot and leaving Zurich a free hand.[3] Lucerne vainly attempted to appeal to the Emperor at Augsburg to intervene, and for all practical purposes Zurich was left in full control. With the purely secular and administrative implications of this fact Zwingli was personally not directly concerned.

When, however, Abbot Kilian, round whose contested election so much had turned, was drowned while crossing the river Ach on his horse on 30 August 1530, he was succeeded, unchallenged on the Catholic side, unrecognised on the Protestant, by Diethelm Blarer von Wartensee,[3] an imperial nominee well suited both for the times and the office. On the following 25 November, the term of office of the Zurich-nominated Protector, Jakob Frei, came to an end. His place was now due to be taken by the nominee of Lucerne, Jakob am Ort, who was, of course, a Catholic. The peace, however, interfered with this, for it had been provided that the protector should be well disposed to evangelical teaching, should take an oath to uphold the constitution, and should allow the monastic tenants to continue their new forms of worship.[4] This he refused to do, and attempts

---

[1] It was in the form of an agreement between Zurich and Glarus with representatives of twenty-nine *Gemeinden* of the St Gall territory. EA 4, 1 b, 644–53, 1493–1499 (Beilage 12), Spillmann *3*, 73, with a facsimile; Näf, *Vadian* II, 315; Müller, 178–81 (for the preliminary negotiations).   [2] Z VI ii, 683–4. See below 375.

[3] Näf, *Vadian* II, 316–17; Müller, 205–6; Spillmann, *2*, 61; *3*, 74; Strickler II, 667 (no. 1673a, b).

[4] 'by göttlichem wort und irem cristenlichen ansechen beliben lassen'. ZWA XIII (1969), 30; Müller, 183.

by Berne to arrange a compromise failed. Lucerne was not prepared to rule, through its representative, over heretical communities; Zurich was determined not to accept a return of the abbot. Frei, in fact, remained in charge. Neither side was prepared for anything like 'parity' or 'recognition'; each hoped to swing the whole Confederation to its viewpoint. Lucerne could appeal to the *Stanser Verkommnis* of 1481 which guaranteed complete independence and equality to each state. The Zwinglians now argued that this was no longer applicable since freedom and power, if misused, could be properly abrogated. A Catholic administration would reimpose Catholicism on the St Gall tenants, and this Zurich could not allow. *Contra iniustitiam non est ius.* The city of St Gall had no option but to support its Zurich ally when in 1530 conflict became unavoidable. It therefore reluctantly joined with Zurich in bringing the pressure of economic blockade to bear on the Inner States. At the same time, because of fear of a Catholic attack from the north east, it constantly urged peace and negotiation. When the Inner States declared war on Zurich in 1531, St Gall was prepared to support the latter, knowing that a Catholic victory would be a gain for the monastery. This was in fact what happened. The help that Zurich received from St Gall, itself threatened by Marx Sittich of Hohenems, was indeed negligible. Thus, while the St Gall situation was partly responsible for the second Kappel war, the outcome of this was a serious setback to the city. Blarer was recognised as abbot, the monastic estates became Catholic again, mass was said in the abbey church, and the Zurich-given constitution was forgotten. Inside the city, Vadian with difficulty saved what had been gained, and the two St Galls, the Protestant free imperial city and the Catholic abbey at its gates, went their separate ways until the French Revolution.

12

Zwingli and Luther

Capito, writing to his friend Blaurer at the end of 1525, said, 'Future generations will laugh at the pleasure our age takes in quarrelling when we raise such disturbance about the very signs that should unite us.'[1] The modern world has in general been as unsympathetic to the eucharistic controversies of the sixteenth century[2] as Gibbon was to those of the sixth – 'the profane of every age have derided the furious contests which the difference of a single diphthong excited between the Homoousians and the Homoiousians'.[3] Yet most of the Christian churches have embodied the orthodox view of the Trinity in their creeds, as Zwingli himself did, accepting the Nicean rejection of the Arian alternative. So, too, public controversy about transubstantiation, the real presence and even the forms of service accompanying mass, eucharist, holy communion, the Last Supper, or the breaking of the bread – every word and phrase with its own undertones – has been singularly muted in the twentieth century, in some measure, no doubt, because organised religion itself has come to a position of defensive alliance against massive public indifference, if not rejection.

Just as convictions of verbal inspiration of the Bible have given way before textual criticism and a proliferation of varying renderings and translations of the Divine Word, so too reliance upon individual proof texts and their hidden meaning has greatly diminished even among theological controversialists. For the sixteenth century it was different: eternal salvation turned upon understanding and agreeing on the meaning of the words of the Bible, and above all on those spoken by Christ himself of himself. This meant that a right attitude to the mass, or its replacement, was indispensable. We can hardly hope, without a strong exercise of imagination, to recapture the intensity and vitality of the sixteenth-century approach to revealed religion. The issue about the eucharist was

---

[1] *Briefwechsel der Brüder Ambrosius und Thomas Blaurer, 1509–1548* bearbeitet von Traugott Schiess, Bd. I (Freiburg i.B., 1908), 125.

[2] E.g. A. L. Rowse: 'The sixteenth century is full of the useless fooleries of disputes about doctrine...' *The England of Elizabeth* (London, 1950) 387.

[3] Gibbon, *Decline & Fall* ed. J. B. Bury (London, 1913) II, 352.

central; to be right about it was to be right with God, and power in this secular world was involved as well.

Every textbook sets out the Catholic belief that at the words of consecration the accidents or perceptible qualities of the bread and wine remain unchanged while the substance miraculously becomes the body and blood of Christ. Similarly, it is well known that Luther rejected this transubstantiation and substituted what came to be loosely called 'consubstantiation' – a word Luther never used – no change in substance, but an addition to the elements of the body and blood of Christ. Zwingli, it has been said, made the elements symbolical only and rejected the real presence altogether. If the differences were as simple as this, many volumes need not have been written and endless hours of dispute would be rendered superfluous. In fact, however, we are taken into realms of faith and conviction that are beyond ratiocination and into metaphysical problems of accidents and substance, of *genera* and *species*, of appearance and reality, into 'the most momentous questions to which the human intellect can address itself... but which "common sense" will undertake to clear up in five minutes'.[1]

Although at times individuals battled about words and seemingly about words only, and there were inevitably clashes of personalities as well as of intellects, basically, within an agreed Christian framework, the protagonists sought truth, and through truth God himself. They were desperately in earnest, for all eternity depended upon a true faith.

God the son, it was agreed, had two natures, the divine, which was ubiquitous and eternal, and the human, which appeared among men in time and took on human limitations. This was accepted by all parties[2] – so too was the absolute need for faith, the special gift of the Holy Spirit, inexplicable in its workings. In this sphere, as in others, there were many scholars who, like Erasmus, when forced to make a reluctant stand, took refuge in the existence of divine mysteries beyond the comprehension of the human intellect; most ordinary people, likewise, were content enough to accept, in obedience and simplicity, what they were taught by Catholic priest, Protestant minister or government authority.

In regard to the dual nature of Christ, both Luther and Zwingli proceeded sufficiently warily to avoid falling into a position held as heretical by the early Church. It was not easy – as the condemnation of Marcion (c. A.D. 144) had demonstrated – but although many attempts were made by Catholic controversialists to show that certain Lutheran or Zwinglian phrases were heterodox, these were not successful. None the less, there

---

[1] H. Rashdall, *The Universities of Europe in the Middle Ages*, ed. F. M. Powicke and A. B. Emden, I (Oxford, 1936), 40.
[2] Except those who, like Servetus, became the nucleus of the later Socinians or Unitarians. Williams, 605ff, 630ff.

was much room for manoeuvre, and in some sense this went on all the time and has continued ever since. Even so acute a theologian as Koehler was unable to find a secure and permanent foothold in the shifting sands and manifold implications of the dual nature. Zwingli was perhaps more worried than he allowed to become apparent by the narratives of Christ's appearances on earth after the resurrection, for then his body was 'glorified'; it was not the same as that which had suffered once and for all upon the cross, bearing and atoning for the sins of the human race. The human nature of Christ died upon the cross; the post-crucifixion appearances were 'supernatural', and, like the Resurrection and Ascension, miraculous. To deny resurrection and ascension was to deny Christianity, to be numbered among the infidels and, unless silent, to suffer death as heretic or blasphemer.

In this body Christ ascended to heaven, and Zwingli made no difficulty about this Ascension; the fact was clearly described in the Acts of the Apostles: the ascended Christ was in Heaven on the right hand of the Father until the Day of Judgement. Both Luther and Zwingli were 'spiritualists' in the sense that neither ever forgot the eternity and the omnipresence of God.[1] Zwingli once cried out in indignation against those for whom 'sitting' was anthropomorphically visualised 'like a bird sitting on a tree'[2] – he was also perfectly well aware that words applicable to the human frame were commonly applied to God 'everlasting, without body, parts or passions, of infinite power, wisdom and goodness'. He also knew that the heaven to which Christ ascended was no finite 'place' but the home of the Father, the glory of God.

While these concepts remained fixed, Zwingli's thought about the nature of the eucharist developed continuously. While priest at Glarus and Einsiedeln, and for his first three years at Zurich, Zwingli accepted, perhaps without deep thought, the transubstantiation miracle of the mass which he celebrated daily. Luther had first explicitly set out his rejection of transubstantiation in 1520[3] while Zwingli equally clearly implied in April 1522,[4] and even later, that he accepted the teaching of the church, although he already had scruples about the administration of the sacrament to the laity in one kind only. This latter issue, which had bulked so large in fifteenth-century Bohemia, was widely accepted in the sixteenth as a matter of indifference theologically (*adiaphoron*) although not of insignificance.

Switzerland for many purposes had been in a kind of imperial back-

---

[1] C. Gestrich, *Zwingli als Theologe, Glaube und Geist beim Zürcher Reformator* (Zürich/Stuttgart, 1967) 20–1. [2] Koehler, *Z & L* I, 497, II, 73.
[3] In *De captivitate Babylonica ecclesiae praeludium. 1520.* WA 6, 497–573, which followed *Eyn Sermon von dem Hochwirdigen Sacrament des Heyligen Waren Leychnams Christi* (1519) WA 2, 742–54. J. Mackinnon, *Luther and the Reformation* (London, 1928) II, 252.
[4] In *Von Erkiesen und Freiheit der Speisen.* Z I, 126. Koehler, *Z & L* I, 16–18. See above, 75–78.

water. Distant metropolitans ignored the practices of remote rural parishes. Hence communion in both kinds had been not unknown until almost within living memory (which was long) and the issue aroused little discussion. Even in January 1523 when he was rejecting the notion of the mass as a sacrifice, Zwingli had not openly declared himself on the transubstantiation issue, although by June of that year he confessed that his view had now become a different one.[1] How different was not yet made clear, but he had now made the faith of the recipient an indispensable part of the sacrament. Faith, intention, and the Word, had each its part to play; a physical object could not bring faith; this must be there already. To this conviction he constantly returned. This was very far removed from the Catholic belief that transubstantiation happened when the priest said the operative words irrespective of the presence or the convictions of anyone else. Both Lutherans and Zwinglians rejected *opus operatum*.

They were agreed, however, that for the believer the elements had the body and blood of Christ within them; exactly how, how far, and for how long, being left undefined. It was the straining for ever closer definition that exacerbated, if it did not cause, the controversies of the next decade. Yet closer definition was essential if there was to be a constructive alternative to transubstantiation and not merely the crude denials of 'common sense', disbelief and infidelity.[2] Zwingli was thinking out some of these implications in 1521. He was early not very happy about the word *sacramentum*, which his classical training made him think of in military and juridical rather than ecclesiastical terms.[3] Equally difficult was the word 'testament', which for Zwingli meant the inheritance actually received by the legal heir, while to Luther it implied simply the formal confirmation of a property already entered upon.

When the same words mean different things to different people the

---

[1] Koehler, *Z & L* I, 23. See above, 150.

[2] Zwingli's opponents, Eck in particular, constantly accused him of being a follower of Wyclif. In fact this was untrue since he had not even read Wyclif's writings, which in any case were more favourable to Luther and were highly metaphysical. H. B. Workman, *John Wyclif* (Oxford, 1926) II, 30–41; K. B. McFarlane, *John Wycliffe and the Beginnings of English Nonconformity* (London, 1952). The reference in Z III, 795 'Viclevum olim et Valdenses etiam hodie in hac esse sententia' is best referred to Zwingli's acquaintance with Luther's *Von Anbeten des Sakraments des heiligen Leichnams Christi*. WA 11, 431–56. A. W. Dieckhoff, *Die Waldenser im Mittelalter* (Göttingen, 1851) 99ff. (Wyclif's *Trialogus* was printed at Basle in 1525).

[3] For St Augustine it was a sign or a token (Ep. 138. '[Signa] quae cum ad res divinas pertinent, sacramenta appellantur.') (MPL 33. 527) a notion repeated by Peter Lombard – 'Quid est sacramentum? Sacramentum est sacrae rei signum' – and constantly quoted later. It appears in the Vulgate Eph. 5, 32. 'Sacramentum hoc magnum est', 'It is a great truth that is hidden here', and, meaning a secret, 'Et enim sacramentum regis abscondere bonum est', 'A king's secret ought to be kept'. Tob. 12. 7. See above, 109–110.

possibilities of a compromise are sometimes present so long as definitions are not called for. In this case, however, definitions were more and more emphatically demanded.

This situation confronted two religious leaders almost exactly of the same age. They were both accomplished scholars, ornaments of their respective universities, and both had received holy orders at the hands of Catholic bishops. They both came of peasant stock but of relatively well-to-do parents, and they both spoke German as their mother tongue.

Luther's Saxon dialect, however, was very different from Zwingli's Toggenburg-acquired pronunciation and vocabulary;[1] the University of Erfurt was unlike that of Basle, Luther's philosophical background and training was nominalist, Zwingli's realist; Luther was very much 'Herr Doktor', a university professor who had been destined to become a canonist, Zwingli was one of the relatively small group of German humanists for whom the universities found a place and livelihood only with very great difficulty and in his case not at all. It is also almost possible to think of Luther as a monarchist and a conservative, of Zwingli as a radical and a republican, and while both had been ordained, Luther had been a member of a Regular order and Zwingli was always a secular priest. Germans tended to despise Swiss, and Swiss resented German patronage.

Both men were convinced that the truth was on their side and that their opponents were wrong; to be wrong was also to be dangerous; and, being wrong, they were therefore enemies. Each was manifestly a little jealous of the other, and Luther, in particular, believed that Zwingli was personally ambitious and anxious to spread his reputation. That there was a touch of vanity about both accentuated their mutual opposition. When Zwingli gently smiled at the serenity (*Durchlauchtigkeit*) of the Lutheran princes, this was proof to Luther that he lacked respect, part of his besetting sin of pride.[2] According to Luther, he had made himself out to be the great giant of Zurich. 'We Zwingel, by the Grace of God Giant and Roland, hero and conqueror in foreign and in German territory, in France and Spain, Apostle of Apostles, Prophet of Prophets, teacher of teachers, master of masters, Scholar of scholars, Lord of Lords, Spirit of Spirits, and so on.'[3] When they met at Marburg Luther commented that his rival had been anxious to show off, to parade his Greek and Hebrew from the pulpit while in fact his German was bad, he was ignorant of grammar and dialectic, his Bible translations were faulty, he had not realised that Luther had

---

[1] Cf. *Luther's Works*, vol. 37. *Word and Sacrament* III, ed. R. H. Fischer (Philadelphia, 1961), 180 'his clumsy, atrocious German'.
[2] Later, Luther said that because of his pride God had taken the spirit of truth away from Zwingli and had given him an envious, proud, lying spirit. Koehler, *Z & L* I, 276.
[3] WA 23. 283; 26. 342, 371-2.

breached the papal fortress unaided. Not even Zwingli's death at Kappel appeased his opponent: it was merely the removal of another fanatic. Zwingli resorted to the sword and received his just reward.[1] Worst of all, Luther proclaimed, Zwingli was no fellow Christian.

While never failing to assert his own independence of judgement, Zwingli was much more generous in his dealings with his rival; again and again he pays tribute both of admiration and respect, but with no apparent effect.

It was while Zwingli was stipendiary priest at the Great Minster that Luther was excommunicated by name, along with his followers, and was publicly outlawed. No similar bull of excommunication was prepared against Zwingli, who, for his part, always insisted that it was the followers of the Pope who were deviationists while he adhered to the one church. Papal agents were as gentle as possible in their dealings in Switzerland while there was any hope of military support for Rome being forthcoming from Zurich, and Zurich men had good commercial reasons for not wishing to be identified as Lutherans. Later, when the church of Zurich was manifestly hostile to the church of Rome, there arose an unjustified fear lest the Lutherans might come to terms with the common enemy. If Luther was unsound upon the doctrine of the eucharist, his followers might be allies of the Catholics.

It is easy to overlook the many major matters upon which Luther and Zwingli were in agreement. Both emphatically rejected the authority of the Pope. Both were agreed upon the principle of *sola scriptura*, and of justification by faith, upon communion in both kinds, upon the rejection of the 'seven' sacraments and tradition, upon the desirability that ministers should marry, upon the irresistible power of the Word. Basically they stood for the same objectives, and they knew it: this was appreciated by the advisers of Charles V, by Philip of Hesse, the most intelligent of the Protestant Princes, and by the clerics of Lucerne, who were at the heart of Swiss Catholicism.

Zwingli undoubtedly formed his opinions by his own independent study of the Bible, and particularly of Erasmus' edition of the New Testament with his notes and paraphrases, before reading any of Luther's writings. Erasmus himself initially went a long way along the symbolical path until he realised that it might lead him into an uncomfortable wilderness instead of the green pastures that he enjoyed, whereupon he professed Catholic orthodoxy. Zwingli pushed things further but by no means fast.

It was, apparently, to Erasmus' fellow-countryman, Cornelisz Hoen

---

[1] WA *Tischreden* I, 94, II, 103, cited O. Farner, *Das Zwinglibild Luthers* (Tübingen, 1931) 22. Farner hardly faced the difficult problem of the historical value of 'Table talk' – speech reported long after the event.

(Honius), that Zwingli early in 1524 owed the first suggestion that the 'is' in the institution words 'This is my body' meant 'signifies'.[1] This is what he himself stated,[2] his attention having been drawn to this exegesis by Rode and Saganus.[3] There was no moment of sudden revelation, no *Turmerlebnis*; a great deal of reflection led to the acceptance and formulation of conclusions. With 'is' glossed as 'signifies', it was possible to differentiate between the bread eaten by the communicant and the Christ received by faith. All that followed was a development, elaboration, ripening and justification of this decision. He could not accept the Lutheran analogy that Christ was in the consecrated bread as heat is in red-hot iron; he now regarded the eucharist as a commemorative meal and something more. What the something more was emerged slowly.

Before 1524 was out, he had started discussions with Oecolampadius on Hoen's letter and on the pamphlets on the eucharist recently issued by Luther's rival, Karlstadt.[4] In these it was urged that in saying '*this* is my body' Christ had pointed to his own body and not to the bread of the Last Supper. Zwingli did not follow him on this point,[5] and later diverged further from the turbulent enthusiast of Wittenberg, but he recognised that Karlstadt's 'spiritual' approach to the eucharist had commendable elements in it. This was one of the causes of the trouble with Luther. Karlstadt was a rival who had to be dealt with if Luther was to succeed, and it was Karlstadt who was reluctantly forced to give way. He remained, however, the Prince of Sectaries, and Luther early grouped Zwingli with him. In spite of the fact that Zwingli plainly indicated his own divergence from Karlstadt in the open letter to Alber,[6] in November 1524, the suspicion was never eliminated.

That participation in the eucharist did not forgive sin was easily agreed; so, too, that Christ had given his life for mankind upon the cross, and thus, and only thus, his body, but there Karlstadt seemed to stop, and there was more behind. Luther had reacted defensively against the dangerous sectary, Karlstadt, whom he had nourished within his bosom – he accused his opponent of twisting Christ's words to suit his argument, 'making a wax nose of them', as he put it. It is of some importance that Luther faced 'spiritualist' opposition first at home in Wittenberg and, partly perhaps because his vanity was stung, he at once launched into denunciation of

[1] Koehler, *Z & L* I, 4, 61, 69; *Z* v, 738–40, 797; Allen v, 276–7 n. 26, vi, 183 n. 18.
[2] *Z* iv, 560.
[3] Hoen's letter on the subject was later printed in Zurich in 1525, by which time it had become a commonplace of Zwinglian exposition. *Z* iv, 512–19, translated in H. A. Oberman, *Forerunners of the Reformation* (New York, 1966) 268–76.
[4] Koehler, *Z & L* I, 67–9; Allen v, 590–9 (nos. 1522, 1523). See above 156 n. 3.
[5] *Z* iii, 330; H. Barge, *Andreas Bodenstein von Karlstadt* 2 Bde. (Leipzig, 1905) ii, 169ff.
[6] *Z* iii, 322(335)–354. Luther's comments (WA 19, 114–25) came in January, 1526.

sectaries and fanatics – *Schwärmerei*. The word 'is', Luther insisted from the outset, could not be altered or interpreted; it imposed itself in its simplicity: it was Christ's natural and not his spiritual body that was present in the sacrament. From this it followed that the consecrated bread might even be worthy of adoration. All this Zwingli could not reconcile with the Johannine 'The spirit alone gives life, the flesh is of no avail', *caro non prodest quicquam* (John 6. 63 (Vulg. 64)), four words which recur with monotonous frequency in the controversy.

Zwingli's view, with slight differences of emphasis, became that of Oecolampadius also, but Erasmus, whose original tendencies had been in very much the same direction, refused to be drawn into controversy and was finally forced into a guarded confession of Catholic orthodoxy. This was early in 1525: for all his rich correspondence and the dispute with Luther over Free Will, the remaining ten years of Erasmus' life were those of a former captain now without a team and unable to obtain a post as manager. In 1526 Leo Jud quoted enough from earlier Erasmian writings to show that Erasmus had directed his readers to a 'spiritual' view and then had retreated.[1] Bucer, Urbanus Rhegius and Erasmus were three prolific writers who raised difficulties rather than solved them, whose constant changes of front and manipulation of language left many bewildered, but who also illustrated the fact that, even in Catholic circles, eucharistic thought had not settled into the neatly labelled compartments that could be distinguished at the end of the century. They, Bucer most of all, were more anxious to arrange a compromise than to explore the depths of the issue. Neither Zwingli nor Luther was prepared to meet truth half way.

In addition to the metaphysical complexities of abstract notions such as eternity, reality, ubiquity, goodness and truth, there were other difficulties about interpretation of the Bible which posed further problems. All sides recognised that there were agreed Greek and Hebrew texts of the Scriptures. They also fully and almost eagerly accepted the actuality of biblical miracles without seeking for any 'explanation' of them. Generally, too, but with less unanimity, there was also agreement that understanding of the Scriptures could be a direct divine gift, that their inward meaning could be revealed to individuals without literary or philosophical training. The Word could effect this in its own way, and the recipient knew that truth had been revealed to him by the operation of the Holy Spirit. This must indeed be tested to eliminate self-deception or the working of the devil, but it could not be rejected.

[1] Koehler, *Z & L* I, 143 – 'Des Hochgelerten Erasmi von Roterdam und Doctor Luthers maynung vom Nachtmal unsers Herren Jesu Christi, neuerlich aussgangen auff den XVIII. Tag Aprellens'.

There was, in addition, the medieval inheritance of the fourfold interpretation of the Scriptures – literal or historical, allegorical, anagogical (mystical) and tropological.[1] Although Zwingli, like other reformers, reverted to the conviction that the literal interpretation was alone of decisive significance, he was reared in this tradition, and knew perfectly well that there was much poetic imagery and much emblematic writing in the Bible. Any seeming contradiction must be reconcilable, difficult passages were to be interpreted by the aid of less difficult ones, and by these alone. Fundamentalist in a sense *sola scriptura* certainly was, but it was also intellectualist. Even Luther, who regarded reason as dangerous and indignantly rejected rationalist explanations of the miraculous or supernatural, accepted the factual accuracy and reconcilability of every episode in the Bible;[2] for him, as for Zwingli, scripture was its own interpreter. Every chapter of the Old Testament foreshadowed the coming of Christ; the poetry of the Psalms contained Christian doctrine. Luther, who translated Erasmus' edition of the Greek New Testament into German in 1522 and completed that of the whole Bible from the Septuagint and Vulgate in 1534, knew it all with the later intimacy of John Bunyan. Zwingli, with his powerful memory and determination that the Bible should be available in Swiss-German to all who could read, was equally acquainted with its every part. Through the Bible, and even through a healthy acceptance of it as a whole, with their respective reservations about certain parts, it came about that the measure of agreement between Luther and Zwingli was far greater than the differences. If, as was undoubtedly the case, Zwingli was further from Rome than the German Reformer, he was also, in many respects, nearer to more modern views of Bible interpretation. None the less he remained a convinced biblicist; the whole of the Bible was literally the word of God.

Between 1523, when Zwingli first made his position clear, and 1525, when the Roman mass ceased to be said in Zurich, discussions about the Last Supper multiplied. In the letter to Alber he had taken up a position between Karlstadt and Luther which was still a little ambiguous.[3] In 1525, however, he explicitly retracted article 18 of his *Schlussreden*[4] and set out his position in the commentary on the true and false religion.[5] He found independent supporters in Oecolampadius and Leo Jud, and he also

---

[1] M. Deanesly, *The Lollard Bible* (Cambridge, 1920) 166; B. Smalley, *The Study of the Bible in the Middle Ages* (Oxford, 1952) 87ff; *The Cambridge History of the Bible* ed. G. W. H. Lampe (Cambridge, 1969) 214ff; H. Caplan, *The four senses of Scripture, Speculum* vol. 4 (1929), 282–90.
[2] Cf. A. Skevington Wood, *Captive to the Word* (Exeter, 1969) 84, 135, 141, 149–55.
[3] Koehler, *Marburg*, 14.   [4] Z II, 111–57.
[5] Z III, 774: 'Retractamus igitur hic, quae illic diximus, tàli lege, ut quae hic damus, anno aetatis nostrae quadragesimo secundo, propendeant eis, quae quadragesimo dederamus.' See below, 304, and above, 205.

recognised that Erasmus was against him. Catholic opposition and condemnation came from Cajetan, Fabri, Eck and Murner, while the divergence of Lutheran and Zwinglian views steadily became more apparent. Luther thought that Zwingli was echoing Karstadt,[1] which was unfair; and Zwingli was unduly suspicious of Luther's supopsedly catholicising tendencies[2] and perhaps over-anxious to assert his own originality.

When Zwingli answered his Zurich-based opponent, Joachim am Grüt, in *Subsidium sive coronis de eucharistia*, this was treated in Wittenberg as anti-Lutheran. All through 1526 the breach widened. The German reformer was now in a specially confident mood: he was secure in the support of his Prince and of other rulers, he was clearly on the side of authority as against rural malcontents or anti-social Anabaptists. Rivalry and opposition he began to resent. Both Luther and Zwingli were anxious to assure the world that they had not read all one another's writings – Zwingli could have echoed Luther's words, 'I have never read one of the pamphlets of my opponents right through... since I could see from the start that they were vague and lacking in precision of speech.'[3]

These opponents were multiplying in 1525 and 1526 when scores of writers were trying to fill the vacuum left by the elimination of transubstantiation. Karlstadt, Oecolampadius, Bucer, Schwenckfeld, Althamer, Billican, Stigler, Bugenhagen, Brenz, Sam, and many more were coming forward in print with explanations, amplifications and analyses of the growing field of controversy. It slowly became apparent that Wittenberg and Zurich were competing for the spiritual (and practical) allegiance of the South German cities – Basle and Strassburg most obviously, but also Augsburg, Nördlingen, Biberach, Memmingen, Ulm, Isny, Kempten, Lindau and Constance. Without them, and particularly while Berne remained officially Catholic, Zurich would be isolated; with their help much of Germany might be won over. With their allegiance went power, and with power also the triumph of truth itself. To personify the differences into Luther–Zwingli rivalry is to oversimplify.

While allies were needed and eagerly sought, concessions were not readily made. Zwingli could easily have obtained a great deal of 'Anabaptist' support had he been willing to abate his hostility to rebaptism, while Luther could have done likewise by concessions to the Catholics. It is to the credit of both that each steadfastly maintained his position. They believed that all Christendom was involved, that one side or the other must be right, and that their differences must be proclaimed rather than resolved by compromise. Zwingli could, indeed, have pressed his

---

[1] 'Zwinglius Turegensis cum Leone Iude in Heluetiis cum Carstadio eadem sentiunt; ita late serpit hoc malum.' (Luther to Nicolaus Hausmann, 17 November 1524). WA *Br.* 3. 373–4 (No. 793).　　[2] Koehler, *Z & L* I, 175, 179.　　[3] WA 25. 27 (18 November 1527).

Lutheran opponents much harder on their 'Romanizing' tendencies than he did, but he was too conscious of the value of Luther's early stand against the Pope to do this during the critical years 1525–9. It was then that Zurich became a reformed powerhouse for South Germany; from it came the teachers and preachers, well equipped with biblical knowledge and exegesis, missionaries of simplicity and congregational participation in church services, active married men for the most part. These showed by their lives that faith implied the duty to spread the Gospel and to set an example by conduct based on its precepts.

They were supported by the steady flow of books and pamphlets from the busy presses of Basle and Zurich. Tribute must be paid to the indefatigable exertions of the printers at the Froschauer printing-works. Again and again, at very short notice they had to set up a treatise or a long memorandum from Zwingli, matter for and from the Zurich council, as well as the Bibles and theological works needed by the ministers. Zwingli complained with reason when he found his books prohibited in Saxony, but there were always supplies ready for the Frankfurt book fair, from whence they spread far and wide.[1] Zwingli had valuable supporters – the ever-faithful Leo Jud, active especially within the city walls of Zurich; Pellican, Bibliander, Bullinger, Blarer at Constance, Vadian at St Gall, Oecolampadius at Basle, Haller at Berne, and in Lutheran Augsburg itself the invaluable Michael Keller. They were for him what Melanchthon, Justus Jonas, Amsdorf, Bugenhagen, Billican, Cruciger, Osiander and John Agricola were for Luther, but there were no defined 'parties' and many, like Bucer, who maintained an independent line.

Zwingli's first full re-statement of his case was made in August 1525, *Subsidium sive coronis de eucharistia*[2] (an addition to, or a summary of, the Eucharist). In it he developed his distinction between the 'natural' body of Christ before the crucifixion, the 'glorified' body which ascended to heaven, and the mystical body which is the church. Only the recognition of the frequent use in the Bible of the trope or figurative use of words, and in particular the metaphorical explanation of the Last Supper, made scripture plain, simple, reasonable and humanly intelligible.[3] Zwingli never failed to insist that faith in Christ, not any action or material, could alone bring salvation; Christ's own words were intelligible if the bread and wine were symbols, to which the recipient brought faith and hope in God.

[1] Koehler, *Z & L* I, 454; G. R. Potter, 'Zwingli and his publisher', *The Library Chronicle* (Philadelphia, 1974) XL, 108–117, 110–16.   [2] Z IV, 440(458)–504.
[3] A good deal was rightly made of the analogy between the Last Supper and the Passover. Unfortunately, perhaps, Zwingli gave publicity to the reinforcement of his thought by a dream on the night of 12–13 April 1525, which brought some scorn and mockery from his opponents. It was the more unfortunate in that the Anabaptists made much of revelation through dreams. Z IV, 442–6, 483; Baur I, 491–2; Koehler, *Z & L* I, 110–11.

At this date, August 1525, as in his earlier (March 1525) commentary on the true and false religion,[1] he was stating his case for his immediate Zurich followers, but his writings were spreading and were bringing answers and refutations from both Catholics and Lutherans. Among these latter was Bugenhagen (Pomeranus), who, with an eye on Strassburg and Swabia, had restated the Lutheran position as opposed to that of Oecolampadius.[2] 'We eat bread', he said, 'and in the bread the true body of Christ'.[3] No symbolism was necessary. Zwingli's answer[4] was brief, and, with a slightly contemptuous satirical glance at the 'schoolmaster' approach of his opponent, repeated his exposition of the biblical use of figures of speech and claimed that not only the Fourth Gospel but also St Augustine, St Chrysostom and St Cyril, together with much early tradition, were on his side. A little intelligence, a little logic and closer attention to the rules of grammar would clinch the matter.[5]

In 1526 Zwingli and Luther were brought into slightly closer, but still indirect, contact. Luther's violent polemic against the peasants had been ill received in northern Switzerland[6] where trouble had been largely avoided. At the same time, the Wittenberg sacramental position had been more positively re-stated in a new version of the *Swabian Syngramma*[7] which was arousing some attention. Zwinglian books and pamphlets were spreading rapidly in spite of attempts to prevent[8] their doing so, and it was becoming clear that it was not just another sectarian movement that had appeared but a challenge to Rome as serious as that of the ninety-five theses. For Luther the devil was manifesting himself in three ways, in the

---

[1] See above, 204–6.
[2] Koehler, *Z & L* I, 194–202; G. Geisenhof, *Bibliotheca Bugenhagiana* (Leipzig, 1908) (*Bugenhagiana. Quellen zur Lebensgeschichte des Joh. Bugenhagen*).
[3] Z IV, 550, 564 n. 1.
[4] *Ad Ioannis Bugenhagii Pomerani epistolam responsio*. There were slight differences from his earlier discussions. Z IV, 546(558)–76 (23 October 1525); Koehler, *Z & L* I, 287–8.
[5] Z IV, 567. 'Nam quae hactenus a grammaticis didicimus, non possunt iure haec verba Christi: "Hoc est corpus meum" in ista transformare: "In isto pane editur corpus Christi." Oportet te indubie vehementer grammaticum esse, si neges panem esse corpus aut carnem; attamen credas in pane te carnem edere, cum Christus nullatenus dixerit: "Edite panem hunc!; nam in eo edetis corpus meum"; sed: "Hoc", quod scilicet praebebat, "est corpus meum". Magister bone, ostendite nobis consimiles locos in scripturis sacris!'
[6] F. Martini, *Das Bauerntum im deutschen Schrifttum von den Anfängen bis zum 16. Jahrhundert* (Halle, 1944) 330–6. See above, 200–3.
[7] Fourteen Swabian Lutheran ministers meeting at Schwäbisch-Hall on 21 October 1525 had subscribed a basically Lutheran confession, *Syngramma Suevicum*, written by Johannes Brenz. This circulated at first in manuscript, then in print, and was translated by Agricola with an introduction by Luther (WA 19, 457–61) and answered by Oecolampadius as *Antisyngramma*. Questions concerning the publication came from Strassburg and Reutlingen. In a letter of 4 January 1526 to the Reutlingers (WA 19, 118–25), not intended for publication but none the less printed, Luther declared the Zwinglian views to be the work of Satan. Koehler, *Z & L* I, 126–7, 293, 299; Z IV, 928–9 n.
[8] Particularly in Silesia (Koehler, *Z & L* I, 274) and in Nuremberg (Z IV, 773).

rebellious spirit of the peasants, in the recalcitrance of the Anabaptists and in the Zwinglian sacramental teaching.[1] Zwingli now decided to state his case again explicitly for a much wider public, this time in German and answering Eck, Fabri and am Grüt among the Catholics, as well as Luther and Bugenhagen.[2] With some skill, he accentuated the division between his opponents. Luther's unalterable case to the end was that he took his stand on the very words of Christ himself. 'Simple words' – of them, Zwingli insisted, Luther had made up an interpretation that could not be more obscure or more incomprehensible.[3] Or, if words were to be taken at their face value only, the church was really built on the Petrine rock, and the most extreme papal claims were thereby valid.

Transubstantiation was written off in a few lines: it rested upon a miracle, and an unconscious miracle is no miracle: the distinction between substance and accidents was brushed on one side with a remark that if the species alone is broken then the substance is not there, and hence transubstantiation becomes untenable. So far there was no divergence between Zwingli and Luther. He then turned to his favourite *spiritus est qui vivicat*, to repeat the indispensable conjunction of faith and the Word: just as bread feeds the body so Christ's body feeds the soul.[4] After this 'spiritual' exegesis, he directed his attention to a consideration which Luther had so far hardly mentioned but which was henceforward to become almost a central theme, that of the ubiquity of Christ. Of Christ's two natures the divine nature never left heaven, for being one with God the Father the divine nature could not ascend to heaven, as his human nature did.[5] The divinity of Christ is and always has been everywhere, the bodily Christ, seen on earth after the resurrection, remains in heaven until the Last Day. Nor does this limit in any way God's omnipotence – God's word itself made it so.[6] Further, those who would have it that Christ's body was eaten in the Last Supper invisibly and insensibly must also believe (with the heretic Marcion) that Christ was not sensible of his sufferings on the cross or that the disciples did not eat in human fashion since Christ had not yet risen when he instituted this thanksgiving.[7] And so, with singular

---

[1] WA 19. 484, 494, 495, 498, 501, 503, 508, 512.
[2] *Ein klare underrichtung vom nachtmal Christi durch Huldrychen Zuingli tütsch (als vormal nie) umb der einvaltigen willen, damit sy mit niemans spytzfündiheit hindergangen mögind werden, beschriben.* Z IV, 773(789)–862. [3] Z IV, 799: 'aller tuncklest und unverstendligost'.
[4] Z IV, 816. 'Das wirt die sel spysen, glych wie s' brot den lychnam spyst.' A notion later adopted by Bucer 'while the bread is eaten by the teeth, the body of Christ is eaten by the mind'. W. P. Stephens, *The Holy Spirit in the theology of Martin Bucer* (Cambridge, 1970) 246. Cf. ARG 64 (1973), 178–9. [5] Z IV, 778, 827–8; Koehler, *Z & L* I, 306–7.
[6] It is a measure of the difference between the approach of the sixteenth century and the twentieth that, for Zwingli, Psalm 89. 34, 'I will not renounce my covenant nor change my promised purpose' was decisive evidence. [7] Z IV, 778, 837.

clarity and a wealth of illustrative quotations from the Bible and the Fathers, he returns to the initial theme: 'this is' means 'this signifies'.

When this was written, in February 1526, the preliminaries for the Baden Conference were already in hand: Zwingli's followers were united – his opponents were divided between those who upheld transubstantiation at its crudest, the Erasmians who accepted it as inexplicable, and the Lutherans who would have it that it was the body of the risen Christ that was eaten in and along with the sacramental bread.[1] After Eck's triumph at Baden Fabri published a refutation of much of Zwingli's teaching, and, allowing for the inevitable exaggerations of the controversialist, did so rather well. Altogether in 1526 the Catholics were engaged in an exercise tending to show that where, very frequently, Zwingli and Luther differed, it was Luther who was on the side of the Catholic angels.[2]

Among the South German unconvinced Lutherans whom Zwingli hoped to win over, was Theobald Billican,[3] previously of Augsburg and now minister at Nördlingen, who firmly rejected the mass as a sacrifice, who emphasised the indispensability of faith on the part of the recipient of the consecrated elements, all of which suited Zwingli admirably, but who also obstinately insisted that there was no metaphor in Christ's words – the bread and wine were also his body. In a letter[4] dated 1 March 1526 and intended for publication, Zwingli reminded him of their common conviction that the Bible must be interpreted by the Bible alone. If Billican's exegesis was correct some explanation was clearly needed why the disciples, who made so much of the miracle of the draught of fishes (John 21. 6–9), had not marvelled at the far greater miracle of the Last Supper.

He then plunges into his own exposition, this time in Latin and in terms suitable to a scholar such as he slightly patronisingly, slightly flatteringly, assumes his correspondent to be. It is a very adroitly constructed argument, theological and philosophical, yet insisting upon its demonstrable reasonableness.[5] To an omnipotent God all things indeed are possible, but God does act against his own words. We are back to the

---

[1] The treatise ends with a jingle and a challenge:
> Sag mir an, ob du's weist,
> Das vatter, sun und geist,
> Fleisch und blût, brot und wyn
> Als sampt ein got mög sin? Z IV, 862.

[2] Koehler, Z & L I, 346–51.

[3] Theobald Gernolt or Gerlacher (c. 1498–1554) studied and taught for a time at Heidelberg, was tutor to J. Brenz, minister at Weil and Nördlingen, and Professor at Marburg. Koehler, Z & L I, 822; Z VIII, 391.

[4] Ad Theobaldi Billicani et Urbani Rhegii epistolas responsio. Z IV, 880(893)–941; Kohler, Z & L I, 62, 248–51, 315–20.

[5] Z IV, 897. Non de istis loquor, quae a sophistis sunt in theologiam inducta, sed quae sacris literis constant quaeque ex iis recte intellectis colliguntur; nam nulla iusta oratio sine argumentis recte constare potest.

two natures, to the body in heaven, to the impossibility that a creature, unlike God, can be everywhere. In the midst of grammatical argument, accompanied by a solemn assurance that this is no dispute about words only, the writer tells us that he is short-sighted,[1] and reminds his reader that divisions do not lead to peace and tranquillity.

In a kind of appendix addressed to Urban Rhegius,[2] then preacher at St Anne's Church, Augsburg, restating the argument in yet other fashion, Zwingli insists that he is no follower of the Englishman Wyclif ('Viclephus Anglicus') and no 'Lutheranus' either. Nor was he responsible for the phrases 'the edible God, the body in the bread' – *esculentus deus, impanatus deus.*[3]

It was all moderate, learned and attractive. Billican and Rhegius were not completely convinced, but after it Nördlingen at least could not be reckoned as an entirely Lutheran city. With Luther the clash was yet to come, especially after the Baden Conference, at which Zwingli's teaching was condemned in his absence and he himself was designated excommunicate by the customary law of the church. There, Fabri had adroitly succeeded in widening the gap between Lutherans, Zwinglians and Catholics, and in making further trouble all round. In October of the same year, Zwingli emphasised, in letters to Esslingen, his divergence from Karlstadt and the pure 'spiritualists' by agreeing that there was a real presence of Christ in the eucharist provided the meaning was properly understood.[4] For Luther, unfortunately, any opponent who was not a Catholic was a sectary, enthusiast or fanatic (*Schwärmer*). Those who disagreed with him on the fundamental matter of the eucharist were even worse, the devil's servants, with whom there could be no compromise. They were 'outside the faith' and he was not prepared to argue with them. All too soon he placed Zwingli with Karlstadt, Müntzer and Schwenckfeld, and in 1526 he again repeated, to his own satisfaction, a refutation of their views.[5] But Zwingli was too acute to be caught this way. He knew that his teaching was his own, independent and different.

Throughout this year a great deal of discussion went on, leading to a growing perception of the need for even greater clarification of the issues

[1] Z IV, 914 'lusciosus'.
[2] Urbanus Rhegius (Urban Rieger, 1489–1541) was educated at Freiburg, lectured on poetry at Ingolstadt, was Cathedral preacher at Augsburg, and a prominent Lutheran from 1524 onwards.
[3] Farel, when minister to the French colony in Strassburg, may have been the first to use these unlikeable terms. Z IV, 933 n. 5; Koehler, Z & L I, 225, 319.
[4] Koehler Z & L I, 353 n. 8. 'Also kann auch Zwingli das "substantive" der Realpräsenz zugeben, wenn es richtig verstanden wird.' G. W. Locher, ZWA XIII (1970), 281–304 esp. 288, 'Die reale Gegenwart Christi bei der Sakramentsfeier wurde von niemand bestritten.'
[5] In *Sermon von dem Sakrament des Leibes und Blutes Christi, wider die Schwarmgeister, 1526.* WA 19, 474–523; Koehler Z & L I, 383–96.

involved. Hence, after a brief controversy with Jacob Strauss,[1] a Lutheran preacher in Schwäbisch Hall whom he arraigned with some justice for ignorance, confusion and megalomania, and further urged on by Capito, Oecolampadius and the indefatigable Bucer,[2] Zwingli offered the hand of qualified friendship and reconciliation to Luther. At the beginning of 1527 active discussion and controversy about the nature of the eucharist was going on in the south German cities. The Lutherans, led by Johannes Brenz, were positively aggressive, almost spoiling for a fight, but there were many who were not satisfied with the Lutheran appeal to semi-magic and acquiescence. Sam at Ulm, for example, pleaded quite independently what amounted to the Zwinglian case,[3] and Urbanus Rhegius at Augsburg discussed the matter in a way that did not quite satisfy either Zwingli or Luther, but came near to both and very far from transubstantiation. In Italy, south Germany and the Low Countries, men were seeking for guidance, and this made a confrontation of the two leaders unavoidable.

'Our opponents', Bucer wrote, 'call us rationalists because we follow our reason and the evidence of the Fathers.'[4] Quite deliberately Luther would not listen to reason. In matters that pertained to God, the supernatural and eternity, human ratiocination broke down; it was enough that God had revealed himself in his son and that the holy scriptures were the sure guide to salvation. Even for Melanchthon, who did so much to systematise Lutheran teaching, there were things that were unknowable. Luther, with his customary violence of language, would speak of 'the whore, reason' while Zwingli would insist that God had endowed men with brains in order that these might be used. To speak of Zwingli the rationalist is as crude as to refer to Luther as the mystic, but there is an element of truth behind both epithets.

Although he was far from avoiding controversy, Zwingli regretted having to dispute with Luther, whereas the latter, conscious of priority and

---

[1] *Antwort über Straussens Büchlein, das Nachtmahl Christi betreffend* (January 1527) Z v, 464–547, which repeated the now familiar arguments but added nothing new. In a vigorous and effective statement Zwingli described his critic as a mere bundle of words – 'ein grössere compophaceloremon der anderhalbschüehiger worten' (Z v, 473–4), but this was unfair. Strauss had been a preacher at Eisenach and a follower of Karlstadt; he later moved to Nuremberg, Hall and Baden-Baden, arguing against the Zwinglians in general and Oecolampadius in particular (Barge II, 72). He was, in fact, a serious opponent who strongly supported the Lutheran preference of faith to reason. He insisted more emphatically than did Luther that Christ's body was of a miraculous nature and therefore its presence after the repetition of the words of consecration was acceptable. He was not far from asserting the Catholic case for transubstantiation, and this made a refutation of his statements the more necessary. There was more in his case than Zwingli's rather superficial treatment of it suggests. Koehler *Z & L* I, 400–23; H. Barge, *Jakob Strauss* (Leipzig, 1937).
[2] Bucer's letter of 8 July 1526 (Z VIII, 646–50) exists (StaA Z E II. 349 fol. 208) in a copy made by Pellican. Staehelin, *Briefe* I, 560 mistakes both the pagination of the printed text and the foliation of the manuscript.   [3] Koehler, *Z & L* I, 446–8.
[4] Z VIII, 649 – quod rationem sequamur et patres homines.

enormously self-confident, neither expected nor desired any rapprochement. In February 1527 Zwingli completed his *Amica exegesis*, 'friendly exposition', one of the most revealing of his many writings, in which he genuinely tried to combine manly independence with reconciliation but found the task impossible.[1] He tried to be tolerant and brotherly but was in too much of a hurry to understand fully the developing subtlety and conviction of Luther's thought. He bases some of his discussion, for example, on the Lutheran reply to the notorious *Assertio septem sacramentorum* written, or at any rate inspired, by Henry VIII in 1521.[2] Since this rejoinder contained more abuse than argument, it was hardly worth powder and shot five years later. Further, the *Amica exegesis* is not based on any close study of Luther's writings, not all of which were in any case available in Zurich, and there was the distraction of the appearance of a new edition of the *Swabian Syngramma* with a commendatory introduction by Luther,[3] and the need to defend Leo Jud against attackers.[4] None the less it is one of Zwingli's most serious and most characteristic writings, appearing at the very height of his powers. In one sense a harmonious note was struck at the outset – justification by faith was willingly conceded. Without faith, discussion was vain – *pro veritate ex fide pugnamus*. Without faith, scripture could not be understood; faith was greater than the biblical words. Having enunciated this convincing sentiment, Zwingli proceeded to concentrate narrowly upon the question of any physical consumption of the body of Christ in the bread of the Communion. Luther, he thought, was making the issue, as he was making the eucharist itself, too prominent.[5] The human spirit could not be strengthened by eating a 'body' (*corpus*) nor could this bring forgiveness of sins or reality to the Gospel. Powerful, essential though the word was, and Zwingli never wavered in his conviction of its power, the word did not bring the body of Christ with it to the bread or make it present therein. Faith could not be confirmed by a physical act, even eating the body of Christ: if it were so, then he who administered the sacrament would be more important than he who received it. Above all, it was faith, trusting belief, that was supremely necessary. Hence it was that the eucharistic bread and wine signified Christ's body and blood. Corpus Christi was the community of the servants of God, the one body corporate of those who worship Christ united

---

[1] *Amica exegesis, id est: expositio eucharistiae et negocii, ad Martinum Lutherum.* Z v, 548(562)–75. The printing was completed in time for a copy to be sent to Luther on 1 April. Z viii, 78. Koehler was right in treating this as the great divide in an unfortunate but necessary controversy. Koehler *Z & L* i, 464–72; ZWA xiii, 285–9.

[2] *Contra Henricum Regem Angliae, 1522* (WA 10. 2, 175(180)–222) E. Doernberg, *Henry VIII and Luther* (London, 1961) 21–3. Zwingli insisted that while Luther had called transubstantiation a blasphemous assertion he had put forward an equally untenable view of his own.

[3] *Zweite Vorrede zum Schwäbischen Syngramm* (1526) WA 19, 524–28; see above, 298 n. 7.

[4] *Z*. v, 549, 552, Koehler, *Z & L* i, 470–1.   [5] Z v, 553.

11-2

in this common meal of thanksgiving and remembrance. Hence, and this was the point upon which Lutherans and Zwinglians remained divided across the ages, unbelievers did not receive the body and blood of Christ spiritually in the sacrament. For Luther, the *impii*, the godless, coming to the Lord's table, received the body of Christ with the bread to their own damnation; for Zwingli, this was utterly wrong. It was for the believer only that Christ was really present,[1] spiritually, not physically, but assuredly present – *dum fides adest homini, habet deum praesentem*.[2] It was therefore perfectly reasonable to describe the symbolical bread as the body of the Lord. Lutheran 'consubstantiation' was shown to approach perilously close to Catholic transubstantiation, while the Zwinglians managed to escape, narrowly perhaps, from the purely 'spiritualist' preachers like the now discredited Karlstadt and the fanciful Schwenckfeld. But, if possible, the *Amica exegesis* pleaded, let there be an end of conflict: 'we return never the better for argument'.[3] He publicly acclaimed Luther as one of the first upholders of the Gospel[4] who, for all his severity and even harshness, was the David and the Jonathan, the Hercules, and the Diomedes, of the Reformation.[5] Mistaken on occasion, as he should recognise, he was yet one through whom the Lord had worked.[6] This was greater magnanimity than Luther ever showed, but it would leave a false impression to emphasise unduly the friendly tone of the whole *Expositio*.

At the same time, Zwingli strenuously insisted upon the independence of his own thought. Long before he had heard of Luther, he had derived the essentials of his teaching from Thomas Wittenbach at Basle, from Erasmus who had, in his earlier days,[7] taught what Luther was later to preach, from the New Testament, copying and learning by heart many of its pages, and from St Augustine. Above all, it was biblical research, careful Bible study in the three languages, that brought him conviction.[8] It was when he came to study Luther's books on the adoration of the sacrament[9] and the answer to Henry VIII that he perceived that Luther's view of the presence of Christ in the sacrament was untenable.[10] It was the

[1] Koehler, *Z & L* I, 483-4, 489.   [2] Z v, 553, 586.
[3] Z v, 567. 'Vides, ut a contentione nunquam redeamus meliores.' Cf. F. Blanke – 'Zu Zwinglis Vorrede an Luther in der Schrift "Amica Exegesis", 1527', ZWA, v (1930) 185-92.
[4] Z v, 613. The words were chosen with care.   [5] Z v, 722-3.   [6] Z v, 750-2.
[7] Especially in 1515-16. Z v, 713 nn. 1, 2, 718, 721 n. 4.
[8] There is revealingly little reference to Hoen in the *Amica exegesis*.
[9] *Von Anbeten des Sakraments des heiligen Leichnams Christi* (1523), WA 11, 417-56; Z v, 647 n. 1; see above 303.
[10] Z v, 652-4. In order to expound his own view, Zwingli tends to exaggerate Luther's acceptance of 'concomitance', the co-existence of Christ's body and blood with the elements. Luther in fact was at once too cautious and too well trained in scholastic philosophy to describe exactly the indescribable, the nature and manner of the presence of Christ in the Last Supper. Both Luther and Zwingli were in agreement (although with varying emphasis)

interpretation of Christ's words, not what was said but what was meant, that constituted the whole central issue. The implications of Christ's 'ubiquity' occupy many pages since for Zwingli the ascended Christ was in heaven until the Last Day, as St Stephen had seen before his death; hence his 'body' could not be everywhere.

Figures of speech, alloeosis, metonomy, catachresis and the rest are fully paraded; miracles, the Passover, circumcision, baptism, are all called in, along with sometimes singularly inappropriate classical allusions to reinforce the insistence that 'this bread' is a figure, a signification, a representation, and a commemoration of Christ's body. If only Luther, through whom a valuable work had been performed, would recognise his mistakes,[1] the future might well be bright. With 'again, farewell most learned Luther' the treatise ends.

The only effect it had upon Luther was to arouse his wrath still further against 'this insolent Swiss', but it advanced the Zwinglian cause in South Germany, soon to be strengthened further when Berne (January 1528) and Basle (April 1529) finally fully accepted the Reformation. Lutheran books and pamphlets circulated freely and openly in Zurich and Basle, but in Saxony, by contrast, Zwingli's writings were suppressed. The plea that it should be otherwise seemed presumptuous in Wittenberg where priority and leadership in the Protestant world should rest. When in April 1527 Luther, disturbed by the apparent harmony of Zurich, Strassburg and Basle, answered both Oecolampadius and the *Amica exegesis*, it was with all too familiar abuse and violent assertion.[2] His opponents were both crazy and possessed of the devil; their teaching was blasphemous, their appeal to reason and common sense was inadequate and objectionable.[3] They were the living representatives of the peasant leader Thomas Müntzer who had been tortured to death at Frankenhausen nearly two years previously – 'Müntzer is dead but his spirit is far from eliminated'.[4] Apart, however, from invective, Luther tried to restate

about the hypostatic union of Christ's humanity and divinity; but Luther, in allowing a measure of 'adoration' of the sacrament, got himself into a difficulty which Zwingli was quick to seize upon: 'If the eucharist is to be adored, it is to be adored because Christ is there as God and man, and this is to concede victory to the Pope...But God alone is to be adored, not flesh and blood.' Z v, 658.

1 Four were set out as a kind of conclusion:
   i. Corpus Christi naturaliter commanducatum in hoc sacramento, fidem confirmat.
   ii. Corpus Christi naturaliter commanducatum peccata remittit.
   iii. Corpus Christi naturaliter adfertur vehiculo verborum prolatorum.
   iv. Corpus Christi cum ad manducandum naturaliter prębeo,
      euangelium familiare facio ei, cui prębeo, et corpus sanguinemque dono.
   (Z v. 754)
2 '*Dass Diese wort Christi, "Das ist mein Leib" noch fest stehen, wider die Schwarmgeister.*' WA 23, 38–283.   3 Koehler, *Z & L* I, 491, 495f.
4 WA 23, 283; Koehler *Z & L* I, 501.

305

his eucharistic beliefs to avoid the charge of simple capernatism or acceptance of transubstantiation. He repeated that on this issue he was impervious to simple reason – 'It is written', and that is enough. From this
position he refused to move. From such opponents he feared the Judas-
kiss of reconciliation, but none the less, after 1526, each side came a little
closer to the other. Both rejected transubstantiation and the mass as
sacrifice. For all his insistence upon the commemorative nature of the Last
Supper and of the bread remaining bread as an outward and visible sign
only, Zwingli also accepted a spiritual real presence in the heart of the
believer which sublimated the meal and its participants. Similarly, Luther,
while holding firmly on to the reality of the presence of Christ, recognised
the need for amplifying, explaining and accepting this as involving more
than 'bread plus'. There were supporters like Burgauer to be encouraged,
and cities like Lindau to be won over. He was also subjected to pressure
from Strassburg and from Bucer whose constant revisions of phraseology
and introduction of mystical notions could not be so brusquely brushed
aside as Zwingli's arguments had been. He was also, possibly, too affected
by Bishop Fisher who, in controversy with Oecolampadius, almost
claimed Luther as an ally.[1] One result of this interesting controversy was
that Luther had to give more thought to the spiritual aspect of the
eucharist; and Zwingli, perhaps, had to consider more carefully its con-
comitants. In any case both sides needed to think out the problem of what
was received at the communion by a disbeliever.[2]

In March 1527 Zwingli offered a tiny piece of olive branch to Luther in
a 'friendly answer' addressed to Wilhelm von Zell and intended to be a
summary of his views.[3] There was no attempt to answer abuse by abuse,
but since the answer also contained the view that it was only through faith
that the Bible could be understood[4] and that Luther had read the scriptures
wrongly, conceding far too much to Rome, it was hardly conciliatory.
Luther's view of the sacrament was neither biblically nor philosophically

[1] John Fisher (c. 1459–1535), Bishop of Rochester, provides an interesting early link between
England and Switzerland. His treatise *De veritate corporis et sanguinis Christi in Eucharistia...
adversus Johannem Oecolampadium*, Cologne, 1527 (also in *Opera Joannis Fischerii* (Würzburg,
1597)), repeats some of the points made by Henry VIII five years previously. Fisher knew the
work of the continental theologians better than most English divines – his treatise was translated into German by Cochlaeus (Koehler *Z & L* I, 241 n. 6) and was a serious defence
of transubstantiation, using sixteenth century terminology. *Discordia Concors*: II, 393–
400.

[2] Koehler *Z & L* I, 541–3.

[3] *Z* v, 763 (771)–94. *Früntlich verglimpfung und ableynung über die predig des treffenlichen
Martini Luthers wider die schwermer, zů Wittemberg gethon unnd beschriben zů schirm des
wåsenlichen lychnams und blůts Christi im sacrament. Zů gůter bewarung von Huldrychen
Zuingli ylends und kurtz begriffen.* Wilhelm von Zell was godfather to Zwingli's younger son
Wilhelm, born 29 January 1526.

[4] *Z* v, 773: 'die gschrifft müss allein durch den glouben verstanden werden'.

tenable, and in this essential matter God had not revealed to him the secret of his meaning.

To this Luther reacted with characteristic violence in a letter to Spalatin in which he mentioned a letter from Zwingli that was filled with pride, obstinacy, slander, hatred and sheer wickedness.[1] Zwingli, who had tried conciliation without concession, and had, with some care, set out his case which he was convinced was scriptural, was greatly hurt by this unreasonable reply. From Oecolampadius came the call for an answer to the Lutheran *Dass diese Worte...*, a reply that should enlighten and encourage their supporters in Basle and Strassburg. Hence the Zwinglian *That these words*[2] became a plain challenge to the Lutheran Goliath. It was written in some heat by a man determined that the world should see and know 'what was black and what was white' plainly fashioned out of God's own words. Again Zwingli emphasised the independence and originality of his own thought, again he firmly restated the implications of Christ's dual nature about which he insisted that his opponent was wretchedly confused. This involved some deep philosophy and theology, from which the writer did not shrink, inflicting the whole (written in German) by dedication upon the Elector, John the Steadfast of Saxony, the Lutheran brother and successor of Frederick 'the Wise'. There was no mistaking the violence of the onslaught – his critic was all too ready to introduce Satan, he was under the illusion that he knew everything whereas in fact he knew little, his logic was weak, he darkened the light and truth of the Gospel, he behaved as if he still wore the monk's cowl. He treated four important points – absolution, purgatory, the intercession of saints and the adoration of images – as if they were matters of indifference, which they were not.[3] Lutheran language was that of the huckster and the horse-dealer, making everything much larger than reality, and this, too often, to the ultimate advantage of the papists. Zwingli himself was always open to conviction – from the Bible, of course – whereas Luther, like the High Priest, was immovable, making God's word almighty in one issue and of no account in others. From internal evidence Zwingli thought that the Gospel according to St Luke was later than those of Matthew and Mark (who were writing primarily for Jews who understood the symbolism of the Passover) and added explanatory matter about the institution of the Last Supper which they had not thought it necessary to insert, an obvious factor which Luther had overlooked. Nor had Luther fully recognised that while Scripture was an infallible complete unity in which no word was unconsidered,

---

[1] WA *Br.* 4, 197; Z v, 795; Z IX, 78 n. 1.
[2] *Das dise wort Iesu Christi: "Das ist min lychnam, der für üch hinggeben wirt", ewiglich den alten eynigen sinn haben werdend, und M. Luter mit sinem letsten büch sinen und des bapsts sinn gar nit gelert noch bewärt hat. Huldrych Zuinglis christenlich antwurt.* Z v, 795 (805)–977.
[3] Z v, 823.

no fact or opinion irreconcilable or contradictory, there were apparently divergent statements which can and must be reconciled; failure to understand is the fault, not of the Word, but of the dullness and inadequacy of his – or our – own intellect. At the same time, each side appealed confidently to particular texts, Zwingli, however, even more than Luther, being prepared to emphasise the need for comprehension of the scriptures as a whole, with, of course, recognition that the law of the Old Testament was superseded by the teaching of the New Testament. In this treatise there were, in accordance with this conviction, long passages about the Passover, the Paschal Lamb, unleavened bread, the various biblical applications of stone, rock, water and the rest.

A good part of the discussion turned on the two natures of Christ, with much illustrative comment, consideration of 'sitting on the right hand of God' and 'ubiquity', all treated possibly too much as matters of dialectic and not doing full justice to the depth of Lutheran theology. Debating points are made freely, but the full implications of God's revelation of himself through his son are glossed over. Instead there is an almost distressing comparison of Luther with a strolling jester visiting fairs, celebrations and consecrations, or a cheapjack who when challenged can cry only 'sectaries' (*Schwärmer*). Having gone so far, and having even accused Luther of falsifying Scripture, in ignorance and not of malice, he could yet recall the earlier Luther whose teaching had been so profitable and whose initial inspiration so admirable – the Elijah of the Reformation.[1] At the end comes an appeal that God may grant Luther both knowledge and truth and avoidance of six manifest errors[2] about the Last Supper.

Having launched this thunderbolt, Zwingli turned once again to Anabaptist opponents, whom he hoped to deal with finally and still more crushingly, and then to the great Berne disputation (6 January 1528), the outcome of which altered the whole political position of Protestantism, and led to the intervention of Philip of Hesse.[3]

After the end of the Peasants' War, the German Catholic princes, led by Duke George of Saxony, planned at Dessau to eliminate the Lutherans, with whom the Zwinglians were linked. The Landgrave of Hesse and the

[1] Apparently Zwingli was the first to use this later much-used analogy. Gussmann II, 241–2. Z v, 965 n. 3 and Zwingli's letter to Myconius 4 January 1520, Z VII, 250–2. Zwingli added, 'You are a man, as I am. God forgive and enlighten us all.' Z v, 957.
[2] Z v, 976–7. These are:
   i. The body (*lychnam*) of Christ, like Christ's divine nature, is everywhere.
   ii. Christ shows himself to us in this sacrament so that we can know where we may find him.
   iii. Christ's body (*lyb*), bodily eaten, takes away sin.
   iv. Christ's body (*fleisch*) is an entirely spiritual body.
   v. Christ's body bodily eaten preserves our body to the Resurrection (*zur urstende*).
   vi. Christ's body (*lyb*) bodily eaten gives or increases faith.
[3] See below 317.

Elector of Saxony replied by a defensive alliance for security, and the eucharistic controversy from then onwards became closely interwoven with German and Swiss politics. The Catholics soon realised that Zwingli and Luther should be kept apart, Zwingli annihilated first, and then what they regarded as his German counterpart. Strangely the situation was rendered more acute by the Pack affair involving all parties. Early in 1528, Dr Otto von Pack, self-styled Canon of Meissen and an official in the Chancery of the Catholic Duke George of Saxony, the rival of the Elector, visited the Prince of Hesse at Kassel. There he informed Philip that a league had been formed of the Archbishops of Mainz and Salzburg, the Bishops of Bamberg and Würzburg, the Elector of Brandenburg and the Dukes of Saxony and Bavaria, with Ferdinand of Austria, to attack the protestant heretics through the Elector of Saxony first, then the Margrave of Hesse, and finally Magdeburg.[1] For all this, he produced documentary evidence and was handsomely rewarded. Philip decided at once that attack was the only effective form of defence, renewed the alliance with the Elector of Saxony, and sent Pack on a mission to Cracow, where he arranged an interview with the Woivode of Transylvania, John I. Zapolya, who was claiming the crown of Hungary (mostly in Turkish occupation in any case) in opposition to Ferdinand. Apparently far exceeding any instructions, Pack negotiated an alliance between Hesse and Transylvania, also to include the Catholic Duke William of Bavaria and a promise by Zapolya to secure 100,000 gulden from his brother-in-law the King of Poland, to be used to hire mercenaries to attack Austria.

The Elector of Saxony, however, was readily persuaded by Luther and Melanchthon not to be an aggressor, and Philip of Hesse was informed of his refusal to move. Philip thereupon produced a copy of the Saxony–Brandenburg treaty. This was at once denounced as an impudent forgery, whereupon Pack was arrested and a full-scale investigation mounted, which entirely confirmed that the whole story was a fabrication. The coalition against the Protestants did not exist, and Philip of Hesse had to reconsider his position. Politically it was a Catholic and imperial triumph and a Protestant setback.[2]

It was almost exactly at this juncture that Luther published his restatement of his sacramental theories in *Vom Abendmahl Christi, Bekenntnis*[3]

---

[1] Hauswirth, *Philipp*, 26, 27–8; Fabian 1, 338–42. ARG 1 (1903) 173ff. H. Schwarz, *Landgraf Philipp von Hessen und die Pack'schen Händel*) Leipzig, 1884) 19–29.

[2] K. Dülfer, *Die Packschen Händel, Darstellung und Quellen* (Marburg, 1958) 36–129 has valuable documentation but no index. Cf. Fabian, 338–9. J. Kühn, 'Landgraf Philipp von Hessen. Der politische Sinn der sogenannten Packschen Händel (1528–1928)' in *Statt und Persönlichkeit. Erich Brandenburg...dargebracht* (Leipzig, 1928) 107–29.

[3] WA 26, 241–509 often called "*Grosses Bekenntnis vom Abendmahl*" (cf. Koehler *Z & L* 1. 619–729) and considered by some his masterpiece.

(March 1528), refuting at one and the same time, without serious differentiation, Wyclif, Oecolampadius, Schwenckfeld and Zwingli. In fact Wyclif, with whose writings Luther was very superficially acquainted, was a stalking-horse for Zwingli, and readers well understood this. What with the plurality of antagonists and Luther's manifest wrath, it is distinctly difficult to disentangle serious argument from mere denunciation. Once again for him the divisions among his opponents are evidence of error;[1] Zwingli was quite as bad as Müntzer, a notorious heretic to be avoided as such, seven times worse than a papist, doomed to an early and violent death, an enthusiast, an ignorant fanatic who did not understand the plain words of scripture.[2] 'For my own part', he said, 'I insist that I cannot regard Zwingli and all his teaching as Christian at all. He neither holds nor teaches any part of the Christian faith rightly and he is seven times more dangerous than when he was a Papist…I publicly maintain before God and the whole world that I neither am nor ever will be connected with Zwingli's doctrine.'

Then, over many pages, for it was a long and serious treatise, came the flat contradiction of the Zwinglian exegesis. 'Is' did not and could not mean 'signifies';[3] there was no need to resort to tropes and metaphors; Christ was a rock, and a new one at that. There was much scholastic concern with definitions, accidents and substance,[4] the occupation of space – *localiter, circumscriptive, diffinitive, repletive* – all furthered by abundant analogies and illustrations. For Luther, flesh and spirit were not separable; flesh and spirit were both equally substances and indivisible. In the light of Zwingli's abandonment of the substantial presence of Christ in the sacrament, Luther was, perhaps reluctantly, forced into the Catholic position of a special miracle in which, in this unique bread and in inexplicable fashion, there was a sacramental union of body and bread. From this he went on to build up the inevitable argument: without the word there could be no eucharistic bread and wine; without bread and wine there could be no body and blood of Christ; without the body and blood of Christ there could ⌐be no New Testament; without the New Testament, no forgiveness of sins, eternal life and blessedness could not be.[5]

---

[1] WA 26, 263-4; Koehler *Z & L* I, 623 acutely remarks that there would not be much difficulty in demonstrating equally distinct differences between Luther, Melanchthon, Brent, Billican and Rhegius.   [2] WA 26, 281-2; Koehler, *Z & L* I, 561-2, 620-1.

[3] WA 26, 271.

[4] With, however, a built-in denial of transubstantiation: 'accidens est substantia nec potest abesse suo subiecto' (WA 26, 282). Luther may have been nearer to the Catholics than to the Zwinglians, but he never recrossed this Rubicon. Equally, he rejected the necessity of administration of the sacrament by an ordained priest – if he leaned very slightly towards *opus operatum*, he rejected *ex opere operantis*.

[5] WA. 26, 478-9. 'Die wort sind das erste, Denn on die wort were der becher und brod nichts, Weiter, on brod und becher were der leib und blut Christi nicht da, On leib und blut Christi

It was Luther's masterpiece, his final statement of his doctrine and convictions.

There was more to it, of course, than the central theme of the Last Supper. Original sin with all its implications – not the 'weakness' as Zwingli saw it – was accepted and expounded; justification was by faith and not by works, hence the self-immolation of the monk was vain and monasteries should make way for theological colleges where men should learn to preach the Gospel. Priests might and should marry: the civil authority was by divine ordinance, and obedience must be yielded to it.[1] There were but two sacraments, holy communion and baptism, the latter for infants, who were thus made members of the community of Christians. The mass was not a sacrifice; matrimony, extreme unction, orders, were no true sacraments; indulgences, purgatory, prayers to the saints, were rejected, and the Pope was Anti-christ. Pictures, images, organs, bells, tapers and lights were matters of indifference which might be tolerated if they were present.[2]

This great exposition was intended to be definitive, Luther's grand apology for his position, and it became a kind of sacramental grammar for his followers. At the time, however, it fell a little flat,[3] for there was nothing in it that had not been said before. Oecolampadius and Zwingli were treated as arch-sectarians and subjected to the abuse and scurrility of which Luther, like many of his age, was a master. Neither grammar nor logic was clearly on the Lutheran side, and the frequent direct attacks on a fellow-reformer at this stage of affairs were unfortunate.

A reply was inevitable and the two defendants, Oecolampadius and Zwingli, consulted together before issuing their answers, printed in Zurich by Froschauer in August 1528.[4]

In sixteenth century fashion, Luther is answered point by point, paragraph by paragraph, hurriedly and almost, when it came to personalities, on a 'knock for knock' basis, although there is a slightly conventional indication of respect and admiration for his opponents, partly perhaps because the treatise was dedicated to the pious[5] princes, John the Steadfast of Saxony[6] and Philip of Hesse. After an agreement that peace is more

were das newe testament nicht da. On das newe testament were vergebung der sunden nicht da...' Z VI ii, 217; Koehler *Z & L* I, 639.   [1] WA. 26, 504.
[2] WA. 26, 507-9.
[3] The sale of this large and relatively expensive volume was disappointing. Capito to Zwingli, 22 April 1528, Z IX, 442.
[4] *Über D. Martin Luters büch, bekentnuss genant, zwo antwurten Joannis Ecolampadii und Huldrychen Zuinglis. Im MDXXVIII. jar,* of which Zwingli's direct share was shown as *Über D. M. Lut[hers] büch, bekentnus genant Antwurt Huldrich Zuinglins.* Z VI ii, 1 (22)-248.   [5] Zwingli avoids the usual salutation 'high-born and serene'.
[6] This prince, by an edict of 17 January 1528, had explicitly forbidden the circulation and reading of Anabaptist, sacramentarian (i.e. Zwinglian) and sectarian writings in his

than desirable and that their discussion is exclusively Bible-based, Zwingli considers first Luther's eucharistic thesis in general, then particular points arising from it, and ends with a relatively brief reference to other matters in dispute. It is a long and closely argued polemic and it is important because, taken along with Luther's treatise, it forms the background to all later discussions.

Having indicated that the treatise with which he is dealing is disorderly, untheological, misleading, and belligerent like its impenitent and invincibly ignorant author, he turns at once to the sacramental issue. Luther, he insists, considered that the power of the word, the recitation of a biblical formula, conjured the spirit into the bread, a position worse than that of his papalist opponents, who required the presence of an ordained priest and his actual or habitual intention to consecrate. For Luther faith was not necessary either in the administrator or the recipient. Before, however, dealing with the complex problem of the unbeliever, Zwingli early switches to a digression which was long but essential to his later argument, about the ubiquity of God and its implications. This is lengthy and difficult enough, but he follows it, after reproaching Luther with too much vain philosophy and scholasticism, by an insistence that the writer is not unduly concerned with mere words but with clarification of their meaning. He then again turns to one of his favourite forms of speech – alloeosis, the transposed attribute, changing attributes of one property or nature of a thing or person to another.[1] Something of this was necessary if Zwingli was to combine, as he did, consistent Trinitarian orthodoxy with a full restatement of the implications of the two natures of Christ. In a final section, he indicates with distinct reservations the considerable area of agreement with his opponent, who has fought manfully and chivalrously against the Pope.

Earnestly and with professional exactness Zwingli sets out his view of the nature and the manner of the real presence of Christ in the Last Supper, all, however, by way of refutation, the refutation in one sense of a nominalist by a realist, although these simple descriptions had become so over-laden with refinements and extensions as hardly to be of descriptive value. The bread in the communion was an outward and visible sign of an inward and spiritual grace,[2] but no more. There was a substantial real

dominions. Zwingli asks, 'Why should your subjects "who form one people and one church with us" be thus left groping in the darkness of error?' Z vi ii, 5, 24, 25, 27 n. 1, 35, 55.
[1] Hence Christ's humanity could sometimes imply or be used for his divinity and vice versa. Zwingli also frequently recognised the use of synecdoche, the part for the whole. C. Nagel, *Zwinglis Stellung zur Schrift* (Freiburg/Leipzig, 1896) 99.
[2] Z vi ii, 200: 'ein sichtbare form oder bild einer unsichtbaren gnad...ein sichtbar zeichen oder form sye der göttlichen gnade, die nit sichtbar ist'. Cf. Koehler, *Z & L* i, 674. As Oecolampadius put it: 'das bey einer sichtbarlichen materie etwas unsichtbarlichs darneben

presence of Christ when the elements were distributed, but in the hearts of the faithful only. Christ was spiritually present, but that was no miracle: Christ was not 'in' the bread, since in his humanity he must be in heaven until the day of judgement. Hence unbelievers could not in any sense, even to their own damnation, receive anything but bread. Similarly the cup could not be the New Testament for the forgiveness of sins since this came from the death of the Saviour.[1] Luther, in his view, gave to Christ's words a sense that they could not bear – his insistence that it was all beyond the powers of reason was not good enough. Page after page of restrained refutation and, equally, constructive thought follow, sometimes showing how dangerously close Luther was to Catholic teaching (which he so emphatically repudiated), sometimes relying upon a combination of biblical exegesis and logical argument that are at any rate impressive. The writer emphatically denies Luther's contention that he so emphasises the manhood of Christ as to take away his divinity, insisting, quite effectively, on his own orthodoxy. Indeed, he tries hard to turn the tables on his opponent, by arguing that God's nature is truth, and hence to attribute to God the possibility that he can do anything contrary to his own word is to attack him as truth.[2] The deductions drawn from this, indeed, depend upon alternative interpretations of texts and passages and we are back to alloeosis, synecdoche, enallage, and the rest. Misunderstanding led to misinterpretation: there is always a qualification. 'We gladly recognise that Christ's body is in the Last Supper in the same way as our bodies are even now in heaven, that is to say, in God's fore-knowledge, election and providence'.[3] For Luther to say that if he has been deceived he has been deceived by God, is to show his own impenetrability – papists and heretics say the same, but for those who read the Bible aright all is plain.[4] Knowledge and faith – faith, of course, indispensable and over-riding, and faith not abiding in any creature, not an opinion, but the gift of God through the Holy Spirit, alone giving peace. Zwingli accepted kinship, but not full agreement, with 'the pious Silesian' (Schwenckfeld), a letter from whom to Duke Albrecht of Prussia he had published without leave (August 1528) causing some embarrassment to its author.[5] For Luther this was merely further evidence of fanaticism (*Schwärmerei*).

verstanden werde'. For a commentary, E. Bizer, *Studien zur Geschichte des Abendmahlstreits im 16. Jahrhundert*[2] (Darmstadt, 1962), (Beiträge zur Förderung christlicher Theologie 2. Reihe 46. Bd.) 12–25.

[1] Z VI ii, 220–7.
[2] Z VI ii, 124, 205. 'Die natur und ard gottes ist, das er warhafft sye...Wer nun gott zügibt, dass er wider syn eigen wort thůge, der lestret inn an syner warheyt'; 'das gott nit möglich ist, wider sin eigen wort ze thůn.'
[3] Z VI ii, 142. [4] Z VI ii, 204–5.
[5] Koehler *Z & L* I, 689–93; Z VI ii, 194, 249–59 (correcting S. G. Schultz, *Caspar Schwenckfeld von Ossig* (Norristown, Pa. 1946) 152–5; Z XI, 505.

Being itself a refutation of another book, *Bekenntnis genannt* does not lend itself to any simple summary. Inevitably there is some logic-chopping, repetition, and a good deal of doctrinal and theological infighting, turning often upon the implications of the two natures of Christ and upon the interpretation of apparently conflicting texts. There is much that has to be understood in the light of the scholastic background of both antagonists, and much also explicable best as the vigorous defence of one knowing himself wrongly attacked. Amid a great deal of earnest and serious – and sometimes arid – theology, comes an explanation that the counter-attack was forced on him when he found his followers accounted heretics and his teaching worthless. Luther could hardly expect to lump them with Mohammedans and then be treated with Christian charity himself.[1]

After further reference to the cup and to the communion as a manifestation of Christian fellowship,[2] Zwingli couples Luther's unrepentant errors with those of the church of Rome, which has never had true Christian faith.[3] And then, quite suddenly, comes a string of points of agreement with his critic. On the perpetual virginity of Mary, on the visible Ascension of Christ, on original sin, there was little need of argument. He regretted that Luther was so indifferent about images, bells, lights, pictures and vestments, repeating his well worn analogy 'if you leave the storks' nests undisturbed they will surely come back to them'. In some churches there were scores of altars; if mass was not to be said, what was the point of these 'sacrilegious blocks of stone'? If only Luther could think it possible that he might be mistaken, all might yet be well, but of this there was no sign. Even St Paul had been in the wrong as against Barnabas; for all his services against the Pope he was far from infallible and should use to better purpose the great strength God had given him and beware lest Satan mislead him through pride. 'On our side we have faith, the Scriptures, the usages of the early Christians and agreement with the doctrine of the earliest exponents of it.'[4]

Somewhat unsatisfactorily for both parties, yet indicative of the widespread speculation on the whole issue which reached its culmination in September 1529, was the fact that neither Luther's *magnum opus* nor Zwingli's laboured refutation of it attracted very much attention.[5] Even Bucer, usually so anxious to join in any controversy, had little to say for

[1] Z vi ii, 235.
[2] And with a reference to the views put forward by Andreas Altkamer at Berne, which was perhaps intended as some acknowledgement that the discussions there were not to be overlooked. [3] Z vi ii, 235. [4] Z vi ii, 247.
[5] Luther not only insisted to Nicolas Hausmann that he had not read it, but that it drove people mad who did so: 'Insanire eos dicunt qui legunt, quod facile credo.' It was not reprinted in the sixteenth century. WA. *Br.* 4, 234 (No. 1131).

the remainder of 1528, when, it seemed, the Catholics were preparing once more to take the offensive.

It was not yet clear where Strassburg stood in the north, or how many south-German cities had fully accepted the Zwinglian view, or what was to be expected from eastern Switzerland.[1] Little wonder that Margrave George of Brandenburg confessed himself puzzled or that Philip of Hesse, having survived the Pack scandal, began to show renewed signs of restlessness.

Obviously there was not going to be agreement by writing. Might discussion be more successful? Might a religious summit-conference do what exchanges of letters and treatises could not? A danger of a biographical approach to history is, very obviously, that of over-emphasising the part played by particular individuals. Luther and Zwingli were impelled powerfully by their environment and the people with whom they were in contact. Luther was a secure and honoured figure in the Electorate of Saxony and more than happy to find civil affairs in the hands of a godly prince whose authority could be exalted. He thus felt that he could to a considerable degree separate religion and politics; he would lead men to the city of God above while others cared for the protection and welfare of the living. Protestantism was safe in Saxony, and in a sense Luther was content that it should be so.

This, however, was impossible elsewhere. Zwingli had been involved in Swiss politics from his youth up, and he could hardly think of government save in terms of that of a Christian community. In Zurich, Berne, Basle, Schaffhausen, Constance and Strassburg, the governing councils must be constantly reminded of their duty, which was to protect the reformed faith. Incessant vigilance was necessary. The Catholic forces were very close to Zurich all the time; Baden and Zug, in Catholic hands, were only twenty miles away, and behind them was the whole weight of the Catholic cause. In fighting for his faith, Zwingli was also fighting to secure a united Protestant Switzerland with allies powerful enough to cover further expansion.[2] He had to fight the crypto-Catholics in his own city and state, and at the same time refute the radical Baptists and the misguided Lutherans. After the triumphant disputation at Berne, Zwingli knew that he could not join forces with Luther. Both Erasmus and Eck had demonstrated that Luther was nearer to them on the central issue of the mass than he was to Zwingli. This had, in fact, important implications.

[1] Hauswirth, *Philipp* 90–1. [2] Cf. Oechsli 3 c. 133–4.

13

Marburg and after

The famous confrontation of Luther and Zwingli in the castle hall of Marburg was brought about for political and personal reasons by Philip of Hesse. An account of this remarkable figure and of his client neighbour, Ulrich of Württemberg, must be deferred to a later chapter.[1] In any case a Lutheran–Zwinglian disputation had been suggested before[2] and had its parallel in more than one meeting with the Anabaptists. Now, even after the successful outcome of the Berne meeting, Zurich remained very much alone, able to maintain its independence but needing help, most obviously from the south German cities, for further advance.

This was realised acutely by Strassburg and by a number of its Zwinglian-inclined counterparts. In his sermon at Berne, Bucer had called for a measure of acceptance of varieties of opinion and practice among evangelicals provided the Bible remained the sole basis of faith. On this premise, neighbourly love might enhance the value of discussion and bring about the internal harmony which was his constant purpose. Differences about the Last Supper need not prevent cooperation, a sentiment repugnant to Luther, who increasingly opposed much that Zwingli stood for, doctrinally and politically. Bucer,[3] on the other hand, pliable and plausible, with a quick and subtle brain, was indefatigable in his efforts to arrange the compromise that never came.

Jacob Sturm, Strassburg's leading politician, supported him. At the Diet of Speier (1526) he had urged on Philip of Hesse the value of the potential help available from the south German cities,[4] and Capito also pressed for cooperation based on mutual understanding. Could they not be Christians rather than Lutherans, Karlstadtians, Zwinglians and Oecolampadians?[5] Active and purposeful contributions to the discussion came from the industrious, if isolated, Schwenckfeld, the learned Bugen-

---

[1] See below, 378–383.
[2] Koehler, *Z & L* II, 1–3.
[3] H. Bornkamm, *Martin Bucers Bedeutung für die europäische Reformationsgeschichte* (Gütersloh, 1952). SVR No. 169 – with bibliography (Bibliographia Bucerana).
[4] Schubert, *Bekenntnisbildung* 8; H. Virck, *Politische Correspondenz der Stadt Strassburg im Zeitalter der Reformation* (Strasburg, 1882) I, 264–8.   [5] Koehler, *Z & L* I, 831.

hagen and the near-Zwinglian Brenz. If the leaders were immovable, their followers were not unwilling to try for understanding.

There were more supporters of the Zwinglian concept of a spiritual acceptance of the body of Christ in the eucharistic bread than was easily apparent.[1] This made the princes and politicians a little more ready to intervene when it became apparent that no agreement was likely if the theologians were left alone. Luther, indeed, insisted that there should be a clear division of functions; ministers of religion should preach the Gospel, be steadfast in prayer and learned in the Scriptures; but politics and temporal affairs were the business of the earthly prince whom God had set over them. This in his case was the smug John of Saxony, well content with his nicely ordered and obedient state and not willing to help to promote religious unity among the Protestants or lead the opposition to the Emperor. For Melanchthon there were but two sides, Lutherans and Catholics, between whom a measure of agreement might be hoped for. If they could be reasonable enough to see that there might be different ways of looking at divine truths, some divergence in dogma and ceremonial might be acceptable. He was much less conciliatory with the Zwinglians, and in some ways he was responsible for the widening breach between the principals.

In 1529 Philip of Hesse perceived that the situation called for action. He was a sincere, if liberal, Christian, at least as much of a theologian as Henry VIII of England (whom he resembles in many respects), and concerned about religious affairs. He understood and appreciated the nature and implications of the eucharistic controversy and the extent to which politics, German politics in particular, were involved. He knew also that any discussion to be of value must be between theologians who were adept at technical terms, but he understood what they said, listened patiently on occasion and inclined to favour the Zwinglian view. He wanted common action combined with respect for differences of opinion. Why was it necessary that what the Bible left uncertain and mysterious should be forced into a particular statement of belief?

Early in 1528 Oecolampadius hinted to Zwingli that the Landgrave would welcome a discussion, and on 22 April a suggestion to this effect came directly from Philip's chancery.[2] While undercover discussions continued, events in 1528 and 1529 made Protestant cooperation more than ever urgently necessary. England could be left out of any calculations since the train of events leading to the breach with Rome started in 1527. The King of France was at last prepared to come to terms with Charles V, and did so finally on 3 August 1529 at Cambrai, promising action against heretics. Pope Clement VII likewise accepted peace at Barcelona (29 June

[1] Koehler, *Z & L* I, 822–7.   [2] Koehler, *Z & L* II, 14–15.

1529), leaving Florence once more to the Medici and acquiescing in the return of Maximilian Sforza to Milan. Charles publicly acknowledged that it was his duty to crush heresy, which for him meant Lutheranism. 'For there are many who, think ill of the Catholic faith and altogether depart from Christian belief and doctrine and it is highly pleasing to his Imperial Majesty that a suitable medicine shall be prepared to deal with this dangerous plague.'[1] The Turkish armies still threatened Vienna, but the worst danger there was past although no one knew it at the time. Charles was at long last likely to be able to devote a little attention to Germany.

In March 1529 the German princes and representatives of the Imperial cities met at the second Diet of Speier and were required to consider the religious situation urgently. This involved directly the Lutherans, who three years previously had received at the same place a large measure of practical immunity since the enforcement of their outlawry as proclaimed at Worms had been postponed until after the meeting of a General Council. The princes had been left free to act as seemed best to them. Now in 1529 the Recess of 11 April 1523 and the resolutions of July 1526 were quashed; the Edict of Worms against Luther and his followers was to come into effect. The result was the famous 'protest', a word often to be repeated later, when six princes[2] and fourteen cities[3] insisted that they would not be bound by a majority decision of the diet because 'in matters which concern God's honour and the salvation and eternal life of our souls every one must stand and give account for himself before God'. 'We hold your resolution null and not binding and we desire, in matters of religion ...so to live, govern and carry ourselves, in our governments as also with and among our subjects and kinsfolk as we trust to answer it before God Almighty.'[4]

It was now apparent that the Emperor meant business and that the Roman mass might soon be heard once more in places from which it had been driven by the pure Gospel. Charles V in 1529 was very different from the youthful monarch who had confronted Luther at Worms. He was experienced and successful and the ally, some thought the master, of

[1] J. du Mont, *Corps Universel Diplomatique* T. IV, Partie ii (Amsterdam, 1726) 6 (No. 1).
[2] John Frederick Elector of Saxony, Philip Landgrave of Hesse, George Margrave of Brandenburg-Anspach, George Prince of Anhalt, Ernest and Francis, Dukes of Brunswick-Lüneburg.
[3] Strassburg, Nuremberg, Weissenburg, Windsheim, Ulm, Lindau, Memmingen, Kempten, Nördlingen, Heilbronn, Reutlingen, Isny – all south German and sympathisers with Zwinglianism – Constance and St Gall.
[4] RTA VII, 1260–5, 1273–88, Kidd, 244–5, Näf, *Vadian* II, 300–1. For a full and in places dramatic narrative of the Diet of Speier see J. Kühn, *Die Geschichte des Speyrer Reichstags, 1529*, SVR Jg. 47 No. 146 (Leipzig, 1929). Its significance was first made clear by Ranke *Ref.* partly translated by S. Austin, ed. R. A. Johnson, *History of the Reformation in Germany* (London, 1905) esp. 552–62 misprinted 652). Cf. P. Joachimsen, *Die Reformation als Epoche der deutschen Geschichte* (Munich, 1951) 184–7.

the papacy. Now at last the moment had come when heresy could be eliminated, the might of the princes humbled, and alienated lands restored to the bishops and abbots who were their rightful owners.

A nucleus of Zwinglians in Zurich and north-east Switzerland, pockets of Anabaptists in some larger cities, Lutherans, Bucerians, and spiritualists could be eliminated piecemeal if Pope and Emperor worked together. Luther, Melanchthon and Elector John of Saxony could not and would not provide a firm core of resistance. Luther's politics were negative; his prince should avoid entangling alliances, and he himself would not be involved in political and military enterprises. At the same time he was lumping together Zwingli, Karlstadt, Leo Jud and Oecolampadius as limbs of the devil, with Bucer as a fallen angel. There seemed to be a complete impasse.

Philip of Hesse, however, could put pressure on the Elector of Saxony and could use both political and religious arguments to secure support from Zurich. His mind was made up; he would arrange a meeting, however great the difficulties.[1] The Elector of Saxony disliked an alliance because it might lead to counter-alliances and because Saxony was well able to defend itself without help and had no need to become involved; in any case the papists were no longer dangerous.[2] And if Luther was reluctant to move, his close friend and adherent, Melanchthon, was willing to enter into a discussion, which had long been wanted by Oecolampadius of Basle. In April 1529, Saxony, Hesse, Strassburg and Ulm were reported to have made a secret defensive alliance, and this, combined with the conclusion of the Christian Alliance between Ferdinand of Austria and the Inner States,[3] made an extension of the Zwinglian *Christliche Burgrecht* to include Strassburg the more attractive. This was important since Philip recognised the key position occupied by Strassburg, a city which John of Saxony disliked as not being Lutheran. Luther, likewise, perceived that the inclusion of Strassburg meant that the league might well be extended to include Ulm, Memmingen, Biberach, Nördlingen and other Swabian cities, which must mean a renewed call for some form of compromise, or at least for further discussions on doctrinal issues on which his mind was made up. The summer of 1529 was alive with rumours, meetings and conferences, in which Bucer, Capito and Oecolampadius were willingly involved. They included gatherings at Schmalkalden, Schleiz, Nuremberg,[4] Rotach and, after the Marburg meeting, at Schwabach on 16–19 October. From Schwabach came another statement of the Lutheran

---

[1] A preliminary discussion of some possible arrangements in December 1528 had culminated in Philip's announcement, 'I will arrange a meeting between Oecolampadius, Luther and their colleagues at my own charges even if it costs 6,000 gulden.' Koehler, *Festgabe*, 364, *Z & L* II, 25.   [2] Koehler, *Z & L* II, 34–5.
[3] See below, 354–5.   [4] Gussmann, I, i, 22.

position which was not unconciliatory and was intended to wean Strassburg away from the Zwinglian camp. The content of these Schwabach articles was in fact agreed by Luther, Melanchthon and Jonas before their meeting with Zwingli, which is what gives them their importance.[1] They also made it clear to the Hessian court that the Lutheran platform was solid and explicit. All the familiar points were reaffirmed – the orthodox Nicean view of the Trinity, salvation by faith, the exclusive and absolute authority of the Bible, the recognition of the two sacraments of Baptism and Holy Communion, child baptism being wholly acceptable. Then came the matters with which the Zwinglians were likely to disagree – original sin was not, as Zwingli maintained, a weakness, a tendency to sin, a negative absence of goodness; it was real sin inherent in human nature. Lutheran 'consubstantiation' was again asserted, negatively and positively.[2] Thus the Lutherans before Marburg were well prepared and knew where to draw the line in any talk of concessions.

Philip of Hesse, for his own part, was more determined than ever to find a theological basis which, as a minimum, would greatly extend his influence, help to restore Duke Ulrich to Württemberg, and, as a maximum, would ensure Protestant domination of the German-speaking lands and the probability that the next Emperor would be Protestant.

Neither Zwingli nor Luther wanted a debate or expected any good to come of it. Nevertheless Philip of Hesse persisted, and it says much for his influence that the Marburg Conference took place at all. He provided the money, the meeting place, the security arrangements; and he sat through hours of debate in technical language which he had never been trained to understand. He very nearly succeeded in bringing about union. Zwingli accepted the invitation in principle early in May,[3] but made it clear that his political master was the Zurich Council, which must be kept informed, although he would come in any event.

The formal invitations to a conference at Marburg were issued by Philip of Hesse from Friedewald on 1 July 1529. They went to Zurich for Zwingli, to Basle for Oecolampadius, to Strassburg for Sturm, Osiander,

---

[1] Koehler, *Z & L* II, 46. The articles were printed in C. W. F. Walch, *Monimenta Medii Aevi* (Göttingen, 1757–64) XVI, 661ff. WA, 30.3.86–91, cf. Schubert, *Bekenntnisbildung* 23; *Die Anfänge der evangelischen Bekenntnisbildung bis 1529/30* (Leipzig, 1928) 32–3; Th. Kolde, *Der Tag von Schleiz und die Entstehung der Schwabacher Artikel* (Gotha, 1896); Koehler, *Festgabe* 365. The Schwabach articles affected the form and content of the Marburg conference. They were later accepted by Saxony, Brunswick-Lüneburg, Anhalt-Bernburg, Nuremberg, Brandenburg-Anspach and the Counts of Mansfeld, but, significantly, not by Strassburg to which they were almost specifically directed, nor by Ulm, Memmingen, Lindau and Constance. Hauswirth, *Philipp*, 117.

[2] Koehler *Z & L* II, 47. Das Abendmahl 'sey nicht allein prot und wein, wie yzo der widerteyl furgibt'...'das sey wahrhaftigklich gegenwertig im prot und wein der ware leyb und plut christi laut der wort Cristi: das ist mein leyb, das ist mein plut.'

[3] After receiving Philip of Hesse's letter of 22 April. Z X, 108–9, 117–18 (7 May).

Marburg and after

Hedio and Bucer,[1] and to Luther and Melanchthon. Luther, apparently, was told only that he would meet Oecolampadius, and learnt later that Zwingli would be there.[2] He still thought that no good could come of such a meeting, and it was with difficulty that the Elector, who could not afford to alienate Philip of Hesse, secured on 23 June his agreement to be present.[3] Luther regarded his sovereign's will as an order, obedience to constituted authority being an essential principle of his own teaching. He was in an uncompromising mood, refused to make any promises in advance, and agreed to attend mainly in order that his opponents should not seem to want peace and unity more than he did.

It was with Luther that the arrival date, Michaelmas Day, Wednesday 29 September, was fixed, and arrangements for his movements were left in the hands of the Saxon authorities. Basically Zwingli was more ready to attend than was Luther, and much more conscious of the political issues involved, but less happy about the journey to Marburg. To get there, he might have to cross Catholic controlled territory; there were Swiss Catholics ready to capture him as a heretic, while in Germany he was liable to arrest as a 'Lutheran'. The route would necessarily lie through either Frankfurt or Strassburg. The latter could be reached by boat along the Rhine, but the 200 miles from thence meant a week on horseback through territory controlled by Duke Lewis of Zweibrücken, Philip's nephew, and then past St Goar into the lower county of Katzenelnbogen where the authority of Philip and Ulrich was operative.

This element of personal danger is worth stressing; Zwingli had refused to participate in the Baden conference because to do so meant a real hazard to his life and he had been able, possibly unwisely, to fall back on the refusal of the Zurich Council to permit his attendance. Marburg was different.[4] The Baden conference was primarily religious, the Marburg

[1] H. Virck, *Politische Correspondenz der Stadt Strassburg im Zeitalter der Reformation* (Strassburg, 1882) I, 382, 384–5.
[2] Schubert, *Bekenntnisbildung*, 15; Staehelin, *Briefe* II, 335–7; Z X, 185–92, 205–6; Koehler, *Z & L* II, 50.
[3] WA Br., 5, 101–5; Koehler, *Rekonstruktion*, 7.
[4] There is a considerable literature connected with the Marburg conference; no biography of Luther fails to mention it. Koehler's fullest and latest views on Marburg are in *Z & L* II, 1–163; he also wrote 'Zum Religionsgespräche von Marburg 1529': *Festgabe für Gerold Meyer von Knonau* (Zurich, 1913) 359–81, which summarises the more detailed narrative in *Das Marburger Religionsgespräch 1529, Versuch einer Rekonstruktion*, SVRG 48 no. 148 (Leipzig, 1929), partly translated in D. J. Ziegler, *Great debates of the Reformation* (New York, 1969); *Das Religionsgespräch zu Marburg* (Tübingen, 1929) (Sammlung gemeinverständlicher Vorträge und Schriften aus dem Gebiet der Theologie und Religionsgeschichte. 140). There are some useful pages in H. von Schubert, *Bekenntnisbildung und Religionspolitik 1529–30 (1524–34). Untersuchungen und Texte* (Gotha, 1910) and *Beiträge zur Geschichte der evangelischen Bekenntnis- und Bündnisbildung 1529/20*, ZKG Bd 30. (Gotha, 1909) 271–351, and *Bündnis und Bekenntnis 1529/30*, SVR. 16. H. 48 (Leipzig, 1908) 1–35. G. May (hg.), *Das*

conference much more political.[1] In 1526 the Reformation had but recently been accepted in Zurich; in 1529 there was good hope of a Zurich-dominated Protestant Switzerland, expansionist and aggressive. If only Berne had been invited and had accepted, this could have happened. Although it is now known that Zwingli was far from being supreme in his state, as Waldmann had been, his personal influence in 1529 was greater than at any time previously. It was partly because this was so that events took the turn they did. It is, however, possible to detect from the Zurich records rumblings of discontent with the régime there. There was some Protestant anti-clericalism as there had been Catholic anti-clericalism, a feeling that the ministers of religion were too powerful and that conformity meant rigidity. There was also a conservative Catholic underground movement, led by those who accepted, but regretted, the abolition of the mass and, with it, perhaps, respect for the patricians. In sixteenth-century conditions, an opposition had to be silent, but it existed none the less. Zwingli therefore had continually to advertise his differences with Rome in order to hold his ground, and this above all on the central theme of the eucharist. Melanchthon seemed to be demonstrating that Lutherans could be turned into Catholics by concessions about inessentials, and that the gap between transubstantiation and Lutheran sacramental teaching was not unbridgeable. This could not be true of Zwingli's doctrine of the Last Supper. For Zwingli to give way on this would be not only to depart from the convictions of a decade, but also to break with his own supporters and introduce a fatal element of weakness into Zurich itself.

The preliminary negotiations were conducted in an atmosphere of almost melodramatic secrecy, with Ulrich Funk as Zwingli's messenger. Precautions were taken to see that no one in Zurich knew of the impending departure of their chief minister: the Great Council was not informed, even Frau Zwingli did not know of her husband's intentions till the last moment. The composition of the Zwinglian party is interesting; their leader brought with him the scholarly printer-publisher Froschauer, a personal friend who could help with the expenses and knew what was at stake but was no theologian; Rudolf Collin whose learning in Hebrew and the Old Testament could be useful; and Funk, who understood better than his companions that it was political and strategic topics that were the essential background to the whole gathering. They left after nightfall on 3 September for Brugg. At Basle, on Sunday 5 September they were

Marburger Religionsgespräch, 1529 (Texte zur Kirchen- und Theologiegeschichte, hg. von G. Ruhbach. 13. Gütersloh, 1970) has a short bibliography.
[1] Hanna Köditz, 'Die gesellschaftlichen Ursachen des Scheiterns des Marburger Religionsgesprächs vom 1. bis 4. Oktober 1529' in: *Zeitschrift für Geschichtswissenschaft*, 2. i (1954) 37–70. This Marxist assessment is interesting but quite unacceptable.

joined by Oecolampadius and Rudolf Frey, and next day the six proceeded by boat to Strassburg.[1] There they received what was almost an official civic welcome, staying with the chief Cathedral preacher, Matthew Zell, whose wife later complained of having had to act for nearly a fortnight as cook and housemaid for nine preoccupied parsons. With their Strassburg supporters, Jacob Sturm,[2] Caspar Hedio, and Bucer, there were nearly two weeks of conferences, sermons and work in the Strassburg libraries. Zwingli also managed a brief meeting with Schwenckfeld.[3] The general political situation was also reviewed and Zwingli was the better informed as a result.[4] He again urged that evangelical disunity might mean that Ferdinand, with the help of Pope, Emperor and Spain, as well as a large fifth column of central Swiss, could swoop down on Zurich and from thence eliminate Protestantism in Switzerland and beyond. No reference was apparently made to the conspicuous absence of anyone from Berne, but the implications were obvious.

Fully in accord, the nine men, with arrangements already made about guides and escorts, left Strassburg on 17 September for Herrenstein, Zweibrücken, Meisenheim, St Goar, Giessen and Marburg, reached on 27 September, ten days riding, mostly through forests.[5]

The Saxon party was at the same time moving in greater comfort along the roads from Wittenberg through Torgau, Jena, Weimar, Erfurt and Gotha, arriving three days after the Swiss to receive an elaborate welcome at the castle. It was an impressive group, Luther, Melanchthon, Justus Jonas, Friedrich Myconius, Caspar Cruciger from Leipzig, Georg Rörer, Osiander, Stephen Agricola, together with some others, including Brenz whom Luther had tried unsuccessfully to persuade to stay away. By now any suggestion of secrecy had been dispelled, and Marburg was full of curious and fashionable visitors, the equivalents of the modern journalists. The language of debate was to be German for the benefit of the Prince and of Duke Ulrich of Württemberg (Zwingli would have preferred Latin), and there was to be a series of sermons in the castle chapel – the parallel is that of the modern press conference.

The first sermon which Zwingli preached at Marburg on 29 September 1529 in the presence of Philip of Hesse was in fact a vigorous and un-

---

[1] A. Waldburger, *Zwinglis Reise nach Marburg zum Gespräch mit Luther, 1529* (Görlitz/Zürich, 1929), 3–5.

[2] *Vir minime mediocris* according to Jonas (*Rekonstruction* 50). Sturm, who was the most influential Protestant in Strassburg, and in close contact with Zwingli, probably thought the same of Jonas. [3] Z vi ii, 254. *Corpus Schwenckfeldianorum* xiv, 96; xviii, 45–6.

[4] Hauswirth, *Philipp*, 147–51; ZWA xi, 540–44; Z x, 300–1, 307–10; Z vi ii, 582–3. New information was available 'uss der rechten kunstkamer'.

[5] EA 4, 1 b, 380–1, 417–18; Z x, 311–12; Koehler, *Z & L* ii, 63 (correcting 26 September to 27).

qualified statement of his views on predestination.[1] More even than Luther, with whom he was in substantial agreement on this matter,[2] and quite as emphatically as Calvin, he insisted upon the insignificance of human effort or will in the light of the purpose of God omnipotent, supreme goodness and truth.

It is a short treatise, but not easily summarised. Omnipotent God must also be omniscient, eternal, unchangeable. In his infallible wisdom, goodness, power and truth, every action is known beforehand; man is but God's instrument for good. There is no such thing as chance, luck or accident; man was created master of the world, endowed with understanding after the fall, body and soul in perpetual conflict, but with God's law available to show his will and purpose. Those who disobey do so by God's will and providence,[3] and in their punishment and suffering for sin they demonstrate God's supreme righteousness.

God knew before he created the world and the first man that Adam would fall; indeed he created man in order that mankind might be saved through Christ upon the cross. Goodness can only be known and recognised if there is evil, just as no one would know the meaning of sweetness without experience of bitterness. With biblical texts and homely analogies the message is conveyed: God who cannot sin brings it about that man both can and does. Why this is so we may wonder, but need not enquire.

It is useless to argue, as the Schoolmen did, that God chooses when he perceives what man will do: on the contrary, the actions of all, even murder, are predetermined, as is the salvation of the elect and the damnation of the reprobate. There is no salvation by works, and God is gracious to whom he will. Faith, the gift of the Holy Spirit, is the first need and mark of the Christian, preceding baptism (in adults), invisible, incomprehensible. And election precedes faith, but when and how is not revealed. Those who are elect necessarily do good works, but these may be done

---

[1] The sermon was preached without notes. In a letter from Kassel of 25 January 1530 Philip asked for the text and received a small treatise representing as faithfully as might be what had been said in the pulpit. This was translated into German by Leo Jud, perhaps under Zwingli's supervision. Z x, 422 and n. 15. Z xi, 338 n. 10. *Ad illustrissimum Cattorum principem Philippum, sermonis de providentia dei Anamnema* (Zürich, Froschauer, 20 August 1530) S iv, 79–144. ZH ii, 81–250. A revised text will appear in Z vi iii (No. 166). For a commentary, Wernle, 246–306.

[2] Luther had set out his views in *De servo arbitrio* (December 1523) in answer to the 'Diatribe' of Erasmus, *De libero arbitrio*. It has been described as 'the greatest piece of theological writing' that ever came from Luther's pen. J. I. Packer and O. R. Johnston, *Martin Luther on the bondage of the will* (London, 1957) 40. WA 18, 600ff.

[3] 'Providentia est perpetuum et immutabile rerum universarum regnum et administratio.' S iv, 84. For fuller treatment Baur ii, 712–13; Wernle ii, 249, 251–2; G. W. Locher, 'Die Prädestinationslehre Huldrych Zwinglis', *Theologische Zeitschrift* 12 (1956), 526–48 and *Grundzüge der Theologie Huldrych Zwinglis in Vergleich mit derjenigen Martin Luthers und Johannes Calvins*. ZWA xii (1967) 470–509, 545–95, esp. 571–2. S. Rother, *Die religiösen und geistigen Grundlagen der Politik Huldrych Zwinglis* (Erlangen, 1956) 25–32, 118–24.

hypocritically by others, and of this only God may judge with certainty. The utmost that we can say is that those who die in disbelief are almost surely damned. Perhaps we may hope that children dying very young are among the elect, but no more than this.

The treatise ends with a denunciation of appeals to chance, luck or any sure guidance by stars or dreams; for the elect, even their wicked actions have good consequences, which cannot be true of the rest of mankind. God, perfect wisdom, must know everything, perfect power, must do everything. Even this statement to Philip, so uncompromising in its determinism, is itself something pre-ordained by God. Calvin, surely, was never more explicit than this. Years later Schwenckfeld went out of his way to refute it in detail.[1]

After a formal introductory speech by Chancellor Johann Feige at daybreak of Friday, 1 October, direct discussions started, Luther meeting Oecolampadius, and Zwingli facing Melanchthon.[2] It was a kind of explanatory meeting in which Zwingli's orthodoxy on such matters as the Trinity and the inspiration of the Bible were found to be acceptable. On the subject of the eucharist the cautious German insisted on the literal interpretation of *hoc est corpus* while also accepting the proposition that faith was essential. The problem of 'ubiquity' was also touched on, Melanchthon conceding that Zwingli had St Augustine, but St Augustine alone of the Fathers, on his side.[3] It was a friendly statement of alternative positions and no more, but the meeting was much more cordial than the later encounter between Luther and Bucer, the latter being greeted with the observation, 'You are from the Evil one.'[4] There was little hope of concord between these two, the one so rigid, the other so flexible. Luther, as is almost too well known, was obstinate or determined from the first, chalking *hoc est corpus meum* on the table in front of him. In the sense that no argument would induce him to abandon his conviction of the bodily real presence of Christ in the eucharist, the outcome was a foregone conclusion; but in fact the Lutheran side may have been more shaken by the arguments they heard than seemed likely. During the opening discussion with Oecolampadius, Luther answered his opponent's insistence upon the limitation of Christ's 'glorified' body to its place in heaven until the day of judgement by appeals to 2 Corinthians 12. 2 and Ephesians 4. 10 (St Paul's vision of Christ), and by the view that place and time were limited human concepts, all places being one with God.

Bucer was not invited to the first direct conference of the leading

[1] *Corpus Schwenckfeldianorum* XII, 882f, 935–41, 955–7.
[2] Z VI ii, 507–9; May, 31–2; Schubert, *Bekenntnisbildung*, 56; Koehler, *Z & L* II, 76–7; R. Stupperich, *Melanchthon* (Berlin, 1960) 64–5.
[3] Koehler, *Z & L* II, 82–3; *Rekonstruktion* 42; May, 32.
[4] 'Du bist des Teufels'. Koehler, *Z & L* II, 83; *Rekonstruktion*, 49; May, 40; Bornkamm, 21.

protagonists at six o'clock on the morning of Saturday, 2 October. This was under the chairmanship of the Prince, with his Chancellor in attendance. Luther, Zwingli, Melanchthon and Oecolampadius exchanged views without any notes being taken by anyone: hence a certain difficulty about reconstructing the exact nature of the discussions. After these preliminary statements, the mornings and afternoons of the two whole days, Saturday and Sunday, were devoted to discussions of the central theme between the principals. Luther was not prepared for any departure from his position, elaborated in the *Bekenntnis* and embodied in the articles of Schwabach, that the Word brought the body of Christ into the bread. Reason and grammar did not apply – Christ's body was eaten; with the acceptance of this truth eternal life, the kingdom of heaven and forgiveness of sins were all involved. It was not for the servant to ask why he should obey an order but simply blindly to do what he was told.

Zwingli could not accept this approach: for him God was not hidden, *absconditus, occultissimus*: as Oecolampadius put it to Luther, 'Where does it say in the Bible that we should close our eyes to its meaning, Herr Doctor?'[1] On the contrary, God's meaning was clear to the believer who would apply his whole powers, however humble his intellect, to the Bible. 'It is the oracles of the demons that are dark, not the words of Christ.'[2] To this Luther answered that there were matters like the virginity of Mary which were not fully comprehensible or explicable intellectually, and the eucharist fell into this category. Nor was he prepared to enter into mathematical hair-splitting, for God was superior to any mathematician.[3] If he were only to ask what is possible, what is certain, he would neither be baptised nor believe in Christ.[4] 'In faith', Luther insisted, 'we eat this body which was given for us; the mouth receives the body of Christ, for the soul believes the words as the body is eaten.'[5] At this point Zwingli resumed his case for the eucharistic metaphor – Christ's words were not beyond human comprehension; quite the contrary. The body of Christ could not be brought through the word to the disbeliever, for faith was of the essence of participation. The word signified the will of God, no more than that: it was for the believer only that God was present, and not for the comfort of the body but of the spirit.

For Luther this was to make Christ's words words of straw, a 'wax nose' which could be twisted into any shape: it was not human words that were spoken but divine ones; behind them was the power and command of

---

[1] Koehler, *Rekonstruktion*, 13.
[2] May, 34; *Rekonstruktion*, 14, 15.
[3] *Rekonstruktion*, 9, 29, 100, 101.
[4] 'Possem non baptizari nec credere in Christum...quia sic nec...accipietis coenam, quia nescitis probitatem.' *Rekonstruktion* 64, 83; *Z & L* II, 89, 91.
[5] *Rekonstruktion* 15, 69.

Christ; hence, faith or no faith, believer or disbeliever, the body of Christ was there present.

This was dangerously like *opus operatum*, a simple, uncompromising repetition of the case set out in *Vom Abendmahl Christi: Bekenntnis*. Not unnaturally, Zwingli was both impatient and annoyed. There was a heated clash over 'the flesh profits nothing' verse of John 6. 63, which Luther refused to accept as effectively apposite but to which Zwingli returned triumphantly. So far from being bad dialectic, 'the passage breaks your neck'. 'Don't be so sure. Necks are not so easily broken', was the often quoted retort, 'you're in Hesse here, not in Switzerland.'[1] Shortly after, a nod from Philip indicated that the second discussion was no more fruitful than the first.

The afternoon session revolved on the same theme. *Verbum prolatum*, the pronunciation of a formula like 'open sesame' did not bring Christ:[2] there was no *manducatio corporalis*; the concept of the body of Christ feeding the soul must be linked to the fact of the resurrection. It looked as if there was no way round, although Luther was prepared to regard the body of Christ as different from all human food, not consumed, not digested along with material provender but permeating the body, preparing it for the resurrection.

Later Zwingli tried to force the pace, again insisting that only the believer could hope to profit by the Last Supper. 'This is' was a way of saying 'this signifies', and any parallel with the bodily ascension of Christ was inadmissible. The afternoon ended where it had begun – for Luther the disbeliever received what the believer received, but to his damnation. For Zwingli the disbeliever received nothing but plain baked bread. This was the point upon which the negotiations broke off: Luther was not prepared for logical argument – *argumenta rationis* – and, as it were, shut his ears. He would not distinguish here between the humanity and the divinity of Christ; he would have no trope or metaphor in the consecration words; if there was to be a technical term it was synecdoche, the bread being 'my body in the bread'. 'Have we got to have everything that you want?' was Zwingli's final Saturday fling.[3]

Luther was, in fact, in the unusual position of acting on the defensive. The Prince of Hesse did not give him the comforting support to which he was accustomed at home. For a long while he had been laying down the law to admiring disciples; his intellect was closed on the eucharistic theme; he had made up his mind, he was not prepared to argue and he was taken aback by the massive logic and ability of his opponent. Zwingli,

---

[1] 'Der locus bricht euch den hals ab.' 'Rühmet nit zu sehr, die Hälse brechen nicht also, Ihr seid in Hessen, nicht in Schweitz.' Koehler, 76. *Z & L* II, 95; *Rekonstruktion*, 19; May, 23, 36.

[2] May, 44.   [3] Koehler, *Z & L* II, 107; *Rekonstruktion*, 31; May, 38.

equally, dared not compromise – to have accepted Luther's position, however modified, would have been to commit political suicide. Luther, unwillingly, grudgingly and without conviction, might perhaps have yielded something, but Zwingli required him to give way on an essential. This he could not do: the operative power of the word he could not abandon.

All the time the drift of the discussion had been moving in the direction of the concept of 'substance', since Zwingli was willing to concede that the body of Christ was present, really present, represented by the bread, for the believer. Further discussion turned upon the meaning and nature of 'presence'. The body of Christ, ran the Zwinglian thesis, is a concrete thing (*finitum*) and therefore must have a place, a local presence,[1] which Luther insisted was irrelevant. Christ was in heaven *and* in the sacrament.[2] An Almighty God could make a body to be in two places at once, a proposition which Zwingli could not deny but turned with the observation that because something can be done it does not necessarily mean that it is done – *arguere a posse ad esse* has no conclusive force.

The final stages dealt with passages from the Fathers and ended with the parties nearer together but not in agreement and with a slightly apologetic remark from Luther – 'I am flesh and blood as well' and Zwingli seriously protesting his regard for his opponent.[3] Luther at the end was prepared to concede that Christ's body 'there' need not be in one particular spot (*localiter*), and Oecolampadius was ready to grant that the real body of Christ was present in faith[4] (*per fidem*), but the gap was not closed. No acceptable formula could be found.

As darkness descended on that fatal first Sunday evening in October, it was apparent they must agree to differ.[5] Zwingli had not succeeded in obtaining the measure of recognition, tolerance and inter-communion for which he had hoped. Luther would not go even as far as this – he was not prepared to accept either the men of Strassburg or the Swiss as brothers[6]

---

[1] Koehler, *Rekonstruktion*, 31; F. W. Schirrmacher, *Briefe und Akten zu den Geschichte des Religionsgespräches zu Marburg* (Halle, 1876), 15; May, 27, 28, 48. 'Vos...Christi corpus localiter ponitis in coena! Dicitis enim: Der leib Christi muss da sein, da, da, ibi est certe adverbum loci.' There is considerable agreement among all the reporters on this passage.

[2] Koehler, *Z & L* II, 101.

[3] Luther wrote on 1 June 1530 that Zwingli had said with tears in his eyes, 'There is no one on earth with whom I would be more willingly in agreement than with those from Wittenberg.' Osiander reported Zwingli as saying that there was no one in Italy or France whom he would more gladly see than Luther. WA *Br.* 5. 340; May, 29; *Rekonstruktion*, 37, 126.

[4] Koehler *Z & L* II, 113 'ibi per fidem esse verum corpus'.

[5] Zwingli, in an informative letter to Vadian (20 October 1529, Z X, 316–18; Vad. *Br.* IV, 192) expressed his certainty that Luther had not proved his case. 'Lutherus impudens et contumax, adperte est victus, sed apud prudentem iudicem et equum, quamvis interim clamaret, se esse invictum etc.'

[6] The words 'You have a different spirit from ours' ('so reymet sich unser gayst und Euer gayst nichts zusammen') were addressed to Bucer, not, as is sometimes said (e.g. J. Atkinson,

and fellow-members of a wider church. He was first over-confident, then abusive: he conceded nothing that mattered, and the Landgrave had failed.

There was, however, more gain than loss. The parties had discussed their differences earnestly and sincerely; they had ceased to call one another heretics, papalists and sectaries. Each side had accepted the three Christian creeds with complete conviction and placed the same interpretation on them. They also accepted the verbal inspiration and indefeasible authority of the Bible. On 4 October the ten disputants set their hands to fifteen articles drafted by Luther.[1] Fourteen of them were agreed; the Trinity in Unity, the Incarnation, the Resurrection and the two natures of Christ, Luther being relieved of the imputation of being Marcionite and Zwingli cleared of Nestorianism. There followed original sin, salvation, justification by faith, the recognition of good works as the natural and necessary outcome of justification, and the special importance of the sermon from a preacher who knew himself called by the Holy Spirit and was accepted by his congregation and fellow ministers. Baptism was a sign of the admission of an infant, through the faith of his parents, to the Christian community. Universal priesthood, a married clergy, the inapplicability of monastic vows, the divine sanction of secular governmental authority and the refusal of tradition where opposed to the Bible, were easily acceptable.

The sting was in the tail. Both sides repudiated transubstantiation, rejected the notion of the eucharist as a sacrifice for dead and living, and insisted upon the administration of the communion in both kinds. But for the Lutherans there was in the eucharist and for all recipients a real bodily presence of Christ, whereas for Zwingli, this presence, however real, was in the hearts of the believers only. The difference was wider than it might seem, an unbridgeable gap of highest import for the future.[2]

Martin Luther and the birth of Protestantism (London, 1968) 277) to Zwingli. The dialogue (from Koehler, *Rekonstruktion*, 38, 129) is worth quoting:
BUCER. Ich bitte: Wollet Ihr mich als Bruder anerkennen oder glaubet Ihr, dass ich irre, auf das ich's verbessere? Zeiget doch an, was Euch missfällt an unserer Lehre.
LUTHER. Ich bin Euer Herr nicht, Euer Richter nicht, Euer Lehrer auch nicht, so reimet sich unser Geist und Euer Geist nichts zusammen, sonder ist offenbar, dass wir nicht einerlei Geist haben. Dann das kann nicht einerlei Geist sein, da man an einem Ort die Wort Christi einfeltigklich glaubt und am andern denselben Glauben tadelt, widerfichtet, lügstrafet und mit allerlei freveln Lästerworten antastet. Darum, wie ich [zu-] vor gesagt hab, befehlen wir Euch dem Urteil Gottes. Lehret, wie Ihrs vor Gott wölt verantwurten.
Koehler, *Z & L* II, 112–13; Bornkamm, 21; ZKG, 77. (1966) 313–14; Staehelin, *Briefe* II, 373.
[1] WA I, 30. 3. 96, 160–71; May, 67; Z VI ii, 521–3; Koehler, *Buch*, 306–12. Three copies were signed, two of which have been preserved, one in Kassel, one in Zurich. WA 30. 3, 101–9.
[2] Art. 15 has been frequently printed, e.g. Kidd, 254–5.
'Concerning the Supper of our Lord Jesus Christ we all believe and are convinced that it should be administered in both kinds according to the institution: that the mass is not a work

There was no confessional alliance, and in spite of the efforts of both Philip and Zwingli there was no military alliance either – on 5 October signs of plague, the English 'sweating sickness', were apparent in Marburg, and the Landgrave hurriedly rode away.[1] Luther returned to Wittenberg, convinced that he had won, that he had shown his opponents to be foolish, stupid and humiliated. From a distance he could still think of Zwingli as basically an arrogant peasant, obstinately wrong.[2]

Each side, in fact, was passionately convinced of its own uprightness and objectivity; each had thought things out, had discovered the way of salvation for all Christians, and having got it exactly right, was not prepared for any dilution, obfuscation or compromise. Luther was convinced that Zwingli was a perfect example of the man overthrown by pride, vainglory and self esteem – 'by that sin fell the angels'. The breach in the papal fortress had been opened for him and having this advantage he merely weakened the attack by his perversity. His double-talk, his wild speculations, his association with and likeness to Karlstadt, prince of sectaries, his boasting of his classical knowledge, were signs that Satan had entered into possession of his soul. In fact, he was both ignorant and disrespectful, his translation of the Bible was either a copy of Luther's own or a perversion of it. He had mixed politics with religion and had succumbed

through which any one may obtain grace for another whether living or dead, that the sacrament of the altar is the sacrament of the true body and blood of Christ and participation in it is in the highest degree necessary for every Christian. Likewise with regard to the use of the sacrament we agree that, like the Word, the sacrament has been handed to us by God's ordinance so that weak consciences may be led by the Holy Spirit to faith and enjoyment of the same.

'Likewise although we have not agreed at this moment whether the true body and blood of Christ be corporeally present in the bread and wine, none the less the one side should behave to the other with Christian charity as far as the conscience of each will allow, and both sides will fervently pray to Almighty God that he will confirm in us true understanding by his spirit.'

The Lutheran formula that Zwingli rejected ran: 'Wir bekennen, das auss vermög diser wort: "Das ist min lib, das ist mein blut" der lib und das blut Christi warhaftlich (hoc est) substantive et essentialiter, non autem quantitative vel qualitative vel localiter, im nachtmal gegenwertig sey und gegeben wird.' Koehler, *Rekonstruktion*, 131; A. W. Dieckhoff, *Der Schlussatz der Marburger Artikel und seine Bedeutung für die richtige Beurteilung des Verhältnisses der Confessionskirchen zur einander* (Rostock, 1872); H. A. van Bakel, *Zwingli oder Luther?* ZKG 52 (1933) 237–62. H. v. Schubert, *Die Anfänge evangelischer Bekenntnisbildung bis 1529/30*, SVRG 143 (Gütersloh, 1968).

[1] Bullinger, *Ref.* II, 232 implied that this caused the failure of the conference and that longer discussions would have been successful. There is no evidence to suggest that this was so. Koehler, *Festgabe*, 370. Bullinger's narrative, while careful and interesting, is highly tendentious and has small evidential value. He was not present. F. Blanke, *Der Junge Bullinger* (Zürich, 1942), 84. S. Hausammann (AKG 77 (1966) insists with some justice that the agreement was only apparent – 'eine Scheinkonkordie' – which each side signed in good faith placing different interpretations on what they signed. By June 1530 Luther was speaking of a 'simulata concordia' WA *Br.* 5. 340.

[2] WA 30. 3. 561; O. Farner, *Das Zwinglibild Luthers* (Tübingen, 1931), 18; J. Pelikan, *Obedient Rebels* (New York, 1964), 141.

330

to the enticement of the former. Unless, by God's grace, Zwingli should see the error of his ways before he died, his false doctrine must lead him to damnation. In most of this Luther was wrong as well as uncharitable in his judgement, but both antagonists were honest and outspoken. They lived for three nights under the same roof, and the Swiss in fact made a better immediate impression than had seemed likely. This image was all too soon blurred over after they parted, but it was something that it had been there at all.

Unfortunate as all this is, the Marburg meeting was of decisive importance. There is much to suggest that after the personal interview each regarded the other more highly even if Luther probably did much later let drop unguarded remarks in conversation which were recalled without their qualifications and thus exaggerated. They respected one another the more after 1529, and Zwingli's life was soon to end abruptly. They had set their hands to a common paper and they ceased to speak of one another as heretics or papalists; they had stated their cases and the eucharistic controversy died down a little – the differences were temporary and the discussion could be re-opened. They agreed not to attack one another publicly without due notice, a provision not very well kept. Zwingli had shown that he was no mere 'rationalist' but a man of deep faith and sincere conviction, one who could and did accept a real presence of Christ in the sacrament. Luther had come to Marburg convinced that his Swiss opponents were not only fanatics but also wild, quarrelsome barbarians. On the latter point, at any rate, he learnt that he was mistaken. Each side had spoken its mind frankly and completely, and each understood the other the better after it. There had been slight signs of real esteem and conciliation which, had Zwingli had more than two years to live, might have burgeoned into something of value. The Landgrave had indeed failed: there was no victor and no vanquished, but there was no united Protestant front either.[1] Nor was there to be later when Zwingli's mantle fell on one who in 1529 was a law student on his way to Bourges – John Calvin.

Luther had lived all his life in the secure traditions of the absolutist state. The prince, now of his own religious convictions, was there to be obeyed willingly and without question.[2] For the common people he had a kind of affectionate contempt: they were there to listen to their betters in church and state and do what the preacher and the government official told them. Democracy, the rule of 'Herr Omnes', was highly undesirable. Zwingli, on the other hand, understood a society based on the intelligent cooperation with the people. In his youth in Toggenburg he had lived in a

---

[1] Koehler, *Marburg*, 42. ZWA v (1930), 81–102, regards the long-term results of the Marburg meeting as impressive – the Württemberg concord (1534), the Wittenberg concord (1536) and perhaps some 'oecumenical' movements derive from it.
[2] Gussmann I i, 25 (and notes, 366, 368).

community in which decisions were taken by the farmers and herdsmen meeting to voice their opinions, and in his manhood he had lived in a city where every artisan could, and did, participate in government through his gild. As a patriotic Confederate, Zwingli not only accepted representative government, Swiss sixteenth-century pattern, but hardly knew any other. This meant that his case must be one that could be explained publicly and could be made intelligible to ordinary people. He had demonstrated that the Pope's religion was the false religion and that his own teaching was at once Bible founded and reasonable. His supporters understood the denial of transubstantiation; what they were not prepared to accept was any Lutheran compromise: if their leader moved in this direction he would lose the indispensable support of a government which, with all its limitations, was 'popular'. Hence his dislike and avoidance of phrases whose meaning was obscure or uncertain. He knew that the Word could not fail him and that he understood it correctly. This was not the case with his Lutheran opponents, and he would not accept any compromise solution. In 1529 he believed he could win over the Lutherans by argument, and then a united Protestant Switzerland would join forces with a Germany converted to his cause. He was sure he had convinced the Prince of Hesse who, as he wrote to Vadian,[1] now agreed to the free circulation of Zwinglian literature and the undisturbed preaching of its adherents. It was not by concession that the reformed churches would survive. And to maintain his position in Zurich, as also in Berne and Schaffhausen, against the Catholic sympathisers, he must reject any formula which could be misinterpreted.[2]

Zwingli returned with all speed to Zurich, which he reached on 19 October, while Luther with his friends reported to the Elector of Saxony what had happened. Philip of Hesse still hoped that Lutherans and Zwinglians, whom he continued to recognise and employ with almost ostentatious impartiality, could agree on political objectives if not on doctrine. He would gladly have taken Zwingli into his service[3] and he remained his friend. While the wordy disputes were continuing at Marburg, Vienna was being besieged, unsuccessfully as it proved, by the Turkish armies of Suleiman I, and Ferdinand, on behalf of the Emperor, was trying frantically to raise money and men to resist the onslaught. As soon, however, as the Turkish tide began to ebb, the German Lutherans had reason to fear a renewal of the attempt to enforce the Edict of Worms. For their own security they now needed external support. Zwingli was more convinced than ever after the Marburg meeting that Pope and Emperor were in close partnership, even that Charles V was hoodwinked by his

[1] Z x, 316–18; ZWA xiii, 293.   [2] Koehler, *Festgabe*, 372.
[3] Z x, 329 n. 1.

associate.[1] Earlier, Zwingli had been willing to cooperate with an Emperor from whom guaranteed security and justice might be expected, but this was no longer the case. The Habsburg menace was, in his view, so serious that all, Philip of Hesse with his allies, France, Venice, the south-German cities and the Christian Civic Union, should now close their ranks. Victory could then be assured.

This was not easy to obtain without concessions. The south-German conference at Schwabach (16–19 October), with its restatement of the Lutheran position, did not secure the adhesion of Strassburg and its supporters.[2] Philip of Hesse began to perceive that his plans for a broad Protestant front under himself as leader were no more acceptable to some of his German associates than they were to Berne and that the evangelical forces were more divided than ever. None the less cooperation in face of probable Catholic aggression was indispensable, and in December there was another meeting at Schmalkalden[3] of a group of princes (including the Elector of Saxony and the Landgrave of Hesse) and cities in an attempt to unite the Protestants. Again, this time partly because Bucer stood by the Zwinglian position, they parted without agreement, and renewed efforts at Biberach and Nuremberg were no more successful. The Swiss Protestant cities were not brought into the discussions, although delegates from Strassburg and Constance, members of the Christian Civic Union, were there. All that was achieved was a negative agreement that the Schwabach articles were not acceptable.[4] There was no common front.

By this time it was becoming apparent that the Emperor himself was preparing to intervene. The summons to the Diet of Augsburg[5] (April–September 1530) was accompanied by an invitation to the Protestants to state their case.[6] This was enhanced at a much lower level by a challenge to debate 404 theses (or counter-theses) put forward by Eck.[7] Statements of belief were hurriedly drafted by, or for, Constance, Memmingen, Heil-

---

[1] Hauswirth, *Philipp*, 151.
[2] Koehler, *Z & L* II, 164–9. See above 319–20.
[3] Schubert, *Bekenntnisbildung*, 117–37.
[4] Koehler *Z & L* II, 177–80.
[5] K. Brandi, *Kaiser Karl V.*[3] (Munich, 1941) 261–72; C. E. Förstemann, *Urkundenbuch zu der Geschichte des Reichstages zu Augsburg im Jahre 1530* Bd. 1 (erster Abschnitt) (Halle, 1833); Gussmann I. 1. 2; F. W. Schirrmacher, *Briefe und Acten zu der Geschichte des Religionsgespräches zu Marburg, 1529 und des Reichstages zu Augsburg, 1530* (Leipzig, 1876); K. Fuchs, 'Zur Politik der protestantischen Reichstände vor der Eröffnung des Augsburger Reichstags von 1530', *Zeitschrift für die Geschichte des Oberrheins*, 118 (1970) 157–74.
[6] The invitation had been 'to allay divisions, to leave all past errors to the judgement of our Saviour, and further, to give a charitable hearing to every man's opinions, thoughts and notions, to weigh them carefully, to bring men to Christian truth and to dispose of everything that has not been rightly explained on both sides'. A slightly different version in Kidd, 258 (21 January 1530).
[7] *Z* VI ii, 791 n. 6; *Z* X, 601; Baur II, 646; Koehler *Z & L* II, 181; K. Rischar, *Johann Eck, auf dem Reichstag zu Augsburg* (Münster, 1968) esp. 84–6. For a translation of the 404 theses see S. M. Jackson (ed.), *Papers of the American Society of Church History* 2. II, 37–81 (New York, 1910).

bronn, Ulm, Nuremberg and the Elector of Saxony, all different and out o line with the Zwinglian case. It was Philip of Hesse who tried to promote Protestant unity and to secure some kind of agreed statement which could be acceptable to the south German cities and to Zurich. In this he found some support from Strassburg, where Sturm was anxious to play down differences within the Protestant camp and to attempt to cover up the gap revealed at Marburg and widened at Schmalkalden. In March 1530 the 'Torgau articles' restated the Lutheran case and these were embodied by Melanchthon into the 'Confessio Augustana'.

The Strassburg party, led by Bucer, Capito and Sturm, worked out a compromise statement, neither fully Zwinglian nor precisely Lutheran, somewhat ambiguous and obscure, but reasonably comprehensive. This was formally accepted on 4 July 1530 by the cities of Constance, Lindau and Memmingen – hence the name, Tetrapolitana[1] – and sent to Augsburg. Although it attracted some attention both then and later, it had been hurriedly compiled; Ulm, Heilbronn, Kempten, Isny and Biberach refused to be associated with it; and it was soon rejected by all parties. Luther, Melanchthon, Oecolampadius, Zwingli, Basle, Zurich and the remaining south German cities all disowned it.[2] The Lutheran case, composed by Melanchthon and revised by Luther himself, who, like Zwingli, was ready to appear in person at Augsburg but was excluded as an 'outlaw', was impressive. It was as moderate as it could be made, emphasised the divergences from the Zwinglians, and became almost the official Lutheran creed.[3] The Lutheran teaching on salvation by faith, marriage of priests, monastic vows, auricular confession and communion in two kinds is set out at length and, in a sense, for the last time. Other German cities sent in their own rather similar statements. Ulm, where Zwingli's friend Sam had once been so influential, was now completely in the Lutheran camp. But neither Philip of Hesse nor Zwingli was in the least prepared to concede defeat. The Landgrave had already, in April 1529, joined in an alliance with Electoral Saxony, Nürnberg, Strassburg and Ulm for the maintenance of their faith and was disappointed that Saxony was singularly reluctant to act. Both Luther and Melanchthon, back in

---

[1] H. A. Niemeyer, *Collectio confessionum in ecclesiis reformatis publicatarum* (Leipzig, 1840) 740ff; E. F. C. Müller, *Die Bekenntnisschriften der reformierten Kirche* (Leipzig, 1903), 55–78; *Martin Bucers deutsche Schriften* Bd. 3, hg. v. R. Stupperich (Gütersloh, 1969), 36–185.

[2] E. Bizer, *Studien zur Geschichte des Abendmahlstreits im 16. Jahrhundert* (Darmstadt, 1962) 28-37; Gussmann I i, 44–6, with notes on 385–7; H. Eells, 'Sacramental negotiations at the Diet of Augsburg 1530', *Princeton Theological Review* 23 (1925) 216–18; Koehler, *Z & L* II, 193–8, 208.

[3] Kidd, 259–89. There are many reprints, e.g. *Die unveränderte Augsburgische Konfession*, hg. v. P. Tschackert (Leipzig, 1901); *Die Bekenntnisschriften der evangelisch-lutherischen Kirche*³ (Göttingen, 1956) 31–137. Charles refused to allow the Augsburg Confession to be printed or copied. Z XI, 279 n. 15.

Wittenberg, were increasingly unwilling to cooperate with Swiss 'fanatics', and said so. And, too, they were opposed to armed combat; they wanted no compromise but no war either.[1]

For Philip the situation was different.[2] Either he must maintain his independent position, politically as well as in religion, or he must submit. He knew that the Emperor was being urged by Campeggio, the Papal legate, to eliminate heresy with fire and sword,[3] and could hardly fail to perceive that the policy of the Catholic advisers of the Emperor was to divide Lutherans from Zwinglians and crush them in detail. Philip of Hesse and Zwingli were ready to fight; the Elector of Saxony and Luther were not. If Philip was to maintain his position in his own territory and support the rights of Ulrich of Württemberg and those of his fellow Protestant princes, he needed above all the aid of the cities, including those of the Christian Civic Union, wealthy, well defended by their walls, advised by patricians of political experience and with soldiers of disciplined valour.

The Diet of Augsburg was opened by Charles in person who showed his faith by walking bare-headed in the hot June sun behind the Host through the streets of the Protestant city on the feast of Corpus Christi (16 June). When he set up a mixed commission[4] to comment on the Augsburg Confession and it was glaringly apparent that no account would be taken of Strassburg or Zurich, the Prince of Hesse, who was ready to accept both the Augsburg Confession and the Tetrapolitana,[5] left in disgust[6] on 6 August. A Catholic confutation of the Augsburg Confession added fuel to the flames.

Zwingli, disappointed at not being invited to Augsburg,[7] was determined that his case should not remain unstated, the more so since Sturm and Oecolampadius urged him to write. He therefore composed his own *Fidei Ratio*[8] during the last days of June. The speed with which it was written is a measure of the deep sincerity and the intensity of conviction behind it. In it he first declares his belief in God the Creator, perfect goodness,

[1] R. Stupperich, *Melanchthon* (Berlin, 1960), 70-1. [2] See below 378–383, 391.
[3] Gussmann, I i, 3.
[4] Of 14 members, 7 Catholic, 7 Protestant, mostly clerics. J. Ficker, *Die Konfutation des Augsburgischen Bekenntnisses, ihre erste Gestalt und ihre Geschichte* (Leipzig, 1891).
[5] Koehler *Z & L* II, 193-4.
[6] H. Grundmann, 'Landgraf Philipp von Hessen auf dem Augsburger Reichstag 1530', in *Aus den Reichstagsakten der 15. und 16. Jahrhunderts* (Göttingen, 1958); also in SVR No. 176 Jg. 63 (Gütersloh, 1959) 6–87.
[7] Z x, 525, 573 n. 7, 629, 633-4, 644; ZWA 5 (1931) 243; Gussmann I i, 30, and notes on 373-4. Luther and Zwingli were not admitted; Erasmus deliberately absented himself. A discussion between the three in 1530 would indeed have been interesting.
[8] Z VI ii, 753-784, 790-817 (in German in ZH Bd. XI (1948) 255-93); ZWA V, 242-58; Baur II, 653ff; F. Blanke, 'Zwinglis "Fidei Ratio" (1530) Entstehung und Bedeutung', ARG 57 (1966) 96-102. It was translated into English by Thomas Cotsforde (STC 26138 (1543), 26139 (1548), 26140 (1555)).

12-2

truth, power, righteousness and wisdom, Father, Son and Holy Spirit, as set out in the Nicene and Athanasian creeds. Then he affirms the incarnation, Christ son of man, son of God for all eternity, with some emphasis on the completeness of his humanity save for his earthly sinlessness. It is all correct and adequate, the accepted teaching of atonement. Christ suffered as man, as God he forgave sins and, having gone so far along the commonplace track, very adroitly, Zwingli introduces his favourite device of alloeosis. In what sense was it that the son of God suffered for us, or the son of man forgave sins?[1] With considerable acuteness he examines the implications of transfers of meaning in the Bible, as well as the difference between body and spirit, matter and mind. Christ, both God and man, suffered death only in his humanity, and from this, important deductions followed.

Zwingli, for example, was no longer, when he wrote in 1530, infralapsarian, for God could not be made dependent upon the action of his own creature, man; God therefore had created man, who would fall, God the son being ready, in time, to take on man's nature and thus redeem what Adam lost.[2] It is indispensable for any understanding of the thought of the age to remember that the direct descent of the human race from Adam was assumed as a certain historical fact with all the consequences that followed from it. For Zwingli, God, holy and merciful, could not be influenced or affected by human action; God being completely just, man must be punished after the fall; completely good, God sent his son in whom goodness and justice were reconciled by his unique sacrifice.[3]

Hence it followed, and here there was no conflict with the Confession of Augsburg, that Christ was the only mediator between God and man; justification by works was eliminated. Zwingli even went some way to meet his critics in his discussion of the implications of original sin for the many infants who died, sometimes unbaptised, within a few days or hours of birth. Earlier he had maintained that babies, sinning unconsciously, were not thereby condemned, but now, as at Marburg, although avoiding as far as possible the phrase 'original sin', which he obviously found difficult to do, he agreed that a weakness, an inescapable proneness to sin, was inborn; the fate of children of heathens, following necessarily the condition of their parents, was completely uncertain. Christian children, part of the visible church of Christ, had better hope.

This led somewhat abruptly to a brief discussion of the meaning of the invisible church,[4] known to God alone, and the visible, sensible church of all who professedly recognised Christ, this visible church including some,

---

[1] I Peter 2. 21, John 3. 13. Z VI ii, 794.
[2] For Zwingli's views on predestination see above, 324–5. Some of his ideas may well have been derived from Lactantius, 'the Christian Cicero', whom he much admired. ZWA XIII (1971), 380.   [3] Z VI, ii, 795–6.   [4] Z VI ii, 800–2.

like Judas, who were not numbered among the elect. Faith was the test: certainty of faith meant certainty of election. The visible church would necessarily include some who were unworthy, none knowing who these were, and the visible Church itself is composed of particular local churches like those of Rome, Augsburg and Lyons.

Then came the restatement, crisp and clear after the Marburg discussion, of the Zwinglian teaching on the sacraments. At this point the treatise takes on a highly 'spiritual' tone. Grace, forgiveness, consideration and help must come as God's gift directly to the spirit of the recipient. It could not be brought (*conferre, adferre, dispensare*) by sensible means, not even by the wind or the word, still less by water, bread and wine or the oil of extreme unction. *Spiritus fuit, qui tulit, non sensibilia* was the basis of Zwingli's confession,[1] the dividing line which allied him, most unwillingly, with some sectaries and divided him from Catholics and Lutherans alike.

He knew the scholastic formulas as well as his opponents – to receive God's grace you must be prepared for it, and this either by self-preparation or by the Holy Spirit. If by preparing ourselves we qualify for grace, then there is no need for that special 'prevenient' grace predisposing to repentance; if we are prepared by the Holy Spirit without a sacrament, then the Holy Spirit brings grace before the sacrament. For Zwingli, the two sacraments of baptism and the eucharist were testimonies of grace already personally received. Thus, whereas for Catholics and Lutherans baptism brings grace, or grace accompanies the action, for Zwingli grace precedes baptism. For children, too, God's promise precedes the baptism of which it is a sign. It is necessary in order that others may know what has come to pass, that there should be a public acknowledgment of an accomplished fact. The sacraments do not, cannot, bring grace or anything else, they are the outward and visible signs of it. The sacraments were indeed honourable and valuable; the Word, brought to the objects, made them so,[2] but this is all that happened.

Briefly brushing off the Anabaptists, and by implication accepting the imperial approval at Speier in April 1529 of their elimination, Zwingli states his own eucharistic convictions. 'I believe that in the holy communion the true body of Christ is present in the mind of the believer.'[3]

---

[1] Z VI ii, 803; Koehler, *Z & L* II, 201.

[2] Zwingli yet again quotes St Augustine 'accedit enim verbum ad elementum, et fit sacramentum'. MPL 35. c. 1840.

[3] Z VI ii, 806. 'Credo, quod in sacra eucharistiae (hoc est: gratiarum actionis) coena verum Christi corpus adsit fidei contemplatione...Sed quod Christi corpus per essentiam et realiter, hoc est: corpus ipsum naturale, in cena aut adsit aut ore dentibusque nostris manducatur, quemadmodum papistae et quidam, qui ad ollas Egiiptiacas respectant, perhibent, id vero non tantum negamus, sed errorem esse, qui verbo dei adversatur, constanter adseveramus.' The words '*fidei contemplatione*' seem to have been used here for the first time. Koehler *Z & L* II, 214, 216–17; Z XI, 41.

'But that the actual, real body of Christ is present in the communion or is consumed by our mouth and teeth as is maintained by the papists and some who long for the flesh pots of Egypt,[1] is something that we not only deny but we consistently maintain that it is an error and contrary to the Scriptures.' There was no change of substance, nor even was (as Luther maintained) the body of Christ objectively present: it was in the grateful conscious remembrance of his death that Christ was present for the believer.

The glorified body of the risen Christ, seated on God's right hand, the manhood of the Saviour, remained in heaven (the earth being thought of as the centre of the universe) and could not be brought down to earth to be eaten. Scripture taught this clearly enough; Christ in his divinity, being God the Son, was everywhere at all times. The bread eaten at the Last Supper, like the Passover lamb, was symbolical only.[2] The soul, being spiritual, could not be nourished by physical substance, and this (for Zwingli) obvious truth was reinforced by the circumstances of the Last Supper itself. The disciples did not receive forgiveness of sins on that occasion, for, had this been so, then the suffering on the cross was in vain. Similarly, it was Christ's earthly and human body that was then present; any other interpretation would imply, with the Marcionites, that Christ's passion was unreal if his body was not as other human bodies.

With many biblical citations and with confident claim of support from St Augustine and St Ambrose, with a reference to his own writings and to a new exposition by Oecolampadius[3] which answered Melanchthon, *Fidei ratio* leaves this central theme as abruptly as it entered, without any suggestion of compromise on this issue with Lutherans or Catholics. That the Emperor ever saw the manifesto addressed to him is unlikely, but he and any other readers were not left in any doubt about the independence and the precision of the statement before them.

The remainder was equally straightforward but more acceptable if not conciliatory. Church ceremonial Zwingli manifestly disliked, but such traditional usages as were neither obviously superstitious nor contrary to the Bible could be tolerated until greater enlightenment[4] prevailed. Then, without undue offence and making allowance for those weak in faith, they should be abolished. Jesus, he noted, had allowed Mary of Bethany to

---

[1] i.e. Lutherans.

[2] Z VI ii, 809–10.

[3] *Quid de eucharistia veteres tum Graeci, tum Latini senserint, Dialogus* (Basle, 1530), replying to Melanchthon's *Sentenciae veterum aliquot scriptorum de Coena Domini* (Wittenberg, 1530), cf. E. Staehelin, *Das theologische Lebenswerk Johannes Oekolampads* (Leipzig, 1939), 608ff; Koehler, *Z & L* II, 204–7.

[4] Z VI ii, 812: 'donec Lucifer magis ac magis allucescat'. The implication seems to have been that the darkness of the Middle Ages was just then (1530) giving way before the dawn of a new era.

anoint his feet[1] (John 12. 3). Images, reverenced and honoured in churches, were explicitly unbiblical and had long before been ejected where Reform penetrated in Switzerland: maintaining this position, he none the less repeated his personal appreciation of pictorial and statuary art when unconnected with undesirable proclivities. Just as there should be no images, so, too, no organ was needed in church, although, personally, Zwingli was both art-lover and talented musician.[2]

There was very little of the olive branch here, but there was more of it in the section dealing with preaching or prophesying. On the importance of the preacher, Lutherans and Zwinglians were agreed, and they were also both opposed to the radical assertion that any illiterate who felt so inspired could demand of right to occupy a pulpit. The exposition of the Word was a serious business, to be undertaken by the successors of the Old Testament prophets, trained and competent – unlike some of the mitred crook-bearing bishops of the old Church. Preaching preceded faith, which came from the Holy Spirit only and was not carried by the word, which could but prepare the worthy recipient. How otherwise was it possible to accept the notorious fact that some heard and were not convinced?[3] The preacher should provide indispensable information, teach, console, serve, care for the sick and the poor, study and expound the Bible. It was a full assignment, and one which Luther, as well as Zwingli and Oecolampadius, imposed upon himself.

Ministers of religion were neither above the government nor wholly subject to it. Here, too, he was more in harmony with the Augsburg Confession than with the Anabaptists, and very briefly but incisively he again faced the problem of the relations of Church and state.[4] The righteousness and justice of God were the province of the magistrate, whose duty it was to see that these were upheld; if, however, a government was despotic and bad, it was none the less to be obeyed until such time as God made it abundantly and unmistakably apparent that the tyrant must be deposed – 'if a chance of liberty should come, take it.' (1 Cor. 7. 21.)

Finally, almost traditionally, Zwingli turned to *memorare novissima*, the Last Things, death, hell and judgement. Purgatory was, for him, as for

---

[1] Zwingli thought (as did Bishop Fisher) that the three Marys, Mary of Bethany, Mary Magdalene and the third unidentified (Luke 7. 36–50; 8. 2) were identical.

[2] 'The devil cannot have all the best tunes' was part of his attitude. J. Schweizer, *Reformierte Abendmahlsgestaltung in der Schau Zwinglis* (Basle, n.d.), deals with some of the liturgical effects of Zwingli's Eucharistic teaching – especially with *Aktion oder Bruch des Nachtmahls* (1525). [3] Z VI ii, 813–14.

[4] For his earlier thought on the subject, see R. C. Walton, *Zwingli's Theocracy* (Toronto, 1967); Jacob Kreutzer, *Zwinglis Lehre von der Obrigkeit*, (Stuttgart, 1909) (Kirchenrechtliche Abhandlungen hg. v. Dr Ulrich Stutz. 57. Heft); Oechsli, *3* and, most valuable, L. von Muralt, 'Zum Problem der Theokratie bei Zwingli, *Discordia Concors* (Basle 1968) II, 369–90; see above 119–121.

Luther and the English church, 'a fond thing, vainly invented, and grounded upon no warranty of Scripture, but rather repugnant to the word of God'.[1] Hence, indulgences and masses said for the repose of the souls of the departed were worthless. The torments of purgatory were figments of the imagination, dwelt upon by priests in order to extract money from the credulous. If by finite torment and suffering the guilt of man's evil deeds could be cleared, Christ's death was in vain and God's grace of no effect. What sort of Christians are they who fear this fire, which is, in any case, but smoke?

But as to hell, where unbelievers, contumacious and wicked persons[2] were punished by eternal flames, 'not only do I believe in it, I know it to be true'. Those who, like the Anabaptists, thought in terms of anything less than eternity,[3] were deceived and deceived others. It was a gloomy ending, but orthodox, as had been the beginning.

On this basis he was confident and ready to fight, over-confident, indeed, but more convinced than ever that he was God's instrument, that his teaching was that of God's word, that Rome could not and would not reform itself but that the Emperor might well be guided by God and come over to the side of reform. Politically it was pathetic – so far from being an eirenicon, it alienated still further Catholics, Lutherans and the Radicals. Uncompromising in its rugged independence, it was, like so much of Zwingli's hurried writings, imperfect and inadequate. *Fidei ratio* could have been his *Christianae religionis institutio*, but it was neither complete nor conciliatory. It had no influence whatever on those to whom it was addressed, although Zwingli seriously hoped for the Emperor's conversion. It came too late to influence either the Augsburg Confession or the Tetrapolitana, and Luther, who had been mollified somewhat by the personal encounter at Marburg, returned to his former attitude of adamantine hostility.[4]

From the Catholic side came a formal refutation[5] written by Eck, but apart from this *Fidei Ratio* was ignored. Eck's reply insisted that Zwingli was no Christian but a Turk, a Tartar, a Hun, a Nebuchadnezer, Antio-

---

[1] Article 22.   [2] Z VI ii, 815: 'perfidi, contumaces ac perduelles'.
[3] 'Apokatastasis panton', lasting only until the day of judgement.
[4] 'Ich bekenne fur mich, das ich den Zwingel fur einen unchristen halte mit aller seiner lere, denn er helt und leret kein stück des Christlichen glaubens recht.' WA 26, 342. Melanchthon likewise regarded Zwingli as of unstable mind. Baur II 668; WA *Br.* 5. 475. cf. O. Farner, *Das Zwinglibild Luthers* (Tübingen, 1931); Geiser, 91; WA 30. III, 561; WA 54, 141–67.
[5] *Repulsio articulorum Zwinglii Caesareae Maiestati oblatorum Johanne Eccio authore 1530 in Julio* (Augsburg, 1530). Zwingli made an effective and telling reply, *Ad illustrissimos Germaniae Principes Augustae congregatos, de convitiis Eccii epistola*, addressed significantly to the princes. S IV, 19–41; Baur II, 676–85; W. Koehler, *Der Augsburger Reichstag von 1530 und die Schweiz* SZG 3 (1953), 169–89. K. Rischar, *Johann Eck auf dem Reichstag zu Augsburg 1530* (Münster i.W., 1968) esp. 106–7.

chus and Heliodorus. In Zurich profanity was supreme; instead of churches they had stables. They had burnt the monastery at Ittingen, received heretics from Rottweil, and fought their fellow countrymen. Zwingli was utterly divided from Luther, had been afraid to come to Baden, and had been the originator of Anabaptism.

Unaffected by all this, still serenely confident, Zwingli returned to politics and to unrealities. Having failed with Charles V, he would win over Francis I, and to do so he would sacrifice some of his earlier and most cherished convictions. He had only fifteen months to live after this manifesto of 1530, and in them he succeeded in undoing much, but not all, of what he had so far accomplished. When he left Marburg in October 1529, Zwingli knew that the German Lutherans would and must go their own way. Hence, he now urged a defensive alliance on a basis of recognition of existing differences – the two ideologies could unite against the Emperor and Rome.[1]

The story of the relations between Luther and Zwingli is one of the saddest in the history of religion. Here were two utterly committed and devout Christian scholars, men of prayer, convinced of every facet of the revelation of God through his son and through the Word, preachers whose first duty it was to call men to repentance. Their faith was all sustaining and their convictions unshakable. Each, too, knew that the followers of the Pope had left the paths laid down for the church by Christ and the Apostles and that a return to the teaching of the scriptures was incumbent upon all.

Each was a minister of religion in the best sense, seeking neither gain nor personal glory, indefatigable in the defence and exposition of the faith. Each served faithfully his temporal lord, whether a German Elector or a Swiss republic. To say that they parted company over the interpretation of four words is true but unhelpful. There could be but one way of eternal salvation through Christ and the forgiveness of the sins of the world which he embodied. To misunderstand his teaching was to imperil the soul. All eternity depended upon the choice of the right path; to be turned aside from it was to become as much the child of wrath and the son of perdition as the man who committed the unforgivable sin of blasphemy against the Holy Spirit. No amount of temperance, justice, fortitude, mercy, helpfulness to others, prayer or works, could compensate. Faith was indispensable, God-given and not to be questioned, but it must be the true faith, certain and sure. The dispute at Marburg was much more than a

---

[1] This was the position taken up by Philip of Hesse, who never explicitly accepted either the Lutheran or the Zwinglian sacramental teaching but who consistently tried to separate politics from dogma. Zwingli went along with this only in so far as the triumph of the evangelical faith was of supreme importance and politics must be used for this purpose. Gussmann I i, 60–2.

dispute about words; the meaning of the Last Supper involved the whole Christian faith. The atheist, the agnostic and the non-Christian may see the disagreement as either meaningless or an intellectual debate about abstractions. To the sixteenth century it was a matter that affected every baptised person; confession of a true faith opened the door to eternal salvation; without it, the door was closed. That, in some measure, was why men were willing to die for their convictions and even to kill those whom they believed to be in the wrong.

There was indeed an element of vanity about both men. Their background, training and human purposes were different, and neither could think it possible that he might be mistaken. Each lacked humility, and their collision kept half the Christian world divided across the ages. The repercussions of the Marburg conference are felt in the twentieth century, for such is the power of history. Luther and Zwingli could not, in the world of 1529, have found harmony, whatever the good will. And it must be said that it was Zwingli's resistance, warmly seconded by Oecolampadius, that may have prevented an *Anschluss* with Rome which, as later events were to prove, could have been disastrous for religious and intellectual freedom.

14

The gathering storm

It is difficult for the twentieth century to comprehend the violence and the deep feelings aroused by the controversies of the sixteenth. Anyone living after 1900 is aware of a mainly secularised and materially oriented world in which varied religious beliefs and gradations of disbelief are universal. Since Zwingli's day the Council of Trent and the wars of religion have been followed by eighteenth-century Enlightenment and nineteenth-century Evolution, Marxism and modernism. Zwingli and Luther were trained in the scholasticism of the later Middle Ages and could no more cast it off than even a comparable religious leader of today can escape from an education in which scientific criticism however superficial, and historical perspective however slight, have had their part. In 1529 the protagonists had all the world to gain: there were possibilities of Protestant union and of a compromise with Rome. The infidel Turk could be expelled and the light of the Gospel brought to Mohammedans, Hindus, Chinese and the Indians of the New World. If, and it was far from unthinkable, all Switzerland was united in a reformed faith to which Lutherans and Anabaptists could adhere, in alliance with a Protestant France and England, Europe might well be of one evangelical conviction.

The Marburg religious summit of 1529, important as it in the history of religion, was nevertheless also conditioned by the state of central European politics and the situation that year in Switzerland. For four years at least Zurich had been the focus of divisions which were political as well as religious. These now came to a head in a series of alliances and groupings which themselves had a considerable history behind them and which greatly enhanced the influence of the new evangelical city-states.

A fifteenth-century Swiss or south German city was at once a fortress, a market and an administrative and judicial centre. It managed its own affairs and usually controlled the countryside around; sometimes, as with Zurich, Basle and Berne, it did so as actual ruler; sometimes, as at Constance and St Gall, there was no outside territory to rule; while such authority as was exercised by smaller places like Bremgarten, Zofingen, Burgdorf and Payerne, was subject to limitations of treaties or custom.

343

German cities had long since learned to cooperate for trade and protection so that, ever since the thirteenth century, civic alliances – a Lombard League, a Hanseatic League, a Swabian League – were almost commonplaces. In Switzerland such local arrangements, known as *Burgrecht*,[1] involved something closely approaching co-citizenship. An independent city had exclusive jurisdiction over its own citizens, one of whose most valued privileges was that they could not be forced to plead before foreign tribunals; reciprocity in this between different cities brought commercial and legal advantages without any loss of internal authority. What was good for trade was also good politics, and, with the steady weakening of imperial or aristocratic authority, much of Switzerland and South Germany was covered with networks of inter-city cooperative agreements. The Swiss Confederation itself was a kind of loose extension of the same principle.

The spread of the Reformation enhanced the authority of the cities where it was accepted, in that they now no longer recognised any concomitant jurisdiction of bishop, abbot or pope, and were able to insist that clerics were just as much subject to their laws and customs as were other inhabitants. At the same time growth of power and wealth tended to intensify the age-long traditional rivalry of town and country; either you were a resident citizen with voting rights, inherited or acquired; or you were a villager, subject to city-made orders which had to be obeyed. In the chief 'civic' states, Basle, Berne, Schaffhausen, Zurich, there were, on the one hand, the nobles and citizens, with voting rights and status, inherited or acquired; on the other, the subjects, whether unfranchised residents or the farmers and labourers in the fields, who had to submit to the directions of the governing council. Contrasted with these civic states were their rural counterparts, Glarus, Uri, Schwyz, Nid-und-Ob-Walden and Zug most obviously, the homes of herdsmen and agriculturalists as distinct from artisans and traders. To this can be added the inevitable rivalry of the mountain-dwellers and those of the plains. In one respect, however, they all agreed. It was everywhere the recognised duty of every government, whether civic or rural, to secure the obedience of all its subjects. In this there was little difference between them. It is important to realise what self-government meant in sixteenth-century Switzerland. If the citizens chose the councils which governed them, so, too, in the country states, every male adult had a nominal voice in the choice of his masters; but, in practice, in town and country alike, a small minority of members of well-known families dominated all administrations. Government, without a police force, over men accusomed to self-help, was not always an easy matter when dealing with obstinate, illiterate and prejudiced country folk

[1] Bender, *Ref.*, esp. 11–38.

whose main aim was to obtain good prices for their produce which the city-dwellers wanted to buy as cheaply as possible.

Divergent as the city-states were from the rural communities, prior to the Reformation the divergences were less in practice than in theory. Both were involved in the intricate network of alliances, treaties, agreements and understandings which held together the Swiss Confederation, with its allies and associates; but the structure was radically changed by the religious controversies of the 1520s. Cooperation became much more difficult when heresy intervened.

It is difficult for an age which finds even profound religious differences hard to understand, while being only too well aware of the passions aroused by race and ideology, to appreciate the detestation with which the heretic was regarded in the sixteenth century by good Catholics. His mistaken views made him a positive danger to society, for he could imperil the souls of his hearers; he was a rotten bough to be cut off, an anti-social figure to be shunned, a limb of Satan, the enemy of God.

What applied to an individual applied also to a community; there must be no association with those who had removed themselves from the church, outside which there was no salvation. If the Evil One was powerful enough to protect them from the extermination which was right and just, so much the worse, but at any rate there was no call to be associated with them in civic alliances or federal pact. Later, these feelings were transferred to the other side, and good Protestants, convinced that the Pope was Antichrist and his followers perverse idolaters, could not consider them as fellow-Christians. To misinterpret revealed religion was worse than to reject it; there was hope for the non-believer, but none for the mis-believer. Hence, a league between a wholly Catholic city such as Lucerne and a Zwinglian St Gall or semi-Lutheran Schaffhausen became increasingly impossible. None the less, there was also a strong consciousness of common Swiss interests, pride in past successes and a recognition of the need for easy exchange of commodities and for protection by mutual defence. These advantages had been painfully acquired; to lose them might mean falling under foreign (i.e. French, Italian or Imperial) domination. Hence there was a strong reluctance to depart from long tried agreements and understandings. If, however, religion were to force the break up of these, then compensation might well be sought elsewhere.

The Swiss Reformation started in the city of Zurich, was adopted by and for the whole state and spread to other cities, St Gall, Berne, Basle, Biel, Schaffhausen. The continuously Catholic states were the naturally conservative country areas which therefore felt an increasing sense of isolation and that the gap between them and the cities was widening. Hence the search for external support. Religious convictions slowly intensified, and thus cooperation between communities which had much to offer one another, such as Fribourg and Berne, when one was Catholic and the other Zwinglian, became increasingly difficult and rare, if not impossible. By 1528 the Catholics were manifestly determined to boycott the Zwinglians, who were becoming more apprehensive of the implications of outlawry as Lutherans, and even of a possible imperial armed attack upon themselves. Consequently both sides sought to defend themselves by renewed or original inter-city agreements, out of which grew a league of civic co-religionists. This extension, being also an assurance of wider Gospel preaching, Zwingli eagerly fostered and forwarded.

The Swiss Confederation was far from forming a coherent entity – it was rather a loose alliance of separate communities. The Swiss Diet consisted of thirteen states the majority of which remained Catholic; if therefore decisions were to depend upon the votes of a majority of states, Catholic control would have been continuously assured. Majority rule, however, had not yet come into fashion. Unanimity was expected if common action was to be taken; otherwise, no decision was reached. Further, the sovereign states were in no sense equal; Berne and Zurich compared with Zug and Uri were like California and Texas compared with Rhode Island and Delaware, equal only in name. Members attended Federal Diets as delegates only, and decisions about actions to be taken was a matter for their masters. No state could be 'expelled from' the Diet, but if Catholic and Protestant delegates could not meet because Catholics would not sit in the same chamber as heretics, then the Confederation would practically be dissolved. How close it came to this after 1530 is a theme upon which Swiss historians do not like to dwell.

The Confederation had come into being as a defensive alliance against a common Habsburg enemy; slowly its members learned the value of limited common action, and this, in turn, not only had enabled the Burgundian threat from Charles the Rash to be beaten, but also demonstrated that, acting together, the states possessed very great military advantages. Defence led inevitably to aggression and to territorial expansion north and south. At different times and under varied conditions Thurgau, Baden, Rapperswil, the Freie Aemter, Uznach, Gaster, Sargans, the Rheintal, the Ultramontane districts, Livinental, Eschantal, Maiental, Locarno, Riviera, Blenio, Bellinzona, Lugano, with the western fragments of Grasburg, Echallens and the county of Neuchâtel (Neuenburg), had passed into common possession. Of these Mandated Territories (*Gemeine Herrschaften*), those in the north-east, Thurgau, Rheintal, Uznach, Gaster and Sargans, offered special problems, the more so since they were all geographically linked with the considerable possessions of the Prince Abbot of St Gall, whose peculiar position has already received some consideration.

It is convenient, and not entirely inaccurate, to speak of the Swiss Confederation as the 'ruler' of these Mandated Territories, although, in fact, this meant certain groups of Confederates at the time of annexation and thus Basle, Schaffhausen and Appenzell, as late arrivals, were non-participants here. To these territories the governing states (meeting in Diet) appointed *Vögte* (Lords Lieutenant, governors or 'bailiffs'), an office taken in turn by nominees of the trustee powers, these officers having dignity, authority and a handsome salary.[1] In addition they could, and did, recruit mercenary soldiers and were appropriately rewarded for this. A Mandated Territory, such as Thurgau, was thus a valued possession. The Five Inner States esteemed their share in these conquests the more highly because of their own relative poverty; they also were insistent that the Catholic faith should prevail there.

After the triumph of Lutheranism in Saxony, it became the custom in Germany for subjects to accept and follow the religion of their rulers, and this, after 1525, slowly came to be the practice in Switzerland as well. Thus when the governments of Berne and Basle decided for Protestantism, the Catholics had to conform, or, like Erasmus, to leave. What, however, if the rulers were themselves divided? Were the inhabitants to change their faith with a change of governor?

A governorship brought both personal prestige and wealth. It was therefore particularly highly coveted in the poor Inner States as eminently desirable. In Zurich and Berne this was only slightly less attractive, for in them other opportunities for enrichment by trade and commerce existed. Hence in any rivalry over the Mandated Territories the Inner States were likely to be more tenacious of their rights of nomination of governors than their rivals, and peculiarly unwilling to relinquish them. If, because the Catholics controlled a majority of states, they could establish the principle that only a Catholic governor could be appointed to control Catholic territory, they would hope for financial as well as political gain. But how far were the northern Mandated Territories one hundred per cent Catholic? Were their inhabitants to be allowed to hear the 'pure word of God' read and expounded?

Zurich after 1525 was certainly not willing to accept any arrangement that prevented the Gospel from being preached freely in any area over which its jurisdiction, even partially or temporarily, stretched. It now seemed deplorable that mass was said at all in an area like Thurgau, and its cessation was called for. Equally, Zurich had consistently opposed mercenary service and was therefore most unwilling that recruiting should go on in such districts. Apart from military aid either for defence or offence, the Swiss Confederates recognised no obligations one to another. Religious

[1] EA 4, 1b, 1601–2.

347

affairs were matters for the individual governments, not for the Confederation.[1] Therefore there neither need be, nor should be, a combined religious policy in the Mandated Territories. This principle had been acceptable enough when unity of belief was taken for granted, but after Zurich had rejected communion with Rome, the picture changed. Zwingli now again maintained that in these districts reformed preaching and worship should be allowed freely, and that if any community (i.e. the adult males) called for a change it should be permitted for its own particular parish (*Gemeinde*). When a majority of these were so converted, the whole district might follow.[2]

There was one important difference of approach between the Zwinglian and the Catholic states. Zwingli did not believe in compulsion in matters of faith – 'der Glaub liess sich nicht mit Gewalt eingehen' – and coercion was not recommended.[3] He was completely convinced that the Gospel had only to be preached for it to prevail, such was the power of the Word. There might, indeed, be a kind of saturation preaching, for there could never be too much of a good thing, but actual physical force was never to be used to bring about conversion. Direct public opposition to the Bible, of course, was a different matter and not to be tolerated. Only too often it was the pensioners, recipients of money from foreign Catholic powers, who were, in Zwingli's view, the chief opponents of the evangelicals. He was therefore the more anxious to secure their elimination as they also represented the mercenary service of which he so much disapproved.

These notions were quite unacceptable to his opponents. They were accustomed to the Inquisition; heretics had always been burnt out. Where they shared a joint responsibility for Mandated Territories they could not connive at the admission of heresy. They insisted that the Confederation had accepted, on occasion, in disputed issues, the prevalence of the wishes of the majority of independent states.[4] Normally the state whose turn it

---

[1] The principle, so congenial to Berne (see above 249, 251, below 375), was re-stated in February 1527. 'Weil die Bünde, laut des Buchstabens, sich nicht auf den Glauben, sondern allein auf äusserliche Dinge beziehen...ohne Rucksicht auf den Glauben'; 'nit uf den glouben und seel, sonders uf beschirmung land, lüt, witwen, weisen, bewarung der eren, handhabung des rechten, beschützung vor gewalt und der glichen üsserlich sachen belangend'. EA 4, 1a, 1050 (No. 420), 1063 (No. 426), cf. G. Meyer von Knonau, *Aus der schweizerischen Geschichte in der Zeit der Reformation und Gegenreformation* HZ 40 (1878) 127.

[2] Berne and Zurich agreed in 1528 (EA 4, 1a, 1521–5, esp. 1524) that where an evangelical preacher was invited by the local *Gemeinde*, he should in the first instance be safe from expulsion, and people who listened to him and heard the Bible read should not be punished.

[3] Haas, *Kappelerkrieg*, 80.

[4] F. Elsener, *Zur Geschichte des Majoritätsprinzips (Pars major und Pars sanior) insbesondere nach schweizerischen Quellen.* ZRG, KA 42 (1956), 73–116, 560–70; 55 (1969) 238–81; P. Brüschweiler, *Die landfriedlichen Simultanverhältnisse im Thurgau* (Frauenfeld, 1932); Vasella 2, 45–8; M. Kopp, *Die Geltung der Mehrheitsprinzips in eidgenössischen Angelegenheiten vom 13. Jahrhundert bis 1848 in seiner Bedeutung für die alte Eidgenossenschaft* (Winterthur, 1959).

was to administer the area undertook all duties and responsibilities. In the event of a conflict of significance all the protecting states should be consulted and, failing unanimity, the wishes of the majority of them should prevail. The application of this principle obviously might be used to prevent any change of religious allegiance. It was far from being a simple matter. Rules acceptable for secular civil affairs were not transferable to matters religious. While the Catholics hoped that a majority opinion in the Diet could be held to prevail, they were not prepared to extend this principle to localities. Zurich argued for majority decisions in the *Gemeinden* of the Mandated Territories to be decisive locally, a view totally unacceptable to its opponents.[1] There was, of course, no freedom for the *Gemeinden* within any state, Catholic or Protestant, to exercise religious local option.[2]

The reformation movement made steady, even rapid, progress in Thurgau.[3] By April 1529 it was reported that a majority of the parishes were in its favour, most spontaneously, some perhaps responding to pressure from Zurich emissaries. Similar, but slower, results were obtained in Toggenburg, Gaster, Sargans, the county of Werdenberg and in the Lordship (*Herrschaft*) of Sax-Forstegg where the local Freiherr was well disposed.

A Zwinglian Thurgau, reinforced by other eastern territories including the lands of the monastery of St Gall – the city of St Gall was increasingly Zwinglian from 1524 – would readily accept Zurich's guidance in other matters, and this in turn would give Zurich control of an area equal in size to, but much more valuable than, the Bernese Oberland. This would mean that Zurich, traditionally the leading state, would be doubled in size, wealth and warrior population. In alliance with Berne and supported by Oecolampadian Basle, the combination would be irresistible. The rest of Switzerland, it would seem, must follow. Zurich would be the pacemaker, then become the dominant partner and finally the controlling force in a Protestant Switzerland.

The implications of this did not escape the keen perception of the cautious councillors of Berne. It would mean that the Aar would become, as it were, a tributary of the Limmat; Saints Felix and Regula would displace the bear. Swiss interests would thus be almost wholly German-orientated, possibilities of expansion westward into French-speaking areas such as Franche-Comté or the Vaud would be at a discount and Bernese soldiers would be used to further the interests of Zurich. Further, since there was no serious hope that Central Switzerland would become Protestant otherwise than by coercion, it might well mean that Berne

---

[1] EA 4, 1a, 1372 (August 1529).   [2] Kägi, 83–6.
[3] Knittel I, 169–245; Kägi, 63–70.

would be engaged in hostilities with Lucerne, Schwyz, Uri, Nidwalden and Obwalden, its immediate neighbours, and probably with Savoy and Valais as well, and this to make Zurich stronger.

On its eastern frontier Berne had a special problem. Keeping a tight hold on the peasants of the comparatively recently acquired Bernese Oberland was not easy at any time; these isolated backward communities constituted a kind of Bernese La Vendée, where bucolic conservatism resisted religious change all the more when it was apparent that the removal of mass-priests and the suppression of monasteries did not bring any relaxation of services, tithe or rent-charge payments.[1] At the same time, clandestine attendance at mass might involve a heavy fine.[2] They very reasonably expected help from across the border and they knew that there were a number of crypto-Catholic well-wishers in the city of Berne itself.

Behind the Inner States lay the enigmatic figure of Ferdinand, Archduke of Austria, brother of Charles V and from 1526 onwards King of Bohemia and Hungary. As ruler of the Tyrol, the Black Forest, Breisgau, Sundgau, Upper and Lower Alsace (*Vorderoesterreich*), with administrative centres at Innsbruck, Ensisheim and Landshut, he represented an immediate Catholic menace on the frontier. Although the Inner States had come into being to resist Habsburg external interference and had become allies of the King of France, they could now increasingly feel that they must turn to this Catholic dynasty for help. Without external aid they might not survive. Ferdinand, too, was in regular communication with the Emperor Charles V.

This latter became more and more the Catholic ogre for Zwingli, although the Zurich tradition had formerly been one of relatively good relations with him. He was also now coming to be regarded by Lucerne and its friends, traditionally so anti-Habsburg, as a supporter, the more so when in 1529 the Pope had learnt the lesson of the sack of Rome (1527) and had accepted the consequence of the defeat of the French in north Italy. The hopes and fears of Catholics and Protestants alike were in fact unnecessary ones, but they influenced events. Charles V neither could nor would waste man-power and resources against recalcitrant Swiss republicans. He had yet to secure his position in Milan, arrange his coronation, deal with the Diet of Speier and keep both the Turks, and events in the New World, in view. The advisers of Ferdinand at Innsbruck were indeed anxious to urge their master to take advantage of any opportunity to forward the Catholic cause, but their physical and financial resources were woefully inadequate. This was what Zurich failed to appreciate.

---

[1] Feller, II, 166–70. H. Specker, *Die Reformationswirren im Berner Oberland 1528. Ihre Geschichte und ihre Folgen* (Fribourg 1951). (SKG 1952 Beiheft 9), 22 Tardent, 127.
[2] Vasella *I*, 308.

Berne was avowedly and publicly a Zwinglian state after the disputation of January 1528, an event that may have saved the Protestant faith in Europe. It was not, however, easy for Berne to bring the new teaching to all its subjects, particularly to the coarse and stupid farmers of the more distant and remote valleys. Enforcement of the new worship was carried out slowly, with caution, mildness and thoroughness, all, as has been seen,[1] characteristic features of Bernese administration. There had indeed been discontent in Haslital accompanied by intervention from Unterwalden, but this had proved abortive.[2] Berne, with an anxious eye on its southern neighbours, had no intention of dropping its demand for an admission of guilty responsibility and suitable reparations from Unterwalden for incitement to revolt. By helping the rebels, Unterwalden had undoubtedly broken Federal agreements, the *Pfaffenbrief* (1370) and the *Stanser Verkommniss* (1481), so that Berne, supported by Zurich, could now demand the exclusion of Unterwalden from meetings of the Federal Diet for ten years and from any share in the control of the Mandated Territories.[3] The Unterwaldner administration retaliated by accusing Berne of wanting to destroy the old Confederation, a charge easily answered by a reminder that the issue was secular, not religious, and by an agreement to submit the matter to conventional arbitration. The arbitrators,[4] after long deliberation, agreed that the attackers had been in the wrong but also that it had been a local spontaneous movement rather than a government sponsored one, and Unterwalden agreed to consider the Bernese as 'pious and honourable Confederates'. Berne was not willing to let the matter rest there. It was indispensable in the conditions of 1528–9 that Berne and Zurich remain united, and therefore Berne would not agree to any arrangement that was unacceptable to Zurich. Zurich was not prepared for any unsatisfactory compromise – as a minimum, rebels who had fled to Unterwalden territory must be returned, defamation of Berne must cease and proper compensation be paid. Zwingli personally in more than one memorandum[5] strongly urged that wider matters involving the spread of the Gospel must be taken into account, including the intrigues of the Five Inner States with Austria. An easy peace would encourage the Catholics to persecute in Gaster, Weesen, Toggenburg and Glarus. The pensioners would strengthen the ties with Ferdinand.[6] Therefore he insisted that Unterwalden must explicitly admit that it had broken the Federal Pact and ask for forgiveness, and there must be no more defamation of reformers. Unterwalden must also drop its alliance with the other Inner States against

[1] See above, 245.   [2] See above, 264.
[3] Feller II, 191. Strictly, Nidwalden alone was involved. Z vi ii, 319–20.
[4] Basle, Schaffhausen, Appenzell and Graubünden. EA 4, 1b, 40; EA 4, 1a, 1467; Z x, 147; Z vi ii, 331, 343; Schmid 9–11.
[5] Z vi ii, 318–44, 361–71.   [6] Z vi ii, 362–3.

Zurich and Berne, stop negotiating with Austria, forbid pension-taking and abandon one turn in appointing to office in the Mandated Territories (specifically in the *Freie Aemter*) and pay costs. If, as it seems, Zwingli's advice was intended to prevent peace[1] and keep the matter open until a settlement was reached over the Mandated Territories, then it was successful, and the Unterwalden incursion proved to be the first link in the chain that led to war. There was also a growing suspicion amounting to conviction[2] that the Five *Orte* were negotiating an extra-Federal and contra-Federal alliance with Austria; and something like this was indeed the case.

The varied civic alliances in which Zurich was involved, originally made for trade and mutual protection, had, with the expansion of evangelical teaching, become more coherent as religious interests and fears had been added to the other unifying forces. Already, as early as January 1525, Zurich, Berne, St Gall, Biel, Mülhausen, Basle, Schaffhausen, Solothurn and Strassburg were prepared to work together to resist the enforcement of the Edict of Worms[3] in their territories, and, with the growing strength of the reform movement, others were willing to join. In 1527 Zwingli was canvassing the potentialities of an alliance of the reformed cities.[4] Now that Berne had become officially Protestant and Oecolampadius was clearly succeeding in his efforts in Basle,[5] the evangelical cities constituted themselves into a formidable and possibly aggressive group, a Christian Civic Union.[6] There had been many such unions during the previous half century for trade, protection and war. In general they involved economic and legal reciprocity for the citizens included and were either indefinite (*ewige*) or for a fixed term of years.

Constance held one of the keys to the Christian Civic Union. This free imperial city had succeeded in throwing off its dependence upon its bishop and from 1500 had wanted nothing better than to become a Swiss state (*gleichberechtigter Ort*). Only thus could its reformed religion be secure and the city avoid absorption into the Habsburg family possessions, which

---

[1] Haas, *Kappelerkrieg*, 68–75; Feller II, 181; Hauswirth, *Philipp*, 124.

[2] EA 4, 1b, 102.

[3] EA 4, 1a, 529 (No. 224), 553 (No. 235); HZ 40 (1878) 131; Bender, *Reformationsbündnisse*, 162–4.

[4] Z VI i, 197–201; Hauswirth, *Philipp*, 88.

[5] The final decisive date is 10 February 1529, when images were removed and the mass forbidden. P. Roth, *Durchbruch und Festsetzung der Reformation in Basel* (Basle, 1942) 30.

[6] *Das Christliche Burgrecht*. Basle, Mülhausen, Biel, Berne, Zurich, St Gall, and from December 1527 Constance, were included. The first meeting of what became the Christian Civic Union was held in Berne between representatives of Berne, Zurich and Constance on 5 and 6 January, immediately after the Berne disputation. The acceptance of exclusively evangelical preaching was implied in the title which does not appear until the agreement of 25 June between Zurich and Berne. Later, meetings of representatives of some or all of the cities were held, often in Aarau, as needed. Z VI ii, 670; EA 4, 1a, 1345, 1521–5; Vasella, 2, 59–61.

in fact happened in 1548. The bishop naturally tended to favour an Austrian alliance, thus securing his own position, while the city council as an evangelical body was anxious to escape from his jurisdiction. At the same time a city without any territory (as was also the case with St Gall) was in no strong military or economic position. If, however, the city could secure the areas under episcopal control, just as if the city of St Gall could embrace the monastic possessions, the situation would be altered, but not entirely to the advantage of Zurich.

The efforts of the brothers Ambrose and Thomas Blaurer from 1523 onwards had secured the acceptance of the Zwinglian reform and Zwingli looked thither for support; the bishop's authority was repudiated, and in 1528 Constance was deprived of imperial protection. In so far as the German cities were Lutheran, Constance was not an acceptable ally to them; and in so far as Constance hoped to absorb Thurgau, it was suspected by Zurich. The Five (Catholic) States were in any event opposed to the admission of an additional 'Civic' member to the Confederation, a veto which included Strassburg as well as Constance, and religion settled the matter.

Zwingli for his part needed support from and in Constance, especially after the setback at Baden.[1] On 18–23 May 1527, men from Zurich, Lindau and Constance met in St Gall at a shooting-match (*Schützenfest*), which was also a social occasion. In August Zwingli advocated an alliance.[2] The outcome, seven months later, was the alliance (*Burgrecht*) of Zurich and Constance, dated 25 December 1527,[3] the text of which was drawn up by Georg Vögeli, town clerk of Constance. The document stated that the alliance was concluded for the honour, advantage and welfare of the Holy Roman Empire. Each party was to act in matters of belief as they would answer to God and his holy word – the formula of the Speier Recess of 1526. If either party were attacked the other would come in arms to its help. Zurich thus had its northern flank covered and, in fact, the alliance was not merely defensive. The defence of the Reformation called for action, and Zurich with Constance could hope to advance further. Any territory occupied or annexed was to be held in common by both sides. Corresponding treaties with Berne, Basle, Schaffhausen, St Gall, Biel and Mülhausen followed.[4] Zurich and Berne insisted that the Gospel was truly

---

[1] F. Blanke, *Zwingli mit Ambrosius Blarer im Gespräch. Der Konstanzer Reformator Ambrosius Blarer 1492–1564*, hg. v. B. Moeller (Constance, 1964) 81–6.

[2] EA 4, 1b, 309; Z VI i, 200–1; Z IX, 187–8.

[3] EA 4, 1a, 1510–16; Bullinger *Ref.* I, 419–25; HZ 40 (1876), 134–51 and H. C. Rublack, *Die Einführung der Reformation in Konstanz* (Gütersloh, 1971), 121–4 analyse the negotiations well.

[4] The main Zwinglian alliances (*Burgrecht*) were:
Berne and Fribourg with Lausanne, 7 December 1525 for 25 years.
Berne and Fribourg with Geneva, 8 February 1526 for 25 years.

353

preached by them, and they were always willing to be better instructed from the Bible. The eight Catholic states had tried to seduce the subjects of the cities from their allegiance. Hence there was to be full co-citizenship between the reformed associates; they would defend their religion and aid one another if attacked. No subject in the Mandated Territories who accepted the Apostles creed and the Bible was to be punished. Monks might leave their monasteries freely and parishes which voted by a majority for the Reformation were not to be prevented from accepting it. Federal alliances were to be retained.

Together these inter-civic alliances involved ever closer cooperation. In January 1529 delegates from Berne, Zurich and Constance inaugurated a series of meetings for the discussion of common interests, and these soon became assemblies or diets of all the cities involved, which were now regularly referred to as the Christian Civic Union (*das Christliche Burgrecht*), particularly after the accession of Basle in March. Aarau became the usual meeting place for these diets, and its choice, apart from geographical convenience, is significant. Berne was determined from the outset not to be involved in any expansive south German alliance which should include Württemberg and Hesse, and to keep the meeting place of the union close at hand.

All this had not escaped the notice of the Inner States, who felt themselves isolated and threatened with exclusion from their federal rights in the Mandated Territories. Hence they were already considering in great secrecy what counter-measures could be taken, and in 1528–9 the possibility of Austrian support was discussed at Lucerne.[1] With Fabri's encouragement, negotiations with Austrian officials, alarmed by Basle's entry into the Christian Civic Union, were opened at Feldkirch on 14 February,[2] and the terms were embodied in a treaty at Waldshut on 22 April 1529, the later notorious 'Christian Alliance' (*die Christliche*

Zurich with Constance, 25 December 1527 for 10 years.
Berne with Constance, 31 January 1528 for 10 years.
Zurich with Berne, 25 June 1528. (This followed the acceptance of the Zwinglian faith by Berne, future alliances being designated 'Christian' – '*das christliche Burgrecht*' – and these extended more widely.)
Zurich and Berne with St Gall (city), 3 November 1528.
Zurich and Berne with Biel, 28 January 1529.
Zurich and Berne with Mülhausen, 17 February 1529.
Zurich and Berne with Basle, 3 March 1529.
Basle with Mülhausen, 17 February 1529.
Basle with Biel, 8 May 1529.
Zurich, Berne and Basle with Schaffhausen, 15 October 1529.
Zurich, Berne and Basle with Strassburg, 5 January 1530.
The documents are in EA 4, 1a, 1505–27; EA 4, 1b, 1463–93.

[1] Escher, *Glaubensparteien* 62–3. Lucerne was actively in favour of this, Uri much less so.
[2] EA 4, 1b, 49–59. Rudolf Collin was able to send a report of the proceedings to Zwingli. Vasella 2, 107; HZ 40 (1878) 150–1.

Vereinigung).[1] The union agreed at Waldshut was superficially entirely defensive in character. The contracting parties undertook to give no offence or occasion for war, and to defend themselves and their faith only in the event of a direct attack. They would support one another in the punishment of heretics, and Austria would assist its allies (but with advice only) in the maintenance of their rights in the Mandated Territories and as co-protectors of St Gall.

If the Catholic states should be attacked, Ferdinand promised to put in the field 6,000 infantry, 400 cavalry and some guns, and to send food supplies. Soldiers might be hired by the Austrian administration at the standard rates, but Austrian poverty made this highly improbable. No conquests were directly envisaged, but it was agreed that any territory within the bounds of the Confederation or its allies that was occupied should become the responsibility of the Five. Any gains made outside the Confederation with the aid of hired Swiss soldiers would fall to Austria, a provision aimed at the city of Constance. The Austrian advisers recognised that the Five States were greatly inferior in effective military power to their rivals but hoped to overcome this, since the adhesion of Valais, Fribourg and Solothurn was anticipated, and there were expectations of assistance from the Bishop of Constance, Count Frederick of Fürstenberg, the Count of Werdenberg, together with Überlingen, Wangen, Ravensburg and Salzburg. The expectations did not materialise and served only to alarm the other side. At the end of April a meeting of representatives of Berne, Glarus, Basle, Solothurn, Schaffhausen, Appenzell, St Gall, Biel, Chur and Constance protested[2] against the Feldkirch treaty, but in vain. The protest could have been serious, but in fact it was ineffective from the start. There was some genuine fear. News that the Emperor was assembling forces against the Turks was taken to mean that these were really intended to be used against the Swiss; men were gathering in Lorraine, a force of 8,000 in Valais was ready to invade Berne, a force of 1,000 could come from the south against the Graubünden. The alliance was, in fact, a rather irresponsible arrangement, but rumour greatly exaggerated its implications[3] and helped on a kind of war fever. Significantly, perhaps, the formation of the 'Christian Alliance' coincided with the renewed activity from the side of St Gall which has already been described[4] and with growing expectations of conflict.

The Gospel-preaching in the Toggenburg district had gone forward

---

[1] EA 4, 1b, 123, and Beilage v, 1467–75; *Archiv für die schweizerische Reformationsgeschichte* (Piusvereins, Solothurn, 1876) III, 573–80; Spillmann *1*, 31; Vasella *2*, 108.
[2] EA 4, 1b, 139–45.
[3] Valais made an alliance with Savoy, accompanied by some unnecessary publicity: 'wir geben nit ein pfifferling um die Zürcher, Berner, die evangelischen sackpfifer'. Escher, *Glaubensparteien* 71; Oechsli *3*, c. 139; EA 4, 1b, 73.   [4] See above, 279–283.

remarkably well[1] in spite of opposition. Those who were won over wanted evangelical ministers and feared prosecution for heresy, from which Zurich alone could save them. The efforts of Johannes Döring and Bernard Künzli of Brunnadern had been successful enough to cause the abbot to complain both to the federal Diet and to the Protecting Powers and in 1528 there had also been a number of cases of iconoclasm, notably at Lichtensteig, and of civil disobedience as well.[2]

In particular there had been trouble in 1528 over the Benedictine monastery of St John (Alt St Johann im Thurtal), a few miles west of Wildhaus and well known to Zwingli, his uncle and his younger brother James having been monks there. The abbot, Johann Steiger von Bütschwil, was notorious for his hostility to the evangelicals around him, and had appealed to Schwyz and Glarus for support against them. When this was not forthcoming, he took the precaution of removing the more valuable of the church ornaments to Feldkirch in order to save them from destruction on 14 September 1528, when the abbey church was wrecked by religious enthusiasts. When punishment of these vandals was demanded by Schwyz, which could in fact involve proceedings against all Zwinglian supporters in Toggenburg, Berne and Zurich refused to countenance it.[3] There this matter rested until after the second Kappel war when the monastery was restored with support from the Abbot of St Gall, and the efforts by Schwyz to extend its authority thither were thwarted. It was not, however, an isolated event.

To cast down graven images had biblical commendation and had been accepted by Zurich as a godly action to be carried out with restraint and deliberation. This was less easy to secure in areas under joint control, and it was difficult to prevent the 'cleansing of the churches' from being used by looters, anxious to steal articles of value, or by enthusiastic youths for whom wanton destruction, easily extending beyond the offending objects, was good sport.[4] Pious Catholics, of course, were deeply offended by the destruction of revered buildings and their contents.

There were other events which exacerbated feelings on both sides. Thurgau was a key area; hence the attention it received from the evangelicals. From the point of view of Zurich, annexation or incorporation would be highly advantageous. If, however, this should prove entirely unaccept-

[1] Z IX, 534–6; Müller, 77–90; G. Egli, Die Reformation im Toggenburg (Schaffhausen, 1955) 115–18.   [2] Müller, 85–7; Kägi, 94.
[3] G. Egli, Die Reformation in Toggenburg, 119; Sabbata, 289; Salat, 186; Z VI ii, 268–71; Escher, Glaubensparteien, 47–8; Strickler I, 666–7 (No. 2105); EA 4, 1a, 1404; Kägi, 20–2, 75–6, 88.
[4] The rough and unrestrained violence of the age receives ample illustration in the sketches that accompany Diebold Schilling. Luzerner Bilderchronik, 1513, bearbeitet v. R. Durrer u. P. Hilber (Geneva, 1932). J. Zemp, Die schweizerischen Bilderchroniken und ihre Architecktur-Darstellungen (Zürich, 1897) 36ff.

able, as in fact it did, then the next best thing for the reformers would be for it to secure independence and self-government (*Rechtsgleichheit*) thus escaping Catholic control. Better still, it might become a full state (*Ort*) of the Confederation, but this the opponents were determined, as with Constance, to prevent. Nor would a Zurich-controlled Thurgau be welcome to Berne.[1] The evangelicals in Thurgau had long complained of oppression by the local administrator (*Landweibel*) Marx Wehrli, an aggressive Catholic whose actions caused great resentment in Zurich and increased the determination there to help their oppressed brethren. In May 1528, in the company of the governor, Heinrich Wirz of Obwalden, Wehrli stayed in the Zurich inn *Zum Roten Schwert*. There he was arrested, found guilty of violence against his evangelical subordinates, and beheaded.[2]

Further outbreaks of iconoclasm occurred in a number of towns and villages of Thurgau,[3] images were quietly removed at Constance, and there was a serious religious riot at Weesen at the end of January 1529.[4] Here the attackers were led by their active minister, Hans Schindler (probably one of Zwingli's former pupils at Glarus), who successfully appealed to Zwingli and Zurich for support. Such encouragement led to further outrages, in Benken, Schänis and Oberkirch, for example, in February.[5] In May a Thurgau peasant was killed in a squabble by an officer of the law, Lanz von Liebenfels, which led to further rioting, and it was with difficulty that Jakob Frei was prevented by Bernese intervention from retaliating in force.[6] In Bremgarten, chief city of the *Freie Aemter*[7] and strategically important, where the Dean had been recently superseded as leading minister by his son, Henry Bullinger, there were similar incidents.[8] All

---

[1] Knittel, I, 152.

[2] Knittel I, 155; Haas, *Kappelerkrieg*, 87; Spillmann *3*, 61; EA 4, 1a, 1315.

[3] Vasella *I*, 308; Knittel I, 177–8, 183. The legal and other implications are studied in Kägi, 127–50 and K. Straub, *Rechtsgeschichte der evangelischen Kirchgemeinden der Landschaft Thurgau unter den eidgenössischen Landfrieden* (Frauenfeld, 1902).

[4] ZWA VII, 231; Z X, 39, 47. Schwyz feared lest the whole of the adjoining 'March' might follow. Valentin Tschudi in his Chronicle (*Chronik*, 55–7) deplored the rapidity of the success of the reformed teaching in Gasterland, in which Weesen was. Zurich did not share in the administration of Gaster or Uznach. W. Ammann, *Die Reformation im Gaster*, ZWA VII (1940), 209–50.

[5] ZWA VII (1940); 233.

[6] Z X, 134; Strickler II, 168 (No. 404); Haas, *Kappelerkrieg*, 88.

[7] The Mandatory Powers in 'die gemeineidgenössischen Vogteien in den Freien Ämtern in Aargau' were Zurich, Lucerne, Zug, Schwyz, Glarus and Unterwalden. Berne and Uri were not directly involved, but Berne could not be oblivious to the future of Bremgarten. The Freie Aemter with the adjoining county of Baden were of special interest to the Inner States as providing a Catholic access to Waldshut and Austrian Alsace. The literal translation of Freie Aemter as 'free offices' is almost meaningless. 'Independent districts' might be better.

[8] Bremgarten, the largest town in the district and a key position strategically, had been secured for the evangelicals by Bullinger's preaching. A holocaust of images took place on 17 May 1529, and the mass was abolished there from 26 April. A. Bucher, *Die Reformation in den*

this, in the spring of 1529, served to increase the determination of the Catholics to maintain and defend their rights. They knew that there were hard realities behind these events, and that Zwingli and others seriously hoped that both Schwyz and Lucerne could become evangelised. This never happened, and it is convenient to group the central states as solidly Catholic, but the complete polarisation of the opposing sides can be exaggerated.[1]

The urge to violence was intensified by active propaganda. In Lucerne the support of the mass and the attacks on the vernacular Bible by Thomas Murner[2] were so violent as to arouse special resentment in Berne and Zurich, the more so in that he had not confined himself to theology. He was urging a fight: long spears and good halberds were ready to defend the faith.[3] When an attempt was made from both Berne and Zurich to persuade the Lucerne authorities to suppress these inflammatory writings it was rejected on the ground that the administration was not concerned with a personal statement by a cleric.[4] In Basle local manifestations of anti-clericalism, particularly by the gildsmen, were serious, and violence was anticipated.[5] At the same time, February 1529, the truce with the Protestants in Germany came to an end. After the Diet of Speier,[6] Luther remained an outlaw and Eck succeeded in securing the explicit condemnation of the Zwinglians, who had so far secured a precarious legal immunity for themselves by their insistence that they were not Lutherans. The persecuting spirit was abroad.

As the war of pamphlets and speeches intensified, complaints became louder. Somewhat curiously, in an age of unbridled scurrility, sixteenth-century governments could on occasion be as sensitive about abuse and denigration as any twentieth-century dictator. A great deal of mud was thrown about, and some of it stuck. Why some epithets should have been considered as especially derogatory it is sometimes hard, across the centuries, to appreciate. Thus the five Catholic states were strangely annoyed by being labelled 'the five little cow sheds or cowpats'.[7]

At the same time, there was no more suggestion of freedom of the press

---

Freien Aemtern und in der Stadt Bremgarten (bis 1531) (Sarnen, 1949–50) 95–6; E. Schulz, *Reformation und Gegenreformation in den Freien-Ämtern* (Zürich, 1899) 12–28; F. Blanke, *Der junge Bullinger* (Zürich, 1942) 119; Haas, *Kappelerkrieg* 89–94.

[1] ZWA VII, 229.   [2] Feller, *Bern* II, 190.
[3] EA 4, 1b, 72–3.   [4] Haas, *Kappelerkrieg*, 28–9, 44.
[5] P. Roth, *Durchbruch und Festsetzung der Reformation in Basel* (Basle, 1942), 17–18, 27–8. There was image-breaking on 10 February followed by the departure of the Cathedral Chapter to Neuchâtel and Freiburg, a revision of the state constitution on 18 February, and full adoption of the Reformation on 1 April.
[6] Above, 318.
[7] Die fünf Sennhüttli, die fünf Kuhdräckli (= Kuhdreckli) EA 4, 1b, 959; Salat, 280; Farner IV, 302; Bullinger, *Ref.* II, 129.

than there was of freedom of religion. It was taken for granted that a government could, and should, exercise control over statements made by its own subjects whether verbally or in writing. To allow verbal violence to pass unrebuked was to accept responsibility for it. What was disliked intensely in 1529 was the indiscriminate and local abuse which spread from the streets to the pulpits, and thus into the sphere of religion.[1] Were there to be no limits to what the evangelical preachers, or their opponents, addressed to their congregations? The dispute about sermonising in the Mandated Territories made bad feeling even worse. Preaching could scarcely be differentiated from Bible-reading when Zwinglian evangelists were expressly enjoined to preach nothing else.

Zwingli, like other Reformers, remained utterly sincere and immovable in his conviction that the power of the word was such that if proclaimed in its purest biblical simplicity it must necessarily prevail. All that was required was that its propagation should not be impeded. Nothing would have surprised him more, could he have envisaged a completely literate society, than that there would be avowed disbelievers, or even papists, in lands where all were free and able to read the Bible in the vernacular. The Bible, of course, was wholly inspired by the Holy Spirit. All parties were agreed on this point; to doubt it was to deny Christ, and this was blasphemy. That the mouth of the blasphemer must be stopped (Leviticus 24. 13–16), again all were agreed. A further deduction was that, provided the evangelical doctrine was freely expounded in the Mandated Territories, the inhabitants would be certain gladly and willingly to accept the new teaching. It could not be otherwise. From this it was assumed to follow that unrestricted access to the undiluted Bible text would convince all its readers that certain Catholic convictions such as the mass as sacrifice, the value of prayers to the saints, monastic vows, clerical celibacy and so forth, were not compatible with it. Therefore they must not be practised where any non-Catholic government was in control, and this without reciprocity. The argument further implied that Protestants must be free to evangelise among Catholic communities but Catholics could not be allowed to celebrate mass for their followers in a Protestant area. On the opposite side, the Catholic states, equally wedded to ancient and accepted church tradition, would not willingly tolerate the presence, let alone the teaching and preaching, of heretics. In such an atmosphere of conflict, it was by no means easy to decide where legitimate preaching began and slander ended. It was particularly in the districts where dual control, Catholic and Protestant, was statutorily involved, that there was no obvious way out. These problems of joint responsibility for administra-

[1] F. Straub, *Zürich und die Bewährung des ersten Landfriedens (1529–1530)* (Zürich, 1970), 158–67, provides numerous examples of this.

tion, freedom of preaching, and prevention of slander, became particularly acute in 1529–30 in the area of the Freie Aemter.

The appointment of the chief administrative officer or governor (*Vogt*) in any division of the Mandated Territories rested with the governments of the occupying powers in rotation. One of the reasons for which Zurich had wanted Unterwalden to be condemned to exclusion from the Federal Diet for ten years after 1528 was that it was the turn of the Unterwalden government to nominate the local governor of the Freie Aemter and the county of Baden in the summer of 1529.[1] It was known that he would inevitably be a Catholic, who would insist upon orthodoxy within his bailiwick and it would be his duty to eliminate heresy and heretics. The Gospel would thus no longer be preached freely there after having made remarkable progress in the previous year. Since the immediate origins of the first Kappel war are to be found in these Freie Aemter, and since the second war followed almost inevitably from the first and led to Zwingli's death and to the collapse of his plans for a united Protestant Switzerland, they deserve a little attention.

The Upper and the Lower Freiamt were small areas of formerly Habsburg territory now ruled by the six states, Zurich, Lucerne, Zug, Glarus, Unterwalden and Schwyz.[2] Berne and Uri were not directly concerned. This little narrow tongue of land between Zurich and Berne was the Silesia of sixteenth-century Switzerland. It was relatively thinly populated by small communities of peasant farmers and graziers, a majority of whom in 1529 had hearkened to the voice of the preachers and had accepted the form of religion favoured by their two mighty neighbours. A minority remained convinced Catholics. If the Freie Aemter were Catholic, Lucerne might hope to add them to its dominions, thus securing an all-Catholic corridor from the Rhine and Habsburg-owned territory to north Italy, thus also separating their opponents. If they remained Protestant, they might well be absorbed between Zurich and Berne or possibly by Berne alone, Zurich being allowed a free hand in the East. When, therefore, it was known in May that Unterwalden intended to nominate a Catholic, Anton Adacker, as local governor,[3] tension grew. Unterwalden had not yet fulfilled its financial and other obligations to Berne, and, it was argued, it could not validly exercise its prerogative until it had done so.[4] In any

---

[1] See above, 5 and the list in EA 4, 1b, Anhang IV, 1601–2.

[2] Z VI ii, 370 n. 7. There were 13 districts in all. The area was sometimes known as *Das Freiamt*, sometimes as *Aemter im Waggenthal*. For a further account of the various names see Oechsli *I*, 212–15.

[3] The *Landvogt* did not reside in the district. He usually appeared twice a year at Muri and Hitzkirch. (Oechsli *I*, 216). He was represented in each local administrative area by a resident *Untervogt*.

[4] Berne insisted (HZ 40 (1878) 141) that Unterwalden had not kept the oath to the Bund and so had no legal rights within it.

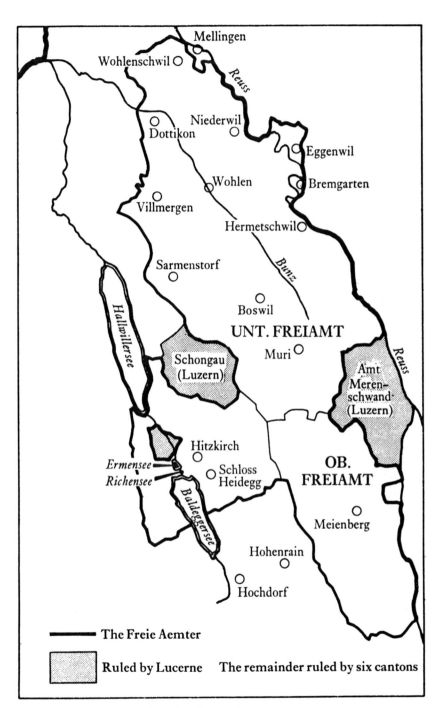

The Freie Aemter, Aargau c. 1530

case Zurich, advised by Zwingli, was determined to protect its co-religion-ists and keep the Unterwalden nominee away. In the phrase of the time, he must be forcibly prevented from 'riding by the interposition of armed guards.[1] This was a high-handed and possibly illegal threat and was probably intended to be a reply to the Catholic–Austrian alliance of Waldshut.

Already, on 22 April, the reformed and uncommitted states (except Fribourg) had met at Zurich. There[2] they had emphasised the need for federal unity and had deplored the indications of an alliance between Ferdinand and the Inner States. An embassy was sent to ask that this be renounced, but it met only with a decisive refusal.[3] The alliance with Ferdinand, they said, was only to counterbalance the Christian Civic Union; it was Zurich that had failed to abide by its federal obligations in Toggenburg and Gaster and was trying to impose minority rule on Thur-gau and Rheintal. Grievances soon multiplied from both sides. The familiar objections to the acceptance of foreign pensions and mercenary service were again brought forward. At Sarnen, capital of Obwalden, the coats of arms of Zurich, Berne, Basle and Strassburg were depicted in April 1529 for all to see on the house of the *Landschreiber* ('clerk to the county council') with four gallows beside them.[4] This, in an illiterate age, was well understood to be a calculated 'insult to the flag', and people were exceedingly sensitive about these things.

The most infuriating action of all, however, was undoubtedly the burning of Jacob Kaiser as a heretic.[5] This fiery preacher, a native of Uznach, otherwise known as Jacob Schlosser, had attracted a good deal of attention by his active promotion of reform in Schwerzenbach, where he had married and presided over the removal of images from the church. He was present at the Berne disputation,[6] and in the spring of 1529 was chosen, possibly irregularly, as parish priest of Oberkirch near Kalt-brunn.[7] As soon as it was known that he had left Zurich territory to take up his new duties, on his way through a wood within the jurisdiction of Uznach, he was arrested by Untervogt Peter Hasler, an agent from Schwyz, almost certainly illegally. Zurich at once protested[8] to the Uznach

[1] Schmid, 16; Lüthi, 44. Berne was anxious to exclude an Unterwalden governor, but had no rights in the Freie Aemter. Bullinger, *Ref.* II, 149–51.
[2] EA 4, 1b, 139–5.   [3] Tardent, 143.
[4] Feller II, 196; Z VI ii, 408, 411; R. Thommen, *Urkundenbuch der Stadt Basel* (Basle, 1908) X, 102; Bullinger, *Ref.* II, 142; Schmid 16; Stumpf 2 II, 40. Brändly, 91 seems wrong in placing the episode in Stans.
[5] EA 4, 1b, 195–6, 202–3. Bullinger, *Ref.* II, 148–9 is the basis for most subsequent accounts. Tschudi, *Chronik* 24 (1888) 69–71 (Nos. 148–52); W. Ammann, *Die Reformation im Gaster*, ZWA VII (1940) 240–3.   [6] Steck & Tobler, 600 (No. 1466).
[7] Oberkirch was in Gasterland which was ruled by Schwyz and Glarus.
[8] EA 4, 1b, 194–6, 202–3; Stumpf 2, II, 49.

authorities, who disclaimed responsibility. This was followed by a visit to Schwyz by Junker Hans Edlibach to demand Kaiser's release, otherwise there would be war. There were threats of reprisals, a formal demand from Glarus that Kaiser should be passed back for trial in Uznach, and further requests for clemency, but on 29 May Kaiser was burnt to death in Schwyz as a heretic. This action aroused immense public indignation. It raised serious issues of jurisdiction, since the rights of the court of Uznach to deal with its own citizens had been flouted[1] and the preacher was carrying out the wishes of his masters, the Zurich Council. The legal right of Schwyz to intervene was very dubious except that it was a Catholic commonplace that heretics should be burnt if apprehended. It was a kind of test-case. If it went unchallenged, it might imply both the exclusion of reformation from a Mandated Territory and a serious check to Zurich's hopes of territorial expansion.

The Catholics, somewhat less effectively, on their side, too, could complain of the treatment meted out to Theodore (Theodul) Schlegel in the previous January. He was abbot of the Premonstratensian house of St Luzi, Chur, and was put to death there on 23 January because of his refusal to refrain from saying mass but nominally for having persuaded Bishop Paul Ziegler of Chur to retire in favour of Gian Angelo de Medici and for supposedly stealing the valuables of the monastery which in fact he had carried to Feldkirch for safety.[2] An outbreak of hostility seemed imminent in spite of the furious diplomatic activity of the last days of May 1529.[3] Uncommitted states and individuals were trying to maintain the exiguous bridge between the northern states and their southern antagonists, but little could be achieved by negotiation. Berne, immovable now in religion, was politically all for moderation, patience and restraint. From Zurich came increasingly urgent calls for action. The threat from the enemy must be met by a short preventive war before the opposed forces could gather.[4] Zug, Schwyz and Unterwalden should be dealt with at once in a way that would ensure the safety of the faithful and the progress of the evangel.

It was to encourage this project that Zwingli produced (25–9 May) his plan for a frontal advance on three fronts which should be conclusive.[5] He had already urged[6] that the occupation of Mellingen and Bremgarten could seriously interfere with food supplies to the south. Similarly, the communications with Austria could be blocked by a garrison at Kaiserstuhl. Berne was to be kept closely informed since her cooperation was indispensable whether their ends were accomplished by negotiation or by force.

---

[1] Z VI ii, 434.   [2] Vasella *I*, 263, 272; Z X, 45–6; Sabbata, 303.   [3] Schmid, 18–20.
[4] Steck & Tobler, 1046–47 (No. 2315, 2316, 2317); Feller, II, 195–8; Escher, *Glaubensparteien*, 89–90; Haas, *Kappelerkrieg*, 134–41; Tardent, 240; Lüthi, 44–7.
[5] *Ratschlag über den Krieg*, Z VI ii, 424(433)–40; EA 4, 1b, 197–9.   [6] Z VI ii, 419–22.

The plan now was that a 'warning' to Lucerne and Uri should announce the opening of hostilities, and at the same time precautions should be taken against an attack on the Freie Aemter by Unterwalden. Toggenburg would support Zurich with 1,500 men who would occupy Uznach and liberate it from the tyranny of Schwyz and the Abbot of St Gall. A further contingent from Rüti would join in the occupation and then secure oaths of allegiance from the men of Gasterland and Weesen (Walensee). Preparations should likewise be made to secure the crossing of the river Linth 'in the March' and to blockade Pfäffikon and Wollerau, in the occupation of Schwyz but formerly controlled by Zurich. There was also some good but gratuitous advice about the use of guns and the choice of a suitable commander. Alternatively an attack could be made on Pfäffikon and Wollerau ('die Höfe') and the March; the Toggenburger would take Gaster and Uznacht and effect a junction at Steiner with a party from Zurich. At the same time, the governor at Kiburg should occupy Kaiserstuhl. It was all set out with the detailed confidence of the amateur strategist, but how much of it was practical was fortunately not put to the test.

The immediate implementation of Zwingli's plans by the Zurich Council was prevented, to his obvious mortification, by the arrival on 3 June of a delegation from Berne led by the statesman-like Niklaus Manuel and Anton Bischoff.[1] The almost proverbial caution of Berne had reason behind it in the summer of 1529. In addition to the continued dispute with Unterwalden about the Oberland invasion and the alliance of the Catholic states with Ferdinand, the possibility of attack from Valais, Savoy, Geneva and the Austrian *Vorderlände* threatened Berne with encirclement. Hence Berne insisted on correct and legal behaviour, and, above all, that there should be no precipitate action. Its representatives urged that the threat by Unterwalden to send Anton Adacker to the monastery of Muri *en route* for the Freie Aemter, protected by 20 horse with 300 Lucerne infantry to follow, was not an adequate reason for a declaration of war to which Berne was opposed. In this, almost his last, speech, after touching on the danger to Berne of an attack on its south flank from Valais and Savoy, Manuel concluded, 'God's word calls only for peace and unity. You cannot really bring faith by means of spears and halberds'.[2]

---

[1] Feller II, 196; Tardent 242–55; Z VI ii, 428; EA 4, 1b, 212–13 (No. 114); Schmid 19; Haas, *Kappelerkrieg*, 138; Stumpf 2 II, 51f; ZWA XII (1968), 701–11; Steck & Tobler, 1047 (No. 2317).

[2] 'Warlich man mag mit spiess und halbarten den glouben nit ingeben.' These words have often been quoted with approval: they were, however, as much out of harmony with the current feeling of the early sixteenth century as they suit the temper of the twentieth. War, for most Swiss, was a normal state of affairs. EA 4, 1b, 212. Feller, II, 196 .ZWA XIII (1971), 403 n. 10 quotes a slightly different version from StA. B XLIV.

Zurich, however, was determined that a southern Catholic deputy should not reach Baden and put into effect the avowed policy of halting evangelisation.[1] Rather than have this happening, Zurich would take action alone, knowing that Berne would thus be obliged reluctantly to acquiesce. On the evening of 4 June, after Zwingli had said that otherwise he would leave Zurich, the fatal decision to risk war was taken.[2] Fighting men had already been enrolled. A contingent under Ulrich Stoll and Heinrich Rahn marched to Bremgarten, and another under Hans Edlibach and Peter Meyer moved into the Freiamt and occupied Muri on 6 June.[3] These actions, technically merely strengthening garrisons already there, were both provocative and precautionary but not illegal.[4] Berne reluctantly acquiesced, but there were no signs of any local enthusiasm for a campaign. Zurich insisted 'We are forced to save the honour of God and his holy word as well as our own and with God's help will overthrow the forces of evil and punish and take reparations for the wrong that has been done.'[5] Relying on the assumption that there was no lawful Abbot of St Gall, and ignoring delaying tactics from Berne, Zurich forces moved towards the monastic estates, Urzach, Thurgau and Rheintal. The blocking of the road to Muri meant that Unterwalden recalled its agent, who thus did not 'ride' after all, but it was too late to affect the situation, and the occupation went forward as planned.[6] This withdrawal was promptly reported to Zurich by Berne with some pleasure; there was now no cause for war, and Bernese help would be forthcoming only if Zurich territory was actually attacked. It made no difference. Zurich was convinced that there was just cause for intervention and that a combined Catholic operation against the evangelicals must be anticipated. Men had started to move and could not be recalled. The Zurich declaration of war on 8 June was accompanied by a carefully worded printed statement of their case.[7]

The evangelical superiority in manpower was manifest – Zurich with her supporters could put 30,000 men into the field, while the Catholics had at best only a third of that number. The latter were taken by surprise, were short of supplies, ill-equipped, and left in the lurch by their allies;

---

[1] Steck & Tobler, 1045 (No. 2313), 1052 (No. 2326); Tardent, 242–3.
[2] Z VI ii, 430–1; Haas, *Kappelerkrieg*, 142; EA 4, 1b, 216; Müller, 110. 'Tünd umb gotzwillen etwas dapfers' was Zwingli's advice on 16 June. Z X, 165.
[3] Haas, *Kappelerkrieg* 144; E. Schultz, *Reformation und Gegenreformation in den Freien-Ämtern* (Zürich, 1899).
[4] Tardent 259; Lüthi 47; ZWA VII, 245.
[5] EA 4, 1b, 225.
[6] Schultz 32–3.
[7] EA 4, 1b, 224–7; Haas, *Kappelerkrieg*, 147; ZWA VII, 244; Bullinger, *Ref.* II, 167–9. Basle followed suit on 13 June. R. Wackernagel, etc., *Urkundenbuch der Stadt Basel* (Basle, 1910) x, 101–2 (No. 88); E. Dürr u. P. Roth, *Aktensammlung zur Geschichte der Basler Reformation* (Basle, 1937) 3; 566–7.

such men as they could gather were at Baar waiting on events. Not a man or a gun came from Austria. The Innsbruck administration was bankrupt, the Austrian governor of Bregenz and the Vorarlberg, Marx Sittich of Hohenems, did not move, although his threats caused momentary alarm in Winterthur. A force of 600 men from Zurich under the governor of Kiburg, Hans Rudolf Lavater, rapidly overran Thurgau, Rheintal and St Gall territory, met with no resistance, and by 11 June oaths of allegiance were being received from all sides. Wil and Uznach were occupied easily on 9 and 10 June by Jacob Werdmüller and Ludwig Tschudi of Glarus, but they found it more difficult to secure firm guarantees of obedience from all the inhabitants.[1] A third contingent under Hans Escher occupied Wädenswil, while the main force of 4,000, with guns, marched from Zurich to Kappel at mid-day on 9 June to threaten the Catholic states with invasion.[2] With them rode Zwingli on a horse, as volunteer and not as army chaplain, with a fine but very unclerical halberd over his shoulder. He wanted a permanent settlement. To a friend he wrote: 'The peace, which so many strive for, means war; the war that we call for means peace, for we thirst for no man's blood but are determined that the effective force of the Oligarchs shall be cut off. If that does not happen neither the truths of the Bible nor the lives of its servants are safe. Our intentions are not cruel ones for what we seek is friendship and the true interests of our country. We hope to save it when, through ignorance, it is in danger of being overthrown. With all our might we strive to secure freedom.'[3]

The Bernese movements are interesting. A strong force of 6,000 men under Sebastian von Diesbach and Kaspar von Mülinen left Berne on 10 June and, halting en route at Langental and Aarau, reached Bremgarten only on 16 June. Although there was no action, the existence of this army was important. Berne was disturbed by the rapidity of Zurich's eastward advance and was not in favour of breaking up the Confederation; Diesbach was believed to have Catholic sympathies, the war was not popular,[4] and the men were anxious to be home for the hay harvest. The small supporting force from Basle was equally unenthusiastic.

Solothurn, Schaffhausen, St Gall, Glarus and other states offered to mediate, and almost as soon as the Zurich force arrived at Kappel the

---

[1] ZWA VII, 245–6; Stumpf, 2, II, 56–8; Haas, *Kappelerkrieg* 153.

[2] The commander of the contingent was Jörg Berger, who soon succeeded Jacob Werdmüller as city treasurer (*Seckelmeister*). For the campaign, Müller, 112–20; Wyss, 118–22; Z X, 149–50; Muralt, *Berger*.

[3] Z X, 147–8; Schmid 17–18. This report (from Myconius) deserves attention. Was Zwingli right? Would not action in 1529 have prevented the war of 1531, with a very different outcome?

[4] 'Wir liegen mit schweren Kosten im Feld, die Zürcher nehmen den Nutzen.' Oechsli 3, cc. 141–2; Z X, 152–8; Feller II, 197; Haas, *Kappelerkrieg* 158–64. 'Der gmein man ist zuo beder syt me frid begirig dann hitzig und lustig zuo kriegen.' Strickler II, 241 (No. 617).

Landammann of Glarus, Hans Aebli, a relative of Zwingli, asked on behalf of Schwyz for an armistice. Next morning he appeared again, renewing his appeal for peace with tears in his eyes. He urged the distress to widows and families of the slain, and at the same time appealed to the unity of the Confederation which had resisted the common enemy in the past so successfully. The soldiers agreed to consider the position, and Zwingli parted from Aebli with the words, 'You must render account of this to God. While the enemy are weak and ill-equipped they speak fair words which you believe and call for peace. But if they are able to rearm they will have no pity on us and there will be no one to make peace.'[1]

Zwingli, who was spoiling for a fight, was now obliged to state the terms on which he would agree to an armistice if this must come, although personally he was opposed to it.[2] First of all, he insisted, they must require that the Bible should be freely preached in the Catholic states, Catholic services, of course, continuing there as usual and the mass remaining forbidden in Zurich-controlled territory. Foreign pensions were to be renounced and those who had received them were to be punished. Reparations must be paid to Zurich for the costs of putting men on a war footing, with compensation to the children of Jacob Kaiser, and no one was to be molested for any part taken in such activities – 'no victimisation'. There must be an end to insults, abuse and mockery, with punishment for those responsible, Thomas Murner being later singled out by name. Alliances with foreign powers (i.e. Ferdinand) must be publicly denounced.

While these suggestions, or requirements, were being considered, the armed men stopped at the frontier.[3] Those from the Catholic states were short of solid food because Zurich had deliberately prevented grain from reaching the mountain inhabitants in order to build up pressure for peace. They had, naturally, ample supplies of milk. At the armistice, the hostile forces confronted each other at Ebertswil on the border near Kappel – to cross it would be an act of hostility. While the commanders were being entertained by Joner in the secularised buildings of the Abbey of Kappel, the southerners, as we may call them, on 10 June placed a huge barrel or vat of milk on the demarcation line, explaining they had no bread to go with it. The northerners produced bread, of which they had plenty, and meat, so that milk soup resulted, each side dipping into the pot in turn. If, however, anyone stretched too far, he got his knuckles cracked, with the words 'eat on your own territory'. Jacob Sturm from Strassburg was

[1] Bullinger, *Ref.* II, 170.
[2] Haas, *Kappelerkrieg*, 169; Schmid, 25; Z VI ii, 448 (451)-3; Z X, 153-4.
[3] There was thus no invasion. Solothurn, the ally of Berne, must otherwise have supported Zurich, but instead was able to help to mediate.

present and was heard to remark: 'You Swiss are wonderful people. Divided, you are yet united and do not forget ancient friendships.'[1]

It took two weeks of hard bargaining in a tent at Kappel, helped along by the mediators, to produce agreement about the terms to be embodied in the 'First Territorial Peace' (*Landfriede*).

The negotiations took place in three stages between 16 June and 25 June.[2] On 16 June Manuel, Imhag, Bischoff and Tremp had preliminary discussions in Zurich before riding to Kappel on the following day. There, further arbitrators from Glarus, Fribourg, Appenzell and Graubünden had arrived to meet the delegates from the Five Inner States, the Christian Civic Union and the army commanders. The preliminary discussions (16–18 June) took place at Steinhausen between the representatives of Berne, Basle, Zurich and the city of St Gall to agree on their demands. Berne was not there prepared to uphold the Zurich condition that pensions and mercenary service should be permanently renounced and that past pensioners should be punished. Manuel further insisted that the Zurich unconditional requirement of freedom of preaching should be modified to a request. The Zurich plea for war damages of 30,000 crowns with continued occupation of Thurgau, Rheintal and St Gall territory until these were paid was left to the decision of the mediators. These latter also agreed with Manuel that the requirement for the abandonment of pensions should be changed into an urgent suggestion, at which point Zwingli intervened in person to insist that this clause should remain mandatory. Zurich and Berne were thus out of step.

Manuel thereupon asked for further instructions from Berne, knowing that his resistance to punishment of the leading pensioners would please his masters. He also indicated that he had reservations about the question of the continuation of the French alliance and about the renunciation of mercenary service and of foreign presents. He further reported that there was likely to be agreement about occupation costs. The answer was to leave him a free hand to negotiate but with no authority to make any binding contract.

Berne was not ready to insist upon freedom of preaching or the punishment of pensioners, and it was in the light of these instructions that the reformed allies discussed the terms to be demanded with the mediators at Kappel. Zwingli now tried to secure agreement with Berne about pensions by an appeal to the people, and was so far successful that the clause about the renunciations of pensions was agreed, although without any mention

---

[1] Bullinger, *Ref.* II, 182–3 (cf. Salat, 229–30) seems to be the original of this story proudly repeated in every Swiss text-book. It seems likely that fraternisation was confined to the 'other ranks' and that the official attitude was one of disapproval. The same men were ruthlessly killing one another two years later, also at Kappel.

[2] For what follows, Tardent 261–77; EA 4, 1b, 265–74.

of punishment for past offenders. General discussions re-opened at Kappel on 20 June when the possibility that the egregious Murner might manage to escape trial by leaving the country was considered. This was all that could be arranged then, and the situation became serious. If the armistice came to an end, fighting was sure to start. There were further discussions between Zurich and Berne, particularly about Unterwalden, Berne insisting upon its submission. Finally at a third round of negotiations from 22 to 25 June, the terms of the first peace of Kappel were reduced to writing.[1] Up to the last moment it seemed as if hostilities must re-open, which was what Zwingli hoped for, because the Catholics were most reluctant to produce the treaty of Waldshut for public destruction, but in the end they gave way.[2]

During the interval the soldiers, armed and prepared for battle, maintained exemplary discipline on each side. The Catholics heard mass, walked in processions and organised a pilgrimage to Einsiedeln; among the Zurich contingent there were sermons and prayer-meetings as in the English 'Model Army' a century later, and there was singularly little of the countryside pilfering which was usually a feature of armies on campaign. The men from Zurich returned home on 26 June to an elaborate public welcome at the Lindenhof arranged by the city gilds, and by the end of the month all the contingents, with banners flying, had marched in triumph or contentment to their respective dispersing points.[3]

Zwingli was bitterly disappointed at the outcome, which also marked a decline in his political influence.[4] Agreement had been the work of the soldiers rather than the politicians, and the compromise reflected the common sense of Berne, guided by Hans Escher, rather than Zurich religious idealism and political ambition. With the peace, in fact, vanished Zwingli's dream of an all-Protestant united Confederation. There was no sign that the people of the Catholic states were ready to turn against either their rulers or their religion, and in 1529 neither side visualised the possibility of a viable Swiss state embracing irreconcilable religious faiths. By then, everything connected with the Roman Catholic church had become wholly evil in Zwingli's eyes so that he thought of its overthrow as necessary, inevitable and even imminent. This conviction clouded his usually acute political judgement.

It is easy to think of Zwingli in the light of his advocacy of a preventive war in 1529 and of his death in action in 1531 with battle-axe and breast

---

[1] Probably the terms were verbally agreed on 24 June, written out on 25 June, and formally sealed on 26 June. For fuller details see below, 371–4.
[2] Feller, II, 198–9; EA 4, 1b, 1478–83; Escher, *Glaubensparteien*, 91; Schmid 32–5.
[3] ZWA x, 537–73 with a good review of the literature; ZWA xII, 257; Stumpf 2, II, 64; Wyss, 128–9; Bullinger, *Ref.* II, 193.
[4] ZWA xII, 254–80, 309–29 esp. 312–13; Z x, 177.

plate, as a 'hawk' or militarist. This, however, is a superficial view. His early experiences in Italy had convinced him of the horrors of warfare, and his reading of the Erasmian literature on war had intensified this conviction. Peace was a desirable state to be sought at all times. There were, none the less, two important qualifications to this end. Armed combat was the affair of the secular state, and it was the duty of a citizen to obey his government and therefore to fight if called upon to do so. A war could be both just and necessary: just, if it was in defence of the word of God or to resist an unprovoked attack; necessary, if by God's will his kingdom could be secured by the sword. In this latter event Zwingli obviously welcomed the prospect of a favourable decision and was prepared to continue to fight until favourable terms had been obtained. Hence his dissatisfaction with the Bernese reluctance to continue in the field in 1529. In 1531 the aggression came from the Catholic camp; Zurich was attacked, and the second war was one of legitimate self-defence in which he could take part as a loyal citizen.

He was right in thinking that for there to be a powerful Switzerland it must be united, but even on this supposition he thought in terms of an earlier generation and miscalculated the real strength of a small confederation. None the less, if everything had gone as Zwingli wished and planned in 1529, the central states must have submitted and the possibility of an effective and strong *confoederatio Helvetica*, enlarged and guided by its cities, could have become a reality. It was a remote chance, but, as it turned out, the only one.

15

Precarious peace

Zurich, supported by Berne and their civic allies, was at war with the Inner States for sixteen days (8–24 June 1529), during which there was no fighting but which resulted in a qualified victory for the attackers. The first Land Peace of Kappel (*der erste Landfriede*), as the agreement which ended the war on 24 June was known, came after over a week of hard bargaining. Its provisions[1] reflected the chief interests involved – the determination of Zurich to extend the evangelical faith and with it to increase its authority in eastern Switzerland, and the anxiety of Berne to keep the confederation in being while at the same time asserting its own authority together with its firm adhesion to a reformed church.

The peace terms were harsh, but were a good deal less severe than Zwingli had wanted. There was not complete submission; the right of each side to maintain its own faith and worship was upheld. The Catholics were not crushed or humiliated; they were not even to be forced to accept evangelical preachers without reciprocity. Instead, the first article called for freedom of belief; no one was to be compelled to adopt a particular faith.[2] In the Mandated Territories the parishes (*Gemeinden*) were to be free to choose their own form of worship, Catholic or Zwinglian, by a majority vote if necessary, after which there should be no further governmental interference.[3]

---

[1] EA 4, 1b, 262, 321–2, 1478–86; Bullinger *Ref.* II, 185–91. There is a useful summary in Z VI ii, 457–9 and a commentary in F. Straub, *Zürich und die Bewährung des ersten Landfriedens* (Zurich, 1970). Also in W. Oechsli, *Quellenbuch zur Schweizergeschichte*[2] (Zürich, 1901) (modernised and abbreviated), 425 (No. 135).

[2] 'Des ersten, von wegen des göttlichen worts, diewyl und niemand zum glouben gezwungen sol werden, dass dann die Oerter und die iren desselben ouch nit genötiget; aber die zuogwandten und vogtyen, wo man mit einandern zuo beherschen hat, belangend, wo die selben die mess abgestellt und die bilder verbrennt oder abgetan, dass die selben an lib, eer und guot nit gestraft söllend werden; wo aber die mess und ander ceremonia noch vorhanden, die söllent nit gezwungen, ouch deheine predicanten, so es durch den merteil nit erkannt würt, geschickt, ufgestellt oder gegeben werden, sunder was under inen den kilchgnossen, die uf oder abzetuon, der glichen mit der spyss, so gott nit verbotten ze essen, gemeret würt, daby sol es biss uff der kilchgnossen gefallen bliben, und dehein teil dem andern sinen glouben weder fechen noch strafen.' EA 4, 1b, 1479. Cf. E. Walder, *Religionsvergleiche des 16. Jahrhunderts* (Berne, 1945) 5. Z X, 195, 203–4, 213–14 n. I.

[3] P. Brüschweiler, *Die landfriedlichen Simultanverhältnisse im Thurgau* (Frauenfeld, 1932), 51–2.

This critical article was, in fact, a model of ambiguity and was differently interpreted by each side. Zwingli thought it secured freedom for his followers to preach the Gospel unhindered anywhere, an interpretation which the Catholics would not accept. In practice, the reformed minorities looked to Zurich and Berne for protection, and Catholic minorities to the five Catholic states.

By the second article, as Zwingli had insisted, the treaty of Waldshut with Ferdinand was abrogated and the Catholic Christian Alliance was dissolved, in spite of its nominally purely defensive character. The actual parchment instrument was exhibited to all by Hans Aebli and then cut into shreds and burnt, to the astonishment of Thomas Platter, who was present at the time.[1]

The matter of foreign pensions and the recruitment of mercenaries outside their own territory by the five Catholic states again received less decisive treatment than Zwingli had asked. There was indeed a clause prohibiting recruiting, but this applied only to land controlled by the reformed cities, who could see to it themselves; and the acceptance of extraneous pensions, while declared undesirable, was left, as Berne wished, to the discretion of each state. By article five it was agreed that affairs involving the whole Confederation should not be discussed in separate Catholic or Protestant diets; these might, however, deal with business affecting themselves only.

War damages or reparations were to be paid as assessed by arbitrators (who reduced a claim for 80,000 gulden to the much more moderate figure of 2,500 'Sonnen-Kronen' each to Berne and Zurich). Berne's claims from Unterwalden were also left to arbitration.[2] Compensation was similarly to be assessed for the dependants of Jacob Kaiser.[3] Continuity for reform in Thurgau, Toggenburg, Rheintal, Gaster and monastic St Gall was thought to be secured by a provision that agreements already made to accept the reformed faith were to be maintained and no one was to be punished for having aided Zurich and Berne. Any future guardian (*Schirmhauptmann*) of monastic property in Thurgau was to be an evangelical.

Thomas Murner,[4] so much disliked, was to be handed over for trial on a

[1] Z x, 181, 209; *Thomas Platter: Lebensbeschreibung*, hg. v. A. Hartmann (Basle, 1944) 84, 85.
[2] EA 4, 1b, 301, 371, 1483–6; Escher, *Glaubensparteien* 121, 169, 181; Bullinger, *Ref.* II, 200, 203; Tardent, 285, 292; ZWA XII (1964), 267, 324. Negotiations about payment went on for a long while: something, but it is difficult to determine how much, was actually received, and how far the use made of the blockade weapon could be justly referred to this condition of the peace is equally debatable.
[3] EA 4, 1b, 1480; Steck & Tobler, 1458 (No. 3207). The arbitrators awarded 100 Kronen a month, charged on Lucerne.
[4] EA 4, 1b, 1481. He was an indefatigable journalist who had set up his own press at Lucerne and whose notorious *Ketzerkalender* was a thoroughly scurrilous performance, like many

charge of inciting to revolt, but apart from this there was to be 'no victimisation', no individual prosecution of adherents to either side. Linked up
with this was a vague and ill-drafted clause demanding the cessation of
slander and defamation[1] and the punishment of perpetrators. Open abuse
of those of contrary faith was to cease and offenders were to be dealt with
by their governments. In the sixteenth century, when virulent personal
denunciation was commonplace, such a provision was hardly capable of
enforcement. It was, none the less, to be used later as a pretext for reopening hostilities.

Even worse was the practical application of the agreement that the
localities should decide by an internal majority (*durch den merteil*) their
doctrinal preference. Apart from uncertainty as to who might 'vote', the
introduction of local option by majority choice in religious affairs was an
almost unheard-of innovation. Unanimity, as has been seen, had been the
normal expectation[2] and it was for the government to decide the religion
of its subjects. Now local assemblies (*Gemeindeversammlungen, Lands-
gemeinden, Landräte*) had to meet, as well as local synods for the clergy, of
which important use was made.[3] If parishes were allowed to come to a
majority decision why not other groups? And what was to happen when,
as in monastic St Gall, the administering authorities were half Catholic,
half Protestant? There was to be no acceptable answer to this for a long while.

More obvious were the clauses dealing with obligations and accomplished facts. Thus tithes and other customary offerings for the upkeep of
the churches and their ministers were to continue to be paid as previously.
Similarly, where altars and images had already been removed, the old
regime was not to return, existing arrangements were to be frozen, and no
one was to be punished for earlier iconoclasm.[4]

others of the age. He had been equally violent in his satirical attacks on Luther. At Strassburg
his activities were such that he was expelled from this unusually tolerant city: Berne was
specially annoyed by his publications, particularly, *Hie würt angezeigt das unchristlich frevel
...einer loblichen herrschaft von Bern* (1528). His later escape *via* Valais to his native Alsace,
and thence to Heidelberg, made possible by the connivance of Lucerne, was much resented.
'Die böseste Zunge in der Eidgenossenschaft war stille geworden' (Brändly, 93). See also
Salat 141, 239; Th. v. Liebenau, *Der Franziskaner Dr. Thomas Murner* (Freiburg, 1913)
238–48; Schmid, 35, 37, 39; P. Scherrer, *Thomas Murners Verhältnis zum Humanismus*
(Basle, 1929); W. Kawerau, *Th. Murner und die deutsche Reformation* (Halle, 1891), *Thomas
Murner und die Kirche des Mittelalters* (Halle, 1890); W. Pfeiffer-Belli, *Thomas Murner im
Schweizer Glaubenskampf. Corpus Catholicorum* 22 (Münster i.W., 1939), 39–86.
[1] A. Blatter, *Schmähungen, Scheltreden, Drohungen. Ein Beitrag zur Geschichte der Volksstim-
mung zur Zeit der schweizer. Reformation* (Basle, 1911) provides samples.
[2] In the *Burgrecht* between Zurich and Berne of 25 June 1528, the possibility of majority
acceptance of evangelical preaching had been agreed on as a working arrangement. EA 4, 1b,
esp. 1334, 1521–5 Art. 8 'Weliche ouch unser gmeinen underthanen das evangelium und
wort gottes mit merer hand ir gmeinen kilchgnossen annemen'. See above, 348–9.
[3] Egli 4, 84–5, 90–4.
[4] EA 4, 1b, 1480–1.

The occupation of Thurgau and monastic St Gall was to continue until these conditions were fulfilled and, by a kind of appendix, the evangelical cities were permitted to maintain an economic blockade against their former opponents should the articles be transgressed or the indemnity remain unpaid.[1] The last article, inserted at the wish of Berne, called for a renewal of the oath of Confederation, to include mention of this peace. In practice it proved impossible to reach agreement on any acceptable formula for this, and after long and inconclusive discussions no such action was possible until 1798.

The results of the first, bloodless, war of Kappel did not satisfy the ambitions and demands of Zurich. There had been no trial of strength; and complete, unrestricted freedom to spread the Zwinglian creed throughout the Confederation had not been secured. Foreign pensions continued to be paid, and hopes of expansion into Aargau by Zurich had not been fulfilled. There were, however, substantial gains in eastern Switzerland. Schaffhausen became entirely Zwinglian,[2] and in Rheintal, Gaster, Weesen, Bremgarten, Mellingen, in the county of Baden, and in a number of parishes in Sargans, reformed majorities were relatively easily secured.[3] Berne remained an ally, but without enthusiasm for the expansionist activities of its neighbour. Its support in June 1529 had been a little reluctant, motivated chiefly by the need for help in the event of a war with Savoy, now acting in cooperation with the five Catholic states.[4] In contrast, the city of St Gall, which had made every effort to assist its ally with provisions, ammunition and a few men, was highly satisfied by the outcome of the war, as was its chief citizen, Vadian.[5] The chapel of St James there was completely wrecked, and the nuns, who had already been forced to abandon their habits, were expelled, their corporate income being confiscated to the city. The walls of the monastic church were whitewashed, verses from the Bible replacing the earlier mural paintings, and a new, enthusiastic Reformed minister, Christopher Schappeler,[6] was installed

---

[1] 'feilen kouf und spiss abschlagen', *Proviantsperre, Proviantabschlag*, i.e. economic sanctions. The harvest in 1529 was bad and this made the threat the more serious. R. Bosch, *Der Kornhandel der Nord-Ost-Innerschweiz und der ennetbirgischen Vogteien im 15. und 16. Jahrhundert* (Zurich, 1913), 109.

[2] J. Wipf, *Reformationsgeschichte der Stadt und Landschaft Schaffhausen* (Zurich, 1929).

[3] The terms of the peace did not apply to Murten, Orbe-Eschellens and Grandson, which Berne continued to administer jointly with Catholic Fribourg. In fact Berne secured the reformation of these areas without much difficulty. Feller II, 355, 359; P. Weissenbach, 'Die Reformation in Bremgarten' (in *Argovia. Jahresschrift der Historischen Gesellschaft des Kantons Aargau* VI (1871), 3–65, with an appendix of documents).

[4] Lüthi, 57–8. See below 385.

[5] Näf, *Vadian* II, 309–10; Müller, 115–16, 192ff; Muralt/Fast, 597, 598.

[6] Müller 192–3; Bullinger *Ref.* II, 115–19. Schappeler had published articles against the Catholics and had sided with the peasants in 1525. O. Clemen, *Flugschriften aus den ersten Jahren der Reformation* II, 4. hg. A. Götze (Leipzig, 1908).

there. At least fourteen church bells were melted down, the metal being used for making a cannon able to fire a stone ball weighing thirteen pounds.

The first peace of Kappel, like many another relatively common-sense arrangement, satisfied neither side. The Catholics had been humiliated by heretics without being defeated, and this rankled. The Zwinglians, equally, were confident that, but for the armistice, they would have crushed their immediate opponents whom they outnumbered. The Gospel would then have been able to make its way unimpeded, and the mass would have given way before it, with the implication of a Zurich-dominated Protestant confederation. The peace was, in fact, in advance of its time. Hardly any one, in 1529, thought it possible for two opposed religious communities to live side by side in peace in the same state. This, it was supposed, and with a good deal of justification, merely meant civil war, which must end in the final triumph of one party. In Switzerland, indeed, a conflict could scarcely be regarded as civil war so loose was the constitution of the federation. Religious affairs were the exclusive concern of each state[1] and others were not involved, but even so the Reformation intensified antagonism. Even limited cooperation was difficult, if not impossible, between 'orthodox' and 'heretics', the adherents of the 'true' and the 'false' religion. All were agreed that it was the duty of a Christian government – *die Christliche Obrichkeit* – to see to it that its subjects were properly instructed in the Christian faith, evangelical or Catholic. The government must be obeyed. To this accepted conviction there were important qualifications. For the Catholics, a government that upheld heresy was detestable and must rightly be eliminated; for the Zwinglians, one that impeded or resisted the promulgation of God's word could be lawfully disobeyed. Thus in areas where the government was in the hands of a plurality of states, as in the Mandated Territories, each side could have a case for intervention in a parish which disobeyed its rulers, i.e. the majority of the controlling states.[2] Zurich could use this argument in eastern Switzerland to its own political advantage.

The first peace of Kappel was an agreement made between the antagonists only and was in no way binding on the other states of the Confederation. The contracting parties, however, agreed that the special local arrangements applied to the Mandated Territories in which they were

---

[1] At a meeting in Zurich in February 1527, followed by another in Berne, it had been accepted that the Confederation dealt 'only with external affairs, mutual help, advice and care for widows and orphans, land and people'. EA 4, 1a, 1050, 1063. It was pointed out that in Germany, in spite of religious dividions, Lutheran and Catholic cities met their allies for political and economic discussions and the cities were summoned to Imperial Diets irrespective of sect. Similar arrangements should be possible for the Swiss. Escher, *Glaubensparteien*, 45.   [2] Haas, *Kappelerkrieg*, 86.

severally involved. It was accepted that two faiths could exist side by side in one district; but within this each village or *Gemeinde* decided its acceptable form of worship to be applicable to all its inhabitants. It was, perhaps, on a very small scale the appearance of the *cuius regio eius religio* principle of 1555. The obscurely worded clause, which permitted preaching of the Gospel generally, was unworkable. If it meant that Zwinglian evangelists were to occupy Catholic pulpits, Lucerne would obviously refuse, the more so since Catholic priests could not administer the sacraments in Zwinglian states. There were local difficulties over the interpretation of the 'majority clause' of the first peace almost from the beginning.[1] At Flums, for example, where Martin Mannhart evangelised actively but not entirely successfully, there was profound disagreement about its application.[2] Again, there was trouble at Rapperswil. Hans Schindler of Weesen complained that he was slandered by the Catholic priest of Rapperswil, Hans Ofner, contrary to the provisions of the treaty, and sought a remedy. Rapperswil refused to hand over Ofner for trial when requested to do so by Zurich, which had no special rights in either Weesen or Rapperswil. Ofner was supported by Uri, Schwyz and Unterwalden, while Glarus refused to intervene. Schindler died before the matter came to a head, but many in Zurich regretted a lost opportunity.[3]

The abandonment of the Christian Alliance by the Catholics was no irreparable disaster. Austria, not for the first or the last time, had proved an unreliable ally, and the lesson was duly learnt. Its evangelical counterpart, the Christian Civic Union, remained in existence but was not notably effective. Constance, indeed, had already been included, but the attempts that were made to secure recognition for Constance as a fourteenth component of the Confederation were unsuccessful.[4] Another city-state member would alter the balance of town and country states; Constance, ruling no territory outside its own walls, had little to offer; it would not be easy for it to be assimilated even into an evangelical Confederation, and in fact the city-states did not cooperate very readily.

Many of these considerations likewise applied to Strassburg, the last city to join the Christian Civic Union. A special relationship had long existed between the Swiss and this free imperial city. When both were in danger of attack by Charles the Rash of Burgundy, Strassburg had sought

---

[1] At Bremgarten, Bullinger, who had certainly been more useful there than he would have been at Marburg, was indefatigable in his evangelical sermons. There was violence at Muri, where the Catholics secured a majority of 40; elsewhere there were frequent arguments about eligibility to vote. Indeed the very notion of voting was hardly a comprehensible one then. Could a servant of the monastery vote in the Alte Landschaft? Were youths of 13 eligible?
[2] Z x, 494, 536–7. See below p. 384 n. 3.
[3] Strickler II, 657 (No. 1641).
[4] See above 352–3; below 385.

and obtained inclusion in the Lower Union (*die Niedere Vereinigung*) with Sigismund of Austria and had thus become the ally of the Swiss in the fifteenth century.[1] The city, under the guidance of Bucer, Capito and Sturm (all of whom had been present at the Berne disputation), had accepted the Reformation without being Lutheran; its position could be described as quasi-Zwinglian. This meant that its situation was somewhat precarious and isolated, but it was in close contact by the Rhine with Basle and so with the other cities of the Christian Civic Union. To Zurich and Basle it could offer a northern bulwark and a link with Hesse. It was vulnerable to attack from the Austrian forces in Alsace and the Black Forest and if forcibly Catholicised might be a threat to Basle. An alliance was obviously advantageous. It could supply grain, provender and gunpowder, and the spiritual and intellectual support of its leading divines was appreciated. Strassburg abolished the mass in February 1529, Basle in April; the first Kappel peace was in June. A meeting at Aarau in July favoured an agreement with Strassburg, which Zwingli visited in September, and this city was belatedly accepted into *Burgrecht* with Zurich and as a full member of the Christian Civic Union on 5 January 1530.[2] The delay had been caused by long discussions about exactly what Strassburg could offer and about precedence which Zurich successfully insisted upon maintaining.[3]

By that time, however, a good deal had happened, involving both Zurich and Zwingli personally. He was now at the height of his intellectual powers, and his position at home was never stronger.[4] It is probably a misuse of words to speak of Zwinglian Zurich as a theocracy,[5] but after the expulsion of the Anabaptists and the abolition of the mass, the external aspect of the city had altered decidedly for the better. There was less swearing, gambling, dancing and drunkenness. A code of compulsory conduct issued in March 1530[6] enforced public morality as well as regular church-going, attendance at sermons, and closing hours for vendors of wine (joined a little incongruously with regulation of weights and measures),

[1] E. Toutey, *Charles le Téméraire et la ligue de Constance* (Paris, 1902) 86–8, 243–4. Mülhausen, a member of the Christian Civil Union, was in a similar position but in the long run had to break away, as did Rottweil where 300 Protestants were expelled. Z vi ii, 672; Oechsli 2, 26–30, 88–94, 116.
[2] EA 4, 1b, 498, 1488–93; Wyss, 149 n. 2; Z vi ii, 468–77; R. Reuss, *Histoire de Strasbourg depuis ses origines jusqu'à nos jours* (Paris, 1922), 129–31.
[3] The question of precedence was settled, 22 Dec. 1529. Strassburg wanted the alliance to be called *Christlich nachbarlicher Verstand*, but this fell flat. Z x, 352, 355–6; Escher, *Glaubensparteien*, 101–7, 140–42; EA 4, 1b, 353; HZ 40. 131.
[4] Hauswirth, *Philipp*, 196. 'Von der Rückkehr aus Marburg bis über die Jahreswende war Zwingli fast unmittelbarer Führer der zürcherischen Aussenpolitik gewesen.'
[5] R. C. Walton, *Zwingli's Theocracy* (Toronto, 1967); L. v. Muralt, 'Zum Problem der Theokratie bei Zwingli', *Discordia Concors* ii, 367–90; Locher, 198.
[6] Egli *1*, 702–11, No. 1656; Bullinger, *Ref.* ii, 276–88.

while prohibiting blasphemy,[1] card-playing, dicing, skittles, chess and other games likely to lead to disorder. A Christian government, Zwingli always insisted, would be a good government because it followed Bible precepts, and Zurich did just that. There were indeed still a good many clerics, but their learning, dress and conduct were strictly checked and regulated; disrespect to them, however, could lead to exclusion from church services, which might well be followed by more tangible penalties Sermons and church-going were a conspicuous feature of civic life. Zwingli constantly accused his Catholic rivals of hypocrisy, but there are some indications that this same fault was not always absent from among his own followers now that they were supreme.

At the same time the Marburg conference, to which, significantly, no representative of Berne had been invited, had left the Zwinglians in a lonely position. The continued theological disharmony had its political repercussions, since after October 1529 cooperation between Lutheran princes and Zwinglian cities was almost bound to be limited strictly to defence.[2] The important political discussions at Marburg further meant that Zwingli was now closely involved in German affairs. His teaching had made remarkable progress among the south-German cities from Constance to Ulm, and he was now directly in touch with the Landgrave Philip of Hesse.[3] This remarkable young ruler, whose contacts with Zwingli at Marburg have already been considered, had succeeded in 1518, scarcely aged fourteen, to almost absolute authority in a powerful and wealthy state stretching from Kassel to Giessen. He had shown from the outset vast energy and ambition, great ability and determination to advance his power still further. Physically rather small, sometimes reckless and aggres-

---

[1] It is characteristic of the age that in 1529 and 1530 two farmers from the Kelleramt were put to death for swearing and for irreverent and careless speech on the way to the Christmas communion service: little comment seems to have been aroused. Farner IV, 398; Egli *I*, 693 (No. 1632), 701 (No. 1654).   [2] Bender, *Ref.*, 155, 173; Schmid, 40.

[3] A good biography of Philip the Magnanimous is a desideratum. The documents in D. C. von Rommel, *Philipp der Grossmüthige, Landgraf von Hessen* (3 Bde., Giessen, 1830), supplemented by W. Heinemeyer, *Quellen und Darstellungen zur Geschichte des Landgrafen Philipp des Grossmütigen* (Marburg, 1954), are useful. P. Hoffmeister, *Das Leben Philipps des Grossmüthigen, Landgrafen von Hessen* (Kassel, 1846) formed the basis for later accounts, including the article by Friedensburg in ADB (1887). The German background is in D. C. v. Rommel, *Geschichte von Hessen* (8 Bde., Marburg, Kassel, 1820–43) III i, III ii. G. Egelhaaf, *Landgraf Philipp der Grossmüthige* (Halle, 1904); *Philipp der Grossmütige. Beiträge zur Geschichte seines Lebens und seiner Zeit*: ed. J. R. Dieterich & B. Müller, Historischer Verein für das Grossherzogtum Hessen (Marburg, 1904), have little about Switzerland. J. W. Wille, *Philipp der Grossmüthige von Hessen und die Restitution Ulrichs von Wirtemberg* (Tübingen, 1882) is valuable, and René Hauswirth, *Landgraf Philipp von Hessen und Zwingli: ihre politischen Beziehungen, 1529–30*, ZWA XI (1962), 499–552, and *Philipp* are essential. They correct and amplify, but do not supersede, Lenz, articles which first decoded the symbols used in the correspondence between Philip and Zwingli. H. J. Hillerbrand, *Landgrave Philipp of Hesse 1504–1567* (St Louis, Missouri, 1967) is a very brief sketch. Fabian, 331–2 has a useful note.

sive, highly class-conscious, and connected by birth and marriage with the ruling princely caste,[1] he was later known as 'the magnanimous', an epithet Zwingli used of him in 1531.[2] As a result, perhaps, of Melanchthon's preaching, he became a sincere and broad-minded evangelical in 1524[3] and the backbone of the opposition to the Catholics and the Habsburgs. Convinced that God had conferred a special, almost unique, position on a 'godly prince', he had made himself the leader of the attack on the knights under Franz von Sickingen, and on the insurgent peasants in 1525. He had profound political sense and real ability, was a good judge of men and was in many ways in marked contrast with his equally influential eastern neighbour, John 'the Steadfast', Elector of Saxony. This deeply religious man was likewise determined to uphold the reformed faith but was by nature mild, lethargic and primarily interested in his own state. Unlike Philip, he had considerable respect for the office and person of the Emperor, and he opposed Philip's efforts to expand his possessions at the expense of the neighbouring bishoprics.

Even so, in 1526 Philip hoped to join with Lutheran Saxony, Brunswick,[4] Mecklenburg, Mansfeld and the Protestant cities, especially Strassburg, Nuremberg, Augsburg and Ulm, in defence of their liberties as set out at the Diet of Speier. Support might reasonably be expected from Frederick I, King of Denmark and Duke of Schleswig-Holstein, a Protestant who could be relied upon to oppose Charles V, whose sister, Isabella, had married the rival claimant Christian II.[5] Brandenburg under Elector Joachim I was indeed still Catholic, but its ruler was neutral and wavering. In any case Philip was capable of keeping religion and politics apart and had no objection to an alliance with the Catholic King of France or with the Catholic Dukes William and Louis of Bavaria, the Wittelsbach rivals of the Habsburgs and strongly opposed to the choice of Ferdinand as King of the Romans, a position Philip was believed to covet for himself. For them, as for Philip, loyalty to an elected Emperor was an outmoded tradition; territorial independence and expansion were what mattered.

At home in all the bewildering family connections and rivalries of Germany,[6] the Prince of Hesse had intelligence enough to look further

---

[1] His (first) wife, Christine, was the daughter of Duke George of Saxony; his sister Elizabeth married Duke George's son John; his daughter Agnes married first Maurice of Saxony and secondly the Elector John Frederick II of Saxony.

[2] Z XI, 559 (June 1531 to Lambert Maigret): 'De Cattorum principe sic intellige: iuvenis quidem est, puta: 28 natus annos, sed super hanc aetatem prudens, magnanimus et constans, apud illum possumus fere quicquid volumus.'

[3] F. Hugh, 'Landgraf Philipp und die Einführung der Reformation in Hessen', *Zeitschrift des Vereins für Hessische Geschichte und Landeskunde* 80 (Kassel, 1900), 210–42. C. L. Manschreck, *Melanchthon* (New York, 1958), 100.

[4] Dukes Ernest and Francis of Braunschweig-Lüneburg-Celle and Henry of Braunschweig-Wolfenbüttel.   [5] K. Brandi, *Kaiser Karl V*[3] (Münich, 1941), 121–2, 166.

[6] See above, 309, 316–18, 331–4.

afield, to the cities, fearful and jealous of the Emperor, and to the Swiss, as a source of military manpower. This was to introduce a new dimension into the situation. Hitherto the Swiss had been regarded with some dislike and distrust as, at best, providing some good infantry for hire who might also be competitors with the German Landsknechts. This was based not so much on German hostility as on their ignorance about and indifference to the Swiss Confederation.[1] For Luther and his Elector, the Swiss were sectaries and revolutionaries whose notions of self-government and citizen-participation in public affairs were as deplorable as their mis-interpretation of the New Testament. Now, with Philip and Zwingli in agreement, Zurich and its supporters were to be directly involved in German affairs for the first time, and the relations of prince and preacher were to be of decisive importance in 1530 and 1531.

One reason for this was that Philip of Hesse was now actively committed to the cause of the restoration of Duke Ulrich of Württemberg.[2] This violent, ostentatious and impetuous prince, highly unpopular in his own duchy, had married in 1511, at the age of 24, Sabina, daughter of Duke Albert IV of Bavaria. They were ill-matched, and the marriage seemed a fruitless failure. The duke then fell in love with Ursula von Thumb, daughter of his Court Comptroller (*Hofmarschall*) and wife of his Master of the Horse (*Stallmeister*), Ludwig von Hutten, who was himself reputed to have made advances to the duchess Sabina. After a strange scene in which the duke was reported to have knelt before his own servant and avowed his love for the latter's wife, he killed Ludwig while hunting with him in the Böblinger Wald on 7 May 1515. Shortly after this, Sabina, who had given birth to a son, Christopher, fled for protection to her brother, Duke of Bavaria. The Hutten family took up arms, the matter was brought before the Emperor Maximilian, who decided that Ulrich should be deprived of his authority (*Regierung*) for six years, pay a fine, and provide an income for Sabina. On his refusal to accept these conditions, he was put to the ban (*Acht*) of the Empire in 1516 and again in 1518, but this had little effect, even when repeated on the accession of Charles V in 1519. At this juncture, two citizens of Reutlingen, a free imperial city, killed one of Ulrich's officials. Thereupon Ulrich, with the help of Swiss soldiers whom he had been able to hire with French money, attacked the city, reducing it to a dependency (*Landstadt*). This was manifestly a renewed act of open war against the Empire; an imperial force, led by William of Bavaria and supported by the Swabian League,

[1] K. Mommsen, *Eidgenossen, Kaiser und Reich* (Basler Beiträge zur Geschichtswissenschaft, Bd. 72. Basle, 1958).
[2] 1487–1550. B. v. Kugler, *Ulrich, Herzog zu Wirtemberg* (Stuttgart, 1865); Do., *Christoph, Herzog zu Wirtemberg*, 2 Bde. (Stuttgart, 1868–72) I, 5–7; Z VIII, 379–80 n. 1.

brought about Ulrich's defeat at Asperg in May. He took refuge in Basle,[1] where he was patronised by Oecolampadius, whose teaching he accepted. 'Saul became Paul.' He was admitted to co-citizenship there, and in 1524 he moved to Zurich, where he met the Great Council and attended Zwingli's sermons. He was much impressed: 'he taught me to pray', he said later.[2] After his expulsion from his duchy, where the rights of his son Christopher were ignored, his territories fell, in 1521, to Charles V's younger brother, Ferdinand. Ulrich, however, with Philip's help, retained a hold on Hohentwiel and upheld Philip's claim to the small but rich county of Katzenelnbogen (which included Darmstadt and St Goar), although the imperial government insisted that he had no legal rights there.[3] He never ceased to hope to regain his possessions with their capital at Stuttgart, all of which would then inevitably become Protestant. This would also break the Catholic–Habsburg ring which surrounded Zurich from the Vorarlberg to Alsace, and although Ulrich's success was not settled in Zwingli's lifetime it was constantly hoped for and anticipated[4] and made Ulrich a much more acceptable neighbour than Ferdinand. As the ally and supporter of Ulrich, Philip of Hesse had a permanent excuse for an attack on the Habsburgs should a favourable occasion arise, and a united Hesse and Württemberg would alter the balance of power in south Germany. It was through Ulrich that Zwingli came to realise the significance of the position.

The initial contact between Philip, Ulrich and Zwingli had been made in 1524,[5] and the parties were now ready to push matters much further. While the first Kappel war was moving to its inconclusive end, the German situation was transformed by the second Diet of Speier in April 1529.[6] Although Charles V had not been present in person, his own European position was steadily improving. The Pope was no longer actively antagonistic, hostilities with France were suspended, Florence was surrounded by imperial forces, and preparations were in train for the coronation of the Emperor at Bologna. After the Protest of Speier, the German princes had reason to fear lest the return of Charles V to Germany

---

[1] A. Feyler, *Die Beziehungen des Hauses Württemberg zur schweizerischen Eidgenossenschaft in der ersten Hälfte des 16. Jahrhunderts* (Zürich, 1905), 247, 251. Z viii. 226. In November 1521 Ulrich had been accepted by Zurich as a citizen.
[2] Farner IV, 340–1; Muralt-Schmid, 28 n. 1; Z VIII, 380.
[3] There was a stronger claim to it by Counts Henry and William of Nassau. Otto Meinardus, *Der katzenelnbogische Erbfolgestreit* (Nassau-Oranische Correspondenzen I, Wiesbaden, 1899); W. Koehler, *Der Katzenelnbogische Erbfolgestreit im Rahmen der allgemeinen Reformationsgeschichte bis zum Jahre 1530* (Mitteilungen des Oberhessischen Geschichtsvereins, N.F. 11 (Giessen, 1902), 1–30).
[4] Jakob Wille, *Philipp der Grossmüttige von Hessen und die Restitution Ulrichs von Wirtemberg 1526–35* (Tübingen, 1882).
[5] Z VIII, 226; ZWA XIII (1969), 152.   [6] See above, 318–19.

might lead to a diminution of their power and, above all, to an edict of restitution depriving them of the episcopal and monastic territories that they had seized. They might soon have to fight the house of Habsburg for their lands and liberties. For this they needed the support of the wealthy cities,[1] including those of south Germany and Switzerland, many of which were now Zwinglian. If these cities could obtain an alliance with the militant Swiss Confederation, so much the better. Out of it might arise a reformed north–south axis from the Baltic to the Mediterranean, embracing Denmark, Holstein, Frisia, Guelders, Lüneburg, Mecklenburg, Brunswick, Brandenburg, Saxony, Hesse, Württemberg, Zweibrücken, Strassburg, Basle, Zurich, Berne, Constance, Schaffhausen, St Gall, and even Venice and France.[2] How unsubstantial all this was, events were soon to prove.

Zwingli had re-established contact with Philip by sending him a copy of *Amica Exegesis* in June 1527,[3] so that the correspondence of 1529–30, of which probably only fragments survive, was facilitated. Both men were sanguine and optimistic by nature, and they soon came to have confidence in each other. Zwingli was naturally pleased and encouraged to receive the attentions of a prince whose faith he could strengthen by his deep conviction of the sure triumph of his cause. He liked to work out on paper alliances that would forward the expansion of the gospel and the influence of Zurich. The state of affairs in central Germany seemed to offer him opportunities for this, just as that in Switzerland could help Philip. Each wanted action as against the essentially negative and passive attitude of Wittenberg and Berne, and neither really succeeded in obtaining it.

Philip of Hesse hoped for a general Protestant alliance against Pope and Emperor which was not just passively defensive. His attempt to unite Lutherans and Zwinglians at Marburg failed, but politically the outlook was a little more hopeful. At Schmalkalden he again tried unsuccessfully to unite Swiss and Germans, but this also was not his fault. Both Zwingli and Philip miscalculated. Zwingli, the preacher, prophet and religious leader, failed to perceive that Philip was not as sincere as he was himself. He likewise did not appreciate the looseness of the Swiss Confederation, which acted only in self-defence or for manifest economic advantage and was now more deeply divided than ever before. He also far too readily assumed that help would be forthcoming from other Protestant cities,

---

[1] Including, particularly, Strassburg, where Sturm had convinced Philip of the value of its support. Saxony, Hesse, Strassburg, Nuremberg and Ulm agreed in principle to a defensive military alliance on 22 April 1529. Kühn, *Speyer*, 233–4.

[2] See below 393–5. Escher, *Glaubensparteien*, 185; Z x, 379, 444; Lenz, 60–1 n. 2. The instructions from Zurich of 28 October 1529 dealing with this (Z vi ii, 607–8; EA 4, 1b, 419–21) are from StaZ. A. 229. 2 (No. 159 Kappelerkrieg). The numbering is not as in the original.   [3] Z ix, 161–2.

particularly Strassburg and Constance. Philip mistakenly thought of Zwingli as responsible for the policy of Zurich, which he was not, and of Zurich as able to dominate the Christian Civic Union, which it did not. Philip wanted to hire Swiss mercenaries for his own personal and political aims in Germany, Zwingli expected Hessian soldiers to join him in overthrowing the Catholic states of Switzerland, and both were wrong.[1]

The situation in Switzerland had been profoundly altered by the adoption of the Reformation by Berne, Basle, St Gall, Schaffhausen and Constance, accompanied by the strengthening and expansion of the Christian Civic Union.[2] Even before this had happened, Zurich had emerged from the partial isolation caused by its opposition to mercenary service and by the religious innovations. It was soon apparent that only the central states, cautiously supported by Fribourg and Solothurn, were inexorably hostile – with Basle, Berne, Glarus, Appenzell, St Gall and Schaffhausen intercourse continued on a basis of common economic and political interests. Consultations with Strassburg and Constance, however, inevitably led to consideration of the state of affairs in south Germany, but to any intervention there or to any entangling alliance Berne was resolutely opposed. Berne, in continuous touch with Catholic Fribourg and Solothurn, never indifferent to what was happening in Lausanne and Geneva, with its eyes fixed on the west and the south, had no interest in Zurich's expansionist ideas, whether for secular interest or for religion, across the Rhine.

However, in 1529 the northern Swiss cities had all finally rejected the church of Rome, and the Zwinglian Reformation was advancing rapidly. This encouraged Zwingli in his conviction of the assured triumph of his Bible-teaching. Now that Berne had adopted the evangelical creed, the avowed hostility of the Inner States might be ignored, and Zurich could seek for allies and even take the offensive. There were openings to be exploited in the Mandated Territories for which Zurich shared responsibility, as well as possibilities in St Gall and among the Zwinglian-minded cities of Swabia. If, however, there was to be something more than this, an evangelical Swiss Confederation, united in opposition to Rome and the Habsburgs, with Zurich at its head, it could only be brought about with the help of Berne. Zwingli now insisted that if, after the humiliation of the Inner States at the first Peace of Kappel, Zurich and Berne had pressed their advantages, their opponents might have been reduced to acquiescence and submission. The thirteen states had indeed been working together for

---

[1] Hauswirth, *Philipp* 245, 256–7. Lortz recognised that 'Philipp und Zwingli waren überhaupt die einzigen protestantischen Führer, die in grösseren politischen Zusammenhängen zu denken fähig und geübt waren.' J. Lortz, *Die Reformation in Deutschland*[4] (Freiburg, 1962) II, 65. [2] Above, 376–7.

over a decade, but with increasing difficulty; the time had come, Zwingli was to argue, for a new united confederation to emerge which was to be coherent and effective. Zurich and Berne together were powerful enough to dominate the others.[1]

This implied agreement as to aims, ends and means. Berne, however, was certainly not prepared to underwrite its ally's ambitions either in eastern Switzerland or north of the Rhine. If, as was apparently taking place, the peace terms were to be pressed to the full and the parishes of the Mandated Territories allowed freedom of choice in matters of religious worship, all the territory between the Limmat and Lake Constance might become Zwinglian. Thus, Zurich's influence in Thurgau, the Rheintal,[2] Gaster and Sargans[3] would amount to a protectorate, and its power would be proportionately enhanced.

This suited neither Berne's interests nor its traditions. Its interests were western, and Zurich's success in the east, added to close connection with south German Protestants, was not to Berne's liking, nor was it necessarily in the interests of the Confederation as a whole. Berne took its federal responsibilities seriously, and was anxious to hold the traditional confederation together and to avoid war. There was no leader of Zwingli's calibre in Berne, nor would one have been tolerated by its ruling class however much its form of government by Bürgermeister and councils resembled that of its neighbour. There was also a tradition of consultation between city and countryside such as did not exist in Zurich, and this helped to make Bernese policy realist, cautious and cool.

In March 1530, the one man who might have kept Zurich and Berne in line died suddenly at the age of 45. This was Zwingli's friend and supporter, Niklaus Manuel, leader of the Bernese Council. With his disappearance, the last chances of happy accord between the two states vanished and Berne reverted to its traditional conservatism. This state in any case refused to be associated with any measures implying the formation of an all-Protestant Confederation by coercion. This became manifest when Zurich accepted what had been discussed at Marburg, an alliance with Hesse. With this the government of Berne was not prepared to be

---

[1] See below, 402.
[2] T. Frey, *Das Rheintal zur Zeit der Glaubensspaltung* (Altstätten, 1947).
[3] Sargans was the responsibility of seven states, and the provisions of the first Peace of Kappel were consistently applied there, but it remained Catholic. At Flums there was an actively evangelical minister, Martin Mannhart, who made himself unpopular by the violence of his denunciation of the Catholic mass, which was still permitted for the minority. When, in February 1530, Gilg (Aegidius) Tschudi from Glarus became Governor and showed signs of supporting the Catholics, there were strong demands that Zurich should intervene to prevent this. Instead, however, Mannhart was removed and provided with a benefice elsewhere directly under Zurich's control, where he continued to give trouble. Farner IV, 419–21; Z X, 494 n. 4, 536 n. 1, 544–5; Straub, 117–30.

associated and this meant that Zwingli's wider aims were impracticable. It also meant that Basle, which had hoped with German help to annex all the territory ruled by its bishop, had to abandon this attempt and, in turn, was less enthusiastic about the other purposes of the Christian Civic Union.[1]

Constance, which Zwingli once called 'the key to Switzerland'[2] and to which Zurich turned hopefully, was no adequate substitute for Berne. It had no territory, and could hardly resist indefinitely the efforts of its bishop to regain his authority there with Austrian help, unless support was forthcoming from the Swiss side, which was not in fact available. Its only hope was to be accepted as a full sovereign member – *gleichberechtigter und ranghoher Ort* – of the Confederation, and this was strenuously resisted by the central states as upsetting the balance of power. Berne would agree to accept Constance only as an ally (*zugewandter Ort*), and even Zurich was hesitant about the wider demand because it might mean recognition of the city's claim to juridical rights in Thurgau, which would conflict with Zurich's ambitions there.[3]

1530 was, in fact, a year of concealed rivalry between Berne and Zurich. Cool, realist, secular-minded and traditionalist, the Bernese patricians had constantly to consider the security of their state and their relations with their own subjects, their neighbours and the Confederation. They were in close contact with the Catholic powers, France and Savoy, and, still nearer at hand, with the hostile communities of Valais and with their immediate obstinately Catholic neighbour Fribourg. Berne, Fribourg and Solothurn joined to defend Geneva when attacked by the Duke of Savoy who, on 19 October 1530, had been obliged to agree to the peace of Saint-Julien.[4] The Vaud was then placed under Berne–Fribourg protection, and free trade with Savoy was promised as well. For security and further possible expansion a proportion of Bernese forces must therefore remain in the west. Hence Berne could not deploy the whole of its force to defend Zurich even if attacked, and it certainly was not prepared to support a preventive war for religion which could also mean that eastern Switzerland came under the control of its already too-powerful neighbour. The Confederation must not be altered out of all recognition for the sake either of religion or of German ambition.

Events in Germany, however, forced the pace. With the opening of 1530 it became ever more obvious, as the Diet of Augsburg came nearer,

[1] Z x, 401 n. 7, 513–14; Escher, *Glaubensparteien*, 142.
[2] Z xi, 559: 'Constantia vero velut clavis est Helvetiae.'
[3] For similar reasons, involving claims to the monastic property, in spite of the fact that St Gall was also a free imperial city and one of the 'protestants' of 1529, Zurich was not prepared to admit it to anything more than a defensive alliance (*Burgrecht*).
[4] EA 4, 1b, 1501–5.

that a religious war was imminent. Gatherings of Lutherans at Schmal-kalden and elsewhere culminated in an offensive and defensive league matching the Christian Civic Union.[1] That this should be expanded was very much Zwingli's wish, but the initiative remained with Hesse. From Zurich, Zwingli hoped, the civic alliance would be expanded to include Strassburg, Constance and Lindau,[2] but it was not easy to move even as far as this. The Prince of Hesse was a genuine Protestant who used the faith to which he was converted for his own political and territorial ends; compared with him Zwingli was an amateur politician, convinced that the security and expansion of his creed involved opposition to Pope and Emperor. Philip's was the master mind, but prince and theologian were equally sanguine. Zwingli's confidence was unshakeable. 'God', he wrote, 'is old but not sick and has strength and wisdom enough for us.'[3]

Proposals for an extended alliance of the cities of the Christian Civic Union to include Philip and Ulrich had been canvassed in 1529 and 1530. There were discussions in February[4] and March, and in April 1530 the Zurich council agreed, by a small majority with several abstentions or absentees, to the principle of cooperation with Hesse, Ulrich, Basle and Berne.[5] The refusal of Berne to participate was followed by further meetings[6] and by the acceptance by Zurich of the principle of an alliance, *christliche Verstand*, with Strassburg, Basle and Hesse even without Berne.[7] In spite of the fact that Constance and St Gall were prepared to cooperate,[8] in October[9] the abstention of Berne was confirmed on the grounds that the conflict between Geneva and Savoy demanded prior attention and that if Philip were defeated by the Emperor Berne might be in danger.

This refusal by Berne to be associated with any alliance or understanding with Hesse was of real significance for Zwingli, Switzerland and Germany. If Berne had been an active and willing associate, the other Zwinglian states would have shown greater interest, which, in turn, through the Swabian cities, must have made a German–Swiss common front a reality. Before this, imperial hostility might well have crumbled and a broadened Schmalkaldic league must have greatly restricted Charles V's activities. It

---

[1] Fabian, 102–3, 181–2.
[2] 'das von oben hinab hie diset Ryns bis gen Strassburg ein volck und püntnus werden.' Z VI i, 201; EA 4, 1b, 309. E. Kobelt, *Die Bedeutung der Eidgenossenschaft für Huldrych Zwingli* MAGZ 45 (134. Nbl. Zurich, 1970) 190.
[3] Z XI, 252. [4] Z X, 445.
[5] Hauswirth, *Philipp*, 208; Escher, *Glaubensparteien*, 146. EA 4, 1b, 964.
[6] EA 4, 1b, 426ff, 570ff, 674ff; Z X, 401 n. 7; Z XI, 21 n. 1, 153 n. 2; Lenz ZKG III, 220ff; Steck & Tobler 1270 (No. 2830).
[7] EA 4, 1b, n. 7. Zwingli continued to encourage Philip: 'Hallt an, frommer achermann, hallt an.' Z XI, 35 (22 July, 1530).
[8] Fabian, 49 n. 12.
[9] EA 4, 1b, 805; Z XI, 200, 211 n. 8; Feller II, 210–11.

would also have implied the acceptance of Zwingli's wish and purpose that the Confederation should become a Zurich–Berne dominated, and therefore Protestant, state. This must have changed the whole outlook and policy of the rulers of Berne and to their potential disadvantage. In all this Berne was more 'Swiss' in outlook than was Zwingli for all his devotion to the Federation. Berne was not a Lutheran state and was not willing to be associated with Lutherans or to participate in any Bucerian compromise which might extend to extra-Swiss affairs. Zurich, however, persisted, and the 'Hessian understanding' or Christian agreement (*Hessische, christliche Verstand*) of Zurich, Basle, Strassburg and Hesse was sealed on 18 November 1530.[1] It was a simple defensive pact along familiar lines, each party agreeing to help its allies in the event of an attack or rebellion. Nothing was said about doctrine, although it was potentially a Protestant grand alliance. In fact it was a paper agreement only. A purely defensive pact, and one without Berne, was of little use to either Philip or Zwingli, who both wanted action.[2] Even the adhesion of Constance made little difference. There was, in fact, no general Protestant front. In Germany, Electoral Saxony, Hesse, Braunschweig-Lüneburg, Braunschweig-Grubenhagen, the Counts of Mansfeld and Anhalt, with Magdeburg and Bremen, formed a Lutheran league at Schmalkalden in December 1530, and at first Zwingli thought that Zurich might be invited to join[3] as Constance did in the summer of 1531 together with most of the south German cities. But the German princes would admit Zwinglians only on the basis of an acceptance of the Tetrapolitana, and this was rejected by both Zurich and Berne, although Basle might have been persuaded to agree.[4] Strassburg had been pressurised into acquiescence, but the Swiss cities rejected it freely.[5] There was no doctrinal compromise with the Lutherans, which, in the event, meant that Swiss neutrality in the later struggles in Germany was assured.[6]

There was also some talk of the formation of two circles, one of princes, with Saxony, Lüneburg and Hesse as chief components, and one or more of cities.[7] The Christian Civic Union could be combined with Strassburg, Constance, Ulm, Isny, Kempten, Biberach, Reutlingen, Memmingen and Lindau, thus forming a powerful block. These cities were indeed prepared

---

[1] EA 4, 1b, 837, 1514–16; Lenz, 222; Schmid, 40–1; Bender, *Ref.*, 172. Zurich was represented by Bürgermeister Röist and Stadtschreiber Beyel. Zwingli was not present. *Politische Correspondenz der Stadt Strassburg im Zeitalter der Reformation*, Bd. I, *1517–1530* bearbeitet v. H. Virck (Strassburg, 1882) 542–4 (No. 839) 550–1 (No. 844). The original document, handed over after the second war, is in the Lucerne archives.
[2] EA 4, 1b, 837, 1514–16; Schmid 40–1; Lenz ZKG III, 240–3; Hauswirth, *Philipp*, 221–6; Bender, *Ref.*, 171–2; Wyss, 151 n. 4; Fabian 211–16; Z XI, 21.
[3] Z XI, 337; Fabian, 102–3, 181–2, 204–5.   [4] Z XI, 350 n. 3, 354–5. See above, 334–5 n. 4.
[5] Z XI, 371 n. 4, 381.   [6] Fabian, 229–32.
[7] Fabian, 102–6; Lenz, 445.

to help to defend one another if attacked, so as not to be crushed separately as Rottweil had been, but no more. Memmingen and Kempten were particularly apprehensive,[1] but, being cities, they all thought in terms of resisting attack only. Princes and cities could neither cohere nor combine, and nothing happened. Moreoever, Zwingli, primarily concerned to promote the cause of the Gospel, which was also the greater glory of Zurich, and Philip, determined to restore Ulrich and thwart the Habsburgs, were drifting apart.

All this followed upon the Diet of Augsburg[2] and the presentation of the Lutheran *Augustana* and Zwingli's own *Fidei ratio*. Notwithstanding his increasing involvement in German as well as Swiss public affairs, Zwingli remained what he had always been – preacher, prophet, minister of religion and theologian. Right as Koehler was[3] to emphasise the deterioration in Zwingli's idealism in the months between the armed encounters of 1529 and 1531, the reformer did not cease to preach and expound the Gospel. After the Marburg discussions, however, he had come to rate the support of Philip of Hesse very highly. Rightly apprehensive for the future of the evangelical faith, he misunderstood and exaggerated the Habsburg menace.[4] The situation, as Bucer pointed out in September 1530, was serious enough.[5] With France and the Empire at peace, northern Italy under imperial control, Florence submissive, Venice satisfied, Charles III of Savoy an ally, Charles V seemed ready to maintain the Catholic faith by fire and sword even if this involved the end of civil and civic liberties, for the sake of uniformity of religion. Zwingli oversimplified the situation and saw in Philip of Hesse a zealot like himself in the cause of truth. In fact Philip was chiefly interested in the limited objective of restoring Ulrich of Württemberg, while the Schmalkaldic League had much wider objectives than the security of Zurich.[6]

In an age when rumours flourished and exact facts were hard to come by, Zwingli readily believed that Ferdinand was collecting forces for an attack on Constance and the Vorarlberg followed by an incursion into Switzerland.[7] As a Catholic prince he would come to extirpate heretics, and as successor to Rudolf I would seek to reoccupy his inheritance across the Rhine. It was also commonly suspected that the formation of an imperial

---

[1] Z x, 523.
[2] See above, 335 and n. 7. Zwingli had confidently expected to be invited. Z x, 525 (No. 1002); Staehelin *Briefe* II, 443–4 (No. 747).
[3] Koehler, *Zwingli*, 198, 219, 229.
[4] Knowing little of the history and politics of the Empire, Zwingli overrated its practical effectiveness. Schmid, 41–2; K. Mommsen, *Eidgenossen, Kaiser und Reich*, BasBeitr. (1958) 72; R. Hauswirth, *Zur Realität des Reiches in der Eidgenossenschaft im Zeitalter der Glaubenskämpfe*, Festgabe Leonhard von Muralt (Zürich, 1970) 152–61, esp. 154–5, 159.
[5] Z xi, 107–10.   [6] ZWA xi, 547.
[7] Haas, *Kappelerkrieg*, 50; Z x, 260–1.

army for use against the Turks was merely a blind to gather a force to crush the Swiss. For Zwingli Pope and Emperor were now identical.[1] Hence his preoccupation with politics, which bulks so largely in his later correspondence.

To see the minister of religion as subordinate to the statesman is as wrong at the end of his life as to make the humanist override the Christian during his formative years. Zwingli remained to the end the singleminded servant of the Gospel that he had always been. His sermons, his pastoral work and his Bible exposition continued unabated. It is easy to overlook, or to relegate to a separate compartment, his continued contribution to the end of his life to the *Prophezei*, especially his translation of and commentaries on Isaiah and Jeremiah.[2] He would carry the Gospel and true religion to all his fellow Swiss. If conditions required the support of the secular arm, or of foreign allies, such was God's will. The Bible did not teach that combat was to be avoided in the cause of righteousness. It was as a prophet, in the Old Testament sense, that Zwingli lived and died.

---

[1]   Babstüm und Keisertüm,
      Die sind beide von Rhom. Z XI, 157.

[2] These are printed with notes by F. Blanke and A. Farner in Z XIV, 5–679 and are of special value in explaining Zwingli's methods of biblical exegesis. They have also some direct contemporary relevance. The commentary on Jeremiah, for example, was dedicated to the city of Strassburg, and in both commentaries there are direct and indirect references to current affairs. The word of God, it was said, was overlaid by 'polita loquacitas', hypocrisy displaced virtue, force prevailed over equity and justice, the 'Catabaptistae' were continuously provocative. Z XIV, 107, 269, 513, 586, 600–1.

16

The last year

The situation in Switzerland in 1530 had become one that called for great forbearance, restraint and statesmanship if the Confederation was to survive at all. The intensification of religious strife, the complex legal situation arising out of the St Gall differences, the exclusion of the Swiss evangelicals from the Schmalkaldic League and the inability to secure the integration of Constance, all put a special responsibility on Zurich. Powerful though Zwingli was there after his return from Marburg, he was far from being dictator or even prime minister. Many books have repeated the unguarded statement of Hans Salat, the ill-informed, prejudiced Catholic chronicler from Lucerne – 'in Zurich Zwingli is mayor, council and gilds rolled into one'.[1] Final authority remained, as it always had, with the great council, the Two Hundred, meeting weekly. Executive authority and church affairs were dealt with by the small council, both bodies having by 1529 become, in spite of some resistance by the 'Constables', exclusively evangelical. There was also a kind of standing advisory sub-committee, *geheime Rat* or *heimlichen Sechs* of leading citizens – a Bürgermeister, representatives of the chief gilds, and Zwingli – entrusted with external negotiations. Its terms of reference were never precisely defined, and the council need not, and often did not, follow its advice. For it Zwingli wrote numerous memoranda which have made his influence appear even greater than it was. His popularity in the pulpit, his numerous friends, vast industry, facility with pen and tongue, ensured attention, most obviously of all in matters of worship and of social conduct. There was also, however, an appreciable minority of anti-clericals, crypto-Catholics and displaced aristocrats, who formed a kind of opposition although

---

[1] 'Vnd was Zwingli in disem handel schon Zürich bürgermeister, schryber, raat ij^c, rums, tantz vnd der gantz gwallt.' *Archiv für die schweizerische Reformationsgeschichte* Bd. 1. hg. Th. Scherer-Boccard etc. (Freiburg, 1869) 43. *Handbuch*, 516 n. 663. Escher, *Glaubensparteien*, 88–9 mistakenly accepted this at its face value and was followed by later writers. What considerable qualifications are now required has been shown by Hauswirth, *Philipp*, 230–50; Jacob, 14, 100; Haas, *Kappelerkrieg* 14–25, 183–4; and E. Fabian, 'Zwingli und der Geheime Rat, 1529–31', in '*Gottesreich und Menschenreich*', *Ernst Staehelin zum 80. Geburtstag* (Basle/Stuttgart, 1969) 151–95. ZWA XIII (1970) 234–44, XII (1964) 35–68.

lacking any obvious leader. In some very important matters affecting external relations, even peace and war, Zwingli's advice was received but not followed; indeed Bullinger later rightly complained that Zwingli was sometimes blamed for policies that were not his own.[1]

The events that followed the first peace of Kappel, itself a watered-down version of Zwingli's requirements, exhibited compromises that were not entirely acceptable to the 'prophet'. They also led to successful resistance to Zurich's expansionist plans and hence, in a measure, were a set-back to Zwinglian evangelism. The extension of the Christian Civic Union beyond the Confederation, the projected alliance with Philip of Hesse and the German Protestants, the controversial outcome of the action against the abbot and monastery of St Gall, and impediments to the Gospel in eastern Switzerland, were all disappointing. There were some who were prepared to tolerate the pensioners and even to come to terms with Lucerne. Zwingli had one of his rare bouts of depression on 26 July 1531, when he appeared before the great council and, with tears in his eyes, offered his resignation. For eleven years, he said, he had preached the Gospel there, confident that it would triumph. He was now willing to leave his post at the Great Minster and go elsewhere. A high-powered delegation persuaded him to withdraw his resignation, but his power was slipping, and he knew it.[2] One relatively minor episode had already illustrated this. After the Marburg conference and the rejection of the Hessian alliance by Berne, another setback to Zwinglian hopes of expansion had taken place. At Marburg there had been mention of the possibility of an approach to Venice so that the Republic of St Mark might become the southern end of the chain of allies associated with the cities of the Christian Civic Union against the Emperor. Philip of Hesse was not impressed but seems to have hoped that a friendly Venice could be induced to provide a loan to hire mercenaries who, supported by Tyrol peasants, would help the cause of the restoration of Ulrich.[3] Zwingli had for some time been in touch with the Reformed peasant agitator, Michael Gaismair, who had been leading the opposition to the Austrian regime in the Tyrol.[4] In the adjoining Graubünden evangelical preaching had made good progress, and the northern group, the League of God's House, had repudiated the authority of the Bishop of Chur. Through the south of the Graubünden ran the river highway of the Valtelline, the northern bracket of the frontiers of Venice, and Milan, and the route from north Italy to Austria. If Venice, already in touch with Gaismair, could be induced to oppose the

[1] Bullinger *Ref.* I, 308.
[2] Bullinger *Ref.* III, 45; Stumpf *I*, 166; Sprüngli, 20; ZWA III, 50–4.
[3] Lenz, 221–4; Z VI ii, 590, 633; Hauswirth *Philipp*, 156, 166–71.
[4] Vasella *4*; Z VI ii, 633–7, 720–32; EA 4, 1b, 489–90; J. Macek (trans. E. Ullmann), *Der Tiroler Bauernkrieg und Michael Gaismair* (Berlin, 1965) 364, 370, 405.

Emperor, it could be made much more difficult for the latter to join forces with Ferdinand. Venice, too, as the ally of France, had been anti-imperialist, as Zurich had now become. The plan was not entirely unreasonable, but the timing of the embassy was disastrous. The envoy sent by Zurich in December 1529 with a letter of introduction[1] written by Zwingli, was the young artisan turned humanist, Rudolf Collin.[2] His instructions were to seek Venetian friendship with Zurich by emphasising earlier amiable contacts and the common interests of city republics (like the Christian Civic Union) and free peoples in resistance to monarchs and tyrants. Quite apart from the fact that Venetian policy was not likely to be moved by such considerations or impressed by a sectional Swiss approach, the whole scheme was misconceived and ill-timed. Five days before Collin was received in audience by Doge Andrea Gritti on 28 December, Venice had made its peace with Charles V at Bologna.[3] Any useful alliance was therefore out of the question; Collin's oration[4] was heard with suitable gravity, a few leading questions were asked and compliments exchanged before he was dismissed with a trifling present that was almost a calculated insult. There was no Venetian alliance and Gaismair soon proved to be an ineffectual supporter who became a discredited refugee and was murdered in 1532. Zwingli was now more convinced than ever of direct danger to Zurich and its neighbours from the mischief-making Emperor.

None the less, his first purpose in life remained to preach the Gospel as he knew and read it – this in turn implied government support and brought additional problems with consequent political implications. How all this involved using worldly weapons for spiritual ends has been seen in connection with St Gall and Philip of Hesse: in 1530–1 France, Venice and North Italy were involved, in each instance unsatisfactorily for Zurich. The Catholic states, likewise, expected to rely upon supports other than simple persuasion. For the defence of the faith, men and money could be expected from Pope and Emperor and from Catholic states outside the Confederation. The vital north–south road to Italy from the Austrian territories at, and north of, Waldshut through Baden and the Freie Aemter to Zug, Lucerne and the St Gotthard, had to be kept under Catholic control for strategic and political as well as religious reasons.

In all these matters Berne was much concerned. There were Catholic

[1] Z VI ii, 633(638)–40.
[2] Z VII, 339–40; Z X, 374. Known as Clivanus (Ambühl), a ropemaker, soldier, priest and Greek scholar who later married and taught Greek in Zurich. K. Furrer, *Rudolf Collin. Ein Characterbild aus der Schweizerischen Reformationsgeschichte. Zeitschrift für wissenschaftliche Theologie* 5 (Halle, 1862) 337–99.
[3] H. Kretschmayr, *Geschichte von Venedig* (Stuttgart, 1934) III, 19, 20.
[4] EA 4 1b, 487–8.

neighbours on all sides, Solothurn, Fribourg, Savoy, Valais, Uri, Unterwalden, Lucerne; and while more than a match for any of these individually, Berne must, and did, take care that they did not combine against her. Although the state had deliberately accepted Zwinglian Protestantism in 1528, and this with characteristic slowness, even reluctance, it had still not been easy, as events proved, to convince its herdsmen-subjects in remote valleys of the necessity for the change. Berne did not willingly alienate its subjects even while expecting obedience from them. She wished above all to maintain the Confederation. Moreover, the rulers knew very well that the other members of the Christian Civic Union, Basle, Biel, Zurich, Schaffhausen, St Gall, Constance, made up an invaluable defensive alliance, but defensive it must remain. They should fight to maintain their way of life but not to impose it on others.

Zurich's active evangelisation of Mandated Territories in the Freie Aemter, monastic St Gall and, with much help from Constance, in Thurgau, was not entirely welcome. It caused discontent and disruption; in so far as it was successful it meant that Zurich gained considerably in wealth and manpower and thus would outmatch the rest. There were disadvantages in having a too-powerful neighbour, however friendly, particularly when the expansionist eyes of this neighbour were turned eastwards and northwards to Germany.

In 1530 Zwingli attempted to secure a special relationship with France. Fearing the danger from a united Catholic front which he had learnt 'uss der rechten Kunstkamer' when on his way to Marburg,[1] he hoped now at least to detach France from the other side. This was not an easy decision. France had close relations with the Swiss,[2] but Zurich had not been associated with the alliance and Zwingli had consistently opposed the payment of rewards and pensions to influential citizens and the recruitment of Swiss soldiers to fight French battles. Now, however, Berne and Zurich were working together and the Habsburg menace seemed to require some revision of policy. The French pensions had in any case gone mostly to the catholic states and had been condemned in principle by the first peace of Kappel. The patricians of Berne were not prepared to leave entirely to the other side such pecuniary advantages as were offered, and Zwingli was obliged to agree that pensions might be accepted by a group or community, although not by individuals.[3]

France was Berne's traditional ally, and there was still hope that its monarch might accept the Reformation.[4] It was not yet apparent that the

---

[1] See above, 323.
[2] See above, 41.　　　　　　　　　　[3] Z XI, 319.
[4] Imbart de la Tour, *Les origines de la réforme* (Paris, 1914) III, 258–72; R. J. Knecht, 'The early Reformation in England and France: a comparison', *History* 57 (1972) 10–12; Z XI, 36, 104.

efforts of Lefèvre d'Etaples, Briçonnet, Farel, Roussel and Margaret of Navarre were of no avail. Francis I would not, indeed, declare himself until his two sons, left as hostages with Spain, were returned, which was not until July 1530, but Zwingli was ever hopeful. The French king was anxious to retain his Swiss allies and to maintain complete freedom of action.[1] Through his agents in Switzerland, Hans Kaltschmid of Kaiserstuhl and Hans Junker of Rapperswil,[2] he insisted that the treaty of Cambrai was not directed against the Swiss[3] and he was ready to discuss closer cooperation. These cautious advances were received with reserve,[4] but as the situation seemed to grow more dangerous, Zwingli and his supporters became more amenable to suggestions. The French did not want a religious civil war in Switzerland which might strengthen Austria and interfere with recruiting plans; and their two representatives in Fribourg, Lambert Meigret and Louis Boisrigault (Daugerant), were instructed to keep the matter open as long as possible.[5]

Zwingli was at first suspicious, particularly since Zurich had rejected the French alliance in 1521. But now that the Swiss Catholics were switching allegiance to the Emperor might not Zurich change its tune? He recognised the worth of a powerful ally with abundance of money and the ability to offer horses and guns to be used for defence against aggression and for upholding the Gospel. A French–Swiss force securing Strassburg, Constance and Württemberg could ensure the safety of Switzerland from Habsburg attack, the more so if support could be secured from John Zapolya in Hungary or from Venice. Freedom for evangelical preaching in France was assumed. An alliance would be of limited duration[6] and acceptable because the emergency, an imperial–Catholic onslaught, was real. For the sake of this he was now prepared to countenance the recruitment of mercenaries in Zurich-controlled territory. Mercenary service was evil and deplorable, but if necessary for the defence of the evangelical cause it could be accepted. The King of France was resisting, as the Swiss had always done, the tyranny of the Holy Roman Empire. Charles V

---

[1] Lenz, 232-4.   [2] Z x, 404-7.

[3] Z x, 405; Z xi, 104 (September 1530): 'Nunquam inducetur rex, ut per se vel per alios arma capiat pro imperatore contra urbes Christiani fęderis etc. Euangelium enim mire crescit inter nobiles in curia regis.'   [4] Z x, 459-60, 474 n. 3.

[5] Meigret (or Maigret) was 'contrôleur général des guerres' and is sometimes called 'general'. The two were frequently employed on missions in western Switzerland, always trying to keep the peace. Meigret was described as 'the French orator in Switzerland...holding frequent conferences with...Zuinglio' (*Calendar of State Papers Spanish*, 1531-3 no. 755). E. Rott, *Histoire de la Représentation diplomatique de la France auprès des cantons suisses*, I (Berne, 1900) 269-81, 380-7. P. Brüschweiler, *Les rapports de Zwingli avec la France* (Paris, 1894) 70-3. Farner, *Zwingli* IV, 448-50. Hauswirth, *Philipp*, 185-7. Koehler, *Zwinglis französischen Bündnisplänen*, ZWA IV, 302-11.

[6] E. Kobelt, *Die Bedeutung der Eidgenossenschaft für Huldrych Zwingli* MAGZ 45 (1970), 88-91.

threatened Swiss and French equally, but together, relying on God's help, they could thwart his ambitious schemes.[1] Once again, the argument was coming close to making the end justify the means, and in this case the concession was worthless. A renewed attempt by Collin to obtain active French help at Solothurn failed,[2] and there was no alliance, to the relief, perhaps, of Berne, which might otherwise have had to change its neutral course.

All this caused Zwingli to send to Francis I, to whom he had dedicated his *Commentary on the true and false religion* in 1525, a fresh defence of his purpose and teachings. This was *Fidei expositio*, the last pamphlet from his pen.[3] Optimistic to the end, he seriously thought that the King of France, about whom he knew singularly little, or his sister, Margaret of Navarre, could be brought over to the evangelical side by the perusal of a treatise, almost a tract. It was an explanation, a defence and an appeal. It opens with a short passage on the Deity, the incarnation, salvation through Christ alone, the ascension and resurrection. The writer's undoubted orthodoxy on the Trinity and his careful exposition of the two natures of Christ are intended to demonstrate that he was no sectary and that every word of his teaching was based on holy writ. Truth daily moves further forward to triumph; the visible church consists of those who accept Christ and is not limited to the Pope and the Catholic bishops.

The little treatise was adroitly constructed. The familiar interpretation of the Last Supper as a symbolical memorial was re-expounded. The bread and wine, ordained and used by Christ at the institution of the eucharist, precious, holy, honourable, signifying Christ as the bread of life, analogous with the one body of the church of which Christ is the head, strengthen and refresh the soul as bread and wine do the human frame and remind the recipient of the death of the Lord.

There is special insistence upon the perpetual virginity of Mary, emphasised the more in a French context, and an indication of aristocracy as the 'best' adjunct of government and of the duty of obedience to constituted authority as incumbent upon all citizens. Taxes must be paid and customary obligations met. The disorderly and disobedient Anabaptists are thoroughly castigated and emphasis is laid on the sanctity of contract as a cement of society. The prophets are there to warn and advise monarchs,

---

[1] Lenz, 235; Koehler, *Buch*, 313–16.
[2] Z XI, 444–5; EA 4, 1b, 1117–18; Fabian, *Q*, 96.
[3] S IV, 44–78, translated in ZH, *Zwingli der Theologe* III. Teil (Zürich, 1948), 300–54; for a summary see Wernle, 328–54. The manuscript copy now in the *Bibliothèque Nationale*, MS. Lat. 3673A, was taken to Paris by Collin. It was not printed until 1536, with an explanatory preface by Bullinger, who called it Zwingli's swan song (ZWA XIII, 463–71). It was translated into German by Leo Jud as *Eyn kurtze klare sũm und erklärung des Christenen gloubẽs | von Huldrychen Zwinglin gepredigt | und unlang vor synem tod zů eynem Christenen Künig geschriben.*

for which plentiful biblical examples, from Saul and David to Herod, were ready at hand. Purgatory had no biblical sanction, and the king might expect to find alongside the saints in the Paradise which he would surely attain, his own predecessors, together with pious heathens including Cato, Scipio, Socrates, Aristides, Antigonus, Numa Pompilius, Camillus, Theseus and Hercules.[1] The inclusion of this latter figure was to be the occasion of some ribald humour from Zwingli's critics later, but the thought behind it was serious. It ends with an appeal to the 'Most Christian King' to allow the Gospel to be preached freely in his dominions. There is no evidence that Francis I ever read it, and it had no influence on the course of events, but it remains the author's last, and not least impressive, apology.

Francis I could not fail to be interested in the course of events in north Italy. There, while he was negotiating with the Emperor, external peace had allowed a local situation of considerable concern to the Swiss to develop. On the ill-defined northern frontier of the duchy of Milan a local adventurer on Lake Como, no longer an ally of France, was seeking to establish himself as an independent prince. This was Gian Giacomo de' Medici,[2] known as 'il Medeghino'. He had obtained possession of the powerful castle – its ruins are still impressive – of Musso, from whence he could threaten communications over the Splügen pass, terrorise the countryside and interfere with traders and travellers. No opportunity to strengthen his position during the warfare in northern Italy was ever missed. Swiss soldiers had been hired or threatened as occasion demanded. One of his brothers, arch-priest of Mazzo, was intriguing to become Bishop of Chur, and his sister Clara was betrothed to Wolf Dietrich of Hohenems, son of the powerful and aggressive Catholic, Marx Sittich.[3] On 14 November 1528 'Musso', as Gian Giacomo was commonly called, asked the Graubünden for safe conduct for his sister through their territory. Fearing that

---

[1] Cf. R. Pfister, *Die Seligkeit erwählter Heiden bei Zwingli* (Zollikon–Zurich, 1952) 45ff, 86ff; ZWA XIII, 471. G. H. Williams in *Essays in memory of E.H. Harbison* (Princeton, 1969) 358–60.

[2] 1495–1555. He was not connected with the Medici of Florence in spite of the family name. His younger brother Giovanni (Gian) Angelo de' Medici became Pope Pius IV (1559–65), and Charles Borromeo was his nephew. H. Zeller-Werdmüller, *Der Krieg gegen den Tyrannen von Musso am Comersee in den Jahren 1531–1532.* Nbl. LXXVIII. der Feuerwerker Gesellschaft in Zürich (Zürich, 1883); F. Bertoliatti, *La guerra di Musso e suoi riflessi sui baliaggi* (Como, 1947) and *Ulrico Zwingli e la guerra di Musso*, Svizzera italiana, 64 (Locarno, 1947) 299–309. E. Weiss, *Basels Anteil am Kriege gegen Giangiacomo de Medici, den Kastellan von Musso 1531–1532* (Basle, 1902) and Vasella *1* add interesting detail.

[3] Marx was a good and experienced general much respected by the Austrian administration whose agent (*Vogt*) he was in Bregenz and Vorarlberg. Z X, 179 n. 4; Z XI, 15 n. 4, 411 n. 2; Vasella *2*, 73; Weiss, 125; L. Welti, *Geschichte der Reichsgrafschaft Hohenems und des Reichshofes Lustenau* (Forschungen zur Geschichte Vorarlbergs u. Liechtensteins, 4. Innsbruck, 1930) 63–82; Do., *Marx Sittich und Wolf Dietrich von Ems* (Schriften zur Vorarlberger Landeskunde, hg. v. B. Bilgeri u. M. Tieffenthaler, 4. Dornbirn, 1952).

this would be used to restore a Catholic bishop to the cathedral of Chur, the Bündner refused, and the bride-to-be had to go to Feldkirch through the central Swiss states.[1] This, of course, did not please the Zwinglians. According to popular belief, all this was part of an elaborate scheme by which Ferdinand of Austria, with the help of the Inner States, could advance against the Swiss Protestants while the Elector of Saxony was neutralised by his rival, Duke George. There was, in fact, little substance in this; Ferdinand was in real danger from the Turks, money was short, and Habsburg policies ranged far beyond Swiss internal disputes. 'Musso' was too insignificant to be a trustworthy ally, and such Austrian encouragement as he received was negligible.

Local castle-building, threats and terrorism, which had been going on for some time, came to a head on 9 March 1531, when two peace emissaries from the Graubünden were killed by Musso's men while on their way from Milan.[2] That this was no accident became apparent when compensation and apology were refused and when it was followed by an invasion of the Valtelline, then unquestionably Graubünden territory. As allies, the Swiss were obliged to protect this area, and the occupation of Morbengo, the key to the Adda, made things worse. Help was now urgently requested[3] and received. Forces from all the Swiss states,[4] with the significant exception of the Catholic Five, came willingly with guns and ammunition to the assistance of their ally. The expedition was entirely within the framework of the Confederation, and volunteers, perhaps hoping for easy loot, were readily forthcoming. It was also part of Zurich's policy of protecting its reformed neighbours against Catholic aggression. In this, and in other ways, it was entirely successful; but the absence of contingents from the five Catholic states was much resented, the more so because of persistent reports that they were helping the other side.[5]

'Musso' found himself almost deserted. Not one of the 8,000 men promised by Wolf Dietrich appeared, nor did any of the 300 landsknechts expected from Ferdinand, nor any Spaniards under Antonio de Leiva; no help came from Venice[6] and only a little money from the Pope. For the Swiss it was almost a parade. The Valtelline was easily reoccupied, fortresses, Morbengo in particular, on Lake Como were taken, and finally the castle of Musso itself surrendered to the Zurich artillery which was

---

[1] Vasella *1*, 211ff. F. Jecklin, *Materialen zur Standes- und Landesgeschichte gem. III. Bünde (Graubünden) 1464–1803* (Basle, 1907) I, 95 (No. 1528).

[2] Bullinger, *Ref.* II, 355; Hauswirth, *Philipp*, 237.

[3] EA 4, 1b, 932; Fabian, *Q*, 85; Strickler III, 135–6 (No. 304).

[4] At least 5,000 in number (Zeller-Werdmüller 3, 6–8; Stumpf 2, 119) including 1,200 from Berne (Feller II, 215) and 1,000 from Zurich under Jörg Göldli (Z XI, 365 n. 10, 394 n. 4, 407 n. 10).

[5] Strickler III, 170–6 (No. 395).   [6] Z XI, 402 n. 1, 417–18.

directed by one 'Master Michael', one of two experts lent by Philip of Hesse.[1] On 7 May Francesco Maria Sforza, Duke of Milan, to the annoyance of the Emperor, arranged terms – an indemnity of 30,000 gulden, destruction of the castle, and security against further attack guaranteed by 1,200 Swiss soldiers who were taken into Milanese pay while a further 800 remained at the cost of their own states.[2] The duke could provide some warships for the lakes, and the final overthrow of the 'tyrant' proved a relatively simple matter. The repute of the Swiss soldiers remained as high as ever, with Zurich suitably represented, facts noted by Zwingli with satisfaction. A final settlement, which did not come until after his death, ensured the safety of the Swiss Mandated Territories in the south, together with the Graubünden.

The episode happened when internal tension was at its height, and each side drew from it the conclusions it wished. Zurich had encouraged the expedition in order to unite the cities of the Christian Civic Union against the Catholics and had been disappointed when the other cities refused to help the Graubünden by an attack on Austria.[3] Zwingli was convinced that other Catholic attacks would follow; in the north, Ferdinand of Austria was preparing to advance from Innsbruck and Ensisheim in support of Marx Sittich of Hohenems and in the south Valais and Savoy were menacing. He also felt certain that the Inner States had deliberately refused to fulfil their obligations in order that they might be in a position to attack Zurich when the latter's best troops were away in the south. It was one of the reasons for calling for a renewal of the blockade.

The Inner States, in fact, found themselves isolated and drew the conclusion that they must fight for survival and could not rely upon help from others. The fears of both sides were not entirely justified, but they were real enough. Zwingli returned to his demand that the Inner States must be taught that they could not repudiate obligations with impunity. If they could be coerced into submission a united evangelical Swiss confederation might come into being. Philip of Hesse could then hope to restore Ulrich of Württemberg with the aid of Swiss Protestants for whose services he would pay. In 1530 Philip had been reluctantly forced to recognise that there was not to be a united Protestant front and that he was the link between Lutherans and Zwinglians whom he would use impartially and to his best advantage.[4] Hence his continued correspondence with Zwingli.

Meanwhile what the first peace of Kappel might mean in practice was

---

[1] Stumpf 2, II, 125; Bullinger, *Ref.* II, 360; Zeller-Werdmüller 3, 9–11; Fabian, *Q*, 93.
[2] EA 4, 1b, 977, 1563–5; Z XI, 461 n. 3; Bertoliatti, *La guerra di Musso*, 117. As often happened, the pay was soon in arrears. Zeller-Werdmüller 3, 19; Jacklin, I, 102 (No. 486).
[3] Schmid, 46.   [4] Hauswirth, *Philipp*, 201–208.

being made abundantly clear in Thurgau. There civil administration rested, as had long been the case, with the responsible powers – Zurich, Glarus, Schwyz, Unterwalden, Zug, Uri and Lucerne. The inhabitants, however, were anxious to secure independent control of church affairs, a large majority of parishes having accepted evangelical teaching, itself the result of considerable efforts at proselytising by determined and forceful preachers. In Appenzell and Rheintal also, local assemblies called for evangelical pastors, and on 13–17 December 1529, in May 1530, in December 1530, and again in May 1531, synods of up to five hundred ministers were addressed at Frauenfeld, by Zwick, Blaurer, Pellican, Collin and Zwingli.[1] In Constance, Diessenhofen and Stein, Zwingli preached to large numbers.[2] When, as in the latter half of 1530, the governor, Philip Brunner, was himself an evangelical from Glarus, the position was such that Zurich reformation decrees were declared operative throughout Thurgau in spite of opposition by the Inner States.[3] All this made it increasingly apparent to these latter that they were being deprived of traditional and accepted rights for the retention of which they might have to fight. Throughout eastern Switzerland evangelisation was accompanied by the same difficulties as earlier in Zurich. The Anabaptists had been active as well, and there were some ministers, such as Fortmüller of Altstätten and the indefatigable Zili of St Gall who objected on biblical grounds to taking an oath to teach and preach according to the Gospel. Others demanded for the local community the right to exclude notorious sinners, the 'ban' so dear to the Anabaptist teaching. In December 1530 there was a considerable gathering of clergy and laity from Rheintal, Toggenburg and Appenzell at St Gall, where they were met in argument by Zwingli and Joner on questions of church discipline.[4] Excommunication was neither necessary nor desirable since the punishment of evil-doers was the province of the police, not of the minister of religion. The texts about the taking of oaths did not exclude their proper administration by the civil authority, a familiar exegesis which brought an accusation that Zwingli twisted texts to make them suit his own views of the relations of church and state.[5] It is pleasant to add that after the debate there was an evening vocal and instrumental concert in the St Gall monastic cloisters at which Zwingli was a performer. A little later, as further evidence that the reformer was still also the humanist, Zwingli patronised a performance of the *Plutus*

[1] Z VI ii, 641–6; Knittel I, 271–2, 347; Egli *4*, I, 83–92 (Zürich, 1899); Kessler, 229; G. R. Potter, 'Zwinglian synods in Eastern Switzerland', *Journal of Ecclesiastical History* 16 (1975). [2] Farner IV, 415–16.
[3] Knittel I, 294–303.
[4] Egli *4*, I, 92; Z XI, 267–8; Sabbata, 275–82.
[5] 'Du heisst nicht allein der Zwingli, sondern auch der Ringli, denn du ringlest und renglest die Schrift, wie Dich gut dünkt.' Mörikofer II, 314. See above, 191.

of Aristophanes in the original Greek. Collin wrote a Latin prologue referring to Zurich as the Athens of the north, George Binder was the producer and Zwingli composed the music. The cast included Hospinian, Wirth, Konrad Meyer von Knonau and Konrad Gessner, then only fifteen, who played the part of Penia (Poverty).[1] It can indeed have been little more than a play-reading on New Year's Day, 1531, before a small and select audience, but it is significant of Zwingli's continued breadth of interest.

The last day of 1530 had seen a further sign of Zurich's ambitions. A force of 600 armed men from St Gall territory occupied Oberriet[2] on 31 December 1530 and obliged the inhabitants to accept orders from Zurich, an action which brought a renewed protest from the Inner States. On 9 January 1531, representatives of the Abbot of St Gall, who was still recognised by the Catholics, appeared at a Federal Diet to complain of unlawful occupation of monastic territory.[3]

This provoked further altercation. The evangelicals complained that their opponents were still in communication with Ferdinand, that they continued to impede the free preaching of God's word, that they were ready to accept foreign gold and that they had failed to fulfil the peace agreement that required them to suppress criticism and slander. There was continued resentment at the manner in which Murner had been allowed to get away in spite of promises to bring him to trial. It was because of their indifference that the Castellan of Musso was a continuing menace. To all this, one Catholic spokesman, Landammann Troger of Uri, rejoined that Zurich was attacking the political independence of Catholic subjects upon whom it was forcing an alien regime and hated heresy. The war of words, if anything, intensified. Catholic priests denounced their opponents as heretical soul-thieves and soul-murderers; the evangelicals retorted with epithets such as flesh-sellers, blood-suckers, mass-men, image-slaves, money guzzlers and idolaters,[4] all this in defiance of the peace terms, which prohibited slander.

If this situation was unacceptable, so too was that in regard to the monastery of St Gall. It had been agreed at Kappel that the protector (*Schirmhauptmann*) of the monastic territories should be a competent, brave, God-fearing man who would uphold the Bible, evangelical doctrine and truth. What this meant to Zurich was well known, and this was to be

[1] Z VII, 197; ZWA I, 11–13; Bullinger, *Ref.* II, 182; Egli *I*, 664–5; A. Hug, *Aufführung einer griechischen Komödie in Zürich am 1. Januar 1531* (Zürich, 1874); H. Fischer, *Conrad Gessner*. Njbl. der Naturforschenden Gesellschaft in Zürich auf das Jahr 1966 (Zürich, 1966) 11.
[2] E. Gagliardi, *Geschichte der Schweiz*, 3 Bde. (Zürich/Leipzig, 1938) II, 567.
[3] EA 4, 1b, 875, 883–4.
[4] Salat 232, 280. 'Tanngrötzli, kuokemen, milchbengel, knöbelbärt, zigerclozen, bluothünd... kätzer, bäpstler, gottlos, sodomiter'.

guaranteed to the inhabitants by the protector appointed, Jacob Frei. This had been done on the assumption that Zurich and Glarus had taken over the territorial rights of the abbot while not depriving Schwyz and Lucerne of their legal participating privileges. The Inner States, however, had never agreed to any such interpretation; for them there was a lawful prince-abbot and the tenants were his serfs or subjects. The revised constitution of May 1530 and the new administrative arrangements under it were rejected. When Frei's term of office came to its end on 25 November 1530, it became the turn of Lucerne to nominate his successor. Since he would not be an evangelical like his predecessor and since Lucerne recognised the legitimacy of the abbot Kilian and the new protector refused to take an oath to uphold the revised constitution, Zurich argued that Frei must remain in control and upheld the refusal of the monastic tenants to take an oath of obedience to the Lucerne nominee. Lucerne then accused Zurich of breaking the federal constitution, and Zurich invoked the clauses of the peace treaty. Here was another discord that could be resolved only by war.

In April and again in May 1531 representatives of the Swiss reformed cities met to discuss the whole situation. From Zurich came the call to attack the central states while it was yet feasible and thus to strike at the arch-enemy Charles V. Berne again opposed war in spite of Catholic provocation by their refusal to join against Musso and by continued public criticism. Instead, Berne suggested pressure by the economic sanctions that had been envisaged in the first peace of Kappel. The northern markets should be closed to Catholic traders, and suppliers of grain, meat, salt, iron and other necessities should be prevented from going south. This should be enough; Berne was all for legality and diplomatic pressure but was utterly opposed to aggression and a preventive war. Zwingli pointed out that a blockade would merely intensify Catholic hostility while at the same time enabling their enemies to strike only when they were ready. In the Lord's cause it was better for soldiers to meet in battle than for children to die of starvation.

Nor could a blockade be effectively fully applied without the help of Glarus, Gaster, Weesen and the Freie Aemter, all most unwilling to participate. From the Catholic side there even came promises to suppress future verbal and written slander, but without guarantees this meant little. Negotiations continued amid growing suspicion and hostility, but efforts at mediation were of little avail.

Zwingli now proposed, to the alarm of the traditionalists of Berne, the creation of what amounted to a new Switzerland. Instead of a loose confederation there should be dyarchy: Zurich and Berne should join to dominate their neighbours. Together they would be the two oxen which should draw the federal cart behind them.[1] Almost certainly it was between 17 and 22 August 1531 that Zwingli wrote the notorious memorandum 'Was Zürich und Bern not ze betrachten sye im fünförtischen handel'.[2]

This sketch or project may have been no more than a paper written for his own clarification and guidance, but it clearly represents the policy for which he now stood and which implied armed coercion. The Five States, it was argued, had shown, in regard to St Gall in particular, unwillingness to carry out their treaty obligations. They expected to use the numerical majority of Catholic states in the Federation to prevent the spread of the Reformation, and they refused to reject mercenary service and the acceptance of foreign pensions. By their corrupt and intolerant administration and by their intrigues with Austria, they had forfeited their federal rights. The *Stanser Verkommnis* implying equal votes in the management of the Mandated Territories must be denounced and withdrawn. It was absurd that Zurich and Berne, controlling two-thirds of the territory of the Confederation (six sevenths with the Mandated Territories), should have their voting power thus restricted. On the principle that *contra iusticiam non est ius* Zwingli maintained that by their own actions the Inner States had severed their bond with the Federation. They had sold governorships to the highest bidder and the governors appointed had fleeced their subjects. To negotiate was no longer possible; an attack was the only way to lower their insufferable pride. They must be reduced to submission as Carthage had been when destroyed by Rome. Since wars are now decided by guns, which they lack, an onslaught must be successful and a new constitution could then be forcibly imposed. It would be a righteous war. The new Swiss Confederation was seen as a sovereign evangelical republic under the joint control of the equal partners, Zurich and Berne acting in harmony and to the public advantage – the other members to be subordinates, consulted and humoured, but also dominated.[3] Implied, although not worked out, was a denial of the sovereignty of the separate states; the will of the majority, who were also the wealthiest and the most powerful, must prevail and a strong state emerge. It was a revolutionary proposal, a fanciful and unworkable scheme with which Berne was never likely to consider association,[4] the more so after Zurich had practically annexed Thurgau, Toggenburg, the Rheintal and the monastic estates of St Gall. Berne, indeed, was later to balance this by the occupation of the

---

[1] 'So werdend sy an der Eidgnoschafft sin glych wie zwen ochsen vor dem wagen, die an einem joch ziehend.' EA 4, 1b, 1043.

[2] S II, 3, 101–7; EA 4, 1b, 1041–5; Koehler, *Buch* 318–26. ZWA VIII, 535–54; ZWA XII, 222–33 (where the first week in August is suggested as the date).

[3] S II, 3, 107; EA 4, 1b, 1045. 'Summa summarum, wer nit ein herr kann sin, ist billich dass er knecht sye.'   [4] J. Courvoisier, *Zwingli* (Geneva, 1947) 184–5.

Vaud, and more successfully so in that this area remained Bernese until the end of the eighteenth century whereas Zurich could not hold on to its gains; but this was to be in the future.

The immediate cause of the second Kappel war was the blockade – economic sanctions by which grain, wine, iron and salt were prevented from reaching Lucerne and its associates.[1] The pretext for the conflict was failure to fulfil the conditions of the first peace of Kappel; the reality was that the north fought to preserve its reformed faith while the central states were determined to maintain their independence and their adherence to Rome and the Pope. Zwingli never doubted that war must be renewed and that fundamental differences could be settled only on the battlefield. Berne hoped that war could be avoided and only reluctantly agreed to blockade as a compromise measure. It was a cruel weapon which hurt the weak more than the strong, and it was in fact rather ineffectively applied by Berne but with greater efficiency by Zurich and its immediate neighbours. Bad harvests in 1529 and 1530 combined to bring it about that little material came north from Lombardy.[2] The central peasantry, unable to sell their beasts, milk and cheese, and unable to buy the salt and grain necessary for their existence, were in real danger of destitution. The people had to secure supplies somehow and would attack in desperation. Zwingli recognised that to do nothing but apply 'sanctions' was to hand over the initiative to the enemy, who would choose the time and the place for attack.[3] If there was a case for a blockade there was a stronger case for open war by force in the battlefield against men, rather than by starving women and children. Hence, in part, his opposition to a policy favoured by Berne and the other evangelical cities. There were mediators ready and willing; France, Graubünden, Valais, Appenzell, Glarus, Fribourg, Solothurn, again and again tried this unsuccessfully.[4] Berne again insisted on negative action – an expedition against the central states, it feared, would alienate the Duke of Milan, whose goodwill had been sought.

Zwingli had kept up the pressure from the pulpit: in his Whitsunday sermon on 28 May he had declared: 'If someone is called a liar to his face, he must defend himself. Not to attack is to invite defeat.'[5] In June Zurich again urged Berne to insist upon the fulfilment of the Kappel peace terms. In July Schwyz retaliated with complaints that it was intolerable that its own subjects in Weesen and Gaster were being forced to support the blockade against them.[6] The war drums were reverberating.

[1] R. Bosch, *Der Kornhandel der Nord-, Ost-Innerschweiz und der ennetbirgischen Vogteien im 15. und 16. Jahrhundert* (Zürich, 1913) 109. [2] Wyss, 150f; Z XI, 193 n. 7.
[3] Bullinger, *Ref.* II, 388; Farner IV, 467.
[4] E.g. at Bremgarten 12–13 June 1531. Feller II, 220; Mörikofer II, 377.
[5] Bullinger, *Ref.* II, 383–8; Farner IV, 467; Schmid, 46ff.
[6] Z XI, 531, EA. 4, 1b, 1070.

In August the Protestant cause seemed more encouraging. Rapperswil and Appenzell declared for the Reformation; in Augsburg Zwingli's teaching was making advances, and Henry VIII consulted with him about his matrimonial problem.[1] The Duke of Milan was asked through Giovanni Domenico Panizzone about the possibilities of an alliance, and a cordial, if non-committal, reply was received from him.[2] It was hardly likely that Catholic Milan and Zwinglian Zurich could work together, but, as with France, Zwingli was ever hopeful. His ebullient self-confidence was restored. The efforts made by Berne to maintain the status quo while relinquishing none of its demands, combined with Zurich's determination to interpret the peace of Kappel to its own advantage, led to a conflict which Zwingli wanted and welcomed.[3] The failure of the arbitrators, the continued Catholic hope of Habsburg and papal help, and the determination of the Inner States to fight rather than allow freedom of preaching, all widened the gap.[4] It was certain that the inhabitants of the Catholic states would not become Zwinglian; they were determined to maintain their traditional federal rights and in this they were supported by the growing suspicion or jealousy of Zurich felt elsewhere. At the same time the cold war of economic blockade was, to Zwingli's dislike, being stepped up. Food sanctions were applied from Bremgarten, Mellingen, Thurgau, Rheingau, Rheintal, Toggenburg, Weesen, Gaster, Sargans, St Gall and the reformed *Gemeinden* of the Freie Aemter. The Graubünden did not directly intervene but their passes were, so far as practicable, closed to traffic[5] and the Duke of Milan also cooperated. Glarus, Fribourg, Appenzell, Solothurn and Strassburg and even France persisted in their efforts at mediation, but both sides continued to ignore them.

Nothing had come of Zurich complaints to a meeting of the Swiss Protestant cities at Aarau of an intensified campaign of denigration,[6] and when Zwingli again drew attention to the persistent attacks on his honour

---

[1] This was done through Grynaeus. Zwingli's letters, in which he apparently accepted the necessity for a divorce from Catherine, have been lost. They were seen by Gilbert Burnet (*History of the Reformation of the Church of England* ed. N. Pocock, Oxford, 1865 I, 160–1) but the library of Richard Smith, in which they were, went to the auction room and was dispersed. The letters may still exist. Z XI, 579–80, 603.

Z XI, 604, 622; Farner IV, 456–8.   [3] Stumpf 2, II, 157–8.

[4] Schmid 50–8; Hauswirth, *Philipp*, 232. Writing to friends in Ulm on 4 June 1531, Zwingli had insisted that the only obstacle to peace was the unwillingness of the Five States to allow evangelical preaching. 'Quinquepagici verbi praedicationem nolunt admittere...Hic senatus respondit: si sperent fore, ut Quinquepagici verbum dei prędicari patiantur et hanc pacis legem servent, qua cavetur, ne fidem nostram persequantur neque apud suos neque apud nostros, iam fore, ut de pace ac conciliatione tractari feramus.' Z XI, 460–2.

[5] Bosch, *Kornhandel* 110; Bucher, 143, 145. Zurich complained that there were leakages via Berne-controlled Lenzburg, while the peasants of the countryside sometimes helped the Catholics to smuggle food from Baden by pretending that it was for home consumption, but these evasions were insignificant.

[6] Z XI, 447; EA 4, 1b, 980–3.

and threats to his person made by Catholic authorities,[1] he was not at all
mollified to be reminded that similar charges were often brought against
their opponents by Protestants and were just as much abuse and slander
as when uttered by Catholics.[2] On a lower level, the Zurich millers and
bakers were complaining that the blockade was ruining their trade with
central Switzerland, and the fact that mass was being secretly heard by
Catholic sympathisers from Zurich in or near to its territories was regarded
as deliberately provocative.[3]

On 10 August Zwingli, Collin and Werner Steiner travelled to Bremgarten to impress, not entirely successfully, on a party of influential
councillors from Berne the urgent need for action. Berne, in fact, was
silently displacing its rival as the chief power among the protestant states,
but this was hardly realised. The appearance of a comet[4] in the sky north
west of St Gall just after sunset on 12 August was regarded in many
quarters as a portent of war, and special prayers were said in the churches.
By less apprehensive ministers of religion it was declared to be a sign of
divine displeasure at the dancing and drinking that had accompanied some
fashionable weddings. A renewal of hostilities was beginning to be taken
for granted, and on 10 September a kind of war council of Lavater,
Johann Schwyzer and Wilhelm Tönig was formed. They could summon
men to arms, but decisions about their use and about war or peace lay as
always with the Great Council. Yet no active steps were taken either for
defence or for offence, in spite of warning from Basle that the Five States
were arming and would yield only to force.[5] A curious semi-paralysis, an
unwillingness to fight, was all too apparent and yet every attempt at
mediation was fruitless. This was the more serious in that, in fact, on
26 September representatives of the Five States had resolved in desperation that an attack on Zurich was their only hope. They must either fight
or starve; they had the advantage of favourable terrain, they could choose
their time, and their soldiers were ready and united.

Exactly the opposite was true of their opponents. Rather vague reports
of possible hostile action reached Zurich and Berne; some attention was
given to them by the latter, but in Zurich, and by Zwingli hmiself, they
were discounted or ignored.[6] There were reports of the arrival of Catholic
volunteers from Valais, Eschental and even Lombardy,[7] but this, for

---

[1] Konrad Hiltbrand of Einsiedeln was specially violent in his denunciation of Zwingli and his
friends. Z XI, 361 n. 3.   [2] Feller II, 218.   [3] Staehelin II, 480-1; Mörikofer II, 348-9.
[4] Halley, who gave his name to the comet, used Kessler's detailed account to establish its orbit.
[5] Bosshart, 274-5 n. 3; Z XI, 582; Staehelin II, 484.
[6] Bucher, 151-2; Sprüngli, 25; Luthi, 67; ZWA XIII, 302.
[7] Escher, *Glaubensparteien* 276-80, 293. A few (at first 200, later more) Italian soldiers of
fortune claiming papal approbation came too late to be of any practical assistance. They
proved far more of an embarrassment to their friends by looting en route and threatening to
return home if not paid than a danger to the other side.

Zwingli, was simply further convincing evidence of a great imperial–papal conspiracy against the adherents of the true religion. By the beginning of October the Catholics knew that they would only lose by delay, and prepared for action, while as late as 3 October the other reformed cities were still urging Zurich to hold back.[1] The preparations indicated, as a contemporary realised, 'the beginning of our downfall'.[2] Glarus declared at once for neutrality; the Graubünden likewise declined to move against Uri or to take any action except to watch and wait; the communities of Valais, for their part, similarly showed no serious signs of an attack on Berne. In Zurich, in spite of Zwingli's warnings and pleadings, no precautions were taken, partly from a desire not to offend Berne by precipitate action, partly from wanton carelessness.

Direct initiative was taken by the Inner States with a move against Ober Freiamt, close to the borders of Lucerne. The district was a commandery of the Teutonic Order, and the local commander was Hans Albrecht von Mülinen, son-in-law of Bürgermeister Diethelm Röist of Zurich and a personal friend of Zwingli.[3] He had cautiously but successfully promoted the evangelical cause in his district, thereby incurring the wrath of Lucerne, which shared the Federal rights over the district and objected to its evangelisation. When hostile forces appeared, occupying (on 8–9 October) Hitzkirch,[4] a reformed house of the Teutonic Order, and pillaging the countryside, he retired to Bremgarten, as directed, in order to avoid a confrontation. News of this was accompanied on 8 October by a report[5] that a considerable force was being concentrated near Baar, and that another body, numbering about 600 men, was gathering in Zug ready to invade the Freie Aemter, where they expected help from sympathisers in Bremgarten.[6] A formal preliminary notification of intention to open hostilities (*Absagbrief*) had been prepared at Lucerne on 4 October.[7] Their

[1] EA 4, 1b, 1178.
[2] Sprüngli, 25; Schmid, 58.
[3] Z IX, 622 n. 1.
[4] Beside being of some strategic importance and housing the French representatives, Meigret and Daugerant (Boisrigault), Hitzkirch had religious significance as well. In May 1529 it had been reported to Lucerne that a majority of the parish wished to remain Catholic but also wanted to hear the word of God. They had, however, only one priest (presented by the Teutonic knights) instead of three. After the first peace of Kappel, the parish decided by a majority in favour of the Reformation, but after 1531 it was re-Catholicised. Th. v. Liebenau, *Reformation und Gegenreformation in Hitzkirch* (Lucerne, 1867).
[5] This was received in Zurich at 4 a.m. on 10 October. P. Schweizer, *Die Schlacht bei Kappel am 11. Oktober 1531*, JSG 41 (1916), 14.
[6] Bucher, 152.
[7] Almost certainly this was not sent. Bullinger, *Ref.* III, 88, is very vague. It, or another which had been agreed at Lucerne (EA 4, 1b, 1179-83, 1188-9; Steck & Tobler (No. 3095), 1397; Stumpf 2, II, 163) arrived on 9 October and included a demand for the exclusion of Zurich from the Confederation.

appeal was to God to decide: their quarrel, they insisted, was with Zurich alone whose exclusion from the Confederation had already been recommended by the Inner States. Zurich had broken the peace by the blockade and had brought foreigners (i.e. Constance and Strassburg) into the affairs of the Confederation.[1] The attackers were at once desperate, enthusiastic and confident of help from Austria.

There was, however, no direct formal violation of Zurich territory. The only force that Zurich had close to the frontier was a small garrison, less than 300 in all, based on Kappel[2] and manifestly no threat to its neighbours. The Zurich Great Council was hurriedly summoned, and the military men were asked for their professional advice. This was, apparently, neither clear nor convincing. They continued to treat the reports they received as either alarmist or exaggerated, and it was not until 7 October that Berne, which reasonably complained of having received no information for three days, was belatedly informed about the situation.[3] Relations were not improved by allegations, not entirely without foundation, that Berne was allowing food supplies to filter across its frontiers and was opposed to a war. The Zurich government was now ready to risk war and resolved to fight, but its ally, Berne, was understandably unwilling to come to its support as long as there was no attack – i.e. no armed violation of Zurich territory. Both sides were 'right', if the word 'right' is a meaningful one on the context. War had been planned by the evangelicals but entered on by the Catholics, driven to desperation by economic pressure and hopeful of powerful external aid. For Zwingli's religious aims and Zurich's political objectives to be attained, the Inner States must be manifestly defeated in battle and their offensive potential eliminated; thus and thus alone, could the evangelical cause triumph. Yet to advance without Bernese support was hazardous and could have been successful only with a disciplined and enthusiastic army. This was exactly what Zurich did not have. They chose the wrong commander, they agreed on impracticable strategy, the tactics were deplorable and the Zurchers who took the field were few in number and unwilling to fight for survival.

The most remarkable fact of all is that Zurich, which had been clamouring for a reopening of hostilities, was now completely unprepared for them. Its army, which in 1529 had been a model of discipline, had deteriorated rapidly after a civilian overhaul.[4] In September, during Zwingli's absence,

---

[1] There was also included an allegation that Zurich had forced the nuns of Hermetswil to reform. Koehler, *Zwingli*, 259; Schmid, 59; Bucher, 153.

[2] Where Joner, as administrator, was living in the monastic buildings and could advise the council on what was happening. He now called for reinforcements.

[3] Anshelm VI, 88.

[4] J. Häne, *Zürcher Militär und Politik im zweiten Kappelerkrieg* (Zürich, 1913) 26–32 for the text of the *Kriegsordnung*.

the number of experienced officers had been reduced,[1] partly to save money, but also to eliminate any opponents of the government by retaining only those regarded as God-fearing lovers of truth acceptable to the new establishment.[2] Rates of pay had been lowered to discourage volunteers. Civilian interference in military affairs, especially by members of the socially rather low Kämbel gild, was resented by many officers to whom the new set-up was distasteful. The normal parades and inspections had not been held, and there was in circulation a certain amount of anti-war or pacifist propaganda attributed to Anabaptist sympathisers. There was little enthusiasm among the soldiers for a war against their own Swiss neighbours with whom they had fought side by side at Marignano and elsewhere.

Inadequate 'intelligence' was added to military confusion: the over-all situation was not understood from Zurich. It was known that hostile Catholic forces were gathering at Zug, but what their intentions were and where the attack would come were matters for conjecture. To secure communications with Berne, some 600 men and four guns were sent to Bremgarten[3] under Heinrich Werdmüller, reasonably enough since the Freie Aemter were menaced. Felix Manz secured the route to Sarmensdorf, and other contingents were sent to Mellingen, Wädenswil (under Jacob Frei) and Gaster.[4] More than this is might have been inadvisable to do since Zurich had agreed with its allies that there should be no fighting unless its territory was actually attacked.

This indeed was what the Five States had decided upon. On 4 October armed men had already converged on Zug, but no notice was taken of this; even when word came from Kappel of what was happening, it was assumed that any attack would be on the Freie Aemter against the lines of communication with Berne. It was also assumed that the local militia would defend the monastery of Kappel if this were attacked, but singularly little attention was paid to hostile troop movements. By 9 October, when reasons for renewing the war were restated at Lucerne, the forces gathering between Zug and Baar were obviously too large to be ignored. The company from Lucerne which had occupied Hitzkirch also threatened Bünzen, while their opponents under Felix Manz fell back on Sarmensdorf.[5] There was still no sense of urgency in Zurich, although it had already been agreed to appoint Hans Rudolf Lavater as commander-in-chief (*Oberster*

---

[1] Including Hans Escher and Jörg Berger, a competent general.
[2] A new council of war, 23 in number, too large to be effective, was set up. ZWA X, 541–5; XII, 311; Schaufelberger, 36–53.
[3] Mellingen and Bremgarten on the Reuss commanding the road to Baden had declared for the reformers in 1529. They were Mandated Territories ruled by Zurich, Lucerne, Schwyz, Unterwalden and Glarus (not including Uri or Berne).
[4] Bucher, 155–7; Bosshart, 275 n.; Schweizer, 15–16.
[5] Egli 2, 24; Sprüngli, 25.

Hauptmann).[1] Forty years old, strikingly handsome, active, eloquent, affable, he had been in papal military service in 1521 and accepted the Zwinglian reform which he forwarded in Thurgau as governor of Kiburg (from 1525) where he was popular. The serious nature of the threat from the south was not realised until the afternoon of 10 October when the Great Council ordered Jörg Göldli of Tiefenau to advance to the defence of Kappel with fewer than 1,000 men mostly collected en route.[2] Göldli, wealthy and well-connected, now forty-five, with a record of service in the Italian campaigns and against 'Musso', was one of the few experienced commanders immediately available.[3] His duties and responsibilities were not defined, and the choice turned out to be unfortunate. As many knew, his younger brother Kaspar, a supporter of mercenary service, had refused to accept the Reformation, had left Zurich in 1523 and was now with the other side. There was even a story in circulation that the brothers met secretly and exchanged information about the disposition of their forces.[4]

Göldli, who had received explicit instructions to avoid an engagement until reinforcements arrived, at once set off with his advance force. Behind him came Peter Fuessli[5] with six guns for which horses had been found

[1] Egli *4*, 150–64; Z XI, 458 n. 3; Wyss, 122 n. 5; Lüthi, 67; Schweizer, 49–50; Sprüngli, 25; NblW no. 86 (1864); Mörikofer, II, 392–3; Bullinger, *Ref.* III, 56–7. He was much more a politician than a soldier: a subsequent investigation into his conduct (Schweizer, 49–50) cleared him of charges of incompetence and neglect, and he was later several times Bürgermeister of Zurich.

[2] Schweizer, 15; Lüthi, 70; Häne, 44; Stumpf *2* II, 165. A considerable literature has gathered round the battle of Kappel. Egli *2* analysed all the contemporary accounts (by Füssli, Huber, Göldli, von Hertenstein, Schönbrunner and Blättler) known to him and criticised the narratives of Salat, Aegidius Tschudi and Bullinger. Bullinger, *Ref.* III, 103–81 was written some thirty years after the event and was chiefly concerned to magnify the achievement of his revered predecessor, but his detailed account was carefully compiled. Other contemporary accounts are in Stumpf *2*; Stumpf *1*; Bosshart; Sprüngli; L. Weisz, *Unbekannte ausländische Quellen zur Geschichte der Kapellerkriege*, Geschichtsfreund 86 (Stans, 1931) 1–133; Do., *Die Geschichte der Kappelerkriege nach Hans Edlibach*, ZSK XXVI (1932) 81–108, 270–87.

As with the battle of Waterloo, argument about detail continues. There is useful matter in Th. von Liebenau, *Beschreibung des II. Cappelerkrieges von Werner Steiner von Zug*, ASG NF 4 (1884), 305–41; P. Schweizer, *Die Schlacht bei Kappel am 11. Oktober 1531*, JSG 41 (1916), 3–50; W. Schaufelberger, 'Kappel – die Hintergründe einer militärischen Katastrophe', SAV 51 (1955), 34–61 (*Festschrift für Hans Georg Wackernagel*); R. Braun, *Zur Militärpolitik Zürichs im Zeitalter der Kappeler Kriege* ZWA X (1958) 537–73; E. Egli, *Zwinglis Tod und seiner Bedeutung für Kirche und Vaterland* (Zürich, 1893).

[3] Wyss, 122; Z XI, 407 n. 10.

[4] Egli *2*, 25; Schweizer, 28–9; Farner IV, 427; Jacob, 167–70; ZWA X, 552. There is no positive evidence for this inherently improbable meeting, but it is significant that the story was repeated and believed.

[5] Fuessli, together with his father (both believed to have Catholic sympathies) had cast 162 guns for Zurich, and he later wrote a short but revealing narrative of the engagement. He was related by marriage to Zwingli's colleague Hans Engelhard, third stipendiary priest in Zurich and an opponent of the war. Egli *2*, 11; Schweizer, 4. Mörikofer's useful narrative (Mörikofer, II, 366) relies too heavily on the facts collected by Aegidius Tschudi in 1560.

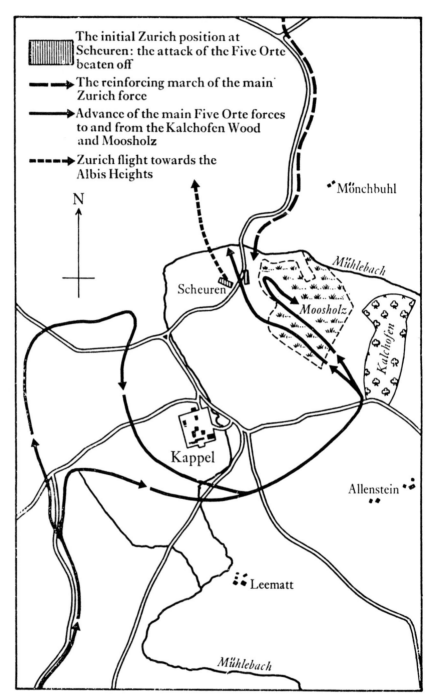

The battle of Kappel, 11 October 1531

410

only after some difficulty and delay. There were two possible positions within sight of Kappel, both on a hill, one at Scheuren, and the other, a little to its rear, at Mönchbühl. Fuessli advised against Scheuren as unsuitable for his guns, but Göldli decided in its favour. It is easy to argue with hindsight that this was wrong; Mönchbühl, although better adapted for defence, or for a retreat, was further from Kappel, was even more marshy, and provided a much inferior view of the opposing forces coming up from Baar. Since Göldli cannot have known the size of the opposition, this was an important consideration. His decision was not necessarily the wrong one, for he could have fallen back on Mönchbühl if necessary; but having taken up a position, he did nothing to improve it, and he neglected to make sure of a possible retreat. He apparently also ignored the existence of a beech wood at Kalchofen on his left which could provide cover for the enemy.[1] Once in place he obstinately refused to change his dispositions – 'Ich will dieser Platz und keinen andern'.[2] Between Scheuren and Mönchbühl ran a little stream, the Mühlebach, crossed by a simple bridge but surrounded by a good deal of sodden, marshy ground across which armoured soldiers could struggle only with much difficulty. Göldli also neglected to send forward scouts to bring information about the enemy, discipline was not very good, he failed to protect his flank, and he accepted battle when his instructions were to avoid it.[3] To apply, however, terms of military tactics to a short fight in which only about 5,000 men were involved in all (as compared with more than ten times this number at Marignano or Mohács), is a little excessive. Kappel, although decisive, was only a skirmish in which but a fraction of the Zurich forces were engaged.

While Göldli's men (*das Fähnlein*) thus moved uncomfortably to the frontier on 10 October, there was some confusion, but still no sense of urgency, in Zurich. The Great Council, some of whose members should have read Zwingli's earlier advice[4] on strategy and could consult him easily enough, spent much of the day in debate. The delay had serious consequences. The challenge, it was agreed, had to be taken up; invasion of Zurich territory would bring help from Berne; men must be sent to Bremgarten, Rapperswil and Gasterland, as well as to meet the threat at Kappel. Lavater wanted to assemble the main force (*das Banner*) at once, but the summons, or call-up, was proclaimed, by tradition, in Ober-

---

[1] Protection could have been obtained, as Ulrich Bonder suggested, by simple trenches or by cutting down trees in the wood. Axes and men were available, but the order was not given.

[2] Egli 2, 24. Egli's account is still unsurpassed, but he loses no opportunity to show his disapproval of Göldli.

[3] Egli 2, 25. 'Seine Aufgabe hiess aber offenbar: "Gewinne Zeit, damit wir uns sammeln – vermeide es, dich schlagen zu lassen".'

[4] See above, 210–12.

winterthur,[1] only in the evening. Many did not know where to report, many more stayed away, and it was not until first light on 11 October that a few hundred men[2] gathered round the colours in Zurich without commissariat or rations, some having walked in overnight. In what was almost a disorderly mob, with Zwingli dressed in green, armed and on horseback among them, they streamed out of the city gate heading for the Albis, with Schwyzer as standard-bearer (*Pannerherr*) and Tönig in charge of the guns (*Schützenhauptmann*).

Göldli had meanwhile had his men out at 4 a.m. before it was light, with hoar-frost on the ground, expecting an attack.[3] When it was possible to see the enemy movements there was a discussion at which Rudolf Ziegler called for a retreat to the greater security of Mönchbühl covered by a party on the left flank guarding the wood,[4] but this was not accepted. At about 9 a.m. the well-rested enemy could be seen approaching Kappel under Markwart Zelger of Unterwalden and Golder of Lucerne, the latter bringing the formal defiance or declaration of war. Their advance force, some 700 strong with some guns, approached the Zurich right wing to seek an open field for attack, and were beaten off by fire from Fuessli's artillery, apparently against Göldli's orders.[5] The attackers then turned back to join the main body, some 7,000 strong, which moved eastwards past Kappel towards Ebertsweilerhöhe and the undefended beech wood of Kalchofen. This right wheel was a hazardous operation. Rudolf Gallmann and Rudolf Schinz begged Göldli to attack – 'Now they are ours; if we attack now they are defeated; if we let them form up and attack us we shall be overwhelmed.'[6] Göldli, however, refused; expecting immediate reinforcement, hoping perhaps to keep the peace in accordance with his original instructions, and it being now too late to withdraw, he awaited the onset of the enemy.[7]

The Zurich main force (*Banner*), such as it was, was indeed on its way. By midday the motley crowd, including some thirty ministers of religion, had reached Hausen where Tönig asked for a rest for the famished and exhausted men. Lavater, Schwyzer and Zwingli insisted on moving forward, and by 3 p.m. the forces joined. There was a hurried discussion about the next move, at which it was agreed, too late in any case, to draw back to Mönchbühl. This involved traversing marshy land, dragging guns

---

[1] T. Müller-Wolfer, *Das Jahrhundert der Glaubenstrennung* (Berne, 1925), 31.

[2] Lavater had expected over 1,000 – estimates vary between 200 and 700.

[3] A story was current (Stumpf 2, 167) that a traitor from Zurich, Hans Andress, in return for money from Heini Schönbrunner of Zug, had reported on the precise size and composition of the Zurich force. It is not incredible, but it made little difference since there was almost no possibility of, or attempt at, concealment.

[4] Egli 2, 27. Rudolf Gallmann flatly refused to move. 'Da, da muoss min kylchhoff sin. Gott lasse mich den tag nimmerme leben, das ich deren lütcn ein tritt wychen wölle.' Bullinger, *Ref.* III, 118.　　　[5] Egli 2, 28.　　　[6] Egli 2, 29.　　　[7] Bullinger, *Ref.* III, 121.

across the Mühlebach stream, in the face of a largely superior force. The enemy was already in possession of the beechwood and out of range of such guns as there were, but at 4 p.m. it was growing dusk and their men were not drawn up in battle order. The leaders were prepared to hold their ground and fight the next day, but Hans Jauch, governor of Uri, supported by about 100 eager warriors, called for an immediate advance through the wood. This small force, with some crossbowmen, threw themselves on the Zurich flank. The few opposing guns were useless, the lead was immediately followed up by a general advance, and within half an hour what could have been a considered withdrawal had become a disgraceful rout.

There were no clear orders, no heroics, no suggestion, as at St Jakob an der Birs, of holding out to the last man. The cowardly Zurchers, who had invited the unnecessary combat, broke and fled, knowing that their short daggers were of little use against the long swords of their opponents. Lavater,[1] Göldli and Fuessli, none of whom was hurt, led the flight. The guns were abandoned, some of the fugitives, impeded by their armour, were drowned in the Mühlebach, and darkness fell on small groups which held out, as Swiss thrust and hacked at Swiss with swords and halberds.[2] One group, which included Zwingli, some officers and some brother clerics, resisted manfully under a hedge or tree, but in vain. Zwingli himself, severely wounded, was recognised by torchlight, refused the ministrations of a confessor, and was killed by Vokinger of Unterwalden.[3] His body was quartered and burnt by Hans Schwendinan of Lucerne, and mixed with dung, to show the intensity of the feeling against the arch-heretic and to prevent his ashes being collected as relics.[4] According to some later reports, he said before dying, 'You may kill the body but you cannot kill the soul', and if this is what his friends thought he should have said, it certainly represented his attitude.[5] There is good reason to believe that Hans Schönbrunner, the Catholic priest who had gone from the Fraumünster to Zug, looked upon him and said, 'Had you but been a Catholic I am sure

---

[1] There was a false report of his death. H. Dommann, *Die Korrespondenz der V Orte im zweiten Kappelerkriege*, Geschichtsfreunde (Stans, 1931), 249, Doc. 12.

[2] Bullinger, *Ref.* III, 126–8; Salat, 308.   [3] Egli 2, 42–3.

[4] As with Joan of Arc, there was a story that Zwingli's heart escaped the flames. ZWA IX (1953), 563–76.

[5] Myconius gave currency to this story. 'Prostratum, aiebam, prementiū multitudine iam tertio, sed in pedes semper restitisse; quarto fixum cuspide sub mento, & in genua prolapsum dixisse: Ecquid hoc infortunii: Age, corpus quidē occidere possunt, animam nō possunt. Atqz his dictis mox obdormiuisse in Domino.' *DD. Ioannis Oecolampadii et Huldrichi Zuinglii epistolarum libri quatuor.* (Basileae, MDXXXVI) Sig. *θ* 2. Bullinger took care to collect all the testimony he could later, and his narrative (*Ref.* III, 136–7, 166–8) is to be preferred to the partial account of Salat, 310–12, who minimises Zwingli's wounds and his courage, and those of Tschudi (ASR I, 44–55) and Kessler (Sabbata, 367–8). A. Erichson, *Zwinglis Tod und dessen Beurtheilung durch Zeitgenossen* (Strassburg, 1883) makes good use of the evidence from contemporary letters.

you would have been a good Confederate.'[1] It was profoundly true: Zwingli was a Christian first and foremost, prepared to be Christ's soldier and to live and die according to his interpretation of the Bible text. Next he was devoted to his country and countrymen, more sincerely and passionately perhaps than most. Zurich, where his ideas triumphed, came third; yet it was for Zurich, rather than for Christ or the Confederation, that he died.

Before midnight, the survivors were trailing into Zurich to tell Zwingli's widow that she had lost as well a son, brother, brother-in-law and other relatives. Among the score or more of clergymen who lay dead on the field were the bodies of Wolfgang Joner of Kappel, Wolfgang Rübli of Einsiedeln, Commander Schmid of Küssnacht, Canon Anton Walder from the Great Minster, and the ministers from Embrach, Egg, Bülach, Buchs, Ottenbach and elsewhere. Were they all, like Zwingli, armed combatants? If not, was their presence entirely necessary or desirable?[2] The confident negative of the twentieth century did not come at all naturally to the sixteenth, which took warfare for granted and expected the clergy to be with the fighting men. Even so, their numbers, considering how few parishioners can have accompanied some of them, are remarkably large. Luther had no doubt that Zwingli was mistaken as usual – 'all who take the sword die by the sword', was his comment[3] on hearing the news. With these men, the chief intellectual and spiritual leaders of the Zwinglian reform were eliminated, and Oecolampadius was soon to follow.

The battle of Kappel was a minor engagement which had enduring and disastrous consequences. With Zwingli there perished some 500 of his own side and perhaps 100 of the enemy. The killing, however, was, perhaps purposely, selective. Of the 500 dead,[4] many were from old Zurich families, including Thumysen (father and two sons), Bluntschli, Meyer, Pfeiffer, Ochsner, Frei, Wyss, Wirz, Walder, Werdmüller, Escher, Funk, Usteri.[5] The former leaders of the Zurich council were seen in the Rathaus no more.

---

[1] Egli 2, 43. L. v. Muralt thought this very probable. Vasella SKG 38 Jg. (1944), 156 discounted Schönbrunner's story.

[2] Cf. L. Weisz, *Nach der Schlacht von Kappel*, 137 Nbl. hg. von der Hülfsgesellschaft in Zürich, 1937, 16–25 – 'Klageschrift eines unbekannten gegen die Predikanten.'

[3] 'Gott hat schon zweimal gestraft; erstlich unter dem Münzer, jetzt unter dem Zwinglin.' WA *Br.* 6. 244, several times repeated e.g. 246 and WA *Tischreden* I. 220, II. 3, 103. A. Erichson, *Zwinglis Tod und dessen Beurteilung durch Zeitgenossen* (Strassburg, 1883), 27–8, 80–1; O. Farner, *Das Zwinglibild Luthers* (Tübingen, 1931) 24. Vadian expressed similar sentiments. Näf, *Vadian* II, 339.

[4] Farner, ZWA x (1955) 201, following Bullinger, *Ref.* III, 142, makes the number killed 383. A greatly exaggerated report reached the Emperor. *Calendar of State Papers Spanish 1531–3* ed. P. de Gayangos (London, 1882) 201 (No. 755) 282 (No. 428).

[5] A. Bernoulli, *Eine zürcherische Verlustliste von der Schlacht Kappel* (Anzeiger für schweizerische Geschichte IV. Bern, 1899) 200–1.

When darkness fell and further pursuit was impossible, the victorious Catholics returned to the battlefield to say five Aves, five paternosters and the creed. They lit campfires and collected their wounded together with three standards, eighteen guns and any valuables left behind by the enemy. They then remained two nights on the battlefield as custom demanded. Their forces were not strong enough to attack the almost impregnable city of Zurich, whose rulers now called in soldiers from Thurgau and Rheintal to join with those of Berne under Sebastian von Diesbach at Bremgarten. These now pushed south with superior numbers. There was, however, little enthusiasm for the campaign. Berne and its friends fulfilled their obligations to help an ally when attacked and to uphold the Zwinglian faith, but this was all.[1] Glarus withdrew from the conflict, and Philip of Hesse regretted that no help could come from his side. There was a general desire for a speedy end to the war, and as the Protestant forces approached Zug, Bernese reluctance to advance further became obvious. Many Bernese returned home, but the remaining Protestant states maintained their forces reasonably adequately.

The army of the Inner States now established itself near Zug in a strongly fortified position on the Zugerberg where it could defy attack, while Berne refused to countenance an advance against Lucerne. Instead, 4,000 men from Zurich, Basle, Schaffhausen and St Gall were sent round the mountain to take the Catholics in the rear. They looted and burnt mercilessly en route before establishing themselves on the heights near Gubel in careless disorder. There they were suddenly attacked just after midnight on 24 October by local inhabitants who joined some Zug soldiers, all making themselves recognisable by white shirts. Surprise was followed by panic, nearly a thousand Protestants were killed, including Jacob Frei,[2] the rest fled in disorder or were captured, leaving their guns and equipment to the enemy.[3] It was Kappel over again. Basle now joined Berne in the search for peace terms, and enemy territory was evacuated. An expeditionary force from the Inner States even made a raid along the shore of the lake of Zurich to within five miles of the city, causing the country people to clamour for peace, while Berne steadfastly refused to advance. On all sides the 'clerics' war' was unpopular.

On 16 November therefore the Zurich council accepted at Deinikon a settlement which guaranteed its political and ecclesiastical independence, and deserted its allies in the Mandated Territories and in St Gall. The Bernese army left the Freie Aemter, and the Catholics promptly compelled all to hear mass once more, while on 24 November Berne and its sup-

---

[1] Lüthi, 76-7.   [2] Stumpf 2, II, 228.
[3] A. Müller, *Die Schlacht auf dem Gubel. Mit besonderer Benützung der neuentdeckten Quellen*, ZSK 17 (1923) 1-28, 81-104, 182-200.

porters agreed to the second peace of Kappel.[1] Each side accepted the principle later expressed as *cuius regio, eius religio*; the *Ort* chose its own form of worship, either the new one (i.e. Zwinglian) or 'our true undoubted Christian faith' (Catholicism). In states where there was a Catholic majority this was to be the sole permitted religion.

In the relevant Mandated Territories, communities which had accepted the evangelical creed were free to continue so to worship; individuals, as well as groups, were free to return to Catholicism, and in a parish with an evangelical majority the Catholic minority were guaranteed freedom of worship and a proportionate share of the church property. Thus, in a grudging and limited way the principle of parity was now accepted in a public treaty, and thus the political unity of a religiously divided Switzerland was made possible. The provision, however, did not apply where there was a Catholic majority, and Mandated Territories administered by Catholic states only were not allowed toleration nor were Rapperswil, Gaster, Weesen, Sargans, Bremgarten, Mellingen and the Freie Aemter (which had been occupied by Catholic forces). The first peace of Kappel was cancelled, and there was to be no further discussion of the Unterwalden incursion, outstanding debts were to be liquidated and Zurich repaid its share of the war indemnity. Civic alliances (*Burgrechte*) contracted outside the Confederation (i.e. the *hessische Bündniss*) were abrogated, including that with Constance, which meant, ultimately, the return of Catholicism there. The abbot of St Gall was restored to his monastery with his territorial jurisdiction and his alliance (*Landrecht*) with Glarus and Schwyz reaffirmed. In his demesne (*Alte Landschaft*) Catholicism was reimposed, but in Toggenburg the principle of parity was accepted. The city of St Gall remained reformed and independent, with Vadian as its leading figure. In Thurgau, where Zwinglian missionary activity had been intense and effective and the parishes were allowed to choose their own form of religion, the Catholic church regained a good deal of ground.

In Zurich itself the exclusive triumph of Zwinglianism was confirmed by the choice on 9 December of Bullinger – who had opposed the war – as Zwingli's successor. He and the other ministers were, however, bidden to keep their sermons to the exposition of the Gospel and to cease to become involved in politics. This applied also to the countryside, where the preachers were chosen by the council, but it was agreed that any one locally objectionable should be withdrawn. There was to be closer consultation with the *Gemeinden* and war was not to be made without their

---

[1] EA 4, 1b, 1567–77; Bullinger, *Ref.* III, 247f. There were separate, but practically identical, agreements between the Inner Five and Zurich (20 Nov.), Berne (24 Nov.), Basle (22 Dec.) and Schaffhausen (31 Jan. 1532). For the literature see E. Walder, *Religionsvergleiche des 16. Jahrhunderts* I, 3–14 Quellen zur neueren Geschichte² hg. v. historischen Seminar der Universität Bern. 7 (Berne, 1960).

knowledge and consent. The aristocratic 'constables' regained influence in the Zurich Council which for the time being withdraw from intervention in federal affairs. The second peace left Switzerland a deeply divided confederation and externally weak for this reason. Neither side was entirely satisfied, but further civil war was averted for a long while.

The death of Zwingli meant the rejection of his external policies. Zurich lost control of Thurgau and thus of eastern Switzerland which reverted to the joint administration as before 1529. The Rhine became Switzerland's permanent northern frontier, community of action between Protestant Switzerland and Lutheran Germany was at an end and Zurich no longer had an effective foreign policy. Basle, Berne, Biel, Schaffhausen, St Gall and Chur remained evangelical, but after 1531 they were on the defensive. Constance had to be relinquished to Austria, the Christian Civic Union was at an end, and Swiss influence in south Germany was greatly diminished. The alliance with Philip of Hesse[1] evaporated, and the Lutheran League of Schmalkalden went its own way to partial failure. Five years after the battle of Kappel, John Calvin was persuaded to stay in Geneva, and Swiss Protestantism ultimately found common ground in the first (*Consensus Tigurinus*, 1549) and in the second Helvetic Confessions (1566). This, however, was the achievement of Zwingli's worthy successors, Bullinger and Leo Jud, and opened a new chapter in Swiss history.

Humanly speaking, the death of Zwingli in October 1531 was unexpected, unnecessary and easily avoidable. There need have been no war, because the forces making for peace were strong, and if the food-blockade had been called off the Catholic forces could readily have been persuaded to go home. A compromise about preaching the Gospel might have been arranged, the entirely minor dispute about war reparations was practically settled already, and although the hard words of slander and abuse that came from both sides undoubtedly aroused resentment, the age was only too accustomed to hearing them.

Having urged war for the sake of religion all through 1530, Zwingli could, perhaps, hardly have absented himself from the column which marched to defeat at Kappel. He fought as a volunteer and against his own countrymen, having spent much of his life deploring warfare and emphasising Swiss solidarity. He was 47 when he died, and he had been in Zurich less than twelve years; had he returned alive from Kappel to continue his work, much must have been very different. His activity was stupendous: to a wide correspondence was added pastoral care, frequent sermons, theological exposition and unceasing controversy. Humanist, divine, and statesman, he became more and more involved in affairs and was often on the move. He could advise the ruler of Hesse as confidently

[1] For whose tribute to Zwingli see Mörikofer II, 420, corrected by Fabian *Q*, 101.

as he could lead the ordinary man from the pulpit, and he was convinced that all Switzerland could be united behind his teaching, and in alliance with the Hessians and the King of France all western Europe might follow. More even than Luther, he was the arch-enemy of Rome and utterly uncompromisingly so. The false religion of the Catholics must be exchanged for his own which was that of the Bible.

A man of prayer and supremely God-fearing, he humbly sought the guidance of the Holy Spirit through God's word in the Scriptures or directly from above. Biblical quotations, texts and phrases permeate every page of his letters and treatises. He was a renowned scholar and he had devoted friends and disciples. His faith was irresistible, unclouded by doubt, utterly submissive to the Divine will. He seriously believed that Pope and Emperor could be overthrown and a new era, almost a reign of the saints, begin. In Switzerland, united and a great power, men would show by hard work, by contentment with a life of agriculture and cattle rearing, and by lives in which religion was predominant, what Christians could offer the world.

Scholar, musician, orator, a loving father and husband, entirely without personal ambition, lacking Calvin's logical mind and Calvin's vanity, far more conscious of social obligations than Luther, he was the prophet of Switzerland. In his republicanism, in his belief in government by discussion in which the ignorant and illiterate would accept the leadership of the educated, all working towards the establishment of God's kingdom on earth, he was Swiss to the core. For all we know, he never travelled further north than Aachen or further south than Milan, and he spoke no language but German and Latin. His thought was moulded by the university scholasticism which he despised, by the rhetoricians of classical Rome whom he imitated, and by the narrow biblicism by which he was enchained. He was a man of action in the best sense: what he had learnt from his books he must use to exhort, advise and implore. The stream of visitors was endless. He was always approachable, always ready to help the unfortunate, constantly encouraging the hesistant, yet prepared to come to terms with the world if Christ's kingdom could be brought nearer or the Gospel message proclaimed for all to hear. Fearless, self-confident, self-reliant, he had the strength that comes to the man who knows that God speaks through him and that he has a message to deliver. From humanist to theologian, from theologian to politician and thence to compromise with secularism in order that his way might triumph, it is a story of conviction that failed. The Catholics were as wrong as Lutherans, Anabaptists and Socinians. Zurich had got things right and was the model polity for the world, and through it, and the religion of its chief pastor, lay the way to the kingdom of God.

Zwingli was right in one assertion – without war there could not have been a Switzerland united in religion. Even before the counter-Reformation, the Catholics were so firmly entrenched in the Inner States, and religion was so closely bound up with the regional interests and independence of the mountain-dwellers that a complete conversion by persuasion alone was most unlikely. The religion of the individual was the religion of the state and a change of religion meant a change of government, a revolution. The Catholics were quite determined to exclude heresy and heretical preachers, while even parity, two religions operating within one state, was a long way off. Zwingli certainly never thought of it save as a possibly unavoidable evil until the forces of righteousness should have finally triumphed.

For him life on earth was a preparation-time for the life to come, the chosen few showing the world by their example how the true Christian should live. He was at one with his religious opponents about the force of prayer, but prayer directly to God and not through an intermediary, the Virgin or the saints; prayer, too, that was spontaneous, unprescribed, and personal rather than corporate. For the true Christian, Christ was an ever-present reality, and it was in certain faith in the love of God, shown through his son, revealed in the New Testament, that the Swiss reformer lived and died. Teacher, scholar, advocate, leader of men, the prophet through whose mouth God spoke to his hearers, Zwingli established his reformed teaching in central Europe with a secure permanence that endured across the ages. In an oecumenical world which accepts few of his premises, his teaching and memory remain an inspiration as well as a fact of history.

Index

Index

Besançon, Archbishop of, 55
Bible, 91–2, 94, 104, 106–7, 113, 122–4, 127–8, 130, 144, 149, 155, 201; authority of, 63, 72, 84, 87–8, 130, 154, 168, 172–3; Baruch (Apocrypha), 113; exegesis, 85, 87, 98, 190–1, 294–5, 300, 307–8, 389n; inspiration of, 64, 175, 287, 359; New Testament, 91, 93, 95, 105, 107, 118, 122, 131, 140, 152, 162, 172, 176, 183, 190, 419; Old Testament 118, 131–3, 135, 140, 162, 172, 190; St Luke and, 20, 83, 118, 358–9; Septuagint, 222; translations of,62, 128–9, 173, 223, 295; Zwingli's use of, 62–4, 111, 135, 173, 295
Bicocca, 90
Biel, 38
Biel, Gabriel, 162
Billican, Theobald, 300
Binder, Georg, 75n, 400
Bischoff, Anton, 364, 368
Bischofszell, 144
Black Forest (Schwarzwald), 59, 377
Blansch (Plank), Dr Martin, 101n
Blarer, Diethelm, von Wartensee, Abbot of St Gall, 285–6
Blaurer (Blarer), Ambrose and Thomas, 260n, 287, 297, 353, 397, 399
Blaurock, Georg vom Haus Jakob, (Cajakob), 177n, 181–2, 185–6, 188, 199, 275
Blenio, 30
Bleuler, Leonhard, 181, 184
Blockade: of Inner States (1530–1), 372, 374, 401, 403, 404, 405
Boisrigault, Louis (Daugerant), 394
Bologna, 31, 32, 41, 392; concordat of (1516), 108
Bombasius, Paul, Cardinal, 42n
Bormio, 33
Bosshart, Max, 181, 184
Bourbon, Charles, Duke of, 127, 138
Brandenburg, Georg, Margrave of, 315
Brandenburg, Joachim I, Elector of, 379
Brant, Sebastian, 15, 16, 17
Breitenmoser, Hans, 269
Breitinger, 184
Bremgarten, 5, 67, 357, 363, 365–6, 405, 411, 415–6
Brennwald, 184
Brenz, Johannes, 298n, 317, 323n
Brethren of the Common Life, 61–2
Brethren, Swiss, 173
Briçonnet, Guillaume, 394
Brieffer, Niklaus, 255
Brötli, Johann, 181, 183–5
Bruggbach, (Brubach), 184
Brun, Rudolf, 48–50, 56
Brunner, Jörg, 248

Brunner, Philip, 399
Bubikon, 55, 199
Bucer, (Butzer), Martin, 152, 241, 256, 258, 294, 302, 319, 325, 328–9, 333, 377
Buchs, 414
Buchstab, Johann, 256, 259
Budaeus, (Budé), Guillaume, 43
Bülach, 59, 414
Bünzen, 408
Bünzli, Gregory, 8, 14, 22, 153
Bütschwil, Johann Steiger von, abbot, 356
Bugenhagen, Johann, (Pomeranus), 298
Bullinger, Heinrich, 7n, 64, 357, 416–17
Bulls, Papal: *Etsi Romani pontifices*, 37; *Decet Romanum*, 71n, 82n; *Exsurge Domine*, 82n
Bundschuh, 120, 200
Burg bei Stein, 145, 146
Burgauer, Benedict, 236n, 259n, 274
Burgrecht, 344, 353
Burgrecht, das christliche, see Union, Christian Civic
Burgundy, Free County of, 3, 30
Burgundy, Duchy of, 3, 8, 37
Burgundy, Charles the Rash, Duke of, 3, 28, 346, 376
Butzbach, Johann, 11

Cajetan, Cardinal (Tommaso de Vio), 71
Calvin, John, 62, 66, 85, 167, 324–5, 417–18
Cambrai, League of (1508), 3; Peace of (1529), 394
Cambridge, 39
Campeggio, Lorenzo, Cardinal, 154, 225, 335
Capito, Wolfgang Fabricius (Köpfel) 43, 334, 377
Castelberger, Andreas (auf den Stülzen), 176, 181, 183, 200
Castiglione, 33
Cato, Distichs of, 7
Celtes, Conrad, 12, 217
Ceporinus (Jakob Wiesendanger of Dynhard), 217n, 222
Cham, Jakob von, 56
Charlemagne, Emperor (St), 47, 56, 115
Charles the Rash, see Burgundy, Duke of
Charles III, of Savoy, see Savoy
Charles V, Holy Roman Emperor, 71, 90, 118, 318, 350, 379, 388, 392, 401
Charles VIII, King of France, 30
Chiasso expedition (1510), 32, 33
Chiavenna, 33
Chieregati, Francesco, Cardinal, 90
Christ, Jesus, 40, 61, 65–6, 87, 105, 108–9, 111–12, 121, 149–150, 196–7, 205, chapters XII, XIII, 299, 314, 308, 312; body of, in heaven, 289, 338; glorified body of, 297, 325;

Index

Index

Glarus, 2, 4, 5, 6, 11, 20, 22–4, 26–31, 34, 37–9, 41, 49, 60, 76, 104, 111, 129, 142, 176, 209, 212, 280, 399, 403

Göldli, Heinrich, 22

Göldli, Jörg (of Tiefenau), 409, 411–13

Göldli, Kaspar, 409

Golder, Hans, *Schultheiss* of Lucerne, 412

Gospel, *see also* Bible, 91–2, 102, 105, 108, 120, 122–3, 125, 128, 133, 135–7, 144, 146, 156, 173, 240–1

Gospel, propagation of: in St Gall, 275; in south Germany, 240; in northern Switzerland, 226

Gottlieben castle, 96, 137

Government, 117–20, 133, 135, 137, 143, 153, 165, 202–3, 206–7, 241, 250, 315, 339, 358–9, 375; and worship, 107, 207, 375; aristocratic, approved, 395; Godless, God-fearing, 205

Governors (*Vögte*), 347; in *Freie Aemter*, 360

Grandson, battle of (1476), 4, 38

Grat, Alexius, 256, 258

Graubünden (Grisons), 28, 33, 212, 391, 397–8

Great Minster (*Grossmünster*), Zurich, 26, 45, 48, 55, 57–8, 60, 65, 73, 76, 78–9, 81, 92–3, 95, 106–7, 115, 129, 144, 162, 171, 178, 185, 220; and Zurich, 55; canons of, 56; school at, 220, reform of, 220

Grebel, Conrad, 18, 27, 52, 58, 132, 177–9, 181–3, 185–6, 194, 196, 199, 200, 275

Grebel, James (Jakob), 58, 242–3

Grebel, Peter, 58

Greek, study and teaching of, 17, 19, 20, 25, 27, 39, 40, 43, 62, 64–5, 92, 100, 102–3, 123, 172–3

Gregory of Nazianzen, St, 26

Gregory I, Pope (590–604), 64, 151

Greifensee, 53, 59

Griesenberg, 144

Gritti, Andrea, Doge of Venice, 392

Grossman, Caspar (Megander), 18, 60, 80, 184–5, 208, 263

Grüningen, 53, 59, 185, 199, 202, 269

Gubel, battle of the, 415

Guicciardini, Francesco, 29

Habsburg, house of, 1, 2, 4, 24, 34, 35, 60, 143, 210, 238, 379, 388; Zwingli's fear of, 333

Habsburg, Rudolf I of, 48

Hätzer, Ludwig, 178, 179, 182–3, 188

Haller, Berchtold, 62, 236, 239, 249, 254

Haller, Johannes, 249n

Hasler, Peter, *Untervogt*, 362

Haslital, 264, 351

Hausen, 412

Hebrew, knowledge and teaching of, 15, 27, 43, 64, 92, 100, 102–3, 123, 172, 196; Zwingli's knowledge of, 192, 223

Hedio, Caspar, 19, 42n, 323

Hegenwald, Erhard, 101n

Heiligenberg, monastery at, 55

Hell, Zwingli's acceptance of, 339–40

Helvidius, 89

Hemmerli, Felix, Canon, 56

Henry VIII, King of England, 31–2, 38, 90, 100, 129, 137, 317, 403; *Assertio septem sacramentorum*, 303; consults Zwingli about divorce, 303, 404

Hercules, 396

heresy, heretics, 71, 103, 126, 148, 166, 180, 187, 209, 225, 227, 230, 250, 266, 329, 335, 345, 348, 362, 375; Zwingli accused of, 83, 228, 238, 413

Hermann, Konrad, 156

Hesse, 354, 377, 386; Christian alliance of (*christliche Verstand*), 386–7, 391, 418; Berne's rejection of, 387; Philip the Magnanimous, Landgrave of, 262, 266, 309, 312, 316–17, 319, 320, 335, 378–81, 388, 391, 398, 415, 417

Heynlin, of Stein, John, 15, 16, 18, 65n

Hilary, St, 23

Hildegard, Abbess (of Fraumünster), 47

Hiltbrand, Konrad, 405n

Hitzkirch, 406, 408

Hochrütiner, Lorenz, 176, 275

Hoen, (Honius), Cornelisz, 158, 292–3

Höngg, 55, 130, 177

Hofmann, Conrad, Canon, 66, 76, 131–2, 220

Hofmeister, Sebastian (Oeconomus), 131n, 155, 180, 186, 212n, 263

Hohenems, Marx Sittich of, 264n, 286, 366, 398

Hohenems, Wolf Dietrich of, 396–7

Hohengeroldseck, Diebold (Theobald) von, administrator of Einsiedeln, 42, 151

Hohenklingen, castle of, 146

Hohenlandenberg, Hugo of, Bishop of Constance, 20, 67, 77, 86, 95, 98–9, 131, 207, 225, 228, 231, 254, 256

Hohenrechberg, Conrad of, Abbot of Einsiedeln, 41–2

Hohensaxe, Gerald of, Abbot of Einsiedeln, 41

Hohentwiel, 381

Hospinian, Rudolf, 400

Hospitallers, 55, 199

Hospitals, 57–9

Hottinger, Hans, 185

Hottinger, Jacob, 183–4

Hottinger, Klaus, 130–1, 176

Huber, Hans, 181, 237

425

Index

Hubmaier, Balthasar (Pacimontanus), 132–3, 156, 179, 180, 185–6, 192
Hug, Heinrich, 240n
Hus, John, Hussites, 63, 80, 96, 109, 138, 167, 230, 238
Huter, Diebold, 256
Hutten, Ludwig von, 380
Hutten, Ulrich von, 90n, 127–8

images, 127, 130, 132–4, 139, 140, 144–5, 205, 212, 254, 259, 261–2; in churches, attacks on, 130, 141, 356, 362; crucifix, Zwingli's views on, 112–13, 115, 140; removed at St Gall, 277; veneration of, 42, 92–5, 260, limitations to, 115
Imhag, 368
indulgences, 19, 44, 66–7, 94, 126, 136
Infralapsarian: Zwingli as, 336
Ingolstadt, 12, 154, 179, 217
Ininger, Wolfgang, 130n
Inner States (Five Orte), 23, 30, 67, 138, 210, 226, 228, 232, 256, 286, 347, 350, 353–4, 372, 399, 408, 415, 419
Innsbruck, 350, 398
Interlaken, monastery at, 263–4
Inzel, zur, monastery at, 258
Italy, Italian 3, 10, 12–13, 17, 28–34, 37, 54, 60, 65, 68, 102, 118, 138, 251, 388, 409
Ittingen (Carthusian monastery): attack on, 144; burnt, 147; rebuilt, 148–9

Jauch, Hans, of Uri, 413
Jerome, St, 19, 26, 43, 64–5, 113, 122
Jetzer, Hans, Dominican at Berne, 246
John, St, the Baptist, 52, 114, 133, 190, 192
Jonas, Justus, 323n
Joner, Wolfgang, Abbot of Kappel, 135, 148, 186, 367, 399, 414
Josephus, 122
Jud, Leo (Keller), 18, 60, 80–1, 87, 92, 128, 130, 132–3, 143, 151, 180–1, 184–6, 208, 274, 295, 303, 417
Jüterbog, 44
Julius II, Pope (1503–13), 31, 34
Junker, Hans, of Rapperswil, 394

Kaiser, Jacob (Schlosser), 362–3, 372
Kaisersberg, Geiler of, 16, 167
Kaiserstuhl, 212, 363
Kalchofen, 411
Kalchrain, monastery at, 144
Kaltschmid, Hans, 394
Kappel, Cistercian monastery, 55, 143, 221, 222n, 268, 367–9; milk soup of, 367–8; first war of, 365–8; first peace of (1529), 285, 368–9, 371–5, 403; second war of,

406–11, unpopularity of, 401, 408, 415; battle of, 409–15; second peace of (1531), 416
Karlstadt, Andrew, of Bodenstein, 152, 154–6, 158, 170, 176, 179, 196, 200
Katzenelnbogen, county of, 321, 381
Keller, Michael (Cellarius), 297
Kempten, 388
Kessler, John, 221, 236, 274
keys, discussion of, 108, 122, 258
Kiburg, 53, 144, 202, 364, 409
Kilchmeyer, Jodocus (Jost), 80
Kilian (German or Köuffi), Abbot of St Gall, 280–5; election, validity of, 280–1
Kleinbasel, 8, 14
Knonau, 53
Knonau, Gerold Meyer von, 218
Knonau, Hans Meyer von, 79
Knonau, Konrad Meyer von, 400
Kolb, Franz, 254
Kontoblatas, Andronicus, 17
Kröwl (Chroil), Wolfgang, 270
Künzli, Bernard, of Brunnadern, 356
Küssnacht, 55, 268
Kunz, Peter, 236

Lactantius, 26, 43
Lambert, Francis, of Avignon, 82n, 248
Landenberg, Caspar von, Abbot of St Gall, 272
Landfriede, see Kappel, peace of
Langenstein, Heinrich von, 12
Latin, Latinity, 6–8, 12–13, 15–20, 24, 26–7, 35–6, 40, 57, 65–6, 81, 86, 98, 100, 102–3, 106, 109, 121, 132–3, 154, 418
La Trémoille, Louis de, 37
Lausanne, diocese and bishops of, 8, 137, 227, 231, 234, 245, 256
Lavater, Hans Rudolf, 52, 202, 366, 405, 408, 411–13
Law, Canon (Corpus Juris Canonici), 77, 97, 107, 207, 214, 281n
Law, Mosaic, 133, 134, 162, 308
Leiden, John of, 169
Leipzig, 71, 155
Lenzburg, 263, 287
Leo II, Pope (682–3), 151
Leo X, Pope (1513–21), 34, 37, 90
letter-writing, 25, 27
Leu, Heinrich, 242
Leutpriester, meaning of, 40n, 45n
libellum, anonymous, Von der Kindertaufe, 193
Lichtensteig, 356
Liebenfels, Lanz von, 357
Limmat, river, 44, 47, 57
Lindau, 212, 334

426

Index

Index

purgatory, 44, 103, 112, 122, 132, 150, 152, 154, 179, 205, 259, 339-40, 396

Rahn, Heinrich, 242, 365
Rapperswil, 5, 23, 209, 212, 376, 411, 416
Ravenna, 31, 33
Ravensburg, 355
realism, 13, 15, 16, 158, 291
Regensberg, 53, 59
Regensburg (Ratisbon), 179; Convention of, 225, 238; Diet of (1528), 255
registers, marriage/baptism, 193, 215-16
Reinhart, Anna, 79-80, 218, 322
relics, 23, 24, 138, 141, 245
Reuchlin, John, 15-17, 217; *Rudimenta Hebraica*, 26, 43
Reutlingen, 156, 380
Rhaetia, see Graubünden
Rhegius, Urbanus (Rieger), 294, 301-2
Rheinau, 59
Rheinfelden, 212
Rheintal, 5, 201, 362, 365-6, 372, 384, 399, 415
Rhellikan, John, 263, 271
Rhenanus, Beatus (Beat Bild), 19, 44, 179
Rhine, river, 14, 59, 179, 201; as frontier, 2-4, 417
Rhodes, island of, 118
Rieden, 55
Riedlingen, 131
Rivoli, 38
Rode, John (Hinne), 158
Röist, Diethelm, 153, 254
Röist, Marx, 38, 44, 52, 58, 100, 183, 278, 406
Rösch, Ulrich, Abbot of St Gall, 6, 273
Röubli, William (Reublin), 52, 178, 180-1, 183-5
Roggenacker, 184
Rome, 3, 10, 17, 22, 31, 34, 39, 40, 41-2, 44, 55, 65, 67-8, 72, 76, 78, 91-2, 94, 98, 104, 106, 227; see also Papacy
Rorschach, 212, 272, 278-9, 283
Rotach, 319
Roussel, Gérard, 394
Rudolfzell, 271
Rübli, Wolfgang, 414
Rüfers, 55
Rüschlikon, 55
Rüti, monastery at, 55, 143, 199, 221, 268; reformed regulations for, 269-70
Rütimann, Burkhart, *Untervogt*, 147-8
Ruppel, Berthold, 15

Sabina, Duchess of Württemberg, 380
sacrament(s), 109-10, 290, 337; see also baptism, eucharist
safe conduct(s), 230, 255

Saints, as mediators, 112-13, 154, 259; days, work on, 77
St Blasien, monastery, looted, 202
St Gall (St Gallen), 4-6, 13, 29, 60, 88, 131, 142, 185, 188, 190, 201, 212, 230, 266, Chapter XI, 399; city of, see also Vadina, 216, 271, 275, 277, 349, 374, 416-17; and Christian Civic Union, 282; church of St Lawrence, 274; monastery at, 5, 271-3, 275, 282-3, 373, relations with city, 272-5, 282, property of, 277, 279, 281, 283-6, 349, 400, 416, abbots of, 4, 28, 85, 416, (election of, 279-81), see also Blarer, Kilian, Röist, Rösch
St Gotthard, 2, 4
St Jakob an der Birs, battle (1448), 30
St John, Benedictine abbey (Alt St Johann im Thurtal), 356; see also Zwingli, uncle of
St Julien, peace of, 385
St Luzi, monastery, 363
St Vitus and St Modestus, Mandate of, 249
Salat, Hans, 390
Salzburg, 355
Sam, Conrad, 260, 296, 302
Sanson, Bernhardin, 44, 66, 67
Sargans, 5, 212, 349, 384, 404, 416
Sarmensdorf, 408
Sarnen, 362
Sattler, Michael, 186, 194n
Savoy: Duchy of, 3, 9, 245, 364, 398; Dukes of, 4, 8, 211, 385, 398 (Charles III)
Sax-Forstegg, 349
Saxony, Electorate of, 47, 63, 72, 108, 387; John the Steadfast, Elector of, 72, 104, 309, 312, 317, 319, 379, 396; Duchy of, 397, Duke George of, 397
Schad, 184
Schänis, 357
Schaffhausen, 4, 38, 98, 131, 138, 142, 185, 201, 209, 212, 239, 267, 275, 366, 374, 382, 417
Schappeler, Christopher (Sertorius), 131, 374
Schatzgeyer, Caspar, 137
Scheuren, 411
Schilling, Conrad, Abbot of Gottstadt, 255
Schindler, Hans, of Weesen, 357, 376
Schiner, Matthias, Cardinal, 32, 33n, 39, 56, 118, 227, 247
Schinz, Rudolf, 412
Schlegel, Theodore (Theodul), 363
Schleitheim, Convention and Confession of (1527), 193
Schleiz, Conference at, 319
Schlieren, 107n
Schmalkalden, Conference at, 319, 333; League of, 386-8, 390, 417

429

Index

Index

Index

Printed in the United Kingdom
by Lightning Source UK Ltd.
135361UK00001B/307-309/P